Neurotheology

" The Neurological Explanation of The Religious Experience "

Edited by Paul F. Kisak

Contents

Chapter 1

Neurotheology

Not to be confused with neuroethology.

Neurotheology, also known as **spiritual neuroscience**,[1] attempts to explain religious experience and behaviour in neuroscientific terms.[2] It is the study of correlations of neural phenomena with subjective experiences of spirituality and hypotheses to explain these phenomena. This contrasts with the Psychology of religion which studies psychological, rather than neural, states.

Proponents of neurotheology say there is a neurological and evolutionary basis for subjective experiences traditionally categorized as spiritual or religious.[3] The field has formed the basis of several popular science books,[4][5][6] but has received criticism from psychologists.[2]

1.1 Introduction

"Neurotheology" is a neologism that describes the scientific study of the neural correlates of religious or spiritual beliefs, experiences and practices. Other researchers prefer to use terms like "spiritual neuroscience" or "neuroscience of religion". Researchers in the field attempt to explain the neurological basis for religious experiences, such as:[7]

- The perception that time, fear or self-consciousness have dissolved

- Spiritual awe

- Oneness with the universe

- Ecstatic trance

- Sudden enlightenment[8]

- Altered states of consciousness

1.2 Terminology

Aldous Huxley used the term *neurotheology* for the first time in the utopian novel *Island*. The discipline studies the cognitive neuroscience of religious experience and spirituality. The term is also sometimes used in a less scientific context or a philosophical context. Some of these uses, according to the mainstream scientific community, qualify as pseudoscience. Huxley used it mainly in a philosophical context.

The use of the term neurotheology in published scientific work is currently uncommon. A search on the citation indexing service provided by Institute for Scientific Information returns five articles. Three of these are published in the journal Zygon: Journal of Religion and Science, while two are published in *American Behavioral Scientist*. Work on the neural basis of spirituality has, however, occurred sporadically throughout the 20th century.

1.3 Theoretical work

In an attempt to focus and clarify what was a growing interest in this field, in 1994 educator and businessman Laurence O. McKinney published the first book on the subject, titled "Neurotheology: Virtual Religion in the 21st Century", written for a popular audience but also promoted in the theological journal *Zygon*.[9] According to McKinney, neurotheology sources the basis of religious inquiry in relatively recent developmental neurophysiology. According to McKinney's theory, pre-frontal development, in humans, creates an illusion of chronological time as a fundamental part of normal adult cognition past the age of three. The inability of the adult brain to retrieve earlier images experienced by an infantile brain creates questions such as "where did I come from" and "where does it all go", which McKinney suggests led to the creation of various religious explanations. The experience of death as a peaceful regression into timelessness as the brain dies won praise from readers as varied as author Arthur C. Clarke, eminent theologian Harvey Cox, and the Dalai Lama and sparked a new interest in the field.

Andrew B. Newberg and others describe neurological processes which are driven by the repetitive, rhythmic stimulation which is typical of human ritual, and which contribute to the delivery of transcendental feelings of connection to a universal unity. They posit, however, that physical stimulation alone is not sufficient to generate transcendental unitive experiences. For this to occur they say there must be a blending of the rhythmic stimulation with ideas. Once this occurs "…ritual turns a meaningful idea into a visceral experience."[10] Moreover, they say that humans are compelled to act out myths by the biological operations of the brain on account of what they call the "inbuilt tendency of the brain to turn thoughts into actions".

The radical Catholic theologian Eugen Drewermann developed a two-volume critique of traditional conceptions of God and the soul and a reinterpretation of religion (Modern Neurology and the Question of God) based on current neuroscientific research.[11]

However, it has also been argued "that neurotheology should be conceived and practiced within a theological framework."[12] Furthermore, it has been suggested that creating a separate category for this kind of research is moot since conventional Behavioural and Social Neurosciences disciplines can handle any empirical investigation of this nature.[13]

Various theories regarding the evolutionary origin of religion and the evolutionary psychology of religion have been proposed.

1.4 Experimental work

1.4.1 Magnetic stimulation studies

Main article: God helmet

During the 1980s Michael Persinger stimulated the temporal lobes of human subjects with a weak magnetic field using an apparatus that popularly became known as the "God helmet"[14] and reported that many of his subjects claimed to experience a "sensed presence" during stimulation.[15] This work has been criticised[2] and has, to date, not been replicated by other researchers.[16][17]

Granqvist et al. claimed that Persinger's work was not "double-blind." Participants were often graduate students who knew what sort of results to expect, and there was the risk that the experimenters' expectations would be transmitted to subjects by unconscious cues. The participants

were frequently given an idea of the purpose of the study by being asked to fill in questionnaires designed to test their suggestibility to paranormal experiences before the trials were conducted. Granqvist et al. failed to replicate Persinger's experiments double-blinded, and concluded that the presence or absence of the magnetic field had no relationship with any religious or spiritual experience reported by the participants, but was predicted entirely by their suggestibility and personality traits. Following the publication of this study, Persinger et al. dispute this.[18] One published attempt to create a "haunted room" using environmental "complex" electromagnetic fields based on Persinger's theoretical and experimental work did not produce the sensation of a "sensed presence" and found that reports of unusual experiences were uncorrelated with the presence or absence of these fields. As in the study by Granqvist et al., reports of unusual experiences were instead predicted by the personality characteristics and suggestibility of participants.[19] One experiment with a commercial version of the God helmet found no difference in response to graphic images whether the device was on or off.[20][21]

1.4.2 Neuropsychology and neuroimaging

The first researcher to note and catalog the abnormal experiences associated with temporal lobe epilepsy (TLE) was neurologist Norman Geschwind, who noted a set of religious behavioral traits associated with TLE seizures.[22] These include hypergraphia, hyperreligiosity, reduced sexual interest, fainting spells, and pedantism, often collectively ascribed to a condition known as Geschwind syndrome.

Vilayanur S. Ramachandran explored the neural basis of the hyperreligiosity seen in TLE using the galvanic skin response (GSR), which correlates with emotional arousal, to determine whether the hyperreligiosity seen in TLE was due to an overall heightened emotional state or was specific to religious stimuli. Ramachandran presented two subjects with neutral, sexually arousing and religious words while measuring GSR. Ramachandran was able to show that patients with TLE showed enhanced emotional responses to the religious words, diminished responses to the sexually charged words, and normal responses to the neutral words. This study was presented as an abstract at a neuroscience conference and referenced in Ramachandran's book, Phantoms in the Brain,[23] but it has never been published in the peer-reviewed scientific press.

Research by Mario Beauregard at the University of Montreal, using fMRI imaging of Carmelite nuns, has purported to show that religious and spiritual experiences include several brain regions and not a single 'God spot'. As Beauregard has said, "There is no God spot in the brain. Spiritual experiences are complex, like intense experiences with other human beings."[24] The neuroimaging was conducted when the nuns were asked to recall past mystical states and not while actually experiencing mystical states; "subjects were asked to remember and relive (eyes closed) the most intense mystical experience ever felt in their lives as a member of the Carmelite Order." [25] A 2011 study by researchers at the Duke University Medical Center found hippocampal atrophy is associated with older adults who report life-changing religious experiences, as well as those who are "born-again Protestants, Catholics, and those with no religious affiliation".[26]

1.4.3   Psychopharmacology

Some scientists working in the field hypothesize that the basis of spiritual experience arises in neurological physiology. Speculative suggestions have been made that an increase of N,N-dimethyltryptamine levels in the pineal gland contribute to spiritual experiences.[27][28] Scientific studies confirming this have yet to be published. It has also been suggested that stimulation of the temporal lobe by psychoactive ingredients of 'Magic Mushrooms' mimics religious experiences.[29] This hypothesis has found laboratory validation with respect to psilocybin.[30][31]

1.5   See also

- Biological psychology
- Bicameralism (psychology)
- Cognitive science of religion
- Daniel Dennett
- Dimethyltryptamine
- Dualism/Materialism/Nondual
- Eight-circuit model of consciousness
- Eugen Drewermann
- Evolutionary origin of religions
- Geschwind syndrome
- God gene
- God helmet
- *God in a Pill?*
- Julian Jaynes
- Meditation

- Music Therapy
- Neuroethics
- Neuroscience
- Neurotechnology
- Oceanic feeling
- Out-of-body experience
- Philosophy of mind
- Philosophy of science
- Psychedelic crisis
- Psychology of religion
- Religious ecstasy
- Religious experience
- Temporal lobe epilepsy
- Theological anthropology
- Third Man factor
- Transpersonal psychology
- Viruses of the Mind
- VMAT2
- *Zen and the Brain*

1.6   References

[1] "David Biello, Searching for God in the Brain, Scientific American, 2007-10-03". Retrieved 2009-03-22.

[2] "Craig Aaen-Stockdale (2012). "Neuroscience for the Soul". The Psychologist 25 (7): 520–523".

[3] Gajilan, A. Chris (2007-04-05). "Are humans hard-wired for faith?". Cable News Network. Retrieved 2007-04-09.

[4] Matthew Alper. *The "God" Part of the Brain: A Scientific Interpretation of Human Spirituality and God.*

[5] James H. Austin. *Zen and the Brain: Toward an Understanding of Meditation and Consciousness.*

[6] James H. Austin. *Zen-Brain Reflections: Reviewing Recent Developments in Meditation and States of Consciousness.*

[7] Burton, Robert A. (2008). "Neurotheology". *On Being Certain. Believing You Are Right Even When You're Not.* New York City: Macmillan Publishers/St. Martin's Press. ISBN 978-1-4299-2611-9. ISBN 1-4299-2611-2(Macmillan Publishers edition). ISBN 0-312-35920-9. ISBN 978-0-312-35920-1(St. Martin's Press edition).

[8] Carr, Robert (2003). *God Men Con Men*. Smriti Books.

[9] Laurence O. McKinney (1994). *Neurotheology: Virtual Religion in the 21st Century*. American Institute for Mindfulness. ISBN 0-945724-01-2.

[10] Newberg, Andrew B.; D'Aquili, Eugene G.; Rause, Vince (2002). *Why God Won't Go Away: Brain Science and the Biology of Belief*. New York: Ballantine Books. p. 90. ISBN 0-345-44034-X.

[11] Eugen Drewermann (2006–2007). *Atem des Lebens: Die moderne Neurologie und die Frage nach Gott. (Modern neurology and the question of God) Vol 1: Das Gehirn. Vol. 2: Die Seele*. Düsseldorf: Patmos Verlag. Vol. 1: 864; Vol. 2: 1072. ISBN 3-491-21000-3. (Vol. 1). ISBN 3-491-21001-1(Vol. 2).

[12] Apfalter, Wilfried (2009). "Neurotheology: What Can We Expect from a (Future) Catholic Version?". *Theology and Science* 7: 163–174. doi:10.1080/14746700902796528.

[13] *"Neurotheology": A semantic trap set by pseudo-science for the unwary scientist*, Dr Milind Ovalekar

[14] Persinger, M A (1983). "Religious and mystical experiences as artifacts of temporal lobe function: a general hypothesis.". *Perceptual and motor skills* **57** (3 Pt 2): 1255–62. doi:10.2466/pms.1983.57.3f.1255. PMID 6664802.

[15] Persinger, MA (2003). "The Sensed Presence Within Experimental Settings: Implications for the Male and Female Concept of Self". *The Journal of Psychology: Interdisciplinary and Applied* **137** (1): 5–16. doi:10.1080/00223980309600595.

[16] Granqvist, P; Fredrikson, M; Unge, P; Hagenfeldt, A; Valind, S; Larhammar, D; Larsson, M (2005). "Sensed presence and mystical experiences are predicted by suggestibility, not by the application of transcranial weak complex magnetic fields". *Neuroscience Letters* **379** (1): 1–6. doi:10.1016/j.neulet.2004.10.057. PMID 15849873. Lay summary – *BioEd Online* (December 9, 2004).

[17] Larsson, M., Larhammarb, D., Fredrikson, M., and Granqvist, P. (2005). "Reply to M.A. Persinger and S. A. Koren's response to Granqvist et al. "Sensed presence and mystical experiences are predicted by suggestibility, not by the application of transcranial weak magnetic fields"". *Neuroscience Letters* **380** (3): 348–350. doi:10.1016/j.neulet.2005.03.059.

[18] Persinger, Michael; et al. (2005). "A response to Granqvist et al. "Sensed presence and mystical experiences are predicted by suggestibility, not by the application of transcranial weak magnetic fields".". *Neuroscience Letters* **380** (1): 346–347. doi:10.1016/j.neulet.2005.03.060. PMID 15862915.

[19] French, CC., Haque, U., Bunton-Stasyshyn, R., Davis, R. (2009). "The "Haunt" project: An attempt to build a "haunted" room by manipulating complex electromagnetic fields and infrasound". *Cortex* **45** (5): 619–629. doi:10.1016/j.cortex.2007.10.011. PMID 18635163.

[20] Gendle, MH & McGrath, MG (2012). "Can the 8-coil shakti alter subjective emotional experience? A randomized, placebo-controlled study.". *Perceptual and Motor Skills* **114** (1): 217–235. doi:10.2466/02.24.pms.114.1.217-235.

[21] Craig Aaen-Stockdale (2012). "Neuroscience for the Soul". *The Psychologist* **25** (7): 520–523. Murphy claims his devices are able to modulate emotional states in addition to enhancing meditation and generating altered states. In flat contradiction of this claim, Gendle & McGrath (2012) found no significant difference in emotional state whether the device was on or off.

[22] Waxman SG, Geschwind N. (1975). "The interictal behavior syndrome of temporal lobe epilepsy.". *Arch Gen Psychiatry* **32** (12): 1580–6. doi:10.1001/archpsyc.1975.01760300118011. PMID 1200777.

[23] Ramachandran, V. and Blakeslee (1998). *Phantoms in the Brain*.

[24] *Harper Collins Publishers Author Interview with mario Beauregard*, HarperCollins.com

[25] Mario Beauregard, Mario Beauregard (26 June 2006). "Neural correlates of a mystical experience in Carmelite nuns" (PDF) (405 (2006)). Neuroscience Letters. Retrieved 2010-05-09.

[26] Owen AD, Hayward RD, Koenig HG, Steffens DC, Payne ME (2011). "Religious factors and hippocampal atrophy in late life". *PLoS ONE* **6** (3): e17006. doi:10.1371/journal.pone.0017006.

[27] Strassman, R (2001). *DMT: The Spiritual Molecule*. Inner Traditions Bear and Company. ISBN 0-89281-927-8.

[28] Hood, Jr., Ralph W. and Jacob A. Belzen (2005). *"Research Methods in the Psychology of Religion", in Handbook Of The Psychology Of Religion And Spirituality, ed. by Raymond F. Paloutzian and Crystal L. Park*. New York: Guilford Press. p. 64. ISBN 1-57230-922-9.

[29] Skatssoon, Judy (2006-07-12). "Magic mushrooms hit the God spot". ABC Science Online. Retrieved 2006-07-13.

[30] Griffiths, Rr; Richards, Wa; Johnson, Mw; McCann, Ud; Jesse, R (2008). "Mystical-type experiences occasioned by psilocybin mediate the attribution of personal meaning and spiritual significance 14 months later.". *Journal of psychopharmacology* **22** (6): 621–32. doi:10.1177/0269881108094300. PMC 3050654. PMID 18593735.

[31] Griffiths, R R; Richards, W A; McCann, U; Jesse, R (2006). "Psilocybin can occasion mystical-type experiences having substantial and sustained personal meaning and spiritual significance.". *Psychopharmacology* **187** (3): 268–83; discussion 284–92. doi:10.1007/s00213-006-0457-5. PMID 16826400.

1.7 Further reading

- Andrew Neher, *The Psychology of Transcendence*, Dover, 2nd ed 1990, ISBN 0-486-26167-0

- Andrew B. Newberg, *The Mystical Mind: Probing the Biology of Religious Experience*, (1999), Fortress Press, Minneapolis, ISBN 0-8006-3163-3

- Patrick McNamara, "The Neuroscience of Religious Experience". Cambridge: Cambridge UP, 2009. ISBN 978-0-521-88958-2

- Thomas B. Roberts, "Chemical Input — Religious Output: Entheogens" Chapter 10 in *Where God and Science Meet: Vol. 3. The Psychology of Religious Experience* edited by Robert McNamara. Westport, CT: Praeger/Greenwood.

- Runehov Anne L.C., "Sacred or Neural? The Potential of Neuroscience to Explain Religious Experience". Göttingen: Vandenhoeck and Ruprecht, 2007. ISBN 978-3-525-56980-1.

- Gerald Wolf, (science-in-fiction novels) *Der HirnGott*; Dr. Ziethen Verlag 2005, Sich Verlag 2008, ISBN 978-3-9811692-8-7. *Glaube mir, mich gibt es nicht*; Sich Verlag 2009, ISBN 978-3-9812628-0-3.

1.8 External links

- The Science Of Spirituality - Is This Your Brain On God? - (NPR article)

- Horizon - God on the Brain

- *Your Brain on Religion: Mystic visions or brain circuits at work?* (Newsweek neurotheology article, May 2001)

- Center for Cognitive Liberty & Ethics neurotheology resource directory

- "This Is Your Brain on God" (*Wired magazine*, November 1999)

- Neurotheology: With God in Mind neurotheology article

- Survey of spiritual experiences, by the University of Pennsylvania

- Neurotheology at DMOZ

- 2006 National Film Board of Canada documentary, *Mystical Brain*

Chapter 2

Nervous system

The **nervous system** is the part of an animal's body that coordinates its voluntary and involuntary actions and transmits signals to and from different parts of its body. Nervous tissue first arose in wormlike organisms about 550 to 600 million years ago. In vertebrate species it consists of two main parts, the central nervous system (CNS) and the peripheral nervous system (PNS). The CNS contains the brain and spinal cord. The PNS consists mainly of nerves, which are enclosed bundles of the long fibers or axons, that connect the CNS to every other part of the body. Nerves that transmit signals from the brain are called *motor* or *efferent* nerves, while those nerves that transmit information from the body to the CNS are called *sensory* or *afferent*. Most nerves serve both functions and are called *mixed* nerves. The PNS is divided into a) somatic and b) autonomic nervous system, and c) the enteric nervous system. Somatic nerves mediate voluntary movement. The autonomic nervous system is further subdivided into the sympathetic and the parasympathetic nervous systems. The sympathetic nervous system is activated in cases of emergencies to mobilize energy, while the parasympathetic nervous system is activated when organisms are in a relaxed state. The enteric nervous system functions to control the gastrointestinal system. Both autonomic and enteric nervous systems function involuntarily. Nerves that exit from the cranium are called cranial nerves while those exiting from the spinal cord are called spinal nerves.

At the cellular level, the nervous system is defined by the presence of a special type of cell, called the neuron, also known as a "nerve cell". Neurons have special structures that allow them to send signals rapidly and precisely to other cells. They send these signals in the form of electrochemical waves traveling along thin fibers called axons, which cause chemicals called neurotransmitters to be released at junctions called synapses. A cell that receives a synaptic signal from a neuron may be excited, inhibited, or otherwise modulated. The connections between neurons can form neural circuits and also neural networks that generate an organism's perception of the world and determine its behavior. Along with neurons, the nervous system contains other specialized cells called glial cells (or simply glia), which provide structural and metabolic support.

Nervous systems are found in most multicellular animals, but vary greatly in complexity.[1] The only multicellular animals that have no nervous system at all are sponges, placozoans, and mesozoans, which have very simple body plans. The nervous systems of the radially symmetric organisms ctenophores (comb jellies) and cnidarians (which include anemones, hydras, corals and jellyfish) consist of a diffuse nerve net. All other animal species, with the exception of a few types of worm, have a nervous system containing a brain, a central cord (or two cords running in parallel), and nerves radiating from the brain and central cord. The size of the nervous system ranges from a few hundred cells in the simplest worms, to around 300 billion cells in African elephants.[2]

The central nervous system functions to send signals from one cell to others, or from one part of the body to others and to receive feedback. Malfunction of the nervous system can occur as a result of genetic defects, physical damage due to trauma or toxicity, infection or simply of ageing. The medical specialty of neurology studies disorders of the nervous system and looks for interventions that can prevent or treat them. In the peripheral nervous system, the most common problem is the failure of nerve conduction, which can be due to different causes including diabetic neuropathy and demyelinating disorders such as multiple sclerosis and amyotrophic lateral sclerosis.

Neuroscience is the field of science that focuses on the study of the nervous system.

2.1 Structure

The nervous system derives its name from nerves, which are cylindrical bundles of fibers (the axons of neurons), that emanate from the brain and spinal cord, and branch repeatedly to innervate every part of the body.[3] Nerves are large enough to have been recognized by the ancient Egyptians,

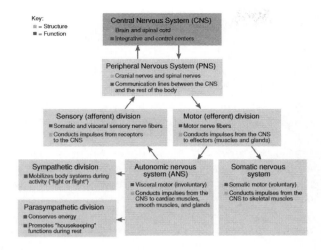

Key:
- ▨ = Structure
- ■ = Function

Central Nervous System (CNS)
- Brain and spinal cord
- ■ Integrative and control centers

Peripheral Nervous System (PNS)
- Cranial nerves and spinal nerves
- ■ Communication lines between the CNS and the rest of the body

Sensory (afferent) division
- ■ Somatic and visceral sensory nerve fibers
- ■ Conducts impulses from receptors to the CNS

Motor (efferent) division
- ■ Motor nerve fibers
- ■ Conducts impulses from the CNS to effectors (muscles and glands)

Sympathetic division
- ■ Mobilizes body systems during activity ("fight or flight")

Autonomic nervous system (ANS)
- ■ Visceral motor (involuntary)
- ■ Conducts impulses from the CNS to cardiac muscles, smooth muscles, and glands

Somatic nervous system
- ■ Somatic motor (voluntary)
- ■ Conducts impulses from the CNS to skeletal muscles

Parasympathetic division
- ■ Conserves energy
- ■ Promotes "housekeeping" functions during rest

Diagram showing the major divisions of the vertebrate nervous system.

Greeks, and Romans,[4] but their internal structure was not understood until it became possible to examine them using a microscope.[5] "It is difficult to believe that until approximately year 1900 it was not known that neurons are the basic units of the brain (Santiago Ramón y Cajall). Equally surprising is the fact that the concept of chemical transmission in the brain was not known until around 1930 (Henry Hallett Dale) and (Otto Loewi). We began to understand the basic electrical phenomenon that neurons use in order to communicate among themselves, the action potential, in the decade of 1950 (Alan Lloyd Hodgkin, Huxley Andrew Huxley and John Eccles). It was in the decade of 1960 that we became aware of how basic neuronal networks code stimuli and thus basic concepts are possible (David H. Hubel, and Torsten Wiesel). The molecular revolution swept across US universities in the decade of 1980. It was in the decade of 1990 that molecular mechanisms of behavioral phenomena became widely known (Eric Richard Kandel)."[6] A microscopic examination shows that nerves consist primarily of axons, along with different membranes that wrap around them and segregate them into fascicles. The neurons that give rise to nerves do not lie entirely within the nerves themselves—their cell bodies reside within the brain, spinal cord, or peripheral ganglia.[3]

All animals more advanced than sponges have nervous systems. However, even sponges, unicellular animals, and non-animals such as slime molds have cell-to-cell signalling mechanisms that are precursors to those of neurons.[7] In radially symmetric animals such as the jellyfish and hydra, the nervous system consists of a nerve net, a diffuse network of isolated cells.[8] In bilaterian animals, which make up the great majority of existing species, the nervous system has a common structure that originated early in the Ediacaran period, over 550 million years ago.[9][10]

2.1.1 Cells

The nervous system contains two main categories or types of cells: neurons and glial cells.

Neurons

The nervous system is defined by the presence of a special type of cell—the neuron (sometimes called "neurone" or "nerve cell").[3] Neurons can be distinguished from other cells in a number of ways, but their most fundamental property is that they communicate with other cells via synapses, which are membrane-to-membrane junctions containing molecular machinery that allows rapid transmission of signals, either electrical or chemical.[3] Many types of neuron possess an axon, a protoplasmic protrusion that can extend to distant parts of the body and make thousands of synaptic contacts.[11] Axons frequently travel through the body in bundles called nerves.

Even in the nervous system of a single species such as humans, hundreds of different types of neurons exist, with a wide variety of morphologies and functions.[11] These include sensory neurons that transmute physical stimuli such as light and sound into neural signals, and motor neurons that transmute neural signals into activation of muscles or glands; however in many species the great majority of neurons participate in the formation of centralized structures (the brain and ganglia) and they receive all of their input from other neurons and send their output to other neurons.[3]

Glial cells

Glial cells (named from the Greek for "glue") are non-neuronal cells that provide support and nutrition, maintain homeostasis, form myelin, and participate in signal transmission in the nervous system.[12] In the human brain, it is estimated that the total number of glia roughly equals the number of neurons, although the proportions vary in different brain areas.[13] Among the most important functions of glial cells are to support neurons and hold them in place; to supply nutrients to neurons; to insulate neurons electrically; to destroy pathogens and remove dead neurons; and to provide guidance cues directing the axons of neurons to their targets.[12] A very important type of glial cell (oligodendrocytes in the central nervous system, and Schwann cells in the peripheral nervous system) generates layers of a fatty substance called myelin that wraps around axons and provides electrical insulation which allows them to transmit action potentials much more rapidly and efficiently.

2.1.2   Anatomy in vertebrates

See also: List of nerves of the human body
The nervous system of vertebrates (including humans) is

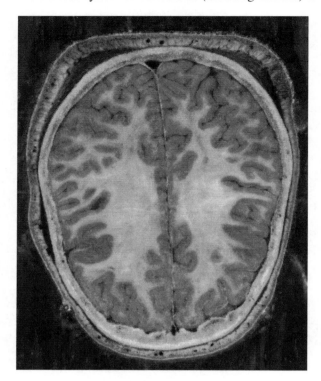

Horizontal section of the head of an adult female, showing skin, skull, and brain with grey matter (brown in this image) and underlying white matter

divided into the central nervous system (CNS) and the peripheral nervous system (PNS).[14]

The (CNS) is the major division, and consists of the brain and the spinal cord.[14] The spinal canal contains the spinal cord, while the cranial cavity contains the brain. The CNS is enclosed and protected by the meninges, a three-layered system of membranes, including a tough, leathery outer layer called the dura mater. The brain is also protected by the skull, and the spinal cord by the vertebrae.

The peripheral nervous system (PNS) is a collective term for the nervous system structures that do not lie within the CNS.[15] The large majority of the axon bundles called nerves are considered to belong to the PNS, even when the cell bodies of the neurons to which they belong reside within the brain or spinal cord. The PNS is divided into somatic and visceral parts. The somatic part consists of the nerves that innervate the skin, joints, and muscles. The cell bodies of somatic sensory neurons lie in dorsal root ganglia of the spinal cord. The visceral part, also known as the autonomic nervous system, contains neurons that innervate the internal organs, blood vessels, and glands. The autonomic nervous

system itself consists of two parts: the sympathetic nervous system and the parasympathetic nervous system. Some authors also include sensory neurons whose cell bodies lie in the periphery (for senses such as hearing) as part of the PNS; others, however, omit them.[16]

The vertebrate nervous system can also be divided into areas called grey matter ("gray matter" in American spelling) and white matter.[17] Grey matter (which is only grey in preserved tissue, and is better described as pink or light brown in living tissue) contains a high proportion of cell bodies of neurons. White matter is composed mainly of myelinated axons, and takes its color from the myelin. White matter includes all of the nerves, and much of the interior of the brain and spinal cord. Grey matter is found in clusters of neurons in the brain and spinal cord, and in cortical layers that line their surfaces. There is an anatomical convention that a cluster of neurons in the brain or spinal cord is called a nucleus, whereas a cluster of neurons in the periphery is called a ganglion.[18] There are, however, a few exceptions to this rule, notably including the part of the forebrain called the basal ganglia.[19]

2.1.3   Comparative anatomy and evolution

Main article: Evolution of nervous systems

Neural precursors in sponges

Sponges have no cells connected to each other by synaptic junctions, that is, no neurons, and therefore no nervous system. They do, however, have homologs of many genes that play key roles in synaptic function. Recent studies have shown that sponge cells express a group of proteins that cluster together to form a structure resembling a postsynaptic density (the signal-receiving part of a synapse).[7] However, the function of this structure is currently unclear. Although sponge cells do not show synaptic transmission, they do communicate with each other via calcium waves and other impulses, which mediate some simple actions such as whole-body contraction.[20]

Radiata

Jellyfish, comb jellies, and related animals have diffuse nerve nets rather than a central nervous system. In most jellyfish the nerve net is spread more or less evenly across the body; in comb jellies it is concentrated near the mouth. The nerve nets consist of sensory neurons, which pick up chemical, tactile, and visual signals; motor neurons, which can activate contractions of the body wall; and intermediate neurons, which detect patterns of activity in the sensory neurons and, in response, send signals to groups of motor neurons. In some cases groups of intermediate neurons are clustered into discrete ganglia.[8]

The development of the nervous system in radiata is relatively unstructured. Unlike bilaterians, radiata only have two primordial cell layers, endoderm and ectoderm. Neurons are generated from a special set of ectodermal precursor cells, which also serve as precursors for every other ectodermal cell type.[21]

Bilateria

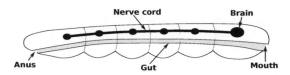

Nervous system of a bilaterian animal, in the form of a nerve cord with segmental enlargements, and a "brain" at the front

The vast majority of existing animals are bilaterians, meaning animals with left and right sides that are approximate mirror images of each other. All bilateria are thought to have descended from a common wormlike ancestor that appeared in the Ediacaran period, 550–600 million years ago.[9] The fundamental bilaterian body form is a tube with a hollow gut cavity running from mouth to anus, and a nerve cord with an enlargement (a "ganglion") for each body segment, with an especially large ganglion at the front, called the "brain".

Even mammals, including humans, show the segmented bilaterian body plan at the level of the nervous system. The spinal cord contains a series of segmental ganglia, each giving rise to motor and sensory nerves that innervate a portion of the body surface and underlying musculature. On the limbs, the layout of the innervation pattern is complex, but on the trunk it gives rise to a series of narrow bands. The top three segments belong to the brain, giving rise to the forebrain, midbrain, and hindbrain.[22]

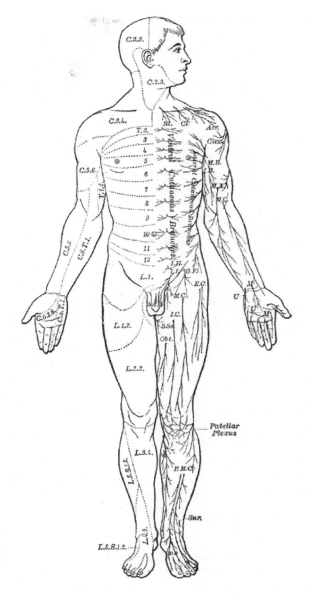

Area of the human body surface innervated by each spinal nerve

Bilaterians can be divided, based on events that occur very early in embryonic development, into two groups (superphyla) called protostomes and deuterostomes.[23] Deuterostomes include vertebrates as well as echinoderms, hemichordates (mainly acorn worms), and Xenoturbellidans.[24] Protostomes, the more diverse group, include arthropods, molluscs, and numerous types of worms. There is a basic difference between the two groups in the placement of the nervous system within the body: protostomes possess a nerve cord on the ventral (usually bottom) side of the body, whereas in deuterostomes the nerve cord is on the dorsal (usually top)

side. In fact, numerous aspects of the body are inverted between the two groups, including the expression patterns of several genes that show dorsal-to-ventral gradients. Most anatomists now consider that the bodies of protostomes and deuterostomes are "flipped over" with respect to each other, a hypothesis that was first proposed by Geoffroy Saint-Hilaire for insects in comparison to vertebrates. Thus insects, for example, have nerve cords that run along the ventral midline of the body, while all vertebrates have spinal cords that run along the dorsal midline.[25]

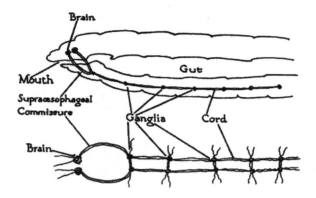

Earthworm nervous system. Top: *side view of the front of the worm.* Bottom: *nervous system in isolation, viewed from above*

Worms

Worms are the simplest bilaterian animals, and reveal the basic structure of the bilaterian nervous system in the most straightforward way. As an example, earthworms have dual nerve cords running along the length of the body and merging at the tail and the mouth. These nerve cords are connected by transverse nerves like the rungs of a ladder. These transverse nerves help coordinate the two sides of the animal. Two ganglia at the head end function similar to a simple brain. Photoreceptors on the animal's eyespots provide sensory information on light and dark.[26]

The nervous system of one very small roundworm, the nematode *Caenorhabditis elegans*, has been completely mapped out in a connectome including its synapses. Every neuron and its cellular lineage has been recorded and most, if not all, of the neural connections are known. In this species, the nervous system is sexually dimorphic; the nervous systems of the two sexes, males and female hermaphrodites, have different numbers of neurons and groups of neurons that perform sex-specific functions. In *C. elegans*, males have exactly 383 neurons, while hermaphrodites have exactly 302 neurons.[27]

Arthropods

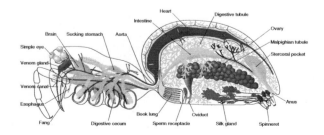

Internal anatomy of a spider, showing the nervous system in blue

Arthropods, such as insects and crustaceans, have a nervous system made up of a series of ganglia, connected by a ventral nerve cord made up of two parallel connectives running along the length of the belly.[28] Typically, each body segment has one ganglion on each side, though some ganglia are fused to form the brain and other large ganglia. The head segment contains the brain, also known as the supraesophageal ganglion. In the insect nervous system, the brain is anatomically divided into the protocerebrum, deutocerebrum, and tritocerebrum. Immediately behind the brain is the subesophageal ganglion, which is composed of three pairs of fused ganglia. It controls the mouthparts, the salivary glands and certain muscles. Many arthropods have well-developed sensory organs, including compound eyes for vision and antennae for olfaction and pheromone sensation. The sensory information from these organs is processed by the brain.

In insects, many neurons have cell bodies that are positioned at the edge of the brain and are electrically passive—the cell bodies serve only to provide metabolic support and do not participate in signalling. A protoplasmic fiber runs from the cell body and branches profusely, with some parts transmitting signals and other parts receiving signals. Thus, most parts of the insect brain have passive cell bodies arranged around the periphery, while the neural signal processing takes place in a tangle of protoplasmic fibers called neuropil, in the interior.[29]

"Identified" neurons

A neuron is called *identified* if it has properties that distinguish it from every other neuron in the same animal—properties such as location, neurotransmitter, gene expression pattern, and connectivity—and if every individual organism belonging to the same species has one and only one neuron with the same set of properties.[30] In vertebrate nervous systems very few neurons are "identified" in this sense—in humans, there are believed to be none—but in simpler nervous systems, some or all neurons may be thus unique. In the roundworm *C. elegans*, whose nervous system is the most thoroughly described of any animal's, every neuron in the body is uniquely identifiable, with the same location and the same connections in every individual worm. One notable consequence of this fact is that the form of the *C. elegans* nervous system is completely specified by the genome, with no experience-dependent plasticity.[27]

The brains of many molluscs and insects also contain substantial numbers of identified neurons.[30] In vertebrates, the best known identified neurons are the gigantic Mauthner cells of fish.[31] Every fish has two Mauthner cells, located in the bottom part of the brainstem, one on the left side and one on the right. Each Mauthner cell has an axon that crosses over, innervating neurons at the same brain level and then travelling down through the spinal cord, making numerous connections as it goes. The synapses generated by a Mauthner cell are so powerful that a single action potential gives rise to a major behavioral response: within milliseconds the fish curves its body into a C-shape, then straightens, thereby propelling itself rapidly forward. Functionally this is a fast escape response, triggered most easily by a strong sound wave or pressure wave impinging on the lateral line organ of the fish. Mauthner cells are not the only identified neurons in fish—there are about 20 more types, including pairs of "Mauthner cell analogs" in each spinal segmental nucleus. Although a Mauthner cell is capable of bringing about an escape response individually, in the context of ordinary behavior other types of cells usually contribute to shaping the amplitude and direction of the response.

Mauthner cells have been described as command neurons. A command neuron is a special type of identified neuron, defined as a neuron that is capable of driving a specific behavior individually.[32] Such neurons appear most commonly in the fast escape systems of various species—the squid giant axon and squid giant synapse, used for pioneering experiments in neurophysiology because of their enormous size, both participate in the fast escape circuit of the squid. The concept of a command neuron has, however, become controversial, because of studies showing that some neurons that initially appeared to fit the description were really only capable of evoking a response in a limited set of circumstances.[33]

2.2 Function

At the most basic level, the function of the nervous system is to send signals from one cell to others, or from one part of the body to others. There are multiple ways that a cell can send signals to other cells. One is by releasing chemicals called hormones into the internal circulation, so that they can diffuse to distant sites. In contrast to this "broadcast" mode of signaling, the nervous system provides "point-to-point" signals—neurons project their axons to specific target areas and make synaptic connections with specific target cells.[34] Thus, neural signaling is capable of a much higher level of specificity than hormonal signaling. It is also much faster: the fastest nerve signals travel at speeds that exceed 100 meters per second.

At a more integrative level, the primary function of the nervous system is to control the body.[3] It does this by extracting information from the environment using sensory receptors, sending signals that encode this information into the central nervous system, processing the information to determine an appropriate response, and sending output signals to muscles or glands to activate the response. The evolution of

a complex nervous system has made it possible for various animal species to have advanced perception abilities such as vision, complex social interactions, rapid coordination of organ systems, and integrated processing of concurrent signals. In humans, the sophistication of the nervous system makes it possible to have language, abstract representation of concepts, transmission of culture, and many other features of human society that would not exist without the human brain.

2.2.1 Neurons and synapses

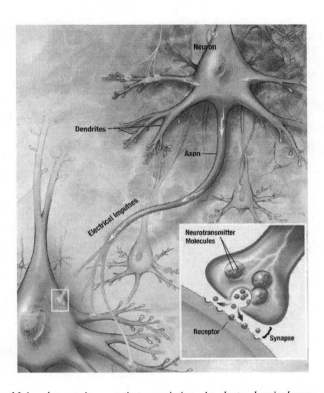

Major elements in synaptic transmission. An electrochemical wave called an action potential travels along the axon of a neuron. When the wave reaches a synapse, it provokes release of a small amount of neurotransmitter molecules, which bind to chemical receptor molecules located in the membrane of the target cell.

Most neurons send signals via their axons, although some types are capable of dendrite-to-dendrite communication. (In fact, the types of neurons called amacrine cells have no axons, and communicate only via their dendrites.) Neural signals propagate along an axon in the form of electrochemical waves called action potentials, which produce cell-to-cell signals at points where axon terminals make synaptic contact with other cells.[35]

Synapses may be electrical or chemical. Electrical synapses make direct electrical connections between neurons,[36] but chemical synapses are much more common, and much more diverse in function.[37] At a chemical synapse, the cell that sends signals is called presynaptic, and the cell that receives signals is called postsynaptic. Both the presynaptic and postsynaptic areas are full of molecular machinery that carries out the signalling process. The presynaptic area contains large numbers of tiny spherical vessels called synaptic vesicles, packed with neurotransmitter chemicals.[35] When the presynaptic terminal is electrically stimulated, an array of molecules embedded in the membrane are activated, and cause the contents of the vesicles to be released into the narrow space between the presynaptic and postsynaptic membranes, called the synaptic cleft. The neurotransmitter then binds to receptors embedded in the postsynaptic membrane, causing them to enter an activated state.[37] Depending on the type of receptor, the resulting effect on the postsynaptic cell may be excitatory, inhibitory, or modulatory in more complex ways. For example, release of the neurotransmitter acetylcholine at a synaptic contact between a motor neuron and a muscle cell induces rapid contraction of the muscle cell.[38] The entire synaptic transmission process takes only a fraction of a millisecond, although the effects on the postsynaptic cell may last much longer (even indefinitely, in cases where the synaptic signal leads to the formation of a memory trace).[11]

There are literally hundreds of different types of synapses. In fact, there are over a hundred known neurotransmitters, and many of them have multiple types of receptors.[39] Many synapses use more than one neurotransmitter—a common arrangement is for a synapse to use one fast-acting small-molecule neurotransmitter such as glutamate or GABA, along with one or more peptide neurotransmitters that play slower-acting modulatory roles. Molecular neuroscientists generally divide receptors into two broad groups: chemically gated ion channels and second messenger systems. When a chemically gated ion channel is activated, it forms a passage that allow specific types of ion to flow across the membrane. Depending on the type of ion, the effect on the target cell may be excitatory or inhibitory. When a second messenger system is activated, it starts a cascade of molecular interactions inside the target cell, which may ultimately produce a wide variety of complex effects, such as increasing or decreasing the sensitivity of the cell to stimuli, or even altering gene transcription.

According to a rule called Dale's principle, which has only a few known exceptions, a neuron releases the same neurotransmitters at all of its synapses.[40] This does not mean, though, that a neuron exerts the same effect on all of its targets, because the effect of a synapse depends not on the neurotransmitter, but on the receptors that it activates.[37] Because different targets can (and frequently do) use different types of receptors, it is possible for a neuron to have excitatory effects on one set of target cells, inhibitory effects on others, and complex modulatory effects on oth-

ers still. Nevertheless, it happens that the two most widely used neurotransmitters, glutamate and GABA, each have largely consistent effects. Glutamate has several widely occurring types of receptors, but all of them are excitatory or modulatory. Similarly, GABA has several widely occurring receptor types, but all of them are inhibitory.[41] Because of this consistency, glutamatergic cells are frequently referred to as "excitatory neurons", and GABAergic cells as "inhibitory neurons". Strictly speaking this is an abuse of terminology—it is the receptors that are excitatory and inhibitory, not the neurons—but it is commonly seen even in scholarly publications.

One very important subset of synapses are capable of forming memory traces by means of long-lasting activity-dependent changes in synaptic strength.[42] The best-known form of neural memory is a process called long-term potentiation (abbreviated LTP), which operates at synapses that use the neurotransmitter glutamate acting on a special type of receptor known as the NMDA receptor.[43] The NMDA receptor has an "associative" property: if the two cells involved in the synapse are both activated at approximately the same time, a channel opens that permits calcium to flow into the target cell.[44] The calcium entry initiates a second messenger cascade that ultimately leads to an increase in the number of glutamate receptors in the target cell, thereby increasing the effective strength of the synapse. This change in strength can last for weeks or longer. Since the discovery of LTP in 1973, many other types of synaptic memory traces have been found, involving increases or decreases in synaptic strength that are induced by varying conditions, and last for variable periods of time.[43] The reward system, that reinforces desired behaviour for example, depends on a variant form of LTP that is conditioned on an extra input coming from a reward-signalling pathway that uses dopamine as neurotransmitter.[45] All these forms of synaptic modifiability, taken collectively, give rise to neural plasticity, that is, to a capability for the nervous system to adapt itself to variations in the environment.

2.2.2 Neural circuits and systems

The basic neuronal function of sending signals to other cells includes a capability for neurons to exchange signals with each other. Networks formed by interconnected groups of neurons are capable of a wide variety of functions, including feature detection, pattern generation and timing,[46] and there are seen to be countless types of information processing possible. Warren McCulloch and Walter Pitts showed in 1943 that even artificial neural networks formed from a greatly simplified mathematical abstraction of a neuron are capable of universal computation.[47]

Historically, for many years the predominant view of the

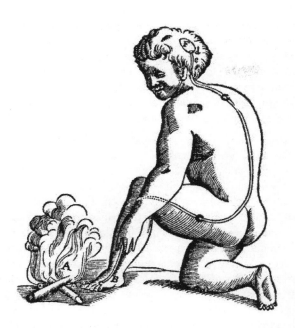

Illustration of pain pathway, from René Descartes's Treatise of Man

chains, and partly in terms of intrinsically generated activity patterns—both types of activity interact with each other to generate the full repertoire of behavior.[53]

Reflexes and other stimulus-response circuits

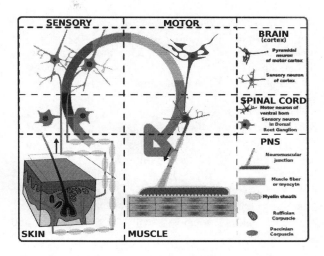

Simplified schema of basic nervous system function: signals are picked up by sensory receptors and sent to the spinal cord and brain, where processing occurs that results in signals sent back to the spinal cord and then out to motor neurons

function of the nervous system was as a stimulus-response associator.[48] In this conception, neural processing begins with stimuli that activate sensory neurons, producing signals that propagate through chains of connections in the spinal cord and brain, giving rise eventually to activation of motor neurons and thereby to muscle contraction, i.e., to overt responses. Descartes believed that all of the behaviors of animals, and most of the behaviors of humans, could be explained in terms of stimulus-response circuits, although he also believed that higher cognitive functions such as language were not capable of being explained mechanistically.[49] Charles Sherrington, in his influential 1906 book *The Integrative Action of the Nervous System*,[48] developed the concept of stimulus-response mechanisms in much more detail, and Behaviorism, the school of thought that dominated Psychology through the middle of the 20th century, attempted to explain every aspect of human behavior in stimulus-response terms.[50]

However, experimental studies of electrophysiology, beginning in the early 20th century and reaching high productivity by the 1940s, showed that the nervous system contains many mechanisms for generating patterns of activity intrinsically, without requiring an external stimulus.[51] Neurons were found to be capable of producing regular sequences of action potentials, or sequences of bursts, even in complete isolation.[52] When intrinsically active neurons are connected to each other in complex circuits, the possibilities for generating intricate temporal patterns become far more extensive.[46] A modern conception views the function of the nervous system partly in terms of stimulus-response

The simplest type of neural circuit is a reflex arc, which begins with a sensory input and ends with a motor output, passing through a sequence of neurons connected in series.[54] This can be shown in the "withdrawal reflex" causing a hand to jerk back after a hot stove is touched. The circuit begins with sensory receptors in the skin that are activated by harmful levels of heat: a special type of molecular structure embedded in the membrane causes heat to change the electrical field across the membrane. If the change in electrical potential is large enough to pass the given threshold, it evokes an action potential, which is transmitted along the axon of the receptor cell, into the spinal cord. There the axon makes excitatory synaptic contacts with other cells, some of which project (send axonal output) to the same region of the spinal cord, others projecting into the brain. One target is a set of spinal interneurons that project to motor neurons controlling the arm muscles. The interneurons excite the motor neurons, and if the excitation is strong enough, some of the motor neurons generate action potentials, which travel down their axons to the point where they make excitatory synaptic contacts with muscle cells. The excitatory signals induce contraction of the muscle cells, which causes the joint angles in the arm to change, pulling the arm away.

In reality, this straightforward schema is subject to numerous complications.[54] Although for the simplest reflexes there are short neural paths from sensory neuron to motor neuron, there are also other nearby neurons that participate in the circuit and modulate the response. Furthermore, there are projections from the brain to the spinal cord that are capable of enhancing or inhibiting the reflex.

Although the simplest reflexes may be mediated by circuits lying entirely within the spinal cord, more complex responses rely on signal processing in the brain.[55] For example, when an object in the periphery of the visual field moves, and a person looks toward it many stages of signal processing are initiated. The initial sensory response, in the retina of the eye, and the final motor response, in the oculomotor nuclei of the brain stem, are not all that different from those in a simple reflex, but the intermediate stages are completely different. Instead of a one or two step chain of processing, the visual signals pass through perhaps a dozen stages of integration, involving the thalamus, cerebral cortex, basal ganglia, superior colliculus, cerebellum, and several brainstem nuclei. These areas perform signal-processing functions that include feature detection, perceptual analysis, memory recall, decision-making, and motor planning.[56]

Feature detection is the ability to extract biologically relevant information from combinations of sensory signals.[57] In the visual system, for example, sensory receptors in the retina of the eye are only individually capable of detecting "points of light" in the outside world.[58] Second-level visual neurons receive input from groups of primary receptors, higher-level neurons receive input from groups of second-level neurons, and so on, forming a hierarchy of processing stages. At each stage, important information is extracted from the signal ensemble and unimportant information is discarded. By the end of the process, input signals representing "points of light" have been transformed into a neural representation of objects in the surrounding world and their properties. The most sophisticated sensory processing occurs inside the brain, but complex feature extraction also takes place in the spinal cord and in peripheral sensory organs such as the retina.

Intrinsic pattern generation

Although stimulus-response mechanisms are the easiest to understand, the nervous system is also capable of controlling the body in ways that do not require an external stimulus, by means of internally generated rhythms of activity. Because of the variety of voltage-sensitive ion channels that can be embedded in the membrane of a neuron, many types of neurons are capable, even in isolation, of generating rhythmic sequences of action potentials, or rhythmic alternations between high-rate bursting and quiescence. When neurons that are intrinsically rhythmic are connected

to each other by excitatory or inhibitory synapses, the resulting networks are capable of a wide variety of dynamical behaviors, including attractor dynamics, periodicity, and even chaos. A network of neurons that uses its internal structure to generate temporally structured output, without requiring a corresponding temporally structured stimulus, is called a central pattern generator.

Internal pattern generation operates on a wide range of time scales, from milliseconds to hours or longer. One of the most important types of temporal pattern is circadian rhythmicity—that is, rhythmicity with a period of approximately 24 hours. All animals that have been studied show circadian fluctuations in neural activity, which control circadian alternations in behavior such as the sleep-wake cycle. Experimental studies dating from the 1990s have shown that circadian rhythms are generated by a "genetic clock" consisting of a special set of genes whose expression level rises and falls over the course of the day. Animals as diverse as insects and vertebrates share a similar genetic clock system. The circadian clock is influenced by light but continues to operate even when light levels are held constant and no other external time-of-day cues are available. The clock genes are expressed in many parts of the nervous system as well as many peripheral organs, but in mammals all of these "tissue clocks" are kept in synchrony by signals that emanate from a master timekeeper in a tiny part of the brain called the suprachiasmatic nucleus.

2.2.3 Mirror neurons

A mirror neuron is a neuron that fires both when an animal acts and when the animal observes the same action performed by another.[59][60][61] Thus, the neuron "mirrors" the behavior of the other, as though the observer were itself acting. Such neurons have been directly observed in primate species.[62] Birds have been shown to have imitative resonance behaviors and neurological evidence suggests the presence of some form of mirroring system.[62][63] In humans, brain activity consistent with that of mirror neurons has been found in the premotor cortex, the supplementary motor area, the primary somatosensory cortex and the inferior parietal cortex.[64] The function of the mirror system is a subject of much speculation. Many researchers in cognitive neuroscience and cognitive psychology consider that this system provides the physiological mechanism for the perception/action coupling (see the common coding theory).[61] They argue that mirror neurons may be important for understanding the actions of other people, and for learning new skills by imitation. Some researchers also speculate that mirror systems may simulate observed actions, and thus contribute to theory of mind skills,[65][66] while others relate mirror neurons to language abilities.[67] However, to date, no widely accepted neural or computational models have been put forward to describe how mirror neuron activity supports cognitive functions such as imitation.[68] There are neuroscientists who caution that the claims being made for the role of mirror neurons are not supported by adequate research.[69][70]

2.3 Development

In vertebrates, landmarks of embryonic neural development include the birth and differentiation of neurons from stem cell precursors, the migration of immature neurons from their birthplaces in the embryo to their final positions, outgrowth of axons from neurons and guidance of the motile growth cone through the embryo towards postsynaptic partners, the generation of synapses between these axons and their postsynaptic partners, and finally the lifelong changes in synapses which are thought to underlie learning and memory.[71]

All bilaterian animals at an early stage of development form a gastrula, which is polarized, with one end called the animal pole and the other the vegetal pole. The gastrula has the shape of a disk with three layers of cells, an inner layer called the endoderm, which gives rise to the lining of most internal organs, a middle layer called the mesoderm, which gives rise to the bones and muscles, and an outer layer called the ectoderm, which gives rise to the skin and nervous system.[72]

In vertebrates, the first sign of the nervous system is the appearance of a thin strip of cells along the center of the back, called the neural plate. The inner portion of the neural plate (along the midline) is destined to become the central nervous system (CNS), the outer portion the peripheral nervous system (PNS). As development proceeds, a fold called the neural groove appears along the midline. This fold deepens, and then closes up at the top. At this point the future CNS appears as a cylindrical structure called the neural tube, whereas the future PNS appears as two strips of tissue called the neural crest, running lengthwise above the neural tube. The sequence of stages from neural plate to neural tube and neural crest is known as neurulation.

In the early 20th century, a set of famous experiments by Hans Spemann and Hilde Mangold showed that the formation of nervous tissue is "induced" by signals from a group of mesodermal cells called the *organizer region*.[71] For decades, though, the nature of the induction process defeated every attempt to figure it out, until finally it was resolved by genetic approaches in the 1990s. Induction of neural tissue requires inhibition of the gene for a so-called bone morphogenetic protein, or BMP. Specifically the protein BMP4 appears to be involved. Two proteins called Noggin and Chordin, both secreted by the mesoderm, are capable of inhibiting BMP4 and thereby inducing ectoderm to turn into neural tissue. It appears that a similar molecular mechanism is involved for widely disparate types of animals, including arthropods as well as vertebrates. In some animals, however, another type of molecule called Fibroblast Growth Factor or FGF may also play an important role in induction.

Induction of neural tissues causes formation of neural precursor cells, called neuroblasts.[73] In drosophila, neuroblasts divide asymmetrically, so that one product is a "ganglion mother cell" (GMC), and the other is a neuroblast. A GMC divides once, to give rise to either a pair of neurons or a pair of glial cells. In all, a neuroblast is capable of generating an indefinite number of neurons or glia.

As shown in a 2008 study, one factor common to all bilateral organisms (including humans) is a family of secreted signaling molecules called neurotrophins which regulate the growth and survival of neurons.[74] Zhu et al. identified DNT1, the first neurotrophin found in flies. DNT1 shares structural similarity with all known neurotrophins and is a key factor in the fate of neurons in Drosophila. Because neurotrophins have now been identified in both vertebrate and invertebrates, this evidence suggests that neurotrophins were present in an ancestor common to bilateral organisms and may represent a common mechanism for nervous system formation.

2.4 Pathology

Main article: Neurology
See also: Psychiatry

The central nervous system is protected by major physical and chemical barriers. Physically, the brain and spinal cord are surrounded by tough meningeal membranes, and enclosed in the bones of the skull and spinal vertebrae, which combine to form a strong physical shield. Chemically, the brain and spinal cord are isolated by the so-called blood–brain barrier, which prevents most types of chemicals from moving from the bloodstream into the interior of the CNS. These protections make the CNS less susceptible in many ways than the PNS; the flip side, however, is that damage to the CNS tends to have more serious consequences.

Although nerves tend to lie deep under the skin except in a few places such as the ulnar nerve near the elbow joint, they are still relatively exposed to physical damage, which can cause pain, loss of sensation, or loss of muscle control. Damage to nerves can also be caused by swelling or bruises at places where a nerve passes through a tight bony channel, as happens in carpal tunnel syndrome. If a nerve is completely transected, it will often regenerate, but for long nerves this process may take months to complete. In addition to physical damage, peripheral neuropathy may be caused by many other medical problems, including genetic conditions, metabolic conditions such as diabetes, inflammatory conditions such as Guillain–Barré syndrome, vitamin deficiency, infectious diseases such as leprosy or shingles, or poisoning by toxins such as heavy metals. Many cases have no cause that can be identified, and are referred to as idiopathic. It is also possible for nerves to lose function temporarily, resulting in numbness as stiffness—common causes include mechanical pressure, a drop in temperature, or chemical interactions with local anesthetic drugs such as lidocaine.

Physical damage to the spinal cord may result in loss of sensation or movement. If an injury to the spine produces nothing worse than swelling, the symptoms may be transient, but if nerve fibers in the spine are actually destroyed, the loss of function is usually permanent. Experimental studies have shown that spinal nerve fibers attempt to regrow in the same way as nerve fibers, but in the spinal cord, tissue destruction usually produces scar tissue that cannot be penetrated by the regrowing nerves.

2.5   References

[1] "Nervous System". *Columbia Encyclopedia*. Columbia University Press.

[2] Herculano-Houzel S, Avelino-de-Souza K, et al. (2014). "The elephant brain in numbers". *Front Neuroanat* **8**: 46. doi:10.3389/fnana.2014.00046. PMC 4053853. PMID 24971054.

[3] Kandel ER, Schwartz JH, Jessel TM, eds. (2000). "Ch. 2: Nerve cells and behavior". *Principles of Neural Science*. McGraw-Hill Professional. ISBN 978-0-8385-7701-1.

[4] Finger S (2001). "Ch. 1: The brain in antiquity". *Origins of neuroscience: a history of explorations into brain function*. Oxford Univ. Press. ISBN 978-0-19-514694-3.

[5] Finger, pp. 43–50

[6] Nikoletseas Michael M. (2010) Behavioral and Neural Plasticity. ISBN 978-1453789452

[7] Sakarya O, Armstrong KA, Adamska M, et al. (2007). Vosshall L, ed. "A post-synaptic scaffold at the origin of the animal kingdom". *PLoS ONE* **2** (6): e506. doi:10.1371/journal.pone.0000506. PMC 1876816. PMID 17551586.

[8] Ruppert EE, Fox RS, Barnes RD (2004). *Invertebrate Zoology* (7 ed.). Brooks / Cole. pp. 111–124. ISBN 0-03-025982-7.

[9] Balavoine G (2003). "The segmented Urbilateria: A testable scenario". *Int Comp Biology* **43** (1): 137–47. doi:10.1093/icb/43.1.137.

[10] Ortega-Hernandez, Javier (29 Feb 2016), *Our 500 million-year-old nervous system fossil shines a light on animal evolution*, The Conversation US, Inc., retrieved 6 Mar 2016

[11] Kandel ER, Schwartz JH, Jessel TM, eds. (2000). "Ch. 4: The cytology of neurons". *Principles of Neural Science*. McGraw-Hill Professional. ISBN 978-0-8385-7701-1.

[12] Allen NJ, Barres BA (2009). "Neuroscience: Glia - more than just brain glue". *Nature* **457** (7230): 675–7. doi:10.1038/457675a. PMID 19194443.

[13] Azevedo FA, Carvalho LR, Grinberg LT, et al. (2009). "Equal numbers of neuronal and nonneuronal cells make the human brain an isometrically scaled-up primate brain". *J. Comp. Neurol.* **513** (5): 532–41. doi:10.1002/cne.21974. PMID 19226510.

[14] Kandel ER, Schwartz JH, Jessel TM, eds. (2000). "Ch. 17: The anatomical organization of the central nervous system". *Principles of Neural Science*. McGraw-Hill Professional. ISBN 978-0-8385-7701-1.

[15] Standring, Susan (Editor-in-chief) (2005). *Gray's Anatomy* (39th ed.). Elsevier Churchill Livingstone. pp. 233–234. ISBN 978-0-443-07168-3.

[16] Hubbard JI (1974). *The peripheral nervous system*. Plenum Press. p. vii. ISBN 978-0-306-30764-5.

[17] Purves D, Augustine GJ, Fitzpatrick D, Hall WC, LaMantia A-S, McNamara JO, White LE (2008). *Neuroscience. 4th ed.* Sinauer Associates. pp. 15–16.

[18] "ganglion" at *Dorland's Medical Dictionary*

[19] Afifi AK (July 1994). "Basal ganglia: functional anatomy and physiology. Part 1". *J. Child Neurol.* **9** (3): 249–60. doi:10.1177/088307389400900306. PMID 7930403.

[20] Jacobs DK1, Nakanishi N, Yuan D; et al. (2007). "Evolution of sensory structures in basal metazoa". *Integr Comp Biol* **47** (5): 712–723. doi:10.1093/icb/icm094. PMID 21669752.

[21] Sanes DH, Reh TA, Harris WA (2006). *Development of the nervous system*. Academic Press. pp. 3–4. ISBN 978-0-12-618621-5.

[22] Ghysen A (2003). "The origin and evolution of the nervous system". *Int. J. Dev. Biol.* **47** (7–8): 555–62. PMID 14756331.

[23] Erwin DH, Davidson EH (July 2002). "The last common bilaterian ancestor". *Development* **129** (13): 3021–32. PMID 12070079.

[24] Bourlat SJ, Juliusdottir T, Lowe CJ, et al. (November 2006). "Deuterostome phylogeny reveals monophyletic chordates and the new phylum Xenoturbellida". *Nature* **444** (7115): 85–8. doi:10.1038/nature05241. PMID 17051155.

[25] Lichtneckert R, Reichert H (May 2005). "Insights into the urbilaterian brain: conserved genetic patterning mechanisms in insect and vertebrate brain development". *Heredity* **94** (5): 465–77. doi:10.1038/sj.hdy.6800664. PMID 15770230.

[26] ADEY WR (February 1951). "The nervous system of the earthworm Megascolex". *J. Comp. Neurol.* **94** (1): 57–103. doi:10.1002/cne.900940104. PMID 14814220.

[27] "Wormbook: Specification of the nervous system".

[28] Chapman RF (1998). "Ch. 20: Nervous system". *The insects: structure and function*. Cambridge University Press. pp. 533–568. ISBN 978-0-521-57890-5.

[29] Chapman, p. 546

[30] Hoyle G, Wiersma CAG (1977). *Identified neurons and behavior of arthropods*. Plenum Press. ISBN 978-0-306-31001-0.

[31] Stein PSG (1999). *Neurons, Networks, and Motor Behavior*. MIT Press. pp. 38–44. ISBN 978-0-262-69227-4.

[32] Stein, p. 112

[33] Simmons PJ, Young D (1999). *Nerve cells and animal behaviour*. Cambridge University Press. p. 43. ISBN 978-0-521-62726-9.

[34] Gray PO (2006). *Psychology* (5 ed.). Macmillan. p. 170. ISBN 978-0-7167-7690-1.

[35] Kandel ER, Schwartz JH, Jessel TM, eds. (2000). "Ch. 9: Propagated signaling: the action potential". *Principles of Neural Science*. McGraw-Hill Professional. ISBN 978-0-8385-7701-1.

[36] Hormuzdi SG, Filippov MA, Mitropoulou G, et al. (2004). "Electrical synapses: a dynamic signaling system that shapes the activity of neuronal networks". *Biochim. Biophys. Acta* **1662** (1–2): 113–37. doi:10.1016/j.bbamem.2003.10.023. PMID 15033583.

[37] Kandel ER, Schwartz JH, Jessel TM, eds. (2000). "Ch. 10: Overview of synaptic transmission". *Principles of Neural Science*. McGraw-Hill Professional. ISBN 978-0-8385-7701-1.

[38] Kandel ER, Schwartz JH, Jessel TM, eds. (2000). "Ch. 11: Signaling at the nerve-muscle synapse". *Principles of Neural Science*. McGraw-Hill Professional. ISBN 978-0-8385-7701-1.

[39] Kandel ER, Schwartz JH, Jessel TM, eds. (2000). "Ch. 15: Neurotransmitters". *Principles of Neural Science*. McGraw-Hill Professional. ISBN 978-0-8385-7701-1.

[40] Strata P, Harvey R (1999). "Dale's principle". *Brain Res. Bull.* **50** (5–6): 349–50. doi:10.1016/S0361-9230(99)00100-8. PMID 10643431.

[41] There are a number of exceptional situations in which GABA has been found to have excitatory effects, mainly during early development. For a review see Marty A, Llano I (June 2005). "Excitatory effects of GABA in established brain networks". *Trends Neurosci.* **28** (6): 284–9. doi:10.1016/j.tins.2005.04.003. PMID 15927683.

[42] Paradiso MA; Bear MF; Connors BW (2007). *Neuroscience: Exploring the Brain*. Lippincott Williams & Wilkins. p. 718. ISBN 0-7817-6003-8.

[43] Cooke SF, Bliss TV (2006). "Plasticity in the human central nervous system". *Brain* **129** (Pt 7): 1659–73. doi:10.1093/brain/awl082. PMID 16672292.

[44] Bliss TV, Collingridge GL (January 1993). "A synaptic model of memory: long-term potentiation in the hippocampus". *Nature* **361** (6407): 31–9. doi:10.1038/361031a0. PMID 8421494.

[45] Kauer JA, Malenka RC (November 2007). "Synaptic plasticity and addiction". *Nat. Rev. Neurosci.* **8** (11): 844–58. doi:10.1038/nrn2234. PMID 17948030.

[46] Dayan P, Abbott LF (2005). *Theoretical Neuroscience: Computational and Mathematical Modeling of Neural Systems*. MIT Press. ISBN 978-0-262-54185-5.

[47] McCulloch WS, Pitts W (1943). "A logical calculus of the ideas immanent in nervous activity". *Bull. Math. Biophys.* **5** (4): 115–133. doi:10.1007/BF02478259.

[48] Sherrington CS (1906). *The Integrative Action of the Nervous System*. Scribner.

[49] Descartes R (1989). *Passions of the Soul*. Voss S. Hackett. ISBN 978-0-87220-035-7.

[50] Baum WM (2005). *Understanding behaviorism: Behavior, Culture and Evolution*. Blackwell. ISBN 978-1-4051-1262-8.

[51] Piccolino M (November 2002). "Fifty years of the Hodgkin-Huxley era". *Trends Neurosci.* **25** (11): 552–3. doi:10.1016/S0166-2236(02)02276-2. PMID 12392928.

[52] Johnston D, Wu SM (1995). *Foundations of cellular neurophysiology*. MIT Press. ISBN 978-0-262-10053-3.

[53] Simmons PJ, Young D (1999). "Ch 1.: Introduction". *Nerve cells and animal behaviour*. Cambridge Univ. Press. ISBN 978-0-521-62726-9.

[54] Kandel ER, Schwartz JH, Jessel TM, eds. (2000). "Ch. 36: Spinal reflexes". *Principles of Neural Science*. McGraw-Hill Professional. ISBN 978-0-8385-7701-1.

[55] Kandel ER, Schwartz JH, Jessel TM, eds. (2000). "Ch. 38: Voluntary movement". *Principles of Neural Science*. McGraw-Hill Professional. ISBN 978-0-8385-7701-1.

[56] Kandel ER, Schwartz JH, Jessel TM, eds. (2000). "Ch. 39: The control of gaze". *Principles of Neural Science*. McGraw-Hill Professional. ISBN 978-0-8385-7701-1.

[57] Kandel ER, Schwartz JH, Jessel TM, eds. (2000). "Ch. 21: Coding of sensory information". *Principles of Neural Science*. McGraw-Hill Professional. ISBN 978-0-8385-7701-1.

[58] Kandel ER, Schwartz JH, Jessel TM, eds. (2000). "Ch. 25: Constructing the visual image". *Principles of Neural Science*. McGraw-Hill Professional. ISBN 978-0-8385-7701-1.

[59] Rizzolatti, Giacomo; Craighero, Laila (2004). "The mirror-neuron system" (PDF). *Annual Review of Neuroscience* **27**: 169–192. doi:10.1146/annurev.neuro.27.070203.144230. PMID 15217330.

[60] Keysers, Christian (2010). "Mirror Neurons" (PDF). *Current Biology* **19** (21): R971–973. doi:10.1016/j.cub.2009.08.026. PMID 19922849.

[61] Keysers, Christian (2011-06-23). *The Empathic Brain*. Kindle.

[62] Rizzolatti, Giacomo; Fadiga, Luciano (1999). "Resonance Behaviors and Mirror Neurons". *Italiennes de Biologie* **137**: 85–100.

[63] Akins, Chana; Klein, Edward (2002). "Imitative Learning in Japanese Quail using Bidirectional Control Procedure". *Animal Learning and Behavior* **30** (3): 275–281. doi:10.3758/bf03192836. PMID 12391793.

[64] Molenberghs P, Cunnington R, Mattingley J (July 2009). "Is the mirror neuron system involved in imitation? A short review and meta-analysis.". *Neuroscience & Biobehavioral Reviews* **33** (1): 975–980. doi:10.1016/j.neubiorev.2009.03.010.

[65] Keysers, Christian; Gazzola, Valeria (2006). "Progress in Brain Research" (PDF). Bcn-nic.nl.

[66] Michael Arbib, *The Mirror System Hypothesis. Linking Language to Theory of Mind*, 2005, retrieved 2006-02-17

[67] Théoret, Hugo; Pascual-Leone, Alvaro (2002). "Language Acquisition: Do as You Hear". *Current Biology* **12** (21): R736–7. doi:10.1016/S0960-9822(02)01251-4. PMID 12419204.

[68] Dinstein I, Thomas C, Behrmann M, Heeger DJ (2008). "A mirror up to nature". *Curr Biol* **18** (1): R13–8. doi:10.1016/j.cub.2007.11.004. PMC 2517574. PMID 18177704.

[69] Hickok, G. (July 21, 2009). "Eight Problems for the Mirror Neuron Theory of Action Understanding in Monkeys and Humans". *Journal of Cognitive Neuroscience* (Press release). p. 1229-1243.

[70] Heyes, Cecilia (2009). "Where do mirror neurons come from?" (PDF). *Neuroscience and Biobehavioral Reviews*.

[71] Kandel ER, Schwartz JH, Jessel TM, eds. (2000). "Ch. 52: The induction and patterning of the nervous system". *Principles of Neural Science*. McGraw-Hill Professional. ISBN 978-0-8385-7701-1.

[72] Sanes DH, Reh TH, Harris WA (2006). "Ch. 1, *Neural induction*". *Development of the Nervous System*. Elsevier Academic Press. ISBN 978-0-12-618621-5.

[73] Kandel ER, Schwartz JH, Jessel TM, eds. (2000). "Ch. 53: The formation and survival of nerve cells". *Principles of Neural Science*. McGraw-Hill Professional. ISBN 978-0-8385-7701-1.

[74] Zhu B, Pennack JA, McQuilton P, Forero MG, Mizuguchi K, Sutcliffe B, Gu CJ, Fenton JC, Hidalgo A (Nov 2008). Bate, Michael, ed. "Drosophila neurotrophins reveal a common mechanism for nervous system formation". *PLoS Biol* **6** (11): e284. doi:10.1371/journal.pbio.0060284. PMC 2586362. PMID 19018662.

2.6 Further reading

- Nervous system William E. Skaggs, Scholarpedia

2.7 External links

- The Nervous System at Wikibooks (human)
- Nervous System at Wikibooks (non-human)
- The Human Brain Project Homepage

Chapter 3

Supernatural

This article is about the philosophical concept. For other uses, see Supernatural (disambiguation).
Not to be confused with Paranormal or Supernatural (U.S. TV series).

The **supernatural** (Medieval Latin: *supernātūrālis*:

One of the many supernatural acts attributed to Jesus, walking on water. Art by François Boucher Cathédrale Saint-Louis (1766) Versailles

supra "above" + *naturalis* "natural", first used: 1520–1530 AD)[1][2] is defined as being incapable to be explained by science or the laws of nature, characteristic or relating to ghosts, gods or other supernatural beings or to appear beyond nature.[3]

3.1 Views

See also: Anthropology of religion

The metaphysical considerations of the existence of the supernatural can be difficult to approach as an exercise in philosophy or theology because any dependencies on its antithesis, the natural, will ultimately have to be inverted or rejected.

One complicating factor is that there is disagreement about the definition of "natural" and the limits of naturalism. Concepts in the supernatural domain are closely related to concepts in religious spirituality and occultism or spiritualism.

> For sometimes we use the word *nature* for that *Author of nature* whom the schoolmen, harshly enough, call *natura naturans*, as when it is said that *nature* hath made man partly corporeal and partly immaterial. Sometimes we mean by the *nature* of a thing the *essence*, or that which the schoolmen scruple not to call the *quiddity* of a thing, namely, the *attribute* or *attributes* on whose score it is what it is, whether the thing be corporeal or not, as when we attempt to define the *nature* of an *angel*, or of a *triangle*, or of a *fluid* body, as such. Sometimes we take *nature* for an internal principle of motion, as when we say that a stone let fall in the air is by *nature* carried towards the centre of the earth, and, on the contrary, that fire or flame does *naturally* move upwards toward heaven. Sometimes we understand by *nature* the established course of things, as when we say that *nature* makes the night succeed the day, *nature* hath made respiration necessary to the life of men. Sometimes we take *nature* for an aggregate of powers belonging to a body, especially a living one, as when physicians say that *nature* is strong or weak or spent, or that in such or such diseases

nature left to herself will do the cure. Sometimes we take nature for the universe, or system of the corporeal works of God, as when it is said of a phoenix, or a chimera, that there is no such thing in *nature*, i.e. in the world. And sometimes too, and that most commonly, we would express by *nature* a semi-deity or other strange kind of being, such as this discourse examines the notion of.

And besides these more absolute acceptions, if I may so call them, of the word *nature*, it has divers others (more relative), as *nature* is wont to be set or in opposition or contradistinction to other things, as when we say of a stone when it falls downwards that it does it by a *natural motion*, but that if it be thrown upwards its motion that way is *violent*. So chemists distinguish vitriol into *natural* and *fictitious*, or made by art, i.e. by the intervention of human power or skill; so it is said that water, kept suspended in a sucking pump, is not in its *natural* place, as that is which is stagnant in the well. We say also that wicked men are still in the state of *nature*, but the regenerate in a state of *grace*; that cures wrought by medicines are natural operations; but the miraculous ones wrought by Christ and his apostles were *supernatural*.[4]

— Robert Boyle, A Free Enquiry into the Vulgarly Received Notion of Nature

The term "supernatural" is often used interchangeably with paranormal or preternatural — the latter typically limited to an adjective for describing abilities which appear to exceed the bounds of possibility.[5] Epistemologically, the relationship between the supernatural and the natural is indistinct in terms of natural phenomena that, *ex hypothesi*, violate the laws of nature, in so far as such laws are realistically accountable.

> Parapsychologists use the term psi to refer to an assumed unitary force underlying the phenomena they study. Psi is defined in the *Journal of Parapsychology* as "a general term used to identify personal factors or processes in nature which transcend accepted laws" (1948: 311) and "which are non-physical in nature" (1962:310), and it is used to cover both extrasensory perception (ESP), an "awareness of or response to an external event or influence not apprehended by sensory means" (1962:309) or inferred from sensory knowledge, and psychokinesis (PK), "the direct influence exerted on a physical system by a subject without any known intermediate

energy or instrumentation" (1945:305).[6]
— Michael Winkelman, Current Anthropology

Many supporters of supernatural explanations believe that past, present, and future complexities and mysteries of the universe cannot be explained solely by naturalistic means and argue that it is reasonable to assume that a non-natural entity or entities resolve the unexplained.

Views on the "supernatural" vary, for example it may be seen as:

- **indistinct from nature**. From this perspective, some events occur according to the laws of nature, and others occur according to a separate set of principles external to known nature. For example, in Scholasticism, it was believed that God was capable of performing any miracle so long as it didn't lead to a logical contradiction. Some religions posit immanent deities, however, and do not have a tradition analogous to the supernatural; some believe that everything anyone experiences occurs by the will (occasionalism), in the mind (neoplatonism), or as a part (nondualism) of a more fundamental divine reality (platonism).

- **incorrectly attributed to nature**. Others believe that all events have natural and only natural causes. They believe that human beings ascribe supernatural attributes to purely natural events, such as lightning, rainbows, floods, and the origin of life.[7][8]

3.2 Demise of

The available evidence suggests that there is a significant decline in belief in the supernatural as a meaningful reality for the majority of people living in modern societies.[9]

3.3 Philosophy

See also: Naturalism (philosophy)

The supernatural is a feature of the philosophical traditions of Neoplatonism[10] and Scholasticism.[11] In contrast, the philosophy of Metaphysical naturalism argues for the conclusion that there are no supernatural entities, object, or powers.

3.4 Religion

Main article: Magic and religion

Most religions include elements of belief in the supernatural (e.g. miraculous works by recognized Saints, the Assumption of Mary, etc.) while also often featuring prominently in the study of the paranormal and occultism.

3.4.1 Christian theology

The patron saint of air travelers, aviators, astronauts, people with a mental handicap, test takers, and poor students is Saint Joseph of Cupertino, who is said to have been gifted with supernatural flight.[12]

Main article: Supernatural order

In Catholic theology, the supernatural order is, according to New Advent, defined as "the ensemble of effects exceeding the powers of the created universe and gratuitously produced by God for the purpose of raising the rational creature above its native sphere to a God-like life and destiny."[13] The *Modern Catholic Dictionary* defines it as "[t]he sum total of heavenly destiny and all the divinely established means of reaching that destiny, which surpass the mere powers and capacities of human nature."[14]

3.4.2 Process theology

Main article: Process theology

Process theology is a school of thought influenced by the metaphysical process philosophy of Alfred North Whitehead (1861–1947) and further developed by Charles Hartshorne (1897–2000).

It is not possible, in process metaphysics, to conceive divine activity as a "supernatural" intervention into the "natural" order of events. Process theists usually regard the distinction between the supernatural and the natural as a by-product of the doctrine of creation *ex nihilo*. In process thought, there is no such thing as a realm of the natural in contrast to that which is supernatural. On the other hand, if "the natural" is defined more neutrally as "what is in the nature of things," then process metaphysics characterizes the natural as the creative activity of actual entities. In Whitehead's words, "It lies in the nature of things that the many enter into complex unity" (Whitehead 1978, 21). It is tempting to emphasize process theism's denial of the supernatural and thereby highlight what the process God cannot do in comparison to what the traditional God can do (that is, to bring something from nothing). In fairness, however, equal stress should be placed on process theism's denial of the natural (as traditionally conceived) so that one may highlight what the creatures cannot do, in traditional theism, in comparison to what they can do in process metaphysics (that is, to be part creators of the world with God).[15]
— Donald Viney, "Process Theism" in *The Stanford Encyclopedia of Philosophy*

3.5 See also

- Magical thinking
- Metaphysical naturalism
- Non-physical entity
- Preternatural

- Religious naturalism

- Supernaturalism

3.6   References

[1] "Supernatural | Define Supernatural at Dictionary.com". Dictionary.reference.com. Retrieved 2013-06-30.

[2] "Online Etymology Dictionary". Etymonline.com. Retrieved 2013-06-30.

[3] "Supernatural | Define Supernatural at Merriam-Webster.com".

[4] Boyle, Robert; Stewart, M.A. (1991). *Selected Philosophical Papers of Robert Boyle*. HPC Classics Series. Hackett. pp. 176–177. ISBN 978-0-87220-122-4. LCCN 91025480.

[5] *The paranormal*. Books.google.com. Retrieved July 26, 2010.

[6] Winkelman, M.; et al. (February 1982). "Magic: A Theoretical Reassessment [and Comments and Replies]". *Current Anthropology* **23** (1): 37–66. doi:10.1086/202778. JSTOR 274255.

[7] Zhong Yang Yan Jiu Yuan; Min Tsu Hsüeh Yen Chiu So (1976). *Bulletin of the Institute of Ethnology, Academia Sinica, Issues 42–44*.

[8] Ellis, B.J.; Bjorklund, D.F. (2004). *Origins of the Social Mind: Evolutionary Psychology and Child Development*. Guilford Publications. p. 413. ISBN 9781593851033. LCCN 2004022693.

[9] https://books.google.co.uk/books?id=Zxc_EDPFgCEC& printsec=frontcover&dq=supernatural&hl=en&sa=X& redir_esc=y#v=onepage&q=supernatural&f=false

[10] "The eventual development of a clear concept of the supernatural in Christian theology was promoted both by dialogues with heretics and by the influence of Neoplatonic philosophy." Benson Saler: *Supernatural as a Western Category*. Ethos 5 (1977): 44

[11] "Saint Thomas's important contribution to the emergence of a technical theology of the supernatural represents a special development of the concept of surpassing effects. Saint Thomas and others of the Scholastics have left us as one of their legacies a dichotomy between the natural and the supernatural that is theologically rooted in the distinction between the Order of Nature and the Order of Grace." Benson Saler: *Supernatural as a Western Category*. Ethos 5 (1977): 47–48

[12] Pastrovicchi, Angelo (1918). Rev. Francis S. Laing, ed. *St. Joseph of Copertino*. St. Louis: B.Herder. p. iv. ISBN 0-89555-135-7.

[13] Sollier, J. "Supernatural Order". Robert Appleton Company. Retrieved 2008-09-11.

[14] Hardon, Fr. John. "Supernatural Order". Eternal Life. Retrieved 2008-09-15.

[15] Viney, Donald (2008). Edward N. Zalta, ed. "Process Theism". *The Stanford Encyclopedia of Philosophy* (Winter 2008 ed.).

3.7   Further reading

- Bouvet, R; Bonnefon, J. F. (2015). *Non-Reflective Thinkers Are Predisposed to Attribute Supernatural Causation to Uncanny Experiences*. Personality and Social Psychology Bulletin.

- McNamara, P; Bulkeley, K. (2015). *Dreams as a Source of Supernatural Agent Concepts*. Frontiers in Psychology.

- Riekki, T; Lindeman, M; Raij, T. T. (2014). *Supernatural Believers Attribute More Intentions to Random Movement than Skeptics: An fMRI Study*. Social Neuroscience 9: 400–411.

- Purzycki, Benjamin G. (2013). *The Minds of Gods: A Comparative Study of Supernatural Agency*. Cognition 129: 163–179.

- Thomson, P; Jaque, S. V. (2014). *Unresolved Mourning, Supernatural Beliefs and Dissociation: A Mediation Analysis*. Attachment and Human Development 16: 499–514.

- Vail, K. E; Arndt, J; Addollahi, A. (2012). *Exploring the Existential Function of Religion and Supernatural Agent Beliefs Among Christians, Muslims, Atheists, and Agnostics*. Personality and Social Psychology Bulletin 38: 1288–1300.

Chapter 4

Religious experience

For the Wayne Proudfoot book, see Religious Experience (book).
See also: Trance

A **religious experience** (sometimes known as a spiritual experience, sacred experience, or mystical experience) is a subjective experience which is interpreted within a religious framework.[1] The concept originated in the 19th century, as a defense against the growing rationalism of Western society.[2] William James popularised the concept.[2]

Many religious and mystical traditions see religious experiences (particularly that knowledge which comes with them) as revelations caused by divine agency rather than ordinary natural processes. They are considered real encounters with God or gods, or real contact with higher-order realities of which humans are not ordinarily aware.[3]

Skeptics may hold that religious experience is an evolved feature of the human brain amenable to normal scientific study.[note 1] The commonalities and differences between religious experiences across different cultures have enabled scholars to categorize them for academic study.[4]

4.1 Definitions

4.1.1 William James' definition

Psychologist and Philosopher William James described four characteristics of mystical experience in *The Varieties of Religious Experience*. According to James, such an experience is:

- **Transient** — the experience is temporary; the individual soon returns to a "normal" frame of mind. It is outside our normal perception of space and time.

- **Ineffable** — the experience cannot be adequately put into words.

- **Noetic** — the individual feels that he or she has learned something valuable from the experience. Gives us knowledge that is normally hidden from human understanding.

- **Passive** — the experience happens to the individual, largely without conscious control. Although there are activities, such as meditation (see below), that can make religious experience more likely, it is not something that can be turned on and off at will.

4.1.2 Norman Habel's definition

Norman Habel defines religious experiences as the structured way in which a believer enters into a relationship with, or gains an awareness of, the sacred within the context of a particular religious tradition (Habel, O'Donoghue and Maddox: 1993).Religious experiences are by their very nature preternatural; that is, out of the ordinary or beyond the natural order of things. They may be difficult to distinguish observationally from psychopathological states such as psychoses or other forms of altered awareness (Charlesworth: 1988). Not all preternatural experiences are considered to be religious experiences. Following Habel's definition, psychopathological states or drug-induced states of awareness are not considered to be religious experiences because they are mostly not performed within the context of a particular religious tradition.

Moore and Habel identify two classes of religious experiences: the immediate and the mediated religious experience (Moore and Habel: 1982).

- **Mediated** — In the mediated experience, the believer experiences the sacred through mediators such as rituals, special persons, religious groups, totemic objects or the natural world (Habel et al.: 1993).

- **Immediate** — The immediate experience comes to the believer without any intervening agency or mediator. The deity or divine is experienced directly

4.1.3 Richard Swinburne's definition

In his book *Faith and Reason*, the philosopher Richard Swinburne formulated five categories into which all religious experiences fall:

- **Public** — a believer 'sees God's hand at work', whereas other explanations are possible e.g. looking at a beautiful sunset

- **Public** — an unusual event that breaches natural law e.g. walking on water

- **Private** — describable using normal language e.g. Jacob's vision of a ladder

- **Private** — indescribable using normal language, usually a mystical experience e.g. "white did not cease to be white, nor black cease to be black, but black became white and white became black."

- **Private** — a non-specific, general feeling of God working in one's life.

Swinburne also suggested two principles for the assessment of religious experiences:

- **Principle of Credulity** — with the absence of any reason to disbelieve it, one should accept what appears to be true e.g. if one sees someone walking on water, one should believe that it is occurring.

- **Principle of Testimony** — with the absence of any reason to disbelieve them, one should accept that eyewitnesses or believers are telling the truth when they testify about religious experiences.

4.1.4 Related terms

Numinous — The German thinker Rudolf Otto (1869–1937) argues that there is one common factor to all religious experience, independent of the cultural background. In his book *The Idea of the Holy* (1923) he identifies this factor as the numinous. The "numinous" experience has two aspects: *mysterium tremendum*, which is the tendency to invoke fear and trembling; and *mysterium fascinans*, the tendency to attract, fascinate and compel. The numinous experience also has a personal quality to it, in that the person feels to be in communion with a holy other. Otto sees the numinous as the only possible religious experience. He states: "There is no religion in which it [the numinous] does not live as the real innermost core and without it no religion would be worthy of the name" (Otto: 1972). Otto does not take any other kind of religious experience such as ecstasy and enthusiasm seriously and is of the opinion that they belong to the 'vestibule of religion'.

Ecstasy — In ecstasy the believer is understood to have a soul or spirit which can leave the body. In ecstasy the focus is on the soul leaving the body and to experience transcendental realities. This type of religious experience is characteristic for the shaman.

Enthusiasm — In enthusiasm — or possession — God is understood to be outside, other than or beyond the believer. A sacred power, being or will enters the body or mind of an individual and possesses it. A person capable of being possessed is sometimes called a medium. The deity, spirit or power uses such a person to communicate to the immanent world. Lewis argues that ecstasy and possession are basically one and the same experience, ecstasy being merely one form which possession may take. The outward manifestation of the phenomenon is the same in that shamans appear to be possessed by spirits, act as their mediums, and even though they claim to have mastery over them, can lose that mastery (Lewis: 1986).

Mystical experience — Mystical experiences are in many ways the opposite of numinous experiences. In the mystical experience, all 'otherness' disappear and the believer becomes one with the transcendent. The believer discovers that he or she is not distinct from the cosmos, the deity or the other reality, but one with it. Zaehner has identified two distinctively different mystical experiences: natural and religious mystical experiences (Charlesworth: 1988). Natural mystical experiences are, for example, experiences of the 'deeper self' or experiences of oneness with nature. Zaehner argues that the experiences typical of 'natural mysticism' are quite different from the experiences typical of religious mysticism (Charlesworth: 1988). Natural mystical experiences are not considered to be religious experiences because they are not linked to a particular tradition, but natural mystical experiences are spiritual experiences that can have a profound effect on the individual.

Spiritual awakening — A spiritual awakening usually involves a realization or opening to a sacred dimension of reality and may or may not be a *religious* experience. Often a spiritual awakening has lasting effects upon one's life. The term "spiritual awakening" may be used to refer to any of a wide range of experiences including being born again, near-death experiences, and mystical experiences such as liberation and enlightenment.

4.2 History

4.2.1 Origins

The notion of "religious experience" can be traced back to William James, who used the term "religious experience" in his book, *The Varieties of Religious Experience*.[5] It is considered to be the classic work in the field, and references to James' ideas are common at professional conferences. James distinguished between institutional religion and personal religion. Institutional religion refers to the religious group or organization, and plays an important part in a society's culture. Personal religion, in which the individual has mystical experience, can be experienced regardless of the culture.

The origins of the use of this term can be dated further back.[2] In the 18th, 19th, and 20th centuries, several historical figures put forth very influential views that religion and its beliefs can be grounded in experience itself. While Kant held that moral experience justified religious beliefs, John Wesley in addition to stressing individual moral exertion thought that the religious experiences in the Methodist movement (paralleling the Romantic Movement) were foundational to religious commitment as a way of life.[6]

Wayne Proudfoot traces the roots of the notion of "religious experience" to the German theologian Friedrich Schleiermacher (1768–1834), who argued that religion is based on a feeling of the infinite. The notion of "religious experience" was used by Schleiermacher and Albert Ritschl to defend religion against the growing scientific and secular citique, and defend the view that human (moral and religious) experience justifies religious beliefs.[2]

The notion of "religious experience" was adopted by many scholars of religion, of which William James was the most influential.[7][note 2]

A broad range of western and eastern movements have incorporated and influenced the emergence of the modern notion of "mystical experience", such as the Perennial philosophy, Transcendentalism, Universalism, the Theosophical Society, New Thought, Neo-Vedanta and Buddhist modernism.[11][12]

Perennial philosophy

Main article: Perennial philosophy

According to the Perennial Philosophy the mystical experiences in all religions are essentially the same. It supposes that many, if not all of the world's great religions, have arisen around the teachings of mystics, including Buddha, Jesus, Lao Tze, and Krishna. It also sees most religious traditions describing fundamental mystical experience, at least

"The Temple of the Rose Cross", Teophilus Schweighardt Constantiens, 1618.

esoterically. A major proponent in the 20th century was Aldous Huxley, who "was heavily influenced in his description by Vivekananda's neo-Vedanta and the idiosyncratic version of Zen exported to the west by D.T. Suzuki. Both of these thinkers expounded their versions of the perennialist thesis",[13] which they originally received from western thinkers and theologians.[14]

Transcendentalism and Unitarian Universalism

Main articles: Transcendentalism and Universalism

Transcendentalism was an early 19th-century liberal Protestant movement, which was rooted in English and German Romanticism, the Biblical criticism of Herder and Schleiermacher, and the skepticism of Hume.[web 1] The Transcendentalists emphasised an intuitive, experiential approach of religion.[web 2] Following Schleiermacher,[15] an individual's intuition of truth was taken as the criterion for truth.[web 2] In the late 18th and early 19th century, the first translations of Hindu texts appeared, which were also read by the Transcendentalists, and influenced their thinking.[web 2] They also endorsed universalist and Unitarianist ideas, leading to Unitarian Universalism, the idea that there must be truth in other religions as well, since a loving God would redeem all living beings, not just

Christians.[web 2][web 3]

New Thought

Main article: New Thought

New Thought promotes the ideas that *Infinite Intelligence*, or God, is everywhere, spirit is the totality of real things, true human selfhood is divine, divine thought is a force for good, sickness originates in the mind, and "right thinking" has a healing effect.[web 4][web 5] New Thought was propelled along by a number of spiritual thinkers and philosophers and emerged through a variety of religious denominations and churches, particularly the Unity Church, Religious Science, and Church of Divine Science.[16] The Home of Truth, which belongs to the New Thought movement has, from its inception as the Pacific Coast Metaphysical Bureau in the 1880s, disseminated the teachings of the Hindu teacher Swami Vivekananda.[web 6]

Theosophical Society

Main article: Theosophical Society
See also: Vipassana movement, Hindu reform movements and Buddhist modernism

The Theosophical Society was formed in 1875 by Helena Blavatsky, Henry Steel Olcott, William Quan Judge and others to advance the spiritual principles and search for Truth known as Theosophy.[17][note 3] The Theosophical Society has been highly influential in promoting interest, both in west and east, in a great variety of religious teachings:

> "No single organization or movement has contributed so many components to the New Age Movement as the Theosophical Society [...] It has been the major force in the dissemination of occult literature in the West in the twentieth century.[17]

The Theosophical Society searched for 'secret teachings' in Asian religions. It has been influential on modernist streams in several Asian religions, notably Hindu reform movements, the revival of Theravada Buddhism, and D.T. Suzuki, who popularized the idea of enlightenment as insight into a timeless, transcendent reality.[web 7][web 8][11] Another example can be seen in Paul Brunton's *A Search in Secret India*, which introduced Ramana Maharshi to a western audience.

Orientalism and the "pizza effect"

Main articles: Pizza effect, Neo-Vedanta and Buddhist modernism

The interplay between western and eastern notions of religion is an important factor in the development of modern mysticsm. In the 19th century, when Asian countries were colonialised by western states, a process of cultural mimesis began.[14][18][2] In this process, Western ideas about religion, especially the notion of "religious experience" were introduced to Asian countries by missionaries, scholars and the Theosophical Society, and amalgamated in a new understanding of the Indian and Buddhist traditions. This amalgam was exported back to the West as 'authentic Asian traditions', and acquired a great popularity in the west. Due to this western popularity, it also gained authority back in India, Sri Lanka and Japan.[14][18][2]

The best-known representatives of this amalgamated tradition are Annie Besant (Theosophical Society), Swami Vivekenanda and Sarvepalli Radhakrishnan (Neo-Vedanta), Anagarika Dharmapala, a 19th-century Sri Lankan Buddhist activist who founded the Maha Bodhi Society, and D.T. Suzuki, a Japanese scholar and Zen-Buddhist. A synonymous term for this broad understanding is nondualism. This mutual influence is also known as the pizza effect.

4.2.2   Criticism

The notion of "experience" has been criticised.[19][20][21]

"Religious empiricism" is seen as highly problematic and was — during the period in-between world wars — famously rejected by Karl Barth.[22] In the 20th century, religious as well as moral experience as justification for religious beliefs still holds sway. Some influential modern scholars holding this liberal theological view are Charles Raven and the Oxford physicist/theologian Charles Coulson.[23]

Robert Sharf points out that "experience" is a typical Western term, which has found its way into Asian religiosity via western influences.[19][note 4] The notion of "experience" introduces a false notion of duality between "experiencer" and "experienced", whereas the essence of kensho is the realisation of the "non-duality" of observer and observed.[25][26] "Pure experience" does not exist; all experience is mediated by intellectual and cognitive activity.[27][28] The specific teachings and practices of a specific tradition may even determine what "experience" someone has, which means that this "experience" is not the *proof* of the teaching, but a *result* of the teaching.[1] A pure consciousness without concepts, reached by "cleansing the doors of perception",[note 5] would be an overwhelming chaos of sensory input without coherence.[30]

4.3 Causes of religious experiences

Meditation

Sufi whirling

See also: Religious practice

Religious practices: traditions offer a wide variety of religious practices to induce religious experiences:

- Extended exercise, often running in a large communal circle, which is used in various tribal and neo-pagan religions.

- Praying[31]

- Music[32]

- Dance, such as Sufi whirling[33]

- Extreme pain, such as mortification of the flesh[34]

- Meditation,[35] Meditative practices are used to calm the mind, and attain states of consciousness such as nirvikalpa samadhi. Meditation can be focused on the breath, concepts, mantras,[36] symbols.

- Questioning or investigating (self)representations/cognitive schemata, such as Self-enquiry, Hua Tou practice, and Douglas Harding's *on having no head*.

- The 12 steps of the Alcoholics Anonymous program[37]

Drugs: religious experiences may also be caused by the use of entheogens, such as:

- Ayahuasca (DMT)[38]

- *Salvia divinorum* (salvinorin A)[39]

- Peyote (mescaline)[40]

- Psilocybin mushrooms (psilocybin)[41]

- *Amanita muscaria* (muscimol)[42]

- Soma

Neurophysiological origins: Religious experiences may have neurophysiological origins. These are studied in the field of neurotheology, and the cognitive science of religion, and include near-death experience[43] and the "Koren helmet"[44] Causes may be:

- Temporal lobe epilepsy,[45] as described in the Geschwind syndrome;

- Stroke[46]

- Profound depression[47] or schizophrenia

4.4 Religious practices

4.4.1 Western

Neoplatonism

Neoplatonism is the modern term for a school of religious and mystical philosophy that took shape in the 3rd century AD, founded by Plotinus and based on the teachings of Plato and earlier Platonists.

Neoplatonism teaches that along the same road by which it descended the soul must retrace its steps back to the supreme Good. It must first of all return to itself. This is accomplished by the practice of virtue, which aims at likeness to God, and leads up to God. By means of ascetic observances the human becomes once more a spiritual and enduring being, free from all sin. But there is still a higher attainment; it is not enough to be sinless, one must become "God", (*henosis*). This is reached through contemplation of the primeval Being, the One — in other words, through an ecstatic approach to it.

It is only in a state of perfect passivity and repose that the soul can recognize and touch the primeval Being. Hence the soul must first pass through a spiritual curriculum. Beginning with the contemplation of corporeal things in their multiplicity and harmony, it then retires upon itself and withdraws into the depths of its own being, rising thence to the *nous*, the world of ideas. But even there it does not find the Highest, the One; it still hears a voice saying, "not we have made ourselves." The last stage is reached when, in the highest tension and concentration, beholding in silence and utter forgetfulness of all things, it is able as it were to lose itself. Then it may see God, the foundation of life, the source of being, the origin of all good, the root of the soul. In that moment it enjoys the highest indescribable bliss; it is as it were swallowed up of divinity, bathed in the light of eternity. Porphyry tells us that on four occasions during the six years of their intercourse Plotinus attained to this ecstatic union with God.

Alcoholics Anonymous Twelfth Step

The twelfth step of the Alcoholics Anonymous program states that "Having had a spiritual awakening as the result of these steps, we tried to carry this message to alcoholics and to practice these principles in all our affairs".[48] The terms "spiritual experience" and "spiritual awakening" are used many times in "The Big Book of Alcoholics Anonymous"[49] which, upon reading, shows that a spiritual experience is needed to bring about recovery from alcoholism.[37]

Christianity

Christian mysticism Main article: Christian mysticism
Christian doctrine generally maintains that God dwells in

Three early Methodist leaders, Charles Wesley, John Wesley, and Francis Asbury, portrayed in stained glass at the Memorial Chapel, Lake Junaluska, North Carolina

all Christians and that they can experience God directly through belief in Jesus,[50] Christian mysticism aspires to apprehend spiritual truths inaccessible through intellectual means, typically by emulation of Christ. William Inge divides this *scala perfectionis* into three stages: the "*purgative*" or ascetic stage, the "*illuminative*" or contemplative stage, and the third, "*unitive*" stage, in which God may be beheld "face to face."[51]

The third stage, usually called contemplation in the Western tradition, refers to the experience of oneself as united with God in some way. The experience of union varies, but it is first and foremost always associated with a reuniting with Divine *love*. The underlying theme here is that God, the perfect goodness,[52] is known or experienced at least as much by the heart as by the intellect since, in the words of 1 John 4:16: "God is love, and he who abides in love abides in God and God in him." Some approaches to classical mysticism would consider the first two phases as preparatory to the third, explicitly mystical experience; but others state that these three phases overlap and intertwine.

Hesychasm Based on Christ's injunction in the Gospel of Matthew to "go into your closet to pray",[53] hesychasm in tradition has been the process of retiring inward by ceasing to register the senses, in order to achieve an experiential knowledge of God (see theoria).

The highest goal of the hesychast is the experiential knowledge of God. In the 14th Century, the possibility of this experiential knowledge of God was challenged by a Calabrian monk, Barlaam, who, although he was formally a member of the Orthodox Church, had been trained in Western

Scholastic theology. Barlaam asserted that our knowledge of God can only be propositional. The practice of the hesychasts was defended by St. Gregory Palamas.

In solitude and retirement the hesychast repeats the Jesus Prayer, "Lord Jesus Christ, son of God, have mercy on me, a sinner." He considers bare repetition of the Jesus Prayer as a mere string of syllables, perhaps with a 'mystical' inner meaning beyond the overt verbal meaning, to be worthless or even dangerous.

4.4.2 Islam

While all Muslims believe that they are on the pathway to God and will become close to God in Paradise — after death and after the "Final Judgment" — Sufis believe that it is possible to become close to God and to experience this closeness while one is alive.[54] Sufis believe in a tripartite way to God as explained by a tradition attributed to the Prophet,"The Shariah are my words (aqwal), the tariqa are my actions (amal), and the haqiqa is my interior states (ahwal)". Shariah, tariqa and haqiqa are mutually interdependent.

The tariqa, the 'path' on which the mystics walk, has been defined as 'the path which comes out of the Shariah, for the main road is called shar, the path, tariq.' No mystical experience can be realized if the binding injunctions of the Shariah are not followed faithfully first. The path, tariqa, however, is narrower and more difficult to walk. It leads the adept, called salik (wayfarer), in his suluk (wandering), through different stations (maqam) until he reaches his goal, the perfect tauhid, the existential confession that God is One.[55]

4.4.3 Asia

Buddhism

In Theravada Buddhism practice is described in the three-fold training of discipline (*śīla*), meditative concentration (*samādhi*), and transcendent wisdom (*prajñā*). Zen-Buddhism emphaises the sole practice of meditation, while Vajrayana Buddhism utilizes a wide variety of practices. While the main aim of meditation and *prajna* is to let go of attachments, it may also result in a comprehension of the Buddha-nature and the inherent lucidity of the mind.

Different varieties of religious experience are described in detail in the *Śūraṅgama Sūtra*. In its section on the fifty skandha-maras, each of the five skandhas has ten skandha-maras associated with it, and each skandha-mara is described in detail as a deviation from correct samādhi. These skandha-maras are also known as the "fifty skandha

The Buddha demonstrating control over fire and water. Gandhara, 3rd century CE

demons" in some English-language publications.[56]

It is also believed that supernormal abilities are developed from meditation, which are termed "higher knowledge" (*abhijñā*), or "spiritual power" (*ṛddhi*). One early description found in the *Samyutta Nikaya*, which mentions abilities such as:[57]

> ... he goes unhindered through a wall, through a rampart, through a mountain as though through space; he dives in and out of the earth as though it were water; he walks on water without sinking as though it were earth; seated cross-legged, he travels in space like a bird; with his hands he touches and strokes the moon and sun so powerful and mighty; he exercises mastery with the body as far as the brahmā world.

Hinduism

According to Sarvepalli Radhakrishnan, "Hinduism is not just a faith. It is the union of reason and intuition that cannot be defined, but is only to be experienced."[58] This emphasis on experience as validation of a religious world-view is a modern development, which started in the 19th century, and was introduced to Indian thought by western Unitarian missionaries.[12] It has been popularized in Neo-Vedanta, which has dominated the popular understanding of Hinduism since the 19th century.[59][note 6] It emphasizes mysticism,[59] Aryan origins and the unity of Hinduism[60] have been emphasised.[61][62][63][59]

Meher Baba

According to the syncretistic Indian spiritual teacher Meher Baba, "Spiritual experience involves more than can be grasped by mere intellect. This is often emphasised by calling it a mystical experience. Mysticism is often regarded as something anti-intellectual, obscure and confused, or impractical and unconnected with experience. In fact, true mysticism is none of these. There is nothing irrational in true mysticism when it is, as it should be, a vision of Reality. It is a form of perception which is absolutely unclouded, and so practical that it can be lived every moment of life and expressed in every-day duties. Its connection with experience is so deep that, in one sense, it is the final understanding of all experience."[64]

4.5 Psychedelic drugs

See also: Ego death, Shamanism and Soma

Dr. R.R. Griffiths and colleagues at Johns Hopkin University had done a double blind study evaluating the psychological effects of psilocybin comparing with methylphenidate(Ritalin). 36 hallucinogen-naive adults were recruited. 22 of the 36 reported mystical experience. The effect persisted even at 2 and 14 months follow-up.[65][66] The group continued to do studies in evaluating the effect with different dosing[67] and the resulting mystical effect on personality.[68]

4.6 Neurophysiology

4.6.1 Psychiatry

A 2012 paper suggested that psychiatric conditions associated with psychotic spectrum symptoms may be possible explanations for revelatory driven experiences and activities such as those of Abraham, Moses, Jesus and Saint Paul.[69]

4.6.2 Neuroscience

Neurology

Visionary religious experiences, and momentary lapses of consciousness, may point toward a diagnosis of Geschwind syndrome. More generally, the symptoms are consistent with features of Temporal Lobe Epilepsy, not an uncommon feature in religious icons and mystics.[70]

Neurotheology

Neurotheology, also known as *biotheology* or *spiritual neuroscience*,[71] is the study of correlations of neural phenomena with subjective experiences of spirituality and hypotheses to explain these phenomena. Proponents of neurotheology claim that there is a neurological and evolutionary basis for subjective experiences traditionally categorized as spiritual or religious.[72]

According to the neurotheologist Andrew B. Newberg, neurological processes which are driven by the repetitive, rhythmic stimulation which is typical of human ritual, and which contribute to the delivery of transcendental feelings of connection to a universal unity. They posit, however, that physical stimulation alone is not sufficient to generate transcendental unitive experiences. For this to occur they say there must be a blending of the rhythmic stimulation with ideas. Once this occurs "...ritual turns a meaningful idea into a visceral experience."[73] Moreover, they say that humans are compelled to act out myths by the biological operations of the brain due to what they call the "inbuilt tendency of the brain to turn thoughts into actions".

Studies of the brain and religious experience

Early studies in the 1950s and 1960s attempted to use EEGs to study brain wave patterns correlated with spiritual states. During the 1980s Dr. Michael Persinger stimulated the temporal lobes of human subjects[74] with a weak magnetic field. His subjects claimed to have a sensation of "an ethereal presence in the room."[75] Some current studies use neuroimaging to localize brain regions active, or differentially active, during religious experiences.[76][77][78] These neuroimaging studies have implicated a number of brain regions, including the limbic system, dorsolateral prefrontal cortex, superior parietal lobe, and caudate nucleus.[79][80][81] Based on the complex nature of religious experience, it is likely that they are mediated by an interaction of neural mechanisms that all add a small piece to the overall experience.[80]

4.7 Integrating religious experience

See also: Training after kenshō

Several psychologists have proposed models in which religious experiences are part of a process of transformation of the self.

Carl Jung's work on himself and his patients convinced him that life has a spiritual purpose beyond material goals. Our main task, he believed, is to discover and fulfil our deep innate potential, much as the acorn contains the potential to become the oak, or the caterpillar to become the butterfly. Based on his study of Christianity, Hinduism, Buddhism, Gnosticism, Taoism, and other traditions, Jung perceived that this journey of transformation is at the mystical heart of all religions. It is a journey to meet the self and at the same time to meet the Divine. Unlike Sigmund Freud, Jung thought spiritual experience was essential to our well-being.[82]

The notion of the numinous was an important concept in the writings of Carl Jung. Jung regarded numinous experiences as fundamental to an understanding of the individuation process because of their association with experiences of synchronicity in which the presence of archetypes is felt.[83][84]

McNamara proposes that religious experiences may help in "decentering" the self, and transform it into an integral self which is closer to an ideal self.[85]

Transpersonal psychology is a school of psychology that studies the transpersonal, self-transcendent or spiritual aspects of the human experience. The *Journal of Transpersonal Psychology* describes transpersonal psychology as "the study of humanity's highest potential, and with the recognition, understanding, and realization of unitive, spiritual, and transcendent states of consciousness" (Lajoie and Shapiro, 1992:91). Issues considered in transpersonal psychology include spiritual self-development, peak experiences, mystical experiences, systemic trance and other metaphysical experiences of living.

4.8 See also

- Altered state of consciousness
- Psychedelic experience
- Argument from religious experience
- Cognitive science of religion
- Enlightenment (spiritual)

- Entheogens
- Higher consciousness
- Kundalini
- Mysticism
- Near death experience
- Neurotheology
- Nirvana
- Numinosum
- Psychology of religion
- Psychonaut
- Religious ecstasy
- Religious Experience Research Centre
- Religious revival
- Revelation
- Samadhi
- Self-knowledge
- Spiritual crisis
- *The Varieties of Religious Experience*
- Theta rhythm
- Transcendence (religion)
- Transpersonal psychology
- Turiya

4.9 Notes

[1] Such study may be said to have begun with the American psychologist and philosopher William James in his 1901/02 Gifford Lectures later published as *The Varieties of Religious Experience*.

[2] James also gives descriptions of conversion experiences. The Christian model of dramatic conversions, based on the role-model of Paul's conversion, may also have served as a model for Western interpretations and expectations regarding "enlightenment", similar to Protestant influences on Theravada Buddhism, as described by Carrithers: "It rests upon the notion of the primacy of religious experiences, preferably spectacular ones, as the origin and legitimation of religious action. But this presupposition has a natural home, not in Buddhism, but in Christian and especially Protestant Christian movements which prescribe a radical

conversion."[8] See Sekida for an example of this influence of William James and Christian conversion stories, mentioning Luther[9] and St. Paul.[10] See also McMahan for the influence of Christian thought on Buddhism.[11]

[3]   (a) To form a nucleus of the universal brotherhood of humanity without distinction of race, creed, sex, caste, or colour.

(b) To encourage the study of comparative religion, philosophy, and science.

(c) To investigate the unexplained laws of nature and the powers latent in man.

[4]   Robert Sharf: "[T]he role of experience in the history of Buddhism has been greatly exaggerated in contemporary scholarship. Both historical and ethnographic evidence suggests that the privileging of experience may well be traced to certain twentieth-century reform movements, notably those that urge a return to *zazen* or *vipassana* meditation, and these reforms were profoundly influenced by religious developments in the west [...] While some adepts may indeed experience "altered states" in the course of their training, critical analysis shows that such states do not constitute the reference point for the elaborate Buddhist discourse pertaining to the "path".[24]

[5]   William Blake: "If the doors of perception were cleansed every thing would appear to man as it is, infinite. For man has closed himself up, till he sees all things thru' narrow chinks of his cavern."[29]

[6]   Also called neo-Hinduism[59]

4.10   References

[1]   Samy 1998, p. 80.

[2]   Sharf 2000.

[3]   The Argument from Religious Experience http://www.philosophyofreligion.info/?page_id=41

[4]   Batson, C. D., Schoenrade, P., & Ventis, W. L. (1993). *Religion and the individual: A social psychological perspective.* Oxford University Press.

[5]   Hori 1999, p. 47.

[6]   Issues in Science and Religion, Ian Barbour, Prentice-Hall, 1966, page 68, 79

[7]   Sharf 2000, p. 271.

[8]   Carrithers 1983, p. 18.

[9]   Sekida 1985, p. 196-197.

[10]   Sekida 1985, p. 251.

[11]   McMahan 2008.

[12]   King 2001.

[13]   King 2002, p. 163.

[14]   King 2002.

[15]   Sharf 1995.

[16]   Melton 1992, p. 16–18.

[17]   Melton, Gordon J. (Sr. ed.) (1990). "Theosophical Society". *New Age Encyclopedia*. Farmington Hills, Michigan: Gale Research. pp. 458–461. ISBN 0-8103-7159-6

[18]   McMahan 2010.

[19]   Sharf 1995a.

[20]   Mohr 2000, p. 282-286.

[21]   Low 2006, p. 12.

[22]   Issues in Science and Religion, Ian Barbour, Prentice-Hall, 1966, page 114, 116-119

[23]   Issues in Science and Religion, Ian Barbour, Prentice-Hall, 1966, p. 126-127

[24]   Sharf 1995b, p. 1.

[25]   Hori 1994, p. 30.

[26]   Samy 1998, p. 82.

[27]   Mohr 2000, p. 282.

[28]   Samy 1998, p. 80-82.

[29]   Quote DB

[30]   Mohr 2000, p. 284.

[31]   "'Exploring the biology of religious experience" NRC online

[32]   "'The Emotional Effects of Music on Religious Experience: A Study of the Pentecostal-Charismatic Style of Music and Worship " Sage Journals

[33]   "'ufis seek ultimate religious experience through mystic trances or altered states of consciousness, often induced through twirling dances " Sufism: New Age Spirituality Dictionary

[34]   "'Self-inflicted Pain in Religious Experience " www.faithfaq.com (URL accessed on July 11, 2006)

[35]   "'Divining the brain" Salon.com (URL accessed on September 20, 2006)

[36]   Daniélou, Alain: Yoga, methods of re-integration

[37]   http://www.aa.org/assets/en_US/en_bigbook_appendiceii.pdf

[38]   "'Psychedelics and Religious Experience " Alan Watts http://deoxy.org/ (URL accessed on July 11, 2006)

[39] "'Those who think of the salvia experience in religious, spiritual, or mystical terms may speak of such things as enlightenment, satori, and "cleansing the doors of perception." " sagewisdom.org (URL accessed on August 26, 2007)

[40] "'A Note on the Safety of Peyote when Used Religiously. " www.csp.org Council on Spiritual Practices (URL accessed on July 11, 2006)

[41] "'Drug's Mystical Properties Confirmed " www.washingtonpost.com (URL accessed on July 11, 2006)

[42] "'The Psychology of Religion: An Empirical Approach. " Conuncil on Spiritual Practices (URL accessed on July 11, 2006)

[43] Moody, Raymond. *Life After Life* ISBN 0-06-251739-2

[44] Persinger, MA; et al. (2010). "The Electromagnetic Induction of Mystical and Altered States Within the Laboratory". *Journal of Consciousness Exploration & Research* **1** (7): 808–830. ISSN 2153-8212.

[45] "'God on the Brain " http://news.bbc.co.uk (URL accessed on March 20, 2003)

[46] "My Stroke of Insight" http://www.ted.com/index.php/talks/jill_bolte_taylor_s_powerful_stroke_of_insight.html (URL accessed on July 2, 2008)

[47] Katie, Byron. *Loving What Is* page xi ISBN 1-4000-4537-1

[48] http://www.aa.org.au/members/twelve-steps.php

[49] http://www.aa.org/pages/en_US/alcoholics-anonymous

[50] John 7:16–39

[51] *Christian Mysticism* (1899 Bampton Lectures)

[52] Theologia Germanica, public domain

[53] Matthew 6:5–6 (King James Version)

[54] Sufism, Sufis, and Sufi Orders: Sufism's Many Paths

[55] Annemarie Schimmel, Mystical Dimensions of Islam (1975) pg.99

[56] Ron Epstein. "Fifty Skandha Demon States: Forward".

[57] Bhikkhu Bodhi. *The Connected Discourses of the Buddha.* 2000. p. 1727

[58] *Bhagavad Gita*, Sarvepalli Radhakrishnan

[59] King 1999.

[60] King 1999, p. 171.

[61] Muesse 2011, p. 3-4.

[62] Doniger 2010, p. 18.

[63] Jouhki 2006, p. 10-11.

[64] Baba, Meher: *Discourses*, Sufism Reoriented, 1967, p. 20

[65] "Psilocybin can occasion mystical-type experiences having substantial and sustained personal meaning and spiritual significance". *Psychopharmacology (Berl.)* **187**: 268–83; discussion 284–92. August 2006. doi:10.1007/s00213-006-0457-5. PMID 16826400.

[66] "Mystical-type experiences occasioned by psilocybin mediate the attribution of personal meaning and spiritual significance 14 months later". *J. Psychopharmacol. (Oxford)* **22**: 621–32. August 2008. doi:10.1177/0269881108094300. PMC 3050654. PMID 18593735.

[67] "Psilocybin occasioned mystical-type experiences: immediate and persisting dose-related effects". *Psychopharmacology (Berl.)* **218**: 649–65. December 2011. doi:10.1007/s00213-011-2358-5. PMC 3308357. PMID 21674151.

[68] "Mystical experiences occasioned by the hallucinogen psilocybin lead to increases in the personality domain of openness". *J. Psychopharmacol. (Oxford)* **25**: 1453–61. November 2011. doi:10.1177/0269881111420188. PMC 3537171. PMID 21956378.

[69] Murray, ED.; Cunningham MG, Price BH. (1). "The role of psychotic disorders in religious history considered". J Neuropsychiatry Clin Neuroscience 24 (4): 410–26. doi: 10.1176/appi.neuropsych.11090214. PMID 23224447

[70] Devinsky, J.; Schachter, S. (2009). "Norman Geschwind's contribution to the understanding of behavioral changes in temporal lobe epilepsy: The February 1974 lecture". *Epilepsy & Behavior* **15** (4): 417–24. doi:10.1016/j.yebeh.2009.06.006. PMID 19640791.

[71] Biello, David (2007-10-03). "Searching for God in the Brain". Scientific American. Archived from the original on 2007-10-11. Retrieved 2007-10-07.

[72] Gajilan, A. Chris (2007-04-05). "Are humans hard-wired for faith?". Cable News Network. Retrieved 2007-04-09.

[73] Newberg, Andrew B.; D'Aquili, Eugene G.; Rause, Vince (2002). *Why God Won't Go Away: Brain Science and the Biology of Belief*. New York: Ballantine Books. p. 90. ISBN 0-345-44034-X.

[74] "'God on the Brain?" BBC

[75] "'This Is Your Brain on God" Wired

[76] Azari, N. P.; Nickel, J.; Wunderlich, G.; Niedeggen, M.; Hefter, H.; Tellmann, L.; Herzog, H.; Stoerig, P.; Birnbacher, D.; Seitz, R. J. (2001). "Neural correlates of religious experience". *The European Journal of Neuroscience* **13** (8): 1649–1652. doi:10.1046/j.0953-816x.2001.01527.x. PMID 11328359.

[77] "' From Brain Imaging Religious Experience to Explaining Religion: A Critique." Ingenta Connect

[78] "' The new science of neurotheology." Wordpress

[79] Newberg, A.; Alavi, A.; Baime, M.; Pourdehnad, M.; Santanna, J.; Aquili, E. (2001). "The measurement of regional cerebral blood flow during the complex cognitive task of meditation: A preliminary SPECT study". *Psychiatry Research: Neuroimaging* **106**: 113–122. doi:10.1016/s0925-4927(01)00074-9.

[80] Azari, N.P.; Missimer, J.; Seitz, R.J. (2005). "Religious experience and emotion: Evidence for distinctive cognitive neural patterns". *International Journal for the Psychology of Religion* **15**: 263–281. doi:10.1207/s15327582ijpr1504_1.

[81] Beauregard, M.; Paquette, V. (2006). "Neural correlates of a mystical experience in Carmelite nuns". *Neuroscience Letters* **405**: 186–190. doi:10.1016/j.neulet.2006.06.060.

[82] Crowley, Vivianne (2000). *Jung: A Journey of Transformation:Exploring His Life and Experiencing His Ideas.* Wheaton Illinois: Quest Books. ISBN 978-0-8356-0782-7.

[83] Jung, C. G. (1980). *C. G. Jung speaking: Interviews and encounters(W. McGuire & R. F. C. Hull Eds.).* London: Pan Books.

[84] Main, R. (2004). *The rupture of time: Synchronicity and Jung's critique of modern western culture.* Hove and New York: Brunner-Routledge.

[85] McNamara 2014.

4.11   Sources

4.11.1   Printed sources

- Carrithers, Michael (1983), *The Forest Monks of Sri Lanka*

- Charlesworth, Max (1988). *Religious experience. Unit A. Study guide 2* (Deakin University).

- Deida, David. *Finding God Through Sex* ISBN 1-59179-273-8

- Doniger, Wendy (2010), *The Hindus: An Alternative History*, Oxford University Press

- Habel, Norman, O'Donoghue, Michael and Maddox, Marion (1993). 'Religious experience'. In: *Myth, ritual and the sacred. Introducing the phenomena of religion* (Underdale: University of South Australia).

- Hori, Victor Sogen (1994), *Teaching and Learning in the Zen Rinzai Monastery. In: Journal of Japanese Studies, Vol.20, No. 1, (Winter, 1994), 5-35* (PDF)

- Jouhki, Jukka (2006), "Orientalism and India" (PDF), *J@RGONIA 8/2006*

- Katie, Byron. *Loving What Is* page xi ISBN 1-4000-4537-1

- King, Richard (1999), *Orientalism and Religion: Post-Colonial Theory, India and "The Mystic East"*, Routledge

- King, Richard (2002), *Orientalism and Religion: Post-Colonial Theory, India and "The Mystic East"*, Routledge eBook

- Lewis, James R.; Melton, J. Gordon (1992), *Perspectives on the New Age*, SUNY Press, ISBN 0-7914-1213-X

- Lewis, Ioan M (1986). *Religion in context: cults and charisma* (Cambridge: Cambridge University Press).

- Low, Albert (2006), *Hakuin on Kensho. The Four Ways of Knowing*, Boston & London: Shambhala

- McMahan, David L. (2008), *The Making of Buddhist Modernism*, Oxford: Oxford University Press, ISBN 9780195183276

- McNamara (2014), *The neuroscience of religious experience* (PDF)

- Mohr, Michel (2000), *Emerging from Nonduality. Koan Practice in the Rinzai Tradition since Hakuin. In: steven Heine & Dale S. Wright (eds.)(2000), "The Koan. texts and Contexts in Zen Buddhism"*, Oxford: Oxford University Press

- Moody, Raymond. *Life After Life* ISBN 0-06-251739-2

- Moore, B and Habel N (1982). Appendix 1. In: *When religion goes to school* (Adelaide: SACAE), pages 184-218.

- Muesse, Mark W. (2011), *The Hindu Traditions: A Concise Introduction*, Fortress Press

- Otto, Rudolf (1972). Chapters 2-5. In: *The idea of the holy* (London: Oxford University Press), pages 5–30. [Originally published in 1923].

- Previous, Peter (1998). Omgaan met het transcendente (Dealing with the transcendent). Open University of the Netherlands.

- Roberts, T. B. (editor) (2001). *Psychoactive Sacramentals: Essays on Entheogens and Religion.* San Francosco: Council on Spiritual Practices.

- Roberts, T. B., and Hruby, P. J. (1995–2002). Religion and Psychoactive Sacraments An Entheogen Chrestomathy. Online archive.

- Roberts, T. B. "Chemical Input — Religious Output: Entheogens." Chapter 10 in *Where God and Science Meet: Vol. 3: The Psychology of Religious Experience* Robert McNamara (editor)(2006). Westport, CT: Praeger/Greenwood.

- Samy, AMA (1998), *Waarom kwam Bodhidharma naar het Westen? De ontmoeting van Zen met het Westen*, Asoka: Asoka

- Sekida, Katsuki (1985), *Zen Training. Methods and Philosophy*, New York, Tokyo: Weatherhill

- Sharf, Robert H. (1995a), "Buddhist Modernism and the Rhetoric of Meditative Experience" (PDF), *NUMEN* **42**

- Sharf, Robert H. (1995b), "Sanbokyodan. Zen and the Way of the New Religions" (PDF), *Japanese Journal of Religious Studies 1995 22/3-4*

- Sharf, Robert H. (2000), *The Rhetoric of Experience and the Study of Religion. In: Journal of Consciousness Studies, 7, No. 11-12, 2000, pp. 267-87* (PDF)

- Vardy, Peter (1990). *The Puzzle of God*. Collins Sons and Co. pp. 99–106.

4.11.2 Web-sources

[1] "Stanford Encyclopdeia of Philosophy, ''Transcendentalism''". Plato.stanford.edu. Retrieved 2013-11-06.

[2] Jone Johnson Lewis. "Jone John Lewis, ''What is Transcendentalism?''". Transcendentalists.com. Retrieved 2013-11-06.

[3] "Barry Andrews, ''The Roots Of Unitarian Universalist Spirituality In New England Transcendentalism ''". Archive.uua.org. 1999-03-12. Retrieved 2013-11-06.

[4] Declaration of Principles (accessed 2008–09)

[5] New Thought info, *Statement of beliefs* (accessed 2008–09)

[6] "tHe HOme of Truth, ''Our History''". Thehomeoftruth.org. Retrieved 2013-11-06.

[7] "Robert H. Sharf, ''Whose Zen? Zen Nationalism Revisited''" (PDF). Retrieved 2013-11-06.

[8] "Hu Shih: Ch'an (Zen) Buddhism in China. Its History and Method". Thezensite.com. Retrieved 2013-11-06.

4.12   Further reading

- William James, *The Varieties of religious Experience*

- Batson, C. D., & Ventis, W. L. (1982). *The religious experience: A social-psychological perspective.* New York: Oxford University Press, ISBN 0-19-503030-3

- Giussani, Luigi (1997). *The Religious Sense*. Mcgill Queens Univ Press, ISBN 978-0773516267

- Simon Dein (2011), *Religious experience: perspectives and research paradigms*, WCPRR June 2011: 3-9

- Ann Taves (1999), *Fits, Trances, and Visions: Experiencing Religion and Explaining Experience from Wesley to James*, Oxford University Press

- McNamara (2006), *Where God and Science Meet: How Brain and Evolutionary Studies Alter Our Understanding of Religion*

- McNamara (2009/2014): *The neuroscience of religious experience*

4.13   External links

- Stanford Encyclopedia of Philosophy, *Religious Experience*

- "Self-transcendence enhanced by removal of portions of the parietal-occipital cortex" Article from the Institute for the Biocultural Study of Religion

- Peru: Hell and Back National Geographic explores the uses of Ayahuasca in Shamanic healing

- Is This Your Brain On God? (May 2009 week long NPR series)

Chapter 5

Cognitive neuroscience

For the academic journal, see Cognitive Neuroscience.

Cognitive neuroscience is an academic field concerned with the scientific study of biological substrates underlying cognition,[1] with a specific focus on the neural substrates of mental processes. It addresses the questions of how psychological/cognitive functions are produced by neural circuits in the brain. Cognitive neuroscience is a branch of both psychology and neuroscience, overlapping with disciplines such as physiological psychology, cognitive psychology, and neuropsychology.[2] Cognitive neuroscience relies upon theories in cognitive science coupled with evidence from neuropsychology, and computational modeling.[2]

Due to its multidisciplinary nature, cognitive neuroscientists may have various backgrounds. Other than the associated disciplines just mentioned, cognitive neuroscientists may have backgrounds in neurobiology, bioengineering, psychiatry, neurology, physics, computer science, linguistics, philosophy, and mathematics.

Methods employed in cognitive neuroscience include experimental paradigms from psychophysics and cognitive psychology, functional neuroimaging, electrophysiology, cognitive genomics, and behavioral genetics. Studies of patients with cognitive deficits due to brain lesions constitute an important aspect of cognitive neuroscience. Theoretical approaches include computational neuroscience and cognitive psychology.

Cognitive neuroscience can look at the effects of damage to the brain and subsequent changes in the thought processes due to changes in neural circuitry resulting from the damage. Also, cognitive abilities based on brain development are studied and examined under the subfield of developmental cognitive neuroscience.

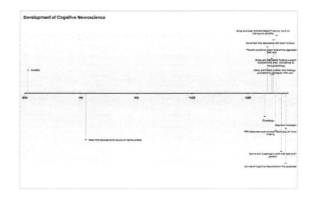

Timeline showing major developments in science that led to the emergence of the field cognitive neuroscience.

5.1 Historical origins

Cognitive neuroscience is an interdisciplinary area of study that has emerged from many other fields, perhaps most significantly neuroscience, psychology, and computer science.[3] There were several stages in these disciplines that changed the way researchers approached their investigations and that led to the field becoming fully established.

Although the task of cognitive neuroscience is to describe how the brain creates the mind, historically it has progressed by investigating how a certain area of the brain supports a given mental faculty. However, early efforts to subdivide the brain proved to be problematic. The phrenologist movement failed to supply a scientific basis for its theories and has since been rejected. The aggregate field view, meaning that all areas of the brain participated in all behavior,[4] was also rejected as a result of brain mapping, which began with Hitzig and Fritsch's experiments [5] and eventually developed through methods such as positron emission tomography (PET) and functional magnetic resonance imaging (fMRI).[6] Gestalt theory, neuropsychology, and the cognitive revolution were major turning points in the creation of cognitive neuroscience as a field, bringing together ideas and techniques that enabled researchers to make more links between behavior and its neural substrates.

5.1.1 Origins in philosophy

Philosophers have always been interested in the mind. For example, Aristotle thought the brain was the body's cooling system and the capacity for intelligence was located in the heart. It has been suggested that the first person to believe otherwise was the Roman physician Galen in the second century AD, who declared that the brain was the source of mental activity,[7] although this has also been accredited to Alcmaeon.[8] However, Galen believed that personality and emotion were not generated by the brain, but rather by other organs. Andreas Vesalius, an anatomist and physician, was the first to believe that the brain and the nervous system are the center of the mind and emotion.[9] Psychology, a major contributing field to cognitive neuroscience, emerged from philosophical reasoning about the mind.[10]

5.1.2 19th century

Phrenology

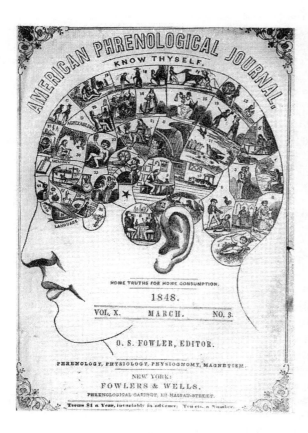

A page from the American Phrenological Journal

Main article: Phrenology

One of the predecessors to cognitive neuroscience was phrenology, a pseudoscientific approach that claimed that behavior could be determined by the shape of the scalp. In the early 19th century, Franz Joseph Gall and J. G. Spurzheim believed that the human brain was localized into approximately 35 different sections. In his book, The Anatomy and Physiology of the Nervous System in General, and of the Brain in Particular, Gall claimed that a larger bump in one of these areas meant that that area of the brain was used more frequently by that person. This theory gained significant public attention, leading to the publication of phrenology journals and the creation of phrenometers, which measured the bumps on a human subject's head. While phrenology remained a fixture at fairs and carnivals, it did not enjoy wide acceptance within the scientific community.[11] The major criticism of phrenology is that researchers were not able to test theories empirically.[3]

Localizationist view

The localizationist view was concerned with mental abilities being localized to specific areas of the brain rather than on what the characteristics of the abilities were and how to measure them.[3] Studies performed in Europe, such as those of John Hughlings Jackson, supported this view. Jackson studied patients with brain damage, particularly those with epilepsy. He discovered that the epileptic patients often made the same clonic and tonic movements of muscle during their seizures, leading Jackson to believe that they must be occurring in the same place every time. Jackson proposed that specific functions were localized to specific areas of the brain,[12] which was critical to future understanding of the brain lobes.

Aggregate field view

According to the aggregate field view, all areas of the brain participate in every mental function.[4]

Pierre Flourens, a French experimental psychologist, challenged the localizationist view by using animal experiments.[3] He discovered that removing the cerebellum in rabbits and pigeons affected their sense of muscular coordination, and that all cognitive functions were disrupted in pigeons when the cerebral hemispheres were removed. From this he concluded that the cerebral cortex, cerebellum, and brainstem functioned together as a whole.[13] His approach has been criticised on the basis that the tests were not sensitive enough to notice selective deficits had they been present.[3]

Emergence of neuropsychology

Perhaps the first serious attempts to localize mental functions to specific locations in the brain was by Broca and Wernicke. This was mostly achieved by studying the effects of injuries to different parts of the brain on psychological functions.[14] In 1861, French neurologist Paul Broca came across a man who was able to understand language but unable to speak. The man could only produce the sound "tan". It was later discovered that the man had damage to an area of his left frontal lobe now known as Broca's area. Carl Wernicke, a German neurologist, found a patient who could speak fluently but non-sensibly. The patient had been the victim of a stroke, and could not understand spoken or written language. This patient had a lesion in the area where the left parietal and temporal lobes meet, now known as Wernicke's area. These cases, which suggested that lesions caused specific behavioral changes, strongly supported the localizationist view.

Mapping the brain

In 1870, German physicians Eduard Hitzig and Gustav Fritsch published their findings about the behavior of animals. Hitzig and Fritsch ran an electric current through the cerebral cortex of a dog, causing different muscles to contract depending on which areas of the brain were electrically stimulated. This led to the proposition that individual functions are localized to specific areas of the brain rather than the cerebrum as a whole, as the aggregate field view suggests.[5] Brodmann was also an important figure in brain mapping; his experiments based on Franz Nissl's tissue staining techniques divided the brain into fifty-two areas.

5.1.3   20th century

Cognitive revolution

At the start of the 20th century, attitudes in America were characterised by pragmatism, which led to a preference for behaviorism as the primary approach in psychology. J.B. Watson was a key figure with his stimulus-response approach. By conducting experiments on animals he was aiming to be able to predict and control behaviour. Behaviourism eventually failed because it could not provide realistic psychology of human action and thought – it was too based in physical concepts to explain phenomena like memory and thought. This led to what is often termed as the "cognitive revolution".[15]

Neuron doctrine

Main article: Neuron doctrine

In the early 20th century, Santiago Ramón y Cajal and Camillo Golgi began working on the structure of the neuron. Golgi developed a silver staining method that could entirely stain several cells in a particular area, leading him to believe that neurons were directly connected with each other in one cytoplasm. Cajal challenged this view after staining areas of the brain that had less myelin and discovering that neurons were discrete cells. Cajal also discovered that cells transmit electrical signals down the neuron in one direction only. Both Golgi and Cajal were awarded a Nobel Prize in Physiology or Medicine in 1906 for this work on the neuron doctrine.[16]

5.1.4   Mid-late 20th century

Several findings in the 20th century continued to advance the field, such as the discovery of ocular dominance columns, recording of single nerve cells in animals, and coordination of eye and head movements. Experimental psychology was also significant in the foundation of cognitive neuroscience. Some particularly important results were the demonstration that some tasks are accomplished via discrete processing stages, the study of attention, and the notion that behavioural data do not provide enough information by themselves to explain mental processes. As a result, some experimental psychologists began to investigate neural bases of behaviour. Wilder Penfield built up maps of primary sensory and motor areas of the brain by stimulating cortices of patients during surgery. Sperry and Gazzaniga's work on split brain patients in the 1950s was also instrumental in the progress of the field.[7]

Brain mapping

New brain mapping technology, particularly fMRI and PET, allowed researchers to investigate experimental strategies of cognitive psychology by observing brain function. Although this is often thought of as a new method (most of the technology is relatively recent), the underlying principle goes back as far as 1878 when blood flow was first associated with brain function.[6] Angelo Mosso, an Italian psychologist of the 19th century, had monitored the pulsations of the adult brain through neurosurgically created bony defects in the skulls of patients. He noted that when the subjects engaged in tasks such as mathematical calculations the pulsations of the brain increased locally. Such observations led Mosso to conclude that blood flow of the brain followed function.[6]

5.2 Emergence of a new discipline

5.2.1 Birth of cognitive science

On September 11, 1956, a large-scale meeting of cognitivists took place at the Massachusetts Institute of Technology. George A. Miller presented his "The Magical Number Seven, Plus or Minus Two" paper while Noam Chomsky and Newell & Simon presented their findings on computer science. Ulric Neisser commented on many of the findings at this meeting in his 1967 book *Cognitive Psychology*. The term "psychology" had been waning in the 1950s and 1960s, causing the field to be referred to as "cognitive science". Behaviorists such as Miller began to focus on the representation of language rather than general behavior. David Marr concluded that one should understand any cognitive process at three levels of analysis. These levels include computational, algorithmic/representational, and physical levels of analysis.[17]

5.2.2 Combining neuroscience and cognitive science

Before the 1980s, interaction between neuroscience and cognitive science was scarce.[18] The term 'cognitive neuroscience' was coined by George Miller and Michael Gazzaniga toward the end of the 1970s.[18] Cognitive neuroscience began to integrate the newly laid theoretical ground in cognitive science, that emerged between the 1950s and 1960s, with approaches in experimental psychology, neuropsychology and neuroscience. (Neuroscience was not established as a unified discipline until 1971[19]). In the very late 20th century new technologies evolved that are now the mainstay of the methodology of cognitive neuroscience, including TMS (1985) and fMRI (1991). Earlier methods used in cognitive neuroscience includes EEG (human EEG 1920) and MEG (1968). Occasionally cognitive neuroscientists utilize other brain imaging methods such as PET and SPECT. An upcoming technique in neuroscience is NIRS which uses light absorption to calculate changes in oxy- and deoxyhemoglobin in cortical areas. In some animals Single-unit recording can be used. Other methods include microneurography, facial EMG, and eye-tracking. Integrative neuroscience attempts to consolidate data in databases, and form unified descriptive models from various fields and scales: biology, psychology, anatomy, and clinical practice.[20] In 2014, Stanislas Dehaene, Giacomo Rizzolatti and Trevor Robbins, were awarded the Brain Prize "for their pioneering research on higher brain mechanisms underpinning such complex human functions as literacy, numeracy, motivated behaviour and social cognition, and for their efforts to understand cognitive and behavioural disorders".[21] Brenda Milner, Marcus Raichle and John

O'Keefe received the Kavli Prize in Neuroscience "for the discovery of specialized brain networks for memory and cognition"[22] and O'Keefe shared the Nobel Prize in Physiology or Medicine in the same year with May-Britt Moser and Edvard Moser "for their discoveries of cells that constitute a positioning system in the brain".[23]

5.3 Recent trends

Recently the foci of research have expanded from the localization of brain area(s) for specific functions in the adult brain using a single technology, studies have been diverging in several different directions [24] such as monitoring REM sleep via polygraphy, a machine that is capable of recording the electrical activity of a sleeping brain. Advances in non-invasive functional neuroimaging and associated data analysis methods have also made it possible to use highly naturalistic stimuli and tasks such as feature films depicting social interactions in cognitive neuroscience studies.[25]

5.4 Topics

- Attention
- Change blindness
- Consciousness
- Decision-making
- Learning
- Memory
- Language
- Mirror neurons
- Social cognition
- Emotions

5.5 Methods

Experimental methods of specific psychology fields include:

- Psychophysics
- Functional magnetic resonance imaging
- Electroencephalography
- Electrocorticography
- Transcranial Magnetic Stimulation
- Computational Modeling

5.6 Related WikiBooks

- wikibooks:Cognitive Psychology and Cognitive Neuroscience

- Wikibook on consciousness

- Cognitive Neuroscience chapter of the Neuroscience WikiBook

- Computational Cognitive Neuroscience wikibook

5.7 See also

5.8 References

[1] Gazzaniga, Ivry and Mangun 2002, cf. title

[2] Gazzaniga 2002, p. xv

[3] Kosslyn, S, M. & Andersen, R, A. (1992). Frontiers in cognitive neuroscience. Cambridge, MA: MIT press.

[4] Cordelia Erickson-Davis. "Neurofeedback Training for Parkinsonian Tremor and Bradykinesia" (PDF). Retrieved 2013-05-23.

[5] G. Fritsch, E. Hitzig, Electric excitability of the cerebrum (Über die elektrische Erregbarkeit des Grosshirns), Epilepsy & Behavior, Volume 15, Issue 2, June 2009, Pages 123-130, ISSN 1525-5050, 10.1016/j.yebeh.2009.03.001.

[6] Marcus E. Raichle. (2009). A brief history of human brain mapping. Trends in Neurosciences. 32 (2) 118-126.

[7] Uttal, W, R. (2011). Mind and brain: A critical appraisal of cognitive neuroscience. Cambridge, MA: MIT Press

[8] Gross, C, G. (1995) Aristotle on the Brain. The Neuroscientist(1) 4.

[9] Smith, C, U. (2013). Cardiocentric neurophysiology. the persistence of a delusion. Journal of the History of Neuroscience 22(1) 6-13.

[10] Hatfield, G. (2002). Psychology, Philosophy, and Cognitive Science: Reflections on the History and Philosophy of Experimental Psychology. Mind and Language. 17(3) 207-232.

[11] Bear et al. 2007, pp. 10-11

[12] Enersen, O. D. 2009

[13] Boring, E.G. (1957). A history of experimental psychology. New York.

[14] Uttal, W, R. (2011). Mind and brain: A critical appraisal of cognitive neuroscience. Cambridge, MA: MIT PressUttal, W, R. (2011). Mind and brain: A critical appraisal of cognitive neuroscience. Cambridge, MA: MIT Press

[15] Mandler, G. (2002) Origins of the cognitive (r)evolution. J. Hist. Behav. Sci. Fall 38(4)339-53.

[16] "The Nobel Prize in Physiology or Medicine 1906".

[17] jungminded.weebly.com/7/post/2013/01/approaches-in-cognitive-pscyhology.html

[18] not available, http://www.petemandik.com/philosophy/papers/brookmadik.com.pdf not available

[19] Society for Neuroscience. Date of the first meeting of the Sociefy for Neuroscience

[20] https://www.boundless.com/psychology/history-psychology/origin-psychology/growth-of-psychology-as-a-science-$-$31/

[21] "The Brain Prize".

[22] http://www.kavliprize.org/prizes-and-laureates/prizes/2014-kavli-prize-laureates-neuroscience

[23] http://www.nobelprize.org/nobel_prizes/medicine/laureates/2014/

[24] Takeo, Watanabe. "Cognitive neuroscience Editorial overview" (PDF).

[25] Hasson, Uri; et al. "Intersubject Synchronization of Cortical Activity During Natural Vision".

5.9 Further reading

- Bear, M. F., Connors, B. W. & Paradiso M. A.(2007). "Neuroscience: Exploring the Brain" (3rd ed.). pp. 10–11. Lippincott Williams & Wilkins, ISBN 0-7817-6003-8

- Churchland, P.S. & Sejnowski, T.J. (1992). *The Computational Brain*, The MIT Press, ISBN 0-262-03188-4.

- Code, C. (1996). *Classic Cases: Ancient & Modern Milestones in the Development of Neuropsychological Science*. In: Code, C. et al. *Classic Cases in Neuropsychology*.

- Enersen, O. D. (2009). *John Hughlings Jackson*. In: Who Named It. http://www.whonamedit.com/doctor.cfm/2766.html Retrieved 14 August 2009

- Gazzaniga, M. S., Ivry, R. B. & Mangun, G. R. (2002). *Cognitive Neuroscience: The biology of the mind* (2nd ed.). New York: W.W.Norton.

- Gazzaniga, M. S., *The Cognitive Neurosciences III*, (2004), The MIT Press, ISBN 0-262-07254-8

- Gazzaniga, M. S., Ed. (1999). *Conversations in the Cognitive Neurosciences*, The MIT Press, ISBN 0-262-57117-X.

- Miller, G. A. (1956). The magical number seven, plus or minus two: Some limits on our capacity for processing information. *Psychological Review*, 63, 81-97

- Sternberg, Eliezer J. *Are You a Machine? The Brain, the Mind and What it Means to be Human.* Amherst, NY: Prometheus Books.

- Ward, Jamie (2015). *The Student's Guide to Cognitive Neuroscience, 3rd Edition.* Psychology Press. ISBN 978-1848722729. External link in |publisher= (help)

- Handbook of Functional Neuroimaging of Cognition By Roberto Cabeza, Alan Kingstone

- Principles of neural science By Eric R. Kandel, James H. Schwartz, Thomas M. Jessell

- The Cognitive Neuroscience of Memory By Amanda Parker, Edward L. Wilding, Timothy J. Bussey

- Neuronal Theories of the Brain By Christof Koch, Joel L. Davis

- Cambridge Handbook of Thinking and Reasoning By Keith James Holyoak, Robert G. Morrison

- Handbook of Mathematical Cognition By Jamie I. D. Campbell

- Cognitive Psychology By Michael W. Eysenck, Mark T. Keane

- Development of Intelligence By Mike Anderson

- Development of Mental Processing By Andreas Demetriou, et. al.

- Memory and Thinking By Robert H. Logie, K. J. Gilhooly

- Memory Capacity By Nelson Cowan

- Proceedings of the Nineteenth Annual Conference of the Cognitive Science

- Models of Working Memory By Akira Miyake, Priti Shah

- Memory and Thinking By Robert H. Logie, K. J. Gilhooly

- Variation in Working Memory By Andrew R. A. Conway, et. al.

- Memory Capacity By Nelson Cowan

- Cognition and Intelligence By Robert J. Sternberg, Jean E. Pretz

- General Factor of Intelligence By Robert J. Sternberg, Elena Grigorenko

- Neurological Basis of Learning, Development and Discovery By Anton E. Lawson

- Memory and Human Cognition By John T. E. Richardson

- Society for Neuroscience. http://www.sfn.org/index.cfm?pagename=about_sfn#timeline Retrieved 14 August 2009

- Keiji Tanaka,"Current Opinion in Neurobiology", (2007)

5.10 External links

- Cognitive Neuroscience Society Homepage

- There's Something about Zero

- What Is Cognitive Neuroscience?, Jamie Ward/Psychology Press

- goCognitive - Educational Tools for Cognitive Neuroscience (including video interviews)

- CogNet, The Brain and Cognitive Sciences Community Online, MIT

- Cognitive Neuroscience Arena, Psychology Press

- Cognitive Neuroscience and Philosophy, CUJCS, Spring 2002

- Whole Brain Atlas Top 100 Brain Structures

- Cognitive Neuroscience Discussion Group

- John Jonides, a big role in Cognitive Neurosciences by Beebrite

- School of Cognitive Science, Jadavpur University

- Introduction to Cognitive Neuroscience

- AgliotiLAB - Social and Cognitive Neuroscience Laboratory founded in 2003 in Rome, Italy

Chapter 6

Cognitive science of religion

Cognitive science of religion is the study of religious thought and behavior from the perspective of the cognitive and evolutionary sciences. The field employs methods and theories from a very broad range of disciplines, including: cognitive psychology, evolutionary psychology, cognitive anthropology, artificial intelligence, cognitive neuroscience, neurobiology, zoology, and ethology.   Scholars in this field seek to explain how human minds acquire, generate, and transmit religious thoughts, practices, and schemas by means of ordinary cognitive capacities.

6.1   History

Although religion has been the subject of serious scientific study since at least the late nineteenth century, the study of religion as a cognitive phenomenon is relatively recent. While it often relies upon earlier research within anthropology of religion[1] and sociology of religion, cognitive science of religion considers the results of that work within the context of evolutionary and cognitive theories. As such, cognitive science of religion was only made possible by the cognitive revolution of the 1950s and the development, starting in the 1970s, of sociobiology and other approaches explaining human behaviour in evolutionary terms, especially evolutionary psychology.

While Dan Sperber foreshadowed cognitive science of religion in his 1975 book *Rethinking Symbolism*, the earliest research to fall within the scope of the discipline was published during the 1980s. Among this work, Stewart E. Guthrie's "A cognitive theory of religion" *Current Anthropology* 21 (2) 1980 was significant for examining the significance of anthropomorphism within religion, work that ultimately led to the development of the concept of the hyperactive agency detection device – a key concept within cognitive science of religion.

The real beginning of cognitive science of religion can be dated to the 1990s, however. During that decade a large number of highly influential books and articles were pub-lished which helped to lay the foundations of cognitive science of religion. These included *Rethinking Religion: Connecting Cognition and Culture* and *Bringing Ritual to Mind: Psychological Foundations of Cultural Forms*, written by E. Thomas Lawson and Robert McCauley, *Naturalness of Religious Ideas* by Pascal Boyer, as well as Guthrie's book-length development of his theories in *Faces in the Clouds*. In the 1990s, these and other researchers, who had been working independently in a variety of different disciplines, discovered each other's work and found valuable parallels between their approaches, with the result that something of a self-aware research tradition began to coalesce. By 2000, the field was well-enough defined for Justin L. Barrett to coin the term 'cognitive science of religion' in his article "Exploring the natural foundations of religion".[2]

Since 2000, cognitive science of religion has grown, similarly to other approaches that apply evolutionary thinking to sociological phenomena. Each year more researchers become involved in the field, with theoretical and empirical developments proceeding at a very rapid pace. The field remains somewhat loosely defined, bringing together as it does researchers who come from a variety of different traditions. Much of the cohesion in the field comes not from shared detailed theoretical commitments but from a general willingness to view religion in cognitive and evolutionary terms as well as from the willingness to engage with the work of the others developing this field. A vital role in bringing together researchers is played by the International Association for the Cognitive Science of Religion, formed in 2006.

6.2   Theoretical basis

See also: Evolutionary psychology of religion

Despite a lack of agreement concerning the theoretical basis for work in cognitive science of religion, it is possible to outline some tendencies. Most significant of these is reliance upon the theories developed within evolutionary psychology. That particular approach to evolutionary explanations of human behaviour is particularly suitable to the cognitive byproduct explanation of religion that is most popular among cognitive scientists of religion. This is because of the focus on byproduct and ancestral trait explanations within evolutionary psychology. A particularly significant concept associated with this approach is modularity of mind, used as it is to underpin accounts of the mental mechanisms seen to be responsible for religious beliefs. Important examples of work that falls under this rubric are provided by research carried out by Pascal Boyer and Justin L. Barrett.

These theoretical commitments are not shared by all cognitive scientists of religion, however. Ongoing debates regarding the comparative advantages of different evolutionary explanations for human behaviour[3] find a reflection within cognitive science of religion with dual inheritance theory recently gaining adherents among researchers in the field, including Armin Geertz and Ara Norenzayan. The perceived advantage of this theoretical framework is its ability to deal with more complex interactions between cognitive and cultural phenomena, but it comes at the cost of experimental design having to take into consideration a richer range of possibilities.

6.3 Main concepts

6.3.1 Cognitive byproduct

The view that religious beliefs and practices should be understood as nonfunctional but as produced by human cognitive mechanisms that are functional outside of the context of religion. Examples of this are the hyperactive agent detection device and the minimally counterintuitive concepts [4] or the process of initiation [5] explaining buddhism and taoism. The cognitive byproduct explanation of religion is an application of the concept of spandrel (biology) and of the concept of exaptation explored by Stephen Jay Gould among others.

6.3.2 Minimally counterintuitive concepts

Concepts that mostly fit human preconceptions but break with them in one or two striking ways. These concepts are both easy to remember (thanks to the counterintuitive elements) and easy to use (thanks to largely agreeing with what people expect). Examples include talking trees and noncorporeal agents. Pascal Boyer argues that many religious entities fit into this category.[6] Upal [7] lablled the fact that minimally counterintuitive ideas are better remem-

bered than intuitive and maximally counterintuitive ideas as the minimal counterintuitiveness effect or the MCI-effect.

6.3.3 Hyperactive agency detection device

Postulated mental mechanism whose function is to identify the activity of agents. Given the relative costs of failing to spot an agent, the mechanism is said to be hyperactive, producing a large number of false positive errors. Stewart E. Guthrie and others have claimed these errors can explain the appearance of supernatural concepts.

6.3.4 Pro-social adaptation

According to the prosocial adaptation account of religion, religious beliefs and practices should be understood as having the function of eliciting adaptive prosocial behaviour and avoiding the free rider problem. Within the cognitive science of religion this approach is primarily pursued by Richard Sosis. David Sloan Wilson is another major proponent of this approach and interprets religion as a group-level adaptation, but his work is generally seen as falling outside the cognitive science of religion.

6.3.5 Costly signaling

Practices that, due to their inherent cost, can be relied upon to provide an honest signal regarding the intentions of the agent. Richard Sosis has suggested that religious practices can be explained as costly signals of the willingness to cooperate. A similar line of argument has been pursued by Lyle Steadman and Craig Palmer. Alternatively, D. Jason Slone has argued that religiosity may be a costly signal used as a mating strategy in so far as religiosity serves as a proxy for "family values."

6.3.6 Dual inheritance

In the context of cognitive science of religion, dual inheritance theory can be understood as attempting to combine the cognitive byproduct and prosocial adaptation accounts using the theoretical approach developed by Robert Boyd and Peter Richerson, among others. The basic view is that while belief in supernatural entities is a cognitive byproduct, cultural traditions have recruited such beliefs to motivate prosocial behaviour. A sophisticated statement of this approach can be found in Scott Atran and Joseph Henrich (2010) "The Evolution of Religion: How Cognitive By-Products, Adaptive Learning Heuristics, Ritual Displays, and Group Competition Generate Deep Commitments to Prosocial Religions" *Biological Theory* 5.1.

6.4   Leading specialists

Researchers in the field include:

- Scott Atran, Directeur de Recherche, Institut Jean Nicod, CNRS, Paris

- Justin L. Barrett, Thrive Professor of Developmental Science and Director of the Thrive Center for Human Development, Fuller Graduate School of Psychology

- Jesse Bering, Associate Professor, Centre for Science Communication, University of Otago

- Pascal Boyer, Henry Luce Professor of Individual and Collective Memory at Washington University in St. Louis

- Armin W. Geertz, Professor at the Religion, Cognition and Culture research unit at Aarhus University

- Jeppe Sinding Jensen, Senior Lecturer at the Religion, Cognition and Culture research unit at Aarhus University

- Jonathan Jong

- Deborah Kelemen, Professor of Psychology, Boston University

- E. Thomas Lawson, Honorary Professor and Research Scientist at the Institute of Cognition and Culture, Queen's University Belfast

- Luther H. Martin, Emeritus Professor at the University of Vermont

- Robert McCauley, Director of the Center for Mind, Brain, and Culture, Emory University

- Uffe Schjoedt, Associate Professor at the Religion, Cognition and Culture research unit at Aarhus University

- D. Jason Slone, Professor of Religious Studies, Georgia Southern University

- Jesper Sørensen, Head of the Religion, Cognition and Culture research unit at Aarhus University

- Dan Sperber, Directeur de Recherche, Institut Jean Nicod, CNRS, Paris

- Ann Taves, professor of religious studies at the University of California, Santa Barbara

- Harvey Whitehouse, professor of social anthropology at the University of Oxford

- Dmitris Xygalatas

- Cristine H. Legare, Associate Professor, The University of Texas at Austin

- Andre L. Souza, Assistant Professor, The University of Alabama

Writers on this topic include:

- J. Anderson Thomson, a Trustee of the Richard Dawkins Foundation for Reason and Science

- Afzal Upal, A Cognitive Scientist at Defence R & D Canada.

- Kelly James Clark, philosopher

- Helen De Cruz, philosopher

6.5   Publications

- Atran, S., & Norenzayan, A. (2004). "Religion's evolutionary landscape: Counterintuition, commitment, compassion, communion". *Behavioral and Brain Sciences* 27, 713-770.

- Barrett, J.L. "Cognitive Science of Religion: What Is It and Why Is It?" *Religion Compass* 2007, vol 1.

- Barrett, J.L. "Exploring the Natural Foundations of Religion." *Trends in Cognitive Sciences* 2000, vol. 4 pp 29–34

- Barrett, J.L. *Why Would Anyone Believe in God?* AltaMira Press, 2004.

- Barrett, J.L. and Jonathan A. Lanman. "The Science of Religious Beliefs." *Religion* 38, 2008. 109-124

- Barrett, Nathaniel F. *Toward an Alternative Evolutionary Theory of Religion: Looking Past Computational Evolutionary Psychology to a Wider Field of Possibilities.* Journal of the American Academy of Religion, September 2010, Vol. 78, No. 3, pp. 583–621.

- Boyer, Pascal. *The Naturalness of Religious Ideas* University of California Press, 1994.

- Boyer, Pascal. *Religion Explained: The Evolutionary Origins of Religious Thought* Basic Books, 2001

- Boyer, Pascal. "Religious Thought and Behavior as By-Products of Brain Functions," *Trends in Cognitive Sciences* 7, pp 119–24

- Boyer, P and Liénard, P. "Why ritualized behavior? Precaution Systems and action parsing in developmental, pathological and cultural rituals .*Behavioral and Brain Sciences* 29: 595-650.

- Cohen, E. *The Mind Possessed. The Cognition of Spirit Possession in the Afro-Brazilian Religious Tradition* Oxford University Press.

- De Cruz, Helen & De Smedt, Johan. (2015). "A natural history of natural theology. The Cognitive Science of Theology and Philosophy of Religion." MIT Press, 2015.

- Geertz, Armin W. (2004). "Cognitive Approaches to the Study of Religion," in P. Antes, A.W. Geertz, R.R. Warne (Eds.) *New Approaches to the Study of Religion Volume 2: Textual, Comparative, Sociological, and Cognitive Approaches.* Berlin: Walter de Gruyter, pp. 347–399.

- Geertz, Armin W. (2008). "From Apes to Devils and Angels: Comparing Scenarios on the Evolution of Religion," in J. Bulbulia et al. (Eds.) *The Evolution of Religion: Studies, Theories, & Critiques* Santa Margarita: Collins Foundation Press, pp. 43–49.

- Guthrie, S. E. (1993). '*Faces in the Clouds: A new theory of religion* New York: Oxford University Press.

- Knight, N., Sousa, P., Barrett, J. L., & Atran, S. (2004). "Children's attributions of beliefs to humans and God". *Cognitive Science* 28(1): 117-126.

- Kress, O. (1993). "A new approach to cognitive development: ontogenesis and the process of initiation". *Evolution and Cognition* 2(4): 319-332.

- Lawson, E. T. "Toward a Cognitive Science of Religion." *Numen* 47(3): 338-349(12).

- Lawson, E. T. "Religious Thought." *Encyclopedia of Cognitive Science* vol 3 (A607).

- Lawson, E. T. and McCauley, RN. *Rethinking Religion: Connecting Cognition and Culture* Cambridge University Press, 1990.

- Legare, C. and Gelman, S. "Bewitchment, Biology, or Both: The Co-existence of Natural and Supernatural Explanatory Frameworks Across Development." *Cognitive Science* 32(4): 607-642.

- Light, T and Wilson, B (eds). *Religion as a Human Capacity: A Festschrift in Honor of E. Thomas Lawson* Brill, 2004.

- McCauley, RN. "The Naturalness of Religion and the Unnaturalness of Science." *Explanation and Cognition* (Keil and Wilson eds), pp 61–85. MIT Press, 2000.

- McCauley, RN and Lawson, E. T. *Bringing Ritual to Mind: Psychological Foundations of Cultural Forms* Cambridge University Press, 2002.

- McCorkle Jr., William W. *Ritualizing the Disposal of the Deceased: From Corpse to Concept* Peter Lang, 2010.

- Norenzayan, A., Atran, S., Faulkner, J., & Schaller, M. (2006). "Memory and mystery: The cultural selection of minimally counterintuitive narratives". *Cognitive Science* 30, 531-553.

- Nuckolls, C. "Boring Rituals," *Journal of Ritual Studies* 2006.

- Pyysiäinen, I. *How Religion Works: Towards a New Cognitive Science of Religion* Brill, 2001.

- Slone, DJ. *Theological Incorrectness: Why Religious People Believe What They Shouldn't* Oxford University Press, 2004.

- Slone, DJ (ed). *Religion and Cognition: A Reader* Equinox Press, 2006.

- Slone, DJ, and Van Slyke, J. *The Attraction of Religion.* Bloomsbury Academic Press. 2015.

- Sørensen, J. "A Cognitive Theory of Magic." AltaMira Press, 2006.

- Sperber, D. *Rethinking Symbolism* Cambridge University Press, 1975.

- Sperber, D. *Explaining Culture* Blackwell Publishers, 1996.

- Talmont-Kaminski, K. (2013). *Religion as Magical Ideology: How the Supernatural Reflects Rationality* Durham: Acumen.

- Taves, A. "Religious Experience Reconsidered: A Building Block Approach to the Study of Religion and Other Special Things" Princeton University Press, 2011.

- Tremlin, T. *Minds and Gods: The Cognitive Foundations of Religion* Oxford University Press, 2006.

- Upal, M. A. (2005). "Towards a Cognitive Science of New Religious Movements," *Cognition and Culture*, 5(2), 214-239.

- Upal, M. A., Gonce, L., Tweney, R., and Slone, J. (2007). Contextualizing counterintuitiveness: How Context Affects Comprehension and Memorability of Counterintuitive Concepts, Cognitive Science, 31(3), 415-439.

- Whitehouse, H. (1995). *Inside the Cult: Religious innovation and transmission in Papua New Guinea* Oxford: Clarendon Press.

- Whitehouse, H. (1996a). "Apparitions, orations, and rings: Experience of spirits" in Dadul. Jeannette Mageo and Alan Howard (eds). *Spirits in Culture, History, and Mind* New York: Routledge.

- Whitehouse, H. (1996b). "Rites of terror: Emotion, metaphor, and memory in Melanesian initiation cults" *Journal of the Royal Anthropological Institute* 2, 703-715.

- Whitehouse, H. (2000). *Arguments and Icons: Divergent modes of religiosity* Oxford: Oxford University Press.

- Whitehouse, H. (2004). *Modes of Religiosity: a cognitive theory of religious transmission* Walnut Creek, CA: AltaMira Press.

- Xygalatas, D and McCorkle Jr., W.W. (eds). *Mental Culture: Classical Social Theory and The Cognitive Science of Religion* Durham: Acumen.

6.6   See also

- Psychology of religion

- International Association for the Cognitive Science of Religion (IACSR)

- Issues in Science and Religion

- Evolutionary epistemology

- Evolutionary origin of religions

- Evolutionary psychology of religion

- Neurotheology

6.7   References

[1] Geertz C. (1966) "Religion as cultural system" In: Banton, M. (ed) *Anthropological approaches to the study of religion* London: Tavistock p 1-46

[2] Barrett, Justin (1 January 2000). "Exploring the natural foundations of religion". *Trends in Cognitive Sciences* **4**: 29–34. doi:10.1016/S1364-6613(99)01419-9.

[3] See Laland K. and Brown D. (2002) *Sense and Nonsense: Evolutionary Perspectives on Human Behavior* Oxford: Oxford University Press for overview.

[4] Minimal counterintuitiveness

[5] Kress, Oliver (1993). "A new approach to cognitive development: ontogenesis and the process of initiation". Evolution and Cognition 2(4): 319-332.

[6] Boyer, Pascal. *The Naturalness of Religious Ideas* University of California Press, 1994.

[7] Upal, M. A. (2010). "An Alternative View of the Minimal Counterintuitiveness Effect", *Journal of Cognitive Systems Research*, 11(2), 194-203.

Chapter 7

Psychology of religion

Psychology of religion consists of the application of psychological methods and interpretive frameworks to religious traditions, as well as to both religious and irreligious individuals. It attempts to accurately describe the details, origins, and uses of religious beliefs and behaviors. Although the psychology of religion first arose as a self-conscious discipline as recently as the late 19th century, all three of these tasks have a history going back many centuries before that.[1]

In contrast to neurotheology, the psychology of religion studies only psychological rather than neural states.

Many areas of religion remain unexplored by psychology. While religion and spirituality play a role in many people's lives, it is uncertain how they lead to outcomes that are at times positive, and at other times negative.

7.1 Overview

The challenge for the psychology of religion is essentially threefold: (1) to provide a thoroughgoing description of the objects of investigation, whether they be shared religious content (e.g., a tradition's ritual observances) or individual experiences, attitudes, or conduct; (2) to account in psychological terms for the rise of such phenomena; and (3) to clarify the outcomes—the fruits, as William James put it—of these phenomena, for individuals and for the larger society.[1]

The first, descriptive task naturally requires a clarification of one's terms, above all, the word religion. Historians of religion have long underscored the problematic character of this term, noting that its usage over the centuries has changed in significant ways, generally in the direction of reification.[2] The early psychologists of religion were fully aware of these difficulties, typically acknowledging that the definitions they were choosing to use were to some degree arbitrary.[3] With the rise of positivistic trends in psychology over the course of the 20th century, especially the demand that all phenomena be measured, psychologists of re-

ligion developed a multitude of scales, most of them developed for use with Protestant Christians.[4] Factor analysis was also brought into play by both psychologists and sociologists of religion, in an effort to establish a fixed core of dimensions and a corresponding set of scales. The justification and adequacy of these efforts, especially in the light of constructivist and other postmodern viewpoints, remains a matter of debate.

In the last several decades, especially among clinical psychologists, a preference for the terms "spirituality" and "spiritual" has emerged, along with efforts to distinguish them from "religion" and "religious." Especially in the United States, "religion" has for many become associated with sectarian institutions and their obligatory creeds and rituals, thus giving the word a negative cast; "spirituality," in contrast, is positively constructed as deeply individual and subjective, as a universal capacity to apprehend and accord one's life with higher realities.[5] In fact, "spirituality" has likewise undergone an evolution in the West, from a time when it was essentially a synonym for religion in its original, subjective meaning.[6] Pargament (1997) suggests that rather than limiting the usage of "religion" to functional terms, a search for meaning, or substantive terms, anything related to the sacred, we can consider the interplay of these two vantage points. He proposes that religion can be considered the process of searching for meaning in relationship with the sacred.[7] Today, efforts are ongoing to "operationalize" these terms, with little regard for their history in their Western context, and with the apparent realist assumption that underlying them are fixed qualities identifiable by means of empirical procedures.[8]

Schnitker and Emmons theorized that the understanding of religion as a search for meaning makes implications in the three psychological areas of motivation, cognition and social relationships. The cognitive aspects relate to God and a sense of purpose, the motivational ones to the need to control, and the religious search for meaning is also weaved into social communities.[9]

7.2   History

7.2.1   William James

American psychologist and philosopher William James (1842–1910) is regarded by most psychologists of religion as the founder of the field.[10] He served as president of the *American Psychological Association*, and wrote one of the first psychology textbooks. In the psychology of religion, James' influence endures. His *Varieties of Religious Experience* is considered to be the classic work in the field, and references to James' ideas are common at professional conferences.

James distinguished between institutional religion and personal religion. Institutional religion refers to the religious group or organization, and plays an important part in a society's culture. Personal religion, in which the individual has mystical experience, can be experienced regardless of the culture. James was most interested in understanding personal religious experience.

In studying personal religious experiences, James made a distinction between *healthy-minded* and *sick-souled* religiousness. Individuals predisposed to healthy-mindedness tend to ignore the evil in the world and focus on the positive and the good. James used examples of Walt Whitman and the "mind-cure" religious movement to illustrate healthy-mindedness in *The Varieties of Religious Experience*. In contrast, individuals predisposed to having a sick-souled religion are unable to ignore evil and suffering, and need a unifying experience, religious or otherwise, to reconcile good and evil. James included quotations from Leo Tolstoy and John Bunyan to illustrate the sick soul.

William James' hypothesis of pragmatism stems from the efficacy of religion. If an individual believes in and performs religious activities, and those actions happen to work, then that practice appears the proper choice for the individual. However, if the processes of religion have little efficacy, then there is no rationality for continuing the practice.

7.2.2   Other early theorists

G.W.F. Hegel

Hegel (1770–1831) described all systems of religion, philosophy, and social science as expressions of the basic urge of consciousness to learn about itself and its surroundings, and record its findings and hypotheses. Thus, religion is only a form of that search for knowledge, within which humans record various experiences and reflections. Others, compiling and categorizing these writings in various ways, form the consolidated worldview as articulated by that religion, philosophy, social science, etc. His work The Phe-

nomenology of Spirit was a study of how various types of writing and thinking draw from and re-combine with the individual and group experiences of various places and times, influencing the current forms of knowledge and worldviews that are operative in a population. This activity is the functioning of an incomplete group mind, where each individual is accessing the recorded wisdom of others. His works often include detailed descriptions of the psychological motivations involved in thought and behavior, e.g., the struggle of a community or nation to know itself and thus correctly govern itself. In Hegel's system, Religion is one of the major repositories of wisdom to be used in these struggles, representing a huge body of recollections from humanity's past in various stages of its development.

Sigmund Freud

Group photo 1909 in front of Clark University.   Front row: Sigmund Freud, G. Stanley Hall, Carl Jung.   Back row: Abraham Brill, Ernest Jones, Sándor Ferenczi.

Sigmund Freud (1856–1939) gave explanations of the genesis of religion in his various writings. In *Totem and Taboo*, he applied the idea of the Oedipus complex (involving unresolved sexual feelings of, for example, a son toward his mother and hostility toward his father) and postulated its emergence in the primordial stage of human development.

In *Moses and Monotheism*, Freud reconstructed biblical history in accordance with his general theory. His ideas were also developed in *The Future of an Illusion*. When Freud spoke of religion as an illusion, he maintained that it "is a fantasy structure from which a man must be set free if he is to grow to maturity."

Freud views the idea of God as being a version of the father image, and religious belief as at bottom infantile and neurotic. Authoritarian religion, Freud believed, is dysfunctional and alienates man from himself.

Carl Jung

The Swiss psychoanalyst Carl Jung (1875–1961) adopted a very different posture, one that was more sympathetic to religion and more concerned with a positive appreciation of religious symbolism. Jung considered the question of the metaphysical existence of God to be unanswerable by the psychologist and adopted a kind of agnosticism.[11]

Jung postulated, in addition to the personal unconscious (roughly adopting Freud's concept), the collective unconscious, which is the repository of human experience and which contains "archetypes" (i.e. basic images that are universal in that they recur regardless of culture). The irruption of these images from the unconscious into the realm of consciousness he viewed as the basis of religious experience and often of artistic creativity. Some of Jung's writings have been devoted to elucidating some of the archetypal symbols, and include his work in comparative mythology.

Alfred Adler

Austrian psychiatrist Alfred Adler (1870–1937), who parted ways with Freud, emphasised the role of goals and motivation in his *Individual Psychology*. One of Adler's most famous ideas is that we try to compensate for inferiorities that we perceive in ourselves. A lack of power often lies at the root of feelings of inferiority. One way that religion enters into this picture is through our beliefs in God, which are characteristic of our tendency to strive for perfection and superiority. For example, in many religions God is considered to be perfect and omnipotent, and commands people likewise to be perfect. If we, too, achieve perfection, we become one with God. By identifying with God in this way, we compensate for our imperfections and feelings of inferiority.

Our ideas about God are important indicators of how we view the world. According to Adler, these ideas have changed over time, as our vision of the world – and our place in it – has changed. Consider this example that Adler offers: the traditional belief that people were placed deliberately on earth as God's ultimate creation is being replaced with the idea that people have evolved by natural selection. This coincides with a view of God not as a real being, but as an abstract representation of nature's forces. In this way our view of God has changed from one that was concrete and specific to one that is more general. From Adler's vantage point, this is a relatively ineffective perception of God because it is so general that it fails to convey a strong sense of direction and purpose.

An important thing for Adler is that God (or the idea of God) motivates people to act, and that those actions do have real consequences for ourselves and for others. Our view of God is important because it embodies our goals and directs our social interactions.

Compared to science, another social movement, religion is more efficient because it motivates people more effectively. According to Adler, only when science begins to capture the same religious fervour, and promotes the welfare of all segments of society, will the two be more equal in peoples' eyes.

Gordon Allport

In his classic book *The Individual and His Religion* (1950), Gordon Allport (1897–1967) illustrates how people may use religion in different ways.[12] He makes a distinction between *Mature religion* and *Immature religion*. Mature religious sentiment is how Allport characterized the person whose approach to religion is dynamic, open-minded, and able to maintain links between inconsistencies. In contrast, immature religion is self-serving and generally represents the negative stereotypes that people have about religion. More recently, this distinction has been encapsulated in the terms "intrinsic religion", referring to a genuine, heartfelt devout faith, and "extrinsic religion", referring to a more utilitarian use of religion as a means to an end, such as church attendance to gain social status. These dimensions of religion were measured on the Religious Orientation Scale of Allport and Ross (1967). A third form of religious orientation has been described by Daniel Batson. This refers to treatment of religion as an open-ended search (Batson, Schoenrade & Ventis, 1993). More specifically, it has been seen by Batson as comprising a willingness to view religious doubts in a positive manner, acceptance that religious orientation can change and existential complexity, the belief that one's religious beliefs should be shaped from personal crises that one has experienced in one's life. Batson refers to extrinsic, intrinsic and quest respectively as religion-as-means, religion-as-end and religion-as-quest, and measures these constructs on the Religious Life Inventory (Batson, Schoenrade & Ventis, 1993).

Erik H. Erikson

Erik Erikson (1902–1994) is best known for his theory of psychological development, which has its roots in the psychoanalytic importance of identity in personality. His biographies of Gandhi and Martin Luther reveal Erikson's positive view of religion. He considered religions to be important influences in successful personality development because they are the primary way that cultures promote the virtues associated with each stage of life. Religious rituals facilitate this development. Erikson's theory has not benefited from systematic empirical study, but it remains an influential and well-regarded theory in the psychological study of religion.

Erich Fromm

The American scholar Erich Fromm (1900–1980) modified the Freudian theory and produced a more complex account of the functions of religion. In his book *Psychoanalysis and Religion* he responded to Freud's theories by explaining that part of the modification is viewing the Oedipus complex as based not so much on sexuality as on a "much more profound desire", namely, the childish desire to remain attached to protecting figures. The right religion, in Fromm's estimation, can, in principle, foster an individual's highest potentialities, but religion in practice tends to relapse into being neurotic.[13]

According to Fromm, humans have a need for a stable frame of reference. Religion apparently fills this need. In effect, humans crave answers to questions that no other source of knowledge has an answer to, which only religion may seem to answer. However, a sense of free will must be given in order for religion to appear healthy. An authoritarian notion of religion appears detrimental.[14]

Rudolf Otto

Rudolf Otto (1869–1937) was a German Protestant theologian and scholar of comparative religion. Otto's most famous work, *The Idea of the Holy* (published first in 1917 as *Das Heilige*), defines the concept of the holy as that which is *numinous*. Otto explained the numinous as a "non-rational, non-sensory experience or feeling whose primary and immediate object is outside the self." It is a mystery (Latin: *mysterium tremendum*) that is both fascinating (*fascinans*) and terrifying at the same time; A mystery that causes trembling and fascination, attempting to explain that inexpressible and perhaps supernatural emotional reaction of wonder drawing us to seemingly ordinary and/or religious experiences of grace. This sense of emotional wonder appears evident at the root of all religious experiences. Through this emotional wonder, we suspend our rational mind for non-rational possibilities.

It also sets a paradigm for the study of religion that focuses on the need to realise the religious as a non-reducible, original category in its own right. This paradigm was under much attack between approximately 1950 and 1990 but has made a strong comeback since then.

7.2.3 Modern thinkers

Autobiographal accounts of 20th-century psychology of religion as a field have been supplied by numerous modern psychologists of religion, primarily based in Europe, but also by several US-based psychologists such as Ralph W. Hood and Donald Capps.[15]

Allen Bergin

Allen Bergin is noted for his 1980 paper "Psychotherapy and Religious Values," which is known as a landmark in scholarly acceptance that religious values do, in practice, influence psychotherapy.[16][17] He received the Distinguished Professional Contributions to Knowledge award from the American Psychological Association in 1989 and was cited as challenging "psychological orthodoxy to emphasize the importance of values and religion in therapy."[18]

Robert Emmons

Robert Emmons offered a theory of "spiritual strivings" in his 1999 book, *The Psychology of Ultimate Concerns*.[19] With support from empirical studies, Emmons argued that spiritual strivings foster personality integration because they exist at a higher level of the personality.

Kenneth Pargament

Kenneth Pargament is noted for his book *Psychology of Religion and Coping* (1997; see article),[20] as well as for a 2007 book on religion and psychotherapy, and a sustained research program on religious coping. He is professor of psychology at Bowling Green State University (Ohio, US), and has published more than 100 papers on the subject of religion and spirituality in psychology. Pargament led the design of a questionnaire called the "RCOPE" to measure Religious Coping strategies.[21] Pargament has distinguished between three types of styles for coping with stress:[22] 1) Collaborative, in which people co-operate with God to deal with stressful events; 2) Deferring, in which people leave everything to God; and 3) Self-directed, in which people do not rely on God and try exclusively to solve problems by their own efforts. He also describes four major stances toward religion that have been adopted by psychotherapists in their work with clients, which he calls the religiously *rejectionist*, *exclusivist*, *constructivist*, and *pluralist* stances.[20][23]

James Hillman

James Hillman, at the end of his book *Re-Visioning Psychology*, reverses James' position of viewing religion through psychology, urging instead that we view psychology as a variety of religious experience. He concludes: "Psychology as religion implies imagining all psychological events as effects of Gods in the soul.[24]"

Julian Jaynes

Julian Jaynes, primarily in his book *The Origin of Consciousness in the Breakdown of the Bicameral Mind*, proposed that religion (and some other psychological phenomena such as hypnosis and schizophrenia) is a remnant of a relatively recent time in human development, prior to the advent of consciousness. Jaynes hypothesized that hallucinated verbal commands helped non-conscious early man to perform tasks promoting human survival. Starting about 10,000 BCE, selective pressures favored the hallucinated verbal commands for social control, and they came to be perceived as an external, rather than internal, voice commanding the person to take some action. These were hence often explained as originating from invisible gods, spirits, ancestors, etc.[25]

7.3 Hypotheses on the role of religion

There are three primary hypotheses on the role of religion in the modern world.

7.3.1 Secularization

The first hypothesis, secularization, holds that science and technology will take the place of religion.[26] Secularization supports the separation of religion from politics, ethics, and psychology. Taking this position even further, Taylor explains that secularization denies transcendence, divinity, and rationality in religious beliefs.[27]

7.3.2 Religious transformation

Challenges to the secularization hypothesis led to significant revisions, resulting in the religious transformation hypothesis.[28] This perspective holds that general trends towards individualism and social disintegration will produce changes in religion, making religious practice more individualized and spiritually focused.[29] This in turn is expected to produce more spiritual seeking, although not exclusive

to religious institutions.[30] Eclecticism, which draws from multiple religious/spiritual systems and New Age movements are also predicted to result.[31][32]

7.3.3 Cultural divide

In response to the religious transformation hypothesis, Ronald Inglehart piloted the renewal of the secularization hypothesis. His argument hinges on the premise that religion develops to fill the human need for security. Therefore, the development of social and economic security in Europe explains its corresponding secularization due to a lack of need for religion.[33] However, religion continues in the third world where social and economic insecurity are rampant. The overall effect is expected to be a growing cultural disparity.[34]

The idea that religiosity arises from the human need for security has also been furthered by studies examining religious beliefs as a compensatory mechanism of control. These studies are motivated by the idea that people are invested in maintaining beliefs in order and structure to prevent beliefs in chaos and randomness[35][36]

In the experimental setting, researchers have also tested compensatory control in regard to individuals' perceptions of external systems, such as religion or government. For example, Kay and colleagues[37] found that in a laboratory setting, individuals are more likely to endorse broad external systems (e.g., religion or sociopolitical systems) that impose order and control on their lives when they are induced with lowered levels of personal control. In this study, researchers suggest that when a person's personal control is lessened, their motivation to believe in order is threatened, resulting in compensation of this threat through adherence to other external sources of control.

7.4 Psychometric approaches to religion

Since the 1960s psychologists of religion have used the methodology of psychometrics to assess ways in which a person may be religious. An example is the Religious Orientation Scale of Allport and Ross,[38] which measures how respondents stand on intrinsic and extrinsic religion as described by Allport. More recent questionnaires include the Age-Universal I-E Scale of Gorsuch and Venable,[39] the Religious Life Inventory of Batson, Schoenrade and Ventis,[40] and the Spiritual Experiences Index-Revised of Genia.[41] The first provides an age-independent measure of Allport and Ross's two religious orientations. The second measures three forms of religious orientation: religion as means (intrinsic), religion as end (extrinsic), and religion as quest. The third assesses spiritual maturity using two factors: Spiritual Support and Spiritual Openness.

7.4.1 Religious orientations and religious dimensions

Further information: Sociology of religion

Some questionnaires, such as the Religious Orientation Scale, relate to different religious orientations, such as intrinsic and extrinsic religiousness, referring to different motivations for religious allegiance. A rather different approach, taken, for example, by Glock and Stark (1965), has been to list different dimensions of religion rather than different religious orientations, which relates to how an individual may manifest different forms of being religious. Glock and Stark's famous typology described five dimensions of religion – the doctrinal, the intellectual, the ethical-consequential, the ritual, and the experiential. In later work these authors subdivided the ritual dimension into devotional and public ritual, and also clarified that their distinction of religion along multiple dimensions was not identical to distinguishing religious orientations. Although some psychologists of religion have found it helpful to take a multidimensional approach to religion for the purpose of psychometric scale design, there has been, as Wulff (1997) explains, considerable controversy about whether religion should really be seen as multidimensional.

7.4.2 Questionnaires to assess religious experience

What we call religious experiences can differ greatly. Some reports exist of supernatural happenings that it would be difficult to explain from a rational, scientific point of view. On the other hand, there also exist the sort of testimonies that simply seem to convey a feeling of peace or oneness – something which most of us, religious or not, may possibly relate to. In categorizing religious experiences it is perhaps helpful to look at them as explicable through one of two theories: the Objectivist thesis or the Subjectivist thesis.

An objectivist would argue that the religious experience is a proof of God's existence. However, others have criticised the reliability of religious experiences. The English philosopher Thomas Hobbes asked how it was possible to tell the difference between talking to God in a dream, and dreaming about talking to God.[42]

The Subjectivist view argues that it is not necessary to think of religious experiences as evidence for the existence of an actual being whom we call God. From this point of view,

the important thing is the experience itself and the effect that it has on the individual.[43]

7.5 Developmental approaches to religion

Main articles: James W. Fowler and Stages of faith development

Many have looked at stage models, like those of Jean Piaget and Lawrence Kohlberg, to explain how children develop ideas about God and religion in general.

The most well known stage model of spiritual or religious development is that of James W. Fowler, a developmental psychologist at the Candler School of Theology, in his *Stages of Faith*.[44] He follows Piaget and Kohlberg and has proposed a holistic staged development of faith (or spiritual development) across the lifespan.

The book-length study contains a framework and ideas which have generated a good deal of response from those interested in religion, so it appears to have face validity. James Fowler proposes six stages of faith development: 1. Intuitive-projective 2. Symbolic Literal 3. Synthetic Conventional 4. Individuating 5. Paradoxical (conjunctive) 6. Universalising. Although there is evidence that children up to the age of twelve years do tend to be in the first two of these stages, adults over the age of sixty-one show considerable variation in displays of qualities of Stages 3 and beyond, most adults remaining in Stage 3 (Synthetic Conventional). Fowler's model has generated some empirical studies, and fuller descriptions of this research (and of these six stages) can be found in Wulff (1991).

Fowler's scientific research has been criticized for methodological weaknesses. Of Fowler's six stages, only the first two found empirical support, and these were heavily based upon Piaget's stages of cognitive development. The tables and graphs in the book were presented in such a way that the last four stages appeared to be validated, but the requirements of statistical verification of the stages were not met. His study was not published in a journal, so was not peer-reviewed. Other critics of Fowler have questioned whether his ordering of the stages really reflects his own commitment to a rather liberal Christian Protestant outlook, as if to say that people who adopt a similar viewpoint to Fowler are at higher stages of faith development. Nevertheless, the concepts Fowler introduced seemed to hit home with those in the circles of academic religion, and have been an important starting point for various theories and subsequent studies.

Other theorists in developmental psychology have suggested that religiosity comes naturally to young children. Specifically, children may have a natural-born conception of mind-body dualism, which lends itself to beliefs that the mind may live on after the body dies. In addition, children have a tendency to see agency and human design where there is not, and prefer a creationist explanation of the world even when raised by parents who do not.[45][46]

Researchers have also investigated attachment system dynamics as a predictor of the religious conversion experience throughout childhood and adolescence. One hypothesis is the correspondence hypothesis,[47] which posits that individuals with secure parental attachment are more likely to experience a gradual conversion experience. Under the correspondence hypothesis, internal working models of a person's attachment figure is thought to perpetuate his or her perception of God as a secure base. Another hypothesis relating attachment style to the conversion experience is the compensation hypothesis,[48] which states that individuals with insecure attachments are more likely to have a sudden conversion experience as they compensate for their insecure attachment relationship by seeking a relationship with God. Researchers have tested these hypotheses using longitudinal studies and individuals' self narratives of their conversation experience. For example, one study investigating attachment styles and adolescent conversions at Young Life religious summer camps resulted in evidence supporting the correspondence hypothesis through analysis of personal narratives and a prospective longitudinal follow-up of Young Life campers, with mixed results for the compensation hypothesis.[49]

7.6 Evolutionary and cognitive psychology of religion

Main articles: Evolutionary psychology of religion and Cognitive science of religion

Evolutionary psychology is based on the hypothesis that, just like the cardiac, pulmonary, urinary, and immune systems, cognition has a functional structure with a genetic basis, and therefore appeared through natural selection. Like other organs and tissues, this functional structure should be universally shared among humans and should solve important problems of survival and reproduction. Evolutionary psychologists seek to understand cognitive processes by understanding the survival and reproductive functions they might serve.

Pascal Boyer is one of the leading figures in the cognitive psychology of religion, a new field of inquiry that is less than fifteen years old, which accounts for the psychological processes that underlie religious thought and practice.

In his book *Religion Explained*, Boyer shows that there is no simple explanation for religious consciousness. Boyer is mainly concerned with explaining the various psychological processes involved in the acquisition and transmission of ideas concerning the gods. Boyer builds on the ideas of cognitive anthropologists Dan Sperber and Scott Atran, who first argued that religious cognition represents a by-product of various evolutionary adaptations, including folk psychology, and purposeful violations of innate expectations about how the world is constructed (for example, bodiless beings with thoughts and emotions) that make religious cognitions striking and memorable.

Religious persons acquire religious ideas and practices through social exposure. The child of a Zen Buddhist will not become an evangelical Christian or a Zulu warrior without the relevant cultural experience. While mere exposure does not cause a particular religious outlook (a person may have been raised a Roman Catholic but leave the church), nevertheless some exposure seems required – this person will never invent Roman Catholicism out of thin air. Boyer says cognitive science can help us to understand the psychological mechanisms that account for these manifest correlations and in so doing enable us to better understand the nature of religious belief and practice.

Boyer moves outside the leading currents in mainstream cognitive psychology and suggests that we can use evolutionary biology to unravel the relevant mental architecture. Our brains are, after all, biological objects, and the best naturalistic account of their development in nature is Darwin's theory of evolution. To the extent that mental architecture exhibits intricate processes and structures, it is plausible to think that this is the result of evolutionary processes working over vast periods of time. Like all biological systems, the mind is optimised to promote survival and reproduction in the evolutionary environment. On this view all specialised cognitive functions broadly serve those reproductive ends.

For Steven Pinker the universal propensity toward religious belief is a genuine scientific puzzle. He thinks that adaptationist explanations for religion do not meet the criteria for adaptations. An alternative explanation is that religious psychology is a by-product of many parts of the mind that evolved for other purposes.

7.7 Religion and prayer

Religious practice oftentimes manifests itself in some form of prayer. Recent studies have focused specifically on the effects of prayer on health. Measures of prayer and the above measures of spirituality evaluate different characteristics and should not be considered synonymous.

Prayer is fairly prevalent in the United States. About 75% of the United States reports praying at least once a week.[50] However, the practice of prayer is more prevalent and practiced more consistently among Americans who perform other religious practices.[51] There are four primary types of prayer in the West. Poloma and Pendleton,[52][53] utilized factor analysis to delineate these four types of prayer: meditative (more spiritual, silent thinking), ritualistic (reciting), petitionary (making requests to God), and colloquial (general conversing with God). Further scientific study of prayer using factor analysis has revealed three dimensions of prayer.[54] Ladd and Spilka's first factor was awareness of self, inward reaching. Their second and third factors were upward reaching (toward God) and outward reaching (toward others). This study appears to support the contemporary model of prayer as connection (whether to the self, higher being, or others).

Dein and Littlewood (2008) suggest that an individual's prayer life can be viewed on a spectrum ranging from immature to mature. A progression on the scale is characterized by a change in the perspective of the purpose of prayer. Rather than using prayer as a means of changing the reality of a situation, a more mature individual will use prayer to request assistance in coping with immutable problems and draw closer to God or others. This change in perspective has been shown to be associated with an individual's passage through adolescence.[55]

Prayer appears to have health implications. Empirical studies suggest that mindfully reading and reciting the Psalms (from scripture) can help a person calm down and focus.[56][57] Prayer is also positively correlated with happiness and religious satisfaction (Poloma & Pendleton, 1989, 1991). A study conducted by Franceis, Robbins, Lewis, and Barnes (2008) investigated the relationship between self-reported prayer frequency and measures of psychoticism and neuroticism according to the abbreviated form of the Revised Eysenck Personality Questionnaire (EPQR-A). The study included a sample size of 2306 students attending Protestant and Catholic schools in the highly religious culture of Northern Ireland. The data shows a negative correlation between prayer frequency and psychoticism. The data also shows that, in Catholic students, frequent prayer has a positive correlation to neuroticism scores.[58] Ladd and McIntosh (2008) suggest that prayer-related behaviors, such as bowing the head and clasping the hands together in an almost fetal position, are suggestive of "social touch" actions. Prayer in this manner may prepare an individual to carry out positive pro-social behavior after praying, due to factors such as increased blood flow to the head and nasal breathing.[59] Overall, slight health benefits have been found fairly consistently across studies.[60]

Three main pathways to explain this trend have been offered: placebo effect, focus and attitude adjustment, and

activation of healing processes.[61] These offerings have been expanded by Breslan and Lewis (2008) who have constructed a five pathway model between prayer and health with the following mediators: physiological, psychological, placebo, social support, and spiritual. The spiritual mediator is a departure from the rest in that its potential for empirical investigation is not currently feasible. Although the conceptualizations of chi, the universal mind, divine intervention, and the like breach the boundaries of scientific observation, they are included in this model as possible links between prayer and health so as to not unnecessarily exclude the supernatural from the broader conversation of psychology and religion.[62] (However, whether the activation of healing processes explanation is supernatural or biological, or even both, is beyond the scope of this study and this article.)

7.8 Religion and ritual

Another significant form of religious practice is ritual.[63] Religious rituals encompass a wide array of practices, but can be defined as the performance of similar actions and vocal expressions based on prescribed tradition and cultural norms.[64] Examples include the Jewish Bar Mitzvah, Christian Holy Eucharist, Hindu Puja, and Muslim Salat and Hajj.

Scheff suggests that ritual provides catharsis, emotional purging, through distancing.[65] This emotional distancing enables an individual to experience feelings with an amount of separation, and thus less intensity. However, the conception of religious ritual as an interactive process has since matured and become more scientifically established. From this view, ritual offers a means to catharsis through behaviors that foster connection with others, allowing for emotional expression.[66] This focus on connection contrasts to the separation that seems to underlie Scheff's view.

Additional research suggests the social component of ritual. For instance, findings suggest that ritual performance indicates group commitment and prevents the uncommitted from gaining membership benefits.[67] Ritual may aid in emphasizing moral values that serve as group norms and regulate societies.[68] It may also strengthen commitment to moral convictions and likelihood of upholding these social expectations.[69] Thus, performance of rituals may foster social group stability.

7.9 Religion and health

Main article: Impacts of religion on health
See also: Handbook of Religion and Health and Religion

and happiness

There is considerable literature on the relationship between religion and health. More than 3000 empirical studies have examined relationships between religion and health, including more than 1200 in the 20th century,[70] and more than 2000 additional studies between 2000 and 2009.[71]

Psychologists consider that there are various ways in which religion may benefit both physical and mental health, including encouraging healthy lifestyles, providing social support networks and encouraging an optimistic outlook on life; prayer and meditation may also help to benefit physiological functioning.[72] The journal "American Psychologist" published important papers on this topic in 2003.[73] Haber, Jacob and Spangler have considered how different dimensions of religiosity may relate to health benefits in different ways.[74]

7.9.1 Religion and physical health

Some studies indicate that religiosity appears to positively correlate with physical health.[75] For instance, mortality rates are lower among people who frequently attend religious events and consider themselves both religious and spiritual.[76] One possibility is that religion provides physical health benefits indirectly. Church attendees present with lower rates of alcohol consumption and improvement in mood, which is associated with better physical health.[77] Kenneth Pargament is a major contributor to the theory of how individuals may use religion as a resource in coping with stress, His work seems to show the influence of attribution theory. Additional evidence suggests that this relationship between religion and physical health may be causal.[78] Religion may reduce likelihood of certain diseases. Studies suggest that it guards against cardiovascular disease by reducing blood pressure, and also improves immune system functioning.[79] Similar studies have been done investigating religious emotions and health. Although religious emotions, such as humility, forgiveness, and gratitude confer health benefits, it is unclear if religious people cultivate and experience those emotions more frequently than non-religious peoples.[80]

However, randomized controlled trials of intercessory prayer have not yielded significant effects on health. These trials have compared personal, focused, committed and organized intercessory prayer with those interceding holding some belief that they are praying to God or a god versus any other intervention. A Cochrane collaboration review of these trials concluded that 1) results were equivocal, 2) evidence does not support a recommendation either in favor or against the use of intercessory prayer and 3) any resources available for future trials should be used to investigate other

questions in health research.[81] In a case-control study done following 5,286 Californians over a 28-year period in which variables were controlled for (i.e. age, race/ethnicity, gender, education level), participants who went to church on a frequent basis (defined as attending a religious service once a week or more) were 36% less likely to die during that period.[82] However, this can be partly be attributed to a better lifestyle since religious people tend to drink and smoke less and eat a healthier diet.

Another study detailing the connection between religion and physical health was done in Israel as a prospective cohort case study. In a study done of almost 4,000 Israelis, over 16 years (beginning in 1970), death rates were compared between the experimental group (people belonging to 11 religious kibbutzim) versus the control group (people belonging to secular kibbutzim). Some determining factors for the groups included the date the kibbutz was created, geography of the different groups, and the similarity in age. It was determined that "belonging to a religious collective was associated with a strong protective effect".[83] Not only do religious people tend to exhibit healthier lifestyles, they also have a strong support system that secular people would not normally have. A religious community can provide support especially through a stressful life event such as the death of a loved one or illness. There is the belief that a higher power will provide healing and strength through the rough times which also can explain the lower mortality rate of religious people vs. secular people.

7.9.2 Religion and personality

Main article: Religion and personality

Some studies have examined whether there is a "religious personality." Research suggests that people who identify as religious are more likely to be high on agreeableness and conscientiousness, and low on psychoticism, but unrelated to other Big Five traits. However, people endorsing fundamentalist religious beliefs are more likely to be low on Openness.[84] Similarly, people who identify as spiritual are more likely to be high on Extroversion and Openness, although this varied based on the type of spirituality endorsed.[85]

7.9.3 Religion and mental health

Evidence suggests that religiosity can be a pathway to both mental health and mental disorder. For example, religiosity is positively associated with mental disorders that involve an excessive amount of self-control and negatively associated with mental disorders that involve a lack of self-control.[86] Other studies have found indications of mental health among both the religious and the secular. For instance, Vilchinsky & Kravetz found negative correlations with psychological distress among religious and secular subgroups of Jewish students.[87] In addition, intrinsic religiosity has been inversely related to depression in the elderly, while extrinsic religiosity has no relation or even a slight positive relation to depression.[88] [89] Religiosity has been found to mitigate the negative impact of injustice and income inequality on life satisfaction.[90][91]

The link between religion and mental health may be due to the guiding framework or social support that it offers to individuals.[92] By these routes, religion has the potential to offer security and significance in life, as well as valuable human relationships, to foster mental health. Some theorists have suggested that the benefits of religion and religiosity are accounted for by the social support afforded by membership in a religious group.[93]

Religion may also provide coping skills to deal with stressors, or demands perceived as straining.[94] Pargament's three primary styles of religious coping are 1) self-directing, characterized by self-reliance and acknowledgement of God, 2) deferring, in which a person passively attributes responsibility to God, and 3) collaborative, which involves an active partnership between the individual and God and is most commonly associated with positive adjustment.[95][96] This model of religious coping has been criticized for its over-simplicity and failure to take into account other factors, such as level of religiosity, specific religion, and type of stressor.[97] Additional work by Pargament involves a detailed delineation of positive and negative forms of religious coping, captured in the BREIF-RCOPE questionnaire which have been linked to a range of positive and negative psychological outcomes.[98][99]

Spirituality has been ascribed many different definitions in different contexts, but a general definition is: an individual's search for meaning and purpose in life. Spirituality is distinct from organized religion in that spirituality does not necessarily need a religious framework. That is, one does not necessarily need to follow certain rules, guidelines or practices to be spiritual, but an organized religion often has some combination of these in place. People who report themselves to be spiritual people may not observe any specific religious practices or traditions.[100] Studies have shown a negative relationship between spiritual well-being and depressive symptoms. In one study, those who were assessed to have a higher spiritual quality of life on a spiritual well-being scale had less depressive symptoms.[101] Cancer and AIDS patients who were more spiritual had lower depressive symptoms than religious patients. Spirituality shows beneficial effects possibly because it speaks to one's ability to intrinsically find meaning in life, strength, and inner peace, which is especially important for very ill patients.[100] Studies have reported ben-

eficial effects of spirituality on the lives of patients with schizophrenia, major depression, and other psychotic disorders. Schizophrenic patients were less likely to be rehospitalized if families encouraged religious practice, and in depressed patients who underwent religiously based interventions, their symptoms improved faster than those who underwent secular interventions. Furthermore, a few cross-sectional studies have shown that more religiously involved people had less instance of psychosis.[102]

Research shows that religiosity moderates the relationship between "thinking about meaning of life" and life satisfaction. For individuals scoring low and moderately on religiosity, thinking about the meaning of life is negatively correlated with life satisfaction. For people scoring highly on religiosity, however, this relationship is positive.[94] Religiosity has also been found to moderate the relationship between negative affect and life satisfaction, such that life satisfaction is less strongly influenced by the frequency of negative emotions in more religious (vs less religious) individuals.[103]

7.9.4 Religion and prejudice

To investigate the salience of religious beliefs in establishing group identity, researchers have also conducted studies looking at religion and prejudice. Some studies have shown that greater religious attitudes may be significant predictors of negative attitudes towards racial or social outgroups.[104][105] These effects are often conceptualized under the framework of intergroup bias, where religious individuals favor members of their ingroup (ingroup favoritism) and exhibit disfavor towards members of their outgroup (outgroup derogation). Evidence supporting religious intergroup bias has been supported in multiple religious groups, including non-Christian groups, and is thought to reflect the role of group dynamics in religious identification. Many studies regarding religion and prejudice implement religious priming both in the laboratory and in naturalistic settings[106][107] with evidence supporting the perpetuation of ingroup favoritism and outgroup derogation in individuals who are high in religiosity.

7.10   Religion and drugs

See also: Entheogen

The American psychologist James H. Leuba (1868–1946), in *A Psychological Study of Religion*, accounts for mystical experience psychologically and physiologically, pointing to analogies with certain drug-induced experiences. Leuba argued forcibly for a naturalistic treatment of religion, which he considered to be necessary if religious psychology were to be looked at scientifically. Shamans all over the world and in different cultures have traditionally used drugs, especially psychedelics, for their religious experiences. In these communities the absorption of drugs leads to dreams (visions) through sensory distortion.

William James was also interested in mystical experiences from a drug-induced perspective, leading him to make some experiments with nitrous oxide and even peyote. He concludes that while the revelations of the mystic hold true, they hold true only for the mystic; for others they are certainly ideas to be considered, but hold no claim to truth without personal experience of such.

7.11 Religion and psychotherapy

Clients' religious beliefs are increasingly being considered in psychotherapy with the goal of improving service and effectiveness of treatment.[108] A resulting development was theistic psychotherapy. Conceptually, it consists of theological principles, a theistic view of personality, and a theistic view of psychotherapy.[109] Following an explicit minimizing strategy, therapists attempt to minimize conflict by acknowledging their religious views while being respectful of client's religious views.[110] This opens up the potential for therapists to directly utilize religious practices and principles in therapy, such as prayer, forgiveness, and grace.

7.11.1 Pastoral psychology

One application of the psychology of religion is in pastoral psychology, the use of psychological findings to improve the pastoral care provided by pastors and other clergy, especially in how they support ordinary members of their congregations. Pastoral psychology is also concerned with improving the practice of chaplains in healthcare and in the military. One major concern of pastoral psychology is to improve the practice of pastoral counseling. Pastoral psychology is a topic of interest for professional journals such as *Pastoral Psychology*, *Journal of Psychology and Christianity*, and *Journal of Psychology and Theology*. In 1984, Thomas Oden severely criticized mid-20th century pastoral care and the pastoral psychology that guided it as having entirely abandoned its classical/traditional sources, and having become overwhelmingly dominated by modern psychological influences from Freud, Rogers, and others.[111] More recently, others have described pastoral psychology as a field that experiences a tension between psychology and theology.[112]

7.11.2 Other views

A 2012 paper suggested that psychiatric conditions associated with psychotic spectrum symptoms may be possible explanations for revelatory driven experiences and activities such as those of Abraham, Moses, Jesus and Saint Paul.[113]

7.12 See also

- Attachment theory and psychology of religion
- Issues in Science and Religion
- Psychology of religion journals
- Magical thinking
- Philosophy of religion
- Social Evolution
- Transpersonal psychology

7.13 References

[1] Wulff, D. M. (2010). Psychology of Religion. In D. A. Leeming, K. Madden, & S. Marian (Eds.), *Encyclopedia of Psychology and Religion* (pp. 732–735). New York; London: Springer.

[2] Smith, W. C. (1963). *The Meaning and End of Religion: A New Approach to the Religious Traditions of Mankind*. New York: Macmillan.

[3] Wulff, D. M. (1999). Psychologists Define Religion: Patterns and Prospects of a Century-Long Quest. In J. G. Platvoet and A. L. Molendijk (Eds.), *The Pragmatics of Defining Religion: Contexts, Concepts, and Contests* (pp. 207–224). Leiden: Brill

[4] Hill, P. C., and Hood, R. W., Jr. (Eds.). (1999). *Measures of Religiosity."* Birmingham, AL: Religious Education Press.

[5] Schlehofer M. M., Omoto A. M., Adelman J. R. (2008). "How Do "Religion" and "Spirituality" Differ? Lay Definitions Among Older Adults". *Journal for the Scientific Study of Religion* **47** (3): 411–425. doi:10.1111/j.1468-5906.2008.00418.x.

[6] Principe W (1983). "Toward Defining Spirituality". *Sciences Religieuses/Studies in Religion* **12**: 127–141.

[7] Pargament, Kenneth I. The Psychology of Religion and Coping: Theory, Research, Practice. New York: Guilford, 1997. Print.

[8] Hill, P. C. (2005). Measurement in the Psychology of Religion and Spirituality: Current Status and Evaluation. In R. F. Paloutzian & C. L. Park (Eds.), *Handbook of the Psychology of Religion and Spirituality*. New York, London: Guilford Press.

[9] Schnitker, Sarah (2013). "Spiritual striving and seeking the sacred: religion as meaningful goal-directed behavior.". *The International Journal For The Psychology Of Religion* **23**: 315–324. doi:10.1080/10508619.2013.795822.

[10] Spilka, Hood, Hunsberger and Gorsuch, 2003, The Psychology of Religion, p. 24

[11] Jung, 'On the Nature of the Psyche', C.W.8, Aphorisms 362, 420.

[12] Leak, Gary K (2002). "Exploratory factor analysis of the religious maturity scale". *BNET UK*. CBS Interactive Inc. Retrieved 22 March 2010.

[13] Fromm, Erich (1950). *Psychoanalysis and Religion*. New Haven, CT, US: Yale University Press. ISBN 0-300-00089-8. Retrieved 10 February 2010.

[14] Burger, Jerry (2007). *Personality*. Stamford, CT, US: Cengage Learning. pp. 122–123. ISBN 0-495-09786-1. Retrieved 10 February 2010.

[15] Belzen, Jacob A., ed. (2012). *Psychology of religion: autobiographical accounts*. New York: Springer. ISBN 978-1-4614-1601-2. OCLC 773924284

[16] Bergin A. E. (1980). "Psychotherapy and religious values". *Journal of Consulting and Clinical Psychology* **48**: 95–105. doi:10.1037/0022-006x.48.1.95.

[17] Slife, B.D. & Whoolery, M. (2003). Understanding disciplinary significance: The story of Allen Bergin's 1980 article on values. In R. Sternberg (Ed.) The anatomy of impact: What has made the great works of psychology great? Washington, D.C.: American Psychological Association.

[18] Bergin Allen E (1990). "Citation – Award for Distinguished Professional Contributions to Knowledge". *American Psychologist* **45** (4): 474. As cited in Swedin E. G. (2003). "Book Review: Eternal Values and Personal Growth: A Guide on Your Journey to Spiritual, Emotional, and Social Wellness, by Allen E Bergin". *AMCAP Journal* **28** (1): 41.

[19] Emmons, Robert A. (1999). *The psychology of ultimate concerns: Motivation and spirituality in personality*. New York: Guilford. ISBN 978-1-57230-935-7.

[20] Kenneth I. Pargament (1997). *The psychology of religion and coping: Theory, research, practice*. New York: Guilford. ISBN 978-1-57230-664-6

[21] Pargament Kenneth I., Koenig Harold G., Perez Lisa M. (2000). "The many methods of religious coping: Development and initial validation of the RCOPE". *Journal of Clinical Psychology* **56** (4): 519–543. doi:10.1002/(SICI)1097-4679(200004)56:4<519::AID-JCLP6>3.0.CO;2-1. PMID 10775045.

[22] Pargament Kenneth I., Kennell Joseph, Hathaway William, Grevengoed Nancy, Newman Jon, Jones Wendy (1988). "Religion and the problem-solving process: Three styles of coping". *Journal for the Scientific Study of Religion* **27** (1): 90–104. doi:10.2307/1387404. JSTOR 1387404.

[23] Brian J. Zinnbauer & Kenneth I. Pargament (2000). Working with the sacred: Four approaches to religious and spiritual issues in counseling. *Journal of Counseling & Development*, v78 n2, pp162–171. ISSN 0748-9633

[24] James Hillman, Re-Visioning Psychology, HarperCollins, NY, 1977, p227

[25] Jaynes, Julian (2000). *The origin of consciousness in the breakdown of the bicameral mind*. Houghton Mifflin. pp. 131–143. ISBN 0-618-05707-2.

[26] Gill, R. (2001). "The future of religious participation and belief in Britain and beyond". In R. K. Fenn. *The Blackwell companion to the sociology of religion*. Oxford: Blackwell. pp. 279–291. ISBN 978-0-631-21241-6. Retrieved 25 April 2010.

[27] Taylor, C. (2007). A secular age. Cambridge, MA: Belknap. ISBN 978-0-674-02676-6. Retrieved 25 April 2010.

[28] Roof, W. C. (1993). A generation of seekers: The spiritual journeys of the baby boom generation. San Francisco: HaperSanFrancisco. ISBN 0-06-066963-2. Retrieved 25 April 2010.

[29] Hill, P. C., Pargament, K. I., Hood, R. W., McCullough, M. E., Swyers, J. P., Larson, D. B.; et al. (2000). "Conceptualizing religion and spirituality: Points of commonality, points of departure" (PDF). *Journal for the Theory of Social Behavior* **30**: 51–77. doi:10.1111/1468-5914.00119. Retrieved 25 April 2010.

[30] Wuthnow, R (1998). After heaven: Spirituality in America since the 1950s. Berkeley, CA: University of California Press. ISBN 978-0-520-22228-1. Retrieved 25 April 2010.

[31] Besecke, K. (2007). "Beyond literalism: Reflexive spirituality and religious meaning". In N. T. Ammerman. *Everyday religion: Observing modern religious lives*. New York: Oxford University. pp. 169–186. ISBN 978-0-19-530541-8. Retrieved 25 April 2010.

[32] Hervieu-Leger, D. (2001). "Individualism, the validation of faith, and the social nature of religion in modernity". In R. K. Fenn. *The Blackwell companion to sociology of religion*. Oxford: Blackwell. pp. 161–175. ISBN 978-0-631-21241-6. Retrieved 25 April 2010.

[33] Casey, M. (1996). *Toward God: The ancient wisdom of the Western prayer*. Liguori, MO: Liguori/ Triumph. p. 25. ISBN 0-89243-890-8. Retrieved 25 April 2010.

[34] Norris, P., Inglehart, R. (2004). *Sacred and secular: Religion and politics worldwide*. Cambridge: Cambridge University Press. ISBN 0-521-83984-X. Retrieved 25 April 2010.

[35] Dechesne, M., Janssen, J., & van Knippenberg, A. (2000). "Derogation and distancing as terror management strategies: the moderating role of need for closure and permeability of group boundaries". *Journal of Personality and Social Psychology* **79** (6): 923–932. doi:10.1037/0022-3514.79.6.923.

[36] Kay, A.C., Jimenez, M.C., Jost, J.T. (2002). "Sour Grapes, Sweet Lemons, and the Anticipatory Rationalization of the Status Quo". *Pers Soc Psychol Bull* **28** (9): 1300–1312. doi:10.1177/01461672022812014.

[37] Kay, A.C., Gaucher, D., Napier, J.L., Callan, M.J., Laurin, K. (2008). "God and the government: Testing a compensatory control mechanism for the support of external systems". *Journal of Personality and Social Psychology* **95** (1): 18–35. doi:10.1037/0022-3514.95.1.18.

[38] Allport, G.W. & J. Michael Ross (1967). "Personal Religious Orientation and Prejudice". *Journal of Personality and Social Psychology* **5** (4): 432–443. doi:10.1037/h0021212.

[39] Gorsuch, R. & Venable (1983). "Development of an Age-Universal I-E Scale". *Journal for the Scientific Study of Religion* (Blackwell Publishing) **22** (2): 181. doi:10.2307/1385677. JSTOR 1385677.

[40] Batson, C.D., Schoenrade, P. & Ventis, L. (1993). *Religion and the Individual.* New York: Oxford University Press. ISBN 0-19-506208-6.

[41] Genia, V. (1997). "The Spiritual Experience Index: Revision and Reformulation". *Review of Religious Research* (Religious Research Association, Inc.) **38** (4): 344–361. doi:10.2307/3512195. JSTOR 3512195.

[42] Southwell, G. "Philosophy of Religion". UK. Retrieved 26 April 2010. |chapter= ignored (help)

[43] Southwell, G. "Philosophy of Religion". UK. Retrieved 26 April 2010. |chapter= ignored (help)

[44] ISBN 0-06-062866-9

[45] Bloom, P. (January 2007). "Religion is natural". *Developmental Science* **10** (1): 147–151. doi:10.1111/j.1467-7687.2007.00577.x.

[46] Evans, E (May 2001). "Cognitive and contextual factors in the emergence of diverse belief systems: creation versus evolution.". *Cogn Psychol* **42** (3): 217–66. doi:10.1006/cogp.2001.0749. PMID 11305883.

[47] Bloom, P. (January 2007). "Religion is natural". *Developmental Science* **10** (1): 147–151. doi:10.1207/s15327582ijpr1404_1.

[48] Kirkpatrick, L.A., Shaver, P.R. (1990). "Attachment theory and religion: Childhood attachments, religious beliefs, and conversion". *Journal for the Scientific Study of Religion* **29**: 315–334. doi:10.2307/1386461.

[49] Sarah A. Schnitkera; Tenelle J. Porterb (7 June 2012). "Attachment Predicts Adolescent Conversions at Young Life". *International Journal for the Psychology of Religion* **22** (3): 198–215. doi:10.1080/10508619.2012.670024.

[50] Bader, C., Dougherty, K., Froese, P., Johnson, B., Mencken, F. C., Park, J.; et al. (2006). "American piety in the 21st century: New insights to the depth and complexity of religion in the US: Selected findings from the Baylor Religion Survey" (PDF). *Waco, TX: Baylor Institute for Studies of Religion.* Retrieved 25 April 2010.

[51] Francis, L. & Evans, T. (2001). "The psychology of Christian prayer: A review of empirical research". In L. Francis, & J. Astley. *Psychological perspectives on prayer.* Leominster, UK: Gracewing. Retrieved 25 April 2010.

[52] Poloma, M. M., & Pendleton, B. F. (1989). "Exploring types of prayer and quality of life: A research note". *Review of Religious Research* **31**: 46–53. doi:10.2307/3511023. Retrieved 25 April 2010.

[53] Poloma, M. M., & Pendleton, B. F. (1991). "The effects of prayer and prayer experiences" (PDF). *Journal of Psychology and Theology* **19**: 71–83. Retrieved 25 April 2010.

[54] Ladd, K. L., & Spilka, B. (2002). "Inward, outward, and upwards: Cognitive aspects of prayer" (PDF). *Journal for the Scientific Study of Religion* **41**: 475–484. doi:10.1111/1468-5906.00131. Retrieved 25 April 2010.

[55] Dein, Simon, and Roland Littlewood. "The Psychology of Prayer and the Development of the Prayer Experience Questionnaire." Mental Health, Religion & Culture 11.1 (2008): 39-52. Print.

[56] Dysinger, L. (2005). *Psalmody and prayer in the in writings of Evagrius Ponticus.* Oxford: Oxford University Press. ISBN 978-0-19-927320-1. Retrieved 25 April 2010.

[57] Kadloubovsky, E., & Palmer, G. E. H., (Trans.). (1992. (Original work published 1951).). *Writings from the 'Philokalia' prayer of the heart.* London: Faber & Faber. Retrieved 25 April 2010. Check date values in: |date= (help)

[58] Francis, Leslie J., Mandy Robbins, Christopher Alan Lewis, and L. Philip Barnes. "Prayer and Psychological Health: A Study among Sixth-form Pupils Attending Catholic and Protestant Schools in Northern Ireland." Mental Health, Religion & Culture 11.1 (2008): 85-92. Print.

[59] Ladd, Kevin L., and Daniel N. McIntosh. "Meaning, God, and Prayer: Physical and Metaphysical Aspects of Social Support." Mental Health, Religion & Culture 11.1 (2008): 23-38. Print.

[60] Nelson, J. M (2009). *Psychology, Religion, and Spirituality.* New York: Springer. p. 456. ISBN 0-387-87572-7. Retrieved 25 April 2010.

[61] Robinson, P. W., Thiel, M., Backus, M., & Meyer, E. (2006). "Matters of spirituality at the end of life in the

pediatric intensive care unit". *Pediatrics* (*Pediatrics*) **118** (3): e719–e729. doi:10.1542/peds.2005-2298. PMID 16950963. Retrieved 25 April 2010.

[62] Breslin, Michael J., and Christopher Alan Lewis. "Theoretical Models of the Nature of Prayer and Health: A Review." Mental Health, Religion & Culture 11.1 (2008): 9-21. Print.

[63] Stark, R., & Clock, C. (1968). *American piety: The nature of religious commitment.* Berkeley, CA: University of California Press. Retrieved 25 April 2010.

[64] Rappaport, R. (1990). *Ritual and religion in the making of humanity.* Cambridge: Cambridge University Press. p. 24. ISBN 0-521-22873-5. Retrieved 25 April 2010.

[65] Scheff, T. J. (1979). *Catharsis in Healing, Ritual, and Drama.* Berkeley, CA: University of California Press. ISBN 978-0-520-04125-7. Retrieved 25 April 2010.

[66] Schumaker, J. F. (1992). *Religion and Mental Health.* New York: Oxford University Press. ISBN 978-0-19-506985-3. Retrieved 25 April 2010.

[67] Sosis, R. (2004). "The adaptive value of religious ritual: Rituals promote group cohesion by requiring members to engage in behavior that is too costly to fake". *American Scientist* **92**: 166–172. doi:10.1511/2004.46.928. Retrieved 25 April 2010.

[68] Reich, K. (1990). "Rituals and social structure: The moral dimension.". In H.-G. Heimbrock, & H. B. Bougewinjinse. *Current studies on rituals: Perspectives for the psychology of religion.* Amsterdam: Rodopi. pp. 121–134. ISBN 978-90-5183-178-8. Retrieved 25 April 2010.

[69] Hinde, R. A. (2005). "Modes theory: Some theoretical considerations.". In H. Whitehouse, & R McCauley. *Mind and religion: Psychological and cognitive foundations of religiosity.* Walnut Creek, CA: AltaMira. pp. 31–55. ISBN 978-0-7591-0619-2. Retrieved 25 April 2010.

[70] Koenig, Harold G.; McCullough, Michael E.; Larson, David B. (2001). *Handbook of Religion and Health* (1st ed.). New York: Oxford University Press. ISBN 978-0-19-511866-7. OCLC 468554547

[71] Koenig, Harold G.; King, Dana E.; Carson, Verna Benner (2012). *Handbook of Religion and Health* (2nd ed.). New York: Oxford University Press. ISBN 9780195335958. OCLC 691927968.

[72] Levin, 2001

[73] see those by Miller and Thoresen (2003) and Powell, Shahabi and Thorsen (2003); see also the article by Oman and Thoresen, in Paloutzian and Park (2005)

[74] Haber, Jacob & Spangler, 2007)

[75] Ellison, C. G., & Levin, J. S. (1998). "The religion-health connection: Evidence, theory, and future directions". *Health education & behavior : the official publication of the Society for Public Health Education* **25** (6): 700–720. doi:10.1177/109019819802500603. PMID 9813743. Retrieved 25 April 2010.

[76] Shahabi, L., Powell, L. H., Musick, M. A., Pargament, K. I., Thoresen, C. E., Williams, D.; et al. (2002). "Correlates of self-perceptions of spirituality in American adults". *Annals of Behavioral Medicine* **24** (1): 59–68. doi:10.1207/s15324796abm2401_07. PMID 12008795.

[77] Koenig, L. B., & Vaillant, G. E. (2009). "A prospective study of church attendance and health over the lifespan". *Health Psychology* **28**: 117–124. doi:10.1037/a0012984. Retrieved 25 April 2010.

[78] Chatters, L. M. (2000). "Religion and health: Public health research and practices". *Annual Review of Public Health* **21**: 335–367. doi:10.1146/annurev.publhealth.21.1.335. Retrieved 25 April 2010.

[79] Seeman, T., Dubin, L. F., & Seeman, M. (2003). "Religiosity/spirituality and health: A critical review of the evidence for biological pathways". *American Psychologist* **58** (1): 53–63. doi:10.1037/0003-066x.58.1.53. Retrieved 25 April 2010.

[80] Emmons RA, Paloutzian RF (2003). "The psychology of religion". *Annual Review of Psychology* **54** (1): 377–402. doi:10.1146/annurev.psych.54.101601.145024. PMID 12171998.

[81] Roberts L, Ahmed I, Hall S, Davison A (2009). "Intercessory prayer for the alleviation of ill health". *The Cochrane Database of Systematic Reviews* (2): CD000368. doi:10.1002/14651858.CD000368.pub3. PMID 19370557.

[82] Strawbridge WJ, Cohen RD, Shema SJ, Kaplan GA (June 1997). "Frequent attendance at religious services and mortality over 28 years". *American Journal of Public Health* **87** (6): 957–61. doi:10.2105/ajph.87.6.957. PMC 1380930. PMID 9224176.

[83] Kark JD, Shemi G, Friedlander Y, Martin O, Manor O, Blondheim SH (March 1996). "Does religious observance promote health? mortality in secular vs religious kibbutzim in Israel". *American Journal of Public Health* **86** (3): 341–6. doi:10.2105/ajph.86.3.341. PMC 1380514. PMID 8604758.

[84] Saroglou, V. (2002). "Religion and the five factors of personality: A meta-analytic review". *Personality and Individual Differences* **32**: 15–25. doi:10.1016/s0191-8869(00)00233-6.

[85] MacDonald DA (February 2000). "Spirituality: description, measurement, and relation to the five factor model of personality". *Journal of Personality* **68** (1): 153–97. doi:10.1111/1467-6494.t01-1-00094. PMID 10820684.

[86] Gartner, J., Larson, D. B., Allen, G. D. (1991). "Religious commitment and mental health: A review of the empirical literature". *Journal of Psychology & Theology* **19**: 6–25. Retrieved 25 April 2010.

[87] Vilchinsky, N, & Kravetz, S. (2005). "How are religious belief and behavior good for you? An investigation of mediators relating religion to mental health in a sample of Israeli Jewish students". *Journal for the Scientific Study of Religion* **44** (4): 459–471. doi:10.1111/j.1468-5906.2005.00297.x. Retrieved 25 April 2010.

[88] Fehring, R.J., Miller, J.F., Shaw, C. (1997). "Spiritual well-being, religiosity, hope, depression, and other mood states in elderly people coping with cancer". *Oncology Nursing Forum* **24**: 663–671.

[89] Nelson, P.B. (1989). "Ethnic differences in intrinsic/extrinsic religious orientation and depression in the elderly". *Archives of Psychiatric Nursing*.

[90] Joshanloo, Mohsen; Weijers, Dan (2015-01-06). "Religiosity Reduces the Negative Influence of Injustice on Subjective Well-being: A Study in 121 Nations". *Applied Research in Quality of Life*: 1–12. doi:10.1007/s11482-014-9384-5. ISSN 1871-2584.

[91] Joshanloo, Mohsen; Weijers, Dan (2015-07-28). "Religiosity Moderates the Relationship between Income Inequality and Life Satisfaction across the Globe". *Social Indicators Research*: 1–20. doi:10.1007/s11205-015-1054-y. ISSN 0303-8300.

[92] Hill, P. C., Pargament, K. I. (2008). "Advanced in the conceptualization and measurement of religion and spirituality: Implications for physical and mental health research". *The American Psychologist* **58** (1): 3–17. doi:10.1037/1941-1022.s.1.3. PMID 12674819.

[93] Graham, J. (Feb 2010). "Beyond beliefs: religions bind individuals into moral communities.". *Personality and Social Psychology Review* **14** (1): 140–50. doi:10.1177/1088868309353415. PMID 20089848.

[94] Joshanloo, Mohsen; Weijers, Dan (2014-01-02). "Does thinking about the meaning of life make you happy in a religious and globalised world? A 75-nation study". *Journal of Psychology in Africa* **24** (1): 73–81. doi:10.1080/14330237.2014.904093. ISSN 1433-0237.

[95] Pargament, K., I. (1997). *The psychology of religion and coping: Theory, research, and practice*. New York: Guilford. pp. 180–182. ISBN 978-1-57230-664-6. Retrieved 25 April 2010.

[96] Bickel, C., Ciarrocchi, J., Sheers, N., & Estadt, B. (1998). "Perceived stress, religious coping styles and depressive affect". *Journal of Psychology & Christianity*. **17**: 33–42. Retrieved 25 April 2010.

[97] Nelson, J. M. (2009). *Psychology, Religion, and Spirituality*. New York: Springer. pp. 326–327. ISBN 0-387-87572-7. Retrieved 25 April 2010.

[98] Ano, Gene G. (Apr 2005). "Religious coping and psychological adjustment to stress: a meta-analysis.". *J Clin Psychol* **61** (4): 461–80. doi:10.1002/jclp.20049. PMID 15503316.

[99] Pargament, Kenneth I. (Apr 2000). "The many methods of religious coping: development and initial validation of the RCOPE.". *J Clin Psychol* **56** (4): 519–43. doi:10.1002/(SICI)1097-4679(200004)56:4<519::AID-JCLP6>3.0.CO;2-1. PMID 10775045.

[100] Nelson, C.J., Rosenfeld, B., Breitbart, W., Galietta, M. (2002). Spirituality, religion, and depression in the terminally ill 43. Psychosomatics. pp. 213–220.

[101] Fehring, R.J., Miller, J.F., Shaw, C. (1997). Spiritual well-being, religiosity, hope, depression, and other mood states in elderly people coping with cancer 24. Oncology Nursing Forum. pp. 663–671.

[102] Koenig, H. G. (2008) Research on religion, spirituality, and mental health: A review. Canadian Journal of Psychiatry.

[103] Joshanloo, Mohsen (2016-04-01). "Religiosity moderates the relationship between negative affect and life satisfaction: A study in 29 European countries". *Journal of Research in Personality* **61**: 11–14. doi:10.1016/j.jrp.2016.01.001.

[104] Hall, D. L. (Feb 2010). "Why don't we practice what we preach? A meta-analytic review of religious racism.". *Personality and Social Psychology Review* **14** (1): 126–39. doi:10.1177/1088868309352179. PMID 20018983.

[105] Whitley, Bernard E. (2009). "Religiosity and Attitudes Toward Lesbians and Gay Men: A Meta-Analysis". *The International Journal for the Psychology of Religion* **19** (1): 21–38. doi:10.1080/10508610802471104.

[106] Hall, D.; Matz, D. & Wood, W. (April 2010). "Priming Christian Religious Concepts Increases Racial Prejudice". *Social Psychological and Personality Science* **1** (2): 119–126. doi:10.1177/1948550609357246.

[107] Jordan P. LaBouffa; W. Rowatt; M. Johnson & C. Finkle (June 18, 2012). "Differences in Attitudes toward Outgroups in Religious and Nonreligious Contexts". *Journal for the Psychology of Religion* **22** (1): 1–9. doi:10.1080/10508619.2012.634778.

[108] Bergin, A. E. (1980). "Psychotherapy and religious values". *Journal of Consulting and Clinical Psychology* **48** (1): 95–105. doi:10.1037/0022-006x.48.1.95. Retrieved 25 April 2010.

[109] Richards, P. S. (2005). "A theistic integrative psychotherapy.". In L. Sperry, & E. P. Shafranske. *Spiritually oriented psychotherapy*. Washington, DC: American Psychological Association. pp. 259–285. Retrieved 25 April 2010.

[110] Richards, P. S., & Bergin, A. (1997). *A spiritual strategy for counseling and psychotherapy*. Washington, DC: American Psychological Association. ISBN 1-55798-434-4. Retrieved 25 April 2010.

[111] Oden, Thomas C. (1984). *Care of souls in the classic tradition*. Philadelphia: Fortress Press. ISBN 978-0-8006-1729-5. (full text online). In Tables 1 through 3, he demonstrated that in pastoral care textbooks, citations to psychologists (such as Freud, Jung, and Rogers) had entirely replaced citations to traditional pastoral care thinkers (such as Augustine, Gregory the Great, and Chrysostom) between the late 19th century and the mid-20th century.

[112] Ermanno Pavesi (2010). "Pastoral psychology as a field of tension between theology and psychology". *Christian Bioethics* **16** (1): 9–29. doi:10.1093/cb/cbq001. ISSN 1744-4195.

[113] Murray ED, Cunningham MG, Price BH (2012). "The role of psychotic disorders in religious history considered". *J Neuropsychiatry Clin Neurosci* **24** (4): 410–26. doi:10.1176/appi.neuropsych.11090214. PMID 23224447.

7.14   Bibliography

- Adler, A., & Jahn, E., *Religion and Psychology*, Frankfurt, 1933.

- Allport, G.W. & Ross, J.M., *Personal Religious Orientation and Prejudice*, Journal of Personality and Social Psychology, 1967.

- Allport, G. W., *The individual and his religion*, New York, Macmillan, 1950.

- Atran, S., *In Gods We Trust: The Evolutionary Landscape of Religion*, New York, Oxford University Press, 2002.

- Batson, C.D., Schoenrade, P. & Ventis, L., *Religion and the Individual*, New York, Oxford University Press, 1993.

- Erikson, E., *Young man Luther: A Study in Psychoanalysis and History*, New York, W. W. Norton, 1958.

- Dykstra C (1986). "Youth and language of faith". *Religious Education* **81**: 164–184. doi:10.1080/0034408600810202.

- Fowler, J. *Stages of Faith*, Harper and Row, San Francisco, 1971.

- Francis, L.J. & Louden, S.H., *The Francis-Louden Mystical Orientation Scale: A Study Among Male Anglican Priests*, Research in the Scientific Study of Religion, 2000.

- Freud, S., *The future of an illusion*, translated by W.D. Robson-Scott, New York, Liveright, 1928.

- Freud, S., *Totem and Taboo: Resemblances Between the Psychic Lives of Savages and Neurotics*, New-York, Dodd, 1928.

- Freud, S., *Moses and Monotheism*, London, The Hogarth Press and The Institute of Psychoanalysis, 1939.

- Fromm, E., *Psychoanalysis and Religion*, New Haven, Yale University, 1950.

- Genia, V., *The Spiritual Experience Index: Revision and Reformulation*, Review of Religious Research, 38, 344–361, 1997.

- Glock, C.Y. & Stark, R., *Religion and Society in Tension*, Chicago, Rand McNally, 1965.

- Gorsuch, R. & Venable, *Development of an Age-Universal I-E Scale*, Journal for the Scientific Study of Religion, 1983.

- Haber J., Jacob R., Spangler J.D.C. (2007). "Dimensions of religion and their relationship to health". *The International Journal for the Psychology of Religion* **17** (4): 265–288. doi:10.1080/10508610701572770.

- Hill, P. C. & Hood, R., *Measures of Religiosity*, Birmingham, Alabama, Religious Education Press,1999.

- Hill, P. C. & Pargament, K., *Advances in the Conceptualisation and Measurement of Spirituality*. American Psychologist, 58, p64–74, 2003.

- Hood, R. W., *The Construction and Preliminary Validation of a Measure of Reported Mystical Experience*, Journal for the Scientific Study of Religion, 1975.

- James, W., *The Varieties of Religious Experience*, Cambridge, Ma., Harvard University, 1985.

- Jung, C. G., *Modern Man in Search of a Soul*, New York, Harcourt Brace, 1933.

- Jung, C. G., *Psychology and Religion*, Yale University Press, 1962.

- Jung, C. G., *Psychology and Religion*, Yale Univ. Press, 1992.

- Jung, C. G., *Psychology and Western Religion*, Princeton Univ. Press, 1984.

- Hood, R. W., *The Construction and Preliminary Validation of a Measure of Reported Mystical Experience*, Journal for the Scientific Study of Religion, 1975.

- Leuba, J. H., *The Psychology of Religious Mysticism*, New York, Harcourt, Brace, 1925.

- Leuba, J. H., *The Psychological Origin and the Nature of Religion*. Wikisource text

- Levin, J. (2001). God, Faith and Spirituality: Exploring the Spirituality-Health Connection. New York: Wiley

- Paloutzian, R. F. & Park, C. L. (2005). Handbook of the Psychology of Religion and Spirituality.

- Saroglou, V. (Ed). (2014). Religion, Personality, and Social Behavior. New York: Psychology Press.

- Miller & Thoresen (2003) American Psychologist

- Powell, L.H., Shahabi, L. & Thoresen, C. (2003). Religion and spirituality.

  Links to physical health. American Psychologist. 58 pp36–52

- Wulff, D. M., *Psychology of Religion: Classic and Contemporary* (2nd ed), New York, Wiley, 1997.

7.14.1 Further reading

- Aziz, Robert (1990). *C.G. Jung's Psychology of Religion and Synchronicity* (10 ed.). The State University of New York Press. ISBN 0-7914-0166-9.

- Bendeck Sotillos, S. (Ed.). (2013). *Psychology and the Perennial Philosophy: Studies in Comparative Religion*. Bloomington, IN: World Wisdom. ISBN 978-1-936597-20-8.

- Fontana, D., *Psychology, Religion and Spirituality*, Oxford, Blackwell, 2003.

- Fuller, A. R. (1994). Psychology & religion: Eight points of view (3rd ed.). Lanham, MD: Littlefield Adams. ISBN 0-8226-3036-2.

- Hood, R. W. Jr., Spilka, B., Hunsberger, B., & Gorsuch, R. (1996). *The psychology of religion: An empirical approach*. New York: Guilford. ISBN 1-57230-116-3

- Jones, David., *The Psychology of Jesus*. Valjean Press: Nashville. ISBN 978-09820757-2-2

- Kugelmann, Robert., *Psychology and Catholicism: Contested Boundaries*, Cambridge University Press, 2011 ISBN 1-107-00608-2

- Levin, J., *God, Faith and Health: Exploring the Spirituality-Health Connection*, New York, Wiley, 2001.

- Loewenthal, K. M., *Psychology of Religion: A Short Introduction*, Oxford, Oneworld, 2000.

- McNamara, R. (Ed.) (2006), *Where God and Science Meet [3 Volumes]: How Brain and Evolutionary Studies Alter Our Understanding of Religion*. Westport, CT: Praeger/Greenwood.

- Paloutzian, R. (1996). *Invitation to the Psychology of Religion*, 2nd Ed. New York: Allyn and Bacon. ISBN 0-205-14840-9.

- Meissner, W., *Psychoanalysis and Religious Experience*, London and New Haven, Yale University Press, 1984.

- Roberts, T. B., and Hruby, P. J. (1995–2002). Religion and Psychoactive Sacraments An Entheogen Chrestomathy. Online archive.

- Tsakiridis, George. Evagrius Ponticus and Cognitive Science: A Look at Moral Evil and the Thoughts. Eugene, OR: Pickwick Publications, 2010.

- Wulff, D. M. (1997). *Psychology of religion: Classic and contemporary* (2nd ed.). New York: John Wiley. ISBN 0-471-03706-0.

7.15 External links

- Religiosity and Emotion

- Psychology of religion pages

- International Association for the Psychology of Religion

- Varieties of Religious Experience, a Study in Human Nature by William James

- Psychology of Religious Doubt

- Psychology of religion in Germany

- International Association for the Scientific Study of Religion

- Centre for Psychology of Religion

Chapter 8

Altered state of consciousness

Not to be confused with Altered level of consciousness.

An **altered state of consciousness** (**ASC**),[1] also called **altered state of mind** or **mind alteration**, is any condition which is significantly different from a normal waking beta wave state. The expression was used as early as 1966 by Arnold M. Ludwig[2] and brought into common usage from 1969 by Charles Tart.[3][4] It describes induced changes in one's mental state, almost always temporary. A synonymous phrase is "altered state of awareness".

8.1 Concept

The term "altered state of consciousness" was introduced and defined by Ludwig in 1966.[5] An altered state of consciousness is any mental state induced by physiological, psychological, or pharmacological maneuvers or agents, which deviates from the normal waking state of consciousness.[5]

Some observable abnormal and sluggish behaviors meet the criteria for altered state of consciousness.[6] Altered states of consciousness can also be associated with artistic creativity[7] or different focus levels. They also can be shared interpersonally and studied as a subject of sociological research.[8]

8.2 Causes

Altered states of consciousness may be caused either accidentally or intentionally:

- Accidental and Pathological
- Intentional:
  - Recreational
  - Meditation
  - Listening to specific brainwave entrainment, such as a Binaural beat

ASC may be caused by psychoactive drug or intoxication,[9][note 1] which may be either accidental or pathological, but can also be intentional.

Sometimes two or more causes lead to altered state of consciousness, for example a psychiatric disorder and consumption of psycho-active substances.

Emotions influence behavior that alters the state of consciousness. Emotions can be influenced by various stimuli.[10][note 2]

Altered states of consciousness can be assessed by observations and imaging of the brain such as computed tomography scan (CT), magnetic resonance imaging (MRI), or electroencephalography (EEG) which records the electrical brain wave activity. Imaging is most important to make a diagnosis when patient's history is unobtainable and the physical examination is not dependable. (Dandan, 2004)

8.3 Accidental and pathological causes

Accidental and pathological causes refer to unforeseen events, or illnesses. According to Dr. Jeffrey R. Avner, professor of clinical pediatrics, a crucial element to understanding accidental and pathological causes to altered states of consciousness (ASC) is that it begins with reduced self-awareness followed by reduced awareness in the environment (2006).[11] When the reduction of self-awareness and environmental awareness take effect, they produce altered states of consciousness. The specific conditions below provide clarity on the types of conditions compromise accidental and pathological causes.

8.3.1 Traumatic experience

The first condition, traumatic experience, is defined as a lesion caused by an external force (Trauma. (n.d.) In Merriam Webster Dictionary online, 2013). Examples include impact to the brain caused by blunt force (i.e., a car accident). The reason a traumatic experience causes altered states of consciousness is because it changes how the brain works. The external impact diverts the blood flow from the front of the brain to other areas. The front of the brain is known as the prefrontal cortex responsible for analytical thought (Kunsman, 2012). When the damage becomes uncontrollable, the patient experiences changes in behavior and impaired self-awareness. This is exactly when an ASC is experienced (Spikman et al. 2013).[12]

8.3.2 Epilepsy

Another common cause is epilepsy, according to Medlineplus[13] epilepsy can be described as a brain disorder that causes seizures (2013). During the seizure it is said that the patient will experience hallucinations and loss of mental control (Revonsuo, Chaplin, and Wedlund, 2008)[14] causing temporary dissociation from reality. A study that was conducted with six epileptic patients and used the functional magnetic resonance imaging (fMRI) detected how the patients did indeed experience hallucinations while a seizure is occurring (Korsnes M, Hugdahl K, Nygard M, Bjornæs H, 2010).[15] This not only altered the patient's behavioral pattern, but also made them dissociate from reality during that particular time frame.

8.3.3 Oxygen deficiency

The next item of interest is oxygen deficiency, questioning how oxygen deficiency impacts the brain is an important part of comprehending why ASC occurs when there is oxygen deprivation in an environment. A study conducted by Edwards, Harris, and Berisher illustrated how 20 navy men were impacted when they were exposed to nitrous oxide for 10 minutes. The study confirmed that inhaling substances other than oxygen results in impaired self-awareness, which can produce ASC (1976).[16]

8.3.4 Infections

In addition to oxygen deprivation or deficiency, infections are a common pathological cause of ASC. A prime example of an infection includes meningitis. The medical website WEBMD [17] states that meningitis is an infection that causes the coverings of the brain to swell. This particular infection occurs in children and young adults. This infection is primarily viral. Viral meningitis causes ASC and its symptoms include fevers and seizures (2010). The Impairment becomes visible the moment seizures begin to occur, this is when the patient enters the altered state of consciousness.

8.3.5 Sleep deprivation

Another type of deprivation that can cause ASC includes sleep deprivation. This refers to the loss of sleep that will provoke possible seizures, caused by fatigue. Sleep deprivation can be chronic or short-term depending on the severity of the patient's condition. Many patients can even report hallucinations, because sleep deprivation impacts the brain as well. A Harvard Medical school study conducted in 2007, also indicated with the use of MRI (magnetic resonance imaging) that a sleep deprived brain was not capable of being in control of its sensorimotor functions.[18] Therefore, there was impairment to the patient's self-awareness. Patients were also prone to be a lot clumsier than if had they not been experiencing sleep deprivation.

8.3.6 Fasting

Coupled with deprivation of sleep and oxygen, another form of deprivation includes fasting. Fasting can occur because of religious purposes or from psychological conditions such as anorexia.[19] Fasting refers to the ability to willingly refrain from food and possibly drinks as well. Anorexia, as previously mentioned, is psychological disorder in which the patient is irrationally afraid of gaining weight. Therefore, he or she restricts the intake of calories on a daily basis. Anorexia can lead to seizures due to malnutrition (Hockenbury, Don, and Hockenbury, Sandra, 2008). The dissociation caused by fasting is not only life-threatening but it is the reason why extended fasting periods can lead to ASC. Thus, the temporary dissociation from reality allows fasting to fall into the category of an ASC following the definition provided by Dr. Avner (2006).

8.3.7 Psychosis

Another pathological cause is psychosis, otherwise known as a psychotic episode. In order to comprehend psychosis, it is important to determine what symptoms it implies. Psychotic episodes often include delusions, paranoia, de-realization, depersonalization, and hallucinations (Revonsuo et al., 2008). Studies have not been able to clearly identify when a person is reaching a higher level of risk for a psychotic episode (Schimmelmann, B., Walger, P., & Schultze-Lutter, F.,2013),[20] but the earlier people are treated for psychosis the more likely they are to avoid the devastating consequences which could lead to a psychotic disorder (Schimmelmann, B., Walger, P., & Schultze-Lutter, F., 2013).[20] Unfortunately, there are very few studies which have thoroughly investigated psychotic episodes, and the ability to predict this disorder remains unclear. (Schimmelmann, B., Walger, P., & Schultze-Lutter,

F., 2013).[20]

Reviewing the previous conditions for accidental and pathological causes, we can come to understand that all of these accidental or pathological causes share the component of reduced self-awareness. Therefore, ASCs cannot only be caused naturally but they can be induced intentionally with methods including hypnosis meditation, amongst others. There are also ASCs which are caused by less recreational purposes; people who utilize illegal substances, or heavy dosages of medications, as well as large amounts of alcohol can indeed comply with the definition of an ASC (Revonsuo et al., 2008).

8.4   Intentional causes

An ASC can sometimes be reached intentionally by the use of sensory deprivation, an isolation tank, lucid dreaming, hypnosis, meditation, and psychoactive drugs.

8.4.1   Psychoactive drugs

An altered state of consciousness may be defined as a short-term change in the general configuration of one's individual experience, such that the rational functioning is clearly altered from one's usual state of consciousness. (Revonsuo, A., Kallio, S., & Sikka, P. 2009) There are many ways that one's consciousness can be altered, and drug use is one of them. Psychoactive drugs aid in altering the state of consciousness. Psychoactive drugs can be defined by a chemical substance that passes through the blood and disturbs brain function, causing changes in awareness, attitude, consciousness, and behavior. (Revonsuo, A., Kallio, S., & Sikka, P. 2009)

Marijuana is a psychoactive drug that is known to alter the state of consciousness. Marijuana alters mental activity, memory, and pain perception. One who is under the influence of marijuana may experience degrees of paranoia, increased sensitivity, and delayed reactions not normal for their usual conscious state.

MDMA (ecstasy) is a drug that also alters one's state of consciousness. The state of consciousness brought about by MDMA ingestion includes a rise in positive feelings and a reduction in negative feelings (Aldridge, D., & Fachner, J. ö. 2005). Users' emotions are increased and inhibitions lowered, often accompanied by a sensation of intimacy or connection with other people.

Opiates are a class of drugs that alter consciousness. Examples of opiates include heroin, morphine, hydrocodone, and oxycodone. Opiates produce analgesia and often feelings of euphoria in users. Opiate abuse may result in decreased production of endorphins in the brain, natural pain relievers whose effects may be heightened by drugs. If one takes a large dose of opiates to compensate for the lack of natural endorphins, the result may be death. (Berridge, V. 2001)

Cocaine alters one's state of consciousness. Cocaine affects the neurotransmitters that nerves use to communicate with each other. Cocaine inhibits the re-uptake of norepinephrine, serotonin, dopamine, and other neurotransmitters in the synapse, resulting in an altered state of consciousness or a "high." (Aldridge, D., & Fachner, J. ö. 2005).

Lysergic Acid Diethylamide, or LSD, activates serotonin receptors (the amine transmitter of nerve urges) in brain matter. LSD acts on certain serotonin receptors, and its effects are most prominent in the cerebral cortex, an area involved in attitude, thought, and insight, which obtains sensory signs from all parts of the body. LSD's main effects are emotional and psychological. The ingester's feelings may alter quickly through a range from fear to ecstasy. (Humphrey, N. 2001) This may cause one to experience many levels of altered consciousness.

Alcohol alters consciousness by shifting levels of neurotransmitters. Neurotransmitters are endogenous chemicals that transmit signals across a synapse from one neuron (nerve cell) to another "target" cell (often another neuron). Neurotransmitters can cause inhibitory or excitatory effects on the "target" cell they are affecting.[21] Alcohol increases the effect of the neurotransmitter GABA (Gamma-Aminobuturic Acid) in the brain. GABA causes slow actions and inaudible verbal communication that often occur in alcoholics (Berridge, V 2001). Alcohol also decreases the excitatory neurotransmitter glutamate. Suppressing this stimulant results in a similar type of physiological slow-down. In addition to increasing the GABA and decreasing the glutamate in the brain, alcohol increases the amount of the chemical dopamine in the brain, which is one of the addictive causes of alcoholism.

8.5   See also

Topics

- Autoscopy

- Anxiety

- Coma

- Convulsion

- Daydream

- Delirium

- Depersonalization

- Derealization
- Dementia
- Ecstasy (emotion)
- Ecstasy (religious)
- Ego death
- Energy (esotericism)
- Euphoria
- Fear
- Flow (psychology)
- Hydrogen narcosis
- Hypnagogia
- Hypnopompia
- Hypnosis
- Hysteria
- Immersion (virtual reality)
- Kundalini syndrome
- Major depressive disorder
- Mania
- Meditation
- Music therapy
- Mysticism
- Mystical psychosis
- New Age
- Near death experience
- Neurotheology
- Nitrogen narcosis
- Out-of-body experience
- Panic
- Parapsychology
- Peak experience
- Presyncope
- Psychedelia
- Psychosis

- Psychedelic drug
- Psychedelic experience
- Psychology of religion
- Psychonautics
- Religious experience
- Runner's high
- Sexual pleasure
- Sleep
- Sleep deprivation
- Sleep paralysis
- Syncope
- Wakefulness

People

- Bonny, Helen
- Castaneda, Carlos
- de Ropp, Robert
- Eisner, Bruce
- Farrell, Joseph Pierce
- Gowan, John Curtis
- Golas, Thaddeus
- Grof, Stanislav
- Huxley, Aldous
- Josephson, Ernst
- Leary, Timothy
- Lilly, John C.
- McKenna, Terence
- Naranjo, Claudio
- Tart, Charles

8.6 Notes

[1] Such as amphetamines, anticholinergic, anticonvulsants, barbiturates, benzodiazepines, clonidine, cocaine, ethanol, haloperidol, narcotics, phenothiazine, salicylates, selective serotonin uptake inhibitors (SSRIs), and tricyclic antidepressants.[9]

[2] Such as music, humor, visual objects, movies, books, romance, words or phrases.

8.7 References

[1] Bundzen PV, Korotkov KG, Unestahl LE (April 2002). "Altered states of consciousness: review of experimental data obtained with a multiple techniques approach". *J Altern Complement Med* **8** (2): 153–65. doi:10.1089/107555302317371442. PMID 12006123.

[2] Ludwig, Arnold M. (September 1966). "Altered States of Consciousness (presentation to symposium on Possession States in Primitive People)". *Archives of General Psychiatry* **15** (3): 225. doi:10.1001/archpsyc.1966.01730150001001. Retrieved 29 September 2010.

[3] Tart, Charles T. (1969). *Altered States of Consciousness: A Book of Readings*. New York: Wiley. ISBN 0-471-84560-4.

[4] Tart, Charles T. (2001). *States of Consciousness*. Backinprint.com. ISBN 0-595-15196-5.

[5] Revonsuo, Kallio, & Sikka, 2009

[6] Dandan, 2004

[7] Lombardo GT (2007). "An inquiry into the sources of poetic vision: Part I – the path to inspiration". *J Am Acad Psychoanal Dyn Psychiatry* **35** (3): 351–71. doi:10.1521/jaap.2007.35.3.351. PMID 17907906.

[8] Spivak D (1999). "Altered states of society: a tentative approach". *A World in Transition: Humankind and Nature* (Dordrecht: Kluwer Academic Publishers): 33–42.

[9] Avner, 2006

[10] Altarriba, 2012

[11] "Altered states of consciousness.". Pediatrics in Review. 27(9):331-8, 2006. Retrieved 5 December 2013.

[12] Spikman, Jacoba M. (2013). "Deficits in Facial Emotion Recognition Indicate Behavioral Changes and Impaired Self-Awareness after Moderate to Severe Traumatic Brain Injury". *PLoS ONE* **8**: 1–7. doi:10.1371/journal.pone.0065581.

[13] "Epilepsy". Retrieved 5 December 2013.

[14] Revonsuo, A., Kallio, S., & Sikka, P. (2009). "What is an altered state of consciousness?". *Philosophical Psychology* **22** (22(2)): 187–204. doi:10.1080/09515080902802850.

[15] Korsnes, M., Hugdahl, K., Nygård, M., & Bjørnæs, H. (2010). "An fMRI study of auditory hallucinations in patients with epilepsy.". *Epilepsia*. Series 4 (51(4)): 610–617. doi:10.1111/j.1528-1167.2009.02338.x.

[16] Edwards, D., Harris, J. A., & Biersner, R. (1976). "Encoding and decoding of connected discourse during altered states of consciousness". *Journal of Psychology* **92** (1): 97–102. doi:10.1080/00223980.1976.9921340.

[17] "Meningitis - Topic Overview". 8 December 2013. Retrieved 5 December 2013.

[18] "Harvard Heart Letter". Harvard Health Publications. 31 May 2012. Retrieved 5 December 2013.

[19] Nogal, Powel; Lewiński,Andrzej (January 2008). "Anorexia Nervosa". *Journal of Endocrinology* **59** (2): 148–155.

[20] Schimmelmann, B., Walger, P., & Schultze-Lutter, F. (2013). "The Significance of At-Risk Symptoms for Psychosis in Children and Adolescents". *Canadian Journal of Psychiatry* **58** (1): 32–40.

[21] "Neurotransmitter" at Dorland's Medical Dictionary

8.8 Sources

• Connor, C., Birchwood, M., Palmer, C., Channa, S., Freemantle, N., Lester, H., & ... Singh, S. (2013). Don't turn your back on the symptoms of psychosis: a proof-of-principle, quasi-experimental public health trial to reduce the duration of untreated psychosis in Birmingham, UK. BMC Psychiatry, 13(1), 1-6. doi: 10.1186/1471-244X-13-67

• Edwards, D., Harris, J. A., & Biersner, R. (1976). Encoding and decoding of connected discourse during altered states of consciousness. Journal of Psychology, 92(1), 97.

• Revonsuo, A., Kallio, S., & Sikka, P. (2009). What is an altered state of consciousness?. Philosophical Psychology, 22(2), 187-204. doi:10.1080/ 09515080902802850

• Englot, D., Rutkowski, M., Ivan, M., Sun, P., Kuperman, R., Chang, E., & ... Auguste, K. (2013). Effects of temporal lobectomy on consciousness-impairing and consciousness-sparing seizures in children. Child's Nervous System, 29(10), 1915-1922. doi:10.1007/s00381-013-2168-7

• Spikman J. M., Milders M. V., Visser-Keizer A. C., Westerhof-Evers H. J., Herben-Dekker M., van der Naalt J. (2013). "Deficits in Facial Emotion Recognition Indicate Behavioral Changes and Impaired Self-Awareness after Moderate to Severe Traumatic Brain Injury". *PLoS ONE* **8** (6): 1–7. doi:10.1371/journal.pone.0065581.

• Meningitis - Topic Overview (December 8, 2010) from: http://children.webmd.com/vaccines/tc/ meningitis-topic-overview

- "Harvard Heart Letter examines the costs of not getting enough sleep – Harvard Health Publications". Health.harvard.edu. 31 May 2012. Retrieved 2012-08-13.

- Avner JR: Altered states of consciousness. Pediatrics in Review. 27(9):331-8, 2006.

- Taheri S, Lin L, Austin D, Young T, Mignot E (2004). "Short Sleep Duration Is Associated with Reduced Leptin, Elevated Ghrelin, and Increased Body Mass Index". *PLoS Med* **1** (3): e62. doi:10.1371/journal.pmed.0010062. PMC 535701. PMID 15602591.

- Nogal Powel, Lewiński Andrzej (2008). "Anorexia Nervosa". *Endokrynologia Polska/Polish Journal of Endocrinology* **59** (2): 148–155.

- Bosinelli Marino (1995). "Mind and consciousness during sleep". *Research report on Behavioural Brain Research* **69**: 195–201. doi:10.1016/0166-4328(95)00003-c.

- Bosinelli Marino, PierCarlaCicogna (2001). "Consciousness during Dreams". *Journal of Consciousness and Cognition* **10**: 26–41.

- Louis Breger. (1967) Function of Dreams. *Journal of Abnormal Psychology Monograph*, Vol 72, No. 5, Part 2 or 2 Parts, 1–28

- Calkins Mary (1893). "Statistics of Dreams". *The American Journal of Psychology* **5** (3): 311–343. doi:10.2307/1410996.

- Dennett Daniel C (1976). "Are Dreams Experiences". *The Philosophical Review* **85** (2): 151–171. doi:10.2307/2183728.

- ValdasNorekia , Windt Jennifer M (2011). "How to integrate dreaming into a general theory of consciousness- A critical review of existing positions and suggestions for future research". *Journal of Consciousness and Cognition* **20**: 1091–1107.

- Aldridge, D., & Fachner, J. ö. (2005). Chapter 7: Music and drug-induced altered states of consciousness. (pp. 82–96)

- Berridge V (2001). "Altered states: Opium and tobacco compared". *Social Research* **68** (3): 655–675.

- Humphrey N (2001). "Introduction: Altered states". *Social Research* **68** (3): 585–587.

- Revonsuo A., Kallio S., Sikka P. (2009). "What is an altered state of consciousness?". *Philosophical Psychology* **22** (2): 187–204. doi:10.1080/09515080902802850.

8.9 Further reading

- Bourguignon, Erika (1973). *Religion, Altered States of Consciousness, and Social Change*. Ohio State Univ. Press, Columbus. ISBN 0-8142-0167-9 Full text

- Hoffman, Kay (1998). *The Trance Workbook: Understanding and Using the Power of Altered States*. Translated by Elfie Homann, Clive Williams, and Dr. Christliebe El Mogharbel. Translation edited by Laurel Ornitz. ISBN 0-8069-1765-2

- James, William (1902). *The Varieties of Religious Experience* ISBN 0-14-039034-0

- Locke, R. G.; Kelly, E. F. (1985). "A Preliminary Model for the Cross-Cultural Analysis of Altered States of Consciousness". *Ethos* **13**: 3–55. doi:10.1525/eth.1985.13.1.02a00010.

- Roberts, T.B. (Ed.) (2001). *Psychoactive Sacramentals: Essays on Entheogens and Religion*. San Francisco: Council on Spiritual Practices. ISBN 1-889725-02-1

- Roberts, T.B. and P.J. Hruby. (1995–2002). *Religion and Psychoactive Sacraments: An Entheogen Chrestomathy* . Online archive ISBN 1-889725-00-5

- Roberts, T.B. "Chemical Input—Religious Output: Entheogens." Chapter 10 of *Where God and Science Meet: Vol. 3: The Psychology of Religious Experience*. Edited by Robert McNamara. Westport, CT: Praeger/Greenwood, 2006. ISBN 0-275-98788-4

- Shear, Jonathan. (2011). "Eastern Approaches to Altered States of Consciousness". Altering consciousness. volume 1: multidisciplinary perspectives.

- Weinel, Jonathan (August 2010). "Bass Drum, Saxophone & Laptop: Real-time psychedelic performance software." *eContact! 12.4 — Perspectives on the Electroacoustic Work / Perspectives sur l'œuvre électroacoustique*. Montréal: Canadian Electroacoustic Community.

- Weinel, Jonathan (2012). "Altered States of Consciousness as an Adaptive Principle for Composing Electroacoustic Music". Unpublished PhD Thesis.

- Wier, Dennis R. (1995) *Trance: From Magic to Technology*. Transmedia. ISBN 1-888428-38-4

Chapter 9

Out-of-body experience

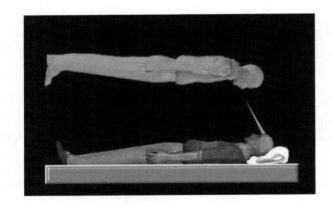

Artist's depiction of the separation stage of an out-of-body experience, which often precedes free movement

An **out-of-body experience** (**OBE** or sometimes **OOBE**) is an experience that typically involves a feeling of floating outside one's body and, in some cases, the feeling of perceiving one's physical body as if from a place outside one's body (autoscopy).

The term *out-of-body experience* was introduced in 1943 by George N. M. Tyrrell in his book *Apparitions*,[1] and was adopted by researchers such as Celia Green[2] and Robert Monroe[3] as an alternative to belief-centric labels such as "astral projection", "soul travel", or "spirit walking". OBEs can be induced by brain traumas, sensory deprivation, near-death experiences, dissociative and psychedelic drugs, dehydration, sleep, and electrical stimulation of the brain,[4] among others. It can also be deliberately induced by some.[5] One in ten people have an OBE once, or more commonly, several times in their life.[6][7]

Neuroscientists and psychologists regard OBEs as dissociative experiences arising from different psychological and neurological factors.[5][8][9][10][11][12][13][14]

9.1 Spontaneous

9.1.1 During/near sleep

Main article: Sleep paralysis

Those experiencing OBEs sometimes report (among other types of immediate and spontaneous experience) a preceding and initiating lucid-dream state. In many cases, people who claim to have had an OBE report being on the verge of sleep, or being already asleep shortly before the experience. A large percentage of these cases refer to situations where the sleep was not particularly deep (due to illness, noises in other rooms, emotional stress, exhaustion from overworking, frequent re-awakening, etc.). In most of these cases subjects perceive themselves as being awake; about half of them note a feeling of sleep paralysis.[15]

9.1.2 Near-death experiences

Main article: Near-death experience

Another form of spontaneous OBE is the near-death experience (NDE). Some subjects report having had an OBE at times of severe physical trauma such as near-drownings or major surgery. Near-death experiences may include subjective impressions of being outside the physical body, sometimes visions of deceased relatives and religious figures, and transcendence of ego and spatiotemporal boundaries.[16] Typically the experience includes such factors as: a sense of being dead; a feeling of peace and painlessness; hearing of various non-physical sounds, an out-of-body experience; a tunnel experience (the sense of moving up or through a narrow passageway); encountering "beings of light" and a God-like figure or similar entities; being given a "life review", and a reluctance to return to life.[17]

9.1.3 Resulting from extreme physical effort

Along the same lines as an NDE, extreme physical effort during activities such as high-altitude climbing and marathon running can induce OBEs. A sense of bilocation may be experienced, with both ground and air-based perspectives being experienced simultaneously.[18]

9.2 Induced

9.2.1 Chemical

- OBEs can be induced by hallucinogens such as ketamine, DMT, MDA, and LSD.[19][20][21][22]

Mental induction

- Falling asleep physically without losing awareness. The "Mind Awake, Body Asleep" state is widely suggested as a cause of OBEs, voluntary and otherwise.[23] Thomas Edison used this state to tackle problems while working on his inventions. He would rest a silver dollar on his head while sitting with a metal bucket in a chair. As he drifted off, the coin would noisily fall into the bucket, restoring some of his alertness.[24] OBE pioneer Sylvan Muldoon more simply used a forearm held perpendicular in bed as the falling object.[25] Salvador Dalí was said to use a similar "paranoiac-critical" method to gain odd visions which inspired his paintings. Deliberately teetering between awake and asleep states is known to cause spontaneous trance episodes at the onset of sleep which are ultimately helpful when attempting to induce an OBE.[26][27][28] By moving deeper and deeper into relaxation, one eventually encounters a "slipping" feeling if the mind is still alert. This slipping is reported to feel like leaving the physical body. Some consider progressive relaxation a passive form of sensory deprivation.

- Deep trance, meditation and visualization. The types of visualizations vary; some common analogies include climbing a rope to "pull out" of one's body, floating out of one's body, getting shot out of a cannon, and other similar approaches. This technique is considered hard to use for people who cannot properly relax. One example of such a technique is the popular Golden Dawn "Body of Light" Technique.[29]

Mechanical induction

- Brainwave synchronization via audio/visual stimulation. Binaural beats can be used to induce specific brainwave frequencies,[30] notably those predominant in various mind awake/body asleep states. Binaural induction of a "body asleep" 4 Hertz brainwave frequency was observed as effective by the Monroe Institute,[31] and some authors consider binaural beats to be significantly supportive of OBE initiation when used in conjunction with other techniques.[32][33] Simultaneous introduction of "mind awake" beta frequencies (detectable in the brains of normal, relaxed awakened individuals) was also observed as constructive. Another popular technology uses sinusoidal wave pulses to achieve similar results, and the drumming accompanying Native American religious ceremonies is also believed to have heightened receptivity to "other worlds" through brainwave entrainment mechanisms.[34]

- Magnetic stimulation of the brain, as with the God helmet developed by Michael Persinger.[35]

- Direct stimulation of the vestibular cortex.[36]

- Electrical stimulation of the brain, particularly the temporoparietal junction (see Blanke study below).

- Sensory deprivation. This approach aims to induce intense disorientation by removal of space and time references. Flotation tanks or pink noise played through headphones are often employed for this purpose.[37]

- Sensory overload, the opposite of sensory deprivation. The subject can for instance be rocked for a long time in a specially designed cradle, or submitted to light forms of torture, to cause the brain to shut itself off from all sensory input. Both conditions tend to cause confusion and this disorientation often permits the subject to experience vivid, ethereal out-of-body experiences.[38]

- Strong g-forces that causes blood to drain from parts of the brain, as experienced for example in high-performance aircraft or high-G training for pilots and astronauts.[39]

- An apparatus that uses a head-mounted display and a touch that confuses the sense of prioroception (and which can also create the sensation of additional limbs).[40]

9.3 Theories of OBEs

9.3.1 Psychological

In the fields of cognitive science and psychology OBEs are considered dissociative experiences arising from different psychological and neurological factors.[5][8][9][10][12][13][14] Scientists consider the OBE to be an experience from a mental state, like a dream or an altered state of consciousness without recourse to the paranormal.[41]

Charles Richet (1887) held that OBEs are created by the subject's memory and imagination processes and are no different from dreams.[42][43] James Hyslop (1912) wrote that OBEs occur when the activity of the subconscious mind dramatizes certain images to give the impression the subject is in a different physical location.[44] Eugèn Osty (1930) considered OBEs to be nothing more than the product of imagination.[45] Other early researchers (such as Schmeing, 1938) supported psychophysiological theories.[46] G. N. M. Tyrrell interpreted OBEs as hallucinatory constructs relating to subconscious levels of personality.[47]

Donovan Rawcliffe (1959) connected the OBE experience with psychosis and hysteria.[48] Other researchers have discussed the phenomena of the OBE in terms of a distortion of the body image (Horowitz, 1970) and depersonalization (Whitlock, 1978).[49][50] The psychologists Nandor Fodor (1959) and Jan Ehrenwald (1974) proposed that an OBE is a defense mechanism designed to deal with the threat of death.[51][52] According to (Irin and Watt, 2007) Jan Ehrenwald had described the out-of-body experience (OBE) "as an imaginal confirmation of the question for immortality, a delusory attempt to assure ourselves that we possess a soul that exists independently of the physical body.[53] The psychologists Donald Hebb (1960) and Cyril Burt (1968) wrote on the psychological interpretation of the OBE involving body image and visual imagery.[54][55] Graham Reed (1974) suggested that the OBE is a stress reaction to a painful situation, such as the loss of love.[56] John Palmer (1978) wrote that the OBE is a response to a body image change causing a threat to personal identity.[57]

Carl Sagan (1977) and Barbara Honegger (1983) wrote that the OBE experience may be based on a rebirth fantasy or reliving of the birth process based on reports of tunnel-like passageways and a cord-like connection by some OBErs which they compared to an umbilical cord.[58][59] Susan Blackmore (1978) came to the conclusion that the OBE is a hallucinatory fantasy as it has characteristics based around imaginary perceptions, perceptual distortions and fantasy-like perceptions of the self (such as having no body).[60][61] Ronald Siegel (1980) also wrote that OBEs are hallucinatory fantasies.[62]

Harvey Irwin (1985) presented a theory of the OBE involving attentional cognitive processes and somatic sensory activity. His theory involved a cognitive personality construct known as psychological absorption and gave instances of the classification of an OBE as examples of autoscopy, depersonalization and mental dissociation.[38] The psychophysiologist Stephen Laberge (1985) has written that the explanation for OBEs can be found in lucid dreaming.[63] David Hufford (1989) linked the OBE experience with a phenomenon he described as a nightmare waking experience, a type of sleep paralysis.[64] Other scientists have also linked OBEs to cases of hypnagogia and sleep paralysis (cataplexy).[65][66]

In case studies fantasy proneness has been shown to be higher among OBErs than those who have not had an OBE.[67] The data has shown a link between the OBE experience in some cases to fantasy prone personality (FPP).[68] In a case study involving 167 participants the findings revealed that those who claimed to have experienced the OBE were "more fantasy prone, higher in their belief in the paranormal and displayed greater somatoform dissociation."[69] Research from studies has also suggested that OBEs are related to cognitive-perceptual schizotypy.[70]

Terence Hines (2003) has written that spontaneous out-of-body experiences can be generated by artificial stimulation of the brain and this strongly suggests that the OBE experience is caused from "temporary, minor brain malfunctions, not by the person's spirit (or whatever) actually leaving the body."[71] In a study review of neurological and neurocognitive data (Bünning and Blanke, 2005) wrote that OBEs are due to "functional disintegration of lower-level multisensory processing and abnormal higher-level self-processing at the temporoparietal junction."[72] Some scientists suspect that OBEs are the result of a mismatch between visual and tactile signals.[73][74]

Richard Wiseman (2011) has noted that OBE research has focused on finding a psychological explanation and "out-of-body experiences are not paranormal and do not provide evidence for the soul. Instead, they reveal something far more remarkable about the everyday workings of your brain and body."[75] A study conducted by Jason Braithwaite and colleagues (2011) linked the OBE to "neural instabilities in the brain's temporal lobes and to errors in the body's sense of itself".[76][77] Braithwaite et al. (2013) reported that the "current and dominant view is that the OBE occurs due to a temporary disruption in multi-sensory integration processes."[78]

9.3.2 Paranormal

Writers within the fields of parapsychology and occultism have written that OBEs are not psychological and that a soul, spirit or subtle body can detach itself out of the body and visit distant locations. Out-of-the-body experiences were known during the Victorian period in spiritualist literature as "travelling clairvoyance". The psychical researcher Frederic Myers referred to the OBE as a "psychical excursion".[79] An early study which described alleged cases of OBEs was the two volume *Phantasms of the Living*, published in 1886 by the psychical researchers Edmund Gurney, Myers and Frank Podmore. The book was largely criticized by the scientific community as the anecdotal reports lacked evidential substantiation in nearly every case.[80][81]

The Theosophist Arthur Powell (1927) was an early author to advocate the subtle body theory of OBEs.[82] Sylvan Muldoon (1936) embraced the concept of an etheric body to explain the OBE experience.[83] The psychical researcher Ernesto Bozzano (1938) had also supported a similar view describing the phenomena of the OBE experience in terms of bilocation in which an "etheric body" can release itself from the physical body in rare circumstances.[84] The subtle body theory was also supported by occult writers such as Ralph Shirley (1938), Benjamin Walker (1977) and Douglas Baker (1979).[85] James Baker (1954) wrote that a mental body enters an "intercosmic region" during the OBE.[86] Robert Crookall in many publications supported the subtle body theory of OBEs.[87][88]

The paranormal interpretation of OBEs has not been supported by all researchers within the study of parapsychology. Gardner Murphy (1961) wrote that OBEs are "not very far from the known terrain of general psychology, which we are beginning to understand more and more without recourse to the paranormal".[89]

In April 1977 a patient from Harborview Medical Center known as Maria claimed to have experienced an out-of-body experience. During her OBE she claimed to have floated outside her body and outside of the hospital. Maria would later tell her social worker Kimberly Clark that during the OBE she had observed a tennis shoe on the third floor window ledge to the north side of the building. Clark would go to the north wing of the building and by looking out of the window could see a tennis shoe on one of the ledges. Clark published the account in 1985. The story has since been used in many paranormal books as evidence a spirit can leave the body.[90]

In 1996, Hayden Ebbern, Sean Mulligan and Barry Beyerstein visited the Medical Center to investigate the story. They placed a tennis shoe on the same ledge and discovered that the shoe was visible from within the building and could have easily been observed by a patient lying in bed. They also discovered the shoe was easily observable from outside the building and suggested that Maria may have overheard a comment about it during her three days in the hospital and incorporated it into her OBE. They concluded "Maria's story merely reveals the naiveté and the power of wishful thinking" from OBE researchers seeking a paranormal explanation.[91] Clark did not publish the description of

the case until seven years after it happened, casting doubt on the story. Richard Wiseman has said that although the story is not evidence for anything paranormal it has been "endlessly repeated by writers who either couldn't be bothered to check the facts, or were unwilling to present their readers with the more skeptical side of the story."[90]

9.4 Studies of OBEs

Early collections of OBE cases had been made by Ernesto Bozzano (Italy) and Robert Crookall (UK). Crookall approached the subject from a spiritualistic position, and collected his cases predominantly from spiritualist newspapers such as the *Psychic News*, which appears to have biased his results in various ways. For example, the majority of his subjects reported seeing a cord connecting the physical body and its observing counterpart; whereas Green found that less than 4% of her subjects noticed anything of this sort, and some 80% reported feeling they were a "disembodied consciousness", with no external body at all.

The first extensive scientific study of OBEs was made by Celia Green (1968).[92] She collected written, first-hand accounts from a total of 400 subjects, recruited by means of appeals in the mainstream media, and followed up by questionnaires. Her purpose was to provide a taxonomy of the different types of OBE, viewed simply as an anomalous perceptual experience or hallucination, while leaving open the question of whether some of the cases might incorporate information derived by extrasensory perception.

In 1999, at the 1st International Forum of Consciousness Research in Barcelona, International Academy of Consciousness research-practitioners Wagner Alegretti and Nanci Trivellato presented preliminary findings of an online survey on the out-of-body experience answered by internet users interested in the subject; therefore, not a sample representative of the general population.[93]

1,007 (85%) of the first 1,185 respondents reported having had an OBE. 37% claimed to have had between two and ten OBEs. 5.5% claimed more than 100 such experiences. 45% of those who reported an OBE said they successfully induced at least one OBE by using a specific technique. 62% of participants claiming to have had an OBE also reported having enjoyed nonphysical flight; 40% reported experiencing the phenomenon of self-bilocation (i.e. seeing one's own physical body whilst outside the body); and 38% claimed having experienced self-permeability (passing through physical objects such as walls). The most commonly reported sensations experienced in connection with the OBE were falling, floating, repercussions e.g. myoclonia (the jerking of limbs, jerking awake), sinking, torpidity (numbness), intracranial sounds, tingling, clairvoyance, oscillation and serenity.

Another reported common sensation related to OBE was temporary or projective catalepsy, a more common feature of sleep paralysis. The sleep paralysis and OBE correlation was later corroborated by the Out-of-Body Experience and Arousal study published in *Neurology* by Kevin Nelson and his colleagues from the University of Kentucky in 2007.[94] The study discovered that people who have out-of-body experiences are more likely to suffer from sleep paralysis.[95]

Also noteworthy, is the Waterloo Unusual Sleep Experiences Questionnaire [96] that further illustrates the correlation. William Buhlman, an author on the subject, has conducted an informal but informative online survey.[97]

In surveys, as many as 85% of respondents tell of hearing loud noises, known as "exploding head syndrome" (EHS), during the onset of OBEs.[98][99]

9.4.1   Miss Z study

In 1968, Charles Tart conducted an OBE experiment with a subject known as Miss Z for four nights in his sleep laboratory. The subject was attached to an EEG machine and a five-digit code was placed on a shelf above her bed. She did not claim to see the number on the first three nights but on fourth gave the number correctly.[100][101] The psychologist James Alcock criticized the experiment for inadequate controls and questioned why the subject was not visually monitored by a video camera.[102] Martin Gardner has written the experiment was not evidence for an OBE and suggested that whilst Tart was "snoring behind the window, Miss Z simply stood up in bed, without detaching the electrodes, and peeked."[103] Susan Blackmore wrote "If Miss Z had tried to climb up, the brain-wave record would have showed a pattern of interference. And that was exactly what it did show."[104]

9.4.2   Neurology and OBE-like experiences

There are several possible physiological explanations for parts of the OBE. OBE-like experiences have been induced by stimulation of the brain. OBE-like experience has also been induced through stimulation of the posterior part of the right superior temporal gyrus in a patient.[105] Positron-emission tomography was also used in this study to identify brain regions affected by this stimulation. The term *OBE-like* is used above because the experiences described in these experiments either lacked some of the clarity or details of normal OBEs, or were described by subjects who had never experienced an OBE before. Such subjects were therefore not qualified to make claims about the authenticity of the experimentally-induced OBE.

English psychologist Susan Blackmore and others suggest that an OBE begins when a person loses contact with sensory input from the body while remaining conscious.[106] The person retains the illusion of having a body, but that perception is no longer derived from the senses. The perceived world may resemble the world he or she generally inhabits while awake, but this perception does not come from the senses either. The vivid body and world is made by our brain's ability to create fully convincing realms, even in the absence of sensory information. This process is witnessed by each of us every night in our dreams, though OBEs are claimed to be far more vivid than even a lucid dream.

Irwin[107] pointed out that OBEs appear to occur under conditions of either very high or very low arousal. For example, Green[108] found that three quarters of a group of 176 subjects reporting a single OBE were lying down at the time of the experience, and of these 12% considered they had been asleep when it started. By contrast, a substantial minority of her cases occurred under conditions of maximum arousal, such as a rock-climbing fall, a traffic accident, or childbirth. McCreery[109][110] has suggested that this paradox may be explained by reference to the fact that sleep can supervene as a reaction to extreme stress or hyper-arousal.[111] He proposes that OBEs under both conditions, relaxation and hyper-arousal, represent a form of "waking dream", or the intrusion of Stage 1 sleep processes into waking consciousness.

Olaf Blanke studies

Research by Olaf Blanke in Switzerland found that it is possible to reliably elicit experiences somewhat similar to the OBE by stimulating regions of the brain called the right temporal-parietal junction (TPJ; a region where the temporal lobe and parietal lobe of the brain come together). Blanke and his collaborators in Switzerland have explored the neural basis of OBEs by showing that they are reliably associated with lesions in the right TPJ region[112] and that they can be reliably elicited with electrical stimulation of this region in a patient with epilepsy.[113] These elicited experiences may include perceptions of transformations of the patient's arms and legs (complex somatosensory responses) and whole-body displacements (vestibular responses).[114][115]

In neurologically normal subjects, Blanke and colleagues then showed that the conscious experience of the self and body being in the same location depends on multisensory integration in the TPJ. Using event-related potentials, Blanke and colleagues showed the selective activation of the TPJ 330–400 ms after stimulus onset when healthy volunteers imagined themselves in the position and visual perspective that generally are reported by people experiencing spontaneous OBEs. Transcranial magnetic stimulation in the same subjects impaired mental transformation of the participant's own body. No such effects were found with stimulation of another site or for imagined spatial transformations of external objects, suggesting the selective implication of the TPJ in mental imagery of one's own body.[116]

In a follow up study, Arzy et al. showed that the location and timing of brain activation depended on whether mental imagery is performed with mentally embodied or disembodied self location. When subjects performed mental imagery with an embodied location, there was increased activation of a region called the "extrastriate body area" (EBA), but when subjects performed mental imagery with a disembodied location, as reported in OBEs, there was increased activation in the region of the TPJ. This leads Arzy et al. to argue that "these data show that distributed brain activity at the EBA and TPJ as well as their timing are crucial for the coding of the self as embodied and as spatially situated within the human body."[117]

Blanke and colleagues thus propose that the right temporal-parietal junction is important for the sense of spatial location of the self, and that when these normal processes go awry, an OBE arises.[118]

In August 2007 Blanke's lab published research in *Science* demonstrating that conflicting visual-somatosensory input in virtual reality could disrupt the spatial unity between the self and the body. During multisensory conflict, participants felt as if a virtual body seen in front of them was their own body and mislocalized themselves toward the virtual body, to a position outside their bodily borders. This indicates that spatial unity and bodily self-consciousness can be studied experimentally and is based on multisensory and cognitive processing of bodily information.[119]

Ehrsson study

In August 2007, Henrik Ehrsson, then at the Institute of Neurology at University College of London (now at the Karolinska Institute in Sweden), published research in *Science* demonstrating the first experimental method that, according to the scientist's claims in the publication, *induced* an out-of-body experience in healthy participants.[120] The experiment was conducted in the following way:

> The study participant sits in a chair wearing a pair of head-mounted video displays. These have two small screens over each eye, which show a live film recorded by two video cameras placed beside each other two metres behind the participant's head. The image from the left video camera is presented on the left-eye display and

the image from the right camera on the right-eye display. The participant sees these as one "stereoscopic" (3D) image, so they see their own back displayed from the perspective of someone sitting behind them.

> The researcher then stands just beside the participant (in their view) and uses two plastic rods to simultaneously touch the participant's actual chest out-of-view and the chest of the illusory body, moving this second rod towards where the illusory chest would be located, just below the camera's view.

> The participants confirmed that they had experienced sitting behind their physical body and looking at it from that location.[73][121]

Both critics and the experimenter himself note that the study fell short of replicating "full-blown" OBEs. As with previous experiments which induced sensations of floating outside of the body, Ehrsson's work does not explain how a brain malfunction might cause an OBE. Essentially, Ehrsson created an illusion that fits a definition of an OBE in which "a person who is awake sees his or her body from a location outside the physical body."[122]

AWARE study

In 2001, Sam Parnia and colleagues investigated out of body claims by placing figures on suspended boards facing the ceiling, not visible from the floor. Parnia wrote "anybody who claimed to have left their body and be near the ceiling during resuscitation attempts would be expected to identify those targets. If, however, such perceptions are psychological, then one would obviously not expect the targets to be identified."[123] The philosopher Keith Augustine, who examined Parnia's study, has written that all target identification experiments have produced negative results.[124] Psychologist Chris French wrote regarding the study "unfortunately, and somewhat atypically, none of the survivors in this sample experienced an OBE."[125]

In the autumn of 2008, 25 UK and US hospitals began participation in a study, coordinated by Sam Parnia and Southampton University known as the AWARE study (AWAreness during REsuscitation). Following on from the work of Pim van Lommel in the Netherlands, the study aims to examine near-death experiences in 1,500 cardiac arrest survivors and so determine whether people without a heartbeat or brain activity can have documentable out-of-body experiences.[126] As part of the study Parnia and colleagues have investigated out of body claims by using hidden targets placed on shelves that could only be seen from above.[126] Parnia has written "if no one sees the pictures, it shows these experiences are illusions or false memories".[126]

In 2014 Parnia issued a statement indicating that the first phase of the project has been completed and the results are undergoing peer review for publication in a medical journal.[127] No subjects saw the images mounted out of sight according to Parnia's early report of the results of the study at an American Heart Association meeting in November 2013. Only two out of the 152 patients reported any visual experiences, and one of them described events that could be verified.[128]

On October 6, 2014 the results of the study were published in the journal *Resuscitation*. Among those who reported a perception of awareness and completed further interviews, 46 per cent experienced a broad range of mental recollections in relation to death that were not compatible with the commonly used term of NDEs. These included fearful and persecutory experiences. Only 9 per cent had experiences compatible with NDEs and 2 per cent exhibited full awareness compatible with OBEs with explicit recall of 'seeing' and 'hearing' events. One case was validated and timed using auditory stimuli during cardiac arrest.[129] According to Caroline Watt "The one 'verifiable period of conscious awareness' that Parnia was able to report did not relate to this objective test. Rather, it was a patient giving a supposedly accurate report of events during his resuscitation. He didn't identify the pictures, he described the defibrillator machine noise. But that's not very impressive since many people know what goes on in an emergency room setting from seeing recreations on television."[130][131]

AWARE Study II

This observational multi centre study is a continuation or enhancement of the previous AWARE Study. The AWARE Study II will collect data from about 1500 patients who experienced cardiac arrest. The patient recruitment will close in May 2017. Once a patient experiencing a cardiac arrest meeting the study inclusion criteria is identified, researchers will attend with portable brain oxygen monitoring devices and a tablet which will display visual images upwards above the patient as resuscitation is taking place. Measurements will be obtained during cardiac arrest and survivors will then be followed up and with their consent will have in-depth, audio recorded interviews. Researchers think that the recollection of memories of what happened during cardiac arrest in certain patients might be related to a better cerebral oxygenation during cardiac arrest in those patients. Images displayed in the tablet above the patient tries to identify whether the "autoscopy" phenomenon observed in some patients is just an illusion or not.[132]

Smith & Messier

A recent functional imaging study reported the case of a woman who could experience out of body experience at will. She reported developing the ability as a child and associated it with difficulties in falling sleep. Her OBEs continued into adulthood but became less frequent. She was able to see herself rotating in the air above her body, lying flat, and rolling in the horizontal plane. She reported sometimes watching herself move from above but remained aware of her unmoving "real" body. The participant reported no particular emotions linked to the experience. "[T]he brain functional changes associated with the reported extra-corporeal experience (ECE) were different than those observed in motor imagery. Activations were mainly left-sided and involved the left supplementary motor area and supramarginal and posterior superior temporal gyri, the last two overlapping with the temporal parietal junction that has been associated with out-of-body experiences. The cerebellum also showed activation that is consistent with the participant's report of the impression of movement during the ECE. There was also left middle and superior orbital frontal gyri activity, regions often associated with action monitoring."[133]

9.4.3   OBE training and research facilities

The Monroe Institute's Nancy Penn Center is a facility specializing in out-of-body experience induction. The Center for Higher Studies of the Consciousness in Brazil is another large OBE training facility. The International Academy of Consciousness in southern Portugal features the Projectarium, a spherical structure dedicated exclusively for practice and research on out-of-body experience.[134] Olaf Blanke's Laboratory of Cognitive Neuroscience has become a well-known laboratory for OBE research.[135]

9.5   Astral projection

Main article: Astral projection

Astral projection is a paranormal interpretation of out-of-body experiences that assumes the existence of one or more non-physical planes of existence and an associated body beyond the physical. Commonly such planes are called *astral*, *etheric*, or *spiritual*. Astral projection is often experienced as the spirit or astral body leaving the physical body to travel in the spirit world or astral plane.[136]

9.6 See also

- Alice in Wonderland syndrome

- Autoscopy

- Depersonalization disorder

- Hallucinations in the sane

- Macropsia

- Near-death experience

- Schizotypy

- Isra and Mi'raj

9.7 Notes

[1] G. N. M. Tyrrell, *Apparitions*, Gerald Duckworth and Co. Ltd, London, 1943, pp. 149. ISBN 978-1169831537

[2] C.E. Green, *Out-of-the-body Experiences*, Hamish Hamilton, London, 1968. ISBN 978-0345248435

[3] Robert Monroe *Journeys Out of the Body*, 1971. ISBN 0-385-00861-9

[4] Aspell, Jane; Blanke, Olaf. (2009). Understanding the out-of-body experience from a neuroscientific perspective in *Psychological Scientific Perspectives on Out of Body and Near Death Experiences* Psychology Research Progress. New York: Nova Science Publishers. ISBN 978-1607417057

[5] Brent, S. B. (1979). Deliberately *induced, premortem, out-of-body experiences: An experimental and theoretical approach*. In B. Kastenbaum (Ed.), *Between life and death* (pp. 89- 123). New York: Springer. ISBN 978-0826125408

[6] Susan Blackmore. (1984). "A Postal Survey of OBEs and Other Experiences".

[7] "(Aug. 24, 2007) First Out-of-body Experience Induced In Laboratory Setting". ScienceDaily. 2007-08-24. Retrieved 2011-10-06.

[8] Gabbard, G. O., & Twemlow, A. W. (1984). *With the eyes of the mind: An empirical analysis of out-of-body states*. New York: Praeger Scientific. ISBN 978-0030689260

[9] Leonard Zusne, Warren H. Jones (1989). *Anomalistic Psychology: A Study of Magical Thinking*. Lawrence Erlbaum Associates. ISBN 0-8058-0508-7

[10] Blanke O, Landis T, Seeck M (2004). "Out-of-body experience and autoscopy of neurological origin". *Brain* **127**: 243–258. doi:10.1093/brain/awh040.

[11] Blanke O, Mohr C (2005). "*Out-of-body experience, heautoscopy, and autoscopic hallucination of neurological origin. Implications for mechanisms of corporeal awareness and self consciousness*". *Brain Research Reviews* **50**: 184–199. doi:10.1016/j.brainresrev.2005.05.008.

[12] Meyerson, Joseph and Gelkopf, Marc (2004). "Therapeutic Utilization of Spontaneous Out-of-Body Experiences in Hypnotherapy". *American Journal of Psychotherapy* **58** (1).

[13] Cheyne, James Allan (Fall 2008). "When Is an OBE Not an OBE? A New Look at Out-of-Body Experiences". *Skeptic*.

[14] Blanke, Olaf (December 2004). "Out Of Body Experiences And Their Neural Basis: They Are Linked To Multisensory And Cognitive Processing In The Brain". *British Medical Journal* **329** (7480): 1414–1415. doi:10.1136/bmj.329.7480.1414. JSTOR 25469629. The reviewed evidence from neurological patients experiencing this striking dissociation between self and body shows that out of body experiences are culturally invariant phenomena that can be investigated scientifically.

[15] "SOBEs". Oberf.org. Retrieved 2011-10-06.

[16] Greyson, Bruce. (2003). *Near-Death Experiences in a Psychiatric Outpatient Clinic Population*. Psychiatr Serv 54: 1649–1651.

[17] Mauro, James. (1992). *Bright lights, big Mystery*. Psychology Today.

[18] Metzinger (citing Alvarado), "Out-of-Body Experiences as the Origin of the Concept of a 'Soul'", Mind & Matter Vol. 3(1), 2005, p. 65.

[19] Siegel Ronald (1980). "The Psychology of Life after Death". *American Psychologist* **35**: 911–931. doi:10.1037/0003-066x.35.10.911.

[20] Bressloff, P. C; Cowan, J. D; Golubitsky, M; Thomas, P J; Wiener, M. (2002). *What geometric visual hallucinations tell us about the visual cortex*. Neural Computation 14: 473-491.

[21] Shermer, Michael. (1997). *Why People Believe Weird Things: Pseudoscience, Superstition, and Other Confusions of Our Time*. Henry Holt and Company . p. 80. ISBN 0-8050-7089-3

[22] Hines, Terence. (2003). *Pseudoscience and the Paranormal* (2nd ed. ed.). Amherst, N.Y.: Prometheus Books. pp. 102-103. ISBN 1-57392-979-4

[23] Focus 10: Mind Awake/Body Asleep. Frederick Aardema (2012). Retrieved June 18, 2012

[24] Pre-Grams of Tomorrow dreams as pathway to a New World Perspective: Forrer, Kurt

[25] Hereward Carrington, Sylvan Muldoon. (1981). *The Projection Of The Astral Body*. Weiser Books. ISBN 978-0-87728-069-9

[26] "Journeys out of the Body", 1972, Robert Monroe, p. 207-210, ISBN 0-285-62753-8

[27] "Astral Dynamics: The Complete Book of Out-of-Body Experiences", 2009, Robert Bruce, p. 208-9, ISBN 978-1-57174-616-0

[28] The Vigil Method. Frederick Aardema (2012). Retrieved June 27, 2012.

[29] "The Art and Practice of Astral Projection", 1974, Ophiel, ISBN 978-0-87728-246-4

[30] "". The Effects of Hemi-Sync on Electrocortical Activity, Sadigh and Kozicky

[31] Campbell, Thomas, 2007, "My Big TOE", p75,79. ISBN 978-0-9725094-6-6

[32] Buhlman, William, 2001, "The Secret of the Soul", p198. ISBN 978-0-06-251671-8

[33] Bruce, Robert, 2009, "Astral Dynamics: The Complete Book of Out-of-Body Experiences", p164. ISBN 978-1-57174-616-0

[34] Haven, Janine. (2006). *At a Glance' Religious and Spiritual Competency for Psychotherapists*. AuthorHouse. ISBN 978-1425906849

[35] "Spirituality & The Brain". Shakti Technology. Retrieved 2011-10-06.

[36] Cheyne J. A., Girard T. A. (2009). "The body unbound: vestibular-motor hallucinations and out-of-body experiences". *Cortex* **45** (2): 201–215. doi:10.1016/j.cortex.2007.05.002. PMID 18621363.

[37] Nicholls, Graham. (2012). *Navigating the Out-of-Body Experience: Radical New Techniques*. Llewellyn Publications. ISBN 978-0738727615

[38] Irwin, Harvey. (1985). *Flight of Mind: A Psychological Study of the Out-Of-Body Experience*. Metuchen, NJ: Scarecrow Press. ISBN 978-0810817371

[39] "Out of Body, Roger". Retrieved 2014-12-12.

[40] "Creating The Illusion Of A Different Body". 2011-02-25. Retrieved 2014-12-12.

[41] Blackmore, Susan. (2002). *Out-of-Body Experiences*. pp. 164-169. In Michael Shermer. *The Skeptic Encyclopedia of Pseudoscience*. ABC-CLIO. ISBN 978-1576076538

[42] Richet, C. (1887). *L 'homme et l'intelligence: Fragments de physiologie et de psychologie* (2nd ed.). Paris: Felix Alcan.

[43] Richet, C. (1922). *Traith de metapsychique*. Paris: Felix Alcan.

[44] Hyslop, J. H. (1912). *A review, a record and a discussion*. Journal of the American Society for Psychical Research, 6, 490-5 16.

[45] Osty, E. (1930). *La vision de soi. Revue metapsychique*. No. 3, 185-197.

[46] Schmeing, K. (1938). *Flugtraiume und "Exkursion des Ich*. Archiv für die Gesamte Psychologie.

[47] Tyrrell, G. N. M. (1953). *Apparitions*. London: Gerald Duckworth. (Originally published, 1942.)

[48] Rawcliffe, D.H. (1959). *Illusions and Delusions of the Supernatural and the Occult*. New York, NY: Dover. (Original work published 1952).

[49] Horowitz, M. J. (1970). *Image formation and cognition*. New York: Appleton-Century-Crofts.

[50] Whitlock, F. A. (1978). *The psychiatry and psychopathology of paranormal phenomena*. Australian and New Zealand Journal of Psychiatry, 12, 1 1-1 9.

[51] Fodor, N. (1959). *The Haunted Mind*. New York: Helix Press.

[52] Ehrenwald, J. (1974). *Out-of-the-body experiences and the denial of death*. Journal of Nervous and Mental Disease, 159, 227-233.

[53] Harvey J. Irwin, Caroline Watt *An Introduction to Parapsychology* 2007, p. 188

[54] Hebb D. O. (1960). "The American Revolution". *American Psychologist* **15**: 735–745. doi:10.1037/h0043506.

[55] Burt, C. (1968). *Psychology and Psychical Research*. London: Society for Psychical Research.

[56] Reed, Graham. (1974). *The Psychology of Anomalous Experience*. Boston: Houghton Mifflin.

[57] Palmer, J. (1978). *The out-of-body experience: A psychological theory*. Parapsychology Review, 9(5), 19-22.

[58] Sagan, C. (1977). *Broca's Brain*. Random House.

[59] Honegger, B. (1983). *The OBE as a near-birth experience*. In Roll, W. G., Beloff, J., and White, R. A. (Eds.), *Research in Parapsychology*. Scarecrow Press. pp. 230-231.

[60] Blackmore, S. (1978). *Parapsychology and out-of-the-body experiences*. London: Transpersonal Books/Society for Psychical Research.

[61] Sheikh, Anees. (1983). *Imagery: Current Theory, Research, and Application*. John Wiley & Sons. p. 372. "Blackmore (1978) reviewed the evidence that indicates that out-of-the-body experiences have the following characteristics that can be expected of hallucinatory fantasies: (1) imaginary perceptions; (2) errors in perception; (3) perceptual distortions (such as seeing through things); (4) instantaneous traveling to distant locations; and (5) fantasy like perceptions of self such as not having a body, having a replica of one's body, and perceiving oneself as a point or a ball of light. She concluded from the data that out-of-the-body experiences should be viewed as hallucinatory fantasies."

[62] Siegel R. K. (1980). "The Psychology of Life After Death". *American Psychologist* **35**: 911–931. doi:10.1037/0003-066x.35.10.911.

[63] LaBerge, S. (1985). *Lucid Dreaming*. Los Angeles: Jeremy P. Tarcher.

[64] Hufford, David. (1989) *The Terror That Comes in the Night: An Experience-Centered Study of Supernatural Assault Traditions (Publications of the American Folklore Society)*. University of Pennsylvania Press. ISBN 978-0812213058

[65] Adler, Shelley. (2010) *Sleep Paralysis: Night-mares, Nocebos, and the Mind-Body Connection (Studies in Medical Anthropology)*. Rutgers University Press. ISBN 978-0813548869.

[66] Mavromatis, Andreas. (2010). *Hypnagogia: The Unique State of Consciousness Between Wakefulness and Sleep*. Thyrsos Press. ISBN 978-0955305214

[67] Myers. S. A., Austrin, H. R., Grisso, J. T., & Nickeson, R. C. (1983). *Personality Characteristics as related to the out-of-body experience*. Journal of Parapsychology, 47. 131-144.

[68] Wilson, S. C., & Barber T. X. (1982). *The fantasy-prone personality: Implications for understanding imagery, hypnosis, and parapsychological phenomena*. In A. A. Sheikh (Ed.) *Imagery: Current theory, Research and Application*. New York: John Wiley.

[69] Gow, K., Lang, T. and Chant, D. (2004). *Fantasy proneness, paranormal beliefs and personality features in out-of-body experiences*. Contemp. Hypnosis, 21: 107–125.

[70] Parra, Alejandro. (2009). *Out-of-Body Experiences and Hallucinatory Experiences: A Psychological Approach*. Journal: Imagination, Cognition and Personality , vol. 29, no. 3, pp. 211-223

[71] Hines, Terence. (2003). *Pseudoscience and the Paranormal*. Prometheus Books. pp. 104-106. ISBN 1-57392-979-4

[72] S. Bünning and O. Blanke. *The out-of body experience: precipitating factors and neural correlates*. Progress in Brain Research, vol. 150, p. 331-50, 2005

[73] "Out-of-body experience recreated". *BBC News*. August 24, 2007. Retrieved May 20, 2010.

[74] Blakeslee, Sandra (2006-10-03). "Out-of-Body Experience? Your Brain Is to Blame". Nytimes.com. Retrieved 2011-10-06.

[75] Wiseman, Richard. (2011). *Paranormality: Why We See What Isn't There*. Macmillan. p. 60. ISBN 978-0-230-75298-6

[76] Braithwaite Jason J., Samson Dana, Apperly Ian, Broglia Emma, Hulleman Johan (2011). "Cognitive correlates of the spontaneous out-of-body experience (OBE) in the psychologically normal population: Evidence for an increased role of temporal-lobe instability, body-distortion processing, and impairments in own-body transformations". *Cortex* **47**: 839–853. doi:10.1016/j.cortex.2010.05.002.

[77] "Out-of-body experiences linked to neural instability and biases in body representation". *Science Daily*.

[78] Braithwaite, J.J., James, K., Dewe, H., Medford, N., Takahashi, C., & Kessler, K. (2013). *Fractionating the unitary notion of dissociation: Disembodied but not embodied dissociative experiences are associated with exocentric perspective-taking*. Frontiers in Neuroscience 7: 719.

[79] Ronald Pearsall. (1972). *The Table-Rappers*. Book Club Associates. p. 197. ISBN 978-0750936842

[80] Alexander Taylor Innes. (1887). *Where Are the Letters? A Cross-Examination of Certain Phantasms*. Nineteenth Century 22: 174-194.

[81] Charles Sanders Peirce. (1958). *Collected Papers of Charles Sanders Peirce, Volume 4*. Harvard University Press. p. 360

[82] Powell, Arthur. (1927). *Astral Body and Other Astral Phenomena*. Kessinger Publishing. ISBN 978-1162570952

[83] Muldoon, S. (1936). *The Case for Astral Projection*. Chicago: Ariel Press. ISBN 978-1162738680

[84] Bozzano, E. (1938). *Discarnate Influences in Human Life*. London: John M. Watkins.

[85] Shirley, Ralph. (1938). *The Mystery of the Human Double: The Case for Astral Projection*. Kessinger Publishing. ISBN 978-0548056035 Walker. Benjamin. (1977). *Beyond the Body: Human Double and the Astral Planes*. Routledge. ISBN 978-0710085818. Baker, Douglas. (1979). *Practical Techniques of Astral Projection*. Red Wheel/Weiser. ISBN 978-0850301410

[86] Baker, James. (1954). *The exteriorization of the mental body : a scientific interpretation of the out-of-the-body experience known as pneumakinesis*. William-Frederick Press. Online

[87] Crookall, R. (1961). *The Study and Practice of Astral Projection*. London: Aquarian Press.

[88] Crookall, R. (1965). *Intimations of Immortality*. Cambridge: James Clarke.

[89] Murphy, G., with Dale, L. (1961). *Challenge of Psychical Research*. New York: Harper & Row.

[90] Wiseman, Richard. (2011). *Paranormality: Why We See What Isn't There*. Macmillan. pp 44-45. ISBN 978-0-230-75298-6

[91] Ebbern, Hayden; Mulligan, Sean; Beyerstein, Barry. (1996). *Maria's Near-Death Experience: Waiting for the Other Shoe to Drop*. Skeptical Inquirer 20: 27-33.

[92] Green, C.E. (1968). *Out-of-the-Body Experiences*. London: Hamish Hamilton.

[93] "preliminary findings". Out-of-body-experience.org. Retrieved 2011-10-06.

[94] "Out-of-body experience and arousal". Neurology.org. 2007-03-06. Retrieved 2011-10-06.

[95] Highfield, Roger. (2007). What really happens in out of body experiences. The Telegraph.

[96] "Waterloo Unusual Sleep Experiences Questionnaire". Watarts.uwaterloo.ca. 1940-06-25. Retrieved 2011-10-06.

[97] "online survey". Astralinfo.org. Retrieved 2011-10-06.

[98] Buhlman, William. "Results of OBE Survey". *The Out of Body Experience*. Retrieved 2011-03-18.

[99] Twemlow SW, Gabbard GO, Jones FC, April (1982). "The out-of-body experience: a phenomenological typology based on questionnaire responses". *American Journal of Psychiatry* **139** (4): 450–455. doi:10.1176/ajp.139.4.450. PMID 7039367.

[100] Zusne, Leonard; Jones, Warren. (1989). *Anomalistic Psychology: A Study of Magical Thinking*. Lawrence Erlbaum Associates. p. 126. ISBN 0-8058-0508-7

[101] Robert Todd Carroll. (2003). *The Skeptic's Dictionary*. Wiley. p. 110. ISBN 0-471-27242-6

[102] Alcock, James. (1981). *Parapsychology-Science Or Magic?: A Psychological Perspective*. Pergamon Press. pp. 130-131. ISBN 978-0080257730

[103] Gardner, Martin. (1989). *How Not To Test A Psychic: 10 Years of Remarkable Experiments with Renowned Clairvoyant Pavel Stepanek*. Prometheus Books. p. 246. ISBN 0-87975-512-1

[104] Blackmore, Susan. (1986). *The Adventures of a Parapsychologist*. Prometheus Books. p. 176. ISBN 0-87975-360-9

[105] De Ridder D, Van Laere K, Dupont P, Menovsky T, Van de Heyning P. Visualizing out-of-body experience in the brain. N Engl J Med. 2007 Nov 1;357(18):1829–33.

[106] Blackmore, S. (1992). *Beyond the body: An investigation of out of body experiences*. Chicago: Academy Chicago Publishers.

[107] Irwin, H.J. (1985). *Flight of Mind: a psychological study of the out-of-body experience*. Metuchen, New Jersey: The Scarecrow Press.

[108] Green C.E. (1968). *Out-of-the-Body Experiences*. London: Hamish Hamilton.

[109] McCreery, C. (1997). Hallucinations and arousability: pointers to a theory of psychosis. In Claridge, G. (ed.): *Schizotypy, Implications for Illness and Health*. Oxford: Oxford University Press.

[110] McCreery, C. (2008). Dreams and psychosis: a new look at an old hypothesis. *Psychological Paper No. 2008–1*. Oxford: Oxford Forum. Online PDF

[111] Oswald, I. (1962). *Sleeping and Waking: Physiology and Psychology*. Amsterdam: Elsevier.

[112] Blanke O., Landis T., Spinelli L., Seeck M. (2004). "Out-of-body experience and autoscopy of neurological origin". *Brain* **127** (2): 243–258. doi:10.1093/brain/awh040.

[113] Blanke, O.; Ortigue, S.; Landis, T.; Seeck, M. (2002). "Stimulating illusory own-body perceptions" (PDF). *Nature* **419** (6904): 269–270. doi:10.1038/419269a. PMID 12239558.

[114] Laboratory of Cognitive Neuroscience at Ecole Polytechnique Federeale de Lausanne: http://lnco.epfl.ch/

[115] Out-of-Body Experiences: All in the Brain? By Jan Holden, EdD, Jeff Long, MD, and Jason MacLurg, MD *Vital Signs* Volume 21, Number 3

[116] Blanke, O., Mohr, C., Michel, C. M., Pascual-Leone, A., Brugger, P., Seeck, M., et al. (2005). Linking out-of-body experience and self processing to mental own-body imagery at the temporoparietal junction. *Journal of Neuroscience*, 25(3); doi:10.1523/JNEUROSCI.2612-04.2005.

[117] Arzy, S.; Thut, G.; Mohr, C.; Michel, C.M.; Blanke, O. (2006). "Neural basis of embodiment: Distinct contributions of temporoparietal junction and extrastriate body area". *Journal of Neuroscience* **26** (31): 8074–8081. doi:10.1523/JNEUROSCI.0745-06.2006. PMID 16885221.

[118] Blanke, O.; Arzy, S. (2005). "The out-of-body experience: Disturbed self-processing at the temporoparietal junction". *Neuroscientist* **11** (1): 16–24. doi:10.1177/1073858404270885. PMID 15632275.

[119] Lenggenhager; et al. (2007). "Video Ergo Sum: Manipulating Bodily Self-Consciousness". *Science* **317**: 1096–1099. doi:10.1126/science.1143439.

[120] Ehrsson H.H. (2007). "The Experimental Induction of Out-of-Body Experiences". *Science* **317**: 1048. doi:10.1126/science.1142175.

[121] First out-of-body experience induced in laboratory setting, August 23, 2007, EurekAlert!

[122] ""Out of Body. Be Back Soon.", EnlightenmentNext, Feb–April 2008". Enlightennext.org. Retrieved 2011-10-06.

[123] Parnia S, Waller D. G, Yeates R, Fenwick P. (2001). "A Qualitative and Quantitative Study of the Incidence, Features and Aetiology of Near-Death Experiences in Cardiac Arrest Survivors". *Resuscitation* **48**: 149–156. doi:10.1016/s0300-9572(00)00328-2.

[124] Keith Augustine. (2008). "Hallucinatory Near-Death Experiences". Internet Infidels. Retrieved 2014-06-03.

[125] French, Chris. (2005). *Near-Death Experiences in Cardiac Arrest Survivors*. Progress in Brain Research 150: 351-367.

[126] Jane Dreaper. (2008). "Study into near-death experiences". BBC News. Retrieved 2014-06-03.

[127] AWARE Study Update 2014. Published online at Horizon Research Foundation.

[128] Bowman, Lee (December 20, 2013). "Scientists looking closer at what happens when body dies; edge closer to new understanding". WEWS-TV. Scripps Howard News Service. Retrieved 2014-05-24.

[129] Parnia *et al.* (2014). "AWARE—AWAreness during REsuscitation—A prospective study". *Resuscitation.*

[130] "One not too impressive study does not prove life after death". Doubtful News.

[131] "No, this study is not evidence for "life after death". James Randi Educational Foundation.

[132] Sam Parnia. "AWARE II (AWAreness during REsuscitation) A Multi-Centre Observational Study of the Relationship between the Quality of Brain Resuscitation and Consciousness, Neurological, Functional and Cognitive Outcomes following Cardiac Arrest" (2014).

[133] Smith AM, Messier C. (2014). *Voluntary out-of-body experience: an fMRI study.* Front Hum Neurosci 8: 70.

[134] IAC. "Projectarium". Iacworld.org. Retrieved 2011-10-06.

[135] Laureys, Steven. (2005). *The Boundaries of Consciousness: Neurobiology and Neuropathology, Volume 150 (Progress in Brain Research).* Elsevier Science. ISBN 978-0444518514

[136] "Astral body in the Historical Terms Glossary from the website of the Parapsychological Association, retrieved August 26, 2007". Parapsych.org. Retrieved 2011-10-06.

9.8   Further reading

- Blackmore Susan (1984). "A psychological theory of the out-of-body experience" (PDF). *Journal of Parapsychology* **48**: 201–218.

- Blackmore, Susan. (1982). *Beyond the Body: An Investigation of Out-of-the-Body Experiences.* London: Heinemann. ISBN 978-0897333443

- Blanke O, Ortigue S, Landis T, Seeck M (2002). "Stimulating illusory own-body peceptions" (PDF). *Nature* **419** (6904): 269–270. doi:10.1038/419269a. PMID 12239558.

- Blanke O, Landis T, Seeck M (2004). "Out-of-body experience and autoscopy of neurological origin". *Brain* **127**: 243–258. doi:10.1093/brain/awh040.

- Blanke O, Mohr C (2005). "Out-of-body experience, heautoscopy, and autoscopic hallucination of neurological origin. Implications for mechanisms of corporeal awareness and self consciousness" (PDF). *Brain Research Reviews* **50**: 184–199. doi:10.1016/j.brainresrev.2005.05.008.

- Blanke O, Arzy S (2005). "The out-of-body experience: Disturbed self-processing at the temporal-parietal junction". *Neuroscientist* **11** (1): 16–24. doi:10.1177/1073858404270885. PMID 15632275.

- Bunning, S; Blanke, O. (2005). *The out-of-body experience: precipitating factors and neural correlates.* In Laureys, S. *The boundaries of consciousness: Neurobiology and neuropathology. Progress in Brain Research,* The Netherlands: Elsevier. 150: 331-350. ISBN 978-0444528766

- Brugger P, Regard M, Landis T (1997). "Illusory reduplication of one's own body: phenomenology and classification of autoscopic phenomena". *Cognitive Neuropsychiatry* **2**: 19–38. doi:10.1080/135468097396397.

- Brugger P (2002). "Reflective mirrors: Perspective-taking in autoscopic phenomena". *Cognitive Neuropsychiatry* **7**: 179–194. doi:10.1080/13546800244000076.

- Cheyne J. A, Girard T. A. (2009). "The body unbound: vestibular-motor hallucination and out of body experiences". *Cortex* **45** (2): 201–215. doi:10.1016/j.cortex.2007.05.002. PMID 18621363.

- Gabbard, G. O; Twemlow, A. W. (1984). *With the eyes of the mind: An empirical analysis of out-of-body states.* New York: Praeger Scientific. ISBN 978-0030689260

- Irwin, Harvey. (1985). *Flight of Mind: A Psychological Study of the Out-Of-Body Experience.* Metuchen, NJ: Scarecrow Press. ISBN 978-0810817371

- Metzinger, Thomas. (2003). *The pre-scientific concept of a 'soul': A neurophenomenological hypothesis about its origin.*

- Reed, Graham. (1988). *The Psychology of Anomalous Experience: A Cognitive Approach.* Prometheus Books. ISBN 978-0879754358

- Schwabe L., Blanke O. (2008). "The Vestibular Component in Out-Of-Body Experiences: A Computational Approach". *Frontiers in Human Neuroscience* **2**: 17. doi:10.3389/neuro.09.017.2008. PMC 2610253. PMID 19115017.

- Terhune D. B. (2009). "The incidence and determinants of visual phenomenology during out-of-body experiences". *Cortex* **45**: 236–242. doi:10.1016/j.cortex.2007.06.007.

9.9   External links

- Visualized Heartbeat Can Trigger 'Out-of-Body Experience'. Association for Psychological Science.

- Out-of-body experience recreated. BBC News.

- Out of body experiences and their neural basis. Olaf Blanke.

- Electrodes trigger out-of-body experience. *Nature.*

- Out-of-body experience: Master of illusion. *Nature.*

- Out-of-body experiences are 'all in the mind'. *New Scientist.*

- Out-of-body experience. *The Skeptic's Dictionary.*

- Out-of-Body Experience? Your Brain Is to Blame. *The New York Times.*

Chapter 10

Religious ecstasy

For related topics, see ecstasy (emotion) and ecstasy (philosophy).

Religious ecstasy is a type of altered state of conscious-

Saint Caterina of Alexandria during her ecstacy by Bernardo Cavallino.

ness characterized by greatly reduced external awareness and expanded interior mental and spiritual awareness, frequently accompanied by visions and emotional (and sometimes physical) euphoria.

Although the experience is usually brief in time,[1] there are records of such experiences lasting several days or even more, and of recurring experiences of ecstasy during one's lifetime.

A person's sense of time and space disappear during a reli-

gious ecstasy forsaking any senses or physical cognizance in its duration. Among venerated Catholic saints who dabble in Christian mysticism, a person's physical stature, human sensory, or perception is completely detached to time and space during an ecstatic experience.

In Islamic Sufism, the experience is referred to as *majzoobiyat*.

10.1 Context

The adjective "religious" means that the experience occurs in connection with religious activities or is interpreted in context of a religion. Marghanita Laski writes in her study "Ecstasy in Religious and Secular Experiences," first published in 1961:

> "Epithets are very often applied to mystical experiences including ecstasies without, apparently, any clear idea about the distinctions that are being made. Thus we find experiences given such names as nature, religious, aesthetic, neoplatonic, sexual etc. experiences, where in some cases the name seems to derive from trigger, sometimes from the overbelief, sometimes from the known standing and beliefs of the mystic, and sometimes, though rarely, from the nature of the experience.

> Ecstasies enjoyed by accepted religious mystics are usually called religious experiences no matter what the nature of the ecstasy or the trigger inducing it."[2]

10.2 Exclusive and inclusive views

Religious people may hold the view that true religious ecstasy occurs only in their religious context (e.g.   as

The religious ecstacy of Saint Teresa of Avila of the Carmelite Order, here portrayed being pierced a thousand times in the heart by a cherub.

Saint Francis of Assisi in Ecstasy. *Caravaggio, oil on panel.*

a gift from the supernatural being whom they follow) and it cannot be induced by natural means (human activities). Trance-like states which are often interpreted as religious ecstasy have been deliberately induced with techniques or ecstatic practices; including, prayer, religious rituals, meditation, breathing exercises, physical exercise, sex, music, dancing, sweating, fasting, thirsting, and

psychotropic drugs. An ecstatic experience may take place in occasion of contact with something or somebody perceived as extremely beautiful or holy. It may also happen without any known reason. The particular technique that an individual uses to induce ecstasy is usually one that is associated with that individual's particular religious and cultural traditions. As a result, an ecstatic experience is usually interpreted within the particular individual religious context and cultural traditions. These interpretations often include statements about contact with supernatural or spiritual beings, about receiving new information as a revelation, also religion-related explanations of subsequent change of values, attitudes and behavior (e.g. in case of religious conversion).

Achieving ecstatic trances is a shamanic activity, inducing ecstasy for such purposes as traveling to heaven or the underworld, guiding or otherwise interacting with spirits, clairvoyance, and healing. Some shamans take drugs from such plants as Ayahuasca, peyote and cannabis (drug) or certain mushrooms in their attempts to reach ecstasy, while others rely on such non-chemical means as ritual, music, dance, ascetic practices, or visual designs as aids to mental discipline.

10.3   Examples

Athletes may follow rituals in preparing for contests, which are dismissed as superstition, but this sports psychology device may help them to attain advantage in an ecstasy-like state.

Yoga provides techniques to attain an ecstasy state called samādhi. According to practitioners, there are various stages of ecstasy, the highest being Nirvikalpa Samadhi. Bhakti Yoga especially, places emphasis on ecstasy as being one of the fruits of its practice.

In Buddhism, especially in the Pali Canon, there are eight states of trance also called absorption. The first four states are Rupa or, materially-oriented. The next four are Arupa or non-material. These eight states are preliminary trances which lead up to final saturation. In Visuddhimagga, great effort and years of sustained meditation are practiced to reach the first absorption, and that not all individuals are able to accomplish it at all.

Modern meditator experiences in the Thai Forest Tradition, as well as other Theravadin traditions, demonstrates that this effort and rarity is necessary only to become completely immersed in the absorptions and experience no other sensations. It is possible to experience the absorptions in a less intense state with much less practice.

In the Dionysian Mysteries, initiates used intoxicants and

other trance-inducing techniques (like dance and music) to remove inhibitions and social constraints, liberating the individual to return to a natural state.

In the monotheistic tradition, ecstasy is usually associated with communion and oneness with God. However, such experiences can also be personal mystical experiences with no significance to anyone but the person experiencing them. Some charismatic Christians practice ecstatic states (such as "being slain in the Spirit") and interpret these as given by the Holy Spirit. The firewalkers of Greece dance themselves into a state of ecstasy at the annual Anastenaria, when they believe themselves under the influence of Saint Constantine.[3] [4][5]

Historically, large groups of individuals have experienced religious ecstasies during periods of Christian revivals, to the point of causing controversy as to the origin and nature of these experiences.[6][7] In response to claims that all emotional expressions of religious ecstasy were attacks on order and theological soundness from the Devil, Jonathan Edwards published his now-famous and influential Treatise on Religious Affections. Here, he argues, religious ecstasy could come from oneself, the Devil, or God, and it was only by observing the fruit, or changes in inner thought and behaviour, that one could determine if the religious ecstasy had come from God.[8]

In hagiography (writings about Christian saints) many instances are recorded in which saints are granted ecstasies. According to the Catholic Encyclopedia[9] religious ecstasy (called "supernatural ecstasy") includes two elements: one, interior and invisible, in which the mind rivets its attention on a religious subject, and another, corporeal and visible, in which the activity of the senses is suspended, reducing the effect of external sensations upon the subject and rendering him or her resistant to awakening. The witnesses of a Marian apparition often describe experiencing these elements of ecstasy.

Modern Witchcraft traditions may define themselves as "ecstatic traditions," and focus on reaching ecstatic states in their rituals. The Reclaiming Tradition and the Feri Tradition are two modern ecstatic Witchcraft examples.[10][11]

As described by the Indian spiritual teacher Meher Baba, God-intoxicated souls known as masts experience a unique type of spiritual ecstasy: "[M]asts are desperately in love with God – or consumed by their love for God. Masts do not suffer from what may be called a disease. They are in a state of mental disorder because their minds are overcome by such intense spiritual energies that are far too much for them, forcing them to lose contact with the world, shed normal human habits and customs, and civilized society and live in a state of spiritual splendor but physical squalor. They are overcome by an agonizing love for God and are drowned in their ecstasy. Only the divine love embodied in a Perfect Master can reach them."[12]

10.4 See also

- Altered state of consciousness
- Ecstasy (philosophy)
- Ecstasy (emotion)
- Enlightenment (spiritual)
- Entheogen
- Eroto-comatose lucidity
- Higher consciousness
- Mast (Sufism)
- Mysticism
- Neurotheology
- Nirvana
- Numinous
- Religious experience
- Sex magic
- Shamanism
- Wajad
- Self-transcendence

10.4.1 Notable individuals or movements

- Anastenaria
- St. Thomas Aquinas experienced an ecstasy during a church service towards the end of his life that caused him to stop writing.
- Dionysus
- St. Teresa of Avila, Roman Catholic mystic, first entered states of ecstasy while studying religious texts when taken ill in a Carmelite cloister.
- Sri Caitanya Mahaprabhu, founder of Gaudiya Vaishnavism, immersed into deeper and deeper stages of ecstasy towards Krishna during the last 24 years of his life
- St. Pio of Pietrelcina
- St. Joseph of Cupertino

- Maulanah Rumi, Mystic Poet

- Hafez, Mystic Poet

- Moinuddin Chishti, Sufi Saint

- Amir Khusrow, Mystic Poet

10.5 References

[1] Marghanita Laski, "Ecstasy. A Study of Some Secular and Religious Experiences." The Cresset Press, London, 1961. p.57

[2] Marghanita Laski, "Ecstasy in Religious and Secular Experiences." Jeremy P. Tarcher, Inc., Los Angeles, 1990, ISBN 0-87477-574-4 p.171

[3] Xygalatas, Dimitris, "Firewalking and the Brain: The Physiology of High-Arousal Rituals", in: Joseph Bulbulia, Richard Sosis, Erica Harris, Russell Genet, Cheryl Genet, and Karen Wyman (eds.) Evolution of Religion: Studies, Theories, and Critiques, Santa Margarita, CA: Collins Foundation Press 2007, pp. 189–195

[4] Xygalatas, Dimitris, 2012. *The Burning Saints. Cognition and Culture in the Fire-walking Rituals of the Anastenaria* London: Equinox ISBN 978-1-84553-976-4

[5] Tomkinson, John L., *Anastenaria*, Anagnosis, Athens, 2003 ISBN 960-87186-7-8 pp 90–99

[6] Chauncy, Charles. Seasonable Thoughts on the State of Religion in New England. 1743

[7] Edwards, Jonathan (1742). *Some Thoughts Concerning the Present Revival in New England and the Way it Ought to be Acknowledged and Promoted.*

[8] *Treatise on Religious Affections* at Google Books

[9] Ecstasy

[10] M. Macha Nightmare, *Reclaiming Tradition Witchcraft*, Witchvox, 2001. Retrieved on 2008-01-13.

[11] Cholla and Gabriel, *Ecstasy and Transgression in the Faery Tradition*, Witch Eye, 2000. Retrieved on 2008-01-13.

[12] Kalchuri, Bhau: *Meher Prabhu: Lord Meher, the Biography of the Avatar of the Age, Meher Baba*, Volume Six, Manifestation, Inc., 1986, p. 2035

Chapter 11

Near-death experience

For other uses, see Near-death experience (disambiguation).
"NDE" redirects here. For other uses, see NDE (disambiguation).
"Near death" redirects here. For the comic book, see Near Death (comics).

A **near-death experience** (NDE) is a personal experience associated with impending death, encompassing multiple possible sensations including detachment from the body, feelings of levitation, total serenity, security, warmth, the experience of absolute dissolution, and the presence of a light.[1][2][3]

Explanatory models for the NDE can be divided into several broad categories, including psychological, physiological, and transcendental explanations.[1][4][5][6] Research from neuroscience considers the NDE to be a hallucinatory state caused by various physiological and psychological factors.[7]

11.1 Characteristics

The equivalent French term *expérience de mort imminente* (experience of imminent death) was proposed by the French psychologist and epistemologist Victor Egger as a result of discussions in the 1890s among philosophers and psychologists concerning climbers' stories of the panoramic life review during falls.[10][11] In 1968 Celia Green published an analysis of 400 first-hand accounts of out-of-body experiences.[12] This represented the first attempt to provide a taxonomy of such experiences, viewed simply as anomalous perceptual experiences, or hallucinations. These experiences were popularized by the work of psychiatrist Raymond Moody in 1975 as the near-death experience (NDE).

Researchers have identified the common elements that define near-death experiences.[13] Bruce Greyson argues that the general features of the experience include impressions of being outside one's physical body, visions of deceased relatives and religious figures, and transcendence of egotic and spatiotemporal boundaries.[14] Many common elements have been reported, although the person's interpretation of these events often corresponds with the cultural, philosophical, or religious beliefs of the person experiencing it.

Another common element in near-death experiences is encountering people, which are generally identified according to the person's individual faith; for instance, in the USA, where 46% of the population believes in guardian angels, they will often be identified as angels or deceased loved ones (or will be unidentified), while Hindus will often identify them as messengers of the god of death.[15][16]

Although the features of NDEs vary from one case to the next, common traits that have been reported by NDErs are as follows:

- A sense/awareness of being dead.[13][17]

- A sense of peace, well-being and painlessness. Positive emotions. A sense of removal from the world.[13][17][18]

- An out-of-body experience. A perception of one's body from an outside position. Sometimes observing doctors and nurses performing medical resuscitation efforts.[13][17][18][19]

- A "tunnel experience" or entering a darkness. A sense of moving up, or through, a passageway or staircase.[13][17][19]

- A rapid movement toward and/or sudden immersion in a powerful light (or "Being of Light") which communicates with the person.[17][18]

- An intense feeling of unconditional love and acceptance.[18]

- Encountering "Beings of Light", "Beings dressed in white", or similar. Also, the possibility of being reunited with deceased loved ones.[13][18][19]

Ascent of the Blessed *by Hieronymus Bosch is associated by some NDE researchers with aspects of the NDE.*[8][9]

- Receiving a life review, commonly referred to as "seeing one's life flash before one's eyes".[13][17][18]

- Receiving knowledge about one's life and the nature of the universe.[18]

- Approaching a border,[17] or a decision by oneself or others to return to one's body, often accompanied by a reluctance to return.[13][18][19]

- Suddenly finding oneself back inside one's body.[20]

- Connection to the cultural beliefs held by the individual, which seem to dictate some of the phenomena experienced in the NDE and particularly the later interpretation thereof.[15]

Kenneth Ring (1980) subdivided the NDE on a five-stage continuum. The subdivisions were:[21]

1. Peace

2. Body separation

3. Entering darkness

4. Seeing the light

5. Entering the light

He stated that 60% experienced stage 1 (feelings of peace and contentment), but only 10% experienced stage 5 ("entering the light").[22]

Clinical circumstances associated with near-death experiences include cardiac arrest in myocardial infarction (clinical death); shock in postpartum loss of blood or in perioperative complications; septic or anaphylactic shock; electrocution; coma resulting from traumatic brain damage; intracerebral hemorrhage or cerebral infarction; attempted suicide; near-drowning or asphyxia; apnea; and serious depression.[23] In contrast to common belief, Kenneth Ring argues that attempted suicides do not lead more often to unpleasant NDEs than unintended near-death situations.[24]

11.1.1 NDE variants

Some NDEs have elements that bear little resemblance to the "typical" near-death experience. Anywhere from one percent (according to a 1982 Gallup poll) to 20 percent of subjects may have distressing experiences and feel terrified or uneasy as various parts of the NDE occur, they visit or view dark and depressing areas or are accosted by what seem to be hostile or oppositional forces or presences.[25]

Persons having bad experiences were not marked by more religiosity or suicidal background. According to one study (Greyson 2006) there is little association between NDEs and prior psychiatric treatment, prior suicidal behavior, or family history of suicidal behavior. There was also little association between NDEs and religiosity, or prior brushes with death, suggesting the occurrence of NDEs is not influenced by psychopathology, by religious denomination or religiosity, or by experiencers' prior expectations of a pleasant dying process or continued postmortem existence.[26] Greyson (2007) also found that the long term recall of NDE incidents was stable and did not change due to embellishment over time.[27]

Bush (2012), a counselor, and board member and former Executive Director to the International Association for Near-Death Studies, holds that not all negative NDE accounts are reported by people with a religious background.[28] Suicide attempters, who should be expected to have a higher rate of psychopathology according to Greyson (1991) did not show much difference from non-suicides in the frequency of NDEs.[29]

11.2 Research

11.2.1 Introduction

Contemporary interest in this field of study was originally spurred by the writings of Raymond Moody such as his book *Life After Life*, which was released in 1975, brought public attention to the topic of NDEs. This was soon to be followed by the establishment of the International Association for Near-Death Studies (IANDS) in 1981. IANDS is an international organization that encourages scientific research and education on the physical, psychological, social, and spiritual nature and ramifications of near-death experiences. Among its publications are the peer-reviewed *Journal of Near-Death Studies* and the quarterly newsletter *Vital Signs*.[30]

As cognitive neuroscience is an interdisciplinary area of study embracing neuroscience, psychology, and computer science,[31] and NDE studies address multiple possible feelings, sensations and their origins, some research on NDEs has been conducted by researchers with credentials in cognitive neuroscience. Cognitive neuroscience addresses the questions of how psychological functions (for example, human feelings and sensations) are produced by neural circuitry (including the human brain).[31] Modern contributions to the research on near-death experiences, however, have come from several academic disciplines that generally do not include neuroscience. There are multiple reasons for this trend.[32] For example, brain activity scans are not typically performed when a patient is undergoing attempts at emergency resuscitation.[33] Claiming that there is no measurable brain activity without having a variety of different EEG, catSCAN, FMRI, etc. is not considered a good scientific practice.[32][33]

Existing research is mainly in the disciplines of medicine, psychology and psychiatry. Heightened brain activity has been recorded in experimental rats directly following cardiac arrest, though there has been no similar research in humans.[34][35][36][37] Individual cases of NDEs in literature have been identified into ancient times.[38] In the 19th century a few efforts moved beyond studying individual cases - one privately done by the Mormons and one in Switzerland. Up to 2005, 95% of world cultures have been documented making some mention of NDEs.[38] A 2001 study by Berlin sociologist Hubert Knoblauch concluded that 4 percent of the German population had been through a near death experience.[39][40][41] Of the survivors of cardiac arrest, between 10% and 20% reported more or less significant near-death experiences.[42][43][44]

Bruce Greyson (psychiatrist), Kenneth Ring (psychologist), and Michael Sabom (cardiologist), helped to launch the field of near-death studies and introduced the study of near-death experiences to the academic setting. From 1975 to 2005, some 2500 self reported individuals in the US had been reviewed in retrospective studies of the phenomena[38] with an additional 600 outside the US in the West,[38] and 70 in Asia.[38] Prospective studies, reviewing groups of individuals and then finding who had an NDE after some time and costing more to do, had identified 270 individuals.[38] In all close to 3500 individual cases between 1975 and 2005 had been reviewed in one or another study. All these studies were carried out by some 55 researchers or teams of researchers.[38] The medical community has been reluctant to address the phenomenon of NDEs, and grant money for research has been scarce.[30] Nevertheless, both Greyson and Ring developed tools usable in a clinical setting. Major contributions to the field include Ring's construction of a "Weighted Core Experience Index"[45] to measure the depth of the near-death experience, and Greyson's construction of the "Near-death experience scale"[46] to differentiate between subjects that are more or less likely to have experienced an NDE. The latter scale is also, according to its author, clinically useful in differentiating NDEs from organic brain syndromes and non-specific stress responses.[46] The NDE-scale was later found to fit the Rasch rating scale model.[47] Greyson[48] has also brought attention to the near-death experience as a focus of clinical attention, while Melvin Morse, head of the Institute for the Scientific Study of Consciousness, and colleagues[19][49] have investigated near-death experiences in a pediatric population.

Neurobiological factors in the experience have been investigated by researchers in the field of medical science and psychiatry.[50] Among the researchers and commentators who tend to emphasize a naturalistic and neurological base for the experience are the British psychologist Susan Blackmore (1993), with her "dying brain hypothesis",[51] and the founding publisher of *Skeptic* magazine, Michael Shermer (1998). More recently, cognitive neuroscientists Jason Braithwaite (2008)[52] from the University of Birmingham and Sebastian Dieguez (2008)[53] and Olaf Blanke (2009)[54] from the Ecole Polytechnique Fédérale de Lausanne, Switzerland have published accounts presenting evidence for a brain-based explanation of near-death experiences.

A study was conducted at Southampton General Hospital involving 63 cardiac arrest survivors who had been resuscitated after being clinically dead with no pulse, no respiration, and fixed dilated pupils—conditions associated with the cessation of brain function (as confirmed by independent studies). According to Dr. Sam Parnia, a Southampton university clinical research fellow and co-author of the study, the rapid loss of brainstem activity during cardiac arrest should make it impossible to sustain lucid processes or form lasting memories."[55]

Seven out of the 63 survivors recalled emotions and visions during their unconscious state, including feelings of peace and joy, time speeding up, heightened senses, lost awareness of body, seeing a bright light, entering another world, encountering a mystical being or deceased relative, and coming to a point of no return. According to Dr. Parnia, the recollections, unlike hallucinations, were "highly structured, narrative, easily recalled and clear." Six percent of the patients met the strict criteria used to diagnose near-death experiences.[55]

There was no difference in oxygen levels or drug treatment between those who had near-death experiences and those who didn't, while the four patients who met the criteria for a true near-death experience actually had higher oxygen levels—contradicting the notion that lack of oxygen is responsible for the experience.[55]

Most top peer-reviewed journals in neuroscience, such as Nature Reviews Neuroscience, Brain Research Reviews, Biological Psychiatry, Journal of Cognitive Neuroscience are generally not publishing research on NDEs. Among the scientific and academic journals that have published, or are regularly publishing, new research on the subject of NDEs are *Journal of Near-Death Studies*, *Journal of Nervous and Mental Disease*, *British Journal of Psychology*, *American Journal of Disease of Children*, *Resuscitation*, *The Lancet*, *Death Studies*, and the *Journal of Advanced Nursing*.

11.2.2   Variance in NDE studies

The prevalence of NDEs has been variable in the studies that have been performed. According to the Gallup and Proctor survey in 1980–1981, of a representative sample of the American population, data showed that 15% described themselves as having had an "unusual experience" when on the verge of death or having a "close call".[56] Knoblauch in 2001 performed a more selective study in Germany and found that 4% of the sample population had an NDE.[57] The information gathered from these studies may nevertheless be subject to the broad timeframe and location of the investigation.

Perera et al., in 2005, conducted a telephone survey of a representative sample of the Australian population, as part of the Roy Morgan Catibus Survey, and concluded that 8.9% of the population had an NDE.[58] In a clinical setting, van Lommel et al. (2001), a cardiologist from Netherlands, studied a group of patients who had suffered cardiac arrests and who were successfully revived. They found that 62 patients (18%) had an NDE, of whom 41 (12%, or 66% of those who had an NDE) described a core experience.

According to Martens[59] the only satisfying method to address the NDE-issue would be an international multicentric data collection within the framework for standardized reporting of cardiac arrest events. The use of cardiac-arrest criteria as a basis for NDE research has been a common approach among the European branch of the research field.[60][61]

11.2.3   Neurobiological and psychological analysis

Psychologist Chris French has summarized psychological and physiological theories that provide a physical explanation for NDEs. One psychological theory proposes that the NDE is a dissociative defense mechanism that occurs in times of extreme danger. A wide range of physiological theories of the NDE have been put forward including those based upon cerebral hypoxia, anoxia, and hypercarbia; endorphins and other neurotransmitters; and abnormal activity in the temporal lobes.[62]

In the 1970s professor of psychiatry Russell Noyes and clinical psychologist Roy Kletti suggested the NDE is a form of depersonalization experienced under emotional conditions such as life-threatening danger and that the NDE can best be understood as a fantasy based hallucination.[63][64][65][66]

In the early 1980s the neuropsychologist Daniel Carr proposed that the NDE has characteristics suggestive of a limbic lobe syndrome and that the NDE can be explained by the release of endorphins and enkephalins in the brain.[67][68] Judson and Wiltshaw (1983) noted how the release of endorphins can lead to blissful or emotional NDEs, whilst naloxone can produce "hellish" NDEs.[69] The first formal neurobiological model for NDE was presented in 1987 by Chilean scientists Juan Sebastián Gómez-Jeria (who holds a PhD in Molecular Physical Chemistry) and Juan Carlos Saavedra-Aguilar (M.D.) from the University of Chile. Their model included endorphins, neurotransmitters of the limbic system, the temporal lobe and other parts of the brain.[70] Extensions and variations of their model came from other scientists such as Louis Appleby (1989) and Karl Jansen (1990).[71][72]

Morse *et al.* 1989 proposed a neurophysiological model in

which serotonin has an important role to play in generating NDEs.[73]

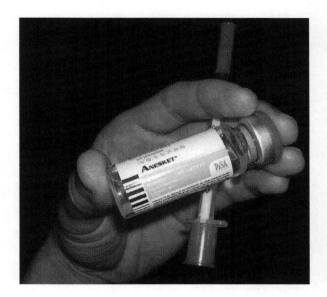

Ketamine by intravenous injection can reproduce all the features of the NDE.

The research of Karl Jansen has revealed how the effects of an NDE can be induced by ketamine. In 1996 he published a paper on the subject which concluded "mounting evidence suggests that the reproduction/induction of NDE's by ketamine is not simply an interesting coincidence... ketamine administered by intravenous injection, in appropriate dosage, is capable of reproducing all of the features of the NDE which have been commonly described in the most cited works in this field."[74]

Whinnery (1997) revealed the similarities between NDEs and G-LOC (G-force induced Loss Of Consciousness) episodes.[75] Based on the observations of G-LOC, Whinnery noted how the experiences often involved "tunnel vision and bright lights, floating sensations, automatic movement, autoscopy, OBEs, not wanting to be disturbed, paralysis, vivid dreamlets of beautiful places, pleasurable sensations, psychological alterations of euphoria and dissociation, inclusion of friends and family, inclusion of prior memories and thoughts, the experience being very memorable (when it can be remembered), confabulation, and a strong urge to understand the experience."[75]

In the 1990s, Rick Strassman conducted research on the psychedelic drug dimethyltryptamine (DMT) at the University of New Mexico. Strassman advanced the hypothesis that a massive release of DMT from the pineal gland prior to death or near-death was the cause of the near-death experience phenomenon. Only two of his test subjects reported NDE-like aural or visual hallucinations, although many reported feeling as though they had entered a state similar to the classical NDE. His explanation for this was the possible lack of panic involved in the clinical setting and possible dosage differences between those administered and those encountered in actual NDE cases. All subjects in the study were also very experienced users of DMT or other psychedelic/entheogenic agents.[76][77][78]

Chris French (2001) stated that at least some reports of NDEs might be based upon false memories.[79]

According to Engmann (2008) near-death experiences of people who are clinically dead are psychopathological symptoms caused by a severe malfunction of the brain resulting from the cessation of cerebral blood circulation.[80] An important question is whether it is possible to "translate" the bloomy experiences of the reanimated survivors into psychopathologically basic phenomena, e.g. acoasms (non-verbal auditory hallucinations), central narrowing of the visual field, autoscopia, visual hallucinations, activation of limbic and memory structures according to Moody's stages. The symptoms suppose a primary affliction of the occipital and temporal cortices under clinical death. This basis could be congruent with the thesis of pathoclisis—the inclination of special parts of the brain to be the first to be damaged in case of disease, lack of oxygen, or malnutrition—established eighty years ago by Cécile and Oskar Vogt.[81]

Research has shown that hypercarbia can induce NDE symptoms such as lights, visions and mystical experiences.[82] Professor of neurology Terence Hines (2003) claimed that near-death experiences are hallucinations caused by cerebral anoxia, drugs, or brain damage.[83] A 2006 study by Lempert *et al.* induced syncopes in 42 healthy subjects using cardiovascular manipulations. They found that the subjects reported NDE experiences such as seeing lights, tunnels, meeting deceased family members and visiting other worlds.[84]

Neuroscientists Olaf Blanke and Sebastian Dieguez (2009) have written that NDE experiences can best be explained by different brain functions and mechanisms without recourse to the paranormal. They suggest that damage to the bilateral occipital cortex and the optic radiation may lead to visual features of NDEs such as seeing a tunnel or lights, and interference with the hippocampus may lead to emotional experiences, memory flashbacks or a life review. They concluded that future neuroscientific studies are likely to reveal the neuroanatomical basis of the NDE which will lead to the demystification of the subject.[85]

Vanhaudenhuyse *et al.* 2009 reported that recent studies employing deep brain stimulation and neuroimaging have demonstrated that out-of-body experiences result from a deficient multisensory integration at the temporoparietal junction and that ongoing studies aim to further identify the functional neuroanatomy of near-death experiences by means of standardized EEG recordings.[86]

Lakhmir Chawla, an Associate Professor of Anesthesiology and Critical Care Medicine and Medicine at George Washington University medical centre argued that near-death experiences are caused by a surge of electrical activity as the brain runs out of oxygen before death.[87] Levels of brain activity were similar to those seen in fully conscious people, even though blood pressure was so low as to be undetectable. The gradual loss of brain activity had occurred in the approximate hour before death, and was interrupted by a brief spurt of action, lasting from 30 seconds to three minutes. Chawla and colleagues from a case series of seven patients wrote "increase in electrical activity occurred when there was no discernable blood pressure, patients who suffer "near death" experiences may be recalling the aggregate memory of the synaptic activity associated with this terminal but potentially reversible hypoxemia."[87]

Research released in 2010 by University of Maribor, Slovenia had put near-death experiences down to high levels of carbon dioxide in the blood altering the chemical balance of the brain and tricking it into 'seeing' things.[88] Of the 52 patients, 11 reported NDEs.[89][90]

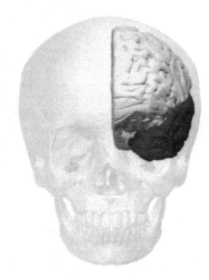

Animation of the human left temporal lobe

NDE subjects have increased activity in the left temporal lobe.[3] Stimulation of the temporal lobe is known to induce hallucinations, out-of-body experiences and memory flashbacks.[91] In an experiment with one patient, electrical stimulation at the left temporoparietal junction lead to an illusion of another person being close to her.[92][93] Chris French has written that the "temporal lobe is almost certain to be involved in NDEs, given that both damage to and direct cortical stimulation of this area are known to produce a number of experiences corresponding to those of the NDE, including OBEs, hallucinations, and memory flashbacks."[62]

In 2011, Alexander Wutzler and his colleagues at the Charité University of Medicine in Berlin, Germany suggested that near-death experiences may be triggered by an increase of serotonin in the brain.[94][95] Charles Q. Choi in an article for the *Scientific American* concluded "scientific evidence suggests that all features of the near-death experience have some basis in normal brain function gone awry."[96]

A 2012 study led by neuroradiologist Renemane reached the conclusion that the NDE is a state of unconsciousness resembling oneiroid syndrome.[97]

In a 2013 study, Marie Thonnard and colleagues suggested that the memories of NDEs are flashbulb memories of hallucinations.[98] The findings were in accordance with a 2014 study published in Frontiers in Human Neuroscience.[99]

11.2.4   REM state

It is suggested that the extreme stress caused by a life-threatening situation triggers brain states similar to REM sleep and that a part of the near death experience is a state similar to dreaming while awake.[100] People who have experienced times when their brains behaved as if they were dreaming while awake are more likely to develop the near death experience.[101]

11.2.5   Lucid dreaming

Some sleep researchers, such as Timothy J. Green, Lynne Levitan and Stephen LaBerge, have noted that NDEs are similar to many reports of lucid dreaming, in which the individual realizes he is in a dream. Often these states are so realistic as to be barely distinguishable from reality.

In a study of fourteen lucid dreamers performed in 1991, people who perform wake-initiated lucid dreams (WILD) reported experiences consistent with aspects of out-of-body experiences such as floating above their beds and the feeling of leaving their bodies.[102] Due to the phenomenological overlap between lucid dreams, near-death experiences, and out-of-body experiences, researchers say they believe a protocol could be developed to induce a lucid dream similar to a near-death experience in the laboratory.[103]

11.2.6   Computational psychology

Modeling of NDEs by S. L. Thaler in 1993[104] using artificial neural networks has shown that many aspects of the core near-death experience can be achieved through simulated neuron death.[105][106][107][108] In the course of such simulations, the essential features of the NDE—life review, novel scenarios (i.e., heaven or hell), and OBE—are observed through the generation of confabulations or false memories, as discussed in Confabulation (neural networks). The key feature contributing to the generation of such confabulatory states are a neural network's inability to differentiate dead from silent neurons.[109] Memories, whether related to direct experience, or not, can be seeded upon arrays of such inactive brain cells.

11.2.7 Effects

NDEs are also associated with changes in personality and outlook on life.[13] Kenneth Ring (professor of psychology) has identified a consistent set of value and belief changes associated with people who have had a near-death experience. Among these changes one finds a greater appreciation for life, higher self-esteem, greater compassion for others, a heightened sense of purpose and self-understanding, desire to learn, elevated spirituality, greater ecological sensitivity and planetary concern, and a feeling of being more intuitive. Changes may also include increased physical sensitivity; diminished tolerance of light, alcohol, and drugs; a feeling that the brain has been "altered" to encompass more; and a feeling that one is now using the "whole brain" rather than a small part.[13] However, not all aftereffects are beneficial[110] and Greyson[111] describes circumstances where changes in attitudes and behavior can lead to psychosocial and psychospiritual problems.[112] Often the problems are those of the adjustment to ordinary life in the wake of the NDE.

11.2.8 Cross-cultural research

Recent research into afterlife conceptions across cultures by religious studies scholar Gregory Shushan[113] analyzes the afterlife beliefs of five ancient civilizations (Old and Middle Kingdom Egypt, Sumerian and Old Babylonian Mesopotamia, Vedic India, pre-Buddhist China, and pre-Columbian Mesoamerica) in light of historical and contemporary reports of near-death experiences, and shamanic afterlife "journeys". It was found that despite numerous culture-specific differences, the nine most frequently recurring NDE elements also recur on a general structural level cross-culturally, which tends to suggest that the authors of these ancient religious texts were familiar with NDEs or similar experiences. Cross-cultural similarity, however, can be used to support both religious and physiological theories, for both rely on demonstrating that the phenomenon is universal.

Studies that have investigated cultural differences in NDEs

summarized by (Augustine, 2003) have argued that the content of the experiences do not vary by culture, except for the identity of the figures seen during the experiences. For example, a Christian may see Jesus, while a Hindu may see Yamaraja, the Hindu king of death.[114]

11.2.9 Van Lommel studies

Pim van Lommel

In 2001, Pim van Lommel, a cardiologist from the Netherlands, and his team conducted a study of near-death experiences (NDEs) in cardiac arrest patients.[60] Of 344 patients who were successfully resuscitated after suffering cardiac arrest, 62 (18%) expressed an intraoperative memory and among these, 41 (12%) experienced core NDEs, which included out-of-body experiences. According to van Lommel, the patients remembered details of their conditions during their cardiac arrest despite being clinically dead with flatlined brain stem activity. Van Lommel concluded that his findings supported the theory that consciousness continued despite lack of neuronal activity in the brain.[60]

Van Lommel's conclusions have been criticized by various authors, one of them being Jason Braithwaite, a Senior Lecturer in Cognitive Neuroscience in the Behavioral Brain

Sciences Centre, University of Birmingham. He issued an in-depth analysis and critique of van Lommel's prospective study published in the medical journal *The Lancet*, concluding that while van Lommel's et al. study makes a useful contribution, it contains several factual and logical errors. Among these errors are van Lommel's misunderstandings and misinterpretations of the dying-brain hypothesis, misunderstandings over the role of anoxia, misplaced confidence in EEG measurements (a flat electroencephalogram (EEG) reading is not evidence of total brain inactivity), etc. Braithwaite concluded with, "it is difficult to see what one could learn from the paranormal survivalist position which sets out assuming the truth of that which it seeks to establish, makes additional and unnecessary assumptions, misrepresents the current state of knowledge from mainstream science, and appears less than comprehensive in its analysis of the available facts."[52]

11.2.10 AWARE study

In 2001, Sam Parnia and colleagues investigated out-of-body claims by placing figures on suspended boards facing the ceiling, not visible from the floor. Parnia wrote "anybody who claimed to have left their body and be near the ceiling during resuscitation attempts would be expected to identify those targets. If, however, such perceptions are psychological, then one would obviously not expect the targets to be identified."[115] The philosopher Keith Augustine, who examined Parnia's study, has written that all target identification experiments have produced negative results.[114] Psychologist Chris French wrote regarding the study "unfortunately, and somewhat atypically, none of the survivors in this sample experienced an OBE."[62]

In the autumn of 2008, 25 UK and US hospitals began participation in a study, coordinated by Sam Parnia and Southampton University known as the AWARE study (AWAreness during REsuscitation). Following on from the work of Pim van Lommel in the Netherlands, the study aims to examine near-death experiences in 1,500 cardiac arrest survivors and so determine whether people without a heartbeat or brain activity can have documentable out-of-body experiences.[116] As part of the study Parnia and colleagues have investigated out of body claims by using hidden targets placed on shelves that could only be seen from above.[116] Parnia has written "if no one sees the pictures, it shows these experiences are illusions or false memories".[116]

In 2014 Parnia issued a statement indicating that the first phase of the project has been completed and the results are undergoing peer review for publication in a medical journal.[117] No subjects saw the images mounted out of sight according to Parnia's early report of the results of the study at an American Heart Association meeting in November

2013. Only two out of the 152 patients reported any visual experiences, and one of them described events that could be verified.[118]

On October 6, 2014 the results of the study were published in the journal *Resuscitation*. Among those who reported a perception of awareness and completed further interviews, 46 per cent experienced a broad range of mental recollections in relation to death that were not compatible with the commonly used term of NDEs. These included fearful and persecutory experiences. Only 9 per cent had experiences compatible with NDEs and 2 per cent exhibited full awareness compatible with OBEs with explicit recall of 'seeing' and 'hearing' events. One case was validated and timed using auditory stimuli during cardiac arrest.[119] According to Dr. Caroline Watt "The one 'verifiable period of conscious awareness' that Parnia was able to report did not relate to this objective test. Rather, it was a patient giving a supposedly accurate report of events during his resuscitation. He didn't identify the pictures, he described the defibrillator machine noise. But that's not very impressive since many people know what goes on in an emergency room setting from seeing recreations on television."[120][121] And according to clinical neurologist Steven Novella, Parnia is "desperately trying to rescue the study by falling back on simply reporting subjective accounts of what people remember long after the event. This type of information is nothing new, and cannot objectively resolve the debate. The results are also completely unimpressive, perfectly consistent with what we would expect given what is already well documented about human memory."[122]

AWARE II – a two-year multicenter observational study of 900-1500 patients experiencing cardiac arrests is currently being prepared, with the closure date set to May 31, 2017.[123]

11.2.11 Afterlife claims and skeptical responses

See also: Consciousness after death

Many individuals who experience an NDE see it as a verification of the existence of an afterlife, and some researchers in the field of near-death studies see the NDE as evidence that human consciousness may continue to exist after death. The transcendental (or survivalist) interpretation of the NDE contends that the experience is exactly what it appears to be to the persons having the experience. According to this interpretation, consciousness can become separated from the brain under certain conditions and glimpse the spiritual realm to which souls travel after death.[62][124]

The transcendental model is in some friction with the dominant view from mainstream neuroscience; that consciousness is a product of, and dependent on, the brain.[125] According to the mainstream neuroscientific view, once the brain stops functioning at brain death, consciousness fails to survive and ceases to exist.[126][127][128]

Several NDE researchers have argued that the NDE poses a major challenge to current scientific thinking regarding the relationship between consciousness and the brain, as argued by Van Lommel:

Other NDE researchers such as Parnia, Fenwick[129] and Greyson,[130] have expressed similar questions and concerns.

These arguments raised by several researchers have been criticized by some scientific skeptics and scientists on several grounds. Chris French (2005, 2009) noted that, "it is clear that the argument that recent findings present a major challenge to modern neuroscience hinges upon the claim that the NDE is actually experienced "during a period of clinical death with flat EEG" as claimed". With respect to the former point he pointed out that it is not at all clear that NDEs actually do occur during a period of flat EEG. Assuming that the patients in question entered a period of flat EEG, French argued that the NDE may have occurred as they entered that state or as they slowly recovered from it. Parnia and Fenwick (2001) had rejected the idea that the NDE may have occurred as the patient is becoming unconscious because they argued that this happens too quickly. But French points out that it is unclear how much time would be required to experience an NDE and that a common feature of altered states of consciousness is time distortion. He argued that this is well illustrated by the life review component of the NDE itself which, although involving a review of a person's entire life, only seems to last a very brief time. And that therefore, "who can say, therefore, that the few seconds of remaining consciousness as an individual enters the state of clinical death is insufficient for the experiences that form the basis of the NDE?".

Parnia and Fenwick (2001) also claimed that the NDE could not occur as a person slowly regains consciousness as this period is characterized by delirium and not by the lucid consciousness reported by NDErs. French again argued that the attribution of confusion is typically made by an outside observer. The subjects themselves may not subjectively feel confused at all. He quoted from an article by Liere and Stickney where they noted that, "Hypoxia quickly affects the higher centers, causing a blunting of the finer sensibilities and a loss of sense of judgment and of self-criticism. The subject feels, however, that his mind is not only quite clear, but unusually keen",[131] and that the subjective claim of great clarity of thought may therefore well be an illusion. French (2005) also noted that "it should be borne in mind that we are always dealing with reports of experiences

Chris French, a notable skeptic of the afterlife claims of NDErs

rather than with the experiences themselves. Memory is a reconstructive process. It is highly likely the final narrative will be much more coherent after the individual has reflected upon it before telling it to others, given the inherently ineffable nature of the experience itself".

And with respect to the latter point, the survivalists have also been criticized by scientists like French and Braithwaite of placing undue confidence in EEG measures. French (2005, 2009) and Braithwaite (2008) claimed that survivalists generally appear to assume that a flat EEG is indicative of total brain inactivity and that therefore the experience of an NDE during such a flatline period would completely undermine the core assumption of modern neuroscience that any complex experience must be based upon a functioning neural substrate.

Even assuming that NDEs actually occur during such periods, the assumption that isoelectric surface EEG recordings are always indicative of total brain inactivity is according to Braithwaite and French wrong. Braithwaite noted that "unless surgically implanted into the brain directly, the EEG principally measures surface cortical activity. The waveforms seen in cortical EEG are largely regarded to come from the synchronistic firing of cortical pyramidal neurons. As such, it is entirely conceivable that deep sub-cortical brain structures could be firing, and even in seizure, in the absence of any cortical signs of this activity."[52][132][133] Braithwaite also noted that Gloor (1986) reviewed evidence indicating that inter-ictal discharges in the hippocampus or amygdala can produce complex meaningful hallucinations without the involvement of the cerebral cortex.[134]

Another argument which, according to Braithwaite (2008), relies upon misplaced confidence in surface EEG measurement was put forward by Fenwick P. and Fenwick E. (1995).[135] They argued that, in cases where the surface EEG recording was not flat, if the NDE was a hallucinatory experience based upon disinhibition, evidence of this disinhibition should be visible in the surface EEG recorded at the time. However, Braithwaite argued that data from a recent study comparing EEG recorded at the scalp with EEG recorded from electrodes surgically implanted in deep sub-cortical regions show conclusively that high-amplitude seizure activity can be occurring in deep brain regions and yet be completely undetectable in the surface EEG.[136] Even more so, a study comparing surface EEG recordings with the fMRI blood-oxygen-level dependent (BOLD) response showed that the surface EEG could fail to detect seizure activity at the level of the cortex that was detected by the BOLD response.[137]

Another argument made by several NDE researchers such as Parnia and Fenwick (2001) for the transcendental model is that the occurrence of anecdotal reports of patients being able to see and recall detailed events occurring during the cardiac arrest that are afterwards verified by hospital staff supports the argument that such perception sometimes do occur during periods of clinical death. NDE researcher Janice Miner Holden found 107 such anecdotal reports in the NDE literature as of 2009, out of which approximately 91% were accurate.[138]

According to French (2005) and Blackmore (1993), when serious attempts at corroboration are attempted, the evidence often turns out to be nowhere near as impressive as it initially appeared.[139] And such cases can possibly (since they had not been ruled out) be accounted for in terms of non-paranormal factors including, "information available at the time, prior knowledge, fantasy or dreams, lucky guesses, and information from the remaining senses. Then there is selective memory for correct details, incorporation of details learned between the end of the NDE and giving an account of it, and the tendency to tell a good story."[140]

According to French (2005) a similar claim to the argument from veridical perceptions are the cases of blind people that during NDEs are able to see even though, in some cases, they may have been blind from birth.[141] According to French (2005), "initial readings of such accounts often give the impression that the experience involves seeing events and surroundings in the same way that sighted people do, but closer reflection upon these cases suggests otherwise." French quoted from an article by NDE researcher Ring where he noted that, "as this kind of testimony builds, it seems more and more difficult to claim that the blind simply see what they report. Rather, it is beginning to appear it is more a matter of their knowing, through a still poorly understood mode of generalized awareness, based on a variety of sensory impressions, especially tactile ones, what is happening around them."[142] French (2005) concluded that, "NDEs in the blind are certainly worthy of study but do not merit any special status in terms of evidential support for spiritual explanations of the phenomenon."

Nevertheless, according to French (2005) future research in the near-death experience should focus on devising ways to distinguish between the two main hypotheses relating to when the NDE is occurring.[62] If it really is occurring when some NDE researchers claim that it is, during a period of flat EEG with no cortical activity, then modern neuroscience would require serious revision.[62] This would also be the case if the OBE, either within the NDE or not, could be shown to be veridical. Attempts to test the veridicality of OBEs using hidden targets (e.g., Parnia and Fenwick (2001) should be welcomed.[62]

11.3 Personal experiences

- *Return from Tomorrow* by George G. Ritchie with Elizabeth Sherrill (1978). At the age of 20, George Ritchie died in an army hospital. Nine minutes later he returned to life. Ritchie's story was the first contact Raymond Moody (who was studying at the University of Virginia, as an undergraduate in Philosophy, at the time) had with NDEs. It inspired Moody to investigate over 150 cases of near-death experiences, in his book *Life After Life*, and two other books that followed.

- *Embraced by the Light* by Betty Eadie (1992). One of the most detailed near-death experiences on record.

- *Saved by the Light* by Dannion Brinkley. Brinkley's experience documents one of the most complete near death experiences, in terms of core experience and additional phenomena from the NDE scale. Brinkley claims to have been clinically dead for 28 minutes and taken to a hospital morgue, but some of his claims are disputed.

- *Placebo* by Howard Pittman (1980). A detailed record of Pittman's near-death experience.

- *The Darkness of God* by John Wren-Lewis (1985). Bulletin of the Australian Institute for Psychical Research No 5. An account of the effects of his NDE after going through the death process several times in one night.

- Three have associated their experiences with their decision to join the Bahá'í Faith: Reinee Pasarow, Ricky Bradshaw, and Marie Watson. Pasarow's published her story as early as 1981.[143] At least one extended talk was video taped and is available online in a couple places.[144] There are also extended partial transcripts.[145] Bradshaw's experience has been reviewed in several books.[146][147][148] Watson, author of *Two Paths* in 1897,[149] says she suffered a car accident in 1890 in Washington DC and reported having a vision and met a guide.[150] She converted to the religion in 1901 and identified the guide as `Abdu'l-Bahá.

- *Dying To Be Me: My Journey from Cancer, to Near Death, to True Healing* by Anita Moorjani, an ethnic Indian woman from Hong Kong, experienced a NDE which has been documented on the Near Death Experience Research Foundation (NDERF) website as one of the most exceptional accounts on their archives. She had end-stage cancer and on February 2, 2006, doctors told her family that she only had a few hours to live. Following her NDE, Anita experienced a remarkable recovery of her health.[151]

- Kiki Carter, a.k.a. Kimberli Wilson, an environmental activist and singer/songwriter, reported a near-death experience in 1983. The day after the experience, her mother, Priscilla Greenwood, encouraged her to write it down. Priscilla Greenwood published the story in September 1983 in a local metaphysical journal. For 24 hours after the experience, Kimberli had an aftervision which was a catalyst for her interest in quantum physics and holograms.[152]

- *90 Minutes in Heaven* by Don Piper, is Piper's account of his own near-death experience. EMTs on the scene determined Piper had been killed instantly after a tractor-trailer had swerved into his lane, crushing his car. Piper survived, however. In the book, he wrote about seeing deceased loved ones and friends as well as magnificent light; he felt a sense of pure peace. Piper had a very difficult and painful recovery, undergoing 34 surgeries.[153]

- *Heaven Is for Real* by Todd Burpo, is a father's account of his son, Colton, and Colton's trip to heaven and back. After discovering that then-four-year-old Colton's appendix has ruptured, he was rushed to the hospital. While unconscious, Colton describes having met Jesus, God, his great-grandfather whom he had never met, and his older sister lost in a miscarriage.[154]

- *Parallel Universes, a Memoir from the Edges of Space and Time* by Linda Morabito Meyer is a NASA scientist's account of several near death experiences at the hands of her parents and William Franklin Mosley of the Temple of the More Abundant Life in Vancouver, British Columbia, Canada. She explained that during these experiences, she visited Heaven, saw Jesus, and was in the presence of God.[155]

- Eben Alexander, M.D., born December, 1953, author of *Proof of Heaven: A Neurosurgeon's Journey into the Afterlife*, which made *The New York Times* Best Seller list for nonfiction.[156] In the book, Alexander describes how he had an intense NDE while in a seven-day coma brought on by an attack of meningitis. Inconsistencies and other issues in his story have led to questions about its veracity.[157]

- Howard Storm. In 1985, Storm travelled to Europe with his wife and university students. After suffering from severe stomach pain, he ended up in a hospital in Paris, where he had a near-death experience. He converted from atheism to Christianity in its aftermath.[158]

- Josh Homme of Queens of the Stone Age elaborated on his near-death experience in an interview with Marc Maron in October 2013. He told Maron that he contracted a methicillin-resistant *Staphylococcus aureus* (MRSA) infection in 2010, which his immune system could not fight due to stress. Due to unexpected complications during knee surgery, the doctors could not oxygenate his blood, and Josh suffered a near-death experience due to asphyxiation. Doctors eventually had to use a defibrillator to revive him. Following this, he was confined to bed rest for three months. The experience left him weakened and unable to produce music for almost two years.[159]

- *The Friend From Mexico, a True Story of Surviving an Intensive Care Unit*[160] by Apostolos Mavrothalassitis (2012) is the author's near-death experience account. Following a mid-air collision while participating in the 2009 Paragliding World Championships, he suffered extensive blood loss during surgery and was put under induced coma for two weeks. During these two weeks he lived a different life, and was not aware of his predicament. The experiences of this period are described extensively in the book.

11.4 In popular culture

Near-death experiences have been a theme in several films, like *Hereafter* by Clint Eastwood (2010) and *Stay* by Marc Forster (2008). It has also been a subject in fantastic literature, for example in the novella *The Baron Bagge* by Alexander Lernet-Holenia (1936).[161] It is also part of books written by Karl May in his novels with the names 'the Hereafter' ('Am Jenseits',1899) and in 'In the Realm of the Silver lion III'('Im Reiche des silbernen Löwen II', 1902).[162]

11.4.1 Films

- *Flatliners* (1990), film starring Kiefer Sutherland, Julia Roberts, Kevin Bacon, and William Baldwin

- *Ghost* (1990), film starring Patrick Swayze, Demi Moore, Whoopi Goldberg; the film received several Academy Awards and Oscar nominations.

- *The Fountain* (2006), film by Darren Aronofsky starring Hugh Jackman

- *Enter the Void* (2009), film by Gaspar Noé

- *If I Stay* (2014), film directed by R.J. Cutter, based on Forman's 2009 novel

- *Heaven Is for Real* (2014), film directed by Randall Wallace and written by Christopher Parker, based on Pastor Todd Burpo and Lynn Vincent's 2010 book of the same name.

11.4.2   Literature

- "The Little Match Girl" (1845), a short story by Hans Christian Andersen

- "To Build a Fire" (1902, revised 1908), two versions of a short story by Jack London

- *Left for Dead: : My Journey Home from Everest* (2000), memoir by Beck Weathers and Stephen G. Michaud, recounting Weathers' near-death experience during the 1996 Mount Everest disaster and its aftermath

- *If I Stay* (2009), novel by Gayle Forman

11.4.3   Television

- *Ghost Whisperer* (September 23, 2005, to May 21, 2010), CBS television series

- *Proof (2015 TV series)* (June 16, 2015, to August 18, 2015), TNT television series

11.5   Known NDE researchers

11.5.1   Maurice S. Rawlings

Maurice S. Rawlings was an American cardiologist who focused on near-death experiences from a Christian point of view. Rawlings was the author of several books, including: "Beyond the line of death - New clear evidence for the existence of Heaven and Hell" (1987), "To Hell and Back - Afterlife" (1996), which were translated into several languages.

11.5.2   Raymond A. Moody

Raymond A. Moody was one of the first to systematically examine the experiences of patients who were clinically dead and revived.[163]

11.5.3   Elisabeth Kübler-Ross

Elisabeth Kübler-Ross interviewed numerous people who were dying and in her work she described the "five stages of dying" which refers to how patients deal with the realization of their impending death. She also focused on near-death experiences.[164] Kübler-Ross was the first to publish interviews with dying patients in 1969.[165]

11.5.4   Bernard Jakoby

Bernard Jakoby is a German NDE researcher who comes to similar conclusions as Moody.

11.5.5   Pim van Lommel

Pim van Lommel is a Dutch author and researcher in the field of near-death studies. He studied medicine at Utrecht University, specializing in cardiology. Lommel is best known for his work on the subject of near-death experiences, including a prospective study published in the medical journal The Lancet.[166]

11.5.6   Sam Parnia

Sam Parnia is an Assistant professor of medicine at the State University of New York at Stony Brook. Parnia is the principal investigator of the AWARE study (AWAreness during REsuscitation), which was launched in 2008, and published in 2014.

11.5.7   Markolf Niemz

Markolf Niemz is a German biophysicist who is also involved with near-death research.[167]

11.5.8   Walter van Laack

Walter van Laack teaches at the University Aachen, Germany, on orthopedics.[167][168][169]

11.5.9 Bruce Greyson

Bruce Greyson is an American psychiatrist and NDE researcher. He is Professor of Psychiatry and Director Division of Perceptual Studies at the University of Virginia and therefore the direct successor to Ian Stevenson. He is a founding member of the International Association for Near-Death Studies (IANDS) and is known for his work in the field of near-death studies.[170] In 1983 he also developed the Greyson questionnaire for the qualification of a near-death experience (known as the "Greyson's NDE scale").[171]

11.6 Further reading

- James Alcock. (1979). *Psychology and Near-Death Experiences*. Skeptical Inquirer 3: 25–41.

- Lee Worth Bailey; Jenny Yates. (1996). *The Near-Death Experience: A Reader*. Routledge. ISBN 0-415-91431-0

- Susan Blackmore. (1993). *Dying to Live: Near-Death Experiences*. Prometheus Books. ISBN 0-87975-870-8

- Jimo Borjigina *et al*. (2013). "Surge of Neurophysiological Coherence and Connectivity in the Dying Brain". Proceedings of the National Academy of Sciences. Volume 110, Issue 35. pp. 14432–14437.

- Birk Engmann.(2014). *Near-Death Experiences. Heavenly Insight or Human Illusion?* Springer International Publishing. ISBN 978-3-319-03727-1

- Chris French. (2005). *Near-Death Experiences in Cardiac Arrest Survivors*. Progress in Brain Research 150: 351367.

- Bruce Greyson, Charles Flynn. (1984). *The Near-Death Experience: Problems, Prospects, Perspectives*. Springfield. ISBN 0-398-05008-2

- Janice Miner Holden, Bruce Greyson, Debbie James, eds. (2009). *The Handbook of Near-Death Experiences: Thirty Years of Investigation*. Praeger. ISBN 978-0-313-35865-4

- Gerd Hövelmann. (1985). *Evidence for Survival from Near-Death Experiences? A Critical Appraisal.* In Paul Kurtz. *A Skeptic's Handbook of Parapsychology.* Prometheus Books. pp. 645–684. ISBN 0-87975-300-5

- Dean Mobbs, Caroline Watt. (2011). *There is Nothing Paranormal About Near-Death Experiences: How Neuroscience Can Explain Seeing Bright Lights, Meeting the Dead, or Being Convinced You Are One of Them*. Trends in Cognitive Sciences. Volume 15, Issue 10. pp. 447–449.

- Mahendra Perera. (2011). *Making Sense of Near-Death Experiences: A Handbook of Clinicians*. Jessica Kingsley Pub. ISBN 978-1-84905-149-1

- Glenn Roberts, John Owen. (1988). *The Near-Death Experience*. British Journal of Psychiatry 153: 607–617.

- Gerald Woerlee. (2005). *Mortal Minds: The Biology of Near Death Experiences*. Prometheus Books. ISBN 1-59102-283-5

- Pim van Lommel. (2010). *Consciousness Beyond Life: The Science of the Near-Death Experience*. HarperOne. ISBN 978-0-06-177725-7

- Carol Zaleski. (1988). *Otherworld Journeys: Accounts of Near-Death Experience in Medieval and Modern Times*. Oxford University Press. ISBN 0-19-503915-7

11.7 See also

- Dr. Raymond Moody

- *Beyond and Back*

- Deathbed phenomena

- Form constant

- Lazarus phenomenon

- Near-death studies

- After-death communication

- Neurotheology

- Out-of-body experience

- Resurrection

11.8 External links

- "Agmatine and Near-Death Experiences"

- "International Association for Near-Death Studies (IANDS)"

- "Near Death Experiences: The Dying Brain"

- "Peace of Mind: Near-Death Experiences Now Found to Have Scientific Explanations". *Scientific American*

- "Why a Near-Death Experience Isn't Proof of Heaven". *Scientific American*

- "Near-Death Experiences". Susan Blackmore

- "Hallucinatory Near-Death Experiences". Internet Infidels

- "Near-Death Experience" (NDE). *Skeptic's Dictionary*

- "Darkness, Tunnels, and Light". *Skeptical Inquirer*

11.9   References

[1] Sleutjes, A. ; Moreira-Almeida, Alexander ; Greyson, B. . *Almost 40 Years Investigating Near-Death Experiences. An Overview of Mainstream Scientific Journals*. The Journal of Nervous and Mental Disease, v. 202, p. 833–836, 2014. Indexed in PubMed.

[2] Roberts, Glenn; Owen, John. (1988). *The Near-Death Experience*. British Journal of Psychiatry 153: 607–617.

[3] Britton, Willoughby B. and Richard R. Bootzin. (2004). *Near-Death Experiences and the Temporal Lobe*. Psychological Science. Vol. 15, No. 4. pp. 254–258.

[4] Linda J. Griffith. "Near-Death Experiences and Psychotherapy" (2009).

[5] Mauro, James. Bright lights, big mystery. Psychology Today, July 1992

[6] Vanhaudenhuyse, A; Thonnard, M; Laureys, S. "Towards a Neuro-scientific Explanation of Near-death Experiences?" (2009).

[7] Olaf Blanke, Sebastian Dieguez. "Leaving Body and Life Behind: Out-of-Body and Near-Death Experience" (2009).

[8] Pim van Lommel (2010). *Consciousness Beyond Life: The science of the near-death experience*. HarperOne. ISBN 978-0-06-177725-7.

[9] Evelyn Elsaesser Valarino (1997). *On the Other Side of Life: Exploring the phenomenon of the near-death experience*. Perseus Publishing. p. 203. ISBN 0-7382-0625-3.

[10] Egger, Victor (1896). « Le moi des mourants », *Revue Philosophique*, XLI : 26–38.

[11] J. Bogousslavsky, M. G. Hennerici, H Bazner, C. Bassetti (Eds.) (2010). *Neurological Disorders in Famous Artists, Part 3*. Karger Publishers. p. 189.

[12] Green, C., *Out-of-the-body Experiences*, London: Hamish Hamilton, 1968.

[13] Mauro, James. "Bright lights, big mystery", *Psychology Today*, July 1992.

[14] Greyson, Bruce (2003) "Near-Death Experiences in a Psychiatric Outpatient Clinic Population". Psychiatric Services, December, Vol. 54 No. 12. The American Psychiatric Association

[15] Holden, Janice Miner (2009). *The Handbook of Near-death Experiences: Thirty Years of Investigation*. Library of Congress Cataloging in Publishing Data. pp. 162, 215.

[16] Kennard, Mary J. "A Visit from an Angel." The American Journal of Nursing 98.3 (1998): 48–51

[17] van Lommel P, van Wees R, Meyers V, Elfferich I. (2001) "Near-Death Experience in Survivors of Cardiac Arrest: A prospective Study in the Netherlands," *The Lancet*, December 15; 358 (9298):2039–45. Table 2.

[18] IANDS Near-Death Experiences: Is this what happens when we die? Durham: International Association for Near-Death Studies.

[19] Morse M., Conner D. and Tyler D. (1985) "Near-Death Experiences in a pediatric population. A preliminary report", American Journal of Disease of Children, n. 139 PubMed abstract PMID 4003364

[20] Moody, Raymond (1975). *Life After Life*. Mockingbird Books. ISBN 978-0-89176-037-5.

[21] Ring, K. (1980). Life at death: A scientific investigation of the near-death experience. New York: Coward, McCann, & Geoghegan., p. 40

[22] Kenneth Ring, quoted in Ketamine—Near Death and Near Birth Experiences Dr Karl Jansen

[23] van Lommel P, van Wees R, Meyers V, Elfferich I. (2001) "Near-Death Experience in Survivors of Cardiac Arrest: A prospective Study in the Netherlands" in The Lancet, December 15; 358(9298):2039–45. Page 2039

[24] Ring, Kenneth. *Heading toward Omega. In search of the Meaning of Near-Death Experience*, 1984, p. 45. "Subsequent research on suicide-related NDEs by Stephen Franklin and myself [Ring] and by Bruce Greyson has also confirmed my earlier tentative findings the NDEs following suicide attempts, however induced, conform to the classic prototype."

[25] Lindley, JH; Bryan, S & Conley, B. (1981). 'Near-death experiences in a Pacific Northwest population: The Evergreen study – Anabiosis 1. p. 109.

[26] Bruce Greyson 2006. *Near-Death Experiences and Spirituality*. Zygon 41:2 393–414

[27] Greyson Bruce. (2007). *Consistency of near-death experience accounts over two decades: are reports embellished over time?* Resuscitation 73: 407–411.

[28] Greyson, Bruce; Bush, Nancy. (1992). *Distressing Near-Death Experiences*. Psychiatry 55: 95–109.

[29] Greyson, Bruce. (1991). *Near-Death Experiences Precipitated by Suicide Attempt.* Journal of Near Death Studies 9(3).

[30] IANDS. "Near-Death Experiences: Is this what happens when we die?" Durham: International Association for Near-Death Studies. Informational brochure available at http://www.iands.org

[31] Kosslyn, S, M. & Andersen, R, A. (1992). Frontiers in cognitive neuroscience. Cambridge, MA: MIT press.

[32] Harris, Sam. "

[33] Mobbs, D. "Response to Greyson et al.: there is nothing paranormal about near-death experiences", Trends in Cognitive Sciences, Volume 16, Issue 9, September 2012, Page 446

[34] Jimo Borjigina *et al.* (2013). "Surge of Neurophysiological Coherence and Connectivity in the Dying Brain". Proceedings of the National Academy of Sciences. Vol. 110, Issue 35. pp. 14432–14437.

[35] "Near-death experiences are 'electrical surge in dying brain'". BBC News.

[36] "Could a final surge in brain activity after death explain near-death experiences?". Nature.

[37] "Near-death experiences exposed: Surge of brain activity after the heart stops may trigger paranormal visions". Daily Mail.

[38] Holden, Janice Miner; Greyson, Bruce; James, Debbie, eds. (Jun 22, 2009). "The Field of Near-Death Studies: Past, Present and Future". *The Handbook of Near-Death Experiences: Thirty Years of Investigation.* Greenwood Publishing Group. pp. 1–16. ISBN 978-0-313-35864-7.

[39] *3,3 Millionen Deutsche mit Nahtoderfahrung.* abgerufen am 24. Mai 2015

[40] *WDR: Planet Wissen: Nahtoderfahrung* video: Minute 0.40, vom 4. Oktober 2013, abgerufen am 24. Mai 2015

[41] *A Report on a Survey of Near-Death Experiences in Germany (2001)* for example: page 2 in the abstract

[42] Bruce Greyson: *Incidence and correlates of near-death experiences in a cardiac care unit* General Hospital Psychiatry, Volume 25 Pages 269–276, published July–August, 2003

[43] Der Spiegel: *Forscher finden Erklärung für Nahtoderlebnis.* 13. August 2013

[44] Sam Parnia, Spearpoint, Fenwick: *Near death experiences, cognitive function and psychological outcomes of surviving cardiac arrest* published April 11, 2006

[45] Ring, K. "Life at death. A scientific investigation of the near-death experience." 1980, New York: Coward McCann and Geoghenan.

[46] Greyson, Bruce (1983) "The Near-Death Experience Scale: Construction, reliability, and validity". Journal of Nervous and Mental Disease, 171, 369–375

[47] Lange R, Greyson B, Houran J. (2004). *A Rasch scaling validation of a 'core' near-death experience.* British Journal of Psychology, Volume: 95 Part: 2 Page: 161–177

[48] Greyson B. (1997)"The near-death experience as a focus of clinical attention". *Journal of Nervous and Mental Disease.* May;185(5):327–34. PubMed abstract PMID 9171810

[49] Morse M, Castillo P, Venecia D, Milstein J, Tyler DC. (1986) "Childhood near-death experiences". *American Journal of Diseases of Children*, Nov;140(11):1110–4.

[50] Mayank and Mukesh, 2004; Jansen, 1995; Thomas, 2004; Fenwick and Fenwick 2008

[51] Bassham, Gregory (2005). *Critical Thinking: A Student's Untroduction* (2nd ed.). Boston: McGraw-Hill. p. 485. ISBN 0-07-287959-9.

[52] Braithwaite, J. J. (2008). "Near Death Experiences: The Dying Brain". Skeptic. Volume 21, Number 2. Retrieved 2014-07–12.

[53] NDE REdux:.

[54] Leaving Body And Life Behind:.

[55] Hope, Jenny. "Near-death patients do see afterlife". *Daily Mail Dot Com.* Associated Newspapers Ltd. Retrieved 20 August 2015.

[56] Gallup, G., and Proctor, W. (1982). Adventures in immortality: a look beyond the threshold of death. New York, McGraw Hill, pp. 198–200. "Have you, yourself, ever been on the verge of death or had a "close call" which involved any unusual experience at that time?". Nationally 15% responded "yes".

[57] Knoblauch, H., Schmied, I. and Schnettler, B. (2001). "Different kinds of Near-Death Experience: a report on a survey of near-death experiences in Germany",*Journal of Near-Death Studies*, 20, 15–29.

[58] Perera, M., Padmasekara, G. and Belanti, J. (2005), "Prevalence of Near Death Experiences in Australia". *Journal of Near-Death Studies*, 24(2), 109–116.

[59] Martens PR (1994) "Near-death-experiences in out-of-hospital cardiac arrest survivors. Meaningful phenomena or just fantasy of death?" *Resuscitation.* Mar; 27(2):171–5. PubMed abstract PMID 8029538

[60] van Lommel P, van Wees R, Meyers V, Elfferich I. (2001) "Near-Death Experience in Survivors of Cardiac Arrest: A prospective Study in the Netherlands" in *The Lancet*, December 15; 358(9298):2039–45. PDF version of article.

[61] Parnia S, Waller DG, Yeates R, Fenwick P (2001) "A qualitative and quantitative study of the incidence, features and aetiology of near death experiences in cardiac arrest survivors". *Resuscitation.* Feb; 48(2):149–56. PubMed abstract PMID 11426476

[62] French, Chris. (2005). *Near-Death Experiences in Cardiac Arrest Survivors.* Progress in Brain Research 150: 351–367.

[63] Noyes, R. (1972) *The experience of dying.* Psychiatry 35: 174–184.

[64] Noyes, R. and Klett, R. (1976) *Depersonalisation in the face of life-threatening danger: an interpretation.* Omega 7: 103–114.

[65] Noyes, R. and Klett, R. (1977) *Depersonalisation in the face of life-threatening danger.* Compr. Psychiat 18: 375–384.

[66] Noyes, R. and Slymen, D. (1978–1979) *The subjective response to life-threatening danger.* Omega 9: 313–321.

[67] Carr, Daniel. (1981). *Endorphins at the Approach of Death.* Lancet 317: 390.

[68] Carr, Daniel. (1982). *Pathophysiology of Stress-Induced Limbic Lobe Dysfunction: A Hypothesis Relevant to Near-Death Experiences.* Anabiosis: The Journal of Near-Death Studies 2: 75–89.

[69] Judson, I. R; Wiltshaw, E. (1983). *A near-death experience.* Lancet 8349: 561–562.

[70] J.C. Saavedra-Aguilar and Juan S. Gómez-Jeria. "A Neurobiological Model for Near-Death Experiences". Journal of Near-Death Studies, 7(4) Summer 1989. Pp. 205–222. http://200.89.70.78:8080/jspui/handle/2250/14775

[71] Appleby, L. (1989). *Near-death experience: Analogous to other stress induced psychological phenomena.* British Medical Journal, 298, 976–977.

[72] • Jansen, K. L. R: (1989). *Near-death experience and the MMDA receptor [Letter].* British Medical Journal, 298, 1708.

     • Jansen, K. L. R. (1989). *The near-death experience [Letter].* British Journal of Psychiatry 154: 883–884.

     • Jansen, K. L. R. (1990). *Neuroscience and the near-death experience: Roles for the NMDA-PCP receptor, the sigma receptor and the endopsychosins.* Medical Hypotheses 31: 25–29.

[73] Morse, M. L; Venecia, D; Milstein, J. (1989). *Near-death experiences: A neurophysiological explanatory model.* Journal of Near-Death Studies 8: 45–53.

[74] Jansen, K. L. R. (1996). *Using ketamine to induce the near-death experience: mechanism of action and therapeutic potential.* In Christian Rätsch, John Baker. *Yearbook for Ethnomedicine and the Study of Consciousness* (Jahrbuch furr Ethnomedizin und Bewubtseinsforschung). Wissenschaft und Bildung. Issue 4. pp. 55–81.

[75] Whinnery, J. E. (1997). *Psychophysiologic correlates of unconsciousness and near-death experiences.* J. Near Death Stud 15: 231–258.

[76] Strassman, Rick (2008). *Inner Paths to Outer Space: Journeys to Alien Worlds through Psychedelics and Other Spiritual Technologies.* Rochester, Vt.: Park Street Press. ISBN 978-1-59477-224-5.

[77] Strassman, Rick (2001). *DMT: The Spirit Molecule: A Doctor's Revolutionary Research into the Biology of Near-Death and Mystical Experiences.* Rochester: Park Street. ISBN 0-89281-927-8.

[78] Earleywine, Mitch (2005). *Mind-Altering Drugs: The Science Of Subjective Experience.* Oxford: Oxford University Press. ISBN 0-19-516531-4.

[79] French, Chris. (2001). *Dying to Know the Truth: Visions of a Dying Brain, or False Memories?.* Lancet 358: 2010–2011.

[80] Engmann, Birk. (2008). *Near-death Experiences: A review on the thesis of pathoclisis, neurotransmitter abnormalities, and psychological aspects.* MMW-Fortschr.Med.Nr.51-52/2008(150.Jg.) pp.42–43. PMID 19156957

[81] Vogt C, Vogt O. (1922). *Erkrankungen der Großhirnrinde im Lichte der Topistik, Pathoklise und Pathoarchitektonik.* Journal für Psychologie und Neurologie; Bd. 28. Joh.-Ambr.- Barth- Verlag. Leipzig. (German).

[82] Shermer, Michael (2002). *The Skeptic Encyclopedia of Pseudoscience.* Santa Barbara, Calif.: ABC-CLIO. pp. 152–157. ISBN 1-57607-653-9.

[83] Hines, Terence (2002). *Pseudoscience and the Paranormal* (2nd ed.). Amherst, N.Y.: Prometheus Books. pp. 101–104. ISBN 1-57392-979-4.

[84] Lempert, T., *et al.* (2006). *Syncope and Near-Death Experience.* Lancet 344: 829–830.

[85] Laureys, Steven; Tononi, Giulio (2009). *The Neurology of Consciousness: Cognitive Neuroscience and Neuropathology* (1st ed.). Amsterdam: Elsevier Academic Press. pp. 225–303. ISBN 978-0-12-374168-4.

[86] Vincent, Jean-Louis (2009). *Intensive Care Medicine.* [S.l.]: Springer New York. pp. 961–968. ISBN 978-0-387-92277-5.

[87] Chawla, L. S., Akst, S., Junker, C., Jacobs, B., & Seneff, M. G. (2009). *Surges of electroencephalogram activity at the time of death: A case series.* Journal of Palliative Medicine 12: 1095–1100.

[88] Zalika Klemenc-Ketis, Janko Kersnik and Stefek Grmec. (2010). *The effect of carbon dioxide on near-death experiences in out-of-hospital cardiac arrest survivors: a prospective observational study.* Critical Care 14 (R56).

[89] , *Carbon Dioxide May Explain 'Near Death Experiences*, Science Daily, 08 April 2010. Accessed 2011-08-25.

[90] James Owen , *Near-Death Experiences Explained?*, National Geographic, 08 April 2010. Accessed 2011-08-25.

[91] Halgren, E.; Walter, R. D; Cherlow, D. G; Crandall, P. H. (1978). *Mental Phenomena Evoked by Electrical Stimulation of the Human Hippocampal Formation and Amygdala.* Brain 101: 83–117.

[92] Arzy S, Seeck M, Ortigue S, Spinelli L & Blanke O. Induction of an illusory shadow person. Nature 2006; 443:287.

[93] Hopkin, Michael (20 September 2006), "Brain Electrodes Conjure up Ghostly Visions", *Nature*, doi:10.1038/news060918-4

[94] Wutzler A, Mavrogiorgou P, Winter C, Juckel G. (2011). *Elevation of Brain Serotonin During Dying.* Neuroscience Letters 498: 20–21.

[95] "Near-death experiences may be triggered by serotonin". *New Scientist.*

[96] "Peace of Mind: Near-Death Experiences Now Found to Have Scientific Explanations". *Scientific American.*

[97] L. Renemane, Z. Straume, B. Kupca, "Psychiatric phenomena among cardiologic patients who have survived a clinical death", European Neuropsychopharmacology, Volume 22, Supplement 2, October 2012, Pages S218-S219, ISSN 0924-977X, 10.1016/S0924-977X(12)70321-8.

[98] "Characteristics of Near-Death Experiences Memories as Compared to Real and Imagined Events Memories". PLOS ONE. 2013. Retrieved 14 April 2013.

[99] ""Reality" of near-death-experience memories: evidence from a psychodynamic and electrophysiological integrated study". Frontiers. 2014. Retrieved 19 June 2014.

[100] Young, Saundra (2009-10-16). "Doctor says near-death experiences are in the mind". *CNN*. Retrieved 2014-05-27.

[101] Nelson, K. R; Mattingly, M; Lee, S. A; Schmitt, F. A. (2006). *Does the arousal system contribute to near death experience?* Neurology 66: 1003–1009.

[102] Lynne Levitan; Stephen LaBerge (1991). "Other Worlds: Out-of-Body Experiences and Lucid Dreams". *Nightlight* (The Lucidity Institute) 3 (2-3).

[103] Green, J. Timothy (1995). "Lucid dreams as one method of replicating components of the near-death experience in a laboratory setting". *Journal-of-Near-Death-Studies* 14: 49. A large phenomenological overlap among lucid dreams, out-of-body experiences, and near-death experiences suggests the possibility of developing a methodology of replicating components of the near-death experience using newly developed methods of inducing lucid dreams. Reports on the literature of both spontaneous and induced near-death-experience-like episodes during lucid dreams suggest a possible protocol.

[104] Thaler, S. L. (1993) 4-2-4 Encoder Death, WCNN'93, Portland: World Congress on Neural Networks, July 11–15. Volume 1.

[105] Yam, P., "Daisy, Daisy" Do computers have near-death experience, *Scientific American*, May 1993.

[106] Strok, D., Dying by design, IEEE Expert, Dec.1993.

[107] Thaler, S. L. (1995). Death of a gedanken creature, Journal of Near-Death Studies, 13(3), Spring 1995.

[108] Thaler, S. L., The death dream and near-death darwinism, Journal of Near-Death Studies, 15(1), Fall 1996.

[109] Thaler, S. L. (1995) "Virtual Input Phenomena" Within the Death of a Simple Pattern Associator, Neural Networks, 8(1), 55–65.

[110] Orne RM. (1995) "The meaning of survival: the early aftermath of a near-death experience". *Research in Nursing & Health.* 1995 Jun; 18(3):239–47. PubMed abstract PMID 7754094

[111] Greyson B. (1997) "The near-death experience as a focus of clinical attention". *Journal of Nervous and Mental Disease.* May; 185(5):327–34. PubMed abstract PMID 9171810

[112] The diagnostic label of "Religious or spiritual problem" is included in DSM-IV under the category of "Other conditions that may be a focus of clinical attention". See American Psychiatric Association (1994) *Diagnostic and Statistical Manual of Mental Disorders, fourth edition.* Washington, D.C.: American Psychiatric Association (Code V62.89, Religious or Spiritual Problem).

[113] Shushan, Gregory (2009). *Conceptions of the Afterlife in Early Civilizations: Universalism, Constructivism, and Near-Death Experience.* London: Continuum. ISBN 978-0-8264-4073-0.

[114] Keith Augustine. (2008). "Hallucinatory Near-Death Experiences". Internet Infidels. Retrieved 2014-06-03.

[115] Parnia, S; Waller, D. G; Yeates, R; Fenwick, P. (2001). *A Qualitative and Quantitative Study of the Incidence, Features and Aetiology of Near-Death Experiences in Cardiac Arrest Survivors.* Resuscitation 48: 149–156.

[116] Jane Dreaper. (2008). "Study into near-death experiences". BBC News. Retrieved 2014-06-03.

[117] AWARE Study Update 2014. Published online at "Horizon Research Foundation".

[118] Bowman, Lee (December 20, 2013). "Scientists looking closer at what happens when body dies; edge closer to new understanding". WEWS-TV. Scripps Howard News Service. Retrieved 2014-05-24.

[119] Parnia *et al.* (2014). "AWARE—AWAreness during REsuscitation—A prospective study". *Resuscitation.*

[120] "One not too impressive study does not prove life after death". Doubtful News.

[121] "No, this study is not evidence for "life after death". James Randi Educational Foundation.

[122] Steven Novella. (2014). "AWARE Results Finally Published – No Evidence of NDE".

[123] Sam Parnia. "AWARE II (AWAreness during REsuscitation) A Multi-Centre Observational Study of the Relationship between the Quality of Brain Resuscitation and Consciousness, Neurological, Functional and Cognitive Outcomes following Cardiac Arrest" (2014).

[124] Murray, Craig D. (2009). *Psychological Scientific Perspectives on Out-of-Body and Near-Death Experiences.* New York: Nova Science Publishers. pp. 187–203. ISBN 978-1-60741-705-7.

[125] James H. Schwartz. *Appendix D: Consciousness and the Neurobiology of the Twenty-First Century.* In Kandel, ER; Schwartz JH; Jessell TM. (2000). *Principles of Neural Science, 4th Edition.*

[126] Piccinini, Gualtiero; Bahar, Sonya. "No Mental Life after Brain Death: The Argument from the Neural Localization of Mental Functions" (2011). University of Missouri – St. Louis.

[127] Bernat JL (8 Apr 2006). "Chronic disorders of consciousness". *Lancet* **367** (9517): 1181–1192. doi:10.1016/S0140-6736(06)68508-5. PMID 16616561.

[128] Laureys, Steven; Tononi, Giulio (2009). *The Neurology of Consciousness: Cognitive Neuroscience and Neuropathology* (1st ed.). Amsterdam: Elsevier Academic Press. p. 20. ISBN 978-0-12-374168-4. In brain death there is irreversible cessation of all functions of the brain including the brainstem. Consciousness is, therefore, permanently lost in brain death.

[129] Sam Parnia, Peter Fenwick. "Near death experiences in cardiac arrest: visions of a dying brain or visions of a new science of consciousness" (2001).

[130] Greyson, B. (2003) Incidence and correlates of near-death experiences in a cardiac care unit. Gen. Hosp. Psychiat., 25: 269–276.

[131] Liere, E.J. and Stickney, J.C. (1963) Hypoxia. University of Chicago Press, Chicago.

[132] Paolin, A., Manuali, A., Di Paola, F., Boccaletto, F., Caputo, P., Zanata, R., Bardin, G.P. and Simini, G. (1995). *Reliability in diagnosis of brain death.* Intens Care Med 21: 657–662.

[133] Bardy, A. H. (2002). *Near-death experiences [letter].* Lancet 359: 2116.

[134] Gloor, P. (1986). Role of the limbic system in perception, memory, and affect: Lessons from temporal lobe epilepsy. In B. K. Doane & K. E. Livingstone (eds.). The limbic system: Functional organisation and clinical disorders. New York: Raven Press.

[135] Fenwick, P., & Fenwick, E. (1995). The truth in the light: An investigation of over 300 near-death experiences. London: Headline.

[136] Tao, J. X., Ray, A., Hawes-Ebersole, S., & Ebersole, J. S. (2005). Intracranial EEG substrates of scalp EEG interictal spikes. Epilepsia, 46, 669–676.

[137] Kobayashi, E., Hawco, C. S., Grova, C., Dubeau, F., & Gotman, J. (2006). Widespread and intense BOLD changes during brief focal electrographic seizures. Neurology, 66, 1049-1055.

[138] Holden, J.M. (2009) Veridical perception in near-death experiences. In The Handbook of Near-Death Experiences (Holden, J.M. et al., eds), pp. 185–211.

[139] Blackmore, S.J. (1993) Dying to Live: Science and the Near-Death Experience. Grafton, London.

[140] Blackmore, S.J. (1996b). Out-of-body experiences. In G. Stein (ed.), The encyclopedia of the paranormal. Amherst, NY: Prometheus Books. Pp. 471–483.

[141] Ring, K. and Cooper, S. (1999) Mindsight: Near-Death and Out-of-Body Experiences in the Blind. William James Center for Consciousness Studies, Palo Alto, CA.

[142] Ring, K. (2001) Mindsight: Eyeless vision in the blind. In: Lorimer D. (Ed.), Thinking Beyond the Brain: A Wider Science of Consciousness. Floris, Edinburgh, pp. 59–70.

[143] Pasarow, R. (1981). "A Personal Account of an NDE". *Vital Signs* **1** (3): 11–14.

[144]
- Pasarow, Reinee (1991). "Is there life after death? New death experience of Renee Pasarow, Part 1" (Shockwave movie). Local Spiritual Assembly of the Bahá'ís of Moorpark, Ca. Retrieved 2013-01-19.
- Pasarow, Reinee (1991). "Is there life after death? New death experience of Renee Pasarow, Part 2" (Shockwave movie). Local Spiritual Assembly of the Bahá'ís of Moorpark, Ca. Retrieved 2013-01-19.
- Pasarow, Reinee (1991). "Near Death Experience of Renee Pasarow" (video). Local Spiritual Assembly of the Bahá'ís of Moorpark, Ca. Retrieved 2013-01-19.

[145] Almeder, Robert F. (1992). *Death and Personal Survival: The Evidence for Life After Death.* Rowman & Littlefield. pp. 170–?. ISBN 9780822630166.

[146] Atwater, PMH (2001). *Coming Back to Life; The After-Effects of the Near-Death Experience* (2001 Revised and Updated ed.). Kensington Pub Corp. pp. 111–112. ISBN 978-0-8065-2303-3.

[147] Atwater, PMH (2007). *The Big Book of Near-Death Experiences; The Ultimate Guide to What Happens When We Die* (2nd, illustrated ed.). Hampton Roads Publishing. pp. 59–60. ISBN 978-1-57174-547-7.

[148] Barnes, Linda L.; Sered, Susan Starr (2005). *Religion and Healing in America* (illustrated ed.). Oxford University Press. pp. 399–400. ISBN 978-0-19-516796-2.

[149] Marie Watson (1897). *The Two Paths*. A.C. Clark.

[150] Watson, Marie (1932). *My Pilgrimage to the Land of Desire*. Executor of the estate of Marie Watson and the Bahá'í Publishing Committee of New York. pp. 13–14.

[151] "Anita M's NDE" NDERF

[152] Kimberli Wilson

[153] *90 Minutes in Heaven* by Don Piper

[154] *Heaven is For Real* by Todd Burpo

[155] "Parallel Universes, a Memoir from the Edges of Space and Time" by Linda A. Morabito

[156] "Best Sellers". *Combined Print & E-Book Nonfiction* (The New York Times). April 25, 2012. Retrieved November 21, 2012.

[157] Jul. 3, 2013 6:45pm Billy Hallowell (2013-07-03). "Did the Famed Neurosurgeon Who Claims He Saw God and Visited Heaven Lie? Article Exposes Alleged Inconsistencies | Video". TheBlaze.com. Retrieved 2015-05-08.

[158] N. E. Bush (2002). Afterward: Making meaning after a frightening near-death experience. *Journal of Near-Death Studies, 21*(2), 99–133. "Among contemporary near-death experiences, the best-known of this type is no doubt that of Howard Storm (2000), self-described as an angry, hostile atheist before a harrowing experience that transmogrified into one of affirmation and transcendence."

[159] "WTF with Marc Maron Podcast – Episode 431 – Josh Homme". Wtfpod.com. Retrieved 2015-03-05.

[160] Mavrothalassitis, Apostolos (2012). *The Friend From Mexico: A True Story of Surviving an Intensive Care Unit*. Translated by David J. Horn. ASIN B00A7VSCJ8. ISBN 978-1-48103-491-3.

[161] compare Dietmar Czycholl (Hg.): *Als ich am gestrigen Tag entschlief. Erfahrungen Wiederbeleber in der Weltliteratur. Eine Anthologie aus drei Jahrtausenden.* Genius Verlag, Oberstaufen 2003 ISBN 3-934719-13-9

[162] Karl May: *Am Jenseits*, Freiburg i.Br. 1912, S. 504 ff. (online auf zeno.org); *Im Reiche des silbernen Löwen*, Band 3, Freiburg i.Br. 1908, S. 270 ff. (online auf zeno.org).

[163] *Video: Dr. Raymond Moody über Nahtod-Erfahrungen* abgerufen am 15. März 2014.

[164] *Video: Elisabeth Kübler-Ross über Nahtoderfahrungen (1981)* , abgerufen am 14. März 2014

[165] *Bild der Wissenschaft: Sind Nahtod-Erfahrungen Bilder aus dem Jenseits?* „Ein helles Licht am Ende eines langen Tunnels, ein Gefühl von Freude und Hoffnung: Davon erzählten Patienten, die einen Herzstillstand erlitten haben, britischen Forschern. Die Wissenschaftler der Universität Southampton werten diese Berichte als die bislang schlüssigsten Hinweise auf ein Leben nach dem Tod, schreibt die deutsche Ärzte-Zeitung. „ abgerufen am 16. März 2014.

[166] van Lommel P, van Wees R, Meyers V, Elfferich I. (2001) „Near-Death Experience in Survivors of Cardiac Arrest: A prospective Study in the Netherlands", *The Lancet*, 358(9298):2039–45, doi:10.1016/S0140-6736(01)07100-8.

[167] *Video: Spiegel-TV: Gibt es ein Leben nach dem Tod? Blick ins Jenseits* siehe Beiträge von Markolf Niemz, von Walter van Laack, vom 9. März 2014

[168] fh-aachen.de vom 19. März 2014

[169] *zdf* Nahtoderfahrungen sind keine Hirnprodukte – ZDF Bericht , abgerufen am 14. März 2014

[170] *Bild der Wissenschaft: Sind Nahtod-Erfahrungen Bilder aus dem Jenseits?* „Ein helles Licht am Ende eines langen Tunnels, ein Gefühl von Freude und Hoffnung: Davon erzählten Patienten, die einen Herzstillstand erlitten haben, britischen Forschern. Die Wissenschaftler der Universität Southampton werten diese Berichte als die bislang schlüssigsten Hinweise auf ein Leben nach dem Tod, schreibt die deutsche Ärzte-Zeitung." und „Eines macht der Forscher Bruce Greyson von der Universität Virginia klar: Menschen mit Nahtod-Erlebnissen sind nicht psychisch krank. Die Änderung des Bewusstseins führt nicht zu bleibenden Schäden, berichtete er in der Fachzeitschrift „Lancet" (Bd. 355, S. 460)." abgerufen am 16. März 2014.

[171] Rense Lange, Bruce Greyson, James Houran: Research Scales Used to Classify an NDE : the Greyson Scale, geladen 13. November 2014

Chapter 12

Near-death studies

Near-death studies is a field of psychology and psychiatry that studies the physiology, phenomenology and after-effects of the near-death experience (NDE). The field was originally associated with a distinct group of North American researchers that followed up on the initial work of Raymond Moody, and who later established the International Association for Near-death Studies (IANDS) and the Journal of Near-Death Studies. Since then the field has expanded, and now includes contributions from a wide range of researchers and commentators worldwide.

12.1 Near-death experience

The near-death experience is an experience reported by people who have come close to dying in a medical or non-medical setting. The aspect of trauma, and physical crises, is also recognized as an indicator for the phenomenon.[1] According to sources[2][3] it is estimated that near-death experiences are reported by five percent of the adult American population. According to IANDS,[4] surveys (conducted in USA, Australia and Germany) suggest that 4 to 15% of the population have had NDEs. Researchers study the role of physiological, psychological and transcendental factors associated with the NDE.[5] These dimensions are also the basis for the three major explanatory models for the NDE.

Some general characteristics of an NDE include subjective impressions of being outside the physical body; visions of deceased relatives and religious figures; transcendence of ego and spatiotemporal boundaries.[6][7] NDE researchers have also found that the NDE may not be a uniquely western experience. Commentators note that several elements and features of the NDE appears to be similar across cultures,[5][7][8][9][10][11] but the details of the experience (figures, beings, scenery), and the interpretation of the experience, varies between cultures.[7][8][10][12] However, a few researchers have challenged the hypothesis that near-death experience accounts are substantially influenced by prevailing cultural models.[13]

12.1.1 Elements of the NDE

According to the *The NDE-scale* [10][14] a near-death-experience includes a few, or several, of the following 16 elements:

1. Time speeds up or slows down.

2. Thought-processes speed up.

3. A return of scenes from the past.

4. A sudden insight, or understanding.

5. A feeling of peace or pleasantness.

6. A feeling of happiness, or joy.

7. A sense of harmony or unity with the universe.

8. Confrontation with a brilliant light.

9. The senses feel more vivid.

10. An awareness of things going on elsewhere, as if by extrasensory perception (ESP).

11. Experiencing scenes from the future.

12. A feeling of being separated from the body.

13. Experiencing a different, unearthly world.

14. Encountering a mystical being or presence, or hearing an unidentifiable voice.

15. Seeing deceased or religious spirits.

16. Coming to a border, or point of no return.

In a study published in *The Lancet* van Lommel and colleagues [7] list ten elements of the NDE: Note a

1. Awareness of being dead.

2. Positive emotions.

3. Out of body experience.

4. Moving through a tunnel.

5. Communication with light.

6. Observation of colours.

7. Observation of a celestial landscape.

8. Meeting with deceased persons.

9. Life review.

10. Presence of border.

12.1.2 After-effects

According to sources the NDE is associated with a number of after-effects,[2][6][7][8][15][16][17][18] or life changing effects.[5][19] The effects, which are often summarized by researchers, include a number of value, attitude and belief changes[8][16] that reflect radical changes in personality,[8] and a new outlook on life and death, human relations, and spirituality.[2][6][15] Many of the effects are considered to be positive [2][19] or beneficial.[6] van Lommel and colleagues conducted a longitudinal follow-up research into transformational processes after NDE's and found a long-lasting transformational effect of the experience.[7]

However, not all after-effects are beneficial. The literature describes circumstances where changes in attitudes and behavior can lead to distress, psychosocial, or psychospiritual problems.[15][16][20]Note b Often the problems have to do with adjustment to the new situation following a near-death experience, and its integration into ordinary life.[16] Another category, so-called distressing or unpleasant near-death experiences, has been investigated by Greyson and Bush.[21]

12.1.3 Explanatory models

Explanatory models for the phenomenology and the elements of the NDE can, according to sources,[2][5][7][22][23][24] be divided into a few broad categories: psychological, physiological, and transcendental. Agrillo,[25] adopting a more parsimonious overview, notes that literature reports two main theoretical frameworks: (1) "biological/psychological" interpretation (in-brain theories), or (2) "survivalist" interpretation (out-of-brain theories). The research on NDEs often include variables from all three models. In a study published in 1990, Owens, Cook and Stevenson[22] presented results that lent support to all of these three interpretations.

Each model contains a number of variables that are often mentioned, or summarized, by commentators:

Psychological theories have suggested that the NDE can be a consequence of mental and emotional reactions to the perceived threat of dying,[5][7][19][22] or a result of expectation.[2] [9][11] Other psychological variables that are considered by researchers include: imagination;[2][11] depersonalization;[2][11] dissociation;[2][11] proneness to fantasy;[2][11] and the memory of being born.[11]

Physiological theories tend to focus on somatic, biological or pharmacological explanations for the NDE, often with an emphasis on the physiology of the brain. Variables that are considered, and often summarized by researchers, include: anoxia;[7][9] cerebral hypoxia;[5][19][26] hypercarbia;[5][19] endorphins;[5][8][9][15][19][26] serotonin[5][8][11][19][26] or various neurotransmitters;[2][11][15] temporal lobe dysfunction or seizures;[2][5][8][9][11][19][26][27] the NMDA receptor;[5][19][26] activation of the limbic system;[5][19] drugs;[5][9][19][26] retinal ischemia;[11] and processes linked to rapid eye-movement (REM) sleep or phenomena generated on the border between sleep and wakefullness.[2][11][27][28][29]

A third model, sometimes called the transcendental explanation,[2][5][7][8][22][23] considers a number of categories, often summarized by commentators, that usually fall outside the scope of physiological or psychological explanations. This explanatory model considers whether the NDE might be related to the existence of a afterlife;[22][23] a changing state of consciousness;[7] mystical (peak) experiences;[5] or the concept of a mind-body separation.[23]

Several researchers in the field, while investigating variables from all three models, have expressed reservations towards explanations that are purely psychological or physiological.[2][7][19][29][30][31] van Lommel and colleagues [7] have argued for the inclusion of transcendental categories as part of the explanatory framework. Other researchers, such as Parnia, Fenwick,[19] and Greyson,[10][31] have argued for an expanded discussion about the mind-brain relationship and the possibilities of human consciousness.

12.2 Research - history and background

Individual cases of NDEs in literature have been identified into ancient times.[32] In the 19th century a few efforts moved beyond studying individual cases - one privately done by Mormons and one in Switzerland. Up to 2005, 95% of world cultures have been documented making some mention of NDEs.[32] From 1975 to 2005, some 2500 self reported individuals in the US had been reviewed in retrospective studies of the phenomena[32] with an additional 600 outside the US in the West,[32] and 70 in Asia.[32]

Prospective studies, reviewing groups of individuals and then finding who had an NDE after some time and costing more to do, had identified 270 individuals.[32] In all close to 3500 individual cases between 1975 and 2005 had been reviewed in one or another study. And all these studies were carried out by some 55 researchers or teams of researchers.[32]

Research on near-death experiences is mainly limited to the disciplines of medicine, psychology and psychiatry. Interest in this field of study was originally spurred by the research of such pioneers as Elisabeth Kübler-Ross (psychiatrist) and Raymond Moody (psychologist and M.D.), but also by autobiographical accounts, such as the books of George Ritchie (psychiatrist).[2][33][34] Kübler-Ross, who was a researcher in the field of Thanatology and a driving force behind the establishment of the Hospice System in the United States, embarked upon the study of near-death experiences in the later part of her career.[35] Raymond Moody, on the other hand, got interested in the subject at the start of his career. In the mid-seventies, while doing his medical residency as a psychiatrist at the University of Virginia, he conducted interviews with Near-Death Experiencers. He later published these findings in the book *Life After Life* (1976).[36] In the book Moody outlines the different elements of the NDE. Features that were picked up by later researchers. The book brought a lot of attention to the topic of NDEs.[8][10]

The late seventies saw the establishment of the *Association for the Scientific Study of Near-Death Phenomena*, an initial group of academic researchers, including John Audette, Raymond Moody, Bruce Greyson, Kenneth Ring and Michael Sabom, who laid the foundations for the field of Near-death studies, and carried out some of the first post-Moody NDE research.[37] The Association was the immediate predecessor of the International Association for Near-death Studies (IANDS), which was founded in the early eighties and which established its headquarters at the University of Connecticut, Storrs.[38] This group of researchers, but especially Ring, was responsible for launching Anabiosis, the first peer-reviewed journal within the field. The journal later became Journal of Near-Death Studies.[2]

However, even though the above mentioned profiles introduced the sucject of NDE's to the academic setting, the subject was often met with academic disbelief,[39] or regarded as taboo.[8] The medical community has been somewhat reluctant to address the phenomenon of NDEs,[8][10] and grant money for research has been scarce.[8] However, both Ring and Sabom made contributions that were influential for the newly established field. Ring published a book in 1980 called *Life at Death: A Scientific Investigation of the Near-Death Experience*.[40] This early research was followed up by new book in 1984 by the title *Head-

ing Toward Omega: In Search of the Meaning of the Near-Death Experience*.[37][41] The early work of Michael Sabom was also bringing attention to the topic within the academic community. Besides contributing material to academic journals,[42] he wrote a book called *Recollections of Death* (1982)[43] which is considered to be a significant publication in the launching of the field.[37]

As research in the field progressed both Greyson and Ring developed measurement tools that can be used in a clinical setting.[14][44] Greyson has also addressed different aspects of the NDE, such as the psychodynamics of the experience,[45] the varieties of NDE,[3] the typology of NDE's[46] and the biology of NDE's.[47] In addition to this he has brought attention to the near-death experience as a focus of clinical attention,[15] suggesting that the aftermath of the NDE, in some cases, can lead to psychological problems.

The 1980's also introduced the research of Melvin Morse, another profile in the field of near-death studies.[48] Morse and colleagues[49][50] investigated near-death experiences in a pediatric population. They found that children reported NDE's that were similar to those described by adults. Morse later published two books, co-authored with Paul Perry, that were aimed at a general audience: *Closer to the light: learning from children's near-death experiences* (1990)[51] and *Transformed by the light: the powerful effect of near-death experiences on people's lives* (1992).[52] Another early contribution to the field was the research of British Neuropsychiatrist Peter Fenwick, who started to collect NDE-stories in the 1980s. In 1987 he presented his findings on a television-program, which resulted in more stories being collected.[53][54] The responses from Near-death experiencers later served as the basis for a book published in 1997, "The Truth in the light", co-authored with his wife Elizabeth Fenwick.[55] Co-operating with other researchers, among others Sam Parnia, Fenwick has also published research on the potential relationship between cardiac arrest and Near-death Experiences.[5][19][26]

Early investigations into the topic of near-death experiences were also being conducted at the University of Virginia, where Ian Stevenson founded the Division of Personality Studies in the late sixties. The division went on to produce research on a number of phenomena that were not considered to be mainstream. In addition to near-death experiences this included: reincarnation and past lives, out-of-body experiences, apparitions and after-death communications, and deathbed visions.[10][56] Stevenson, whose main academic interest was the topic of reincarnation and past lives,[57][58] also made contributions to the field of near-death studies.[22][59] In a 1990-study, co-authored with Owens & Cook, the researchers studied the medical records of 58 people who believed they had been near death. The authors judged 28 candidates to actually have been close to dying, while 30 candidates, who merely thought they were about to die, were judged to not have been in any medical danger. Both groups reported similar experiences, but the first group reported more features of the core NDE-experience than the other group.[8][22]

Recently, the work of Jeffrey Long has also attracted attention to the topic of NDE's in both the academic, and the popular field.[60][61] In 2010 he released a book, co-authored with Paul Perry, called *Evidence of the Afterlife: The Science of Near-Death Experiences*. In the book Long presented results from research conducted over the last decade.[62] Research has also entered into other fields of interest, such as the mental health of military veterans. Goza studied NDE's among combat veterans. She found, among other things, that combat soldiers reported different, and less intense near-death experiences, compared to NDErs in the civilian population.[63][64]

The first decades of Near-death research were characterized by retrospective studies.[2][5][7][19][23][65][66] However, the 2000s marked the beginning of prospective studies in the field, both on the European and the American continent.

In a study from 2001, conducted at Southampton General Hospital, Parnia and colleagues found that 11.1% of 63 cardiac-arrest survivors reported memories of their unconscious period. Several of these memories included NDE-features.[5]Note c This study was the first in a series of new prospective studies using cardiac arrest criteria, and it was soon to be followed by the study of van Lommel and colleagues, also published in 2001. Pim van Lommel (cardiologist) was one of the first researchers to bring the study of NDE's into the area of Hospital Medicine. In 1988 he launched a prospective study that spanned 10 Dutch hospitals. 344 survivors of cardiac arrest were included in the study.[29] 62 patients (18%) reported NDE. 41 of these patients (12%) described a core experience. The aim of the study was to investigate the cause of the experience, and assess variables connected to frequency, depth, and content.[7]

Prospective studies were also taking place in the U.S. Schwaninger and colleagues [67] collaborated with Barnes-Jewish Hospital, where they studied cardiac arrest patients over a three-year period (April 1991 - February 1994). Only a minority of the patients survived, and from this group 30 patients were interviewable. Of these 30 patients 23% reported an NDE, while 13% reported an NDE during a prior life-threatening illness. Greyson [30] conducted a 30-month survey of patients admitted to the cardiac in-patient service of the University of Virginia Hospital. He found that NDE's were reported by 10% of patients with cardiac arrest and 1% of other cardiac patients.

In 2008 the University of Southampton announced the start of a new research-project named The AWARE (AWAreness during REsuscitation) study. The study was launched by the University of Southampton, but included collaboration with medical centres within the UK, mainland Europe and North America. The object of the study was to study the brain, and consciousness, during cardiac arrest, and to test the validity of out of body experiences and reported claims of lucidity (the ability to see and hear) during cardiac arrest.[18][68][69]

The first clinical paper from this project, described as a 4-year multi-center observational study, was published in 2014.[70][71][72][73][74][75] The study found that 9% of patients who completed stage 2 interviews reported experiences compatible with NDEs.

12.2.1 Psychometrics

Several psychometric instruments have been adapted to near-death research. Ring developed the *Weighted Core Experience Index* in order to measure the depth of NDE's,[14] and this instrument has been used by other researchers for this purpose.[76] The instrument has also been used to measure the impact of near-death experiences on dialysis patients.[77] According to some commentators[2] the index has improved consistency in the field. However, Greyson notes that although the index is a pioneering effort, it is not based on statistical analysis, and has not been tested for internal coherence or reliability.[14] In 1984 Ring developed an instrument called the *Life Changes Inventory* (LCI) in order to quantify value changes following an NDE. The instrument was later revised and standardized and a new version, the LCI-R, was published in 2004.[78]

Greyson [14] developed *The Near-Death Experience Scale*. This 16-item Scale was found to have high internal consistency, split-half reliability, and test-retest reliability [6][14] and was correlated with Ring's *Weighted Core Experience Index*. Questions formulated by the scale address such dimensions as: cognition (feelings of accelerated thought, or "life-review"), affect (feelings of peace and joy), paranormal experience (feelings of being outside of the body, or a perception of future events) and transcendence (experience of encountering deceased relatives, or experiencing an unearthly realm). A score of 7 or higher out of a possible 32 was used as the standard criterion for a near-death experience.[6] The scale is, according to the author,[6][14] clinically useful in differentiating NDEs from organic brain syndromes and nonspecific stress responses. The NDE-scale was later found to fit the Rasch rating scale model.[79] The instrument has been used to measure NDE's among cardiac arrest survivors,[5][70] coma survivors,[80] out-of-hospital cardiac arrest patients/survivors,[24][81][82] substance misusers,[83] and dialysis patients.[77]

In the late 1980s Thornburg developed the *Near-Death Phenomena Knowledge and Attitudes Questionnaire*.[84] The questionnaire consists of 23 true/false/undecided response items assessing knowledge, 23 Likert scale items assessing general attitudes toward near-death phenomena, and 20 Likert scale items assessing attitude toward caring for a client who has had an NDE.[85] Knowledge and attitude portions of the instrument were tested for internal consistency. Content validity was established by using a panel of experts selected from nursing, sociology, and psychology.[84] The instrument has been used to measure attitudes toward, and knowledge of, near-death experiences in a college population,[86] among clergy,[87] among registered psychologists,[84] and among hospice nurses.[85]

Greyson has also used mainstream psychological measurements in his research, for example *The Dissociative Experiences Scale*;[16] a measure of dissociative symptoms, and *The Threat Index*;[88] a measure of the threat implied by one's personal death.

12.3 Near death studies community

12.3.1 Research Organizations and Academic locations

The field of near-death studies includes several communities that study the phenomenology of NDE's. The largest of these communities is IANDS, an international organization based in Durham, North-Carolina, that encourages scientific research and education on the physical, psychological, social, and spiritual nature and ramifications of near-death experiences. Among its publications we find the peer-reviewed *Journal of Near-Death Studies*, and the quarterly newsletter *Vital Signs*.[89][90] The organization also maintains an archive of near-death case histories for research and study.[91]

Another research organization, the Louisiana-based Near Death Experience Research Foundation, was established by radiation oncologist Jeffrey Long in 1998.[60][61][92] The foundation maintains a web-site, also launched in 1998, and a database of more than 1,600 cases, which is currently the world's largest collection of near-death reports. The reports come directly from sources all across the world.[61]

A few academic locations have been associated with the activities of the field of near-death studies. Among these we find the University of Connecticut (US),[6] Southampton University (UK),[68] University Of North Texas (US) [63] and the Division of Perceptual Studies at the University of Virginia (US).[10][13][66]

12.3.2 Conferences

IANDS holds conferences, at regular intervals, on the topic of near-death experiences. The first meeting was a medical seminar at Yale University, New Haven (CT) in 1982. This was followed by the first clinical conference in Pembroke Pines (FL), and the first research conference in Farmington (CT) in 1984. Since then conferences have been held in major U.S. cities, almost annually.[93] Many of the conferences have addressed a specific topic, defined in advance of the meeting. In 2004 participants gathered in Evanston (IL) under the headline:"Creativity from the light".[33][94] A few of the conferences have been arranged at academic locations. In 2001 researchers and participants gathered at Seattle Pacific University.[95] In 2006 the University of Texas MD Anderson Cancer Center became the first medical institution to host the annual IANDS conference.[96]

The first international medical conference on near-death experiences was held in 2006.[29] Approximately 1.500 delegates, including people who claim to have had NDEs, were attending the one-day conference in Martigues, France. Among the researchers attending the conference were anaesthetist and intensive care doctor Jean-Jacques Charbonnier, and pioneering researcher Raymond Moody.[97]

12.3.3 Relevant publications

IANDS publishes the quarterly *Journal of Near-Death Studies*, the only scholarly journal in the field. The Journal is cross-disciplinary, is committed to an unbiased exploration of the NDE and related phenomena, and welcomes different theoretical perspectives and interpretations that are based on scientific criteria, such as empirical observation and research.[98] IANDS also publishes *Vital Signs*, a quarterly newsletter that is made available to its members and that includes commentary, news and articles of general interest.

One of the first introductions to the field of near-death studies was the publication of a general reader: *The Near-Death Experience: Problems, Prospects, Perspectives*. The book was published in 1984 and was an early overview of the field.[99] In 2009 Praeger Publishers published the *The handbook of near-death experiences: thirty years of investigation*, a comprehensive critical review of the research carried out within the field of near-death studies.[32][100] 2011 marked the publication of *Making Sense of Near-Death Experiences: A Handbook for Clinicians.* [101] The book is a multi-author text which describes how the NDE can be handled in psychiatric and clinical practice.[102]

12.4 Reception, criticism and skeptical views

Skepticism towards the findings of near-death studies, and the validity of the near-death experience as a subject for scientific study, has been widespread. According to Knapton, in the *The Telegraph*,[103] the subject was, until recently, considered to be controversial. Both scientists and medical professionals have, in general, tended to be skeptical.[8][104][105] According to commentators in the field [39] the early study of Near-death experiences was met with "academic disbelief". Acceptance of NDE's as a legitimate topic for scientific study has improved,[8] but the process has been slow.[10]

Skeptics have remarked that it is difficult to verify many of the anecdotal reports that are being used as background material in order to outline the features of the NDE.[8][60] Martens [82] noted the "lack of uniform nomenclature", and "the failure to control the studied population with an elimination of interfering factors", as examples of criticism directed towards near-death research.

Internet Infidels paper editor, and commentator, Keith Augustine has criticized near-death research for oversimplifying the role of culture in afterlife beliefs. He has also exposed weaknesses in methodology, paucity of data, and gaps in arguments. Instead of a transcendental model of NDE's, which he does not find plausible, he suggests that NDE's are products of individuals' minds rather than windows into a transcendental reality.[106][107] His criticism has been answered by Greyson[107] who suggests that the materialist model favored by Augustine is supported by even fewer data than the "mind-brain separation model" favored by many researchers within the field of near-death studies.

The findings of NDE-research has been contested by several writers in the fields of psychology and neuroscience. Susan Blackmore [60] has contested the findings of NDE-research, and has instead argued in favour of a neurological explanation. Psychologist Christopher French [23][65] has reviewed several of the theories that have originated from the field of Near-death studies. This includes theories that present a challenge to modern neuroscience by suggesting a new understanding of the mind-brain relationship in the direction of transcendental, or paranormal, elements. In reply to this French argues in favour of the conventional scientific understanding, and introduces several non-paranormal factors, as well as psychological theory, that might explain those near-death experiences that defy conventional scientific explanations. However, he does not rule out a future revision of modern neuroscience, awaiting new and improved research procedures.

Jason Braithwaite, a Senior Lecturer in Cognitive Neuroscience in the Behavioural Brain Sciences Centre, University of Birmingham, issued an in-depth analysis and critique of the survivalist's neuroscience of some NDE researchers, concluding, "it is difficult to see what one could learn from the paranormal survivalist position which sets out assuming the truth of that which it seeks to establish, makes additional and unnecessary assumptions, misrepresents the current state of knowledge from mainstream science, and appears less than comprehensive in its analysis of the available facts."[108]

But criticism of the field has also come from commentators within its own ranks. In an open letter to the NDE-community Ring has pointed to the "issue of possible religious bias in near-death studies". According to Ring the field of near-death studies, as well as the larger NDE-movement, has attracted a variety of religious and spiritual affiliations, from a number of traditions, which makes ideological claims on behalf of NDE-research. In his view this has compromised the integrity of research and discussion.[37]

12.5 See also

- IANDS
- Near-death experience
- Journal of Near-Death Studies
- Transpersonal psychology
- Parapsychology
- Bruce Greyson
- Pam Reynolds' NDE

12.6 Notes

a.^ van Lommel et.al, 2001: Table 2

b.^ The diagnostic label of "Religious or spiritual problem" is included in DSM-IV under the category of "Other conditions that may be a focus of clinical attention". See American Psychiatric Association (1994) "Diagnostic and Statistical Manual of Mental Disorders", fourth edition. Washington, D.C.: American Psychiatric Association (Code V62.89, Religious or Spiritual Problem).

c.^ Reported memories were assessed by the Greyson NDE Scale.

12.7   References

[1] Sommers MS. "The near-death experience following multiple trauma". *Crit Care Nurse.* 1994 Apr;14(2):62-6.

[2] Griffith, Linda J. "Near-Death Experiences and Psychotherapy," *Psychiatry* (Edgmont). 2009 October; 6(10): 35–42.

[3] Greyson B. "Varieties of near-death experience". *Psychiatry.* 1993 Nov;56(4):390-9.

[4] IANDS. "Near-death experiences: Key Facts". Informational Brochure published by the International Association for Near-death Studies. Durham, NC. Updated 7.24.07

[5] Parnia S, Waller DG, Yeates R, Fenwick P. "A qualitative and quantitative study of the incidence, features and aetiology of near death experiences in cardiac arrest survivors". *Resuscitation.* Feb;48(2):149-56, 2001 PubMed abstract PMID 11426476

[6] Greyson, Bruce. "Near-Death Experiences in a Psychiatric Outpatient Clinic Population". *Psychiatric Services,* Dec., Vol. 54 No. 12. The American Psychiatric Association, 2003

[7] van Lommel P, van Wees R, Meyers V, Elfferich I. "Near-Death Experience in Survivors of Cardiac Arrest: A prospective Study in the Netherlands". *The Lancet.* December 15, 2001 ; 358(9298):2039-45. PMID 11755611

[8] Mauro, James. *Bright lights, big mystery.* Psychology Today, July 1992

[9] Blackmore, "Susan J. Near-death experiences". "Journal Of The Royal Society of Medicine", Volume 89 February 1996

[10] Graves, Lee. "Altered States. Scientists analyze the near-death experience". *The University of Virginia Magazine,* Summer 2007 Feature

[11] Facco, Enrico & Agrillo, Christian. Near-death experiences between science and prejudice. Frontiers in Human Neuroscience. 2012; 6: 209.

[12] Belanti, John; Perera, Mahendra and Jagadheesan, Karuppiah. "Phenomenology of Near-death Experiences: A Cross-cultural Perspective". *Transcultural Psychiatry,* 2008 45: 121.

[13] Athappilly G, Greyson B, Stevenson I. "Do Prevailing Societal Models Influence Reports of Near-Death Experiences? A Comparison of Accounts Reported Before and After 1975". *The Journal of Nervous and Mental Disease,* Volume 194, Number 3, March 2006.

[14] Greyson, Bruce. "The near-death experience scale. Construction, reliability, and validity". *Journal of Nervous and Mental Disease,* Jun;171(6):369-75, 1983

[15] Greyson, Bruce. "The near-death experience as a focus of clinical attention". *Journal of Nervous and Mental Disease,* May;185(5):327-34, 1997

[16] Greyson, B. "Dissociation in people who have near-death experiences: out of their bodies or out of their minds?" *The Lancet.* Feb 5;355(9202):460-3, 2000

[17] Yang, C. Paul; Lukoff, David; Lu, Francis. "Working with Spiritual Issues". *Psychiatric Annals,* 36:3, March 2006.

[18] Weintraub, Pamela. "Seeing the Light". *Psychology Today,* September/October 2014

[19] Parnia S, Fenwick P. "Near death experiences in cardiac arrest: visions of a dying brain or visions of a new science of consciousness". *Resuscitation.* 2002 Jan;52(1):5-11

[20] Orne RM. "The meaning of survival: the early aftermath of a near-death experience". *Research in Nursing & Health.* 1995 Jun;18(3):239-47. PubMed abstract PMID 7754094

[21] Greyson B, Bush NE. "Distressing near-death experiences". *Psychiatry.* 1992 Feb;55(1):95-110.

[22] Owens J, Cook E W, Stevenson I. "Features of "near-death experience" in relation to whether or not patients were near death." *The Lancet,* Volume 336, Issue 8724, 10 November 1990, Pages 1175–1177.

[23] French, Christopher C. "Near-death experiences in cardiac arrest survivors", in S. Laureys (Ed.) (2005) *Progress in Brain Research,* Vol. 150

[24] Klemenc-Ketis Z, Kersnik J, Grmec S. "The effect of carbon dioxide on near-death experiences in out-of-hospital cardiac arrest survivors: a prospective observational study". *Crit Care.* 2010;14(2):R56.

[25] Agrillo, Christian. Near-Death Experience: Out-of-Body and Out-of-Brain? *Review of General Psychology,* 2011, Vol. 15, No. 1, 1–10.

[26] Parnia S, Spearpoint K, Fenwick PB. "Near death experiences, cognitive function and psychological outcomes of surviving cardiac arrest". *Resuscitation.* 2007 Aug;74(2):215-21.

[27] Britton W. B., Bootzin R. R. "Near-death experiences and the temporal lobe". *Psychol. Sci.* 15, 254–258, 2004

[28] Ruttimann, Jacqueline. "Are near-death experiences a dream?" *Nature magazine,* Published online 10 April 2006

[29] Williams, Daniel. "At the Hour Of Our Death". *TIME Magazine.* Friday, Aug. 31, 2007

[30] Greyson, Bruce. "Incidence and correlates of near-death experiences in a cardiac care unit." *General Hospital Psychiatry,* 25 (2003) 269–276

[31] Greyson, Bruce. "Implications of near-death experiences for a postmaterialist psychology". *Psychology of Religion and Spirituality,* Vol 2(1), Feb 2010, 37-45.

[32] Holden, Janice Miner; Greyson, Bruce; James, Debbie, eds. (Jun 22, 2009). "The Field of Near-Death Studies: Past, Present and Future". *The Handbook of Near-Death Experiences: Thirty Years of Investigation*. Greenwood Publishing Group. pp. 1–16. ISBN 978-0-313-35864-7.

[33] Anderson, Jon. "Shedding light on life at death's door". *Chicago Tribune*, published online May 13, 2004

[34] Slayton, Jeremy. "Death Notice: George Gordon Ritchie Jr dies". *Richmond Times Dispatch*, published online Wednesday, October 31, 2007

[35] Noble, Holcomb B. "Elisabeth Kübler-Ross, 78, Dies; Psychiatrist Revolutionized Care of the Terminally Ill." *New York Times*, August 26, 2004

[36] Moody Raymond A. (1976). *Life after life : the investigation of a phenomenon - survival of bodily death*. Harrisburg, Pa. : Stackpole Books.

[37] Ring, Kenneth. Religious Wars in the NDE Movement: Some Personal Reflections on Michael Sabom's Light & Death. *Journal of Near-Death Studies*, 18(4) Summer 2000

[38] New York Times staff. Connecticut Guide; Near-death Symposium. *New York Times*, April 25, 1982

[39] Bush, Nancy Evans. "Is Ten Years a Life Review?" *Journal of Near-Death Studies*, 10(1) Fall 1991

[40] Ring, K. (1980a). *Life at death: A scientific investigation of the near-death experience*. New York, NY: Coward, McCann and Geoghegan.

[41] Ring, K. (1984). *Heading toward omega: In search of the meaning of the near-death experience.*New York, NY: William Morrow.

[42] Sabom, M. B. The near-death experience. *JAMA* 1980 Jul 4;244(1):29-30.

[43] Sabom, M. (1982). Recollections of death: A medical investigation. New York, NY: Harper and Row.

[44] Ring, Kenneth. (1980) *Life at death. A scientific investigation of the near-death experience*. New York: Coward McCann and Geoghenan.

[45] Greyson, Bruce. "The psychodynamics of near-death experiences." *Journal of Nervous and Mental Disease*, 1983 Jun;171(6):376-81.

[46] Greyson B. "A typology of near-death experiences." *Am J Psychiatry*. 1985 Aug;142(8):967-9.

[47] Greyson B. "Biological aspects of near-death experiences". *Perspect Biol Med*. 1998 Autumn;42(1):14-32.

[48] Maryles, Daisy. Behind the bestsellers. *Publishers Weekly*. 240.20 (May 17, 1993): p17. From Literature Resource Center.

[49] Morse M, Conner D, Tyler D. "Near-death experiences in a pediatric population. A preliminary report". *American Journal of Diseases of Children*, Jun;139(6):595-600, 1985

[50] Morse M, Castillo P, Venecia D, Milstein J, Tyler DC. "Childhood near-death experiences". *American Journal of Diseases of Children*, Nov;140(11):1110-4, 1986

[51] Morse, Melvin (with Paul Perry) (1990) *Closer to the light : learning from children's near-death experiences*. New York : Villard Books

[52] Morse, Melvin (with Paul Perry) (1990) *Transformed by the light : the powerful effect of near-death experiences on people's lives*. New York : Villard Books

[53] Wheatley, Jane (6 October 2006). "Life goes on... but even after death?". *Irish Independent*. Retrieved 10 August 2013.

[54] Mensel, Lars. "I'm no longer afraid of death". Conversation by Lars Mensel with Peter Fenwick. *The European*, published online 10.03.2013.

[55] Fenwick, Peter and Fenwick, Elizabeth (1997). *The truth in the light: an investigation of over 300 near-death experiences*. New York : Berkley Books

[56] Fox, Margalit. "Ian Stevenson Dies at 88; Studied Claims of Past Lives". *New York Times*, February 18, 2007

[57] Wallis, David. "Conversations/Dr. Ian Stevenson; You May Be Reading This In Some Future Past Life". *New York Times*, September 26, 1999

[58] Cadoret, Remi J. "Book Forum: European Cases of the Reincarnation Type". *Am J Psychiatry* 162:823-824, April 2005

[59] Stevenson I, Cook EW. Involuntary memories during severe physical illness or injury. *Journal of Nervous and Mental Disease*. 1995 Jul;183(7):452-8.

[60] Beck, Melinda. "Seeking Proof in Near-Death Claims". *The Wall Street Journal (Health Journal)*, October 25, 2010

[61] MacDonald, G. Jeffrey. "Scientists probe brief brushes with the afterlife". *The Christian Century*, Jan 12, 2011

[62] Fitzpatrick, Laura. *Is There Such a Thing as Life After Death?*. TIME magazine, published online Friday, Jan. 22, 2010

[63] UNT (University of North Texas) News. "UNT research produces new findings on combat soldiers' near-death experiences". Published online Monday, July 11, 2011

[64] Goza, Tracy H. "Combat Near-Death Experiences: An Exploratory, Mixed-Methods Study". Doctoral Dissertation, University of North Texas, August 2011

[65] French, Christopher. "Commentary." *The Lancet* 358, pp. 2010-11, 2001

[66] Greyson, Bruce. An Overview of Near-Death Experiences. *Missouri Medicine*, November/December 2013

[67] Schwaninger J, Eisenberg PR, Schechtman KB, Weiss AN. A Prospective Analysis of Near-Death Experiences in Cardiac Arrest Patients. *Journal of Near-Death Studies*, 20(4), Summer 2002

[68] University of Southampton Press Release. "World's largest-ever study of near-death experiences". 10 September 2008. Ref: 08/165

[69] Stephey, M.J. "What Happens When We Die?". *TIME Magazine*, Thursday, Sep. 18, 2008

[70] Parnia S, et al. AWARE—AWAreness during REsuscitation — A prospective study. *Resuscitation* (2014).

[71] University of Southampton News Release. *Results of world's largest Near Death Experiences study published.* Ref: 14/181, 07 October 2014

[72] Stony Brook University News. "Stony Brook Professor Leads World's Largest Medical Study on the State of Mind and Consciousness at the Time of Death". Published online, October 9, 2014

[73] Cai, S. "Study finds awareness after death in patients". *The Johns Hopkins News-Letter*, published online October 23rd, 2014

[74] Lichfield, Gideon. "The Science of Near-Death Experiences. Empirically investigating brushes with the afterlife". *The Atlantic*, April 2015

[75] Robb, Alice. The Scientists Studying Life After Death Are Not Total Frauds. *The New Republic*, published online October 8, 2014

[76] Lester, David. "Depth of Near-Death Experiences and Confounding Factors". *Perceptual and Motor Skills*, 2003,96, 18.

[77] Lai et al. "Impact of near-death experiences on dialysis patients: a multicenter collaborative study". *Am J Kidney Dis.* 2007 Jul;50(1):124-32, 132.e1-2.

[78] Greyson, Bruce; Ring, Kenneth. "The Life Changes Inventory - Revised." *Journal of Near-Death Studies*, Vol 23(1), 2004, 41-54.

[79] Lange R, Greyson B, Houran J. "A Rasch scaling validation of a 'core' near-death experience". *British Journal of Psychology*. Volume: 95 Part: 2 Page: 161-177, 2004

[80] Thonnard M, Charland-Verville V, Brédart S, Dehon H, Ledoux D, Laureys S, Vanhaudenhuyse A. Characteristics of near-death experiences memories as compared to real and imagined events memories. *PLoS One*. 2013;8(3):e57620. Mar 27.

[81] Klemenc-Ketis Z. "Life changes in patients after out-of-hospital cardiac arrest: the effect of near-death experiences". *Int J Behav Med*. 2013 Mar;20(1):7-12.

[82] Martens PR. "Near-death-experiences in out-of-hospital cardiac arrest survivors. Meaningful phenomena or just fantasy of death?" *Resuscitation*. 1994 Mar;27(2):171-5.

[83] Corazza O, Schifano F. "Near-death states reported in a sample of 50 misusers". *Subst Use Misuse*. 2010 May;45(6):916-24.

[84] Walker, Barbara & Russell, Robert D. "Assessing psychologists' knowledge and attitudes toward near-death phenomena". *Journal of Near-Death Studies*, Vol. 8, Number 2, 103-110

[85] Barnett, Linda. "Hospice Nurses' Knowledge and Attitudes Toward the Near-Death Experience". *Journal of Near-Death Studies*, 9(4), Summer 1991

[86] Ketzenberger, Kay E. & Keim, Gina L. "The Near-Death Experience: Knowledge and Attitudes of College Students". *Journal of Near-Death Studies*, Volume 19, Number 4, 227-232

[87] Bechtel, Lori J.; Chen, Alex; Pierce, Richard A.; Walker, Barbara A. "Assessment of clergy knowledge and attitudes toward near-death experiences". *Journal of Near-Death Studies*, Vol 10(3), 1992, 161-170.

[88] Greyson, Bruce. "Reduced death threat in near-death experiencers". *Death Studies*, Vol. 16, Issue 6, 1992.

[89] IANDS. *Near-Death Experiences: Is this what happens when we die?* Durham: International Association for Near-Death Studies. Informational brochure REV 4/11. Available at www.iands.org.

[90] IANDS: *Vital Signs*. Accessed 2011-02-06.

[91] IANDS: NDE Archives. Accessed 2011-02-06.

[92] Adler, Jerry. "Back From the Dead". *Newsweek*, July 23, 2007

[93] "IANDS Fact Sheet, As of December, 2010. Accessed 2012-02-09.

[94] Gordon, Scott. "Evanston's brush with death." *The Daily Northwestern*, published online June 30, 2004

[95] Forgrave, Reid. "A glimpse of the 'other side': Seattle conference unites near-death individuals". *The Seattle Times*, published online Friday, July 27, 2001

[96] Hopper, Leigh. "Conference to shed light on 'near-death' experiences". *The Houston Chronicle*, published online October 25, 2006

[97] Cosmos Magazine Staff. "Near-death experiences go under the French microscope". *Cosmos Magazine*, Sunday, 18 June 2006. Cosmos Media Pty Ltd

[98] IANDS *Journal of Near-Death Studies*. Accessed 2011-02-06.

[99] Bruce Greyson (Editor), Charles P. Flynn (Editor) (1984) *The Near-Death Experience: Problems, Prospects, Perspectives.* Charles C Thomas Pub Ltd

[100] Holden, Jan. M. "UNT Faculty Member Dr. Janice Minor Holden Publishes The Handbook of Near-Death Experiences: Thirty Years of Investigation". *University of North Texas Counseling Program News*, Vol. 1, Issue 2, Summer/Fall 2010

[101] Mahendra Perera, Karuppiah Jagadheesan, Anthony Peake (editors) (2011) *Making Sense of Near-Death Experiences: A Handbook for Clinicians.* Jessica Kingsley Publishers, 176 pp

[102] Russell, Rebecca. "Book reviews: Making Sense of Near-Death Experiences: A Handbook for Clinicians". *The British Journal of Psychiatry* (2012) 201: 415

[103] Knapton, Sarah. First hint of 'life after death' in biggest ever scientific study. *The Telegraph*, published online 07 Oct 20

[104] Petre, Jonathan. *Soul-searching doctors find life after death. The Telegraph*, published online 22 Oct 2000

[105] O'Connor, Anahad. "Following a Bright Light to a Calmer Tomorrow". *New York Times*, published online April 13, 2004

[106] Augustine, K. "Psychophysiological and cultural correlates undermining a survivalist interpretation of near-death experiences". *Journal of Near Death Studies*, 26 (2):89-125 (2007).

[107] Greyson, Bruce. "Commentary on 'Psychophysiological and Cultural Correlates Undermining a Survivalist Interpretation of Near-Death Experiences' ". *Journal of Near-Death Studies*, 26(2), Winter 2007

[108] Braithwaite, J. J. "Towards a Cognitive Neuroscience of the Dying Brain". The Skeptic, Volume 21, Issue 2 (2008).

12.8 External links

- The International Association for Near-Death Studies, Inc.

- University of Virginia Health System - Division of Perceptual Studies

- Links to 290 online NDE Scientific Papers

Chapter 13

Deathbed phenomena

Not to be confused with Near-death experience.

Deathbed phenomena refers to a range of paranormal experiences claimed by people who are dying. There are many examples of deathbed phenomena in both non-fiction and fictional literature, which suggests that these occurrences have been noted by cultures around the world for centuries, although scientific study of them is relatively recent. In scientific literature such experiences have been referred to as death-related sensory experiences (DRSE).[1] Dying patients have reported to staff working in hospices they have experienced comforting visions.[2][3]

Scientists consider deathbed phenomena and visions to be hallucinations.[4][5][6]

13.1   Deathbed visions

Deathbed visions have been described since ancient times, however the first systematic study was not conducted until the 20th century.[7] They have also been referred to as veridical hallucinations, visions of the dying and pre-death visions.[1] The physician William Barrett, author of the book *Death-Bed Visions* (1926), collected anecdotes of people who had claimed to have experienced visions of deceased friends and relatives, the sound of music and other deathbed phenomena.[8] Barrett was a Christian spiritualist and believed the visions were evidence for spirit communication.[9]

In a study conducted between 1959 and 1973 by the parapsychologists Karlis Osis and Erlendur Haraldsson, they reported that 50% of the tens of thousands of individuals they studied in the United States and India had experienced deathbed visions.[7] Osis and Haraldsson and other parapsychologists such as Raymond Moody have interpreted the reports as evidence for an afterlife.[10][11]

The neurologist Terence Hines has written that the proponents of the afterlife interpretation grossly underestimate the variability among the reports. Hines also criticized their methodology of collecting the reports:

> The way in which the reports are collected poses another serious problem for those who want to take them seriously as evidence of an afterlife. Osis and Haraldsson's (1977) study was based on replies received from ten thousand questionnaires sent to doctors and nurses in the United States and India. Only 6.4 percent were returned. Since it was the doctors and nurses who were giving the reports, not the patients who had, presumably, actually had the experience, the reports were secondhand. This means they had passed through two highly fallible and constructive human memory systems (the doctor's or nurse's and the actual patient's) before reaching Osis and Haraldsson. In other cases (i.e., Moody 1977) the reports were given by the patients themselves, months and years after the event. Such reports are hardly sufficient to argue for the reality of an afterlife.[6]

The skeptical investigator Joe Nickell has written deathbed visions (DBVs) are based on anecdotal accounts that are unreliable. Nickell discovered contradictions and inconsistencies in various DBVs reported by the paranormal author Carla Wills-Brandon.[12]

Research within the Hospice & Palliative Care fields have studied the impact of deathbed phenomena on the dying, their families, and palliative staff. In 2009, a questionnaire was distributed to 111 staff in an Irish hospice program asking if they had encountered staff or patients who had experienced DBP. The majority of respondents that they had been informed of a deathbed vision by a patient or the patient's family. They reported that the content of these visions often seemed to be comforting to the patient and their family.[13] Another study found that DBPs are commonly associated with peaceful death and are generally under-reported by patients and families due to fear of embarrassment and disbelief from medical staff.[14]

In response to this qualitative data, there is a growing movement within the palliative care field that emphasizes "compassionate understanding and respect from those who provide end of life care" in regards to DBPs.[15]

13.2 Scientific evaluation

According to Ronald K. Siegel, noted American psychopharmacologist and researcher, there is a high degree of similarity between deathbed visions and drug-induced hallucinations. Hallucinations caused by drugs frequently contain images of otherworldly beings and deceased friends and relatives.[4] Some scientists who have studied cases of deathbed phenomena have described the visual, auditory, and sensed presences of deceased relatives or angelic beings during the dying process as hallucinations. These hallucinations are theorized to occur due to a number of explanations including but not limited to cerebral hypoxia, confusion, delirium, body systems failures (e.g., renal, hepatic, pulmonary), and a mental reaction to stress.[16]

When the body is injured, or if the heart stops, even if only for a short period, the brain is deprived of oxygen. A short period of cerebral hypoxia can result in the impairment of neuronal function. It is theorized that this neuronal impairment accounts for deathbed visions.[17][18]

13.3 See also

- Deathbed confession

- Deathbed conversion

13.4 References

[1] Ethier, A. (2005). *Death-related sensory experiences.* Journal of Pediatric Oncology Nursing 22: 104-111.

[2] Brayne S, Farnham C, Fenwick P. (2006). *Deathbed phenomena and their effect on a palliative care team: a pilot study.* American Journal of Hospice and Palliative Medicine 23: 17-24.

[3] Lawrence M, Repede E. (2013). *The incidence of deathbed communications and their impact on the dying process.* American Journal of Hospice and Palliative Care 30: 632-639.

[4] Siegel, Ronald. (1980). *The Psychology of Life after Death.* American Psychologist 35: 911-931.

[5] Houran, J. & Lange, R. (1997). *Hallucinations that comfort: contextual mediation of deathbed visions.* Perceptual and Motor Skills 84: 1491-1504.

[6] Hines, Terence (2003). *Pseudoscience and the Paranormal.* Prometheus Books. p. 102. ISBN 978-1573929790

[7] Blom, Jan. (2009). *A Dictionary of Hallucinations.* Springer. pp. 131-132. ISBN 978-1441912220

[8] Barrett, William. (1926). *Death-Bed Visions.* Methuen & Company Limited. ISBN 978-0850305203

[9] Oppenheim, Janet. (1985). *The Other World: Spiritualism and Psychical Research in England, 1850-1914.* Cambridge University Press. p. 365. ISBN 978-0521265058

[10] Moody, Raymond. (1975). *Life After Life.* Mockingbird Books. ISBN 978-0553122206

[11] Osis, K. and Haraldsson, E. (1977). *At The Hour of Death.* Avon. ISBN 978-0380018024

[12] Nickell, Joe. (2002). *"Visitations": After-Death Contacts. Skeptical Inquirer.* Volume 12. Retrieved November 6, 2013.

[13] MacConville U, McQuillan, R. Surveying deathbed phenomena. Irish Medical Times. 2010, May 6.

[14] Fenwick P, Lovelace H, Brayne S. Comfort for the dying: five year retrospective and one year prospective studies of end of life experiences. Arch of Gerontology & Geriatrics. 2010;51:173-179.

[15] Fenwick P, Brayne S. End-of-life experiences: Reaching out for compassion, communication, and connection – meaning of deathbed visions and coincidences. Am J of Hospice & Pall Med. 2011;28(1):7-15.

[16] Brayne S, Lovelace H, Fenwick P. End-of-life experiences and the dying process in a Gloucestershire nursing home as reported by nurses and care assistants. Am J of Hospice & Pall Med. 2008;25(3):195-206.

[17] Brierley, J. and D. Graham. (1984). *Hypoxia and Vascular Disorders of the Central Nervous System.* In *Greenfield's Neuropathology* edited by J. Adams, J. Corsellis, and L. Duchen. 4th edition. New York: Wiley. pp. 125–207.

[18] French, Chis. (2009). *Near-death experiences and the brain.* In Craig Murray, ed. *Psychological scientific perspectives on out-of-body and death-near experiences.* New York: Nova Science Publishers. pp. 187-203. ISBN 978-1607417057

13.5 External links

- Near-Death Experiences and the Brain by Chris French

- Deathbed Phenomena: Real or Imagined?

Chapter 14

God gene

The **God gene** hypothesis proposes that a specific gene, called vesicular monoamine transporter 2 (VMAT2), predisposes humans towards spiritual or mystic experiences. The idea has been postulated by geneticist Dean Hamer, the director of the Gene Structure and Regulation Unit at the U.S. National Cancer Institute, and author of the 2005 book *The God Gene: How Faith is Hardwired into our Genes.*

The God gene hypothesis is based on a combination of behavioral genetic, neurobiological and psychological studies. The major arguments of the hypothesis are: (1) spirituality can be quantified by psychometric measurements; (2) the underlying tendency to spirituality is partially heritable; (3) part of this heritability can be attributed to the gene VMAT2;[1] (4) this gene acts by altering monoamine levels; and (5) spiritual individuals are favored by natural selection because they are provided with an innate sense of optimism, the latter producing positive effects at either a physical or psychological level.

14.1 Scientific criticism

Although it is always difficult to determine the many interacting functions of a gene, VMAT2 appears to be involved in the transport of monoamine neurotransmitters across the synapses of the brain. PZ Myers argues: "It's a pump. A teeny-tiny pump responsible for packaging a neurotransmitter for export during brain activity. Yes, it's important, and it may even be active and necessary during higher order processing, like religious thought. But one thing it isn't is a 'god gene.'"[2]

Carl Zimmer claimed that VMAT2 can be characterized as a gene that accounts for less than one percent of the variance of self-transcendence scores. These, Zimmer says, can signify anything from belonging to the Green Party to believing in ESP. Zimmer also points out that the God Gene theory is based on only one unpublished, unreplicated study.[3] However Hamer notes that the importance of the VMAT2 finding is not that it explains all spiritual or religious feelings, but rather that it points the way toward one neurobiological pathway that may be important.

14.2 Religious response

John Polkinghorne, an Anglican priest, member of the Royal Society and Canon Theologian at Liverpool Cathedral, was asked for a comment on Hamer's theory by the British national daily newspaper, *The Daily Telegraph*. He replied: "The idea of a God gene goes against all my personal theological convictions. You can't cut faith down to the lowest common denominator of genetic survival. It shows the poverty of reductionist thinking." [4][5]

Walter Houston, the chaplain of Mansfield College, Oxford, and a fellow in theology, told the *Telegraph*: "Religious belief is not just related to a person's constitution; it's related to society, tradition, character—everything's involved. Having a gene that could do all that seems pretty unlikely to me."

Hamer responded that the existence of such a gene would not be incompatible with the existence of a personal God: "Religious believers can point to the existence of God genes as one more sign of the creator's ingenuity—a clever way to help humans acknowledge and embrace a divine presence."[5]

Hamer repeatedly notes in his book that, "This book is about whether God genes exist, not about whether there is a God."[6]

14.3 See also

- Neurotheology

- Origin of religion

- Cognitive science of religion

14.4 References

[1] Hamer, Dean (2005). *The God Gene: How Faith Is Hard-wired Into Our Genes.* Anchor Books. ISBN 0-385-72031-9.

[2] Myers, PZ (2005-02-13). "No god, and no 'god gene', either". Pharyngula. Archived from the original on October 3, 2009.

[3] Zimmer, Carl (October 2004). "Faith-Boosting Genes: A search for the genetic basis of spirituality". *Scientific American.*

[4] The 'God Gene' Sales Stunt Archived August 13, 2007, at the Wayback Machine.

[5] Geneticist claims to have found 'God gene' in humans

[6] Hamer, Dean (2005). *The God Gene: How Faith Is Hard-wired Into Our Genes.* Anchor Books. Page 16

- *The God Gene: How Faith is Hardwired into our Genes* by Dean Hamer. Published by Doubleday, ISBN 0-385-50058-0.

14.5 External links

- *Daily Telegraph* report
- Carl Zimmer's review

Chapter 15

God helmet

The **God Helmet** is an experimental apparatus originally called the **Koren helmet** after its inventor Stanley Koren. It was developed by Koren and neuroscientist Michael Persinger to study creativity, religious experience and the effects of subtle stimulation of the temporal lobes.[1] Reports by participants of a "sensed presence" while wearing the God helmet brought public attention and resulted in several TV documentaries.[2] The device has been used in Persinger's research in the field of neurotheology, the study of the neural correlations of religion and spirituality. The apparatus, placed on the head of an experimental subject, generates very weak magnetic fields, that Persinger refers to as "complex." Like other neural stimulation with low-intensity magnetic fields, these fields are approximately as strong as those generated by a land line telephone handset or an ordinary hair dryer, but far weaker than that of an ordinary refrigerator magnet and approximately a million times weaker than transcranial magnetic stimulation.[3]

Persinger reports that many subjects have reported "mystical experiences and altered states"[4] while wearing the God Helmet. The foundations of his theory have been criticised in the scientific press.[5] Anecdotal reports by journalists,[6] academics[7][8] and documentarists[9] have been mixed and several effects reported by Persinger have not yet been independently replicated. One attempt at replication published in the scientific literature reported a failure to reproduce Persinger's effects and the authors proposed that the suggestibility of participants, improper blinding of participants or idiosyncratic methodology could explain Persinger's results.[10] Persinger argues that the replication was technically flawed,[8][11] but the researchers have stood by their replication.[12] More recently, other researchers [13] have published a replication of one God Helmet experiment.[14]

15.1 Development

The God Helmet was not specifically designed to elicit visions of God,[1] but to test several of Persinger's hypotheses about brain function. The first of these is the Vectorial Hemisphericity Hypothesis,[15] which proposes that the human sense of self has two components, one on each side of the brain, that ordinarily work together but in which the left hemisphere is usually dominant.[16][17] Persinger argues that the two hemispheres make different contributions to a single sense of self, but under certain conditions can appear as two separate 'selves'. Persinger and Koren designed the God Helmet in an attempt to create conditions in which contributions to the sense of self from both cerebral hemispheres is disrupted.

The second experimental hypothesis was that when communication between the left and right senses of self is disturbed, as they report it is while wearing the God Helmet, the usually-subordinate 'self' in the right hemisphere intrudes into the awareness of the left-hemispheric dominant self,[17] causing what Persinger refers to as "interhemispheric intrusions".[15]

The third hypothesis was that "visitor experiences" could be explained by such "interhemispheric intrusions" caused by a disruption in "vectorial hemisphericity".[18] Persinger theorises that many paranormal experiences,[19] feelings of having lived past lives,[20] felt presences of non-physical beings,[21] ghosts,[22] muses,[23] and other "spiritual beings", are examples of interhemispheric intrusions.

The God Helmet experiments were also intended, though not specifically designed (see above), to validate the idea that religious and mystic experiences are artifacts of temporal lobe function.[24]

15.2 The device

Persinger uses a modified snowmobile helmet that incorporates solenoids placed over the temporal lobes. This device produces magnetic fields that Persinger describes as "weak but complex"[25][26] (1 microTesla).[27] The pattern of fluctuation in these magnetic fields is derived from physiological sources, for example patterns that appear in EEG traces taken from limbic structures.[28] The purpose of exposing magnetic fields patterned after neurophysiological sources, such as the burst-firing profile of the amygdala, is to enhance the probability of activating the structure from which the signal was derived.[29] Only one of the coils on each side of the helmet is active at any one time, and the active coil changes constantly, "rotating" counterclockwise over each temporal lobe. Persinger's God Helmet sessions consist of two stimulations, applied one after the other.[28] The first of these uses a signal "tailored from a Chirp Signal sequence,[28] applied over right temporal lobe. In the second phase of the procedure, both temporal lobes are stimulated, with a pattern derived from the amygdala.[28][29]

The sessions are conducted with the subject seated in an acoustic chamber.[30] The acoustic chamber is also a Faraday cage,[28] shielding out all EMF emissions and radiation except the Earth's magnetic field. Persinger reports that this shielding allows him to use the apparatus to investigate the effects of geomagnetism on the human brain.[31][32]

15.2.1 Comparison with TMS

Neither the God Helmet, nor technologies derived from it, are examples of transcranial magnetic stimulation (TMS), which uses magnetic fields on the order of one million times stronger than those used in Persinger's lab.[3] Despite this, Persinger reports similar effect sizes with his apparatus.[4] The magnetic fields employed in TMS and in Persinger's experiments are also very different. TMS uses single, paired, and repetitive pulses of high intensity to penetrate the cranium.[33] In contrast, Persinger's apparatus uses weak complex magnetic signals patterned after physiological processes, such as one derived from limbic burst firing.[29][34]

15.3 Experiences

Most reports from Persinger's lab consist of people sensing "presences"; people often interpreted these to be that of angels, a deceased being known to the subject, or a group of beings of some kind. There have also been reports in which the participant has experienced what they perceive as God.[35] Persinger reports that "at least" 80 percent of his participants experience a presence beside them in the room,[36] whilst about one percent report an experience of "God",[37] and others report less evocative experiences of "another consciousness or sentient being".[38]

15.3.1 Anecdotal reports

The scientist and science writer Richard Dawkins, appearing in the BBC science documentary series *Horizon*, did not have a 'sensed presence' experience,[39] but instead felt at times 'slightly dizzy', 'quite strange' and had sensations in his limbs and changes in his breathing. He summarised his experience as follows: "It pretty much felt as though I was in total darkness, with a helmet on my head and pleasantly relaxed".[7] Persinger explained Dawkins' limited results in terms of his low score on a psychological scale measuring temporal lobe sensitivity.[40]

In contrast, the experimental psychologist, and former parapsychology researcher, Susan Blackmore said: "When I went to Persinger's lab and underwent his procedures I had the most extraordinary experiences I've ever had... I'll be surprised if it turns out to be a placebo effect."[8]

Jack Hitt, a journalist from *Wired* magazine, visited Persinger's lab in 1999 and expressed confusion over Persinger's post-stimulation debriefing ("One question: Did the red bulb on the wall grow larger or smaller? There was a red bulb on the wall? I hadn't noticed.") and reported: "Many other questions suggest that there were other experiences I should have had, but to be honest, I didn't. In fact, as transcendental experiences go, on a scale of 1 to 10, Persinger's helmet falls somewhere around, oh, 4. Even though I did have a fairly convincing out-of-body experience, I'm disappointed relative to the great expectations and anxieties I had going in."[41]

15.4 Replication and debate

One pair of researchers succeeded in replicating[13] the effects of one of Persinger's early studies.[14] They reported that their experiment had ruled out suggestibility as an explanation for Persinger's effects, and that analysis of their subjects' verbal reports revealed significant differences between the speech of subjects and controls, as well as less robust effects for suggestion and expectation.

In December 2004 *Nature* reported that a group of Swedish researchers led by Pehr Granqvist, a psychologist at Uppsala University in Sweden, had attempted to replicate Persinger's experiments under double-blind conditions, and were not able to reproduce the effect.[8] The study was published in *Neuroscience Letters* in 2005.[10] Granqvist *et al* concluded that the presence or absence of the magnetic field had no relationship with any religious or spiritual experience reported by the participants, but was predicted entirely by their suggestibility and personality traits. Persinger, however, took issue with the Swedish attempt to replicate his work. "They didn't replicate it, not even close," he says.[8] He argued that the Swedish group did not expose the subjects to magnetic fields for long enough to produce an effect. Granqvist *et al.* respond that Persinger agreed with their proposed methodology beforehand[42][43] and they stand by their replication.[12]

The theoretical basis for the God helmet, especially the connection between temporal lobe function and mystic experiences,[44][45] has also been questioned.[5]

15.5   Related devices and studies

Persinger and colleagues also developed a device nicknamed "The Octopus" which uses solenoids around the whole brain, in a circle just above subject's ears. Commercial versions of the God helmet, Octopus and associated devices are sold by Persinger's research associate Todd Murphy, and he reports that his devices are able to modulate emotional states in addition to enhancing meditation and generating altered states. One experiment found no changes in emotional responses to photographs whether the device was on or off,[46] although the researchers concluded that "additional investigations ... are warranted."[47] Persinger and colleagues report significant changes in subjects' EEG during stimulation with a Shakti system.[48] In one report by Persinger's lab, these changes were correlated with an out-of-body experience.[49]

One published attempt to test Persinger's theories regarding the psychological effects of environmental magnetic fields, used whole-body exposure to magnetic fields and ultrasound in freely-moving participants to create a "haunted room" within which it was hoped subjects would sense a "presence." The study found that reports of unusual experiences were unrelated with the presence or absence of "complex" environmental electromagnetic fields similar to Persinger's. They concluded that the effects were likely due to suggestibility, though they did not directly measure it.[50]

15.6   See also

- Michael Persinger
- Neuroepistemology
- Neurotheology
- Third Man factor

15.7   References

[1] Ruttan, L. A., Persinger, M. A. & Koren, S. (1990). "Enhancement of Temporal Lobe-Related Experiences During Brief Exposures to MilliGauss Intensity Extremely Low Frequency Magnetic Fields". *Journal of Bioelectricity* 9 (1): 33–54. doi:10.3109/15368379009027758.

[2] Science Channel clip of God Helmet

[3] Craig Aaen-Stockdale (2012). "Neuroscience for the Soul". *The Psychologist* 25 (7): 520–523. the magnetic fields generated by the God helmet are far too weak to penetrate the cranium and influence neurons within. Transcranial magnetic stimulation (TMS) uses field strengths of around 1.5 tesla in order to induce currents strong enough to depolarise neurons through the skull and cause them to fire. Persinger's apparatus, on the other hand has a strength ... 5000 times weaker than a typical fridge magnet. Granqvist argues that there is simply no way that this apparatus is having any meaningful effect on the brain, and I'm inclined to agree.

[4] Persinger, MA; et al. (2010). "The Electromagnetic Induction of Mystical and Altered States Within the Laboratory". *Journal of Consciousness Exploration & Research* 1 (7): 808–830. ISSN 2153-8212.

[5] Craig Aaen-Stockdale (2012). "Neuroscience for the Soul". *The Psychologist* 25 (7): 520–523. Persinger's theory is based on the literature on religiosity in temporal lobe epileptics ... a literature that I argue above is both flawed and outdated.

[6] Wired magazine article

[7] Online video excerpt, see 2:00 to 3:26

[8] Roxanne Khamsi (December 9, 2004). "Electrical brainstorms busted as source of ghosts". BioEd Online.

[9] Incomplete filmography for Dr. M.A. Persinger

[10] Granqvist, P; Fredrikson, M; Unge, P; Hagenfeldt, A; Valind, S; Larhammar, D; Larsson, M (2005). "Sensed presence and mystical experiences are predicted by suggestibility, not by the application of transcranial weak complex magnetic fields". *Neuroscience Letters* 379 (1): 1–6. doi:10.1016/j.neulet.2004.10.057. PMID 15849873. Lay summary – *BioEd Online* (December 9, 2004).

[11] Persinger, M; Koren, S (2005). "A response to Granqvist et al. "Sensed presence and mystical experiences are predicted by suggestibility, not by the application of transcranial weak magnetic fields"". *Neuroscience Letters* 380 (3): 346–347. doi:10.1016/j.neulet.2005.03.060. PMID 15862915.

[12] Larsson, M., Larhammarb, D., Fredrikson, M., and Granqvist, P. (2005). "Reply to M.A. Persinger and S. A. Koren's response to Granqvist et al. "Sensed presence and mystical experiences are predicted by suggestibility, not by the application of transcranial weak magnetic fields"". *Neuroscience Letters* 380 (3): 348–350. doi:10.1016/j.neulet.2005.03.059.

[13] Tinoca,, Carlos A;; Ortiz,, João PL; (2014). "Magnetic Stimulation of the Temporal Cortex: A Partial "God Helmet" Replication Study". *Journal of Consciousness Exploration & Research* 5 (3): 234—257. Lay summary.

[14] Richards, P M; Persinger, M A; Koren, S A (1993). "Modification of activation and evaluation properties of narratives by weak complex magnetic field patterns that simulate limbic burst firing.". *The International journal of neuroscience* **71** (1-4): 71—85. Lay summary – *" subjects exposed to a computer-generated wave form, designed to simulate neuronal burst firing, generated narratives dominated by more pleasantness and less activation than a reference group.".*

[15] Persinger, M A (1993). "Vectorial cerebral hemisphericity as differential sources for the sensed presence, mystical experiences and religious conversions". *Perceptual and motor skills* **76** (3 Pt 1): 915–30. doi:10.2466/pms.1993.76.3.915. PMID 8321608.

[16] Persinger, Michael A; Healey, Faye (2002). "Experimental facilitation of the sensed presence: possible intercalation between the hemispheres induced by complex magnetic fields". *The Journal of Nervous and Mental Disease* **190** (8): 533–41. doi:10.1097/00005053-200208000-00006. PMID 12193838.

[17] Persinger, Michael A; Bureau, YR; Peredery, OP; Richards, PM (1994). "The sensed presence within experimental settings: implications for the male and female concept of self". *The Journal of psychology* **78** (3 Pt 1): 999–1009. PMID 8084725. Lay summary – *Popular article about the "sensed presence".*

[18] Persinger, M A (1989). "Geophysical variables and behavior: LV. Predicting the details of visitor experiences and the personality of experients: the temporal lobe factor". *Perceptual and motor skills* **68** (1): 55–65. doi:10.2466/pms.1989.68.1.55. PMID 2648314.

[19] Persinger, M A (1993). "Paranormal and religious beliefs may be mediated differentially by subcortical and cortical phenomenological processes of the temporal (limbic) lobes". *Perceptual and motor skills* **76** (1): 247–51. doi:10.2466/pms.1993.76.1.247. PMID 8451133.

[20] Persinger MA, MA (1996). "Feelings of past lives as expected perturbations within the neurocognitive processes that generate the sense of self: contributions from limbic lability and vectorial hemisphericity". *Perceptual and Motor Skills* **83** (3, pt 2): 1107–21. doi:10.2466/pms.1996.83.3f.1107. PMID 9017718.

[21] Persinger, M A (1992). "Enhanced incidence of "the sensed presence" in people who have learned to meditate: support for the right hemispheric intrusion hypothesis". *Perceptual and motor skills* **75** (3 Pt 2): 1308–10. doi:10.2466/PMS.75.8.1308-1310. PMID 1484802.

[22] Persinger, M A; Tiller, S G; Koren, S A (2000). "Experimental simulation of a haunt experience and elicitation of paroxysmal electroencephalographic activity by transcerebral complex magnetic fields: induction of a synthetic "ghost"?". *Perceptual and motor skills* **90** (2): 659–74. doi:10.2466/PMS.90.2.659-674. PMID 10833767.

[23] Persinger MA, MA; Makarec K., K (1992). "The feeling of a presence and verbal meaningfulness in context of temporal lobe function: factor analytic verification of the muses?". *Brain and Cognition* **20** (2): 217–26. doi:10.1016/0278-2626(92)90016-F. PMID 1449754.

[24] Persinger, M A (1991). "Religious and mystical experiences as artifacts of temporal lobe function: a general hypothesis". *Perceptual and motor skills* **57** (3 Pt 2): 1255–62. doi:10.2466/pms.1983.57.3f.1255. PMID 6664802.

[25] Booth, J. N.; Koren, S. A.; Persinger, M. A. (2008). "Increased Theta Activity in Quantitative Electroencephalographic (QEEG) Measurements During Exposure to Complex Weak Magnetic Fields". *Electromagnetic Biology and Medicine* **27** (4): 426–36. doi:10.1080/15368370802493719. PMID 19037792.

[26] Tsang, E. W.; Koren, S. A.; Persinger, M. A. (2004). "Power increases within the gamma range over the frontal and occipital regions during acute exposures to cerebrally counterclockwise rotating magnetic fields with specific derivatives of change". *International Journal of Neuroscience* **114** (9): 1183–93. doi:10.1080/00207450490475643. PMID 15370182.

[27] Healey, F; Persinger, MA; Koren, SA. (1996). "Enhanced hypnotic suggestibility following application of burst-firing magnetic fields over the right temporoparietal lobes: a replication". *International Journal of Neuroscience* **3–4** (3): 201–7. doi:10.3109/00207459609070838. PMID 9003980.

[28] Persinger, M A (2001). "The neuropsychiatry of paranormal experiences". *The Journal of neuropsychiatry and clinical neurosciences* **13** (4): 515–24. doi:10.1176/appi.neuropsych.13.4.515. PMID 11748322.

[29] Richards PM, Persinger MA, Koren SA (1993). "Modification of Activation and Evaluation Properties of Narratives by Weak Complex Magnetic Field Patterns that Simulate Limbic Burst Firing". *International Journal of Neuroscience* **71** (1-4): 71–85. doi:10.3109/00207459309000594.

[30] Persinger, M A (1999). "Increased emergence of alpha activity over the left but not the right temporal lobe within a dark acoustic chamber: differential response of the left but not the right hemisphere to transcerebral magnetic fields". *International journal of psychophysiology : official journal of the International Organization of Psychophysiology* **34** (2): 163–9. doi:10.1016/S0167-8760(99)00069-0. PMID 10576400.

[31] Booth, J N; Koren, S A; Persinger, M A (2005). "Increased feelings of the sensed presence and increased geomagnetic activity at the time of the experience during exposures to transcerebral weak complex magnetic fields". *The International journal of neuroscience* **115** (7): 1053–79. doi:10.1080/00207450590901521. PMID 16051550.

[32] Churchill, D R; Persinger, M A; Thomas, A W (1994). "Geophysical variables and behavior: LXXVII. Increased geomagnetic activity and decreased pleasantness of spontaneous narratives for percipients but not

agents". *Perceptual and motor skills* **79** (1 Pt 2): 387–92. doi:10.2466/pms.1994.79.1.387. PMID 7808872.

[33] Auvichayapat, P; Auvichayapat, N (2009). "Basic principle of transcranial magnetic stimulation". *Journal of the Medical Association of Thailand* **92** (11): 1560–6. PMID 19938752.

[34] Meli, Salvatore C.; Persinger, Michael A. (2009). "Red Light Facilitates the Sensed Presence Elicited by Application of Weak, Burst-Firing Magnetic Fields Over the Temporal Lobes". *International Journal of Neuroscience* **119** (1): 68–75. doi:10.1080/00207450802507689. PMID 19116832.

[35] Persinger, MA (2001). "The neuropsychiatry of paranormal experiences". *The Journal of Neuropsychiatry & Clinical Neurosciences* **13** (4): 515–524. doi:10.1176/appi.neuropsych.13.4.515. PMID 11748322.

[36] St-Pierre, LS, Persinger, MA (2006). "Experimental Facilitation of the Sensed Presence Is Predicted By The Specific Patterns of the Applied Magnetic Fields, Not By Suggestibility: Re-analysis of 19 Experiments". *International Journal of Neuroscience* **116** (9): 1079–1095. doi:10.1080/00207450600808800. PMID 16861170.

[37] "Email quoted here".

[38] Booth, J. N.; Persinger, M. A. (2009). "Discrete Shifts Within the Theta Band Between the Frontal and Parietal Regions of the Right Hemisphere and the Experiences of a Sensed Presence". *Journal of Neuropsychiatry* **21** (3): 279–83. doi:10.1176/appi.neuropsych.21.3.279.

[39] Video footage, see 3:04-7 and 3:32-43

[40] BBC Article

[41] Jack Hitt (Nov 1999). "This Is Your Brain on God". *Wired* **7** (11).

[42] "Email between Persinger and Granqvist November 2004".

[43] http://oldwebsite.laurentian.ca/neurosci/_news/news.htm

[44] Persinger, MA (1983). "Religious and mystical experiences as artifacts of temporal lobe function: a general hypothesis". *Perceptual and motor skills* **57** (3 Pt 2): 1255–62. doi:10.2466/pms.1983.57.3f.1255. PMID 6664802.

[45] Persinger, MA (1993). "Paranormal and religious beliefs may be mediated differentially by subcortical and cortical phenomenological processes of the temporal (limbic) lobes". *Perceptual and motor skills* **76** (1): 247–51. doi:10.2466/pms.1993.76.1.247. PMID 8451133.

[46] Craig Aaen-Stockdale (2012). "Neuroscience for the Soul". *The Psychologist* **25** (7): 520–523. Murphy claims his devices are able to modulate emotional states in addition to enhancing meditation and generating altered states. Gendle & McGrath (2012) found no significant difference in emotional responses to photographs whether the device was on or off.

[47] Gendle, MH & McGrath, MG (2012). "Can the 8-coil shakti alter subjective emotional experience? A randomized, placebo-controlled study.". *Perceptual and Motor Skills* **114** (1): 217–235. doi:10.2466/02.24.pms.114.1.217-235.

[48] Tsang EW, Koren SA, Persinger MA. (2004). "Electrophysiological and Quantitative Electroencephalographic Measurements After Treatment By Transcerebral Magnetic Fields Generated By Compact Disc Through A Computer Sound Card: The Shakti Treatment". *International Journal of Neuroscience* **114**: 1013, 1024. doi:10.1080/00207450490461323.

[49] Saroka KS, Mulligan BP, Persinger MA, Murphy, TR. (2010). "Experimental elicitation of an Out-of-Body Experience and concomitant cross-hemispheric electroencephalographic coherence". *NeuroQuantology* **8**: 466–477. doi:10.14704/nq.2010.8.4.302.

[50] French, CC., Haque, U., Bunton-Stasyshyn, R., Davis, R. (2009). "The "Haunt" project: An attempt to build a "haunted" room by manipulating complex electromagnetic fields and infrasound". *Cortex* **45** (5): 619–629. doi:10.1016/j.cortex.2007.10.011. PMID 18635163.

15.8   External links

- Neurotheology: With God in Mind — Article describing neurotheology and Dr. Persinger's work with the God helmet

- God on the Brain, BBC, 2003

Chapter 16

G-LOC

For the video game, see G-LOC: Air Battle.
Not to be confused with Glock.

G-force induced loss of consciousness (abbreviated as **G-LOC**, pronounced 'GEE-lock') is a term generally used in aerospace physiology to describe a loss of consciousness occurring from excessive and sustained g-forces draining blood away from the brain causing cerebral hypoxia. The condition is most likely to affect pilots of high performance fighter and aerobatic aircraft or astronauts but is possible on some extreme amusement park rides. G-LOC incidents have caused fatal accidents in high performance aircraft capable of sustaining high *g* for extended periods. High-G training for pilots of high performance aircraft or spacecraft often includes ground training for G-LOC in special centrifuges, with some profiles exposing pilots to 9 *g*s for a sustained period.

16.1 Effects of *g*-forces

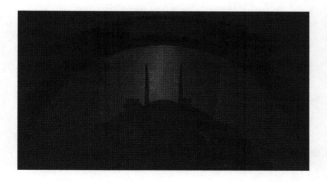

A simulation of the effects of g-forces on humans. As time progresses, tunnel vision occurs and nearly progresses to complete blackout.

Under increasing positive *g*-force, blood in the body will tend to move from the head toward the feet. For higher intensity or longer duration, this can manifest progressively as:

- Greyout - a loss of color vision

- Tunnel vision - loss of peripheral vision, retaining only the center vision

- Blackout - a complete loss of vision but retaining consciousness.

- G-LOC - where consciousness is lost.

Under negative *g*, blood pressure will increase in the head, running the risk of the dangerous condition known as redout, with too much blood pressure in the head and eyes.

Because of the high level of sensitivity that the eye's retina has to hypoxia, symptoms are usually first experienced visually. As the retinal blood pressure decreases below globe pressure (usually 10–21 mm Hg), blood flow begins to cease to the retina, first affecting perfusion farthest from the optic disc and retinal artery with progression towards central vision. Skilled pilots can use this loss of vision as their indicator that they are at maximum turn performance without losing consciousness. Recovery is usually prompt following removal of *g*-force but a period of several seconds of disorientation may occur. Absolute incapacitation is the period of time when the aircrew member is physically unconscious and averages about 12 seconds. Relative incapacitation is the period in which the consciousness has been regained, but the person is confused and remains unable to perform simple tasks. This period averages about 15 seconds. Upon regaining cerebral blood flow, the G-LOC victim usually experiences myoclonic convulsions (often called the 'funky chicken') and oftentimes full amnesia of the event is experienced.[1] Brief but vivid dreams have been reported to follow G-LOC. If G-LOC occurs at low altitude, this momentary lapse can prove fatal and even highly experienced pilots can pull straight to a G-LOC condition without first perceiving the visual onset warnings that would normally be used as the sign to back off from pulling any more *g*s.

The human body is much more tolerant of *g*-force when it is applied laterally (across the body) than when applied longitudinally (along the length of the body). Unfortunately most sustained *g*-forces incurred by pilots is applied longitudinally. This has led to experimentation with prone pilot aircraft designs which lies the pilot face down or (more successfully) reclined positions for astronauts.

16.2   Thresholds

The *g* thresholds at which these effects occur depend on the training, age and fitness of the individual. An un-trained individual not used to the *G*-straining maneuver can black out between 4 and 6 *g*, particularly if this is pulled suddenly. A trained, fit individual wearing a *g* suit and practicing the straining maneuver can, with some difficulty, sustain up to 9*g* without loss of consciousness.

16.3   See also

- G-suit
- Redout
- g-forces

16.4   References

[1] http://goflightmedicine.com/pulling-gs/

16.5   External links

- G-LOC, Could It Happen To You?

Chapter 17

Deep brain stimulation

Deep brain stimulation (**DBS**) is a neurosurgical procedure introduced in 1987,[1] involving the implantation of a medical device called a neurostimulator (sometimes referred to as a 'brain pacemaker'), which sends electrical impulses, through implanted electrodes, to specific parts of the brain (brain nucleus) for the treatment of movement and affective disorders. DBS in select brain regions has provided therapeutic benefits for otherwise-treatment-resistant movement and affective disorders such as Parkinson's disease, essential tremor, dystonia, chronic pain, major depression and obsessive–compulsive disorder (OCD).[2] Despite the long history of DBS,[3] its underlying principles and mechanisms are still not clear.[4][5] DBS directly changes brain activity in a controlled manner, its effects are reversible (unlike those of lesioning techniques), and it is one of only a few neurosurgical methods that allow blinded studies.[2]

The Food and Drug Administration (FDA) approved DBS as a treatment for essential tremor in 1997, for Parkinson's disease in 2002,[6] dystonia in 2003,[7] and OCD in 2009.[8] DBS is also used in research studies to treat chronic pain, PTSD,[9][10] and has been used to treat various affective disorders, including major depression; neither of these applications of DBS have yet been FDA-approved. While DBS has proven effective for some patients, potential for serious complications and side effects exists.

17.1 Components and placement

The deep brain stimulation system consists of three components: the implanted pulse generator (IPG), the lead, and the extension. The IPG is a battery-powered neurostimulator encased in a titanium housing, which sends electrical pulses to the brain to interfere with neural activity at the target site. The lead is a coiled wire insulated in polyurethane with four platinum iridium electrodes and is placed in one or two different nuclei of the brain. The lead is connected to the IPG by the extension, an insulated wire that runs below the skin, from the head, down the side of the neck, behind

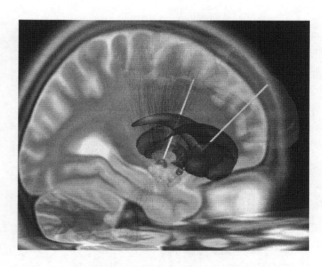

Reconstruction of DBS electrodes. Shown are the subthalamic nucleus (orange), red nucleus (green), the substantia nigra (yellow), the internal (cyan) and external pallidum (blue) and the striatum (red). Structural fibertracts traversing through this volume are visualized with color-coded fibers and cortical regions that they terminate in are visualized with translucent colors.[11]

the ear to the IPG, which is placed subcutaneously below the clavicle or, in some cases, the abdomen.[12] The IPG can be calibrated by a neurologist, nurse, or trained technician to optimize symptom suppression and control side-effects.[13]

DBS leads are placed in the brain according to the type of symptoms to be addressed. For non-Parkinsonian essential tremor, the lead is placed in the ventrointermediate nucleus (VIM) of the thalamus; for dystonia and symptoms associated with Parkinson's disease (rigidity, bradykinesia/akinesia, and tremor), the lead may be placed in either the globus pallidus internus or the subthalamic nucleus; for OCD and Depression to the nucleus accumbens; for incessant pain to the posterior thalamic region or periaqueductal gray; for Parkinson plus patients to two nuclei simultaneously, subthalamic nucleus and tegmental nucleus of pons, with the use of two pulse generators; and for epilepsy treatment to the anterion thalamic nucleus.[14]

All three components are surgically implanted inside the body. Lead implantation may take place under local anesthesia or with the patient under general anesthesia ("asleep DBS") such as for dystonia. A hole about 14 mm in diameter is drilled in the skull and the probe electrode is inserted stereotactically. During the awake procedure with local anesthesia, feedback from the patient is used to determine optimal placement of the permanent electrode. During the asleep procedure, intraoperative MRI guidance is used for direct visualization of brain tissue and device.[15] The installation of the IPG and extension leads occurs under general anesthesia.[16] The right side of the brain is stimulated to address symptoms on the left side of the body and vice versa.

17.2   Applications

17.2.1   Parkinson's disease

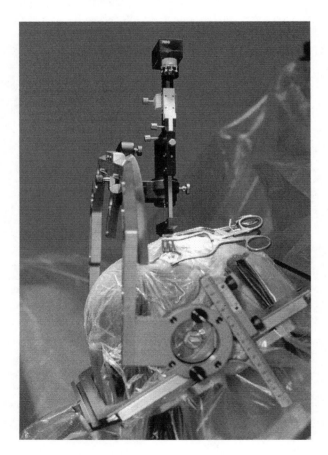

Insertion of electrode during surgery using a stereotactic frame

Parkinson's disease is a neurodegenerative disease whose primary symptoms are tremor, rigidity, bradykinesia, and postural instability.[17] DBS does not cure Parkinson's, but it can help manage some of its symptoms and subsequently improve the patient's quality of life.[18] At present, the procedure is used only for patients whose symptoms cannot be adequately controlled with medications, or whose medications have severe side-effects.[12] Its direct effect on the physiology of brain cells and neurotransmitters is currently debated, but by sending high frequency electrical impulses into specific areas of the brain it can mitigate symptoms[19] and/or directly diminish the side-effects induced by Parkinsonian medications,[20] allowing a decrease in medications, or making a medication regimen more tolerable.

There are a few sites in the brain that can be targeted to achieve differing results, so each patient must be assessed individually, and a site will be chosen based on their needs. Traditionally, the two most common sites are the subthalamic nucleus (STN) and the globus pallidus interna (GPi), but other sites, such as the caudal zona incerta and the pallidofugal fibers medial to the STN, are being evaluated and showing promise.[21]

DBS is approved in the United States by the Food and Drug Administration for the treatment of Parkinson's.[6] DBS carries the risks of major surgery, with a complication rate related to the experience of the surgical team. The major complications include hemorrhage (1–2%) and infection (3–5%).[22]

17.2.2   Chronic pain

Stimulation of the periaqueductal gray and periventricular gray for nociceptive pain, and the internal capsule, ventral posterolateral nucleus, and ventral posteromedial nucleus for neuropathic pain has produced impressive results with some patients, but results vary and appropriate patient selection is important. One study[23] of seventeen patients with intractable cancer pain found that thirteen were virtually pain-free and only four required opioid analgesics on release from hospital after the intervention. Most ultimately did resort to opioids, usually in the last few weeks of life.[24] DBS has also been applied for phantom limb pain.[25]

17.2.3   Major depression

Deep brain stimulation has been used in a small number of clinical trials to treat patients suffering from a severe form of treatment-resistant depression (TRD).[26] A number of neuroanatomical targets have been utilised for deep brain stimulation for TRD including the subgenual cingulate gyrus, posterior gyrus rectus,[27] nucleus accumbens,[28] ventral capsule/ventral striatum, inferior thalamic peduncle, and the lateral habenula.[26] A recently proposed target of DBS intervention in depression is the superolateral branch of the medial forebrain bundle (slMFB), its stimulation lead to surprisingly rapid antidepressant effects in very treatment resistant patients.[29]

The small patient numbers in the early trials of deep brain stimulation for TRD currently limit the selection of an optimal neuroanatomical target.[26] There is insufficient evidence to support DBS as a therapeutic modality for depression; however, the procedure may be an effective treatment modality in the future.[30] In fact, beneficial results have been documented in the neurosurgical literature, including a few instances in which deeply depressed patients were provided with portable stimulators for self-treatment.[31][32][33]

A systematic review of DBS for treatment-resistant depression and obsessive–compulsive disorder identified 23 cases—nine for OCD, seven for treatment-resistant depression, and one for both. It found that "about half the patients did show dramatic improvement" and that adverse events were "generally trivial" given the younger psychiatric patient population than with movements disorders.[34] The first randomized controlled study of DBS for the treatment of treatment resistant depression targeting the ventral capsule/ventral striatum area did not demonstrate a significant difference in response rates between the active and sham groups at the end of a 16-week study.[35]

DBS for treatment-resistant depression can be as effective as antidepressants, with good response and remission rates, but adverse effects and safety must be more fully evaluated. Common side-effects include "wound infection, perioperative headache, and worsening/irritable mood [and] increased suicidality".[36]

17.2.4   Tourette syndrome

Further information: Treatment of Tourette syndrome

Deep brain stimulation has been used experimentally in treating adults with severe Tourette syndrome that does not respond to conventional treatment. Despite widely publicized early successes, DBS remains a highly experimental procedure for the treatment of Tourette's, and more study is needed to determine whether long-term benefits outweigh the risks.[37][38][39][40] The procedure is well tolerated, but complications include "short battery life, abrupt symptom worsening upon cessation of stimulation, hypomanic or manic conversion, and the significant time and effort involved in optimizing stimulation parameters".[41] As of 2006, there were five reports in patients with TS; all experienced reduction in tics and the disappearance of obsessive-compulsive behaviors.[41]

The procedure is invasive and expensive, and requires long-term expert care. Benefits for severe Tourette's are not con-clusive, considering less robust effects of this surgery seen in the Netherlands. Tourette's is more common in pediatric populations, tending to remit in adulthood, so in general this would not be a recommended procedure for use on children. Because diagnosis of Tourette's is made based on a history of symptoms rather than analysis of neurological activity, it may not always be clear how to apply DBS for a particular patient. Due to concern over the use of DBS in the treatment of Tourette syndrome, the Tourette Syndrome Association (renamed in 2015 to Tourette Association of America) convened a group of experts to develop recommendations guiding the use and potential clinical trials of DBS for TS.[42]

Robertson reported that DBS had been used on 55 adults until 2011, and remained an experimental treatment at that time,[38] and recommended that the procedure "should only be conducted by experienced functional neurosurgeons operating in centres which also have a dedicated Tourette syndrome clinic".[38] According to Malone et al (2006), "Only patients with severe, debilitating, and treatment-refractory illness should be considered; while those with severe personality disorders and substance abuse problems should be excluded."[41] Du et al (2010) say that "As an invasive therapy, DBS is currently only advisable for severely affected, treatment-refractory TS adults".[39] Singer (2011) says that "pending determination of patient selection criteria and the outcome of carefully controlled clinical trials, a cautious approach is recommended".[37] Viswanathan A et al (2012) say that DBS should be used in patients with "severe functional impairment that can not be managed medically".[43]

17.2.5   Other clinical applications

Results of DBS in dystonia patients, where positive effects often appear gradually over a period of weeks to months, indicate a role of functional reorganization in at least some cases.[44] The procedure has been tested for effectiveness in people with epilepsy that is resistant to medication.[45] DBS may control or eliminate epileptic seizures with programmed or responsive stimulation.

DBS of the septal areas of patients with schizophrenia have resulted in enhanced alertness, cooperation, and euphoria.[46] Patients with narcolepsy and psychomotor seizures have also reportedly experienced euphoria and sexual thoughts with self-elicited DBS of the septal areas.[32]

17.3   Adverse effects

While DBS is helpful for some patients, there is also the potential for neuropsychiatric side-effects, including apathy, hallucinations, compulsive gambling, hypersexuality, cognitive dysfunction, and depression. However, these may be temporary and related to correct placement and calibration of the stimulator and so are potentially reversible.[47]

Because the brain can shift slightly during surgery, there is the possibility that the electrodes can become displaced or dislodged. This may cause more profound complications such as personality changes, but electrode misplacement is relatively easy to identify using CT. There may also be complications of surgery, such as bleeding within the brain. After surgery, swelling of the brain tissue, mild disorientation, and sleepiness are normal. After 2–4 weeks, there is a follow-up to remove sutures, turn on the neurostimulator, and program it.

As with all surgery there is the risk of infection and bleeding during and after a surgery. The foreign object placed may be rejected by the body or calcification of the implant might take place.

17.4   Mechanisms

The exact mechanism of action of DBS is not known.[48] There are a variety of classes of hypotheses to explain the mechanisms of DBS:[49][50]

1. Depolarization blockade: Electrical currents block the neuronal output at or near the electrode site.

2. Synaptic inhibition: This causes an indirect regulation of the neuronal output by activating axon terminals with synaptic connections to neurons near the stimulating electrode.

3. De-synchronization of abnormal oscillatory activity of neurons.

4. Antidromic activation either activating/blockading distant neurons or blockading slow axons.[5]

Deep brain stimulation represents an advance on previous treatments which involved pallidotomy (i.e., surgical ablation of the globus pallidus) or thalamotomy (i.e., surgical ablation of the thalamus).[51] Instead, a thin lead with multiple electrodes is implanted in the globus pallidus, nucleus ventralis intermedius thalami (Vim) or the subthalamic nucleus and electric pulses are used therapeutically. The lead from the implant is extended to the neurostimulator under the skin in the chest area.

17.5   See also

- Brain implant

- Electroconvulsive therapy

- Electroencephalography

- Robert Galbraith Heath

- Neuroprosthetics

- Organization for Human Brain Mapping

- Psychosurgery

- Responsive neurostimulation device (RNS)

- Transcranial magnetic stimulation

- *The Terminal Man*, a sci-fi book

- Vagus nerve stimulation

17.6   Notes

[1] "The History of Deep Brain Stimulation". *The Parkinson's Appeal for Deep Brain Stimulation.*

[2] Kringelbach ML, Jenkinson N, Owen SLF, Aziz TZ (2007). "Translational principles of deep brain stimulation". *Nature Reviews Neuroscience* **8** (8): 623–635. doi:10.1038/nrn2196. PMID 17637800.

[3] Gildenberg PL (2005). "Evolution of neuromodulation". *Stereotact Funct Neurosurg* **83** (2–3): 71–79. doi:10.1159/000086865. PMID 16006778.

[4] Hammond C., Ammari R, Bioulac B, Garcia L (2008). "Latest view on the mechanism of action of deep brain stimulation". *Mov Disord* **23**: 2111–21. doi:10.1002/mds.22120.

[5] García MR, Pearlmutter BA, Wellstead PE, Middleton RH (2013). "A Slow Axon Antidromic Blockade Hypothesis for Tremor Reduction via Deep Brain Stimulation". *PLoS ONE* **8** (9): e73456. doi:10.1371/journal.pone.0073456.

[6] U.S. Department of Health and Human Services. FDA approves implanted brain stimulator to control tremors. Retrieved February 10, 2015.

[7] 'Brain pacemaker' treats dystonia. KNBC TV, April 22, 2003. Retrieved October 18, 2006.

[8] "FDA Approves Humanitarian Device Exemption for Deep Brain Stimulator for Severe Obsessive-Compulsive Disorder". *fda.gov.*

[9] "Deep brain stimulation of the amygdala alleviates post-traumatic stress disorder symptoms in a rat model". *J Psychiatr Res* **44**: 1241–5. 2010. doi:10.1016/j.jpsychires.2010.04.022. PMID 20537659.

[10] Amygdala deep brain stimulation is superior to paroxetine treatment in a rat model of posttraumatic stress disorder / 2013

[11] Horn A, Kühn A (2015). "Lead-DBS: a toolbox for deep brain stimulation electrode localizations and visualizations". *NeuroImage* **107**: 127–35. doi:10.1016/j.neuroimage.2014.12.002. PMID 25498389.

[12] National Institute of Neurological Disorders and Stroke. Deep brain stimulation for Parkinson's Disease information page. Retrieved November 23, 2006.

[13] Volkmann J, Herzog J, Kopper F, Deuschl G (2002). "Introduction to the programming of deep brain stimulators". *Mov Disord* **17**: S181–187. doi:10.1002/mds.10162. PMID 11948775.

[14] Deep brain stimulation. Surgery Encyclopedia. Retrieved January 25, 2007.

[15] Starr PA, Martin AJ, Ostrem JL, Talke P, Levesque N, Larson PS (Mar 2010). "Subthalamic nucleus deep brain stimulator placement using high-field interventional magnetic resonance imaging and a skull-mounted aiming device: technique and application accuracy". *J Neurosurg* **112** (3): 479–90. doi:10.3171/2009.6.JNS081161. PMID 19681683.

[16] Deep Brain Stimulation, Department of Neurological Surgery, University of Pittsburgh. Retrieved May 13, 2008.

[17] Ropper (2005), p. 916

[18] Kleiner-Fisman G, Herzog J, Fisman DN, et al. (Jun 2006). "Subthalamic nucleus deep brain stimulation: summary and meta-analysis of outcomes". *Mov Disord* **21** (Suppl 14): S290–304. doi:10.1002/mds.20962. PMID 16892449.

[19] Moro E, Lang AE (Nov 2006). "Criteria for deep-brain stimulation in Parkinson's disease: review and analysis". *Expert Review of Neurotherapeutics* **6** (11): 1695–705. doi:10.1586/14737175.6.11.1695. PMID 17144783.

[20] Apetauerova D, Ryan RK, Ro SI, Arle J, et al. (Aug 2006). "End of day dyskinesia in advanced Parkinson's disease can be eliminated by bilateral subthalamic nucleus or globus pallidus deep brain stimulation". *Movement Disorders* **21** (8): 1277–9. doi:10.1002/mds.20896. PMID 16637040.

[21] Plaha P, Ben-Shlomo Y, Patel NK, Gill SS (July 2006). "Stimulation of the caudal zona incerta is superior to stimulation of the subthalamic nucleus in improving contralateral parkinsonism". *Brain* **129** (Pt 7): 1732–47. doi:10.1093/brain/awl127. PMID 16720681.

[22] Doshi PK (April 2011). "Long-term surgical and hardware-related complications of deep brain stimulation". *Stereotact Funct Neurosurg* **89** (2): 89–95. doi:10.1159/000323372. PMID 21293168.

[23] Young RF & Brechner T. Electrical stimulation of the brain for relief of intractable pain due to cancer. *Cancer.* 1986;57:1266–72.

[24] Johnson MI, Oxberry SG & Robb K. Stimulation-induced analgesia. In: Sykes N, Bennett MI & Yuan C-S. *Clinical pain management: Cancer pain.* 2nd ed. London: Hodder Arnold; 2008. ISBN 978-0-340-94007-5. p. 235–250.

[25] Kringelbach Morten L, et al. (2007). "Deep brain stimulation for chronic pain investigated with magnetoencephalography". *NeuroReport* **18** (3): 223–228. doi:10.1097/wnr.0b013e328010dc3d.

[26] Anderson RJ, Frye MA, Abulseoud OA, et al. (September 2012). "Deep brain stimulation for treatment-resistant depression: efficacy, safety and mechanisms of action". *Neurosci Biobehav Rev* **36** (8): 1920–33. doi:10.1016/j.neubiorev.2012.06.001. PMID 22721950.

[27] Accolla, Ettore A.; Aust, Sabine; Merkl, Angela; Schneider, Gerd-Helde; Kühn, Andrea A.; Bajbouj, Malek; Draganski, Bogdan. "Deep brain stimulation of the posterior gyrus rectus region for treatment resistant depression". *Journal of Affective Disorders* **194**: 33–37. doi:10.1016/j.jad.2016.01.022.

[28] Schlaepfer, TE; et al. (2008). "Deep brain stimulation to reward circuitry alleviates anhedonia in refractory major depression". *Neuropsychopharmacology* **33** (2): 368–77. doi:10.1038/sj.npp.1301408. PMID 17429407.

[29] Schlaepfer, TE; et al. (2013). "Rapid effects of deep brain stimulation for treatment-resistant major depression". *Biological Psychiatry* **73** (12): 1204–12. doi:10.1016/j.biopsych.2013.01.034. PMID 23562618.

[30] *Curr Opin Psychiatry.* 2009 May;22(3):306–11

[31] Delgado, Jose (1986). *Physical Control of the Mind: Toward a Psychocivilized Society.* New York: Harper and Row.

[32] Faria, MA (2013). "Violence, mental illness, and the brain – A brief history of psychosurgery: Part 3 – From deep brain stimulation to amygdalotomy for violence behavior, seizures, and pathological aggression in humans". *Surg Neurol Int 2013;4(1):91-91* **4**: 91. doi:10.4103/2152-7806.115162. PMC 3740620. PMID 23956934.

[33] Robison, RA; Taghva A; Liu CY; Apuzzo ML (2012). "Surgery of the mind, mood and conscious state: an idea in evolution". *World Neurosurg* **77**: 662–686. doi:10.1016/j.wneu.2012.03.005.

[34] Lakhan SE, Callaway H (Mar 2010). "Deep brain stimulation for obsessive-compulsive disorder and treatment-resistant depression: systematic review". *BMC Research Notes* **3** (1): 60. doi:10.1186/1756-0500-3-60. PMC 2838907. PMID 20202203.

[35] "A Randomized Sham-Controlled Trial of Deep Brain Stimulation of the Ventral Capsule/Ventral Striatum for Chronic Treatment-Resistant Depression". *Biological Psychiatry* **78**: 240–248. doi:10.1016/j.biopsych.2014.11.023.

doi:10.1002/1097-0142(19860315)57:6<1266::aid-cncr2820570634>3.0.co;2-q. PMID 3484665.

[36] Moreines JL, McClintock SM, Holtzheimer PE (Jan 2011). "Neuropsychologic effects of neuromodulation techniques for treatment-resistant depression: a review". *Brain Stimul* **4** (1): 17–27. doi:10.1016/j.brs.2010.01.005. PMC 3023999. PMID 21255751.

[37] Singer HS (Mar 2005). "Tourette syndrome and other tic disorders". *Handb Clin Neurol.* 2011;100:641–57. DOI 10.1016/B978-0-444-52014-2.00046-X PMID 21496613. Also see Singer HS. "Tourette's syndrome: from behaviour to biology"". *Lancet Neurol* **4** (3): 149–59. doi:10.1016/S1474-4422(05)01012-4. PMID 15721825.

[38] Robertson MM (February 2011). "Gilles de la Tourette syndrome: the complexities of phenotype and treatment". *Br J Hosp Med (Lond)* **72** (2): 100–7. PMID 21378617.

[39] Du JC, Chiu TF, Lee KM, et al. (Oct 2010). "Tourette syndrome in children: an updated review". *Pediatr Neonatol* **51** (5): 255–64. doi:10.1016/S1875-9572(10)60050-2. PMID 20951354.

[40] Tourette Syndrome Association. Statement: Deep Brain Stimulation and Tourette Syndrome. Retrieved November 22, 2005.

[41] Malone DA Jr, Pandya MM (2006). "Behavioral neurosurgery". *Adv Neurol* **99**: 241–7. PMID 16536372.

[42] Mink JW, Walkup J, Frey KA, et al. (November 2006). "(November 2006). "Patient selection and assessment recommendations for deep brain stimulation in Tourette syndrome"". *Mov Disord* **21** (11): 1831–8. doi:10.1002/mds.21039. PMID 16991144.

[43] Viswanathan A, Jimenez-Shahed J, Baizabal Carvallo JF, Jankovic J (2012). "Deep brain stimulation for Tourette syndrome: target selection". *Stereotact Funct Neurosurg* **90** (4): 213–24. doi:10.1159/000337776. PMID 22699684.

[44] Krauss JK (2002). "Deep brain stimulation for dystonia in adults. Overview and developments". *Stereotactic and Functional Neurosurgery* **78** (3–4): 168–182. doi:10.1159/000068963. PMID 12652041.

[45] Wu C, Sharan AD (Jan–Feb 2013). "Neurostimulation for the treatment of epilepsy: a review of current surgical interventions". *Neuromodulation* **16** (1): 10–24. doi:10.1111/j.1525-1403.2012.00501.x. PMID 22947069.

[46] "Pleasure and brain activity in man: Deep and surface electroencephalograms during orgasm." Author Dr. Robert G. Health . Journal of Nervous and Mental Disease, Vol 154(1), Jan 1972, 3-18. DOI 10.1097/00005053-197201000-00002

[47] Burn DJ, Tröster AI (September 2004). "Neuropsychiatric complications of medical and surgical therapies for Parkinson's disease". *J Geriatr Psychiatry Neurol* **17** (3): 172–80. doi:10.1177/0891988704267466. PMID 15312281.

[48] Mogilner A.Y., Benabid A.L., Rezai A.R. (2004). "Chronic Therapeutic Brain Stimulation: History, Current Clinical Indications, and Future Prospects". In Markov, Marko; Paul J. Rosch. *Bioelectromagnetic medicine.* New York, N.Y: Marcel Dekker. pp. 133–51. ISBN 0-8247-4700-3.

[49] McIntyre CC, Thakor NV (2002). "Uncovering the mechanisms of deep brain stimulation for Parkinson's disease through functional imaging, neural recording, and neural modeling". *Crit Rev Biomed Eng* **30** (4-6): 249–81. doi:10.1615/critrevbiomedeng.v30.i456.20. PMID 12739751.

[50] Herrington TM, Cheng JJ, Eskandar EM (2016). "Mechanisms of deep brain stimulation". *J. Neurophysiol.* **115** (4-6): 1. doi:10.1152/jn.00281.2015. PMID 26510756.

[51] Machado A, Rezai AR, Kopell BH, Gross RE, Sharan AD, Benabid AL (June 2006). "Deep brain stimulation for Parkinson's disease: surgical technique and perioperative management". *Mov. Disord.* **21** (Suppl 14): S247–58. doi:10.1002/mds.2095910.1002/mds.20959. PMID 16810722.

17.7   References

- Appleby BS, Duggan PS, Regenberg A, Rabins PV (2007). "Psychiatric and neuropsychiatric adverse events associated with deep brain stimulation: A meta-analysis of ten years' experience". *Movement Disorders* **22** (12): 1722–1728. doi:10.1002/mds.21551. PMID 17721929.

- Gildenberg Philip L (2005). "Evolution of neuromodulation". *Stereotact Funct Neurosurg* **83** (2–3): 71–79. doi:10.1159/000086865. PMID 16006778.

- Kringelbach ML, Jenkinson N, Owen SLF, Aziz TZ (2007). "Translational principles of deep brain stimulation". *Nature Reviews Neuroscience* **8** (8): 623–635. doi:10.1038/nrn2196. PMID 17637800.

- Schlaepfer TE, Bewernick BH, Kayser S, Hurlemann R, Coenen VA (2014). "Deep Brain Stimulation of the Human Reward System for Major Depression-Rationale, Outcomes and Outlook". *Neuropsychopharmacology* **39** (6): 1303–1314. doi:10.3109/15622975.2013.869619. PMID 24506290.

- Diamond A, Shahed J, Azher S, Dat-Vuong K, Jankovic J (May 2006). "Globus pallidus deep brain stimulation in dystonia". *Mov. Disord.* **21** (5): 692–5. doi:10.1002/mds.20767. PMID 16342255.

- Richter E.O., Lozano A.M. (2004). "Deep Brain Stimulation for Parkinson's Disease in Movement Disorders". In Markov, Marko; Paul J. Rosch. *Bioelectromagnetic medicine*. New York, N.Y: Marcel Dekker. pp. 265–76. ISBN 0-8247-4700-3.

17.8 External links

- **Video:** Deep brain stimulation to treat Parkinson's disease

- **Video:** Deep brain stimulation therapy for Parkinson's disease

- The Perils of Deep Brain Stimulation for Depression. Author Danielle Egan. September 24, 2015.

Chapter 18

Consciousness after death

This article is about the neuroscience of consciousness and death. For beliefs about life after death, see Afterlife.

Consciousness after death is a common theme in society

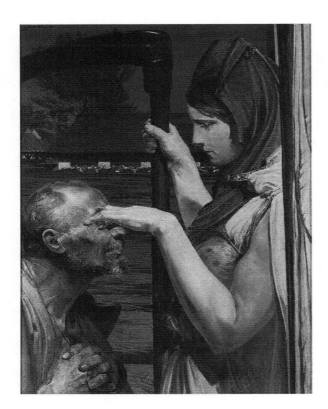

Śmierć ("Death"), a 1902 painting by Jacek Malczewski

and culture in the context of life after death. Scientific research has established that the mind and consciousness are closely connected with the physiological functioning of the brain, the cessation of which defines brain death. However, many people believe in some form of life after death, which is a feature of many religions.

18.1 Neuroscience

Neuroscience is a large interdisciplinary field founded on the premise that all of behavior and all of the cognitive processes that constitute the mind have their origin in the structure and function of the nervous system, especially in the brain. According to this view, the mind can be regarded as a set of operations carried out by the brain.[1][2][3][4][5]

There are multiple lines of evidence that support this view. They are here briefly summarized along with some examples.

- **Neuroanatomical correlates**: In the field of neuroimaging, neuroscientists can use various functional neuroimaging methods to measure an aspect of brain function that correlates with a particular mental state or process.

- **Experimental manipulations**: Neuroimaging (correlational) studies cannot determine whether neural activity plays a causal role in the occurrence of mental processes (correlation does not imply causation) and they cannot determine if the neural activity is either necessary or sufficient for such processes to occur. Identification of causation and necessary and sufficient conditions requires explicit experimental manipulation of that activity. If manipulation of brain activity changes consciousness, then a causal role for that brain activity can be inferred.[6][7] Two of the most common types of manipulation experiments are loss-of-function and gain-of-function experiments. In a loss-of-function (also called "necessity") experiment, a part of the nervous system is diminished or removed in an attempt to determine if it is necessary for a certain process to occur, and in a gain-of-function (also called "sufficiency") experiment, an aspect of the nervous system is increased relative to normal.[8] Manipulations of brain activity can be performed in several ways:

Pharmacological **manipulation**

using various drugs which alter neural activity by interfering with neurotransmission, resulting in alterations in perception, mood, consciousness, cognition, and behavior. Psychoactive drugs are divided into different groups according to their pharmacological effects; euphoriants which tend to induce feelings of euphoria, stimulants that induce temporary improvements in either mental or physical functions, depressants that depress or reduce arousal or stimulation and hallucinogens which can cause hallucinations, perception anomalies, and other substantial subjective changes in thoughts, emotion, and consciousness.

Electrical and magnetical stimulations using various electrical methods and techniques like transcranial magnetic stimulation. In a comprehensive review of electrical brain stimulation (EBS) results obtained from the last 100 years neuroscientist Aslihan Selimbeyoglu and neurologist Josef Parvizi compiled a list of many different subjective experiential phenomena and behavioral changes that can be caused by electrical stimulation of the cerebral cortex or subcortical nuclei in awake and conscious human subjects.[9]

Optogenetic manipulation where light is used to control neurons which have been genetically sensitised to light.

- **Symptoms of brain damage**: Examining case studies (like the case of Phineas Gage) and lesion studies are the only sources of knowledge regarding what happens to the mind when the brain is damaged. Various symptoms have been documented.[10][11]

- **Mental development/brain development correlation**: The brain grows and develops in an intricately orchestrated sequence of stages, and this development is correlated with the development of various mental capabilities.[12][13][14] Impairments in the growth and development of the brain also result in various neurodevelopmental disorders.

18.2   Death

Main article: Death
See also: Neural correlates of consciousness and disorders of consciousness

Death was once defined as the cessation of heartbeat (cardiac arrest) and of breathing, but the development of CPR and prompt defibrillation have rendered that definition inadequate because breathing and heartbeat can sometimes be restarted. Events that were causally linked to death in the past no longer kill in all circumstances; without a functioning heart or lungs, life can sometimes be sustained with a combination of life support devices, organ transplants and artificial pacemakers.

It may also be suggested that it is not possible for oneself or one's consciousness to know, understand, define, or conclude that oneself is already dead, especially when volition and perception - as well as speech and action are generally accepted as integral and a prerequisite of knowledge and thought, hence death in an absolute sense is usually declared by a second party other than the deceased. Today, where a definition of the moment of death is required, doctors and coroners usually turn to "brain death" or "biological death" to define a person as being dead; brain death being defined as the complete and irreversible loss of brain function (including involuntary activity necessary to sustain life).[15][16][17][18]

According to the current neuroscientific view, consciousness fails to survive brain death and, along with all other mental functions, is irrecoverably lost.[19]

18.3   Near-death experiences (NDEs)

Main article: Near-death experiences

A near-death experience (NDE) refers to a personal experience associated with impending death, encompassing multiple possible sensations including detachment from the body, feelings of levitation, total serenity, security, warmth, the experience of absolute dissolution, and the presence of a light.[20][21]

Explanatory models for the NDE can be divided into several broad categories, including psychological, physiological, and transcendental explanations.[22][23][24] Research from neuroscience considers the NDE to be a hallucination caused by various neurological factors such as cerebral anoxia, hypercarbia, abnormal activity in the temporal lobes or brain damage,[25] while some NDE researchers in the field of near-death studies advocate for a transcendental explanation.[26][27]

18.4 See also

- Biogerontology, the science of biological aging
- Death anxiety (psychology)
- Disorders of consciousness, including brain death
- Dualism (philosophy of mind)
- Eternal oblivion
- Information-theoretic death
- Life extension
- Neural correlates of consciousness
- Self
- Senescence, biological aging
- Thanatophobia, fear of death
- Unconsciousness

18.5 References

[1] Kandel, ER; Schwartz JH; Jessell TM; Siegelbaum SA; Hudspeth AJ. "Principles of Neural Science, Fifth Edition" (2012).

[2] Squire, L. et al. "Fundamental Neuroscience, 4th edition" (2012).

[3] O. Carter Snead. "Neuroimaging and the "Complexity" of Capital Punishment" (2007).

[4] Eric R. Kandel, M.D. "A New Intellectual Framework for Psychiatry" (1998).

[5] "Neuroscience Core Concepts: The Essential Principles of Neuroscience". *BrainFacts.org: Explore the Brain and Mind.*

[6] Farah, Martha J.; Murphy, Nancey (February 2009). "Neuroscience and the Soul". *Science* **323** (5918): 1168. doi:10.1126/science.323.5918.1168a. Retrieved 20 November 2012.

[7] Max Velmans, Susan Schneider. "The Blackwell Companion to Consciousness" (2008). p. 560.

[8] Matt Carter, Jennifer C. Shieh. "Guide to Research Techniques in Neuroscience" (2009).

[9] Aslihan Selimbeyoglu, Josef Parvizi. "Electrical stimulation of the human brain: perceptual and behavioral phenomena reported in the old and new literature" (2010). Frontiers in Human Neuroscience.

[10] "Severe TBI Symptoms"

[11] "Symptoms of Brain Injury"

[12] "Cognitive Development and Aging: A Life Span Perspective"

[13] "Adolescent Brains Are A Work In Progress"

[14] "Blossoming brains"

[15] "Brain death". *Encyclopedia of Death and Dying.* Retrieved 25 March 2014.

[16] Young, G Bryan. "Diagnosis of brain death". *UpToDate.* Retrieved 25 March 2014.

[17] Goila, A.; Pawar, M. (2009). "The diagnosis of brain death". *Indian Journal of Critical Care Medicine* **13** (1): 7–11. doi:10.4103/0972-5229.53108. PMC 2772257. PMID 19881172.

[18] Machado, C. (2010). "Diagnosis of brain death". *Neurology International* **2**. doi:10.4081/ni.2010.e2.

[19] Laureys, Steven; Tononi, Giulio. (2009). *The Neurology of Consciousness: Cognitive Neuroscience and Neuropathology.* Academic Press. p. 20. ISBN 978-0-12-374168-4

[20] Roberts, Glenn; Owen, John. (1988). *The Near-Death Experience.* British Journal of Psychiatry 153: 607-617.

[21] Britton, Willoughby B. and Richard R. Bootzin. (2004). *Near-Death Experiences and the Temporal Lobe.* Psychological Science. Vol. 15, No. 4. pp. 254-258.

[22] Linda J. Griffith. "Near-Death Experiences and Psychotherapy" (2009).

[23] Mauro, James. Bright lights, big mystery. Psychology Today, July 1992

[24] Vanhaudenhuyse, A; Thonnard, M; Laureys, S. "Towards a Neuro-scientific Explanation of Near-death Experiences?" (2009).

[25] Olaf Blanke, Sebastian Dieguez. "Leaving Body and Life Behind: Out-of-Body and Near-Death Experience" (2009).

[26] Sam Parnia, Peter Fenwick. "Near death experiences in cardiac arrest: visions of a dying brain or visions of a new science of consciousness" (2001).

[27] Murray, Craig D. (2009). *Psychological Scientific Perspectives on Out-of-Body and Near-Death Experiences.* New York: Nova Science Publishers. pp. 187–203. ISBN 978-1-60741-705-7.

18.6 Further reading

- Martin, Michael; Augustine, Keith. (2015). *The Myth of an Afterlife: The Case against Life After Death.* Rowman & Littlefield. ISBN 978-0-8108-8677-3

- Laureys, Steven; Tononi, Giulio. (2009). *The Neurology of Consciousness: Cognitive Neuroscience and Neuropathology.* Academic Press. ISBN 978-0-12-374168-4

- "What Happens to Consciousness When We Die". *Scientific American.*

- "Death Is Not Final". *Intelligence Squared.*

Chapter 19

Monism

For the academic journal, see The Monist.

Monism is the view that attributes oneness or single-

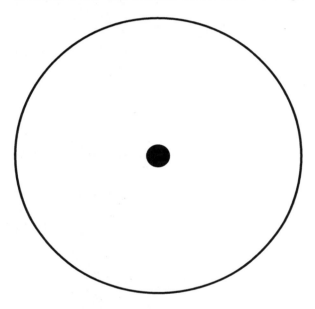

The circled dot was used by the Pythagoreans and later Greeks to represent the first metaphysical being, the Monad or The Absolute.

ness (Greek:μόνος) to a concept (e.g., existence). *Substance monism* is the philosophical view that a variety of existing things can be explained in terms of a single reality or substance.[1] Another definition states that all existing things go back to a source that is distinct from them (e.g., in Neoplatonism everything is derived from The One).[2] This is often termed *priority monism*, and is the view that only one thing is ontologically basic or prior to everything else.

Another distinction is the difference between substance and existence monism, or *stuff monism* and *thing monism*.[3] Substance monism posits that only one kind of stuff (e.g., matter or mind) exists, although many things may be made out of this stuff. Existence monism posits that, strictly speaking, there exists only a single thing (e.g., the universe), which can only be artificially and arbitrarily divided into many things.

19.1 Definitions

There are two sorts of definitions for monism:

1. The wide definition: a philosophy is monistic if it postulates unity of origin of all things; all existing things go back to a source that is distinct from them.[2]

2. The restricted definition: this requires not only unity of origin but also unity of substance and essence.[2]

Although the term "monism" originated in Western philosophy to typify positions in the mind–body problem, it has also been used to typify religious traditions. In modern Hinduism, the term "absolute monism" is being used for Advaita Vedanta.[4][5]

19.2 History

The term "monism" was introduced in the 18th century by Christian von Wolff[6] in his work *Logic* (1728),[7] to designate types of philosophical thought in which the attempt was made to eliminate the dichotomy of body and mind[8] and explain all phenomena by one unifying principle, or as manifestations of a single substance.[6]

The mind–body problem in philosophy examines the relationship between mind and matter, and in particular the relationship between consciousness and the brain. The problem was addressed by René Descartes in the 17th century, resulting in Cartesian dualism, and by pre-Aristotelian philosophers,[9][10] in Avicennian philosophy,[11] and in earlier Asian and more specifically Indian traditions.

It was later also applied to the theory of absolute identity set forth by Hegel and Schelling.[12] Thereafter the term was more broadly used, for any theory postulating a unifying principle.[12] The opponent thesis of dualism also was broadened, to include pluralism.[12] According to Urmson, as a result of this extended use, the term is "systematically ambiguous".[12]

According to Jonathan Schaffer, monism lost popularity due to the emergence of Analytic philosophy in the early twentieth century, which revolted against the neo-Hegelians. Carnap and Ayer, who were strong proponents of positivism, "ridiculed the whole question as incoherent mysticism".[13]

The mind–body problem has reemerged in social psychology and related fields, with the interest in mind–body interaction[14] and the rejection of Cartesian mind–body dualism in the *identity thesis*, a modern form of monism.[15] Monism is also still relevant to the philosophy of mind,[12] where various positions are defended.[16][17]

19.3 Philosophical monism

19.3.1 Types of monism

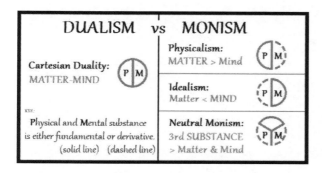

A diagram with neutral monism compared to Cartesian dualism, physicalism and idealism.

Different types of monism include:[12][18]

1. Substance monism, "the view that the apparent plurality of substances is due to different states or appearances of a single substance"[12]

2. Attributive monism, "the view that whatever the number of substances, they are of a single ultimate kind"[12]

3. Partial monism, "within a given realm of being (however many there may be) there is only one substance"[12]

4. Existence monism, "the view that there is only one concrete object token (The One, "Tò "Ev" or the Monad)"[19]

5. Priority monism, "the whole is prior to its parts" or "the world has parts, but the parts are dependent fragments of an integrated whole"[18]

6. Property monism, "the view that all properties are of a single type (e.g., only physical properties exist)"

7. Genus monism, "the doctrine that there is a highest category; e.g., being" [18]

Views contrasting with monism are:

- Metaphysical dualism, which asserts that there are two ultimately irreconcilable substances or realities such as Good and Evil, for example, Manichaeism,[2]

- Metaphysical pluralism, which asserts three or more fundamental substances or realities.[2]

- Nihilism, negates any of the above categories (substances, properties, concrete objects, etc.).

Monism in modern philosophy of mind can be divided into three broad categories:

1. Idealist, phenomenalism, or mentalistic monism, which holds that only mind or spirit is real[2]

2. Neutral monism, which holds that one sort of thing fundamentally exists,[20] to which both the mental and the physical can be reduced[8]

3. Material monism (also called Physicalism and materialism), which holds that only the physical is real, and that the mental or spiritual can be reduced to the physical[2][20]

   a. Eliminative Materialism, according to which everything is physical and mental things do not exist[20]

   b. Reductive physicalism, according to which mental things do exist and are a kind of physical thing[20][note 1]

Certain positions do not fit easily into the above categories, such as functionalism, anomalous monism, and reflexive monism. Moreover, they do not define the meaning of "real".

19.3.2 Monistic philosophers

Pre-Socratic

While the lack of information makes it difficult in some cases to be sure of the details, the following pre-Socratic philosophers thought in monistic terms:[21]

- Thales: Water.

- Anaximander: Apeiron (meaning 'the undefined infinite'). Reality is some, one thing, but we cannot know what.

- Anaximenes: Air.

- Heraclitus: Change, symbolized by fire (in that everything is in constant flux).

- Parmenides argued that Being or Reality is an unmoving perfect sphere, unchanging, undivided.[22]

Post-Socrates

- Neopythagorians such as Apollonius of Tyana centered their cosmologies on the Monad or One.

- Stoics taught that there is only one substance, identified as God.

- Middle Platonism under such works as Numenius taught that the Universe emanates from the Monad or One.

- Neoplatonism is Monistic. Plotinus taught that there was an ineffable transcendent god, 'The One,' of which subsequent realities were emanations. From The One emanates the Divine Mind (Nous), the Cosmic Soul (Psyche), and the World (Cosmos).

Modern

- Giordano Bruno[23][24]

- Baruch de Spinoza

- Gottfried Wilhelm Leibniz

- Alexander Bogdanov

- Hegel

- F. H. Bradley

- Schopenhauer

- Ernst Haeckel[25][26]

- Jonathan Schaffer

19.4 Religious monism

19.4.1 Pantheism

Main article: Pantheism

Pantheism is the belief that everything composes an all-encompassing, immanent God,[27] or that the universe (or nature) is identical with divinity.[28] Pantheists thus do not believe in a personal or anthropomorphic god, but believe that interpretations of the term differ.

Pantheism was popularized in the modern era as both a theology and philosophy based on the work of the 17th century philosopher Baruch Spinoza,[29] whose *Ethics* was an answer to Descartes' famous dualist theory that the body and spirit are separate.[30] Spinoza held that the two are the same, and this monism is a fundamental quality of his philosophy. He was described as a "God-intoxicated man," and used the word God to describe the unity of all substance.[30] Although the term pantheism was not coined until after his death, Spinoza is regarded as its most celebrated advocate.[31]

H.P. Owen (1971: 65) claimed that

> Pantheists are 'monists'...they believe that there is only one Being, and that all other forms of reality are either modes (or appearances) of it or identical with it.[32]

Pantheism is closely related to monism, as pantheists too believe all of reality is one substance, called Universe, God or Nature. Panentheism, a slightly different concept (explained below), however is dualistic.[33] Some of the most famous pantheists are the Stoics, Giordano Bruno and Spinoza.

19.4.2 Panentheism

Main article: Panentheism

Panentheism (from Greek πᾶν (pân) "all"; ἐν (en) "in"; and θεός (theós) "God"; "all-in-God") is a belief system that posits that the divine (be it a monotheistic God, polytheistic gods, or an eternal cosmic animating force) interpenetrates every part of nature, but is not one with nature. Panentheism differentiates itself from pantheism, which holds that the divine is synonymous with the universe.[34]

In panentheism, there are two types of substance, "pan" the universe and God. The universe and the divine are not ontologically equivalent. God is viewed as the eternal animating force within the universe. In some forms of panentheism, the cosmos exists within God, who in turn "transcends", "pervades" or is "in" the cosmos.

While pantheism asserts that 'All is God', panentheism claims that God animates all of the universe, and also transcends the universe. In addition, some forms indicate that the universe is contained within God,[34] like in the concept of Tzimtzum. Much Hindu thought is highly characterized by panentheism and pantheism.[35][36] Hasidic Judaism merges the elite ideal of nullification to paradoxical transcendent Divine Panentheism, through intellectual articulation of inner dimensions of Kabbalah, with the populist emphasis on the panentheistic Divine immanence in everything and deeds of kindness.

Paul Tillich has argued for such a concept within Christian theology, as has liberal biblical scholar Marcus Borg and mystical theologian Matthew Fox, an Episcopal priest.[note 2]

19.4.3 Pandeism

Main article: Pandeism

Pandeism or pan-deism (from Ancient Greek: πᾶν *pan* "all" and Latin: *deus* meaning "god" in the sense of deism), is a term describing beliefs coherently incorporating or mixing logically reconcilable elements of pantheism (that "God", or a metaphysically equivalent creator deity, is identical to Nature) and classical deism (that the creator-god who designed the universe no longer exists in a status where it can be reached, and can instead be confirmed only by reason). It is therefore most particularly the belief that the creator of the universe actually became the universe, and so ceased to exist as a separate entity.[37][38]

Through this synergy pandeism claims to answer primary objections to deism (why would God create and then not interact with the universe?) and to pantheism (how did the universe originate and what is its purpose?).

19.4.4 Asian traditions

Characteristics

The central problem in Asian (religious) philosophy is not the body-mind problem, but the search for an unchanging Real or Absolute beyond the world of appearances and changing phenomena,[39] and the search for liberation from dukkha and the liberation from the cycle of rebirth.[40] In Hinduism, substance-ontology prevails, seeing Brahman as the unchanging real beyond the world of appearances.[41] In Buddhism process ontology is prevalent,[41] seeing reality as empty of an unchanging essence.[42][43]

Characteristic for various Asian religions is the discernment of levels of truth,[44] an emphasis on intuitive-experiential understanding of the Absolute[45][46][47][48] such as jnana,

bodhi and kensho, and an emphasis on the integration of these levels of truth and its understanding.[49][50]

Hinduism

Main articles: Hinduism, Hindu philosophy and Hindu denominations

Vedas   Main article: Vedas

The Vedas are a large body of texts originating in ancient India. The texts constitute the oldest layer of Sanskrit literature and the oldest scriptures of Hinduism.[51]

According to Sehgal, "the Vedas and the Upanishads preach and propagate neither pantheism nor polytheism but monotheism and monism".[52] There are many Gods, but they represent different aspects of the same Reality.[53] Monism and monotheism are found intertwined. In many passages ultimate Reality is represented as immanent, while in other passages ultimate Reality is represented as transcendent.[54] Monism sees Brahma as the ultimate Reality, while monotheism represents the personal form Brahman.[54]

Jeaneane D. Fowler too discerns a "metaphysical monotheism"[55] in the Vedas. The Vedas contain sparse monism. The Nasadiya Sukta of the Rigveda speaks of the One being-non-being that 'breathed without breath'. The manifest cosmos cannot be equated with it, "for "That" is a limitless, indescribable, absolute principle that can exist independently of it - otherwise it cannot be the Source of it."[56] It is the closest the Vedas come to monism,[56] but Fowler argues that this cannot be called a "superpersonal monism",[56] nor "the quintessence of monistic thought",[56] because it is "more expressive of a panentheistic, totally transcendent entity that can become manifest by its own power. It exists in itself, unmanifest, but with the potential for all manifestations of the cosmos".[56]

Vedanta   Main article: Vedanta

Vedanta is the inquiry into and systematisation of the Vedas and Upanishads, to harmonise the various and contrasting ideas that can be found in those texts. Within Vedanta, different schools exist:[57]

- Advaita Vedanta, absolute monism, of which Adi Shankara is the best-known representative;[58]

Adi Shankara with Disciples, *by Raja Ravi Varma (1904)*

- Vishishtadvaita, qualified monism, is from the school of Ramanuja;[59]

- Shuddhadvaita, in-essence monism, is the school of Vallabha;

- Dvaitadvaita, differential monism, is a school founded by Nimbarka;

- Dvaita, dualism, is a school founded by Madhvacharya is probably the only Vedantic System that is opposed to all types of monism. It believes that God is eternally different from souls and matter in both form and essence.

Advaita Vedanta   Main article: Advaita Vedanta

Monism is most clearly identified in Advaita Vedanta,[60] though Renard points out that this may be a western interpretation, bypassing the intuitive understanding of a nondual reality.[61]

In Advaita Vedanta, Brahman is the eternal, unchanging, infinite, immanent, and transcendent reality which is the Divine Ground of all matter, energy, time, space, being, and everything beyond in this Universe. The nature of Brah-

man is described as transpersonal, personal and impersonal by different philosophical schools.[62]

Advaita Vedanta gives an elaborate path to attain moksha. It entails more than self-inquiry or bare insight into one's real nature. Practice, especially Jnana Yoga, is needed to "destroy one's tendencies (vAasanA-s)" before real insight can be attained.[63]

Advaita took over from the Madhyamika the idea of levels of reality.[64] Usually two levels are being mentioned,[65] but Shankara uses sublation as the criterion to postulate an ontological hierarchy of three levels:[66][67]

- Pāramārthika (paramartha, absolute), the absolute level, "which is absolutely real and into which both other reality levels can be resolved".[67] This experience can't be sublated by any other experience.[66]

- Vyāvahārika (vyavahara), or samvriti-saya[65] (empirical or pragmatical), "our world of experience, the phenomenal world that we handle every day when we are awake".[67] It is the level in which both *jiva* (living creatures or individual souls) and *Iswara* are true; here, the material world is also true.

- Prāthibhāsika (pratibhasika, apparent reality, unreality), "reality based on imagination alone".[67] It is the level in which appearances are actually false, like the illusion of a snake over a rope, or a dream.

Vaishnava   Main article: Vaishnavism

All Vaishnava schools are panentheistic and view the universe as part of Krishna or Narayana, but see a plurality of souls and substances within Brahman. Monistic theism, which includes the concept of a personal god as a universal, omnipotent Supreme Being who is both immanent and transcendent, is prevalent within many other schools of Hinduism as well.

Tantra   Main article: Tantra

Tantra sees the Divine as both immanent and transcendent. The Divine can be found in the concrete world. Practices are aimed at transforming the passions, instead of transcending them.

Modern Hinduism   Main article: Hindu reform movements

The colonisation of India by the British had a major impact on Hindu society.[68] In response, leading Hindu intellectuals started to study western culture and philosophy, integrating several western notions into Hinduism.[68] This modernised Hinduism, at its turn, has gained popularity in the west.[45]

A major role was played in the 19th century by Swami Vivekananda in the revival of Hinduism,[69] and the spread of Advaita Vedanta to the west via the Ramakrishna Mission. His interpretation of Advaita Vedanta has been called Neo-Vedanta.[70] In Advaita, Shankara suggests meditation and Nirvikalpa Samadhi are means to gain knowledge of the already existing unity of *Brahman* and *Atman*,[71] not the highest goal itself:

> [Y]oga is a meditative exercise of withdrawal from the particular and identification with the universal, leading to contemplation of oneself as the most universal, namely, Consciousness. This approach is different from the classical Yoga of complete thought suppression.[71]

Vivekananda, according to Gavin Flood, was "a figure of great importance in the development of a modern Hindu self-understanding and in formulating the West's view of Hinduism."[72] Central to his philosophy is the idea that the divine exists in all beings, that all human beings can achieve union with this "innate divinity",[73] and that seeing this divine as the essence of others will further love and social harmony.[73] According to Vivekananda, there is an essential unity to Hinduism, which underlies the diversity of its many forms.[73] According to Flood, Vivekananda's view of Hinduism is the most common among Hindus today.[74] This monism, according to Flood, is at the foundation of earlier Upanishads, to theosophy in the later Vedanta tradition and in modern Neo-Hinduism.[75]

Buddhism

Main article: Buddhism

Monism in Buddhism According to the Pāli Canon, both pluralism (*nānatta*) and monism (*ēkatta*) are speculative views. A Theravada commentary notes that the former is similar to or associated with nihilism (*ucchēdavāda*), and the latter is similar to or associated with eternalism (*sassatavada*).[76] See middle way.

In the Madhyamaka school of Mahayana Buddhism, the ultimate nature of the world is described as *Śūnyatā* or "emptiness", which is inseparable from sensorial objects or anything else. That appears to be a monist position, but the Madhyamaka views - including variations like *rangtong* and *shentong* - will refrain from asserting any ultimately existent entity. They instead deconstruct any detailed or conceptual assertions about ultimate existence as resulting in absurd consequences. The Yogacara view, a minority school now only found among the Mahayana, also rejects monism.

Levels of truth Within Buddhism, a rich variety of philosophical[77] and pedagogical models[78] can be found. Various schools of Buddhism discern levels of truth:

- The Two truths doctrine of the Madhyamaka

- The Three Natures of the Yogacara

- Essence-Function, or Absolute-relative in Chinese and Korean Buddhism

- The Trikaya-formule, consisting of

  - The *Dharmakāya* or *Truth body* which embodies the very principle of enlightenment and knows no limits or boundaries;

  - The *Sambhogakāya* or *body of mutual enjoyment* which is a body of bliss or clear light manifestation;

  - The *Nirmāṇakāya* or *created body* which manifests in time and space.[79]

The Prajnaparamita-sutras and Madhyamaka emphasize the non-duality of form and emptiness: "form is emptiness, emptiness is form", as the heart sutra says.[80] In Chinese Buddhism this was understood to mean that ultimate reality is not a transcendental realm, but equal to the daily world of relative reality. This idea fitted into the Chinese culture, which emphasized the mundane world and society. But this does not tell how the absolute is present in the relative world:

> To deny the duality of samsara and nirvana, as the Perfection of Wisdom does, or to demonstrate logically the error of dichotomizing conceptualization, as Nagarjuna does, is not to address the question of the relationship between samsara and nirvana -or, in more philosophical terms, between phenomenal and ultimate reality [...] What, then, is the relationship between these two realms?[80]

This question is answered in such schemata as the Five Ranks of Tozan,[81] the Oxherding Pictures, and Hakuin's Four ways of knowing.[82]

19.4.5 Abrahamic faiths

Judaism

Main article: Judaism

Jewish thought considers God as separate from all physical, created things (transcendent) and as existing outside of time (eternal).[note 3][note 4]

According to Chasidic Thought (particularly as propounded by the 18th century, early 19th century founder of Chabad, Shneur Zalman of Liadi), God is held to be immanent within creation for two interrelated reasons:

1. A very strong Jewish belief is that "[t]he Divine life-force which brings [the universe] into existence must constantly be present... were this life-force to forsake [the universe] for even one brief moment, it would revert to a state of utter nothingness, as before the creation..." [83]

2. Simultaneously, Judaism holds as axiomatic that God is an absolute unity, and that he is Perfectly Simple - thus if his sustaining power is within nature, then his essence is also within nature.

The Vilna Gaon was very much against this philosophy, for he felt that it would lead to pantheism and heresy. According to some this is the main reason for the Gaon's ban on Chasidism.

According to Maimonides,[84] God is an incorporeal being that caused all other existence. In fact, God is defined as the necessary existent that caused all other existence. According to Maimonides, to admit corporeality to God is tantamount to admitting complexity to God, which is a contradiction to God as the First Cause and constitutes heresy. While Hasidic mystics considered the existence of the physical world a contradiction to God's simpleness, Maimonides saw no contradiction.[note 5]

Christianity

See also: Christian anthropology

Creator-creature distinction   Much of Christianity strongly maintains the Creator-creature distinction as fundamental. Many Christians maintain that God created the universe ex nihilo and not from His own substance, so that the creator is not to be confused with creation, but rather transcends it (metaphysical dualism) (cf. Genesis). Even the more immanent concepts and theologies are to be defined together with God's omnipotence, omnipresence and omniscience, due to God's desire for intimate contact with his own creation (cf. Acts 17:27). Another use of the term "monism" is in Christian anthropology to refer to the innate nature of humankind as being holistic, as usually opposed to bipartite and tripartite views.

Rejection of radical dualism   In *On Free Choice of the Will*, Augustine argued, in the context of the problem of evil, that evil is not the opposite of good, but rather merely the absence of good, something that does not have existence in itself. Likewise, C. S. Lewis described evil as a "parasite" in *Mere Christianity*, as he viewed evil as something that cannot exist without good to provide it with existence. Lewis went on to argue against dualism from the basis of moral absolutism, and rejected the dualistic notion that God and Satan are opposites, arguing instead that God has no equal, hence no opposite. Lewis rather viewed Satan as the opposite of Michael the archangel. Due to this, Lewis instead argued for a more limited type of dualism.[85] Other theologians, such as Greg Boyd, have argued in more depth that the Biblical authors held a "limited dualism", meaning that God and Satan do engage in real battle, but only due to free will given by God, for the duration God allows.[86]

Theosis   In Roman Catholicism and Eastern Orthodoxy, while human beings are not ontologically identical with the Creator, they are nonetheless capable with uniting with his Divine Nature via theosis, and especially, through the devout reception of the Holy Eucharist. This is a supernatural union, over and above that natural union, of which St. John of the Cross says, "it must be known that God dwells and is present substantially in every soul, even in that of the greatest sinner in the world, and this union is natural." Julian of Norwich, while maintaining the orthodox duality of Creator and creature, nonetheless speaks of God as "the true Father and true Mother" of all natures; thus, he indwells them substantially and thus preserves them from annihilation, as without this sustaining indwelling everything would cease to exist.

Christian Monism   Some Christian theologians are avowed monists, such as Paul Tillich. Since God is he "in whom we live and move and have our being" (Book of Acts 17.28), it follows that everything that has being partakes in God.

Islam

Main article: Islam

Quran Although Vincent J. Cornell argue that the Quran also provides a monist image of God by describing the reality as a unified whole, with God being a single concept that would describe or ascribe all existing things. But most argue that Semitic religious scriptures especially Quran see Creation and God as two separate existence. It explains everything been created by God and under his control, but at the same time distinguishes God and creation as having independent existence from each other.

Sufism Main article: Sufism

Sufi mystics advocate monism. One of the most notable being the 13th-century Persian poet Rumi (1207–73) in his didactic poem *Masnavi* espoused monism.[87][88] Rumi says in the Masnavi,

> In the shop for Unity (wahdat); anything that you see there except the One is an idol.[87]

The most influential of the Islamic monists was the Sufi philosopher Ibn Arabi (1165-40). He developed the concept of 'unity of being' (Arabic: *waḥdat al-wujūd*), a pantheistic monoist philosophy. Born in al-Andalus, he made an enormous impact on the Muslim world, where he was crowned "the great Master". In the centuries following his death, his ideas became increasingly controversial.

19.4.6 Bahá'í

Main article: Bahá'í Faith and the unity of religion

Although the Bahá'í teachings have a strong emphasis on social and ethical issues, there exist a number of foundational texts that have been described as mystical.[89] Some of these include statements of a monist nature (e.g., *The Seven Valleys* and the *Hidden Words*). The differences between dualist and monist views are reconciled by the teaching that these opposing viewpoints are caused by differences in the observers themselves, not in that which is observed. This is not a 'higher truth/lower truth' position. God is unknowable. For man it is impossible to acquire any direct knowledge of God or the Absolute, because any knowledge that one has, is relative.[90]

19.4.7 Non-dualism

Main article: Nondualism

According to nondualism, many forms of religion are based on an experiential or intuitive understanding of "the Real".[91] Nondualism, a modern reinterpretation of these religions, prefers the term "nondualism", instead of monism, because this understanding is "nonconceptual", "not graspable in an idea".[91][note 6][note 7]

To these nondual traditions belong Hinduism (including Vedanta, some forms of Yoga, and certain schools of Shaivism), Taoism, Pantheism, Rastafari and similar systems of thought.

19.5 See also

- Cosmic pluralism
- Dialectical monism
- Dualism
- Eliminative materialism
- Henosis
- Holism
- Indefinite monism
- Monistic idealism
- Ontological pluralism

19.6 Notes

[1] Such as Behaviourism,[8] Type-identity theory[8] and Functionalism[8]

[2] See Creation Spirituality

[3] For a discussion of the resultant paradox, see *Tzimtzum*.

[4] See also Negative theology.

[5] See the "Guide for the Perplexed", especially chapter I:50.

[6] In Dutch: "Niet in een denkbeeld te vatten".[91]

[7] According to Renard, Alan Watts has explained the difference between "non-dualism" and "monism" in *The Supreme Identity*, Faber and Faber 1950, p.69 and 95; *The Way of Zen*, Pelican-edition 1976, p.59-60.[92] According to Renard, Alan Watts has been one of the main contributors to thepopularisation of the notion of "nondualism".[91]

19.7   References

[1] Cross & Livingstone 1974.

[2] Brugger 1972.

[3] Strawson, G. (2014 in press): "Nietzsche's metaphysics?". In: Dries, M. & Kail, P. (eds): "Nietzsche on Mind and Nature". Oxford University Press. PDF of draft

[4] Chande 2000, p. 277.

[5] Dasgupta 1992, p. 70.

[6] "monism", Columbia Electronic Encyclopedia, 6th Edition. Retrieved 29 October 2014.

[7] jrank.org, *Monism*

[8] Luke Mastin (2008),*Monism*

[9] Robert M. Young (1996). "The mind-body problem". In RC Olby, GN Cantor, JR Christie, MJS Hodges, eds. *Companion to the History of Modern Science* (Paperback reprint of Routledge 1990 ed.). Taylor and Francis. pp. 702–11. ISBN 0415145783.

[10] Robinson, Howard (Nov 3, 2011). Edward N. Zalta, ed, ed. "Dualism". *The Stanford Encyclopedia of Philosophy (Winter 2011 Edition)*.

[11] Henrik Lagerlund (2010). "Introduction". In Henrik Lagerlund, ed. *Forming the Mind: Essays on the Internal Senses and the Mind/Body Problem from Avicenna to the Medical Enlightenment* (Paperback reprint of 2007 ed.). Springer Science+Business Media. p. 3. ISBN 9048175305.

[12] Urmson 1991, p. 297.

[13] Schaffer 2010.

[14] Fiske 2010, p. 195.

[15] Fiske 2010, p. 195-196.

[16] Mandik 2010.

[17] McLaughlin 2009.

[18] Schaffer, Jonathan, Monism: The Priority of the Whole, http://www.jonathanschaffer.org/monism.pdf

[19] Schaffer, Jonathan, "Monism", The Stanford Encyclopedia of Philosophy (Summer 2015 Edition), Edward N. Zalta (ed.), URL=http://plato.stanford.edu/archives/sum2015/entries/monism/

[20] Mandik 2010, p. 76.

[21] Abernethy & Langford pp.1-7.

[22] Abernethy & Langford pp.8,9.

[23] *De la causa, principio e Uno, London, 1584*

[24] *De monade (De monade, numero et figura liber consequens quinque de minimo magno et mensura), Frankfurt, 1591*

[25] *Wonders of Life* by Ernst Haeckel.

[26] The Evolution of Man: A Popular Scientific Study, Volume 2 by Ernst Heinrich Philipp August Haeckel.

[27] *Encyclopedia of Philosophy ed. Paul Edwards*. New York: Macmillan and Free Press. 1967. p. 34.

[28] *The New Oxford Dictionary Of English*. Oxford: Clarendon Press. 1998. p. 1341. ISBN 0-19-861263-X.

[29] Picton, James Allanson (1905). *Pantheism: its story and significance*. Chicago: Archibald Constable & CO LTD. ISBN 978-1419140082.

[30] Plumptre, Constance (1879). *General sketch of the history of pantheism, Volume 2*. London: Samuel Deacon and Co. pp. 3–5, 8, 29. ISBN 9780766155022.

[31] Shoham, Schlomo Giora (2010). *To Test the Limits of Our Endurance*. Cambridge Scholars. p. 111. ISBN 1443820687.

[32] H.P. Owen, 1971, p.65

[33] Crosby, Donald A. (2008). Living with Ambiguity: Religious Naturalism and the Menace of Evil. New York: State University of New York Press. pp. 124. ISBN 0-7914-7519-0.

[34] Erwin Fahlbusch, Geoffrey William Bromiley, David B. Barrett (1999). *The Encyclopedia of Christianity pg. 21*. Wm. B. Eerdmans Publishing. ISBN 0-8028-2416-1.

[35] Britannica - Pantheism and Panentheism in non-Western cultures

[36] Whiting, Robert. Religions for Today Stanley Thomes (Publishers) Ltd. P. VIII. ISBN 0-7487-0586-4.

[37] Sean F. Johnston (2009). *The History of Science: A Beginner's Guide p. 90*. ISBN 1-85168-681-9.

[38] Alex Ashman, *BBC News*, "Metaphysical Isms".

[39] Nakamura 1991.

[40] Puligandla 1997.

[41] Puligandla 1997, p. 50.

[42] Kalupahana 1992.

[43] Kalupahana 1994.

[44] Loy 1988, p. 9-11.

[45] Rambachan 1994.

[46] Hawley 2006.

[47] Sharf 1995.

[48] renard 2010, p. 59.

[49] Renard 2010, p. 31.

[50] Maezumi 2007.

[51] Radhakrishnan 1957, p. 3.

[52] Sehgal 1999, p. 1372.

[53] Sehgal 1999.

[54] Sehgal 1999, p. 1373.

[55] Fowler 2002, p. 39.

[56] Fowler 2002, p. 43.

[57] Wilhelm Halbfass (1995), Philology and Confrontation: Paul Hacker on Traditional and Modern Vedanta, State University of New York Press, ISBN 978-0791425824, pages 137-143

[58] Flood 1996, p. 239.

[59] Jeaneane Fowler (2012), The Bhagavad Gita: A Text and Commentary for Students, Sussex Academic Press, ISBN 978-1845193461, page xxviii

[60] Momen 2009, p. 191.

[61] renard 2010.

[62] Brodd, Jefferey (2003). World Religions. Winona, MN: Saint Mary's Press. ISBN 978-0-88489-725-5.

[63] James Swartz, *What is Neo-Advaita?*

[64] Renard 2010, p. 130.

[65] Renard 2010, p. 131.

[66] Puligandla 1997, p. 232.

[67] advaita-vision.org, *Discrimination*

[68] Michaels 2004.

[69] Dense 1999, p. 191.

[70] Mukerji 1983.

[71] Comans 1993.

[72] Flood 1996, p. 257.

[73] Flood 1996, p. 258.

[74] Flood 1996, p. 259.

[75] Flood 1996, p. 85.

[76] David Kalupahana, *Causality: The Central Philosophy of Buddhism.* The University Press of Hawaii, 1975, page 88. The passage is SN 2.77.

[77] Williams 1994.

[78] Buswell 1994.

[79] Welwood, John (2000). *The Play of the Mind: Form, Emptiness, and Beyond*, accessed January 13, 2007

[80] Liang-Chieh 1986, p. 9.

[81] Kasulis 2003, p. 29.

[82] Low 2006.

[83] http://www.chabad.org/library/archive/LibraryArchive2.asp?AID=7988

[84] See Foundations of the Law, Chapter 1

[85] Lewis, C.S, "God and Evil" in "God in the Dock: Essays in Theology and Ethics", ed. W. Hooper (Grand Rapids, Mich, Eerdsmans, 1970), p. 21-24

[86] Boyd, Gregory. A, "God at War" (Downers Grove, IL, InterVarsity Press, 1971) p. 185

[87] Reynold Nicholson *Rumi*

[88] Cyprian Rice, O.P., (1964) *The Persian Sufism* George Allen, London

[89] Daphne Daume, Louise Watson, ed. (1992). "The Bahá'í Faith". *Britannica Book of the Year*. Chicago: Encyclopædia Britannica. ISBN 0-85229-486-7.

[90] Momen, Moojan (1988). *Studies in the Bábí and Bahá'í Religions vol. 5, chapter: A Basis For Bahá'í Metaphysics*. Kalimat Press. pp. 185–217. ISBN 0-933770-72-3.

[91] Renard 2010, p. 59.

[92] Renard 2010, p. 59, p.285 note 17.

19.8 Sources

- Abernethy, George L; Langford, Thomas A. (1970), *Introduction to Western Philosophy:Pre-Socratics to Mill*, Belmont,CA: Dickenson

- Brugger, Walter (ed) (1972), *Diccionario de Filosofía*, Barcelona: Herder, art. **dualismo**, **monismo**, **pluralismo**

- Buswell, Robert E. JR; Gimello, Robert M. (editors) (1994), *Paths to Liberation. The Marga and its Transformations in Buddhist Thought*, Delhi: Motilal Banarsidass Publishers

- Chande, M.B. (2000), *Indian Philosophy In Modern Times*, Atlantic Publishers & Dist

- Cross, F.L.; Livingstone, E.A. (1974), *The Oxford Dictionary of the Christian Church*, OUP, art. **monism**

- Dasgupta, Surendranath (1992), *A history of Indian philosophy part 1*, Motilall Banarsidass

- Dense, Christian D. Von (1999), *Philosophers and Religious Leaders*, Greenwood Publishing Group

- Fiske, Susan T.; Gilbert, DanielT.; Lindzey, Gardner (2010), *Handbook of Social Psychology, Volume 1*, John Wiley & Sons

- Flood, Gavin (1996), *An Introduction to Hinduism*, Cambridge University Press, ISBN 0-521-43878-0

- Fowler, Jeaneane D. (2002), *Perspectives of Reality: An Introduction to the Philosophy of Hinduism*, Sussex Academic Press

- Hawley, michael (2006), *Sarvepalli Radhakrishnan (1888—1975)*

- Hori, Victor Sogen (1999), *Translating the Zen Phrase Book. In: Nanzan Bulletin 23 (1999)* (PDF)

- Kalupahana, David J. (1992), *The Principles of Buddhist Psychology*, Delhi: ri Satguru Publications

- Kalupahana, David J. (1994), *A history of Buddhist philosophy*, Delhi: Motilal Banarsidass Publishers Private Limited

- Kasulis, Thomas P. (2003), *Ch'an Spirituality. In: Buddhist Spirituality. Later China, Korea, Japan and the Modern World; edited by Takeuchi Yoshinori*, Delhi: Motilal Banarsidass

- Liang-Chieh (1986), *The Record of Tung-shan*, Kuroda Institute

- Low, Albert (2006), *Hakuin on Kensho. The Four Ways of Knowing*, Boston & London: Shambhala

- Maezumi, Taizan; Glassman, Bernie (2007), *The Hazy Moon of Enlightenment*, Wisdom Publications

- Mandik, Pete (2010), *Key Terms in Philosophy of Mind*, Continuum International Publishing Group

- McLaughlin, Brian; Beckermann, Ansgar; Walter, Sven (2009), *The Oxford Handbook of Philosophy of Mind*, Oxford University Press

- Michaels, Axel (2004), *Hinduism. Past and present*, Princeton, New Jersey: Princeton University Press

- Momen, Moojan (2009) [Originally published as *The Phenomenon of Religion* in 1999], *Understanding Religion: A Thematic Approach*, Oxford, UK: Oneworld Publications, ISBN 978-1-85168-599-8

- Nakamura, Hajime (1991), *Ways of Thinking of Eastern Peoples: India, China, Tibet, Japan*, Delhi: Motilal Banarsidass Publishers Private Limited

- Puligandla, Ramakrishna (1997), *Fundamentals of Indian Philosophy*, New Delhi: D.K. Printworld (P) Ltd.

- Radhakrishnan, Sarvepalli; Moore, Charles A. (1957), *A Sourcebook in Indian Philosophy* (12th Princeton Paperback ed.), Princeton University Press, ISBN 0-691-01958-4

- Rambachan, Anatanand (1994), *The Limits of Scripture: Vivekananda's Reinterpretation of the Vedas*, University of Hawaii Press

- Renard, Philip (1999), *Ramana Upanishad*, Utrecht: Servire

- Schaffer, Jonathan (2010), "Monism: The Priority of the Whole" (PDF), *Philosophical Review 119.1: 31-76)*

- Sehgal, Sunil (1999), *Encyclopaedia of Hinduism: T-Z, Volume 5*, Sarup & Sons

- Sharf, Robert H. (1995), "Buddhist Modernism and the Rhetoric of Meditative Experience" (PDF), *NUMEN, vol.42 (1995)*

- Urmson, James Opie (1991), *The Concise Encyclopedia of Western Philosophy and Philosophers*, Routledge

- White (ed.), David Gordon (2000), *Introduction. In: Tantra in practice*, Princeton and Oxford: Princeton University Press

- Williams, Paul (1994), *Mahayana Buddhism*, Routledge, ISBN 0-415-02537-0

19.9 External links

- "Monism". *Stanford Encyclopedia of Philosophy.*

- Monism at PhilPapers

- Monism at the Indiana Philosophy Ontology Project

- Catholic Encyclopedia - Monism

- Hinduism's Online Lexicon - (search for Monism)

- The Monist

Chapter 20

Subitism

The term **subitism** points to sudden enlightenment, the idea that insight is attained all at once.[1] The opposite approach, that enlightenment can be achieved only step by step, through an arduous practice, is called gradualism.[2]

20.1 Etymology

The application of the term to Buddhism is derived from the French *illumination subite* (sudden awakening), contrasting with 'illumination graduelle' (gradual awakening). It gained currency in this use in English from the work of sinologist Paul Demiéville. His 1947 work 'Mirror of the Mind' was widely read in the U.S. It inaugurated a series by him on subitism and gradualism. [web 1]

20.2 Early Buddhism

20.2.1 *Dhyana* and insight

A core problem in the study of early Buddhism is the relation between *jhana/dhyana* and insight.[3][4][5][note 1] The Buddhist tradition has incorporated two traditions regarding the use of dhyana.[4] There is a tradition that stresses attaining insight (bodhi, prajna, kensho) as the means to awakening and liberation. But it has also incorporated the yogic tradition, as reflected in the use of jhana, which is rejected in other sutras as not resulting in the final result of liberation.[3][6][5] The problem was famously voiced in 1936 by Louis de La Vallee Poussin, in his text *Musila et Narada: Le Chemin de Nirvana*.[7][note 2]

Schmithausen, in his often-cited article *On some Aspects of Descriptions or Theories of 'Liberating Insight' and 'Enlightenment' in Early Buddhism,* notes that the mention of the four noble truths as constituting "liberating insight", which is attained after mastering the Rupa Jhanas, is a later addition to texts such as Majjhima Nikaya 36.[8][4][3] Schmithausen discerns three possible roads to liberation as

described in the suttas. Vetter adds a fourth possibility, which pre-dates these three:[9]

1. The four Rupa Jhanas themselves constituted the core liberating practice of early buddhism, c.q. the Buddha;[10]

2. Mastering the four Rupa Jhanas, where-after "liberating insight" is attained;

3. Mastering the four Rupa Jhanas and the four Arupa Jhanas, where-after "liberating insight" is attained;

4. Liberating insight itself suffices.

This problem has been elaborated by several well-known scholars, including Tilman Vetter,[3] Johannes Bronkhorst,[6] and Richard Gombrich.[5]

20.2.2 Dhyana

According to Tilmann Vetter, the core of earliest Buddhism is the practice of *dhyāna*.[3] Vetter notes that "penetrating abstract truths and penetrating them successively does not seem possible in a state of mind which is without contemplation and reflection."[11] Vetter further argues that the eightfold path constitutes a body of practices which prepare one, and lead up to, the practice of *dhyana*.[12]

Bronkhorst agrees that *dhyana* was a Buddhist invention,[4] whereas Norman notes that "the Buddha's way to release [...] was by means of meditative practices."[13] Gombrich also notes that a development took place in early Buddhism resulting in a change in doctrine, which considered *prajna* to be an alternative means to "enlightenment".[14]

20.2.3 Insight

According to Johannes Bronkhorst,[4] Tillman Vetter,[3] and K.R. Norman,[13] *bodhi* was at first not specified. K.R. Norman:

It is not at all clear what gaining *bodhi* means. We are accustomed to the translation "enlightenment" for *bodhi*, but this is misleading [...] It is not clear what the buddha was awakened to, or at what particular point the awakening came.[13]

According to Norman, *bodhi* may basically have meant the knowledge that *nibbana* was attained,[15][16] due to the practice of *dhyana*.[13][3]

Bronkhorst notes that the conception of what exactly this "liberating insight" was developed throughout time. Whereas originally it may not have been specified, later on the four truths served as such, to be superseded by *pratityasamutpada*, and still later, in the Hinayana schools, by the doctrine of the non-existence of a substantial self or person.[17] And Schmithausen notices that still other descriptions of this "liberating insight" exist in the Buddhist canon:

"that the five Skandhas are impermanent, disagreeable, and neither the Self nor belonging to oneself";[note 3] "the contemplation of the arising and disappearance (*udayabbaya*) of the five Skandhas";[note 4] "the realisation of the Skandhas as empty (*rittaka*), vain (*tucchaka*) and without any pith or substance (*asaraka*).[note 5][18]

Discriminating insight into transiency as a separate path to liberation was a later development.[19][20] This may have been to due an over-literal interpretation by later scholastics of the terminology used by the Buddha,[21] or to the problems involved with the practice of *dhyana*, and the need to develop an easier method.[22] According to Vetter it may not have been as effective as *dhyana*, and methods were developed to deepen the effects of discriminating insight.[22] It was also paired to *dhyana*, resulting in the well-known *sila-samadhi-prajna* scheme.[22] According to Vetter this kind of preparatory *"dhyana"* must have been different from the practice introduced by the Buddha, using kasina-exercises to produce a "more artificially produced dhyana", resulting in the cessation of apperceptions and feelings.[23] It also lead to a different understanding of the eightfold path, since this path does not end with insight, but rather starts with insight. The path was no longer seen as a sequential development resulting in *dhyana*, but as a set of practices which had to be developed simultaneously to gain insight.[24]

20.3 Theravada

The distinction between sudden and gradual is also apparent in the differentiation between vipassana and samatha.

According to Gombrich, the distinction between vipassana and samatha did not originate in the suttas, but in the *interpretation* of the suttas.[25]

20.4 Mahayana

The emphasis on insight is also discernible in the Mahayana-tradition, which emphasises prajna:

[T]he very title of a large corpus of early Mahayana literature, the *Prajnaparamita*, shows that to some extent the historian may extrapolate the trend to extol insight, *prajna*, at the expense of dispassion, *viraga*, the control of the emotions.[26]

Although Theravada and Mahayana are commonly understood as different streams of Buddhism, their practice too may reflect emphasis on insight as a common denominator:[note 6]

20.4.1 Chinese Buddhism

The distinction between sudden and gradual awakening was first introduced in China in the beginning of the 5th century CE by Tao Sheng.[28]

Chan

The term is used in Chan Buddhism to denote the doctrinal position that enlightenment (kenshō, bodhi or satori) is instantaneous, sudden and direct, not attained by practice through a period of time, and not the fruit of a gradual accretion or realisation. Aspects of Dzogchen and Mahamudra may be referred to as subitist, as well as the Rinzai school.

Huineng   In the 8th century the distinction became part of a struggle for influence at the Chinese court by Shenhui, a student of Huineng. Hereafter "sudden enlightenment" became one of the hallmarks of Chan Buddhism, though the sharp distinction was softened by subsequent generations of practitioners.[29]

This softening is reflected in the *Platform Sutra*, a text ascribed to Huineng but composed by later writers of various schools.[29]

While the Patriarch was living in Bao Lin Monastery, the Grand Master Shen Xiu was preaching in Yu Quan Monastery of Jing Nan.

At that time the two Schools, that of Hui Neng of the South and Shen Xiu of the North, flourished side by side. As the two Schools were distinguished from each other by the names "Sudden" (the South) and "Gradual" (the North), the question which sect they should follow baffled certain Buddhist scholars (of that time). (Seeing this), the Patriarch addressed the assembly as follows:

So far as the *Dharma* is concerned, there can be only one School. (If a distinction exists) it exists in the fact that the founder of one school is a northern man, while the other is a southerner. While there is only one *dharma*, some disciples realize it more quickly than others. The reason why the names 'Sudden' and 'Gradual' are given is that some disciples are superior to others in mental dispositions. So far as the Dharma is concerned, the distinction of 'Sudden' and 'Gradual' does not exist.[web 2]

Rivalry between schools While Southern School placed emphasis on sudden enlightenment, it also marked a shift in doctrinal basis from the *Laṅkāvatāra Sūtra* to the prajnaparamita tradition, especially the *Diamond Sutra*. The Laṅkāvatāra Sūtra, which endorses the Buddha-nature, emphasized purity of mind, which can be attained in gradations. The *Diamond Sutra* emphasizes śūnyatā, which "must be realized totally or not at all".[30]

Once this dichotomy was in place, it defined its own logic and rhetorics, which are also recognizable in the distinction between Caodong (Sōtō) and Linji (Rinzai) schools.[31] But it also leads to a "sometimes bitter and always prolix sectarian controversy between later Ch'an and Hua-yen exegetes".[32] In the Huayan classification of teachings, the sudden approach was regarded inferior to the Perfect Teaching of Huayan. Guifeng Zongmi, fifth patriarch of Huayan and Chan master, devised his own classification to counter this subordination.[33] To establish the superiority of Chan, Jinul, the most important figure in the formation of Korean Seon, explained the sudden approach as not pointing to mere emptiness, but to *suchness* or the dharmadhatu.[34]

Later interpretations Guifeng Zongmi, fifth-generation successor to Shenhui, also softened the edge between sudden and gradual. In his analysis, sudden awakening points to seeing into one's true nature, but is to be followed by a gradual cultivation to attain buddhahood.[2]

This is also the standpoint of the contemporary Sanbo Kyodan, according to whom kensho is at the start of the path to full enlightenment.[35]

This gradual cultivation is also recognized by Dongshan Liangjie, who described the Five Ranks of enlightenment]].[web 3] Other example of depiction of stages on the path are the Ten Bulls, which detail the steps on the Path, The Three Mysterious Gates of Linji, and the Four Ways of Knowing of Hakuin Ekaku.[36] This gradual cultivation is described by Chan Master Sheng Yen as follows:

Ch'an expressions refer to enlightenment as "seeing your self-nature". But even this is not enough. After seeing your self-nature, you need to deepen your experience even further and bring it into maturation. You should have enlightenment experience again and again and support them with continuous practice. Even though Ch'an says that at the time of enlightenment, your outlook is the same as of the Buddha, you are not yet a full Buddha.[37]

Hua-yen

In the Fivefold Classification of the Huayan school and the Five Periods and Eight Teachings of the Tiantai-school the sudden teaching was given a high place, but still inferior to the Complete or Perfect teachings of these schools.

20.4.2 Korean Seon

Chinul, a 12th-century Korean Seon master, followed Zongmi, and also emphasized that insight into our true nature is sudden, but is to be followed by practice to ripen the insight and attain full Buddhahood.[38]

In contemporary Korean Seon, Seongcheol has defended the stance of "sudden insight, sudden cultivation". Citing Taego Bou (太古普愚: 1301-1382) as the true successor of the Linji Yixuan (臨濟義玄) line of patriarchs rather than Jinul (知訥: 1158-1210), he advocated Hui Neng's original stance of 'sudden enlightenment, sudden cultivation' (Hangul: 돈오돈수, Hanja: 頓悟頓修) as opposed to Jinul's stance of 'sudden enlightenment, gradual cultivation' (Hangul: 돈오점수, Hanja: 頓悟漸修).[39] Whereas Jinul had initially asserted that with enlightenment comes the need to further one's practice by gradually destroying the karmic vestiges attained through millions of rebirths, Huineng and Seongcheol maintained that with perfect enlightenment, all karmic remnants disappear and one becomes a Buddha immediately.[40][41][42][43]

20.5 Neo-Vedanta

20.5.1 Ramana maharshi - Akrama mukti

Ramana Maharshi made a distinction between *akrama mukti*, "sudden liberation", as opposed to the *krama mukti*, "gradual liberation" as in the Vedanta path of jnana yoga:[web 4][note 7]

> 'Some people,' he said, 'start off by studying literature in their youth. Then they indulge in the pleasures of the world until they are fed up with them. Next, when they are at an advanced age, they turn to books on Vedanta. They go to a guru and get initiated by him and then start the process of sravana, manana and nididhyasana, which finally culminates in samadhi. This is the normal and standard way of approaching liberation. It is called krama mukti [gradual liberation]. But I was overtaken by akrama mukti [sudden liberation] before I passed through any of the above-mentioned stages.'[web 4]

20.5.2 Inchegeri Sampradaya

The teachings of Bhausaheb Maharaj, the founder of the Inchegeri Sampradaya, have been called "the Ant's way", [note 8] the way of meditation,[web 7] while the teachings of Siddharameshwar Maharaj and his disciples Nisargadatta Maharaj and Ranjit Maharaj have been called "the Bird's Way",[note 9] the direct path to Self-discovery:[web 7]

> The way of meditation is a long arduous path while the Bird's Way is a clear direct path of Self investigation, Self exploration, and using thought or concepts as an aid to understanding and Self-Realization. Sometimes this approach is also called the Reverse Path. What Reverse Path indicates is the turning around of one's attention away from objectivity to the more subjective sense of one's Beingness.[note 10] With the Bird's Way, first one's mind must be made subtle. This is generally done with some initial meditaion on a mantra or phrase which helps the aspirant to step beyond the mental/conceptual body, using a concept to go beyond conceptualization.[web 7]

The terms appear in the Varaha Upanishad, Chapter IV:

> 34. (The Rishi) Suka is a Mukta (emancipated person). (The Rishi) Vamadeva is a Mukta. There are no others (who have attained emancipation) than through these (viz., the two paths of these two Rishis). Those brave men who follow the path of Suka in this world become Sadyo-Muktas (viz., emancipated) immediately after (the body wear away);

> 35. While those who always follow the path of Vamadeva (i.e., Vedanta) in this world are subject again and again to rebirths and attain Krama (gradual) emancipation, through Yoga, Sankhya and Karmas associated with Sattva (Guna).
> 36. Thus there are two paths laid down by the Lord of Devas (viz.,) the Suka and Vamadeva paths. The Suka path is called the bird's path; while the Vamadeva path is called the ant's path.[web 8]

20.6 See also

- Enlightenment in Buddhism
- Enlightenment (spiritual)
- Jinul
- Mushi-dokugo ("self-enlightenment")
- Subitizing
- Shattari
- Illuminationism

20.7 Notes

[1] Bodhi, prajna, vipassana, kensho

[2] See Louis de La Vallée Poussin, *Musial and Narad*. Translated from the French by Gelongma Migme Chödrön and Gelong Lodrö Sangpo.

[3] Majjhima Nikaya 26

[4] Anguttara Nikaya II.45 (PTS)

[5] Samyutta Nikaya III.140-142 (PTS)

[6] Warder: "In the Sthaviravada [...] progress in understanding comes all at once, 'insight' (*abhisamaya*) does not come 'gradually' (successively - *anapurva*)".[27]

[7] Rama P. Coomaraswamy: "[Krama-mukti is] to be distinguished from jîvan-mukti, the state of total and immediate liberation attained during this lifetime, and videha-mukti, the state of total liberation attained at the moment of death."[44] See [web 5] for more info on "gradual liberation".

[8] *Pipeelika Mārg,*[45] or *Pipilika Marg ,*[web 6]

[9] *Bihangam Mārg,*[45] or *Vihangam Marg,*[web 6]

[10] Compare Jinul's "tracing back the radiance".Buswell, Robert E. (1991), *Tracing Back the Radiance: Chinul's Korean Way of Zen*, University of Hawaii Press, ISBN 978-0-8248-1427-4

20.8 References

[1] McRae 1991.

[2] Gregory 1991.

[3] Vetter 1988.

[4] Bronkhorst 1993.

[5] Gombrich 1997.

[6] bronkhorst 1993.

[7] Bronkhorst 1993, p. 133-134.

[8] Schmithausen 1981.

[9] Vetter 1988, p. xxi-xxii.

[10] Vetter & 1988 xxi-xxxvii.

[11] Vetter 1988, p. xxvii.

[12] Vetter 1988, p. xxx.

[13] Norman 1997, p. 29.

[14] gombrich 1997, p. 131.

[15] Norman 1997, p. 30.

[16] Vetter 1988, p. xxix, xxxi.

[17] Bronkhorst 1993, p. 100-101.

[18] Bronkhorst 1993, p. 101.

[19] Vetter 1988, p. xxxiv-xxxvii.

[20] Gombrich 1997, p. 131.

[21] Gombrich 1997, p. 96-134.

[22] Vetter 1988, p. xxxv.

[23] Vetter 1988, p. xxxvi.

[24] Vetter 1988, p. xxxvi-xxxvii.

[25] Gombrich 1997, p. 96-144.

[26] Gombrich 1997, p. 133.

[27] Warder 2000, p. 284.

[28] Lai 1991, p. 169.

[29] McRae 2003.

[30] Kasulis 2003, pp. 26–28.

[31] McRae 2003, p. 123.

[32] Buswell 1993, p. 234.

[33] Gregory 1993.

[34] Buswell 1991, p. 240-241.

[35] Kapleau 1989.

[36] Low 2006.

[37] Yen 2006, p. 54.

[38] Buswell 1989, p. 21.

[39] 퇴옹 성철. (1976). *한국불교의 법맥*. 해인사 백련암 (Korea): 장경각. (Toeng Seongcheol. (1976). *Hanguk Bulgyo Ei Bupmaek*. Haeinsa Baekryun'am (Korea): Jang'gyung'gak.) ISBN 89-85244-16-7

[40] 퇴옹 성철. (1987). *자기를 바로 봅시다*. 해인사 백련암 (Korea): 장경각. (Toeng Seongcheol. (1987). *Jaghireul Baro Bopshida*. Haeinsa Baekryun'am (Korea): Jang'gyung'gak.) ISBN 89-85244-11-6

[41] 퇴옹 성철. (1988). *영원한 자유*. 해인사 백련암 (Korea): 장경각. (Toeng Seongcheol. (1988). *Yongwonhan Jayou*. Haeinsa Baekryun'am (Korea): Jang'gyung'gak.) ISBN 89-85244-10-8

[42] 퇴옹 성철. (1987). *선문정로*. 해인사 백련암 (Korea): 장경각. (Toeng Seongcheol. (1987). *Seon Mun Jung Ro*. Haeinsa Baekryun'am (Korea): Jang'gyung'gak.) ISBN 89-85244-14-0

[43] 퇴옹 성철. (1992). *백일법문*. 해인사 백련암 (Korea): 장경각. (Toeng Seongcheol. (1992). *Baek Il Bupmun*. Haeinsa Baekryun'am (Korea): Jang'gyung'gak.) ISBN 89-85244-05-1, ISBN 89-85244-06-X

[44] Coomaraswamy 2004.

[45] Prasoon 2009, p. 8.

20.9 Sources

20.9.1 Published sources

- Bronkhorst, Johannes (1993), *The Two Traditions Of Meditation In Ancient India*, Motilal Banarsidass Publ.

- Buswell, R. E. (1989). "Chinul's Ambivalent Critique of Radical Subitism in Korean Sŏn". *Journal of the International Association of Buddhist Studies* **12** (2): 20–44.

- Buswell, Robert E. (1991), *The "Short-cut" Approach of* K'an-hua Meditation: The Evolution of a Practical Subitism in Chinese Ch'an Buddhism. In: Peter N. Gregory (editor) (1991), *Sudden and Gradual. Approaches to Enlightenment in Chinese Thought*, Delhi: *Motilal Banarsidass Publishers Private Limited*

- Buswell, Robert E (1993), *Ch'an Hermeneutics: A Korean View. In: Donald S. Lopez, Jr. (ed.)(1993)*, Buddhist Hermeneutics, Delhi: Motilal Banarsidass

- Coomaraswamy, Rama P. (2004), *The Essential Ananda K. Coomaraswamy*, World Wisdom, Inc

- Faure, Bernard (2003), *Chan Buddhism in Ritual Context*, Routledge, ISBN 0-415-29748-6

- Gregory, Peter N. (1991), *Sudden Enlightenment Followed by Gradual Cultivation: Tsung-mi's Analysis of Mind. In: Peter N. Gregory (editor)(1991)*, Sudden and Gradual. Approaches to Enlightenment in Chinese Thought, Delhi: Motilal Banarsidass Publishers Private Limited

- Gombrich, Richard F. (1997), *How Buddhism Began. The Conditioned Genesis of the Early Teachings*, New Delhi: Munshiram Manoharlal Publishers Pvt. Ltd.

- Kapleau, Philip (1989), *The three pillars of Zen*

- Kasulis, Thomas P. (2003), *Ch'an Spirituality. In: Buddhist Spirituality. Later China, Korea, Japan and the Modern World; edited by Takeuchi Yoshinori*, Delhi: Motilal Banarsidass

- Lai, Whalen (1991), *Tao Sheng's Theory of Sudden Enlightenment Re-examined. In: Peter N. Gregory, ed. (1991)*, Sudden and Gradual. Approaches to Enlightenment in Chinese Thought, Delhi: Motilal Banarsidass Publishers Private Limited, pp. 169–200

- Low, Albert (2006), *Hakuin on Kensho. The Four Ways of Knowing*, Boston & London: Shambhala

- McRae, John (1991), *Shen-hui and the Teaching of Sudden Enlightenment in Early Ch'an Buddhism. In: Peter N. Gregory (editor)(1991)*, Sudden and Gradual. Approaches to Enlightenment in Chinese Thought, Delhi: Motilal Banarsidass Publishers Private Limited

- McRae, John (2003), *Seeing Through Zen. Encounter, Transformation, and Genealogy in Chinese Chan Buddhism*, The University Press Group Ltd, ISBN 978-0-520-23798-8

- Norman, K.R. (1992), *The Four Noble Truths. In: "Collected Papers", vol 2:210-223*, Pali Text Society, 2003

- Prasoon, Shrikant (2009), *Knowing Sant Kabir*, Pustak Mahal

- Schmithausen, Lambert (1981), *On some Aspects of Descriptions or Theories of 'Liberating Insight' and 'Enlightenment' in Early Buddhism". In: Studien zum Jainismus und Buddhismus (Gedenkschrift für Ludwig Alsdorf), hrsg. von Klaus Bruhn und Albrecht Wezler, Wiesbaden 1981, 199-250*

- Vetter, Tilmann (1988), *The Ideas and Meditative Practices of Early Buddhism*, BRILL

- Warder, A.K. (2000), *Indian Buddhism*, Delhi: Motilal Banarsidass Publishers

- Yen, Chan Master Sheng (1996), *Dharma Drum: The Life and Heart of Ch'an Practice*, Boston & London: Shambhala

20.9.2   Web-sources

[1] Bernard Faure, *Chan/Zen Studies in English: The State Of The Field*

[2] The Sudden School and the Gradual School. Chapter VIII

[3] The Five Ranks of Tozan

[4] David Godman (23 june 2008), *More on Bhagavan's death experience*

[5] Swami Krishnananda, *The Attainment of Liberation: Progressive Salvation*

[6] http://nondualite.free.fr, *Shri Sadguru Siddharameshwar Maharaj*

[7] sadguru.us, *The Bird's way*

[8] swamji.com, *Seven Bhumikas*

20.10   External links

- Gary L. Ray, *The Northern Ch'an School And Sudden Versus Gradual Enlightenment Debates In China And Tibet*

- Wei Chueh, *Gradual Cultivation And Sudden Enlightenment*

20.11   Further reading

- Vetter, Tilmann (1988), *The Ideas and Meditative Practices of Early Buddhism*, BRILL

- Faure, Bernard (1991), *The Rhetoric of Immediacy. A Cultural Critique of Chan/Zen Buddhism.* Princeton, New Jersey: Princeton University Press. ISBN 0-691-02963-6

- Peter N. Gregory (editor)(1991), *Sudden and Gradual. Approaches to Enlightenment in Chinese Thought.* Delhi: Motilal Banarsidass Publishers Private Limited

- McRae, John (2003), *Seeing through Zen. Encounter, Transformation, and Genealogy in Chinese Chan Buddhism.* The University Press Group Ltd . ISBN 978-0-520-23798-8

Chapter 21

Christian anthropology

This article is about Christian anthropology. For other uses, see Anthropology (disambiguation).

In the context of Christian theology, **Christian anthro-**

The Creation of Adam *in the Sistine Chapel*

pology refers to the study of the human ("anthropology") as it relates to God. It differs from the social science of anthropology, which primarily deals with the comparative study of the physical and social characteristics of humanity across times and places.

One aspect studies the innate nature or constitution of the human, known as the *nature of humankind*. It is concerned with the relationship between notions such as body, soul and spirit which together form a person, based on their descriptions in the Bible. There are three traditional views of the human constitution – trichotomism, dichotomism and monism (in the sense of anthropology).[1]

21.1 Early Christian writers

21.1.1 Gregory of Nyssa

The reference source for Gregory's anthropology is his treatise *De opificio hominis*.[2][3] His concept of man is founded on the ontological distinction between the created and uncreated. Man is a material creation, and thus limited, but infinite in that his immortal soul has an indefinite capacity to grow closer to the divine.[4] Gregory believed that the soul is created simultaneous to the creation

of the body (in opposition to Origen, who speculated on the soul's preexistence), and that embryos were thus persons. To Gregory, the human being is exceptional being created in the image of God.[5] Humanity is theomorphic both in having self-awareness and free will, the latter which gives each individual existential power, because to Gregory, in disregarding God one negates one's own existence.[6] In the *Song of Songs*, Gregory metaphorically describes human lives as paintings created by apprentices to a master: the apprentices (the human wills) imitate their master's work (the life of Christ) with beautiful colors (virtues), and thus man strives to be a reflection of Christ.[7] Gregory, in stark contrast to most thinkers of his age, saw great beauty in the Fall: from Adam's sin from two perfect humans would eventually arise myriad.[7]

21.1.2 Augustine of Hippo

Augustine of Hippo was one of the first Christian ancient Latin authors with very clear anthropological vision. He saw the human being as a perfect unity of two substances: soul and body.[8] He was much closer in this anthropological view to Aristotle than to Plato.[9][10] In his late treatise On Care to Be Had for the Dead sec. 5 (420 AD) he insisted that the body is essential part of the human person:

> In no wise are the bodies themselves to be spurned. (...) For these pertain not to ornament or aid which is applied from without, but to the very nature of man.[11]

Augustine's favourite figure to describe *body-soul* unity is marriage: *caro tua, coniux tua – your body is your wife*.[12] Initially, the two elements were in perfect harmony. After the fall of humanity they are now experiencing dramatic combat between one another.

They are two categorically different things. The body is a three-dimensional object composed of the four elements, whereas the soul has no spatial dimensions.[13] Soul is a kind of substance, participating in reason, fit for ruling the body.[14] Augustine was not preoccupied, as Plato and Descartes were, with going too much into details in efforts to explain the metaphysics of the soul-body union. It sufficed for him to admit that they were metaphysically distinct. To be a human is to be a composite of soul and body, and that the soul is superior to the body. The latter statement is grounded in his hierarchical classification of things into those that merely exist, those that exist and live, and those that exist, live, and have intelligence or reason.[15][16]

According to N. Blasquez, Augustine's dualism of substances of the body and soul doesn't stop him from seeing the unity of body and soul as a substance itself.[10][17] Following ancient philosophers he defined man as an *rational mortal animal – animal rationale mortale*.[18][19]

21.2 Terms or components

21.2.1 Body

See also: Human body

The body (Greek σῶμα *soma*) is the corporeal or physical aspect of a human being. Christians have traditionally believed that the body will be resurrected at the end of the age.

Rudolf Bultmann states the following:[20]

> "That *soma* belongs inseparably, constitutively, to human existence is most clearly evident from the fact that Paul cannot conceive even of a future human existence after death, `when that which is perfect is come' as an existence without *soma* – in contrast to the view of those in Corinth who deny the resurrection (1 Cor. 15, especially vv. 35ff.)."[21]

"Man does not have a *soma*; he is a *soma*"

21.2.2 Soul

See also: Soul in the Bible, nephesh and psyche (psychology)

The semantic domain of Biblical soul is based on the Hebrew word *nepes*, which presumably means "breath" or "breathing being".[22] This word never means an immortal soul[23] or an incorporeal part of the human being[24] that can survive death of the body as the spirit of dead.[25] This word usually designates the person as a whole[26] or its physical life. In the Septuagint *nepes* is mostly translated as *psy-*

che (ψυχή) and, exceptionally, in the Book of Joshua as *empneon* (ἔμπνεον), that is "breathing being".[27]

The New Testament follows the terminology of the Septuagint, and thus uses the word *psyche* with the Hebrew semantic domain and not the Greek,[28] that is an invisible power (or ever more, for Platonists, immortal and immaterial) that gives life and motion to the body and is responsible for its attributes.

In Patristic thought, towards the end of the 2nd century *psyche* was understood in more a Greek than a Hebrew way, and it was contrasted with the body. In the 3rd century, with the influence of Origen, there was the establishing of the doctrine of the inherent immortality of the soul and its divine nature.[29] Origen also taught the transmigration of the souls and their preexistence, but these views were officially rejected in 553 in the Fifth Ecumenical Council. Inherent immortality of the soul was accepted among western and eastern theologians throughout the middle ages, and after the Reformation, as evidenced by the Westminster Confession.

On the other hand, a number of modern Protestant scholars have adopted views similar to conditional immortality, including Edward Fudge and Clark Pinnock; however the majority of adherents hold the traditional doctrine.> In the last six decades, conditional immortality, or better "immortality by grace" (κατὰ χάριν ἀθανασία, *kata charin athanasia*), of the soul has also been widely accepted among Eastern Orthodox theologians, by returning to the views of the late 2nd century, where immortality was still considered as a gift granted with the value of Jesus' death and resurrection.[30] The Seventh-day Adventist Church has held to conditional immortality since the mid-19th century.

21.2.3 Spirit

See also: Spirit

The spirit (Hebrew *ruach*, Greek πνεῦμα, *pneuma*, which can also mean "breath") is likewise an immaterial component. It is often used interchangeably with "soul", *psyche*, although trichotomists believe that the spirit is distinct from the soul.

> "When Paul speaks of the *pneuma* of man he does not mean some higher principle within him or some special intellectual or spiritual faculty of his, but simply his self, and the only questions is whether the self is regarded in some particular aspect when it is called *pneuma*. In the first place, it apparently is regarded in the same way as when it is called *psyche* – viz. as the self that lives in man's attitude, in the orientation of his will."[31]

21.2.4 Flesh

See also: Flesh

"Flesh" (Greek σάρξ, *sarx*) is usually considered synonymous with "body", referring to the corporeal aspect of a human being. The apostle Paul contrasts flesh and spirit in Romans 7–8.

21.3 Constitution or nature of the person

Christian theologians have historically differed over the issue of how many distinct components constitute the human being.

21.3.1 Two parts (Dichotomism)

Main articles: Bipartite (theology) and Dualism (philosophy of mind)

The most popular view, affirmed by a large number of lay faithful and theologians from many Christian traditions, is that the human being is formed of two components: material (body/flesh) and spiritual (soul/spirit). The soul or spirit departs from the body at death, and will be reunited with the body at the resurrection.

21.3.2 Three parts (Trichotomism)

Main article: Tripartite (theology)

A significant minority of theologians across the denominational and theological spectrum, in both the East and the West, have held that human beings are made up of three distinct components: body or flesh, soul, and spirit. This is known technically as trichotomism. The biblical texts typically used to support this position are 1 Thessalonians 5:23 and Hebrews 4:12.[32]

21.3.3 One part (Monism)

See also: Monism

Modern theologians increasingly hold to the view that the human being is an indissoluble unity.[32] This is known as holism or monism. The body and soul are not considered separate components of a person, but rather as two facets of a united whole.[33] It is argued that this more accurately represents Hebrew thought, whereas body-soul dualism is more characteristic of classical Greek Platonist and Cartesian thought. Monism is the official position of the Seventh-day Adventist Church, which adheres to the doctrine of "soul sleep". Monism also appears to be more consistent with certain physicalist interpretations of modern neuroscience, which has indicated that the so-called "higher functions" of the mind are dependent upon or emergent from brain structure, not the independent workings of an immaterial soul as was previously thought.[34]

An influential exponent of this view was liberal theologian Rudolf Bultmann. Oscar Cullmann was influential in popularizing it.

21.4 Origin of humanity

See also: Creationism and Theistic evolution

The Bible teaches in the book of Genesis the humans were created by God. Some Christians believe that this must have involved a miraculous creative act, while others are comfortable with the idea that God worked through the evolutionary process.

21.4.1 God's image in the human

Main article: Image of God

The book of Genesis also teaches that human beings, male and female, were created in the image of God. The exact meaning of this has been debated throughout church history (see Image of God).

21.4.2 Origin/transmission of the soul

There are two opposing views about how the soul originates in each human being. *Creationism* teaches that God creates a "fresh" soul within each human embryo at or some time shortly after conception. Note: This is not to be confused with creationism as a view of the origins of life and the universe.

Traducianism, by contrast, teaches that the soul is inherited from the individual's parents, along with his or her biological material.

21.5 Sinful nature

Main article: Original sin

Christian theology traditionally teaches the corruption of human nature. However, there have been a range of views held throughout church history. Pelagius taught that human nature is not so corrupt that we cannot overcome sin. Arminians believe that our nature is corrupt, but that free will can still operate. Saint Augustine believed that all humans are born into the sin and guilt of Adam, and are powerless to do good without grace. John Calvin developed the doctrine of total depravity. The Catholic Church teaches that "Adam and Eve transmitted to their descendants human nature wounded by their own first sin and hence deprived of original holiness and justice." (CCC 417)

21.6 Death and Afterlife

See also: afterlife

Christian anthropology has implications for beliefs about death and the afterlife. The Christian church has traditionally taught that the soul of each individual separates from the body at death, to be reunited at the resurrection. This is closely related to the doctrine of the immortality of the soul. For example, the Westminster Confession (chapter XXXII) states:

> "The bodies of men, after death, return to dust, and see corruption: but their souls, which neither die nor sleep, having an immortal subsistence, immediately return to God who gave them"

21.6.1 Intermediate state

Main article: Intermediate state

The question then arises: where exactly does the disembodied soul "go" at death? Theologians refer to this subject as the intermediate state. The Old Testament speaks of a place called *sheol* where the spirits of the dead reside. In the New Testament, *hades*, the classical Greek realm of the dead, takes the place of *sheol*. In particular, Jesus teaches in Luke 16:19–31 (Lazarus and Dives) that *hades* consists of two separate "sections", one for the righteous and one for the unrighteous. His teaching is consistent with intertestamental Jewish thought on the subject.[35]

Fully developed Christian theology goes a step further; on the basis of such texts as Luke 23:43 and Philippians 1:23, it has traditionally been taught that the souls of the dead are received immediately either into heaven or hell, where they will experience a foretaste of their eternal destiny prior to the resurrection. (Roman Catholicism teaches a third possible location, Purgatory, though this is denied by Protestants and Eastern Orthodox.)

> "the souls of the righteous, being then made perfect in holiness, are received into the highest heavens, where they behold the face of God, in light and glory, waiting for the full redemption of their bodies. And the souls of the wicked are cast into hell, where they remain in torments and utter darkness, reserved to the judgment of the great day." (*Westminster Confession*)

Some Christian groups which stress a monistic anthropology deny that the soul can exist consciously apart from the body. For example, the Seventh-day Adventist Church teaches that the intermediate state is an unconscious sleep; this teaching is informally known as "soul sleep".

21.6.2 Final state

In Christian belief, both the righteous and the unrighteous will be resurrected at the last judgment. The righteous will receive incorruptible, immortal bodies (1 Corinthians 15), while the unrighteous will be sent to the "Lake of Fire" or "Gehenna". Traditionally, Christians have believed that hell will be a place of eternal physical and psychological punishment. In the last two centuries, annihilationism and universalism have become more popular.

21.7 See also

- Human nature, Person
- Philosophical anthropology
- Theological anthropology
- List of important publications in anthropology
- Christian psychology

21.8 References

[1] Erickson, Millard (1998). *Christian Theology* (2 ed.). p. 537. ISBN 0-8010-2182-0.

[2] The Greek text: PG 44, 123–256; SCh 6, (1944) Jean-Jacques Courtiau (ed.)

[3] Étienne Gilson, p. 56

[4] Maspero & Mateo Seco, p. 38

[5] Maspero & Mateo Seco, p. 39

[6] Maspero & Mateo Seco, p. 41

[7] Maspero & Mateo Seco, p. 42

[8] Cf. A. Gianni, pp.148–149

[9] Hendrics, E., p. 291.

[10] Massuti, E., p.98.

[11] *De cura pro mortuis gerenda* CSEL 41, 627[13–22]; PL 40, 595: *Nullo modo ipsa spernenda sunt corpora. (...)Haec enim non ad ornamentum vel adiutorium, quod adhibetur extrinsecus, sed ad ipsam naturam hominis pertinent*; *Contra Faustum*, 22.27; PL 44,418.

[12] *Enarrationes in psalmos*, 143, 6; CCL 40, 2077 [46] – 2078 [74]); *De utilitate ieiunii*, 4,4–5; CCL 46, 234–235.

[13] *De quantitate animae* 1.2; 5.9

[14] *De quantitate animae* 13.12: *Substantia quaedam rationis particeps, regendo corpori accomodata.*

[15] *On the free will (De libero arbitrio)* 2.3.7–6.13

[16] cf. W.E. Mann, p.141-142

[17] *El concepto del substantia segun san Agustin*, pp. 305–350.

[18] *De ordine*, II, 11.31; CCL 29, 124 [18]; PL 32,1009; De quantitate animae, 25,47–49; CSEL 89, 190–194; PL 32, 1062–1063

[19] Cf. Ch. Couturier SJ, p. 543

[20] Bultmann, Rudolf (1953). *Theologie des Neuen Testaments* (in German). Tübingen: Mohr. pp. 189–249. (English translation *Theology of the New Testament* 2 vols, London: SCM, 1952, 1955)

[21] Bultmann, I: 192

[22] *Hebrew-English Lexicon*, Brown, Driver & Briggs, Hendrickson Publishers.

[23] *Baker's Evangelical Dictionary of Biblical Theology.*

[24] *Dictionary of Biblical Theology*, Father Xavier Leon Dufour, 1985.

[25] *New International Dictionary.*

[26] New Dictionary of Biblical Theology

[27] "A careful examination of the βiblical material, particularly the words nefesh, neshama, and ruaḥ, which are often too broadly translated as "soul" and "spirit," indicates that these must not be understood as referring to the psychical side of a psychophysical pair. A man did not possess a nefesh but rather was a nefesh, as Gen. 2:7 says: "wayehi ha-adam le-nefesh ḥayya" (". . . and the man became a living being"). Man was, for most of the biblical writers, what has been called "a unit of vital power," not a dual creature separable into two distinct parts of unequal importance and value. While this understanding of the nature of man dominated biblical thought, in apocalyptic literature (2nd century BCE–2nd century CE) the term nefesh began to be viewed as a separable psychical entity with existence apart from body.... The biblical view of man as an inseparable psychosomatic unit meant that death was understood to be his dissolution."—Britannica, 2004.

[28] *Exegetical Dictionary of the New Testament*

[29] The early Hebrews apparently had a concept of the soul but did not separate it from the body, although later Jewish writers developed the idea of the soul further. Old Testament references to the soul are related to the concept of breath and establish no distinction between the ethereal soul and the corporeal body. Christian concepts of a body-soul dichotomy originated with the ancient Greeks andwere introduced into Christian theology at an early date by St. Gregory of Nyssa and by St. Augustine.—*Britannica*, 2004

[30] *Immortality of the Soul*, George Florovsky.

[31] Bultmann, I:206

[32] Bruce Milne. *Know The Truth*. IVP. pp. 120–122.

[33] "The traditional anthropology encounters major problems in the Bible and its predominantly holistic view of human beings. Genesis 2:7 is a key verse: 'Then the LORD God formed man from the dust of the ground and breathed into his nostrils the breath of life, and the man became a living being' (NRSV). The 'living being' (traditionally, 'living soul') is an attempt to translate the Hebrew *nephesh hayah,* which indicates a 'living person' in the context. More than one interpreter has pointed out that this text does not say that the human being *has* a soul but rather *is* a soul. H. Wheeler Robinson summarized the matter in his statement that 'The Hebrew conceived man as animated body and not as an incarnate soul.'" (Martin E. Tate, "The Comprehensive Nature of Salvation in Biblical Perspective," *Evangelical review of theology,* Vol. 23.)

[34] AJ Gijsbers (2003). "The Dialogue between Neuroscience and Theology" (PDF). ISCAST.

[35] D. K. Innes, "Sheol" in *New Bible Dictionary*, IVP 1996.

21.9   Bibliography

- Agaësse, Paul, SJ (2004). *L'anthropologie chrétienne selon saint Augustin : image, liberté, péché et grâce.*

Paris: Médiasèvres. p. 197. ISBN 2-900388-68-6.

- Blasquez, N, *El concepto del substantia segun san Agustin*, ""Augustinus" 14 (1969), pp. 305–350; 15 (1970), pp. 369–383; 16 (1971), pp. 69–79.

- Bainvel, J. "Ame. Doctrine des trois premiers siècles; Développement de la doctrine du IVe au XIIIe s.". *Dictionnaire de Théologie Catholique* **1**. pp. 977–1006.

- Bultmann, Rudolf (1953). *Theologie des Neuen Testaments* (in German). Tübingen: Mohr. pp. 189–249. (English translation *Theology of the New Testament* 2 vols, London: SCM, 1952, 1955). The leading scholarly reference supporting a holistic anthropology (similar to soul sleep)

- Cullmann, Oscar. *Immortality of the soul or resurrection of the dead?: the witness of the New Testament.* Archived from the original on 2009-10-26.

- Gianni, A., *Il problema antropologico*, Roma 1965.

- Gilson, Étienne, Gregory of Nyssa, Anthropology, in: *History of Christian Philosophy in the Middle Ages*, (1980 reprinted 1985), London: Sheed & Ward, pp. 56–59, ISBN 0-7220-4114-4.

- Couturier, Charles, SJ, *La structure métaphysique de l'homme d'après saint Augustin*, in: *Augustinus Magister. Congrès International Augustinien. Communications*, (1954), Paris, vol. 1, pp. 543–550

- Hendrics, E. *Platonisches und Biblisches Denken bei Augustinus*, in: 'Augustinus Magister. Congrès International Augustinien. Communications*, (1954), Paris , vol. 1.

- Jewitt, R. (1971). *Paul's Anthropological Terms.* Leiden: Brill.

- Kümmel, W. G. (1948). *Das Bild des Menschen im Neuen Testament* (in German). Zürich: Zwingli. (English translation *Man in the NT*. London: Epworth, 1963)

- Ladd, George Eldon (1974). *A Theology of the New Testament*. Grand Rapids, MI: Eerdmans. pp. 457–78.

- Karpp, Heinrich (1950). *Probleme altchristlicher Anthropologie. Biblische Anthropologie und philosophische Psychologie bei den Kirchen-vatern des dritten Jahrhunderts.* Gütersloh: G. Bertelsmann Verlag.

- Mann, W. E., *Inner-Life Ethics*, in:Matthews, G. B., ed. (1999). *The Augustinian Tradition*. Philosophical Traditions. Berkeley-Los Angeles-London: University of California Press. pp. 138–152. ISBN 0-520-20999-0.

- Masutti, Egidio, *Il problema del corpo in San Agostino*, Roma: Borla, 1989, p. 230, ISBN 88-263-0701-6

- Rondeau, Marie Josèphe (1962). "Remarques sur l'anthropologie de saint Hilaire". *Studia Patristica* (Berlin: Akademie-Verlag). 6 (Papers presented to the Third International Conference on Patristic Studies held at Christ Church, Oxford, 1959, Part IV Theologica, Augustiniana, ed. F. L. Cross): 197–210.

- Steenberg, M. C. (2009). *Of God and Man : theology as anthropology from Irenaeus to Athanasius*. London: T & T Clark.

21.10 External links

- Mick Pope, Losing our Souls?

Chapter 22

Hypergraphia

Not to be confused with Hypergraphy.

Hypergraphia is a behavioral condition characterized by

An example of what hypergraphia may look like

the intense desire to write. Forms of hypergraphia can vary in writing style and content. It is a symptom associated with temporal lobe changes in epilepsy, which is the cause of the Geschwind syndrome, a mental disorder.[1] Structures that may have an effect on hypergraphia when damaged due to temporal lobe epilepsy are the hippocampus and Wernicke's area. Aside from temporal lobe epilepsy, chemical causes may be responsible for inducing hypergraphia.

22.1 Characteristics

Patients with hypergraphia exhibit a wide variety of writing styles and content. While some write in a coherent, logical manner, others write in a more jumbled style (sometimes in a specific pattern).

22.1.1 Writing style

Waxman and Geschwind were the first to describe hypergraphia. The patients they observed displayed extensively compulsive detailed writing, sometimes with literary creativity. The patients kept diaries, which some used to meticulously document minute details of their everyday activities, write poetry, or create lists. Case 1 of their study wrote lists of her relatives, her likes and dislikes, and the furniture in her apartment. Besides lists, the patient wrote poetry, often with a moral or philosophical undertone. She described an incident in which she wrote the lyrics of a song she learned when she was 17 several hundred times and another incident in which she felt the urge to write a word over and over again. Another patient wrote aphorisms and certain sentences in repetition.[2]

A patient from a separate study experienced "continuously rhyming in his head" for five years after a seizure and said that he "felt the need to write them down."[3] The patient did not talk in rhyme, nor did he read poetry. Language capacity and mental status were normal for this patient, except for recorded right temporal spikes on electroencephalograms. This patient had right hemisphere epilepsy. Functional MRI scans of other studies suggest that rhyming behavior is produced in the left hemisphere, but Mendez proposed that hyperactive electrical activity of the right hemisphere may induce a release of writing and rhyming abilities in the left hemisphere.[3]

22.1.2 Writing content

In addition to writing in different forms (poetry, books, repeating one word, etc.), hypergraphia patients differ in the complexity of their writings. While some writers (see Alice Flaherty and Dyane Leshin-Harwood, author of "Birth of a New Brain - Healing from Postpartum Bipolar Disorder" who had postpartum hypergraphia/bipolar, peripartum onset) use their hypergraphia to help them write extensive papers and books, most patients do not write things with sub-

Macro and micrographic writing by the same epileptic

22.2.1 Temporal lobe epilepsy

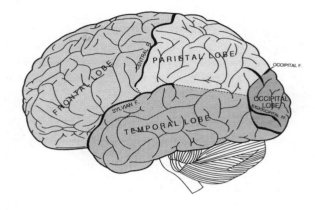

Image of the temporal lobe

stance. Flaherty defines hypergraphia, as a result of temporal lobe epilepsy, as a condition that "increase[s] idea generation, sometimes at the expense of quality."[4] Patients hospitalized with temporal lobe epilepsy and other disorders causing hypergraphia have written memos and lists of random categories (like their favorite songs) and recorded their dreams in extreme length and detail.[4] Some patients who also suffer from temporal lobe epilepsy record the times and locations of each seizure compiled into a giant list.[2]

There are many accounts of patients writing in nonsensical patterns including writing in a center-seeking spiral starting around the edges of a piece of paper.[5] In one case study, a patient even wrote backwards, so that the writing could only be interpreted with the aid of a mirror.[2] Sometimes the writing can consist of scribbles and frantic, random thoughts that are quickly jotted down on paper very frequently. Grammar can be present, but the meaning of these thoughts is generally hard to grasp and the sentences are loose.[5] In some cases, patients write extremely detailed accounts of events that are occurring or descriptions of where they are.[5]

22.2 Causes

Some studies have suggested that hypergraphia is related to bipolar disorder, hypomania, and schizophrenia.[6] Although creative ability was observed in the patients of these studies, signs of creativity were observed, not hypergraphia specifically. Therefore, it is difficult to say with absolute certainty that hypergraphia is a symptom of these psychiatric illnesses because creativity in patients with bipolar disorder, hypomania, or schizophrenia may manifest into something aside from writing. However, other studies have shown significant accounts between hypergraphia and temporal lobe epilepsy[7] and chemical causes.

Hypergraphia is a symptom of temporal lobe epilepsy, a condition of reoccurring seizures caused by excessive neuronal activity, but it is not a common symptom among patients. Less than 10 percent of patients with temporal lobe epilepsy exhibit characteristics of hypergraphia. Temporal lobe epilepsy patients may exhibit irritability, discomfort, or an increasing feeling of dread if their writing activity is disrupted.[8] To elicit such responses when interrupting their writing suggests that hypergraphia is a compulsive condition, resulting in an obsessive motivation to write.[6] A temporal lobe epilepsy may influence frontotemporal connections in such a way that the drive to write is increased in the frontal lobe, beginning with the prefrontal and premotor cortex planning out what to write, and then leading to the motor cortex (located next to the central fissure) executing the physical movement of writing.[6]

Most temporal lobe epilepsy patients who suffer from hypergraphia can write words, but not all may have the capacity to write complete sentences that have meaning.[5]

22.2.2 Chemical

Certain drugs have been known to induce hypergraphia including donepezil. In one case study, a patient taking donepezil reported an elevation in mood and energy levels which led to hypergraphia and other excessive forms of speech (such as singing).[9] Six other cases of patients taking donepezil and experiencing mania have been previously reported. These patients also had cases of dementia, cognitive impairment from a cerebral aneurysm, bipolar I disorder, and/or depression. Researchers are unsure why donepezil can induce mania and hypergraphia. It could potentially result from an increase in acetylcholine levels, which would have an effect on the other neurotransmitters in the brain.[9]

Another potential cause of hypergraphia is from one of the body's neurotransmitters, dopamine (DA). Dopamine has been known to decrease latent inhibition, which causes a decrease in the ability to habituate to different stimuli. Low latent inhibition leads to an excessive level of stimulation and could contribute to the onset of hypergraphia and general creativity. This research implies that there is a direct correlation between the levels of DA between neuronal synapses and the level of creativity exhibited by the patient. DA agonists increase the levels of DA between synapses which results in higher levels of creativity, and the opposite is true for DA antagonists.[4]

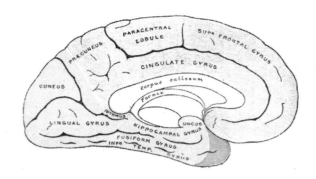

Image of the hippocampal gyrus

22.3   Pathophysiology

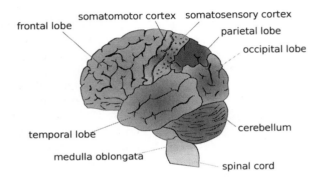

Image of the brain lobes, including the temporal lobe and somatomotor (primary motor) cortex.

Several regions of the brain are involved in the act of writing. Primary areas are the superior parietal cortex and the frontal lobe, the region of the brain that plans out movement.[10] An area of the frontal lobe that is especially active is Exner's area, located in the premotor cortex.[10] The physical motion of the hand is controlled by the primary motor cortex, also located in the frontal lobe, and the right cerebellum.[10] Writing creatively and generating ideas, on the other hand, is controlled by the limbic system, specifically involving the activity of the hippocampus, which is important in the retrieval of long-term memories.[11] Words and ideas are cognized and understood by the temporal lobes, and these temporal lobes are connected to the limbic system.[10]

Although hypergraphia cannot be isolated to one specific part of the brain, some areas are known to have more of an effect than others. The hippocampus has been found to play a role in the occurrence of temporal lobe epilepsy and schizophrenia. In one study, rats induced with temporal lobe epilepsy showed an increase in dopamine neural activity in the hippocampus. Because hypergraphia has been linked to temporal lobe epilepsy and schizophrenia, the hippocampus could have an effect on hypergraphia as well.[12] In another study, patients with bilateral hippocampal atrophy (BHA) showed signs of having Geschwind syndrome, including hypergraphia.[13]

While epilepsy-induced hypergraphia is usually lateralized to the left cerebral hemisphere in the language areas, hypergraphia associated with lesions and other brain damage usually occurs in the right cerebral hemisphere.[14] Lesions to the right side of the brain usually cause hypergraphia because they can disinhibit language function on the left side of the brain.[4] Hypergraphia has also been known to be caused by right hemisphere strokes and tumors.[5][15]

Lesions to Wernicke's area (in the left temporal lobe) can increase speech output, which can sometimes manifest itself in writing.[4]

22.4   Society and culture

Hypergraphia was one of the central issues in the 1999 trial of Alvin Ridley for the imprisonment and murder of his wife Virginia Ridley.[16] The mysterious woman, who had died in bed of apparent suffocation, had remained secluded in her home for 27 years in the small town of Ringgold, Georgia, USA. Her ten thousand page journal, which provided abundant evidence that she suffered from epilepsy and had remained housebound of her own will, was instrumental in the acquittal of her husband.[16]

Vincent van Gogh and Fyodor Dostoevsky are reported to have been affected by hypergraphia.[17] It has been suggested that the poet Robert Burns was a sufferer.[18]

Lewis Carroll, the author of *Alice in Wonderland*, is said to have had hypergraphia.[19] In his lifetime he wrote over 98,000 letters varying in format. Some were written backwards, in rebus, and in patterns, such as "The Mouse's Tale" in the aforementioned book.

22.5 See also

- Automatic writing
- Free writing
- Graphomania

22.6 References

[1] Devinsky J, Schachter S (August 2009). "Norman Geschwind's contribution to the understanding of behavioral changes in temporal lobe epilepsy: the February 1974 lecture". *Epilepsy Behav* (Biography, History article) **15** (4): 417–24. doi:10.1016/j.yebeh.2009.06.006. PMID 19640791.

[2] Waxman, SG; Geschwind, N (March 2005). "Hypergraphia in temporal lobe epilepsy. 1974.". *Epilepsy & behavior : E&B* **6** (2): 282–91. doi:10.1016/j.yebeh.2004.11.022. PMID 15710320.

[3] Mendez, MF (Fall 2005). "Hypergraphia for poetry in an epileptic patient". *The Journal of neuropsychiatry and clinical neurosciences* **17** (4): 560–1. doi:10.1176/appi.neuropsych.17.4.560. PMID 16388002.

[4] Flaherty AW (December 2005). "Frontotemporal and dopaminergic control of idea generation and creative drive". *J. Comp. Neurol.* (Review) **493** (1): 147–53. doi:10.1002/cne.20768. PMC 2571074. PMID 16254989.

[5] Yamadori A, Mori E, Tabuchi M, Kudo Y, Mitani Y (October 1986). "Hypergraphia: a right hemisphere syndrome". *J. Neurol. Neurosurg. Psychiatr.* **49** (10): 1160–4. doi:10.1136/jnnp.49.10.1160. PMC 1029050. PMID 3783177.

[6] Flaherty, AW (March 2011). "Brain illness and creativity: mechanisms and treatment risks". *Canadian journal of psychiatry. Revue canadienne de psychiatrie* **56** (3): 132–43. PMID 21443820.

[7] Sachdev, H S; Waxman, S G (1981). "Frequency of hypergraphia in temporal lobe epilepsy: an index of interictal behaviour syndrome.". *Journal of neurology, neurosurgery, and psychiatry* **44** (4): 358–60. doi:10.1136/jnnp.44.4.358. PMID 7241165. Lay summary. Patients with temporal lobe epilepsy tended to reply more frequently to a standard questionnaire, and wrote extensively (mean: 1301 words) as compared to others (mean: 106 words). The incidence of temporal lobe epilepsy was 73% in patients exhibiting hypergraphia compared to 17% in patients without this trait. These findings suggest that hypergraphia may be a quantitative index of behaviour change in temporal lobe epilepsy.

[8] van Vugt P, Paquier P, Kees L, Cras P (November 1996). "Increased writing activity in neurological conditions: a review and clinical study". *J. Neurol. Neurosurg. Psychiatr.* **61** (5): 510–4. doi:10.1136/jnnp.61.5.510. PMC 1074050. PMID 8937347.

[9] Wicklund S, Wright M (2012). "Donepezil-induced mania". *J Neuropsychiatry Clin Neurosci* **24** (3): E27. doi:10.1176/appi.neuropsych.11070160. PMID 23037669.

[10] Planton S, Jucla M, Roux FE, Démonet JF (2013). "The "handwriting brain": A meta-analysis of neuroimaging studies of motor versus orthographic processes". *Cortex* **49** (10): 2772–87. doi:10.1016/j.cortex.2013.05.011. PMID 23831432.

[11] Shah C, Erhard K, Ortheil HJ, Kaza E, Kessler C, Lotze M (May 2013). "Neural correlates of creative writing: an fMRI study". *Hum Brain Mapp* **34** (5): 1088–101. doi:10.1002/hbm.21493. PMID 22162145.

[12] Cifelli P, Grace AA (12 July 2011). "Pilocarpine-induced temporal lobe epilepsy in the rat is associated with increased dopamine neuron activity". *The International Journal of Neuropsychopharmacology* **15** (07): 957–964. doi:10.1017/S1461145711001106.

[13] van Elst LT, Krishnamoorthy ES, Bäumer D, et al. (June 2003). "Psychopathological profile in patients with severe bilateral hippocampal atrophy and temporal lobe epilepsy: evidence in support of the Geschwind syndrome?". *Epilepsy & behavior : E&B* **4** (3): 291–7. doi:10.1016/s1525-5050(03)00084-2. PMID 12791331.

[14] Ishikawa, T; Saito, M; Fujimoto, S; Imahashi, H (September 2000). "Ictal increased writing preceded by dysphasic seizures.". *Brain & development* **22** (6): 398–402. doi:10.1016/s0387-7604(00)00163-7. PMID 11042425.

[15] Imamura, T; Yamadori, A; Tsuburaya, K (January 1992). "Hypergraphia associated with a brain tumour of the right cerebral hemisphere.". *Journal of neurology, neurosurgery, and psychiatry* **55** (1): 25–7. doi:10.1136/jnnp.55.1.25. PMID 1548492.

[16] Brownlee 2006.

[17] The brains behind writer's block

[18] Robert Burns and the Medical Profession Retrieved : 2014-01-11

[19] Flaherty, *The Midnight Disease* p 26

22.7 Further reading

- Pickover, C. A. (1999). *Strange brains and genius: The secret lives of eccentric scientists and madmen*. New York: William Morrow. ISBN 0-688-16894-9

- Schachter, S. C., Holmes, G. L., & Kasteleijn-Nolst Trenité, D. (2008). *Behavioral aspects of epilepsy: Principles and practice*. New York: Demos. ISBN 1-933864-04-4

- Flaherty, Alice Weaver (2004). *The Midnight Disease: The Drive to Write, Writer's Block, and the Creative Brain.* Houghton Mifflin Harcourt. ISBN 0-618-23065-3.

Chapter 23

Geschwind syndrome

Geschwind syndrome, also known as **Gastaut-Geschwind**, is a group of behavioral phenomena evident in some people with temporal lobe epilepsy. It is named for one of the first individuals to categorize the symptoms, Norman Geschwind, who published prolifically on the topic from 1973 to 1984.[1] There is controversy surrounding whether it is a true neuropsychiatric disorder.[2] Temporal lobe epilepsy causes chronic, mild, interictal (i.e. between seizures) changes in personality, which slowly intensify over time.[1] Geschwind syndrome includes five primary changes; hypergraphia, hyperreligiosity, atypical (usually reduced) sexuality, circumstantiality, and intensified mental life.[3] Not all symptoms must be present for a diagnosis.[2]

Only a subset of people with epilepsy in general and temporal lobe epilepsy in particular present with features of Geschwind syndrome[4] and a recent review concluded that the evidence for a link between temporal lobe epilepsy and hyperreligiosity "isn't terribly compelling."[5]

23.1 Features

23.1.1 Hypergraphia

Hypergraphia is the tendency for extensive and compulsive writing, and has been observed in Temporal Lobe Epilepsy patients who have had multiple seizures.[6] Those with hypergraphia have extreme attention to detail in their writing. Some patients keep diaries and write down meticulous details about their everyday lives. In certain cases, the writing of patients has demonstrated extreme interest in religious topics. Also, these individuals tend to have poor penmanship. The novelist Fyodor Dostoyevsky showed symptoms of Geschwind syndrome, including hypergraphia.[7]

23.1.2 Hyperreligiosity

Some individuals may exhibit increased, usually intense, religious feelings and philosophical interests,[8] and partial (temporal lobe) epilepsy patients with frequent numinous-like auras have greater ictal and interictal spirituality.[9] Some seizures include ecstatic experiences.[10] It has been reported that many religious leaders exhibit this form of epilepsy.[11][12] These religious feelings can motivate beliefs within any religion, including Voodoo,[13] Christianity, Islam,[14] and others. There are reports of patients converting between religions.[15] A few patients internalize their religious feelings: when asked if they are religious they say they are not.[16]

23.1.3 Atypical sexuality

People with Geschwind syndrome reported higher rates of atypical or altered sexuality.[17] In approximately half of individuals hyposexuality (i.e. decreased libido) is reported.[18][19] Cases of hypersexuality have also been reported.[20]

23.1.4 Circumstantiality

Individuals that demonstrate circumstantiality (or *Viscosity*) tend to continue conversations for a long time and talk receptively.[21]

23.2 See also

- Ramakrishna

- Fyodor Dostoyevsky

- Cosmic Consciousness

- Oceanic feeling

23.3   References

[1] Devinsky, J.; Schachter, S. (2009). "Norman Geschwind's contribution to the understanding of behavioral changes in temporal lobe epilepsy: The February 1974 lecture". *Epilepsy & Behavior* **15** (4): 417–24. doi:10.1016/j.yebeh.2009.06.006. PMID 19640791.

[2] Benson, D. F. (1991). "The Geschwind syndrome". *Advances in neurology* **55**: 411–21. PMID 2003418.

[3] Tebartz Van Elst, L.; Krishnamoorthy, E. S.; Bäumer, D.; Selai, C.; von Gunten, A.; Gene-Cos, N.; Ebert, D.; Trimble, M. R. (2003). "Psychopathological profile in patients with severe bilateral hippocampal atrophy and temporal lobe epilepsy: Evidence in support of the Geschwind syndrome?". *Epilepsy & Behavior* **4** (3): 291–297. doi:10.1016/S1525-5050(03)00084-2.

[4] Benson, D.F. & Hermann, B.P. (1998) Personality disorders. In J. Engel Jr. & T.A. Pedley (Eds.) Epilepsy: A comprehensive textbook. Vol. II (pp.2065–2070). Philadelphia: Lippincott–Raven.

[5] Craig Aaen-Stockdale (2012). "Neuroscience for the Soul". *The Psychologist* **25** (7): 520–523.

[6] Tremont, Geoffrey; Smith, Megan M; Bauer, Lyndsey; Alosco, Michael L; Davis, Jennifer D; Blum, Andrew S; LaFrance, W Curt (2012). "Comparison of personality characteristics on the bear-fedio inventory between patients with epilepsy and those with non-epileptic seizures.". *The Journal of neuropsychiatry and clinical neurosciences* **24** (1): 47–52. doi:10.1176/appi.neuropsych.11020039.

[7] Hughes, John R (2005). "The idiosyncratic aspects of the epilepsy of Fyodor Dostoevsky.". *Epilepsy and behavior* **7** (3): 531–8. doi:10.1016/j.yebeh.2005.07.021. PMID 16194626.

[8] Devinsky, Julie; Schachter, Steven (2009). "Norman Geschwind's contribution to the understanding of behavioral changes in temporal lobe epilepsy: the February 1974 lecture.". *Epilepsy & behavior* **15** (4): 417–24. doi:10.1016/j.yebeh.2009.06.006. PMID 19640791.

[9] Dolgoff-Kaspar, R (et al.) (2011). "Numinous-like auras and spirituality in persons with partial seizures.". *Epilepsia* **52** (3): 640–6. doi:10.1111/j.1528-1167.2010.02957.x. PMID 21395568. Epilepsy patients with frequent numinous-like auras have greater ictal and interictal spirituality of an experiential, personalized, and atypical form, which may be distinct from traditional, culturally based religiosity.

[10] Picard, Fabienne; Kurth, Florian (2014). "Ictal alterations of consciousness during ecstatic seizures.". *Epilepsy & Behavior* **30**: 58–61. doi:10.1016/j.yebeh.2013.09.036. PMID 24436968. Lay summary. Patients with ecstatic epileptic seizures report an altered consciousness, which they describe as a sense of heightened perception of themselves - they "feel very present"- and an increased vividness of sensory perceptions.

[11] Muhammed, Louwai (2013). "A retrospective diagnosis of epilepsy in three historical figures: St Paul, Joan of Arc and Socrates.". *Journal of medical biography* **21** (4): 208–11. doi:10.1177/0967772013479757.

[12] Nakken, Karl O; Brodtkorb, Eylert (2011). "[Epilepsy and religion].". *Tidsskrift for den Norske lægeforening : tidsskrift for praktisk medicin, ny række* **131** (13-14): 1294–7. doi:10.4045/tidsskr.10.1049.

[13] Carrazana E. (et al.) (1999). "Epilepsy and Religious Experiences: Voodoo Possession". *Epilepsia* **40** (2): 239–241. doi:10.1111/j.1528-1157.1999.tb02081.x. Lay summary – *Epileptic seizures have a historical association with religion, primarily through the concept of spirit possession. Five cases where epileptic seizures were initially attributed to Voodoo spirit possession are presented. The attribution is discussed within the context of the Voodoo belief system.*

[14] Stephen, M.D. Salloway (1997). "The Neural Substrates of Religious Experience". *The Neuropsychiatry of Limbic and Subcortical Disorders*. American Psychiatric Publications. ISBN 0880489421.

[15] Dewhurst, K; Beard, A W (1970). "Sudden religious conversions in temporal lobe epilepsy.". *The British journal of psychiatry : the journal of mental science* **117** (540): 497–507. doi:10.1192/bjp.117.540.497.

[16] Waxman, Stephen G, MD; Geschwind, Norman, MD (1972). "The Interictal Behavior Syndrome of Temporal Lobe Epilepsy". *Archives of General Psychiatry* **32** (12): 1580–1586. doi:10.1001/archpsyc.1975.01760300118011. Lay summary – *"Although the patient denied being religious, his writings contained numerous religious references, and some pages were adorned with religious symbols".*

[17] Gerhard J. Luef (2008). "Epilepsy and sexuality". *Seizure* **17** (2): 127–130. doi:10.1016/j.seizure.2007.11.009. Lay summary – *Men and women with epilepsy frequently complain, if asked, of sexual dysfunction and appear to have a higher incidence of sexual dysfunction than persons with other chronic neurologic illnesses.*

[18] Harden, Cynthia L (2006). "Sexuality in men and women with epilepsy.". *CNS spectrums* **11** (8 Suppl 9): 13–8. PMID 16871133.

[19] L Tebartz van Elsta (et al.) (2003). "Psychopathological profile in patients with severe bilateral hippocampal atrophy and temporal lobe epilepsy: evidence in support of the Geschwind syndrome?". *Epilepsy & Behavior* **3** (4): 291–297. doi:10.1016/s1525-5050(03)00084-2. Lay summary – *specific symptoms that characterize the Geschwind syndrome like hypergraphia and hyposexuality might be pathogenically related to hippocampal atrophy.*

[20] Rees, Peter M; Fowler, Clare J; Maas, Cornelis (2007). "Sexual function in men and women with neurological disorders.". *Lancet* **369** (9560): 512–25. doi:10.1016/s0140-6736(07)60238-4. PMID 17292771.

[21] Devinsky, Orrin; Vorkas, Charles; Barr, William (2006). "Personality disorders in epilepsy". *Psychiatric Issues in Epilepsy: A Practical Guide to Diagnosis and Treatment.* Lippincott Williams & Wilkins. ISBN 078178591X.

Chapter 24

Hypoactive sexual desire disorder

Hypoactive sexual desire disorder (HSDD) or **inhibited sexual desire** (ISD) is considered a sexual dysfunction and is characterized as a lack or absence of sexual fantasies and desire for sexual activity, as judged by a clinician. For this to be regarded as a disorder, it must cause marked distress or interpersonal difficulties and not be better accounted for by another mental disorder, a drug (legal or illegal), or some other medical condition. A person with ISD will not start, or respond to their partner's desire for, sexual activity.[1] Other terms used to describe the phenomenon include sexual aversion and sexual apathy.[1]

HSDD was listed under the Sexual and Gender Identity Disorders of the DSM-IV.[2] In the DSM-5, it was split into **male hypoactive sexual desire disorder**[3] and **female sexual interest/arousal disorder**.[4] It was first included in the DSM-III under the name inhibited sexual desire disorder,[5] but the name was changed in the DSM-III-R.

There are various subtypes. HSDD can be general (general lack of sexual desire) or situational (still has sexual desire, but lacks sexual desire for current partner), and it can be acquired (HSDD started after a period of normal sexual functioning) or lifelong (the person has always had no/low sexual desire.)

HSDD has garnered much criticism, primarily by asexual activists. They point out that HSDD puts asexuality in the same position homosexuality was from 1974-1987. Back then, the DSM recognised 'ego-dystonic homosexuality' as a disorder, defined as having sexual interest in the same sex and it causing distress. Despite the DSM itself officially recognizing this as unnecessarily pathologizing homosexuality and removing it as a disorder in 1987.[6]

24.1 Causes

Low sexual desire alone is not equivalent to HSDD because of the requirement in HSDD that the low sexual desire causes marked distress and interpersonal difficulty and because of the requirement that the low desire is not better accounted for by another disorder in the DSM or by a general medical problem. It is therefore difficult to say exactly what causes HSDD. It is easier to describe, instead, some of the causes of low sexual desire.

In men, though there are theoretically more types of HSDD/low sexual desire, typically men are only diagnosed with one of three subtypes.

- Lifelong/generalised: The man has little or no desire for sexual stimulation (with a partner or alone) and never had.

- Acquired/situational: The man was previously sexually interested in his present partner but now lacks sexual interest in this partner but has desire for sexual stimulation (i.e. alone or with someone other than his present partner.)

- Acquired/generalised: The man previously had sexual interest in his present partner, but lacks interest in sexual activity, partnered or solitary.

Though it can sometimes be difficult to distinguish between these types, they do not necessarily have the same etiology. The cause of lifelong/generalized HSDD is unknown. In the case of acquired/generalized low sexual desire, possible causes include various medical/health problems, psychiatric problems, low levels of testosterone or high levels of prolactin. One theory suggests that sexual desire is controlled by a balance between inhibitory and excitatory factors.[7] This is thought to be expressed via neurotransmitters in selective brain areas. A decrease in sexual desire may therefore be due to an imbalance between neurotransmitters with excitatory activity like dopamine and norepinephrine and neurotransmitters with inhibitory activity, like serotonin.[8] The, New York-based, "New View Campaign" organization has expressed skepticism about too much emphasis on explanations based on neurotransmitters because emphasis on such explanations have been made largely by "educational" efforts funded by Boehringer-Ingelheim while it was attempting to get the FDA to approve a drug affecting neuro-transmitters for treatment for HSDD.[9] Low sexual desire can also be a side effect of various medications. In the case of acquired/situational HSDD, possible causes include intimacy difficulty, relationship problems, sexual addiction, and chronic illness of the man's partner. The evidence for these is somewhat in question. Some claimed causes of low sexual desire are based on empirical evidence. However, some are based merely on clinical observation.[10] In many cases, the cause of HSDD is simply unknown.[11]

There are some factors that are believed to be possible causes of HSDD in women. As with men, various medical problems, psychiatric problems (such as mood disorders), or increased amounts of prolactin can cause HSDD. Other hormones are believed to be involved as well. Additionally, factors such as relationship problems or stress are believed to be possible causes of reduced sexual desire in women.[12] According to one recent study examining the affective responses and attentional capture of sexual stimuli in women with and without HSDD, women with HSDD do not appear to have a negative association to sexual stimuli, but rather a weaker positive association than women without HSDD [13]

24.2 Diagnosis

In the DSM-5, male hypoactive sexual desire disorder is characterized by "persistently or recurrently deficient (or absent) sexual/erotic thoughts or fantasies and desire for sexual activity", as judged by a clinician with consideration for the patient's age and cultural context.[3] Female sexual interest/arousal disorder is defined as a "lack of, or significantly reduced, sexual interest/arousal", manifesting as at least three of the following symptoms: no or little interest in sexual activity, no or few sexual thoughts, no or few attempts to initiate sexual activity or respond to partner's initiation, no or little sexual pleasure/excitement in 75%−100% of sexual experiences, no or little sexual interest in internal or external erotic stimuli, and no or few genital/nongenital sensations in 75%−100% of sexual experiences.[4]

For both diagnoses, symptoms must persist for at least six months, cause clinically significant distress, and not be better explained by another condition. Simply having lower desire than one's partner is not sufficient for a diagnosis. Self-identification of a lifelong lack of sexual desire as asexuality precludes diagnosis.[3][4]

24.3 Treatment

24.3.1 Counseling

HSDD, like many sexual dysfunctions, is something that people are treated for in the context of a relationship. Theoretically, one could be diagnosed with, and treated for, HSDD without being in a relationship. However, relationship status is the most predictive factor accounting for distress in women with low desire and distress is required for a diagnosis of HSDD.[14] Therefore, it is common for both partners to be involved in therapy. Typically, the therapist tries to find a psychological or biological cause of the HSDD. If the HSDD is organically caused, the clinician may try to deal with that. If the clinician believes it is rooted in a psychological problem, they may recommend therapy for that. If not, treatment generally focuses more on relationship and communication issues, improved communication (verbal and nonverbal), working on non-sexual intimacy, or education about sexuality may all be possible parts of treatment. Sometimes problems occur because people have unrealistic perceptions about what normal sexuality is and are concerned that they do not compare well to that, and this is one reason why education can be important. If the clinician thinks that part of the problem is a result of stress, techniques may be recommended to more effectively deal with that. Also, it can be important to understand why the low level of sexual desire is a problem for the relationship because the two partners may associate different meaning with sex but not know it.[15]

In the case of men, the therapy may depend on the subtype of HSDD. Increasing the level of sexual desire of a man with lifelong/generalized HSDD is unlikely. Instead the focus may be on helping the couple to adapt. In the case of acquired/generalized, it is likely that there is some biological reason for it and the clinician may attempt to deal with that. In the case of acquired/situational, some form of psychotherapy may be used, possibly with the man alone and possibly together with his partner.[10]

24.3.2 Medication

Testosterone supplementation is effective in the short-term.[16] Its long-term safety, however, is unclear.[16]

A few studies suggest that the antidepressant, bupropion, can improve sexual function in women who are not depressed, if they have HSDD.[17]

Flibanserin is the first medication approved for the treatment of HSDD. It is only slightly effective over placebo, having been found to increase the number of satisfying sexual events per month by 0.5 to 1.[18][19] The side effects of dizziness, sleepiness, and nausea occur about three to four times more often.[19] Overall improvement is slight to none.[19]

24.4 History

In the early versions of the DSM, there were only two sexual dysfunctions listed: frigidity (for women) and impotence (for men).

In 1970, Masters and Johnson published their book *Human Sexual Inadequacy*[20] describing sexual dysfunctions, though these included only dysfunctions dealing with the function of genitals such as premature ejaculation and impotence for men, and anorgasmia and vaginismus for women. Prior to Masters and Johnson's research, female orgasm was assumed by some to originate primarily from vaginal, rather than clitoral, stimulation. Consequently, feminists have argued that "frigidity" was "defined by men as the failure of women to have vaginal orgasms".[21]

Following this book, sex therapy increased throughout the 1970s. Reports from sex-therapists about people with low sexual desire are reported from at least 1972, but labeling this as a specific disorder did not occur until 1977.[22] In that year, sex therapists Helen Singer Kaplan and Harold Lief independently of each other proposed creating a specific category for people with low or no sexual desire. Lief named it "Inhibited Sexual Desire," and Kaplan named it "Hypoactive Sexual Desire." The primary motivation for this was that previous models for sex therapy assumed certain levels of sexual interest in one's partner and that problems were only caused by abnormal functioning/non-functioning of the genitals or performance anxiety but that therapies based on those problems were ineffective for people who did not sexually desire their partner.[23] The following year, 1978, Lief and Kaplan together made a proposal to the APA's taskforce for sexual disorders for the DSM III, of which Kaplan and Lief were both members. The diagnosis of Inhibited Sexual Desire (ISD) was added to the DSM when the 3rd edition was published in 1980.[24]

For understanding this diagnosis, it is important to recognize the social context in which it was created. In some cultures, low sexual desire may be considered normal and high sexual desire is problematic. For example, sexual desire may be lower in East Asian populations than Euro-Canadian/American populations.[25] In other cultures, this may be reversed. Some cultures try hard to restrain sexual desire. Others try to excite it. Concepts of "normal" levels of sexual desire are culturally dependent and rarely value-neutral. In the 1970s, there were strong cultural messages that sex is good for you and "the more the better." Within this context, people who were habitually uninterested in sex, who in previous times may not have seen this as a problem, were more likely to feel that this was a situation that needed to be fixed. They may have felt alienated by dominant messages about sexuality and increasingly people went to sex-therapists complaining of low sexual desire. It was within

this context that the diagnosis of ISD was created.[26]

In the revision of the DSM-III, published in 1987 (DSM-III-R), ISD was subdivided into two categories: Hypoactive Sexual Desire Disorder and Sexual Aversion Disorder (SAD).[27] The former is a lack of interest in sex and the latter is a phobic aversion to sex. In addition to this subdivision, one reason for the change is that the committee involved in revising the psychosexual disorders for the DSM-III-R thought that term "inhibited" suggests psychodynamic etiology (i.e. that the conditions for sexual desire are present, but the person is, for some reason, inhibiting their own sexual interest.) The term "hypoactive sexual desire" is more awkward, but more neutral with respect to the cause.[28] The DSM-III-R estimated that about 20% of the population had HSDD.[29] In the DSM-IV (1994), the criterion that the diagnosis requires "marked distress or interpersonal difficulty" was added.

The DSM-5, published in 2013, split HSDD into *male hypoactive sexual desire disorder* and *female sexual interest/arousal disorder*. The distinction was made because men report more intense and frequent sexual desire than women.[3] According to Lori Brotto, this classification is desirable compared to the DSM-IV classification system because: (1) it reflects the finding that desire and arousal tend to overlap (2) it differentiates between women who lack desire before the onset of activity, but who are receptive to initiation and or initiate sexual activity for reasons other than desire, and women who never experience sexual arousal (3) it takes the variability in sexual desire into account. Furthermore, the criterion of 6 symptoms be present for a diagnosis helps safeguard against pathologizing adaptive decreases in desire.[30] [31]

24.5 Criticism

HSDD, as currently defined by the DSM has come under criticism of the social function of the diagnosis.

- HSDD could be seen as part of a history of the medicalization of sexuality by the medical profession to define normal sexuality.[32] It may also over pathologize normal variation in sexuality because the parameters of normality are unclear. This lack of clarity is partly due to the fact that the terms "persistent" and "recurrent" do not have clear operational definitions.[25]

- HSDD may function to pathologize asexuals, though their lack of sexual desire may not be maladaptive.[33] Because of this, some members of the asexual community lobbied the mental health community working on the DSM-5 to regard asexuality as a legitimate sexual orientation rather than a mental disorder.[34]

Other criticisms focus more on scientific and clinical issues.

- HSDD is such a diverse group etiologically that it functions as little more than a starting place for clinicians to assess people.[35]

- The requirement that low sexual desire causes distress or interpersonal difficulty has been criticized. It has been claimed that it is not clinically useful because if it is not causing any problems, the person will not seek out a clinician.[35] One could claim that this criterion (for all of the sexual dysfunctions, including HSDD) decreases the scientific validity of the diagnoses or is a cover-up for a lack of data on what constitutes normal sexual function.[36]

- The distress requirement is also criticized because the term "distress" lacks a clear definition.[37]

24.5.1 DSM-IV criteria

Prior to the publication of the DSM-5, the DSM-IV criteria were criticized on several grounds. It was suggested that a duration criterion should be added because lack of interest in sex over the past month is significantly more common than lack of interest lasting six months.[38] Similarly, a frequency criterion (i.e., the symptoms of low desire be present in 75% or more of sexual encounters) has been suggested.[39][40]

The current framework for HSDD is based on a linear model of human sexual response, developed by Masters and Johnson and modified by Kaplan consisting of desire, arousal, orgasm. The sexual dysfunctions in the DSM are based around problems at any one or more of these stages.[15] Many of the criticisms of the DSM-IV framework for sexual dysfunction in general, and HSDD in particular, claimed that this model ignored the differences between male and female sexuality. Several criticisms were based on inadequacy of the DSM-IV framework for dealing with female's sexual problems.

- Increasingly, evidence shows that there are significant differences between male and female sexuality. Level of desire is highly variable from female to female and there are some females who are considered sexually functional who have no active desire for sex, but they can erotically respond well in contexts they find acceptable. This has been termed "responsive desire" as opposed to spontaneous desire.[15]

- The focus on merely the physiological ignores the social, economic and political factors including sexual violence and lack of access to sexual medicine or education throughout the world affecting females and their sexual health.[41]

- The focus on the physiological ignores the relationship context of sexuality despite the fact that these are often the cause of sexual problems.[41]

- The focus on discrepancy in desire between two partners may result in the partner with the lower level of desire being labeled as "dysfunctional," but the problem really sits with difference between the two partners.[37] However, within couples the assessment of desire tends to be relative. That is, individuals make judgments by comparing their levels of desire to that of their partner.[39]

- The sexual problems that females complain of often do not fit well into the DSM-IV framework for sexual dysfunctions.[41]

- The DSM-IV system of sub-typing may be more applicable to one sex than the other.[10]

- Research indicates a high degree of comorbidity between HSDD and female sexual arousal disorder. Therefore, a diagnosis combining the two (as the DSM-5 eventually did) might be more appropriate.[42]

24.6   See also

- Hypersexuality
- Sexual dysfunction
- Diagnostic and Statistical Manual of Mental Disorders
- Sexual arousal disorder
- Sexual anhedonia

24.7   References

[1] University of Maryland, Medical Centre: Inhibited sexual desire

[2] *Diagnostic and Statistical Manual of Mental Disorders* (4th ed.). Washington DC: American Psychiatric Association. 2000.

[3] American Psychiatric Association, ed. (2013). "Male Hypoactive Sexual Desire Disorder, 302.71 (F52.0)". *Diagnostic and Statistical Manual of Mental Disorders, Fifth Edition*. American Psychiatric Publishing. p. 440-443.

[4] American Psychiatric Association, ed. (2013). "Female Sexual Interest/Arousal Disorder, 302.72 (F52.22)". *Diagnostic and Statistical Manual of Mental Disorders, Fifth Edition*. American Psychiatric Publishing. p. 433-437.

[5] *Diagnostic and Statistical Manual of Mental Disorders* (3rd ed.). Washington DC: American Psychiatric Association. 1980.

[6] Alison Ritter: Appropriate services for gay, lesbian, bisexual and transgender people: More than just gender sensitive? page 5

[7] Janssen, E., Bancroft J. (2006). "The dual control model: The role of sexual inhibition & excitation in sexual arousal and behavior". In Janssen, E. *The Psychophysiology of Sex*. Bloomington IN: Indiana University Press.

[8] Clayton AH (July 2010). "The pathophysiology of hypoactive sexual desire disorder in women". *Int J Gynaecol Obstet* 110 (1): 7–11. doi:10.1016/j.ijgo.2010.02.014. PMID 20434725.

[9] "New View Campaign. Fact Sheet: Marketing" (PDF). Newviewcampaign.org. Retrieved 2013-08-16.

[10] Maurice, William (2007). "Sexual Desire Disorders in Men". In Leiblum, Sandra. *Principles and Practice of Sex Therapy* (4th ed.). New York: The Guilford Press.

[11] Balon, Richard (2007). "Toward an Improved Nosology of Sexual Dysfunction in DSM-V". *Psychiatric Times* 24 (9).

[12] Warnock JJ (2002). "Female hypoactive sexual desire disorder: epidemiology, diagnosis and treatment". *CNS Drugs* 16 (11): 745–53. doi:10.2165/00023210-200216110-00003. PMID 12383030.

[13] Brauer M, van leeuwen M, Janssen E, Newhouse SK, Heiman JR, Laan E (September 2011). "Attentional and Affective Processing of Sexual Stimuli in Women with Hypoactive Sexual Desire Disorder". *Archives of Sexual Behaviour*. doi:10.1007/s10508-011-9820-7.

[14] Rosen RC, Shifren JL, Monz BU, Odom DM, Russo PA, Johannes CB (June 2009). "Correlates of sexually-related personal distress in women with low sexual desire". *Journal of Sexual Medicine* 6 (6): 1549–1560. doi:10.1111/j.1743-6109.2009.01252.x.

[15] Basson, Rosemary (2007). "Sexual Desire/Arousal Disorders in Women". In Leiblum, Sandra. *Principles and Practice of Sex Therapy* (4th ed.). New York: The Guilford Press.

[16] Wierman, ME; Arlt, W; Basson, R; Davis, SR; Miller, KK; Murad, MH; Rosner, W; Santoro, N (Oct 2014). "Androgen therapy in women: a reappraisal: an endocrine society clinical practice guideline.". *The Journal of Clinical Endocrinology and Metabolism* 99 (10): 3489–510. doi:10.1210/jc.2014-2260. PMID 25279570.

[17] Foley KF, DeSanty KP, Kast RE (September 2006). "Bupropion: pharmacology and therapeutic applications". *Expert Rev Neurother* 6 (9): 1249–65. doi:10.1586/14737175.6.9.1249. PMID 17009913.

[18] "Joint Meeting of the Bone, Reproductive and Urologic Drugs Advisory Committee (BRUDAC) and the Drug Safety and Risk Management (DSaRM) Advisory Committee" (PDF). June 4, 2015. Retrieved 5 June 2015.

[19] Jaspers, L; Feys, F; Bramer, WM; Franco, OH; Leusink, P; Laan, ET (1 April 2016). "Efficacy and Safety of Flibanserin for the Treatment of Hypoactive Sexual Desire Disorder in Women: A Systematic Review and Meta-analysis.". *JAMA internal medicine* 176 (4): 453–62. PMID 26927498.

[20] Masters, William; Johnson, Virginia (1970). *Human Sexual Inadequacy*. Boston: Little Brown.

[21] Koedt, A. (1970). "The myth of the vaginal orgasm". In Escoffier, J. *Sexual revolution*. New York: Thunder's Mouth Press. pp. 100–9. ISBN 1-56025-525-0.

[22] Irvine, Janice (2005). *Disorders of Desire*. Philadelphia: Temple University Press. p. 265.

[23] Kaplan, Helen Singer (1995). *The Sexual Desire Disorders*. New York: Taylor & Francis Group. pp. 1–2, 7.

[24] Kaplan 1995, pp. 7–8

[25] Brotto LA, Chik HM, Ryder AG, Gorzalka BB, Seal B (December 2005). "Acculturation and sexual function in Asian women". *Archives of Sexual Behaviour* 34 (6): 613–626. doi:10.1007/s10508-005-7909-6.

[26] Leiblum, Sandra; Rosen, Raymond (1988). *Sexual Desire Disorders*. The Guilford Press. p. 1.

[27] Irvine 2005, p. 172

[28] Apfelbaum, Bernard (1988). "An Ego Analytic Perspective on Desire Disorders". In Lieblum, Sandra; Rosen, Raymond. *Sexual Desire Disorders*. The Guilford Press.

[29] American Psychological Association (1987)

[30] Brotto LA (2010). "The DSM Diagnostic Criteria for Hypoactive Sexual Desire Disorder in Women". *Archives of Sexual Behaviour* 39 (2): 221–239. doi:10.1007/s10508-009-9543-1. PMID 19777334.

[31] Brotto LA (June 2010). "The DSM Diagnostic Criteria for Hypoactive Sexual Desire Disorder in Men". *Archives of Sexual Behaviour* 7 (6): 2015–2030. doi:10.1111/j.1743-6109.2010.01860.x.

[32] Irvine 2005, pp. 175–6

[33] Prause N, Graham CA (June 2007). "Asexuality: classification and characterization" (PDF). *Arch Sex Behav* 36 (3): 341–56. doi:10.1007/s10508-006-9142-3. PMID 17345167.

[34] Asexuals Push for Greater Recognition. http://abcnews.go.com/Health/MindMoodNews/story?id=6656358&page=1

[35] Bancroft J, Graham CA, McCord C (2001). "Conceptualizing women's sexual problems". *J Sex Marital Ther* **27** (2): 95–103. doi:10.1080/00926230152051716. PMID 11247236.

[36] Althof SE (2001). "My personal distress over the inclusion of personal distress". *J Sex Marital Ther* **27** (2): 123–5. doi:10.1080/00926230152051761. PMID 11247205.

[37] Bancroft J, Graham CA, McCord C (2001). "Conceptualizing Women's Sexual Problems". *Journal of Sex & Marital Therapy* **27** (2): 95–103. doi:10.1080/00926230152051716. PMID 11247236.

[38] Mitchell KR, Mercer CH (September 2009). "Prevalence of Low Sexual Desire among Women in Britain: Associated Factors". *The Journal of Sexual Medicine* **6** (9): 2434–2444. doi:10.1111/j.1743-6109.2009.01368.x. PMID 19549088.

[39] Balon R (2008). "The DSM Criteria of Sexual Dysfunction: Need for a Change". *Journal of Sex and Marital Therapy* **34** (3): 186–97. doi:10.1080/00926230701866067. PMID 18398759.

[40] Segraves R, Balon R, Clayton A (2007). "Proposal for Changes in Diagnostic Criteria for Sexual Dysfunctions". *Journal of Sexual Medicine* **4** (3): 567–580. doi:10.1111/j.1743-6109.2007.00455.x. PMID 17433086.

[41] Tiefer L, Hall M, Tavris C (2002). "Beyond dysfunction: a new view of women's sexual problems". *J Sex Marital Ther* **28** (Suppl 1): 225–32. doi:10.1080/00926230252851357. PMID 11898706.

[42] Graham, CA (September 2010). "The DSM Diagnostic Criteria for Female Sexual Arousal Disorder". *Archives of Sexual Behaviour* **39** (2): 240–255. doi:10.1007/s10508-009-9535-1. PMID 19777335.

24.8   Further reading

- Montgomery, KA (Jun 2008). "Sexual Desire Disorders". *Psychiatry (Edgmont)* **5** (6): 50–55. PMC 2695750. PMID 19727285.

- Basson, R; Leiblum, S; Brotto, L; Derogatis, L; Fourcroy, J; Fugl-Meyer, K; Graziottin, A; Heiman, JR; Laan, E; Meston, C; Schover, L; van Lankveld, J; Schultz, WW (Dec 2003). "Definitions of women's sexual dysfunction reconsidered: advocating expansion and revision.". *Journal of psychosomatic obstetrics and gynaecology* **24** (4): 221–9. doi:10.3109/01674820309074686. PMID 14702882.

- Warnock, JJ (2002). "Female hypoactive sexual desire disorder: epidemiology, diagnosis and treatment.". *CNS Drugs* **16** (11): 745–53. doi:10.2165/00023210-200216110-00003. PMID 12383030.

- Basson, R (10 May 2005). "Women's sexual dysfunction: revised and expanded definitions". *Canadian Medical Association Journal* **172** (10): 1327–1333. doi:10.1503/cmaj.1020174. PMC 557105. PMID 15883409.

- Nappi, RE; Wawra, K; Schmitt, S (Jun 2006). "Hypoactive sexual desire disorder in postmenopausal women.". *Gynecological endocrinology: the official journal of the International Society of Gynecological Endocrinology* **22** (6): 318–23. doi:10.1080/09513590600762265. PMID 16785156.

24.9   External links

- Hypoactive Sexual Desire Disorder, symptoms, types, and treatment

Chapter 25

Syncope (medicine)

For other uses, see Syncope.
"Fainting" redirects here. For other uses, see Faint.

Syncope, also known as **fainting**, **passing out** and **swooning**, is defined as a short loss of consciousness and muscle strength, characterized by a fast onset, short duration, and spontaneous recovery. It is due to a decrease in blood flow to the entire brain usually from low blood pressure. Some causes have prodromal symptoms before the loss of consciousness occurs. These symptoms may include lightheadedness, sweating, pale skin, blurred vision, nausea, vomiting, and feeling warm, among others. Syncope may also be associated with a short episode of muscle twitching. If a person does not completely lose consciousness and muscle strength it is referred to as presyncope. It is recommended that presyncope be treated the same as syncope.[1]

Causes range from non-serious to potentially fatal. There are three broad categories of causes: heart or blood vessel related, reflex also known as neurally mediated, and orthostatic hypotension. Issues with the heart and blood vessels are the cause in about 10% and typically the most serious while neurally mediated is the most common. Heart related causes may include an abnormal heart rhythm, problems with the heart valves or heart muscle and blockages of blood vessels from a pulmonary embolism or aortic dissection among others. Neurally mediated syncope occurs when blood vessels expand and heart rate decreases inappropriately. This may occur from either a triggering event such as exposure to blood, pain or strong feelings or a specific activity such as urination, vomiting, or coughing. This type of syncope may also occur when an area in the neck known as the carotid sinus is pressed. The final type of syncope is due to a drop in blood pressure from standing up. This is often due to medications that a person is taking but may also be related to dehydration, significant bleeding or infection.[1]

A medical history, physical examination, and electrocardiogram (ECG) are the most effective ways to figure out the underlying cause. The ECG is useful to detect an abnormal heart rhythm, poor blood flow to the heart muscle, and other electrical issue such as long QT syndrome and Brugada's. Heart related causes also often have little history of a prodrome. Low blood pressure and a fast heart rate after the event may indicate blood loss or dehydration, while low blood oxygen levels may be seen following the event in those with pulmonary embolism. More specific tests such as implantable loop recorders, tilt table testing or carotid sinus massage may be useful in uncertain cases. Computer tomography (CT) is generally not required unless specific concerns are present. Other causes of similar symptoms that should be considered including seizure, stroke, concussion, low blood oxygen, low blood sugar, drug intoxication and some psychiatric disorders among others. Treatment depends on the underlying cause. Those who are considered at high risk following investigation may be admitted to hospital for further monitoring of the heart.[1]

Syncope affects about three to six out of every thousand people each year.[1] It is more common in older people and females. It is the reason for one to three percent of visits to emergency departments and admissions to hospital. Up to half of women over the age of 80 and a third of medical students describe at least one event at some point in their life.[2] Of those presenting with syncope to an emergency department, about 4% died in the next 30 days.[1] The risk of a bad outcome, however, depends very much on the underlying cause.[3]

25.1 Differential diagnosis

25.1.1 Central nervous system ischaemia

The central ischaemic response is triggered by an inadequate supply of oxygenated blood in the brain.

The respiratory system may contribute to oxygen levels through hyperventilation, though a sudden ischaemic episode may also proceed faster than the respiratory system can respond. These processes cause the typical symptoms of fainting: pale skin, rapid breathing, nausea and weakness of the limbs, particularly of the legs. If the ischaemia is intense or prolonged, limb weakness progresses to collapse. An individual with very little skin pigmentation may appear to have all color drained from his or her face at the onset of an episode. This effect combined with the following collapse can make a strong and dramatic impression on bystanders.

The weakness of the legs causes most sufferers to sit or lie down if there is time to do so. This may avert a complete collapse, but whether the sufferer sits down or falls down, the result of an ischaemic episode is a posture in which less blood pressure is required to achieve adequate blood flow. It is unclear whether this is a mechanism evolved in response to the circulatory difficulties of human bipedalism or merely a serendipitous result of a pre-existing circulatory response
.

Vertebro-basilar arterial disease

Arterial disease in the upper spinal cord, or lower brain, causes syncope if there is a reduction in blood supply, which may occur with extending the neck or after drugs to lower blood pressure.

25.1.2 Vasovagal

Main article: Vasovagal syncope

Vasovagal (situational) syncope is one of the most common types which may occur in response to any of a variety of triggers, such as scary, embarrassing or uneasy situations, during blood drawing, or moments of sudden unusually high stress. There are many different syncope syndromes which all fall under the umbrella of vasovagal syncope related by the same central mechanism, such as urination ("micturition syncope"), defecation ("defecation syncope"), and others related to trauma and stress.

Vasovagal syncope can be considered in two forms:

- Isolated episodes of loss of consciousness, unheralded by any warning symptoms for more than a few moments. These tend to occur in the adolescent age group, and may be associated with fasting, exercise, abdominal straining, or circumstances promoting vaso-dilation (e.g., heat, alcohol). The subject is invariably upright. The tilt-table test, if performed, is generally negative.

- Recurrent syncope with complex associated symptoms. This is neurally mediated syncope (NMS). It

is associated with any of the following: preceding or succeeding sleepiness, preceding visual disturbance ("spots before the eyes"), sweating, lightheadedness. The subject is usually but not always upright. The tilt-table test, if performed, is generally positive. It is relatively uncommon.

A pattern of background factors contributes to the attacks. There is typically an unsuspected relatively low blood volume, for instance, from taking a low-salt diet in the absence of any salt-retaining tendency. Heat causes vasodilation and worsens the effect of the relatively insufficient blood volume. That sets the scene, but the next stage is the adrenergic response. If there is underlying fear or anxiety (e.g., social circumstances), or acute fear (e.g., acute threat, needle phobia), the vaso-motor centre demands an increased pumping action by the heart (flight or fight response). This is set in motion via the adrenergic (sympathetic) outflow from the brain, but the heart is unable to meet requirement because of the low blood volume, or decreased return. The high (ineffective) sympathetic activity is always modulated by vagal outflow, in these cases leading to excessive slowing of heart rate. The abnormality lies in this excessive vagal response. The tilt-table test typically evokes the attack.

Much of this pathway was discovered in animal experiments by Bezold (Vienna) in the 1860s. In animals, it may represent a defence mechanism when confronted by danger ("playing possum").

Avoiding what brings on the syncope and possibly greater salt intake is often all that is needed.[4]

Psychological factors also have been found to mediate syncope. It is important for general practitioners and the psychologist in their primary care team to work closely together, and to help patients identify how they might be avoiding activities of daily living due to anticipatory anxiety in relation to a possible faint and the feared physical damage it may cause. Fainting in response to a blood stimulus, needle or a dead body are common and patients can quickly develop safety behaviours to avoid any recurrences of a fainting response. See link for a good description of psychological interventions and theories.[5]

An evolutionary psychology view is that some forms of fainting are non-verbal signals that developed in response to increased inter-group aggression during the paleolithic. A non-combatant who has fainted signals that she or he is not a threat. This would explain the association between fainting and stimuli such as bloodletting and injuries seen in blood-injection-injury type phobias such as trypanophobia as well as the gender differences.[6]

Deglutition (Swallowing) syncope

Syncope may occur during deglutition. Manisty et al. note: "Deglutition syncope is characterised by loss of consciousness on swallowing; it has been associated not only with ingestion of solid food, but also with carbonated and ice-cold beverages, and even belching."[7]

25.1.3   Cardiac

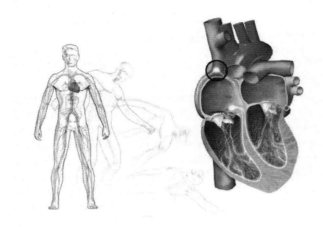

Syncope from Bradycardia

Cardiac arrhythmias

The most common cause of cardiac syncope is cardiac arrhythmia (abnormal heart rhythm) wherein the heart beats too slowly, too rapidly, or too irregularly to pump enough blood to the brain. Some arrhythmias can be life-threatening.

Two major groups of arrhythmias are bradycardia and tachycardia. Bradycardia can be caused by heart blocks. Tachycardias include SVT (supraventricular tachycardia) and VT (ventricular tachycardia). SVT does not cause syncope except in Wolff-Parkinson-White syndrome. Ventricular tachycardia originate in the ventricles. VT causes syncope and can result in sudden death. Ventricular tachycardia, which describes a heart rate of over 100 beats per minute with at least three irregular heartbeats as a sequence of consecutive premature beats, can degenerate into ventricular fibrillation, which is rapidly fatal without cardiopulmonary resuscitation (CPR) and defibrillation.

Typically, tachycardic-generated syncope is caused by a cessation of beats following a tachycardic episode. This condition, called tachycardia-bradycardia syndrome, is usually caused by sinoatrial node dysfunction or block or atrioventricular block.[8]

Obstructive cardiac lesion

Aortic stenosis and mitral stenosis are the most common examples. Aortic stenosis presents with repeated episodes of syncope. A pulmonary embolism can cause obstructed blood vessels. High blood pressure in the arteries supplying the lungs (pulmonary artery hypertension) can occur during pulmonary embolism. Rarely, cardiac tumors such as atrial myxomas can also lead to syncope.

Structural cardiopulmonary disease

These are relatively infrequent causes of faints. The most common cause in this category is fainting associated with an acute myocardial infarction or ischemic event. The faint in this case is primarily caused by an abnormal nervous system reaction similar to the reflex faints. In general, faints caused by structural disease of the heart or blood vessels are particularly important to recognize, as they are warning of potentially life-threatening conditions. Among other conditions prone to trigger syncope (by either hemodynamic compromise or by a neural reflex mechanism, or both), some of the most important are hypertrophic cardiomyopathy, acute aortic dissection, pericardial tamponade, pulmonary embolism, aortic stenosis, and pulmonary hypertension.

Other cardiac causes

Sick sinus syndrome, a sinus node dysfunction, causing alternating bradycardia and tachycardia. Often there is a long pause asystole between heartbeat.

Adams-Stokes syndrome is a cardiac syncope that occurs with seizures caused by complete or incomplete heart block. Symptoms include deep and fast respiration, weak and slow pulse and respiratory pauses that may last for 60 seconds.

Subclavian steal syndrome arises from retrograde (reversed) flow of blood in the vertebral artery or the internal thoracic artery, due to a proximal stenosis (narrowing) and/or occlusion of the subclavian artery.

Aortic dissection (a tear in the aorta) and cardiomyopathy can also result in syncope.[9]

Various medications, such as beta blockers, may cause bradycardia induced syncope.[8]

25.1.4   Blood pressure

*Orthostatic (postural) hypotensive faint*s are as common or perhaps even more common than vasovagal syncope. Orthostatic faints are most often associated with movement from lying or sitting to a standing position, standing up too quickly, or being in a very hot room. The classic example of a combination of these is seen in the frequent fainting by medical students in the operating theatre during observation of surgery.[10]

Apparently healthy individuals may experience minor symptoms ("lightheadedness", "greying-out") as they stand up if blood pressure is slow to respond to the stress of upright posture. If the blood pressure is not adequately maintained during standing, faints may develop. However, the resulting "transient orthostatic hypotension" does not necessarily signal any serious underlying disease.

The most susceptible individuals are elderly frail individuals, or persons who are dehydrated from hot environments or inadequate fluid intake. More serious orthostatic hypotension is often the result of certain commonly prescribed medications such as diuretics, β-adrenergic blockers, other anti-hypertensives (including vasodilators), and nitroglycerin. In a small percentage of cases, the cause of orthostatic hypotensive faints is structural damage to the autonomic nervous system due to systemic diseases (e.g., amyloidosis or diabetes) or in neurological diseases (e.g., Parkinson's disease).

25.1.5   Other causes

Factors that influence fainting are fasting long hours, taking in too little food and fluids, low blood pressure, hypoglycemia, high g-force, emotional distress, and lack of sleep.

One theory in evolutionary psychology is that fainting at the sight of blood might have evolved as a form of playing dead which increased survival from attackers and might have slowed blood loss in a primitive environment.[11] "Blood-injury phobia", as this is called, is experienced by about 15% of people.[12]

Fainting can occur in "cough syncope".[13] following severe fits of coughing, such as that associated with pertussis or "whooping cough."

25.2   Diagnostic approach

For people with uncomplicated syncope (without seizures and a normal neurological exam) computed tomography or MRI is not indicated.[14] Likewise, using carotid ultrasonography on the premise of identifying carotid artery disease as a cause of syncope also is not indicated.[15] Although sometimes investigated as a cause of syncope, carotid artery problems are unlikely to cause that condition.[15]

A hemoglobin count may indicate anemia or blood loss. However, this has been useful in only about 5% of patients evaluated for fainting.[16]

An electrocardiogram (ECG) records the electrical activity of the heart. It is estimated that from 20%−50% of patients have an abnormal ECG. However, while an ECG may identify conditions such as atrial fibrillation, heart block, or a new or old heart attack, it typically does not provide a definite diagnosis for the underlying cause for fainting.[17]

Sometimes, a Holter monitor may be used. This is a portable ECG device that can record the wearer's heart rhythms during daily activities over an extended period of time. Since fainting usually does not occur upon command, a Holter monitor can provide a better understanding of the heart's activity during fainting episodes.

The tilt table test is performed to elicit orthostatic syncope secondary to autonomic dysfunction (neurogenic).

For patients with more than two episodes of syncope and no diagnosis on "routine testing", an insertable cardiac monitor might be used. It lasts 28–36 months. Smaller than a pack of gum, it is inserted just beneath the skin in the upper chest area. The procedure typically takes 15 to 20 minutes. Once inserted, the device continuously monitors the rate and rhythm of the heart. Upon waking from a "fainting" spell, the patient places a hand held pager size device called an Activator over the implanted device and simply presses a button. This information is stored and retrieved by their physician and some devices can be monitored remotely.

25.2.1   San Francisco syncope rule

The San Francisco syncope rule was developed to isolate people who have higher risk for a serious cause of syncope. High risk is anyone who has: congestive heart failure, hematocrit <30%, electrocardiograph abnormality, shortness of breath, or systolic blood pressure <90 mm Hg.[18] The San Francisco syncope rule however was not validated by subsequent studies.[19]

25.3   Management

Recommended acute treatment of vasovagal and orthostatic (hypotension) syncope involves returning blood to the brain by positioning the person on the ground, with legs slightly elevated or leaning forward and the head between the knees for at least 10–15 minutes, preferably in a cool and quiet place. For individuals who have problems with chronic fainting spells, therapy should focus on recognizing the triggers and learning techniques to keep from fainting. At the appearance of warning signs such as lightheadedness, nausea, or cold and clammy skin, counter-pressure maneuvers that involve gripping fingers into a fist, tensing the arms, and crossing the legs or squeezing the thighs together can be used to ward off a fainting spell. After the symptoms have passed, sleep is recommended. If fainting spells occur often without a triggering event, syncope may be a sign of an underlying heart disease. In case syncope is caused by cardiac disease, the treatment is much more sophisticated than that of vasovagal syncope and may involve pacemakers and implantable cardioverter-defibrillators depending on the precise cardiac cause.

25.4   Society and culture

Fainting in women was a commonplace trope or stereotype in Victorian England and in contemporary and modern depictions of the period. This may have been partly due to genuine ill health (the respiratory effects of corsets are frequently cited), but it was fashionable for women to affect an aristocratic frailty and create a scene by fainting at a dramatic moment. Falling-out is a culture-bound syndrome primarily reported in the southern United States and the Caribbean.

Some individuals occasionally or frequently play the "fainting game" (also referred to in the US as the "choking game"), which involves the deliberate induction of syncope via voluntary restriction of blood flow to the brain, an action that can result in acute or cumulative brain damage and even death.[20]

25.5   Etymology

The term is derived from the Late Latin *syncope*, from Ancient Greek συγκοπή (*sunkopē*), from σύν (*sin*, "together, thoroughly") and κόπτειν (*koptein*, "strike, cut off").

25.6   See also

- Voodoo death

25.7   References

[1] Peeters, SY; Hoek, AE; Mollink, SM; Huff, JS (April 2014). "Syncope: risk stratification and clinical decision making.". *Emergency medicine practice* **16** (4): 1–22; quiz 22–3. PMID 25105200.

[2] Kenny, RA; Bhangu, J; King-Kallimanis, BL (2013). "Epidemiology of syncope/collapse in younger and older Western patient populations.". *Progress in cardiovascular dis-*

eases **55** (4): 357–63. doi:10.1016/j.pcad.2012.11.006. PMID 23472771.

[3] Ruwald, MH (August 2013). "Epidemiological studies on syncope--a register based approach.". *Danish medical journal* **60** (8): B4702. PMID 24063058.

[4] Kaufmann, H; Bhattacharya, K (May 2002). "Diagnosis and treatment of neurally mediated syncope.". *The neurologist* **8** (3): 175–85. PMID 12803689.

[5] Gaynor D, Egan J (2011). "Vasovagal syncope (the common faint): what clinicians need to know". *The Irish Psychologist* **37** (7): 176–9. hdl:10147/135366.

[6] Bracha HS (July 2006). "Human brain evolution and the 'Neuroevolutionary Time-depth Principle:' Implications for the Reclassification of fear-circuitry-related traits in DSM-V and for studying resilience to warzone-related posttraumatic stress disorder". *Prog. Neuropsychopharmacol. Biol. Psychiatry* **30** (5): 827–53. doi:10.1016/j.pnpbp.2006.01.008. PMID 16563589.

[7] Manisty C, Hughes-Roberts Y, Kaddoura S (July 2009). "Cardiac manifestations and sequelae of gastrointestinal disorders". *Br J Cardiol* **16** (4): 175–80. Retrieved 11 May 2013.

[8] Freeman, Roy (2011). "Chapter 20: Syncope". In Longo, Dan L.; Kasper, Dennis L.; Jameson, J. Larry; Fauci, Anthony S.; Hauser, Stephen L.; Loscalzo, Joseph. *Harrison's Principles of Internal Medicine* (Textbook) (18th ed.). New York, NY: The McGraw-Hill Companies. pp. 171–177. ISBN 978-0-07-174889-6.

[9] Nallamothu BK, Mehta RH, Saint S, et al. (October 2002). "Syncope in acute aortic dissection: diagnostic, prognostic, and clinical implications". *Am. J. Med.* **113** (6): 468–71. doi:10.1016/S0002-9343(02)01254-8. PMID 12427495.

[10] Jamjoom AA, Nikkar-Esfahani A, Fitzgerald JE (2009). "Operating theatre related syncope in medical students: a cross sectional study". *BMC Med Educ* **9**: 14. doi:10.1186/1472-6920-9-14. PMC: 2657145. PMID 19284564.

[11] https://www.psychologytoday.com/blog/brain-babble/201302/why-do-some-people-faint-the-sight-blood

[12] "Swoon at the Sight of Blood? Why the sight of blood might make you faint -- and what you can do about it.". Retrieved 2015-08-15.

[13] Dicpinigaitis PV, Lim L, Farmakidis C (February 2014). "Cough syncope.". *Respiratory Medicine* **108** (2): 244–51. doi:10.1016/j.rmed.2013.10.020. PMID 24238768.

[14] Moya A, Sutton R, Ammirati F, et al. (November 2009). "Guidelines for the diagnosis and management of syncope (version 2009)". *Eur. Heart J.* **30** (21): 2631–71. doi:10.1093/eurheartj/ehp298. PMC: 3295536. PMID 19713422.

[15] American Academy of Neurology (February 2013), "Five Things Physicians and Patients Should Question", *Choosing Wisely: an initiative of the ABIM Foundation* (American Academy of Neurology), retrieved August 1, 2013, which cites:

(a) • Strickberger, S. A.; Benson, D. W.; Biaggioni, I.; Callans, D. J.; Cohen, M. I.; Ellenbogen, K. A.; Epstein, A. E.; Friedman, P.; Goldberger, J.; Heidenreich, P. A.; Klein, G. J.; Knight, B. P.; Morillo, C. A.; Myerburg, R. J.; Sila, C. A.; American Heart Association Councils On Clinical Cardiology (2006). "AHA/ACCF Scientific Statement on the Evaluation of Syncope: From the American Heart Association Councils on Clinical Cardiology, Cardiovascular Nursing, Cardiovascular Disease in the Young, and Stroke, and the Quality of Care and Outcomes Research Interdisciplinary Working Group; and the American College of Cardiology Foundation: In Collaboration with the Heart Rhythm Society: Endorsed by the American Autonomic Society". *Circulation* **113** (2): 316–327. doi:10.1161/CIRCULATIONAHA.105.170274. PMID 16418451.

• Moya, A.; European Society of Cardiology (ESC); Sutton, R.; European Heart Rhythm Association (EHRA); Ammirati, F.; and Heart Rhythm Society (HRS); Blanc, J.-J.; Endorsed by the following societies; Brignole, M.; European Society of Emergency Medicine (EuSEM); Moya, J. B.; European Federation of Internal Medicine (EFIM); Sutton, J.-C.; European Union Geriatric Medicine Society (EUGMS); Ammirati, J.; Blanc, K.; European Neurological Society (ENS); Brignole, A.; European Federation of Autonomic Societies (EFAS); Dahm, M.; Deharo, M.; Gajek, T.; Gjesdal, R. R.; Krahn, F.; Massin, A.; Pepi, J. G.; Pezawas, E. P.; Ruiz Granell, W.; Sarasin, H.; Ungar, D. G.; et al. (2009). "Guidelines for the diagnosis and management of syncope (version 2009): The Task Force for the Diagnosis and Management of Syncope of the European Society of Cardiology (ESC)". *European Heart Journal* **30** (21): 2631–2671. doi:10.1093/eurheartj/ehp298. PMC: 3295536. PMID 19713422.

• NICE (August 2010), *Transient loss of consciousness in adults and young people (CG109)*, NICE, retrieved 24 October 2013

[16] Grubb (2001) p.83

[17] Grubb (2001) pp.83-84

[18] Quinn J, McDermott D, Stiell I, Kohn M, Wells G (May 2006). "Prospective validation of the San Francisco Syncope Rule to predict patients with serious outcomes". *Ann Emerg Med* **47** (5): 448–54. doi:10.1016/j.annemergmed.2005.11.019. PMID 16631985. Lay summary – *Journal Watch* (July 21, 2006).

[19] Birnbaum A, Esses D, Bijur P, Wollowitz A, Gallagher EJ (August 2008). "Failure to validate the San Francisco Syncope Rule in an independent emergency department population". *Ann Emerg Med* **52** (2): 151–9. doi:10.1016/j.annemergmed.2007.12.007. PMID 18282636.

[20] "'Choking Game' Becoming Deadly Fad For Adolescents". WJZ-TV Baltimore. 2005-11-04. Archived from the original on 2007-12-19. Retrieved 2008-02-13.

25.8 External links

- Syncope (medicine) at DMOZ

- 2004 European Society of Cardiology Guidelines on Management (Diagnosis and Treatment) of Syncope.

- Tilt table test

- The San Francisco syncope rule

Chapter 26

Pedant

Not to be confused with pendant.

A **pedant** is a person who is excessively concerned with formalism, accuracy, and precision, or one who makes an ostentatious and arrogant show of learning.

26.1 Etymology

The English language word "pedant" comes from the French *pédant* (used in 1566 in Darme & Hatzfeldster's *Dictionnaire général de la langue française*) or its older mid-15th century Italian source *pedante*, "teacher, schoolmaster". (Compare the Spanish *pedante*.) The origin of the Italian *pedante* is uncertain, but several dictionaries suggest that it was contracted from the medieval Latin *pædagogans*, present participle of *pædagogare*, "to act as pedagogue, to teach" (Du Cange).[1] The Latin word is derived from Greek παιδαγωγός, *paidagōgós*, παιδ- "child" + ἄγειν "to lead", which originally referred to a slave who escorted children to and from school but later meant "a source of instruction or guidance".[2][3]

26.2 Connotation

The term in English is typically used with a negative connotation to refer to someone who is over-concerned with minutiae and whose tone is condescending.[4] Thomas Nashe wrote in *Have with you to Saffron-walden* (1596), page 43: "O, tis a precious apothegmaticall [terse] Pedant, who will finde matter inough to dilate a whole daye of the first inuention [invention] of Fy, fa, fum". However, when the word was first used by Shakespeare in *Love's Labour's Lost* (1598), it simply meant "teacher".

26.3 Medical conditions

Obsessive–compulsive personality disorder is in part characterized by a form of pedantry that is excessively concerned with the correct following of rules, procedures, and practices.[5] Sometimes the rules that OCPD sufferers obsessively follow are of their own devising, or are corruptions or reinterpretations of the letter of actual rules.

Pedantry can also be an indication of specific developmental disorders. In particular, people with Asperger syndrome often have behaviour characterized by pedantic speech.[6]

26.4 Quotations

- "A Man who has been brought up among Books, and is able to talk of nothing else, is what we call a Pedant. But, methinks, we should enlarge the Title, and give it to every one that does not know how to think out of his Profession and particular way of Life." —Joseph Addison, *Spectator* (1711)[7]

- "Nothing is as peevish and pedantic as men's judgements of one another." —Desiderius Erasmus[8]

- "The pedant is he who finds it impossible to read criticism of himself without immediately reaching for his pen and replying to the effect that the accusation is a gross insult to his person. He is, in effect, a man unable to laugh at himself." —Sigmund Freud, *The Ego and the Id*

- "Servile and impertinent, shallow and pedantic, a bigot and sot" —Thomas Macaulay, describing James Boswell

- "The term, then, is obviously a relative one: my pedantry is your scholarship, his reasonable accuracy, her irreducible minimum of education and someone else's ignorance."—H. W. Fowler, *Modern English Usage*

- "Pedantic, I?" —Alexei Sayle

- "Never argue with a pedant over nomenclature. It wastes your time and annoys the pedant." —Lois McMaster Bujold

- "If you're the kind of person who insists on this or that 'correct' use... abandon your pedantry as I did mine. Dive into the open flowing waters and leave the stagnant canals be... Above all, let there be pleasure!" —Stephen Fry

- "Ben is a crossword-doer, a dictionary-lover, a pedant." —Julian Barnes

26.5 Pedants in literature and fiction

- Barton Fink in *Barton Fink* (feature film)

- Charles Kinbote in *Pale Fire* (novel)

- Paul Bates in *Midnight in Paris* (feature film)

- Sheldon Cooper in *The Big Bang Theory* (TV series)

- Maura Isles in *Rizzoli and Isles* (TV series)

- Temperance "Bones" Brennan in *Bones* (TV series)

- Ogier P in Jean-Paul Sartre's *Nausea* (novel)

- Edward Casaubon in George Eliot's *Middlemarch* (novel)

26.6 References

[1] "pedant". *The American Heritage Dictionary of the English Language* (Fifth ed.). Houghton Mifflin Harcourt Publishing Company. 2014. Retrieved 27 March 2015.

[2] *pedant, n. and adj. The Oxford English Dictionary* (Draft ed.) (Oxford University Press). September 2008.

[3] Harper, Douglas. "pedant". *Online Etymology Dictionary*.

[4] pedantic definition | Dictionary.com Accessed on 2008-12-29

[5] Anankastic personality disorder. International Statistical Classification of Diseases and Related Health Problems 10th Revision (ICD-10).

[6] "Asperger's Syndrome: Guidelines for Assesment and Intervention". Web.archive.org. 2007-04-07. Archived from the original on April 7, 2007. Retrieved 2013-07-25.

[7] Addison, Joseph (30 June 1711). "Saturday, June 30, 1711". *Spectator*. Archived from the original on 3 November 2004. Retrieved 27 March 2015.

[8] Croucher, Rowland. "Desiderius Erasmus Quotes". John Mark Ministries. Retrieved 2013-07-25.

Chapter 27

Neuroimaging

This article is about imaging. For imagery and creating maps, see Brain mapping and Outline of brain mapping.

Neuroimaging or **brain imaging** is the use of vari-

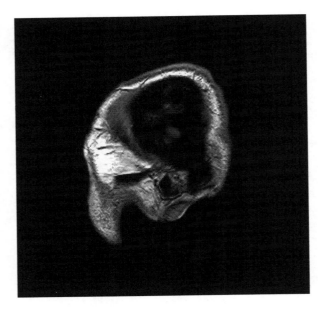

Para-sagittal MRI of the head in a patient with benign familial macrocephaly.

Magnetic resonance image (MRI) of a head, from top to base of the skull

ous techniques to either directly or indirectly image the structure, function/pharmacology of the nervous system. It is a relatively new discipline within medicine and neuroscience/psychology.[1] Physicians who specialize in the performance and interpretation of neuroimaging in the clinical setting are neuroradiologists.

Neuroimaging falls into two broad categories:

- Structural imaging, which deals with the structure of the nervous system and the diagnosis of gross (large scale) intracranial disease (such as tumor), and injury, and

- Functional imaging, which is used to diagnose

metabolic diseases and lesions on a finer scale (such as Alzheimer's disease) and also for neurological and cognitive psychology research and building brain-computer interfaces.

Functional imaging enables, for example, the processing of information by centers in the brain to be visualized directly. Such processing causes the involved area of the brain to increase metabolism and "light up" on the scan. One of the more controversial uses of neuroimaging has been research into "thought identification" or mind-reading.

27.1 History

Main article: History of neuroimaging

The first chapter of the history of neuroimaging traces back to the Italian neuroscientist Angelo Mosso who invented the 'human circulation balance', which could non-invasively measure the redistribution of blood during emotional and intellectual activity.[2] However, even if only briefly mentioned by William James in 1890, the details and precise workings of this balance and the experiments Mosso performed with it have remained largely unknown until the recent discovery of the original instrument as well as Mosso's reports by Stefano Sandrone and colleagues.[3]

In 1918 the American neurosurgeon Walter Dandy introduced the technique of ventriculography. X-ray images of the ventricular system within the brain were obtained by injection of filtered air directly into one or both lateral ventricles of the brain. Dandy also observed that air introduced into the subarachnoid space via lumbar spinal puncture could enter the cerebral ventricles and also demonstrate the cerebrospinal fluid compartments around the base of the brain and over its surface. This technique was called pneumoencephalography.

In 1927 Egas Moniz introduced cerebral angiography, whereby both normal and abnormal blood vessels in and around the brain could be visualized with great precision.

In the early 1970s, Allan McLeod Cormack and Godfrey Newbold Hounsfield introduced computerized axial tomography (CAT or CT scanning), and ever more detailed anatomic images of the brain became available for diagnostic and research purposes. Cormack and Hounsfield won the 1979 Nobel Prize for Physiology or Medicine for their work. Soon after the introduction of CAT in the early 1980s, the development of radioligands allowed single photon emission computed tomography (SPECT) and positron emission tomography (PET) of the brain.

More or less concurrently, magnetic resonance imaging (MRI or MR scanning) was developed by researchers including Peter Mansfield and Paul Lauterbur, who were awarded the Nobel Prize for Physiology or Medicine in 2003. In the early 1980s MRI was introduced clinically, and during the 1980s a veritable explosion of technical refinements and diagnostic MR applications took place. Scientists soon learned that the large blood flow changes measured by PET could also be imaged by the correct type of MRI. Functional magnetic resonance imaging (fMRI) was born, and since the 1990s, fMRI has come to dominate the brain mapping field due to its low invasiveness, lack of radiation exposure, and relatively wide availability.

In the early 2000s the field of neuroimaging reached the stage where limited practical applications of functional brain imaging have become feasible. The main application area is crude forms of brain-computer interface.

27.2 Indications

Neuroimaging follows a neurological examination in which a physician has found cause to more deeply investigate a patient who has or may have a neurological disorder.

One of the more common neurological problems which a person may experience is simple syncope.[4][5] In cases of simple syncope in which the patient's history does not suggest other neurological symptoms, the diagnosis includes a neurological examination but routine neurological imaging is not indicated because the likelihood of finding a cause in the central nervous system is extremely low and the patient is unlikely to benefit from the procedure.[5]

Neuroimaging is not indicated for patients with stable headaches which are diagnosed as migraine.[6] Studies indicate that presence of migraine does not increase a patient's risk for intracranial disease.[6] A diagnosis of migraine which notes the absence of other problems, such as papilledema, would not indicate a need for neuroimaging.[6] In the course of conducting a careful diagnosis, the physician should consider whether the headache has a cause other than the migraine and might require neuroimaging.[6]

Another indication for neuroimaging is CT-, MRI- and PET-guided stereotactic surgery or radiosurgery for treatment of intracranial tumors, arteriovenous malformations and other surgically treatable conditions.[7][8][9][10]

27.3 Brain imaging techniques

27.3.1 Computed axial tomography

Main article: CT head

Computed tomography (CT) or *Computed Axial Tomography* (CAT) scanning uses a series of x-rays of the head taken from many different directions. Typically used for quickly viewing brain injuries, CT scanning uses a computer program that performs a numerical integral calculation (the inverse Radon transform) on the measured x-ray series to estimate how much of an x-ray beam is absorbed in a small volume of the brain. Typically the information is presented as cross sections of the brain.[11]

27.3.2 Diffuse optical imaging

Diffuse optical imaging (DOI) or diffuse optical tomography (DOT) is a medical imaging modality which uses near infrared light to generate images of the body. The technique measures the optical absorption of haemoglobin, and relies on the absorption spectrum of haemoglobin varying with its oxygenation status. High-density diffuse optical tomography (HD-DOT) has seen setbacks due to limited resolution. Early results have been promising, a comparison and validation of diffuse optical imaging against the standard of functional magnetic resonance imaging (fMRI) has been lacking. HD-DOT has adequate image quality to be useful as a surrogate for fMRI.[12]

27.3.3 Event-related optical signal

Event-related optical signal (EROS) is a brain-scanning technique which uses infrared light through optical fibers to measure changes in optical properties of active areas of the cerebral cortex. Whereas techniques such as diffuse optical imaging (DOT) and near infrared spectroscopy (NIRS) measure optical absorption of haemoglobin, and thus are based on blood flow, EROS takes advantage of the scattering properties of the neurons themselves, and thus provides a much more direct measure of cellular activity. EROS can pinpoint activity in the brain within millimeters (spatially) and within milliseconds (temporally). Its biggest downside is the inability to detect activity more than a few centimeters deep. EROS is a new, relatively inexpensive technique that is non-invasive to the test subject. It was developed at the University of Illinois at Urbana-Champaign where it is now used in the Cognitive Neuroimaging Laboratory of Dr. Gabriele Gratton and Dr. Monica Fabiani.

27.3.4 Magnetic resonance imaging

Main article: MRI of brain and brain stem
 Magnetic resonance imaging (MRI) uses magnetic fields and radio waves to produce high quality two- or three-dimensional images of brain structures without use of ionizing radiation (X-rays) or radioactive tracers.

27.3.5 Functional magnetic resonance imaging

Functional magnetic resonance imaging (fMRI) and arterial spin labeling (ASL) relies on the paramagnetic properties of oxygenated and deoxygenated hemoglobin to see images of changing blood flow in the brain associated with neural activity. This allows images to be generated that reflect which brain structures are activated (and how) during performance of different tasks or at resting state. According to the oxygenation hypothesis, changes in oxygen usage in regional cerebral blood flow during cognitive or behavioral activity can be associated with the regional neurons as being directly related to the cognitive or behavioral tasks being attended.

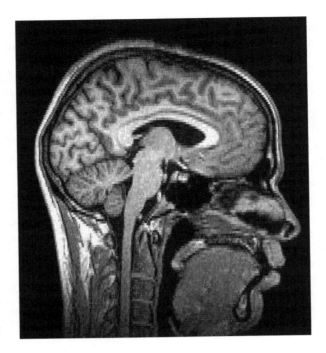

Sagittal MRI slice at the midline.

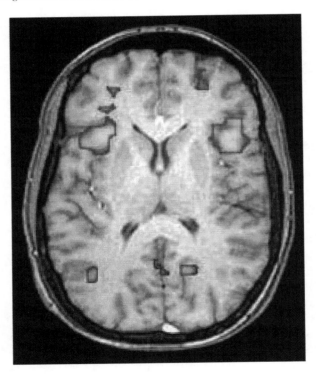

Axial MRI slice at the level of the basal ganglia, showing fMRI BOLD signal changes overlaid in red (increase) and blue (decrease) tones.

Most fMRI scanners allow subjects to be presented with different visual images, sounds and touch stimuli, and to make different actions such as pressing a button or moving a joystick. Consequently, fMRI can be used to reveal brain structures and processes associated with perception, thought and action. The resolution of fMRI is about 2-3 millimeters at present, limited by the spatial spread of the hemodynamic response to neural activity. It has largely superseded PET for the study of brain activation patterns. PET, however, retains the significant advantage of being able to identify specific brain receptors (or transporters) associated with particular neurotransmitters through its ability to image radiolabelled receptor "ligands" (receptor ligands are any chemicals that stick to receptors).

As well as research on healthy subjects, fMRI is increasingly used for the medical diagnosis of disease. Because fMRI is exquisitely sensitive to oxygen usage in blood flow, it is extremely sensitive to early changes in the brain resulting from ischemia (abnormally low blood flow), such as the changes which follow stroke. Early diagnosis of certain types of stroke is increasingly important in neurology, since substances which dissolve blood clots may be used in the first few hours after certain types of stroke occur, but are dangerous to use afterwards. Brain changes seen on fMRI may help to make the decision to treat with these agents. With between 72% and 90% accuracy where chance would achieve 0.8%,[13] fMRI techniques can decide which of a set of known images the subject is viewing.[14]

27.3.6   Magnetoencephalography

Magnetoencephalography (MEG) is an imaging technique used to measure the magnetic fields produced by electrical activity in the brain via extremely sensitive devices such as superconducting quantum interference devices (SQUIDs). MEG offers a very direct measurement of neural electrical activity (compared to fMRI for example) with very high temporal resolution but relatively low spatial resolution. The advantage of measuring the magnetic fields produced by neural activity is that they are likely to be less distorted by surrounding tissue (particularly the skull and scalp) compared to the electric fields measured by electroencephalography (EEG). Specifically, it can be shown that magnetic fields produced by electrical activity are not affected by the surrounding head tissue, when the head is modeled as a set of concentric spherical shells, each being an isotropic homogeneous conductor. Real heads are non-spherical and have largely anisotropic conductivities (particularly white matter and skull). While skull anisotropy has negligible effect on MEG (unlike EEG), white matter anisotropy strongly affects MEG measurements for radial and deep sources.[15] Note, however, that the skull was assumed to be uniformly anisotropic in this study, which is not true for a real head: the absolute and relative thicknesses of diploë and tables layers vary among and within the skull bones. This makes it likely that MEG is

also affected by the skull anisotropy,[16] although probably not to the same degree as EEG.

There are many uses for MEG, including assisting surgeons in localizing a pathology, assisting researchers in determining the function of various parts of the brain, neurofeedback, and others.

27.3.7   Positron emission tomography

Positron emission tomography (PET) measures emissions from radioactively labeled metabolically active chemicals that have been injected into the bloodstream. The emission data are computer-processed to produce 2- or 3-dimensional images of the distribution of the chemicals throughout the brain.[17] The positron emitting radioisotopes used are produced by a cyclotron, and chemicals are labeled with these radioactive atoms. The labeled compound, called a *radiotracer*, is injected into the bloodstream and eventually makes its way to the brain. Sensors in the PET scanner detect the radioactivity as the compound accumulates in various regions of the brain. A computer uses the data gathered by the sensors to create multicolored 2- or 3-dimensional images that show where the compound acts in the brain. Especially useful are a wide array of ligands used to map different aspects of neurotransmitter activity, with by far the most commonly used PET tracer being a labeled form of glucose (see Fludeoxyglucose (18F) (FDG)).

The greatest benefit of PET scanning is that different compounds can show blood flow and oxygen and glucose metabolism in the tissues of the working brain. These measurements reflect the amount of brain activity in the various regions of the brain and allow to learn more about how the brain works. PET scans were superior to all other metabolic imaging methods in terms of resolution and speed of completion (as little as 30 seconds), when they first became available. The improved resolution permitted better study to be made as to the area of the brain activated by a particular task. The biggest drawback of PET scanning is that because the radioactivity decays rapidly, it is limited to monitoring short tasks.[18] Before fMRI technology came online, PET scanning was the preferred method of functional (as opposed to structural) brain imaging, and it continues to make large contributions to neuroscience.

PET scanning is also used for diagnosis of brain disease, most notably because brain tumors, strokes, and neuron-damaging diseases which cause dementia (such as Alzheimer's disease) all cause great changes in brain metabolism, which in turn causes easily detectable changes in PET scans. PET is probably most useful in early cases of certain dementias (with classic examples being Alzheimer's disease and Pick's disease) where the early damage is too diffuse and makes too little difference in brain volume and gross structure to change CT and standard MRI images enough to be able to reliably differentiate it from the "normal" range of cortical atrophy which occurs with aging (in many but not all) persons, and which does *not* cause clinical dementia.

27.3.8 Single-photon emission computed tomography

Single-photon emission computed tomography (SPECT) is similar to PET and uses gamma ray-emitting radioisotopes and a gamma camera to record data that a computer uses to construct two- or three-dimensional images of active brain regions.[19] SPECT relies on an injection of radioactive tracer, or "SPECT agent," which is rapidly taken up by the brain but does not redistribute. Uptake of SPECT agent is nearly 100% complete within 30 to 60 seconds, reflecting cerebral blood flow (CBF) at the time of injection. These properties of SPECT make it particularly well-suited for epilepsy imaging, which is usually made difficult by problems with patient movement and variable seizure types. SPECT provides a "snapshot" of cerebral blood flow since scans can be acquired after seizure termination (so long as the radioactive tracer was injected at the time of the seizure). A significant limitation of SPECT is its poor resolution (about 1 cm) compared to that of MRI. Today, SPECT machines with Dual Detector Heads are commonly used, although Triple Detector Head machines are available in the marketplace. Tomographic reconstruction, (mainly used for functional "snapshots" of the brain) requires multiple projections from Detector Heads which rotate around the human skull, so some researchers have developed 6 and 11 Detector Head SPECT machines to cut imaging time and give higher resolution.[20][21]

Like PET, SPECT also can be used to differentiate different kinds of disease processes which produce dementia, and it is increasingly used for this purpose. Neuro-PET has a disadvantage of requiring use of tracers with half-lives of at most 110 minutes, such as FDG. These must be made in a cyclotron, and are expensive or even unavailable if necessary transport times are prolonged more than a few half-lives. SPECT, however, is able to make use of tracers with much longer half-lives, such as technetium-99m, and as a result, is far more widely available.

27.3.9 Cranial Ultrasound

Cranial ultrasound is usually only used in babies, whose open fontanelles provide acoustic windows allowing ultrasound imaging of the brain. Advantages include absence of ionising radiation and the possibility of bedside scanning, but the lack of soft-tissue detail means MRI may be preferred for some conditions.

27.3.10 Comparison of imaging types

Magnetic Resonance Imaging (MRI) depends on magnetic activity in the brain and does not use X-rays, so it is considered more safe than imaging techniques that do use X-rays. SPECT uses gamma rays, which are characteristically more safe than other imaging systems using alpha or beta rays. Both PET and SPECT scans require the injection of radioactive materials, but the half-lives of isotopes used in SPECT can be more easily managed.

27.4 See also

- Brain mapping
  - Outline of brain mapping
- Connectogram
- Functional integration (neurobiology)
- Functional near-infrared spectroscopy
- Functional neuroimaging
- History of neuroimaging
- Human brain
  - Cognitive neuroscience
  - Outline of the human brain
- List of neuroimaging software
- List of neuroscience databases
- Magnetic resonance imaging
- Magnetoencephalography
- Medical image computing
- Medical imaging
- Neuroimaging journals
- Statistical parametric mapping
- Transcranial magnetic stimulation
- Voxel-based morphometry

27.5 References

[1] Filler, Aaron (12 July 2009). "The History, Development and Impact of Computed Imaging in Neurological Diagnosis and Neurosurgery: CT, MRI, and DTI". *Nature Precedings*. doi:10.1038/npre.2009.3267.5.

[2] Sandrone; et al. (2012). "Angelo Mosso". *Journal of Neurology* **259**: 2513–2514. doi:10.1007/s00415-012-6632-1. PMID 23010944.

[3] Sandrone; et al. (2013). "Weighing brain activity with the balance: Angelo Mosso's original manuscripts come to light". *Brain* **137**: 621–633. doi:10.1093/brain/awt091. PMID 23687118.

[4] Miller, T. H.; Kruse, J. E. (2005). "Evaluation of syncope". *American family physician* **72** (8): 1492–1500. PMID 16273816.

[5] American College of Physicians (September 2013), "Five Things Physicians and Patients Should Question", *Choosing Wisely: an initiative of the ABIM Foundation* (American College of Physicians), retrieved 10 December 2013, which cites

- American College of Radiology; American Society of Neuroradiology (2010), "ACR-ASNR practice guideline for the performance of computed tomography (CT) of the brain", *Agency for Healthcare Research and Quality* (Reston, VA, USA: American College of Radiology), retrieved 9 September 2012

- *Transient loss of consciousness in adults and young people: NICE guideline*, National Institute for Health and Clinical Excellence, 25 August 2010, retrieved 9 September 2012

- Moya, A.; European Society of Cardiology (ESC); Sutton, R.; European Heart Rhythm Association (EHRA); Ammirati, F.; and Heart Rhythm Society (HRS); Blanc, J.-J.; Endorsed by the following societies; Brignole, M.; European Society of Emergency Medicine (EuSEM); Moya, J. B.; European Federation of Internal Medicine (EFIM); Sutton, J.-C.; European Union Geriatric Medicine Society (EUGMS); Ammirati, J.; Blanc, K.; European Neurological Society (ENS); Brignole, A.; European Federation of Autonomic Societies (EFAS); Dahm, M.; Deharo, M.; Gajek, T.; Gjesdal, R. R.; Krahn, F.; Massin, A.; Pepi, J. G.; Pezawas, E. P.; Ruiz Granell, W.; Sarasin, H.; Ungar, D. G.; et al. (2009). "Guidelines for the diagnosis and management of syncope (version 2009): The Task Force for the Diagnosis and Management of Syncope of the European Society of Cardiology (ESC)". *European Heart Journal* **30** (21): 2631–2671. doi:10.1093/eurheartj/ehp298. PMC 3295536. PMID 19713422.

[6] American Headache Society (September 2013), "Five Things Physicians and Patients Should Question", *Choosing Wisely: an initiative of the ABIM Foundation* (American Headache Society), retrieved 10 December 2013, which cites

- Lewis, D. W.; Dorbad, D. (2000). "The utility of neuroimaging in the evaluation of children with migraine or chronic daily headache who have normal neurological examinations". *Headache* **40** (8): 629–632. doi:10.1046/j.1526-4610.2000.040008629.x. PMID 10971658.

- Silberstein, S. D. (2000). "Practice parameter: Evidence-based guidelines for migraine headache (an evidence-based review): Report of the Quality Standards Subcommittee of the American Academy of Neurology". *Neurology* **55** (6): 754–762. doi:10.1212/WNL.55.6.754. PMID 10993991.

- Health Quality, O. (2010). "Neuroimaging for the evaluation of chronic headaches: An evidence-based analysis". *Ontario health technology assessment series* **10** (26): 1–57. PMC 3377587. PMID 23074404.

[7] Thomas DG, Anderson RE, du Boulay GH (January 1984). "CT-guided stereotactic neurosurgery: experience in 24 cases with a new stereotactic system". *Journal of Neurology, Neurosurgery & Psychiatry* **47** (1): 9–16. doi:10.1136/jnnp.47.1.9. PMC 1027634. PMID 6363629.

[8] Heilbrun MP, Sunderland PM, McDonald PR, Wells TH Jr, Cosman E, Ganz E (1987). "Brown-Roberts-Wells stereotactic frame modifications to accomplish magnetic resonance imaging guidance in three planes". *Applied Neurophysiology* **50** (1-6): 143–152. doi:10.1159/000100700. PMID 3329837.

[9] Leksell L, Leksell D, Schwebel J (January 1985). "Stereotaxis and nuclear magnetic resonance". *Journal of Neurology, Neurosurgery & Psychiatry* **48** (1): 14–18. doi:10.1136/jnnp.48.1.14. PMC 1028176. PMID 3882889.

[10] Levivier M, Massager N, Wikler D, Lorenzoni J, Ruiz S, Devriendt D, David P, Desmedt F, Simon S, Van Houtte P, Brotchi J, Goldman S (July 2004). "Use of stereotactic PET images in dosimetry planning of radiosurgery for brain tumors: clinical experience and proposed classification". *Journal of Nuclear Medicine* **45** (7): 1146–1154. PMID 15235060.

[11] Jeeves, Malcolm A. (1994). *Mind Fields: Reflections on the Science of Mind and Brain*. Grand Rapids, MI: Baker Books., p. 21

[12] Eggebrecht, AT; White, BR; Ferradal, SL; Chen, C; Zhan, Y; Snyder, AZ; Dehghani, H; Culver, JP (Jul 16, 2012). "A quantitative spatial comparison of high-density diffuse optical tomography and fMRI cortical mapping.". *NeuroImage* **61** (4): 1120–8. doi:10.1016/j.neuroimage.2012.01.124. PMID 22330315.

[13] Smith, Kerri (March 5, 2008). "Mind-reading with a brain scan". *Nature News* (Nature Publishing Group). Retrieved 2008-03-05.

[14] Keim, Brandon (March 5, 2008). "Brain Scanner Can Tell What You're Looking At". *Wired News* (CondéNet). Retrieved 2015-09-16.

[15] Wolters, C.H.; Anwander, A.; Tricoche, X.; Weinstein, D.; Koch, M.A.; MacLeod, R.S. (31 March 2006). "Influence of tissue conductivity anisotropy on EEG/MEG field and return current computation in a realistic head model: A simulation and visualization study using high-resolution finite element modeling". *NeuroImage* **30** (3): 813–826. doi:10.1016/j.neuroimage.2005.10.014. PMID 16364662.

[16] Ramon, Ceon; Haueisen, Jens; Schimpf, Paul H (1 January 2006). "Influence of head models on neuromagnetic fields and inverse source localizations.". *BioMedical Engineering OnLine* **5** (1): 55. doi:10.1186/1475-925X-5-55. PMC 1629018. PMID 17059601.

[17] Lars-Goran Nilsson and Hans J. Markowitsch (1999). *Cognitive Neuroscience of Memory*. Seattle: Hogrefe & Huber Publishers., page 57

[18] Lars-Goran Nilsson and Hans J. Markowitsch (1999). *Cognitive Neuroscience of Memory*. Seattle: Hogrefe & Huber Publishers., pg. 60

[19] Philip Ball *Brain Imaging Explained*

[20] "SPECT Systems for Brain Imaging". Retrieved July 24, 2014.

[21] "SPECT Brain Imaging". Retrieved January 12, 2016.

27.6   External links

- The Whole Brain Atlas @ Harvard

- The McConnell Brain Imaging Center, McGill University

- The American Society of Neuroimaging (ASN).

- A Neuroimaging portal

- BrainMapping.org, *a free BrainMapping community information portal*

- Lecture notes on mathematical aspects of neuroimaging by Will Penny, University College London

- "Transcranial Magnetic Stimulation".   by Michael Leventon in association with MIT AI Lab.

- NeuroDebian - a complete operating system targeting neuroimaging

Chapter 28

Return from Tomorrow

For the episode of Star Trek: The Original Series,
see Return to Tomorrow.

Return From Tomorrow is a book by George G. Ritchie
in which he describes a near-death experience in an Army
hospital at the age of 20, in which he was legally dead for
nine minutes, and the effect it had on him.

28.1 Further reading

- George G. Ritchie and Elizabeth Sherrill, *Return from
  Tomorrow*. Old Tappan, NJ: F.H. Revell, 1978. ISBN
  0-8007-8412-X.

28.2 External links

- An article about George G. Ritchie's NDE

Chapter 29

Life After Life (book)

This article is about the 1975 nonfiction book. For the 2013 novel, see Life After Life (novel).

Life After Life is a 1975 book written by psychiatrist Raymond Moody. It is a report on a qualitative study in which Moody interviewed 150 people who had undergone near-death experiences (NDEs). The book presents the author's composite account of what it is like to die.[1][2] On the basis of his collection of cases, Moody identified a common set of elements in NDEs:[3]

- • (a) an overwhelming feeling of peace and well-being, including freedom from pain.
- • (b) the impression of being located outside one's physical body.
- • (c) floating or drifting through darkness, sometimes described as a tunnel.
- • (d) becoming aware of a golden light.
- • (e) encountering and perhaps communicating with a "being of light".
- • (f) having a rapid succession of visual images of one's past.
- • (g) experiencing another world of much beauty.[3]

Life After Life sold more than 13 million copies,[4] was translated into a dozen foreign languages[5] and became an international best seller, which made the subject of NDEs popular and opened the way for many other studies.[6][7]

29.1 Reception

Scientists have written that Moody's alleged evidence for an afterlife is flawed, logically and empirically.[8] The psychologist James Alcock has noted that "[Moody] appears to ignore a great deal of the scientific literature dealing with hallucinatory experiences in general, just as he quickly glosses over the very real limitations of his research method."[9]

The philosopher Paul Kurtz has written that Moody's evidence for the NDE is based on personal interviews and anecdotal accounts and there has been no statistical analyses of his data. According to Kurtz "there is no reliable evidence that people who report such experiences have died and returned, or that consciousness exists separate from the brain or body."[10]

29.2 References

[1] Clifton D. Bryant (2003). Handbook of Death and Dying Sage, p.138.

[2] Michael Marsh. Review: Beyond Death: The Rebirth of Immortality *The Hastings Center Report*, Vol. 7, No. 5 (Oct., 1977), pp. 40—42.

[3] Harvey J. Irwin and Caroline Watt. An introduction to parapsychology McFarland, 2007, p. 159.

[4] Towards the light *The Age*, March 23, 2004.

[5] Louis E. LaGrand (1999), *Messages and miracles: extraordinary experiences of the bereaved*, St. Paul, MN: Llewellyn Worldwide, p. 9, ISBN 1-56718-406-5

[6] Harvey J. Irwin, Caroline Watt (2007). An introduction to parapsychology McFarland, p. 158.

[7] Duane S. Crowther (2005). Life Everlasting Cedar Fort, p. 19.

[8] Barry Beyerstein. (1990). *Evaluating the Anomalous Experience*. In Kendrick Frazier. *The Hundredth Monkey and Other Paradigms of the Paranormal*. Prometheus Books. pp. 43–53. ISBN 0-87975-655-1

[9] James Alcock. (1981). *Psychology and Near-Death Experiences*. In Kendrick Frazier. *Paranormal Borderlands of Science*. Prometheus Books. pp. 153–169. ISBN 0-87975-148-7

[10] Paul Kurtz. (1991). *Toward a New Enlightenment: The Philosophy of Paul Kurtz*. Transaction Publishers. p. 349. ISBN 1-56000-118-6

29.3 External links

- Official website

- The Raymond Moody Institute

- NDE episodes from the book *Life After Life* by Dr. R. Moody

Chapter 30

Betty Eadie

Betty (Jean) Eadie (born 1942) is a prominent American author of several books on near-death experiences (NDEs). Her best-known book is the No. 1 New York Times best-selling book *Embraced by the Light* (1992). It describes her near-death experience. It is arguably the most detailed near-death account on record. It was followed by *The Awakening Heart* (1996), which was also a best-seller. *The Ripple Effect* (1999) and *Embraced by the Light: Prayers and Devotions for Daily Living* (2001) were both published independently.

30.1   Early life and career

Eadie, who is part Native American, was born in Valentine, Nebraska and raised on the Rosebud Indian Reservation in South Dakota. When she was four, Betty's parents separated and she was placed in St. Francis Indian School, one of the American Indian boarding schools at the time along with six of her siblings. While in high school she dropped out to care for a younger sister, then later returned to receive her diploma, eventually pursuing a college degree. She also converted to The Church of Jesus Christ of Latter-day Saints (LDS Church), in which she says she was largely inactive until her NDE, after which she became active and served church callings in her ward in Seattle.[1]

After her NDE, Betty began volunteering her time at a cancer research center comforting dying patients and their families. She then studied hypnotherapy, graduating at the top of her class, and later opened her own clinic. After "Embraced" was published, Betty gave up her hypnotherapy practice and began traveling extensively throughout the United States, Canada, Great Britain and Ireland, speaking on death and the afterlife. Today, after more than 37 years of NDE studies, Betty J. Eadie continues to collect and evaluate near-death accounts, as well as giving speeches and lectures.

30.2   NDE account

In her NDE account, Eadie reports many phenomena similar to other NDE accounts, such as going through a dark tunnel, seeing a bright light and experiencing a Life review, as well as features unique to her story. In 1973, while recovering from a surgical operation at age 31, Eadie reported she first felt herself fading to lifelessness, then felt a surge of energy followed by a "pop" and feeling of release, a sense of freedom and movement unhindered by inertia or gravity. She was met by three angelic beings who spoke with her about her prior existence and hitherto suppressed memories in order to participate in earthly experience. She traveled to terrestrial locations such as her home merely by thinking about them, returned to her hospital, and then passed on through a dark tunnel-like medium in which she reported sensing other beings in a transitory preparatory stage.

Exiting the tunnel, Eadie approached an intense white light and met in heaven the embrace of Jesus Christ, during which encounter she reported a strong sense of love and a high-speed transfer of answers to her many questions. Possessing a corporeal identity of an ethereal kind, she visited numerous places, persons, and phenomena such as natural settings and gardens beyond the character of the conventionally material, and was taken on a tour of sorts to learning experiences that she said felt equivalent to weeks or months.

In addition to discussing traditional Christian subjects such as prayer, creation, and the Garden of Eden, Eadie reported visiting a library of the mind in which it became possible to know anything or anyone in history or the present in minute and unambiguous detail, as well as being able to observe individuals on Earth and being taken to distant reaches and civilizations of the universe.

Warned initially upon arrival that she had died prematurely, Eadie was at last told she must return in order to fulfill the personal mission allocated her, though its specific character, like numerous other details, were removed from her memory, in order, she said she was told, to prevent difficulties in her fulfilling it. Upon protesting, she was made to understand the reason behind the necessity for her return and reluctantly agreed to do so, though exacting a promise that she would not be made to stay on earth longer than necessary. Her return to material corporeality she reported as extremely heavy-feeling and unpleasant, initially intermittent in phases, and accompanied not long after by a demonic visitation that was cut short by an angelic reappearance.

Eadie's doctor reportedly verified her clinical death on a return visit to the hospital, attributing it to a hemorrhage during a nurses' shift change, and took great interest in her recollections. Independent verification of the length of her decease was not possible, but she speculated it could have lasted up to four hours based on her memory of certain details preceding and following it.

Some elements of her account seem on their face inconsistent, such as the idea of an elaborately interdependent universal plan and the human ability to fail at it, but this for example she attributed to the permissible scope of free will within a larger divine control.[2]

30.3 After

Subsequent to her experience, she spoke of it very little and suffered a long-term depression, which she attributed to the anticlimactic nature of returning to corporeality after experiencing the heaven of afterlife. She slowly became involved in near-death groups and studies and gave talks, going on subsequently to write her account in book form, which met with runaway success.

While her account incorporated elements of traditional Christianity, it also met with a certain degree of resistance as well, largely to its teaching (as she reported she was given it) that some denominations might approximate truth better than others but that different teachings were more appropriate for certain individuals at their given stage of spiritual development, and that therefore judgment should not be passed on them for where they were. Unlike many fundamentalist Christians,[3] and despite her own strict Catholic upbringing as recounted in her book, and her conversion to The Church of Jesus Christ of Latter-day Saints (LDS Church), after receiving her near-death experience, Eadie refers to God as "he" instead of "He" and insists that all religions are necessary for each person, claiming that each religion is necessary for each person because of their different levels of spiritual enlightenment, contrary to the views shared by many Christians worldwide that only Christianity is the one true valid religion. Curiously, Eadie also claims that after her encounter with Jesus, she learned that Christ and God were in fact two separate entities, a view conflicting with that of her Protestant-taught tradition of the Holy Trinity. This is, however, in keeping with the teachings of the LDS Church.

In addition, unlike some other Near-Death Experiencers, Eadie claims that reincarnation as it is typically thought of does not truly exist. [4] Eadie claims she was told that only a few return to this earth more than once, that some are sent back as teachers to help others.[5] She taught similar withholding of censure on individuals for things like atheism and homosexuality and rejected a common traditional image of hell as an eternity of suffering, suggesting that her life review experience, in which she was made to live and feel the full positive and negative consequences of her cumulative actions in intense detail, including their effects on all around her, were a more than adequate equivalent and probably what the term truly signified.

She also stressed that her key lesson was that life's purpose was to learn love and to grow through the exercise of free will, including making mistakes. Other teachings she said she was given included the idea that there were few if any true accidents, that human lives and paths were chosen, agreed to, and prepared for in advance, with memory of such details suppressed and veiled. Suicide she said she was told was wrong because it deprived people of opportunities to learn and grow, and that there was always hope in life.

30.4 Sequels

The Awakening Heart is Eadie's second book and also became a NYT Bestseller in which she describes her challenges and experience that followed her NDE up through the time that *Embraced By The Light* was published, as well as giving additional details about her NDE that were not included in her first book.[6] *The Ripple Effect* pursued these further, incorporating discussion of the numerous letters she began to receive in response from readers, as well as discussing other NDE contacts she later developed. Eadie formed her own Publishing house,[7] Onjinjinkta Publishing,[8] through which she published her third book and her fourth book, *Embraced By The Light Prayers and Devotions for Daily Living*, as well as various works from other authors.

Because of their appeal to the innate human desire for an understanding of afterlife, her works led to a strong reader response which she initially attempted to answer in detail but became forced to limit. To meet some of this demand, she developed a website for general information and inspirational materials, as well as distribution of her books and related materials.

During a 2004 interview on Coast to Coast AM radio with George Noory, she said she was disappointed following her first book's publication that she was not permitted to return to the Celestial realm, but that while she could not presently know the full scope of her earthly purpose, she understood a film based on *Embraced* would also follow.

Her husband, Joe, worked in aerospace computing and deceased in 2011. Together they had eight children, and as of 2011, fifteen grandchildren and 7 great-grandchildren.

30.5   See also

- Near-death experience

- Raymond Moody

30.6   References

[1] Introvigne, Massimo (1996, Fall).   "Embraced by the Church? Betty Eadie, Near-Death Experiences, and Mormonism."*Dialogue: A Journal of Mormon Thought, 29*(3), 99–119.

[2] Eadie, Betty J. (1992). *Embraced by the Light.* Placerville, CA: Gold Leaf Press.

[3] http://www.allanturner.com/ss01.html

[4] "We understood that memories would be contained in the cells of our new bodies. This was an idea that was completely new to me. I learned that all thoughts and experiences in our lives are recorded in our subconscious minds. They are also recorded in our cells, so that, not only is each cell imprinted with a genetic coding, it is also imprinted with every experience we have ever had. Further, I understood that these memories are passed down through the genetic coding to our children. These memories then account for many of the passed on traits in families, such as addictive tendencies, fears, strengths, and so on. I also learned that we do not have repeated lives on this earth; when we seem to "remember" a past life, we are actually recalling memories contained in these cells." *Embraced by the Light* (Hardcover Edition) (pg. 93)

[5] "Often, when I am asked what I understand about reincarnation, I think about this little girl. Life on earth is like going away to college. Our spirits stay here until we graduate, then we leave the campus and go on to further our development elsewhere. Some graduating students can return if they have acquired enough knowledge to return as teachers." Betty J. Eadie, *The Awakening Heart: My Continuing Journey to Love*, p.157. Pocket Books, 1996

[6] Eadie, Betty J., *The Awakening Heart*, cover matter, Pocket Books, 1996 ISBN 0-671-55868-4

[7] "Media Talk; Inspirational Author Founds Her Own Press," The New York Times: Archives, By Karen Angel July 13, 1998

[8] Open Library, Onjinjinkta Publishing, *Publisher*, openlibrary.org

30.7   External links

- The Official Betty J. Eadie Website

- Embraced By The Light by Betty J. Eadie

- Near-Death Experience Research Foundation

- A Special Report: What Is Betty Eadie Hiding? Christian Research Institute Journal

Chapter 31

Saved by the Light

Saved by the Light (Villard Books, 1994, Harper Torch 1995 ISBN 0-06-100889-3) is a book by Dannion Brinkley describing his near-death experience (NDE). It is co-authored by Paul Perry. Brinkley was struck by lightning and was clinically dead for approximately twenty-eight minutes. Upon reviving, he told a tale of a dark tunnel, a crystal city, and a "cathedral of knowledge" where thirteen angels shared with him over a hundred revelations about the future, some of which he claims come true. The claims made have subsequently been challenged.[1]

Within two weeks of publication, another 5000 copies were printed.[2] The book was on *The New York Times*' bestseller charts for over 25 weeks.[3]

The book was adapted for a 1995 FOX TV film of the same name starring Eric Roberts. Since originally airing, it has been in regular circulation on the Lifetime television network.

31.1 References

[1] Rivernburg, Roy (1995-03-24). "Blinded by the Light? : Tales of near-death experiences--from visions of God to meeting Elvis--fascinate millions of us. But as the stories increase, so does the criticism.". *Los Angeles Times*. Retrieved 2016-03-25.

[2] Colford, Paul D. (1994-03-24). "'How We Die' Becomes Surprise Hit". *Los Angeles Times*. Retrieved 2016-03-25.

[3] Kelly, Leslie (1995-01-23). "Incredible Journey Author's near-death experience brings an enlightened view of life". *The Spokesman-Review*. Retrieved 2016-03-25.

31.2 External links

- *Saved by the Light* at the Internet Movie Database

Chapter 32

Placebo (at funeral)

An obsolete usage of the word **placebo** was to mean someone who came to a funeral, claiming (often falsely) a connection with the deceased to try to get a share of any food and/or drink being handed out. This usage originated from the phrase "placebo Domino in regione vivorum" in the Roman Catholic Church's Office of the Dead ritual.

32.1 Origin and significance of "placebo Domino in regione vivorum"

By the eighth century, the Christian Church in the West had an established form and content of its Office of the Dead ritual, taking the relevant verse from the Vulgate. At the end of each recited passage, the congregation made a response (antiphon) to each recitation. The celebrant's first recitation was Psalm 116:1–9 (Psalm 114:1–9 in the Septuagint), and the congregation's first responding antiphon was verse 9 of that Psalm.[1]

Psalm 114:9 in the Vulgate says,[2] "placebo Domino in regione vivorum" ("I will please the Lord in the land of the living"); the equivalent verse in English bibles is Psalm 116:9, "I will walk before the Lord in the land of the living".

The Vulgate verse follows the Greek Septuagint in meaning. The Christian scholar John Chrysostom (347–407) understood the verse to mean that "those who had departed [from this life] accompanied by good deeds ... [would] abide forever in high honor", and it was from this perspective that he chose to read the Septuagint as saying, "I shall be pleasing in the sight of the Lord in the land of the living" (εὐαρεστήσω ἐναντίον κυρίου ἐν χώρᾳ ζώντων), (Hill 1998, p. 87). See also Popper (1945), Shapiro (1968), Lasagna (1986), Aronson (1999), Jacobs (2000), and Walach (2003).

The numbers of the Psalms are different in the Vulgate from those used in most English bibles: for example, the Vulgate Psalm 114 is Hebrew Psalm 116. See Composition of the Book of Psalms.

32.2 "Placebo singers" in French custom

In France, it was the custom for the mourning family to distribute largesse to the congregation immediately following the Office of the Dead ritual. As a consequence, distant relatives and other, unrelated, parasites would attend the ceremony, simulating great anguish and grief in the hope of, at least, being given food and drink.

The practice was so widespread that these parasites were soon recognized as the personification of all things useless, and were considered to be archetypical simulators. Because the grief simulators' first collective act was to chant "placebo Domino in regione vivorum", they were collectively labelled (in French) as either "placebo singers" or "singers of placebo"; they were so labelled because they sang the word "placebo", *not* because they were "choral placaters", using their song to please.

32.3 Adoption of the expression in English

By the time of Chaucer's Canterbury Tales (circa 1386), the disparaging English expression "placebo singer", meaning a parasite or a sycophant, was well established in the English language. In Chaucer's Parson's Tale, for example, the Parson speaks of how flatterers (those who continuously "sing Placebo") are "the Devil's Chaplains". (Perhaps Charles Darwin had Chaucer's Parson in mind when he wrote: "What a book a Devil's Chaplain might write on the clumsy, wasteful, blundering low and horridly cruel works of nature.")

The English word "placebo" also denoted a sycophant; this use seems to have arisen among those otherwise unaware of the words's origin but who knew that the word is Latin for "I will please".

Chaucer's Merchant's Tale contains a character called

198

Placebo, and other significantly named characters:

- January: the old, blind knight, with hair as white as snow.

- May: his beautiful, lusty, and extremely young wife (and, thus, a January–May marriage).

- Justinus (the "noble man"): his correct and thoughtful brother, who strongly advised against the marriage of January to May (which also involved a considerable transfer of money, land, and wealth to May).

- Placebo (the "Yes man"): his sycophantic, flattering brother, who never once raised objection to any of January's thoughts, and actively supports January's proposal.

This may have helped to give "placebo" the English medical meaning of "simulator".

32.4   Indian equivalent

In India, similar act of placebo is performed at funerals, especially in Rajasthan, by professional mourners called Rudali. They are usually females, wearing black drapery and perform the acts of crying on death of a person. In case, the deceased was a husband, Rudali wipe off the vermillion of the widow and remove all her decorative jewelleries which are the symbols of a married woman. The most important among these ornaments to remove is the mangalsutra.

This act of placebo has been an age old tradition. It is mostly prevalent among the Rajput and Jat clans on northern India.

32.5   See also

- Ormerod hoax

32.6   References

[1] http://www.hebrewoldtestament.com/B19C116.htm#V9 or Green (1997), p.502.

[2]   • Rahlfs (1935), p.128.

Chapter 33

90 Minutes in Heaven

For the film, see 90 Minutes in Heaven (film).

90 Minutes in Heaven is a 2004 New York Times best-selling[1] Christian book written by Don Piper with Cecil Murphey.[2] The book documents the author's near-death experience in 1989. *90 Minutes in Heaven* remained on the *New York Times* best-seller list for more than five years[1] and has sold over six million copies.[1][3][4][5] The book has also been adapted into a feature-length film, released in theaters on September 11, 2015.[6][7]

33.1 Summary

On January 18, 1989, Baptist minister Don Piper was on his way home from a conference in Texas when a semi-trailer truck struck his Ford Taurus while crossing a bridge. Piper describes that he was crushed by the roof of his car, the steering wheel impaled his chest, and the dashboard collapsed on his legs. When paramedics arrived, they could not find any sign of life in Piper and covered him with a tarp as a fellow pastor prayed over him while waiting for the medical examiner to arrive.[8] According to Piper, he went straight to Heaven and experienced things he describes as amazing and beautiful, including meeting family members such as his great-grandmother and joining a Heavenly Choir that proceeded into the Gates of Heaven. Piper, an ordained minister since 1985, has recounted his narrative before 3,000 live audiences that included more than 1.5 million people[1] and appeared on numerous television and radio programs.[8]

33.2 See also

- *23 Minutes in Hell*, 2006 book by Bill Wiese recounting what the author believes were his experiences in Hell in 1998

- Eben Alexander, author of the 2012 book *Proof of Heaven: A Neurosurgeon's Journey into the Afterlife*

- *The Boy Who Came Back From Heaven*, a fabricated account of a near-death experience

- *Heaven Is for Real: A Little Boy's Astounding Story of His Trip to Heaven and Back*, 2010 book by Todd Burpo and Lynn Vincent about a near-death experience reported by Burpo's then-four-year-old son, Colton

- Howard Storm, author of the book *My Descent Into Death* about his near-death experience

- Pam Reynolds case

33.3 References

[1] "Piper's '90 Minutes in Heaven' back on 'New York Times' best-seller list". *Christian Retailing*. 25 April 2014.

[2] Robert Gottlieb (23 October 2014). "To Heaven and Back!". *New York Review of Books*.

[3] "90 Minutes in Heaven". More than 4 million copies sold!

[4] Tim Challies. "Heaven Tourism". *challies.com*.

[5] Challies, Tim. "Book Review - 90 Minutes in Heaven". Challies. Retrieved 7 December 2014.

[6] Driver, Ben. "90 Minutes in Heaven' headed to big screen". *The Baptist Standard*. Retrieved 10 May 2015.

[7] Driver, Ben. "Family Christian Entertainment 'To Be the Disney' of Faith-Based Films As '90 Minutes In Heaven' Enters Production". *Christian Post*. Retrieved 10 May 2015.

[8] Inbar, Michael (2009-09-28). "New study: What really happens when you die?". *TODAY: Health*. msnbc.com. Retrieved 29 December 2010.

33.4 Further reading

- Piper, Don; Murphey, Cecil (2004-09-01). *90 Minutes in Heaven*. Grand Rapids, Michigan: Revell Books. ISBN 978-0-8007-5949-0.

33.5 External links

- Website for the book

- Critical Review on book

Chapter 34

Heaven Is for Real

For the film of the same name, see Heaven Is for Real (film).

Heaven is for Real: A Little Boy's Astounding Story of His Trip to Heaven and Back is a 2010 *New York Times* best-selling Christian book written by Todd Burpo and Lynn Vincent. It was published by Thomas Nelson Publishers. The book documents the report of a near-death experience by Burpo's three-year-old son Colton. The book recounts the experiences that Colton relates from visits which he said he made to heaven during a near-death experience.

By April 2012 over one million ebooks had been sold,[1] and by 2014 over 10 million copies had been sold.[2] A movie based on the book was released on April 16, 2014, earning $101 million at the box office.[3]

34.1 Summary

In the book, Todd Burpo, pastor of Crossroads Wesleyan Church in Imperial, Nebraska, writes that during the months after his son, Colton, had emergency surgery in 2003 at the age of three,[4] Colton began describing events and people that seemed impossible for him to have known about. Examples include knowledge of an unborn sister miscarried by his mother and details of a great-grandfather who had died 30 years before Colton was born.[5] Colton also explained how he personally met Jesus riding a rainbow-colored horse and sat in Jesus' lap while angels sang songs to him.[6][7] He also saw Mary kneeling before the throne of God and at other times standing beside Jesus.[8]

34.2 Response

34.2.1 Sales

Within ten weeks of its November 2010 release, the book debuted at No. 3 on the *New York Times* bestseller list.

By January 2011, there were 200,000 copies in print. The book hit No. 1, remaining in the top 10 for some weeks. It became the No. 1 best-selling non-fiction paperback.[9][10]

34.2.2 Criticism

A variety of Christians have expressed criticism or concern about the book's content and message. *The Berean Call*, a Christian ministry and newsletter, criticized the book for its "extra-biblical" and "problematic" claims, as well as the lack of any medical evidence that the boy was clinically dead during the surgery.[11] Author and pastor John MacArthur has criticized the book for presenting an un-Biblical perspective on the afterlife.[12] In an interview with *The New Yorker* magazine, Vincent expressed concern that Christians would find the book to be a "hoax" if she included people in heaven having wings.[13][14]

In 2015, Alex Malarkey publicly disavowed the book *The Boy Who Came Back from Heaven*, stating that his near-death experience described in that book was fictional[15] and condemned Christian publishers and bookstores for selling popular "heaven tourism" books, which he said "profit from lies."[16][17] Following Malarkey's statement, Colton Burpo expressed that "People have their doubts about my story," but said he stood by the book.[18]

34.3 Film adaptation

Main article: Heaven Is for Real (film)

In May 2011, Sony Pictures acquired the film rights of the book. The film was released on April 16, 2014 starring Connor Corum, Margo Martindale, Greg Kinnear, Kelly Reilly, Thomas Haden Church, and Jacob Vargas.[19] As of July 2014, Rotten Tomatoes rated it at 46%. Critics praised the script and cast, but they were critical of heavy-handed exposition.[20]

34.4 See also

- *The Boy Who Came Back from Heaven*, a fabricated account[16][17] of a near-death experience

- *23 Minutes in Hell*

- *90 Minutes in Heaven*

- *Miracles from Heaven*

- *Proof of Heaven*

- Howard Storm (author)

34.5 References

[1] "Heaven Is For Real reaches one million e-books sold". Thomas Nelson Corporate.

[2] Christine D. Johnson (11 Dec 2014). "'Heaven Is for Real' hits major sales milestone". *Christian Retailing*. Archived from the original on 18 Dec 2014.

[3] "Heaven Is for Real". boxofficemojo.com. Retrieved November 4, 2014.

[4] Schiffer, Kathy (27 April 2014). "Heaven Is For Real: Secrets Colton Burpo Didn't Tell You in the Book or the Movie". *Seasons of Grace*. Retrieved 18 January 2015. Colton is the child who, at the age of three, nearly died and who visited heaven while he was in surgery.

[5] Thomson, Cask J. (27 March 2011). "The Boy Who Allegedly Went to Heaven and Returned". *WordswithMeaning!org*.

[6] "The angels sang to Colton". The North Platte Telegraph. January 13, 2011. Retrieved January 14, 2011.

[7] "Kathie Lee and Hoda with the Scoop" (Video(11:23)). *The Today Show*. NBC.

[8] Thibault, Joanne (4 June 2011). "Near-death experience led to heaven's door". *Winnipeg Free Press*. Todd is even able to report to Christian friends that Colton "saw Mary kneeling before the throne of God and at other times standing beside Jesus."

[9] Sehgal, Parul (6 April 2014). "Best Sellers" (Paperback Nonfiction). New York Times.

[10] BOSMAN, JULIE (11 March 2011). "Celestial Sales for Boy's Tale of Heaven". The New York Times. Retrieved 21 December 2014.

[11] "Is "Heaven Is for Real" for Real?: An Exercise In Discernment". The Berean Call. Retrieved November 15, 2013.

[12] "Are Visits to Heaven for Real?". Retrieved April 19, 2014.

[13] Ariel Levy (15 Oct 2012). "Lives of the Saints". *New Yorker*.

[14] Phil Johnson (18 Oct 2012). "The Burpo-Malarkey Doctrine". *Grace to you*.

[15] "Alex Malarkey, Little Boy Who 'Came Back from Heaven,' Reveals Hoax : People.com". *PEOPLE.com*. Retrieved 18 January 2015.

[16] Mark Woods (15 Jan 2015). "'The boy who came back from heaven' Alex Malarkey says best-selling book is false". *Christianity Today*.

[17] Vencent Funaro (15 Jan 2015). "Boy Who Claimed He Visited Heaven Reads Bible and Recants Story; LifeWay to Pull Book From Stores". *Chrsitian Post*.

[18] Carey Lodge (17 Jan 2015). "Colton Burpo stands by Heaven is for Real". *Christianity Today*.

[19] "Heaven Is For Real". *The "Heaven is Real" page on the Sony Pictures website*. The Sony Pictures website. Retrieved 10 April 2014.

[20] "Heaven Is for Real (2014)". Rotten Tomatoes. Retrieved July 21, 2014.

34.6 External links

- Heaven Is for Real on Facebook

- *The Christian Post* article on near-death experiences (Criticism about near-death experiences.)

Chapter 35

Parallel Universes: A Memoir from the Edges of Space and Time

Parallel Universes, A Memoir from the Edges of Space and Time is a non-fiction Christian book and a personal and science memoir written by Linda Morabito Meyer, the NASA discoverer of the volcanic activity on Jupiter's Io. The book documents the author's several near-death experiences and purported visits to Heaven between 1954 and 1956; the author's quest to uncover a hidden past from 2003 to 2011; and the events of the author's major NASA science discovery in 1979.[1]

35.1   Summary

During the time the memoir was compiled, a fifty-year-old mystery in Morabito Meyer's life was solved. She discovered that her parents had been members of the Temple of the Abundant Life in Vancouver, British Columbia, Canada, run by a convicted criminal who was wanted on outstanding warrants in the United States. William Franklin Wolsey was masquerading as a Bishop in this cult, and was the target of investigative reporting by the Vancouver Sun newspaper.[2] The author's memories of horrific childhood abuse documented in the book, corresponded to the events reported in the news in 1959, at the time she learned about the cult in 2011. This information is summarized in the book's epilogue. Her memories included near death experiences as a result of her parents' involvement with William Franklin Wolsey, in which she remembers visiting Heaven and seeing Jesus. Meyer maintains that William Franklin Wolsey was responsible for the deaths of four children she witnessed. Meyer, who moved with her parents to the United States in 1961, became an Astronomer and working for NASA's Jet Propulsion Laboratory on NASA's Voyager mission to Jupiter, discovered the volcanic activity on Jupiter's moon Io in 1979. The memoir interleaves the author's noteworthy science, personal, and religious experiences.

The book interweaves three journeys told in the author's words. She expresses her love of astronomy, which led her to make the discovery of the volcanic activity on Jupiter's moon Io in 1979. The discovery is considered the largest of NASA's planetary exploration program.[3]

She expresses the horror of a childhood marred by her parents' involvement with a Vancouver, British Columbia, Canada cult between the years of 1954 and 1956. To aid victims of childhood abuse, the author highlights a treatment used for post traumatic stress disorder.[4]

35.2   Kindle release

On November 16, 2010, Linda Morabito Meyer provided an early version of the book in Amazon Kindle electronic format, with the ability for the public to update the book through Amazon.com at no charge, as Morabito Meyer's investigation into her past was completed.[5] The Kindle version was updated to match the final version of the book released in paperback on October 13, 2011.[6]

35.3   References

[1] Linda Morabito website.

[2] http://www.time.com/time/magazine/article/0,9171,826164,00.html

[3] Time Magazine

[4] EMDR.

[5] Kindle

[6] Daily Press>

35.4   Further reading

- Morabito, Meyer, Linda (2011-10-13). *Parallel Universes, A Memoir from the Edges of Space and Time*. Heavens an Imprint of SciRel Publishing. ISBN 978-0-615-54881-4.

35.5   External links

- Official site

- Promotional site

- Interview with Linda Morabito by Bob McCauley on Superwire.

Chapter 36

Eben Alexander (author)

This article is about the neurosurgeon and author. For his great-grandfather, see Eben Alexander.

Warning: Page using Template:Infobox person with unknown parameter "genre" (this message is shown only in preview).

Warning: Page using Template:Infobox person with unknown parameter "influences" (this message is shown only in preview).

Warning: Page using Template:Infobox person with unknown parameter "period" (this message is shown only in preview).

Warning: Page using Template:Infobox person with unknown parameter "influenced" (this message is shown only in preview).

Warning: Page using Template:Infobox person with unknown parameter "subject" (this message is shown only in preview).

Warning: Page using Template:Infobox person with unknown parameter "pseudonym" (this message is shown only in preview).

Eben Alexander III (born December 11, 1953) is an American neurosurgeon and the author of the book *Proof of Heaven: A Neurosurgeon's Journey into the Afterlife*, in which he describes his 2008 near-death experience and asserts that science can and will determine that the brain does not create consciousness and that consciousness survives bodily death.

36.1 Early life, family, and education

Alexander is the adopted descendant of a family of scholars, jurists, and physicians.[1] He attended Phillips Exeter Academy (class of 1972), University of North Carolina at Chapel Hill (A.B., 1975), and the Duke University School of Medicine (M.D., 1981).

Alexander was an Intern in General Surgery at Duke University Medical Center, a resident at Duke, Newcastle (U.K.) General Hospital. He was a resident and research fellow at Brigham and Women's Hospital[2] and Massachusetts General Hospital and is certified by the American Board of Neurological Surgery and the American College of Surgeons (F.A.C.S.).

36.2 Career

36.2.1 Academic and clinical appointments

Alexander has taught at Duke University Medical Center, Brigham and Women's Hospital, Harvard Medical School, University of Massachusetts Medical School, and the University of Virginia Medical School.

He has had hospital appointments at Brigham and Women's Hospital, Boston Children's Hospital, Dana–Farber Cancer Institute, Massachusetts General Hospital, University of Massachusetts Medical Center, and Lynchburg (Virginia) General Hospital-CentraHealth.[3]

36.2.2 Professional activities

Alexander is a member of the American Medical Association and various other professional societies. He has been on the editorial boards of various journals.

36.3 *Proof of Heaven*

36.3.1 Content

Alexander is the author of the 2012 autobiographical book *Proof of Heaven: A Neurosurgeon's Journey into the Afterlife*, in which he asserts that his out of body and near-death experience (NDE) while in a meningitis-induced coma in 2008 proves that consciousness is independent of the brain, that death is a transition, and that an eternity of perfect splendor awaits us beyond the grave – complete with angels, clouds, butterflies, and deceased relatives, one of whom included a beautiful girl in peasant dress whom Alexander later identifies as his deceased sister.[4][5] He further asserts that the current understanding of the mind

> "now lies broken at our feet "— for "What happened to me destroyed it, and I intend to spend the rest of my life investigating the true nature of consciousness and making the fact that we are more, much more, than our physical brains as clear as I can, both to my fellow scientists and to people at large."

Alexander's book was excerpted in a *Newsweek* magazine cover story in October 2012.[6] (In May 2012, Alexander had provided a slightly more technical account of the events described in his book in an article, "My Experience in Coma", in *AANS Neurosurgeon*, the trade publication of the American Association of Neurological Surgeons.)[7] Since the release of the book, he has lectured around the world in churches, hospitals, medical schools, and academic symposia, besides appearing on TV shows including *Super Soul Sunday* with Oprah Winfrey.[8][9]

As of September 21, 2014, *Proof of Heaven* has been on the *The New York Times* Best Seller list for 97 weeks.[10]

Alexander has further expanded on his NDE experiences, and his scientific interpretation of them, in journals including the quarterly publication of the Congress of Neurological Surgeons[11] and the Journal of the Missouri State Medical Association.[12]

36.3.2 Criticism and reaction

In a 2013 investigation of Alexander's story and medical background, *Esquire* magazine reported that before the publication of *Proof of Heaven*, Alexander had been terminated or suspended from multiple hospital positions, and had been the subject of several malpractice lawsuits, including at least two involving the alteration of medical records to cover up a medical error.[13][14] The magazine also found what it claimed were discrepancies with regard to Alexander's version of events in the book. Among the discrepancies, according to an account of the *Esquire* article in *Forbes*, was that "Alexander writes that he slipped into the coma as a result of severe bacterial meningitis and had no higher brain activity, while a doctor who cared for him says the coma was medically induced and the patient was conscious, though hallucinating".[14][13][15]

Alexander responded: "I wrote a truthful account of my experiences in *Proof of Heaven* and have acknowledged in the book both my professional and personal accomplishments and my setbacks. I stand by every word in this book and have made its message the purpose of my life. *Esquire's* cynical article distorts the facts of my 25-year career as a neurosurgeon and is a textbook example of how unsupported assertions and cherry-picked information can be assembled at the expense of the truth."[15]

Alexander's book has been criticized by scientists, including Sam Harris who described Alexander's NDE account as "alarmingly unscientific," and that "everything – *absolutely everything* – in Alexander's account rests on repeated assertions that his visions of heaven occurred while his cerebral cortex was 'shut down', 'inactivated', 'completely shut down', 'totally offline', and 'stunned to complete inactivity'. The evidence he provides for this claim is not only inadequate – it suggests that he doesn't know anything about the relevant brain science."[16] "Even in cases where the brain is alleged to have shut down, its activity must return if the subject is to survive and describe the experience. In such cases, there is generally no way to establish that the NDE occurred while the brain was offline."[17] Neurologist and writer Oliver Sacks agreed with Harris, saying that "to deny the possibility of any natural explanation for an NDE, as Dr. Alexander does, is more than unscientific – it is antiscientific."..."The one most plausible hypothesis in Dr. Alexander's case...is that his NDE occurred not during his coma, but as he was surfacing from the coma and his cortex was returning to full function. It is curious that he does not allow this obvious and natural explanation, but instead insists on a supernatural one."[18] In 2012 Alexander responded to critics in a second *Newsweek* article.[19]

36.4 *The Map of Heaven*

Alexander's second book, *The Map of Heaven: How Science, Religion, and Ordinary People Are Proving the Afterlife*, was published in October 2014. Alexander once again asserts his belief that there is an afterlife, and that consciousness is independent of the brain. To support his views, he cites the writings of philosophers, scientists, and religious leaders throughout history, and also shares letters from readers who have told him about spiritual experiences that match his own as described in *Proof of Heaven*.[20]

Excerpts from *The Map of Heaven* ran in UK newspaper *The Daily Mail* in October 2014.[21][22][23]

The Map of Heaven became a *New York Times* bestseller the week ending October 18, 2014.[24]

36.5   See also

- *23 Minutes in Hell*

- *90 Minutes in Heaven*

- *Heaven is for Real*

- *To Heaven and Back*

- Howard Storm (author)

- Pam Reynolds case

36.6   References

[1] "Renown neurosurgeon Eben Alexander Dies at 91(2004)". Wake Forest Baptist Medical Center. Retrieved April 30, 2014.

[2] "Dr. Eben Alexander – NDE". NDE Stories. Retrieved January 5, 2014.

[3] Dittrich Aug 2013.

[4] Alexander, Eben (2012), *Proof of Heaven: A Neurosurgeon's Journey into the Afterlife*, Simon & Schuster, pg 169.

[5] Alexander, Eben (2012), *Proof of Heaven: A Neurosurgeon's Journey into the Afterlife*, Simon & Schuster, pg 40.

[6] Alexander, Eben (October 8, 2012), "Heaven Is Real: A Doctor's Experience With the Afterlife", *Newsweek*.

[7] Eben Alexander III (2012). "My Experience in Coma". *AANS Neurosurgeon* **21** (2). Retrieved November 23, 2012.

[8] Ingrid Peschke (2013-10-24). "Dr. Eben Alexander Says It's Time for Brain Science to Graduate From Kindergarten". Huffington Post. Retrieved 2014-06-14.

[9] "Dr. Eben Alexander Shares What God Looks Like". OWN TV. Retrieved 2014-06-14.

[10] "Best Sellers". *Paperback Nonfiction* (The New York Times). September 21, 2014. Archived from the original on October 1, 2014. Retrieved October 1, 2014.

[11] Alexander, Eben. "Becoming Conscious: A Neurosurgeon Discusses his Transformational Experience". *Congress of Neurological Surgeons* (Spring 2016).

[12] Alexander, Eben. "Near Death Experiences, the Mind-Body Debate & the Nature of Reality". *The Journal of the Missouri State Medical Association* (January/February 2015): 17–21.

[13] Dittrich, Luke (August 2013). "The Prophet: An Investigation of Eben ALexander, Author of the Blockbuster "Proof of Heaven"". *Esquire* (New York City: Hearst Communications, Inc.). pp. 88–95, 125–126, 128. Page 95: "On August 6, 2008, the patient filed a $3 million lawsuit against Alexander, accusing him of negligence, battery, spoliation, and fraud. The purported cover-up, the changes Alexander had made to the surgical report, was a major aspect of the suit. Once again, a lawyer was accusing Alexander of altering the historical record when the historical record didn't fit the story he wanted to tell."

[14] "Was 'Proof of Heaven' author hallucinating?". *Daily Mail* (London). July 3, 2013. Retrieved July 13, 2013. *Daily Mail* Online, Published July 2, 2013. Includes photos of the *Esquire* magazine August 2013 cover and the article's author, contributing editor Luke Dittrich, and a response from Alexander on the controversy.

[15] Jeff Bercovici. "Esquire Unearths 'Proof of Heaven' Author's Credibility Problems". Forbes. Retrieved July 13, 2013.

[16] Harris, Sam (October 12, 2012), "This Must Be Heaven" @ SamHarris.com.

[17] Sam Harris (November 11, 2012). "Science on the Brink of Death". Retrieved November 26, 2012.

[18] Sacks, Oliver, "Seeing God in the Third Millennium", *The Atlantic Monthly* (December 12, 2012).

[19] Eben Alexander (November 18, 2012). "The Science of Heaven". *Newsweek*. Retrieved August 31, 2015.

[20] http://books.simonandschuster.com/Map-of-Heaven/ Eben-Alexander/9781476766393

[21] Alexander, Eben (17 October 2014). "What Heaven's Really Like - By a Leading Brain Surgeon Who Says He's Been There". *[The Daily Mail]*. Retrieved 28 October 2014.

[22] Alexander, Eben (19 October 2014). "Are these glimpses of the after-life? Top brain surgeon who claims he saw heaven while in a coma reveals the stories of others who say they have had similar life-changing experiences". *The Daily Mail*. Retrieved 28 October 2014.

[23] Alexander, Eben (20 October 2014). "The wife who came back to earth as a butterfly: The poignant moment that a grieving husband lost his scepticism about the after-life". *The Daily Mail*. Retrieved 28 October 2014.

[24] "New York Times". *New York Times*. 2 Nov 2014. Archived from the original on October 28, 2014. Retrieved 28 Oct 2014.

36.7   External links

- Official website

Chapter 37

Beyond and Back

Beyond And Back is a 1978 documentary and "death-sploitation flick"[2][3] released by Sunn Classic Pictures that deals with the subject of near death experiences.

37.1 Production notes

Beyond And Back was produced by Sunn Classic Pictures, a Utah-based independent film company that specialized in releasing low-budget message movies to non-urban audiences. Along with such features as *In Search of Noah's Ark* (1976) and *In Search of Historic Jesus* (1979), the film was one of a series of releases from the company that attempted to present convincing scientific evidence for Christian theology.[3]

Based in part on a book by evangelist Ralph Wilkerson, the idea for *Beyond And Back* was suggested to Sunn Pictures by a freelance writer who submitted a treatment for the film after reading about the film studio in Writer's Digest.[4] The film's screenwriter, Stephen Lord, was a respected television screenwriter, having written scripts for such notable sci-fi/horror programs as *The Outer Limits* and *Kolchak: The Night Stalker*. Directing chores went to James L. Conway, who had helmed Sunn's speculative fiction vehicle *The Lincoln Conspiracy* the previous year. The movie was filmed by cinematographer Henning Schellerup, a veteran of late '60s and early '70s porn films such as *Come One, Come All* (1970) and *Heterosexualis* (1973).

37.2 Promotion

Since *Beyond And Back* never received a traditional wide release, it was able to largely avoid scrutiny from the national media. Sunn Classic Pictures mostly screened its films in smaller towns and non-urban areas. It was also popular at drive-in movie theaters. This approach "avoided the audiences and the critical media in Los Angeles and New York... if the film failed in any single market, negative word

of mouth did not spread to the next locale."[5]

Wasser's assertion has, however, been disputed: "Wow, I saw it when I was 6. Saw it in Brooklyn."[6]

37.3 Born-again Christian background and content

Filmed entirely on location in Utah, *Beyond And Back* was produced by Charles E. Sellier Jr. At the time of the film's release, Sellier noted that he:

> "Believe(s) God wants me to do the films I do, otherwise He wouldn't have made me a success."[7]

37.4 Critical and box office reception

The New York Times' film critic Janet Maslin criticized the film for its inability to answer the many questions it raised, adding:

> "Do you know real malarkey when you hear it? What would you consider a fair price for the Brooklyn Bridge?".[8]

In his January 1979 *Chicago Sun-Times* review, Roger Ebert gave the film one star, noting that it:

> "Gives turkeys a bad name. It exists on about the same cinematic level as an Army training film or one of those junior high chemistry movies in which the experiments never quite worked."[9]

The film appears on rogerebert.com, "Ebert's Most Hated" list, as well as in his 2000 book, *I Hated, Hated, Hated This Movie*.

Produced very inexpensively, the film was a major commercial success. It earned nearly $24 million in U.S. box office receipts and was one of the top 30 top-earning films in the U.S. for 1978.[1][10]

37.5 See also

- Near-death experiences

37.6 References

[1] Beyond and Back, Worldwide Box Office. Worldwide Box Office. Retrieved November 29, 2013.

[2] http://www.movli.com/movie/beyond-and-back-15299

[3] *Beyond and Back*, AMC Movie Guide. AMC. Retrieved July 14, 2014.

[4] Frederick Wasser, Cinema Journal, Winter 1995

[5] (Wasser, 1995)

[6] Chris71, http://www.freedocumentary.tv/beyond-and-back/

[7] *TV Guide*, January 28, 1978.

[8] http://www.nytimes.com/movie/review?res=980CE7DE1530E632A2575BC1A9649C946990D6CF

[9] http://www.rogerebert.com/reviews/beyond-and-back-1979

[10] Beyond and Back, Box Office Information. The Numbers. Retrieved November 29, 2013.

37.7 External links

- *Beyond and Back* at the Internet Movie Database
- *Beyond and Back* at AllMovie
- Brad Crandall at the Internet Movie Database
- Sunn Classic Pictures at the Internet Movie Database
- Beyond And Back (1978), Full-length documentary at FreeDocumentary.tv

Chapter 38

Lazarus syndrome

This article is about the medical phenomenon. For the TV movie, see The Lazarus Syndrome.
Not to be confused with Lazarus sign.

Lazarus syndrome or **autoresuscitation after failed cardiopulmonary resuscitation**[1] is the spontaneous return of circulation after failed attempts at resuscitation.[2] Its occurrence has been noted in medical literature at least 38 times since 1982.[3][4] Also called **Lazarus phenomenon**, it takes its name from Lazarus who, in the New Testament of The Bible, was raised from the dead by Jesus.[5]

Occurrences of the syndrome are extremely rare and the causes are not well understood. One hypothesis for the phenomenon is that a chief factor (though not the only one) is the buildup of pressure in the chest as a result of cardiopulmonary resuscitation (CPR). The relaxation of pressure after resuscitation efforts have ended is thought to allow the heart to expand, triggering the heart's electrical impulses and restarting the heartbeat.[2] Other possible factors are hyperkalemia or high doses of epinephrine.[5]

38.1 Cases

- Daphne Banks overdosed on drugs in Huntingdon, England on 31 December 1996. She was declared dead at Hinchingbrooke Hospital early the next day. She was found snoring at a mortuary 34 hours later.[6]

- A 27-year-old man in the UK collapsed after overdosing on heroin and cocaine. Paramedics gave him an injection, and he recovered enough to walk to the ambulance. He went into cardiac arrest in transit. After 25 minutes of resuscitation efforts, the patient was verbally declared dead. About a minute after resuscitation ended, a nurse noticed a rhythm on the heart monitor and resuscitation was resumed. The patient recovered fully.[5]

- A 66-year-old man suffering from a suspected abdominal aneurysm who, during treatment for this condition, suffered cardiac arrest and received chest compressions and defibrillation shocks for 17 minutes. Vital signs did not return; the patient was declared dead and resuscitation efforts ended. Ten minutes later, the surgeon felt a pulse. The aneurysm was successfully treated and the patient fully recovered with no lasting physical or neurological problems.[2]

- According to a 2002 article in the journal *Forensic Science International*, a 65-year-old prelingually deaf Japanese male was found unconscious in the foster home he lived in. Cardiopulmonary resuscitation was attempted on the scene by home staff, emergency medical personnel and also in the emergency department of the hospital and included appropriate medications and defibrillation. He was declared dead after attempted resuscitation. However, a policeman found the person moving in the mortuary after 20 minutes. The patient survived for 4 more days.[7]

- Judith Johnson, 61, went into cardiac arrest at Beebe Medical Center in Lewes, Delaware, United States, in May 2007. She was given "multiple medicines and synchronized shocks", but never regained a pulse. She was declared dead at 8:34 p.m. but was discovered in the morgue to be alive and breathing. She sued the medical center where it happened for damages due to physical and neurological problems stemming from the event.[4]

- Michael Wilkinson, 23, was found collapsed in Preston, England on 1 February 2009. He was sent to Royal Preston Hospital in Lancashire where medical staff gave him drugs and worked on him for 15 minutes before declaring him dead. Half an hour later, a pulse was found. He survived for two days, and a post-mortem examination found an undiagnosed heart condition.[8]

- A 45-year-old woman in Colombia was pronounced dead, as there were no vital signs showing she was

211

alive. Later, a funeral worker noticed the woman moving and alerted his co-worker that the woman should go back to the hospital.[9][10]

- A 65-year-old man in Malaysia came back to life two-and-a-half hours after doctors at Seberang Jaya Hospital, Penang, pronounced him dead. He died three weeks later.[11]

- Anthony Yahle, 37, in Bellbrook, Ohio, USA, was breathing abnormally at 4 a.m. on 5 August 2013, and could not be woken. He was given CPR, and first responders shocked him several times and found a heartbeat. That afternoon, he coded for 45 minutes at Kettering Medical Center and was pronounced dead. When his son arrived at the hospital, he noticed a heartbeat on the monitor that was still attached. Resuscitation efforts resumed, and the patient was revived.[12]

- Walter Williams, 78, from Lexington, Mississippi, United States, was at home when his hospice nurse called a coroner who arrived and declared him dead at 9 p.m. on 26 February 2014. Once at a funeral home, he was found to be moving, possibly resuscitated by a defibrillator implanted in his chest.[13] The next day he was well enough to be talking with family, but died fifteen days later.[14]

38.2 Implications

The Lazarus phenomenon raises ethical issues for physicians, who must determine when medical death has occurred, resuscitation efforts should end, and postmortem procedures such as autopsies and organ harvesting may take place.[2]

Medical literature has recommended observation of a patient's vital signs for five to ten minutes after cessation of resuscitation before certifying death.[5]

38.3 See also

- Lazarus sign

- Lazarus taxon

- Near-death experience

- Premature burial

- Suspended animation

- The Lazarus Phenomenon Documentary

38.4 References

[1] Hornby K, Hornby L, Shemie SD (May 2010). "A systematic review of autoresuscitation after cardiac arrest". *Crit. Care Med.* **38** (5): 1246–53. doi:10.1097/CCM.0b013e3181d8caaa. PMID 20228683.

[2] Ben-David M.D., Bruce; et al. (2001). "Survival After Failed Intraoperative Resuscitation: A Case of "Lazarus Syndrome"". *Anesthesia & Analgesia* **92** (3): 690–692. doi:10.1213/00000539-200103000-00027. PMID 11226103. Retrieved 2014-07-28.

[3] Adhiyaman, Vedamurthy; Adhiyaman, Sonja; Sundaram, Radha. "The Lazarus phenomenon". *National Center for Biotechnology Information*. Journal of the Royal Society of Medicine. Retrieved 4 January 2014.

[4] "Woman Declared Dead, Still Breathing in Morgue". Fox News. 2008-10-07. Retrieved 2014-07-28.

[5] Walker, A.; H. McClelland; J. Brenchley (2001). "The Lazarus Documentary following recreational drug use". *Emerg Med J* **18** (1): 74–75. doi:10.1136/emj.18.1.74. PMC 1725503. PMID 11310473. Retrieved 2014-07-28.

[6] Derbyshire, David (16 October 2012). "Lazarus Syndrome: Or how - as one British woman's just proved - waking from the dead is more common than you think". *MailOnline* (London). Archived from the original on 2013-05-20.

[7] Maeda, H; Fujita, M. Q.; Zhu, B. L.; Yukioka, H; Shindo, M; Quan, L; Ishida, K (2002). "Death following spontaneous recovery from cardiopulmonary arrest in a hospital mortuary: 'Lazarus phenomenon' in a case of alleged medical negligence". *Forensic Science International* **127** (1–2): 82–7. doi:10.1016/s0379-0738(02)00107-x. PMID 12098530.

[8] "Lazarus syndrome man pronounced dead comes back to life for two days". *MailOnline* (London). 11 June 2009. Retrieved 1 March 2014.

[9] "Embalmer finds 'dead' woman really alive". Bogota: NBC News. 2010-02-17. Retrieved 2014-07-28.

[10] Salazar, Hernando. "¿Colombiana experimentó Síndrome de Lázaro?". *BBC Online* (in Spanish). Retrieved 26 December 2010.

[11] Vinesh, Derrick (26 April 2011). "Resurrection man dies". *The Star Online*. Retrieved 2014-07-28.

[12] Lupkin, Sydney (22 August 2013). "Ohio Man Declared Dead Comes Back to Life". Retrieved 4 January 2014.

[13] McLaughlin, Eliott (28 February 2014). "Dead Mississippi man begins breathing in embalming room, coroner says". *CNN*. Retrieved 28 February 2014.

[14] Ford, Dana (13 March 2014). "Mississippi man who awoke in body bag dies two weeks later". *CNN*. Retrieved 13 March 2014.

Chapter 39

Mediumship

Séance conducted by John Beattie, Bristol, England, 1872

Mediumship is the practice of certain people—known as mediums—to purportedly mediate communication between spirits of the dead and living human beings.[1][2]

Attempts to contact the dead date back to early human history, with mediumship gaining in popularity during the 19th century. Investigations during this period revealed widespread fraud—with some practitioners employing techniques used by stage magicians—and the practice started to lose credibility.[3][4] The practice still continues into the 21st century, with high-profile fraud uncovered as recently as the 2000s.[5]

Scientific researchers have attempted to ascertain the validity of claims of mediumship. An experiment undertaken by the British Psychological Society led to the conclusion that the test subjects demonstrated no mediumistic ability.[6]

Several different variants of mediumship exist; arguably the best-known forms involve a spirit allegedly taking control of a medium's voice and using it to relay a message, or where the medium simply "hears" the message and passes it on. Other forms involve materializations of the spirit or the presence of a voice, and telekinetic activity.

The practice is associated with several religious-belief systems such as Vodoun, Spiritualism, Spiritism, Candomblé, Voodoo, Umbanda and some New Age groups.

39.1 Concept

In Spiritism and Spiritualism the medium has the role of an intermediary between the world of the living and the world of spirit. Mediums claim that they can listen to and relay messages from spirits, or that they can allow a spirit to control their body and speak through it directly or by using automatic writing or drawing.

Spiritualists classify types of mediumship into two main categories: "mental" and "physical":

- Mental mediums allegedly "tune in" to the spirit world by listening, sensing, or seeing spirits or symbols.

- Physical mediums are believed to produce materialization of spirits, apports of objects, and other effects such as knocking, rapping, bell-ringing, etc. by using "ectoplasm" created from the cells of their bodies and those of seance attendees.

During seances, mediums are said to go into trances, varying from light to deep, that permit spirits to control their minds.[7]

Channeling can be seen as the modern form of the old mediumship, where the "channel" (or channeller) allegedly receives messages from "teaching-spirit", an "Ascended Master", from God, or from an angelic entity, but essentially through the filter of his own waking consciousness (or "Higher Self").[8][9]

39.2   History

Main article: Spiritualism

Attempts to communicate with the dead and other living human beings, aka spirits, have been documented back to early human history. The story of the Witch of Endor (In the most recent edition of the NIV witch is rendered medium in the passage) tells of one who raised the spirit of the deceased prophet Samuel to allow the Hebrew king Saul to question his former mentor about an upcoming battle, as related in the *First book of Samuel* in the Jewish Tanakh (the *Old Testament*).

Mediumship became quite popular in the 19th-century United States and the United Kingdom after the rise of Spiritualism as a religious movement. Modern Spiritualism is said to date from practices and lectures of the Fox sisters in New York State in 1848. The trance mediums Paschal Beverly Randolph and Emma Hardinge Britten were among the most celebrated lecturers and authors on the subject in the mid-19th century. Allan Kardec coined the term Spiritism around 1860.[10] Kardec claimed that conversations with spirits by selected mediums were the basis of his *The Spirits' Book* and later, his five-book collection, *Spiritist Codification*.

Some scientists of the period who investigated spiritualism also became converts. They included chemist Robert Hare, physicist William Crookes (1832–1919) and evolutionary biologist Alfred Russel Wallace (1823–1913).[11][12] Nobel laureate Pierre Curie took a very serious scientific interest in the work of medium Eusapia Palladino.[13] Other prominent adherents included journalist and pacifist William T. Stead (1849–1912)[14] and physician and author Arthur Conan Doyle (1859–1930).[15]

After the exposure of the fraudulent use of stage magic tricks by physical mediums such as the Davenport Brothers and the Bangs Sisters, mediumship fell into disrepute. However, the religion and its beliefs continue in spite of this, with physical mediumship and seances falling out of practice and platform mediumship coming to the fore.

In the late 1920s and early 1930s there were around one quarter of a million practising Spiritualists and some two thousand Spiritualist societies in the UK in addition to flourishing microcultures of platform mediumship and 'home circles'.[16] Spiritualism continues to be practiced, primarily through various denominational spiritualist churches in the United States, Canada, Australia and the United Kingdom. In the United Kingdom, over 340 spiritualist churches and centres open their doors to the public and free demonstrations of mediumship are regularly performed.[17]

39.3   Terminology

39.3.1   Spirit guide

Main article: Spirit guide

In 1958, the English-born Spiritualist C. Dorreen Phillips wrote of her experiences with a medium at Camp Chesterfield, Indiana: "In Rev. James Laughton's séances there are many Indians. They are very noisy and appear to have great power. [...] The little guides, or doorkeepers, are usually Indian boys and girls [who act] as messengers who help to locate the spirit friends who wish to speak with you."[18]

39.3.2   Spirit operator

A spirit who uses a medium to manipulate psychic "energy" or "energy systems."

39.3.3   Demonstrations of mediumship

In old-line Spiritualism, a portion of the services, generally toward the end, is given over to demonstrations of mediumship through contact with the spirits of the dead. A typical example of this way of describing a mediumistic church service is found in the 1958 autobiography of C. Dorreen Phillips. She writes of the worship services at the Spiritualist Camp Chesterfield in Chesterfield, Indiana: "Services are held each afternoon, consisting of hymns, a lecture on philosophy, and demonstrations of mediumship."[18]

Today "demonstration of mediumship" is part of the church service at all churches affiliated with the National Spiritualist Association of Churches (NSAC) and the Spiritualists' National Union (SNU). Demonstration links to NSAC's Declaration of Principal #9. "We affirm that the precepts of Prophecy and Healing are Divine attributes proven through Mediumship."

Colin Evans who claimed spirits lifted him into the air was exposed as a fraud.

39.3.4 Mental mediumship

Main article: Séance

"Mental mediumship" is communication of spirits with a medium by telepathy. The medium mentally "hears" (clairaudience), "sees" (clairvoyance), and/or feels (clairsentience) messages from spirits. Directly or with the help of a spirit guide, the medium passes the information on to the message's recipient(s). When a medium is doing a "reading" for a particular person, that person is known as the "sitter."

39.3.5 Trance mediumship

"Trance mediumship" is often seen as a form of mental mediumship.

Most trance mediums remain conscious during a communication period, wherein a spirit uses the medium's mind to communicate. The spirit or spirits using the medium's mind influences the mind with the thoughts being conveyed.

The medium allows the ego to step aside for the message to be delivered. At the same time, one has awareness of the thoughts coming through and may even influence the message with one's own bias. Such a trance is not to be confused with sleepwalking, as the patterns are entirely different. Castillo (1995) states,

> Trance phenomena result from the behavior of intense focusing of attention, which is the key psychological mechanism of trance induction. Adaptive responses, including institutionalized forms of trance, are 'tuned' into neural networks in the brain.[19]

In the 1860s and 1870s, trance mediums were very popular. Spiritualism generally attracted female adherents, many who had strong interests in social justice. Many trance mediums delivered passionate speeches on abolitionism, temperance, and women's suffrage.[20] Scholars have described Leonora Piper as one of the most famous trance mediums in the history of Spiritualism.[3][21][22]

In the typical deep trance, the medium may not have clear recall of all the messages conveyed while in an altered state; such people generally work with an assistant. That person selectively wrote down or otherwise recorded the medium's words. Rarely did the assistant record the responding words of the sitter and other attendants. An example of this kind of relationship can be found in the early 20th century collaboration between the trance medium Mrs. Cecil M. Cook of the William T. Stead Memorial Center in Chicago (a religious body incorporated under the statutes of the State of Illinois) and the journalist Lloyd Kenyon Jones. The latter was a non-medium Spiritualist who transcribed Cook's messages in shorthand. He edited them for publication in book and pamphlet form.[23]

39.3.6 Physical mediumship

Main article: Séance

Physical mediumship is defined as manipulation of energies and energy systems by spirits. This type of mediumship is claimed to involve perceptible manifestations, such as loud raps and noises, voices, materialized objects, apports, materialized spirit bodies, or body parts such as hands, legs and feet. The medium is used as a source of power for such spirit manifestations. By some accounts, this was achieved by using the energy or ectoplasm released by a medium, see Spirit photography.[24][25] The last physical medium to be tested by a committee from *Scientific American* was Mina Crandon in 1924.

Most physical mediumship is presented in a darkened or dimly lit room. Most physical mediums make use of a tra-

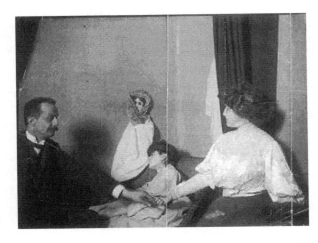

A photograph of the medium Linda Gazzera with a doll as fake ectoplasm.

ditional array of tools and appurtenances, including spirit trumpets, spirit cabinets, and levitation tables.

39.3.7 Direct voice

Direct voice communication is the claim that spirits speak independently of the medium, who facilitates the phenomenon rather than produces it. The role of the medium is to make the connection between the physical and spirit worlds. Trumpets are often utilised to amplify the signal, and directed voice mediums are sometimes known as "trumpet mediums". This form of mediumship also permits the medium to participate in the discourse during séances, since the medium's voice is not required by the spirit to communicate. Leslie Flint was one of the best known exponents of this form of mediumship.[26]

39.3.8 Channeling

In the later half of the 20th century, Western mediumship developed in two different ways. One type involved psychics or sensitives who speak to spirits and then relay what they hear to their clients.[27] The other incarnation of non-physical mediumship is a form of channeling in which the channeler goes into a trance, or "leaves their body", allowing a spiritual entity to borrow their body, who then talks through them.[28] When in a trance the medium appears to come under the control of the spirit of a departed soul, sometimes entering into a cataleptic state,[29] although modern channelers may not. Some channelers open the eyes when channeling, and remain able to walk and behave normally. The rhythm and the intonation of the voice may also change completely.

A widely known channeler of this variety is J. Z. Knight,

who claims to channel the spirit of Ramtha, a 30 thousand-year-old man. Others purport to channel spirits from "future dimensions", ascended masters,[30] or, in the case of the trance mediums of the Brahma Kumaris, God.[31] Other notable channels are Jane Roberts for Seth, Esther Hicks for Abraham,[32] and Carla L. Rueckert for Ra.[33][34]

39.4   Psychic senses

In spiritualism, psychic senses used by mental mediums are sometimes defined differently from in other paranormal fields. A medium is said to have psychic abilities but not all psychics function as mediums. [35] The term *clairvoyance*, for instance, may be used by Spiritualists to include seeing spirits and visions instilled by spirits. The Parapsychological Association defines "clairvoyance" as information derived directly from an external physical source.[36]

- Clairvoyance or "clear seeing", is the ability to see anything that is not physically present, such as objects, animals or people. This sight occurs "in the mind's eye". Some mediums say that this is their normal vision state. Others say that they must train their minds with such practices as meditation in order to achieve this ability, and that assistance from spiritual helpers is often necessary. Some clairvoyant mediums can see a spirit as though the spirit has a physical body. They see the bodily form as if it were physically present. Other mediums see the spirit in their mind's eye, or it appears as a movie or a television programme or a still picture like a photograph in their mind.

- Clairaudience or "clear hearing", is usually defined as the ability to hear the voices or thoughts of spirits. Some mediums hear as though they are listening to a person talking to them on the outside of their head, as though the Spirit is next to or near to the medium, and other mediums hear the voices in their minds as a verbal thought.

- Clairsentience or "clear sensing", is the ability to have an impression of what a spirit wants to communicate, or to feel sensations instilled by a spirit.

- Clairsentinence or "clear feeling" is a condition in which the medium takes on the ailments of a spirit, feeling the same physical problem which the spirit person had before death.

- Clairalience or "clear smelling" is the ability to smell a spirit. For example, a medium may smell the pipe tobacco of a person who smoked during life.

- Clairgustance or "clear tasting" is the ability to receive taste impressions from a spirit.

- Claircognizance or "clear knowing", is the ability to know something without receiving it through normal or psychic senses. It is a feeling of "just knowing". Often, a medium will claim to have the feeling that a message or situation is "right" or "wrong."

39.5 Explanations

39.5.1 Paranormal belief

Spiritualists believe that phenomena produced by mediums (both mental and physical mediumship) are the result of external spirit agencies.[37] The psychical researcher Thomson Jay Hudson in *The Law of Psychic Phenomena* (1892) and Théodore Flournoy in his book *Spiritism and Psychology* (1911) wrote that all kinds of mediumship could be explained by suggestion and telepathy from the medium and that there was no evidence for the spirit hypothesis. The idea of mediumship being explained by telepathy was later merged into the "super-ESP" hypothesis of mediumship which is currently advocated by some parapsychologists.[38]

In their book *How to Think About Weird Things: Critical Thinking for a New Age*, authors Theodore Schick and Lewis Vaughn have noted that the spiritualist and ESP hypothesis of mediumship "has yielded no novel predictions, assumes unknown entities or forces, and conflicts with available scientific evidence."[39]

39.5.2 Scientific skepticism

Scientists who study anomalistic psychology consider mediumship to be the result of fraud and psychological factors. Research from psychology for over a hundred years has revealed that where there is not fraud, mediumship and Spiritualist practices can be explained by hypnotism, magical thinking and suggestion.[40][41] Trance mediumship which is claimed by the Spiritualists to be caused by discarnate spirits speaking through the medium have been proven in cases to be alternate personalities from the medium's subconscious mind.[42]

Magicians such as Joseph Rinn have staged 'fake' séances in which the sitters have claimed to have observed genuine supernatural phenomena.[43] Albert Moll studied the psychology of séance sitters. According to (Wolffram, 2012) "[Moll] argued that the hypnotic atmosphere of the darkened séance room and the suggestive effect of the experimenters' social and scientific prestige could be used to explain why seemingly rational people vouchsafed occult phenomena."[44] The psychologists Leonard Zusne and Warren Jones in their book *Anomalistic Psychology: A Study of Magical Thinking* (1989) wrote that spirits con-

trols are the "products of the medium's own psychological dynamics."[45]

The medium may obtain information about their sitters by secretly eavesdropping on sitter's conversations or searching telephone directories, the internet and newspapers before the sittings.[46] Mediums are known for employing a technique called cold reading and obtain information from the sitter's behavior, clothing, posture, and jewellery.[47][48]

The psychologist Richard Wiseman has written:

> Cold reading also explains why psychics have consistently failed scientific tests of their powers. By isolating them from their clients, psychics are unable to pick up information from the way those clients dress or behave. By presenting all of the volunteers involved in the test with all of the readings, they are prevented from attributing meaning to their own reading, and therefore can't identify it from readings made for others. As a result, the type of highly successful hit rate that psychics enjoy on a daily basis comes crashing down and the truth emerges – their success depends on a fascinating application of psychology and not the existence of paranormal abilities.[49]

In a series of fake séance experiments (Wiseman *et al.* 2003) paranormal believers and disbelievers were suggested by an actor that a table was levitating when, in fact, it remained stationary. After the seance, approximately one third of the participants incorrectly reported that the table had moved. The results showed a greater percentage of believers reporting that the table had moved. In another experiment the believers had also reported that a handbell had moved when it had remained stationary and expressed their belief that the fake séances contained genuine paranormal phenomena. The experiments strongly supported the notion that in the séance room, believers are more suggestible than disbelievers for suggestions that are consistent with their belief in paranormal phenomena.[50]

39.6 Fraud

There have been many instances of fraud and trickery in mediumship practices from its earliest beginnings to contemporary times.[51] Séances take place in darkness so the poor lighting conditions can become an easy opportunity for fraud. Physical mediumship that has been investigated by scientists has been discovered to be the result of deception and trickery.[52] Ectoplasm a supposed paranormal substance was revealed to be made from cheesecloth, butter, muslin and cloth. Mediums would also stick cut-out faces from magazines and newspapers onto cloth or on

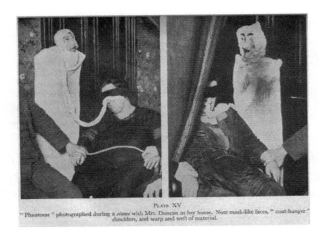

PLATE XV
" Phantoms " photographed during a *séance* with Mrs. Duncan at her home. Note mask-like faces, " coat-hanger " shoulders, and warp and weft of material.

Helen Duncan in a séance with dolls.

other props and use plastic dolls in their séances to pretend to their audiences spirits were contacting them.[53] Lewis Spence in his book *An Encyclopaedia of Occultism* (1960) wrote:

> A very large part is played by fraud in spiritualistic practices, both in the physical and psychical, or automatic, phenomena, but especially in the former. The frequency with which mediums have been convicted of fraud has, indeed, induced many people to abandon the study of psychical research, judging the whole bulk of the phenomena to be fraudulently produced.[54]

In Britain, the Society for Psychical Research has investigated mediumship phenomena. Critical SPR investigations into purported mediums and the exposure of fake mediums has led to a number of resignations by Spiritualist members.[55][56] On the subject of fraud in mediumship Paul Kurtz wrote:

> No doubt a great importance in the paranormal field is the problem of fraud. The field of psychic research and spiritualism has been so notoriously full of charlatans, such as the Fox sisters and Eusapia Palladino—individuals who claim to have special power and gifts but who are actually conjurers who have hoodwinked scientists and the public as well—that we have to be especially cautious about claims made on their behalf.[57]

Magicians have a long history of exposing the fraudulent methods of mediumship. Early debunkers included Chung Ling Soo, Henry Evans and Julien Proskauer.[58] Later magicians to reveal fraud were Joseph Dunninger, Harry Houdini and Joseph Rinn.[59]

Henry Slade

39.6.1   1800s

Many 19th century mediums were discovered to be engaged in fraud.[60] While advocates of mediumship claim that their experiences are genuine, the *Encyclopædia Britannica* article on spiritualism notes in reference to a case in the 19th century that "...one by one, the Spiritualist mediums were discovered to be engaged in fraud, sometimes employing the techniques of stage magicians in their attempts to convince people of their clairvoyant powers." The article also notes that "the exposure of widespread fraud within the spiritualist movement severely damaged its reputation and pushed it to the fringes of society in the United States."[61]

At a séance in the house of the solicitor John Snaith Rymer in Ealing in July 1855, a sitter Frederick Merrifield observed that a "spirit-hand" was a false limb attached on the end of the medium Daniel Dunglas Home's arm. Merrifield also claimed to have observed Home use his foot in the séance room.[62]

The poet Robert Browning and his wife Elizabeth attended a séance on 23, July 1855 in Ealing with the Rymers.[63] During the séance a spirit face materialized which Home claimed was the son of Browning who had died in infancy. Browning seized the "materialization" and discovered it to be the bare foot of Home. To make the deception worse, Browning had never lost a son in infancy. Browning's son Robert in a letter to *The Times*, December 5, 1902 referred to the incident "Home was detected in a vulgar fraud."[64][65] The researchers Joseph McCabe and Trevor H. Hall exposed the "levitation" of Home as nothing more than him moving across a connecting ledge between two iron balconies.[66]

The psychologist and psychical researcher Stanley LeFevre Krebs had exposed the Bangs Sisters as frauds. During a séance he employed a hidden mirror and caught them tampering with a letter in an envelope and writing a reply in it under the table which they would pretend a spirit had written.[67] The British materialization medium Rosina Mary Showers was caught in many fraudulent séances throughout her career.[68] In 1874 during a séance with Edward William Cox a sitter looked into the cabinet and seized the spirit, the headdress fell off and was revealed to be Showers.[69]

In a series of experiments in London at the house of William Crookes in February 1875, the medium Anna Eva Fay managed to fool Crookes into believing she had genuine psychic powers. Fay later confessed to her fraud and revealed the tricks she had used.[70] Frank Herne a British medium who formed a partnership with the medium Charles Williams was repeatedly exposed in fraudulent materialization séances.[71] In 1875 he was caught pretending to be a spirit during a séance in Liverpool and was found "clothed in about two yards of stiffened muslin, wound round his head and hanging down as far as his thigh."[72] Florence Cook had been "trained in the arts of the séance" by Herne and was repeatedly exposed as a fraudulent medium.[73]

The medium Henry Slade was caught in fraud many times throughout his career. In a séance in 1876 in London Ray Lankester and Bryan Donkin snatched his slate before the "spirit" message was supposed to be written, and found the writing already there.[74] Slade also played an accordion with one hand under the table and claimed spirits would play it. The magician Chung Ling Soo revealed how Slade had performed the trick.[75]

The British medium Francis Ward Monck was investigated by psychical researchers and discovered to be a fraud. On November 3, 1876 during the séance a sitter demanded that Monck be searched. Monck ran from the room, locked himself in another room and escaped out of a window. A pair of stuffed gloves was found in his room, as well as cheesecloth, reaching rods and other fraudulent devices in his luggage.[76] After a trial Monck was convicted for his fraudulent mediumship and was sentenced to three months in prison.[77]

In 1876, William Eglinton was exposed as a fraud when the psychical researcher Thomas Colley seized a "spirit" materialization in his séance and cut off a portion of its cloak. It

Eva Carrière with cardboard cut out figure King Ferdinand of Bulgaria.

was discovered that the cut piece matched a cloth found in Eglinton's suitcase.[78] Colley also pulled the beard off the materialization and it was revealed to be a fake, the same as another one found in the suitcase of Eglinton.[79] In 1880 in a séance a spirit named "Yohlande" materialized, a sitter grabbed it and was revealed to be the medium Mme. d'Esperance herself.[80]

In September 1878 the British medium Charles Williams and his fellow-medium at the time, A. Rita, were detected in trickery at Amsterdam. During the séance a materialized spirit was seized and found to be Rita and a bottle of phosphorus oil, muslin and a false beard were found amongst the two mediums.[81] In 1882 C. E. Wood was exposed in a séance in Peterborough. Her Indian spirit control "Pocka" was found to be the medium on her knees, covered in muslin.[82]

In 1880 the American stage mentalist Washington Irving Bishop published a book revealing how mediums would use secret codes as the trick for their clairvoyant readings.[83] The Seybert Commission was a group of faculty at the University of Pennsylvania who in 1884-1887 exposed fraudulent mediums such as Pierre L. O. A. Keeler and Henry

Slade.[84] The Fox sisters confessed to fraud in 1888. Margaret Fox revealed that she and her sister had produced the "spirit" rappings by cracking their toe joints.[85]

In 1891 at a public séance with twenty sitters the medium Cecil Husk was caught leaning over a table pretending to be a spirit by covering his face with phosphor material.[86] The magician Will Goldston also exposed the fraud mediumship of Husk. In a séance Goldston attended a pale face materialization appeared in the room. Goldston wrote "I saw at once that it was a gauze mask, and that the moustache attached to it was loose at one side through lack of gum. I pulled at the mask. It came away, revealing the face of Husk."[87] The British materialization medium Annie Fairlamb Mellon was exposed as a fraud on October 12, 1894. During the séance a sitter seized the materialized spirit, and found it to be the Mellon on her knees with white muslin on her head and shoulders.[88]

The magician Samri Baldwin exposed the tricks of the Davenport brothers in his book *The Secrets of Mahatma Land Explained* (1895).[89] The medium Swami Laura Horos was convicted of fraud several times and was tried for rape and fraud in London in 1901. She was described by the magician Harry Houdini as "one of the most extraordinary fake mediums and mystery swindlers the world has ever known".[90]

In the late 19th century the fraudulent methods of spirit photographers such as David Duguid and Edward Wyllie were revealed by psychical researchers.[91] Hereward Carrington documented various methods (with diagrams) how the medium would manipulate the plates before, during, and after the séance to produce spirit forms.[92] The ectoplasm materializations of the French medium Eva Carrière were exposed as fraudulent. The fake ectoplasm of Carrière was made of cut-out paper faces from newspapers and magazines on which fold marks could sometimes be seen from the photographs.[93] Cut out faces that she used included Woodrow Wilson, King Ferdinand of Bulgaria, French president Raymond Poincaré and the actress Mona Delza.[94]

The séance trick of the Eddy Brothers was revealed by the magician Chung Ling Soo in 1898. The brothers utilized a fake hand made of lead, and with their hands free from control would play musical instruments and move objects in the séance room.[95] The physiologist Ivor Lloyd Tuckett examined a case of spirit photography that W. T. Stead had claimed was genuine. Stead visited a photographer who had produced a photograph of him with deceased soldier known as "Piet Botha". Stead claimed that the photographer could not have come across any information about Piet Botha, however, Tuckett discovered that an article in 1899 had been published on Pietrus Botha in a weekly magazine with a portrait and personal details.[96]

The trance medium Leonora Piper was investigated by psychical researchers and psychologists in the late 19th and early 20th century. In an experiment to test if Piper's "spirit" controls were purely fictitious the psychologist G. Stanley Hall invented a niece called Bessie Beals and asked Piper's 'control' to get in touch with it. Bessie appeared, answered questions and accepted Dr. Hall as her uncle.[97] The psychologist Joseph Jastrow wrote that Piper pretended to be controlled by spirits and fell into simple and logical traps from her comments.[98] Science writer Martin Gardner concluded Piper was a cold reader that would "fish" for information from her séance sitters.[99] The physiologist Ivor Lloyd Tuckett who examined Piper's mediumship in detail wrote it could be explained by "muscle-reading, fishing, guessing, hints obtained in the sitting, knowledge surreptitiously obtained, knowledge acquired in the interval between sittings and lastly, facts already within Mrs. Piper's knowledge."[100]

39.6.2   1900s

In March 1902 in Berlin, police officers interrupted a séance of the German apport medium Frau Anna Rothe. Her hands were grabbed and she was wrestled to the ground. A female police assistant physically examined Rothe and discovered 157 flowers as well as oranges and lemons hidden in her petticoat. She was arrested and charged with fraud.[101] Another apport medium Hilda Lewis known as the "flower medium" confessed to fraud.[102]

The psychical researchers W. W. Baggally and Everard Feilding exposed the British materialization medium Christopher Chambers as a fraud in 1905. A false moustache was discovered in the séance room which he used to fabricate the spirit materializations.[103] The British medium Charles Eldred was exposed as a fraud in 1906. Eldred would sit in a chair in a curtained off area in the room known as a "séance cabinet". Various spirit figures would emerge from the cabinet and move around the séance room, however, it was discovered that the chair had a secret compartment that contained beards, cloths, masks, and wigs that Eldred would dress up in to fake the spirits.[104]

The spirit photographer William Hope tricked William Crookes with a fake spirit photograph of his wife in 1906. Oliver Lodge revealed there had been obvious signs of double exposure, the picture of Lady Crookes had been copied from a wedding anniversary photograph, however, Crookes was a convinced spiritualist and claimed it was genuine evidence for spirit photography.[105]

In 1907, Hereward Carrington exposed the tricks of fraudulent mediums such as those used in slate-writing, table-turning, trumpet mediumship, materializations, sealed-letter reading and spirit photography.[106] Between 1908-

1914 the Italian medium Francesco Carancini was investigated by psychical researchers and they discovered that he used phosphorus matches to produce "spirit lights" and with a freed hand would move objects in the séance room.[107]

In 1908 at a hotel in Naples, the psychical researcher Everard Feilding attended a series of séances with Eusapia Palladino. In a report Feilding claimed genuine supernatural activity had occurred in the séances, this report became known as the Feilding report.[108] In 1910, Feilding returned to Naples, but this time accompanied with the magician William S. Marriott. Unlike the 1908 sittings, Feilding and Marriott detected her cheating, just as she had done in America. Her deceptions were obvious. Palladino evaded control and was caught moving objects with her foot, shaking the curtain with her hands, moving the cabinet table with her elbow and touching the séance sitters. Milbourne Christopher wrote regarding the exposure "when one knows how a feat can be done and what to look for, only the most skillful performer can maintain the illusion in the face of such informed scrutiny."[109]

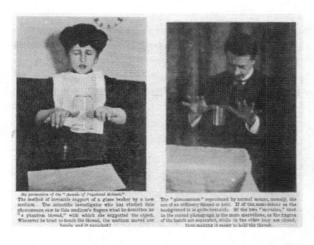

Stanisława Tomczyk (left) and the magician William Marriott (right) who duplicated by natural means her levitation trick of a glass beaker.

In 1910 at a séance in Grenoble, France the apport medium Charles Bailey produced two live birds in the séance room. Bailey was unaware that the dealer he had bought the birds from was present in the séance and he was exposed as a fraud.[110] The psychical researcher Eric Dingwall observed the medium Bert Reese in New York and claimed to have discovered his billet reading tricks.[111] The most detailed account at exposing his tricks (with diagrams) was by the magician Theodore Annemann.[112]

The Polish medium Stanisława Tomczyk's levitation of a glass beaker was exposed and replicated in 1910 by the magician William Marriott by means of a hidden thread.[113] The Italian medium Lucia Sordi was exposed in 1911, she was bound to a chair by psychical researchers but would

free herself during her séances. The tricks of another Italian medium Linda Gazzera were revealed in the same year, she would release her hands and feet from control in her séances and use them. Gazzera would not permit anyone to search her before a séance sitting, as she concealed muslin and other objects in her hair.[114]

In 1917, Edward Clodd analyzed the mediumship of the trance medium Gladys Osborne Leonard and came to the conclusion that Leonard had known her séance sitters before she had held the séances, and could have easily obtained such information by natural means.[115] The British psychiatrist Charles Arthur Mercier wrote in his book *Spiritualism and Sir Oliver Lodge* (1917) that Oliver Lodge had been duped into believing mediumship by trickery and his spiritualist views were based on assumptions and not scientific evidence.[116]

In 1918, Joseph Jastrow wrote about the tricks of Eusapia Palladino who was an expert at freeing her hands and feet from the control in the séance room.[117] In the séance room Palladino would move curtains from a distance by releasing a jet of air from a rubber bulb that she had in her hand.[118] According to the psychical researcher Harry Price "Her tricks were usually childish: long hairs attached to small objects in order to produce 'telekinetic movements'; the gradual substitution of one hand for two when being controlled by sitters; the production of 'phenomena' with a foot which had been surreptitiously removed from its shoe and so on."[119]

In the 1920s the British medium Charles Albert Beare duped the Spiritualist organization the Temple of Light into believing he had genuine mediumship powers. In 1931 Beare published a confession in the newspaper *Daily Express*. In the confession he stated "I have deceived hundreds of people.... I have been guilty of fraud and deception in spiritualistic practices by pretending that I was controlled by a spirit guide.... I am frankly and whole-heartedly sorry that I have allowed myself to deceive people."[120] Due to the exposure of William Hope and other fraudulent spiritualists, Arthur Conan Doyle in the 1920s led a mass resignation of eighty-four members of the Society for Psychical Research, as they believed the Society was opposed to spiritualism.[121]

Between 8 November and 31 December 1920 Gustav Geley of the Institute Metapsychique International attended fourteen séances with the medium Franek Kluski in Paris. A bowl of hot paraffin was placed in the room and according to Kluski spirits dipped their limbs into the paraffin and then into a bath of water to materialize. Three other series of séances were held in Warsaw in Kluski's own apartment, these took place over a period of three years. Kluski was not searched in any of the séances. Photographs of the molds were obtained during the four series of experiments and were published by Geley in 1924.[122][123] Harry Houdini replicated the Kluski materialization moulds by using his hands and a bowl of hot paraffin.[124]

The British direct-voice medium Frederick Tansley Munnings was exposed as a fraud when one of his séance sitters turned the lights on which revealed him to be holding a trumpet by means of a telescopic extension piece and using an angle piece to change the auditory effect of his voice.[125] Richard Hodgson held six sittings with the medium Rosina Thompson and came to the conclusion she was a fraud as he discovered Thompson had access to documents and information about her séance sitters.[126]

On 4 February 1922, Harry Price with James Seymour, Eric Dingwall and William Marriott had proven the spirit photographer William Hope was a fraud during tests at the British College of Psychic Science. Price wrote in his SPR report "William Hope has been found guilty of deliberately substituting his own plates for those of a sitter... It implies that the medium brings to the sitting a duplicate slide and faked plates for fraudulent purposes."[127] The medium Kathleen Goligher was investigated by the physicist Edmund Fournier d'Albe. On July 22, 1921 in a séance he observed Goligher holding the table up with her foot. He also discovered that her ectoplasm was made of muslin. During a séance d'Albe observed white muslin between Goligher's feet.[128]

The Danish medium Einer Nielsen was investigated by a committee from the Kristiania University in Norway, 1922 and discovered in a séance that his ectoplasm was fake.[129] In 1923 the Polish medium Jan Guzyk was exposed as a fraud in a series of séances in Sorbonne in Paris. Guzyk would use his elbows and legs to move objects around the room and touch the sitters. According to Max Dessoir the trick of Guzyk was to use his "foot for psychic touches and sounds".[130]

The psychical researchers Eric Dingwall and Harry Price re-published an anonymous work written by a former medium entitled *Revelations of a Spirit Medium* (1922) which exposed the tricks of mediumship and the fraudulent methods of producing "spirit hands".[131] Originally all the copies of the book were bought up by spiritualists and deliberately destroyed.[132] In 1923, the magician Carlos María de Heredia revealed how fake spirit hands could be made by using a rubber glove, paraffin and a jar of cold water.[133] In 1922, Harry Price, James Seymour, Eric Dingwall and William Marriott exposed the fraud of the spirit photographer William Hope. Price wrote in his report "William Hope has been found guilty of deliberately substituting his own plates for those of a sitter... It implies that the medium brings to the sitting a duplicate slide and faked plates for fraudulent purposes."[127]

The Hungarian medium Ladislas Lasslo confessed that all

of his spirit materializations were fraudulent in 1924. A séance sitter was also found to be working as a confederate for Lasslo.[134][135]

Mina Crandon with her "spirit hand" which was discovered to be a made from a piece of carved animal liver.

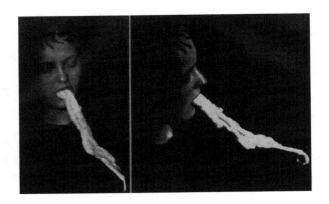

Stanisława P. with ectoplasm.

The Austrian medium Rudi Schneider was investigated in 1924 by the physicists Stefan Meyer and Karl Przibram. They caught Rudi freeing his arm in a series of séances.[136] Rudi claimed he could levitate objects but according Harry Price a photograph taken on April 28, 1932 showed that Rudi had managed to free his arm to move a handkerchief from the table.[137] According to Warren Jay Vinton, Schneider was an expert at freeing himself from control in the séance room.[138] Oliver Gatty and Theodore Besterman who examined the mediumship of Schneider concluded there is "no good evidence that Rudi Schneider possesses supernormal powers."[139]

The spiritualists Arthur Conan Doyle and W. T. Stead were

duped into believing Julius and Agnes Zancig had genuine psychic powers. Both Doyle and Stead wrote that the Zancigs performed telepathy. In 1924 Julius and Agnes Zancig confessed that that their mind reading act was a trick and published the secret code and all the details of the trick method they had used under the title of *Our Secrets!!* in a London Newspaper.[140]

In 1925, Samuel Soal claimed to have taken part in a series of séances with the medium Blanche Cooper who contacted the spirit of a soldier Gordon Davis and revealed the house that he had lived in. Researchers later discovered fraud as the séances had taken place in 1922, not 1925. The magician and paranormal investigator Bob Couttie revealed that Davis was alive, Soal lived close to him and had altered the records of the sittings after checking out the house. Soal's co-workers knew that he had fiddled the results but were kept quiet with threats of libel suits.[141]

Mina Crandon claimed to materialize a "spirit hand", but when examined by biologists the hand was discovered to be made from a piece of carved animal liver.[142] The German apport medium Heinrich Melzer was discovered to be a fraud in 1926. In a séance psychical researchers found that Melzer had small stones attached to the back of his ears by flesh coloured tape.[143] Psychical researchers who investigated the mediumship of Maria Silbert revealed that she used her feet and toes to move objects in the séance room.[144]

In 1930 the Polish medium Stanisława P. was tested at the Institut Metapsychique in Paris. French psychical researcher Eugéne Osty suspected in the séance that Stanislawa had freed her hand from control. Secret flashlight photographs that were taken revealed that her hand was free and she had moved objects on the séance table.[145] It was claimed by spiritualists that during a series of séances in 1930 the medium Eileen J. Garrett channeled secret information from the spirit of the Lieutenant Herbert Carmichael Irwin who had died in the R101 crash a few days before the séance. Researcher Melvin Harris who studied the case wrote that the information described in Garrett's séances were "either commonplace, easily absorbed bits and pieces, or plain gobblede- gook. The so-called secret information just doesn't exist."[146]

In the 1930s Harry Price (director of the National Laboratory of Psychical Research) had investigated the medium Helen Duncan and had her perform a number of test séances. She was suspected of swallowing cheesecloth which was then regurgitated as "ectoplasm".[147] Price had proven through analysis of a sample of ectoplasm produced by Duncan, that it was made of cheesecloth.[148] Helen Duncan would also use a doll made of a painted papier-mâché mask draped in an old sheet which she pretended to her sitters was a spirit.[149] The photographs taken by Thomas

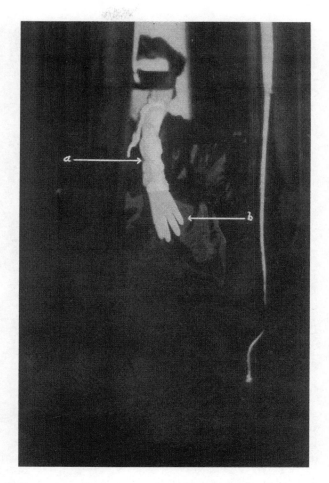

Helen Duncan with fake ectoplasm, analysed by Harry Price to be made of cheesecloth and a rubber glove.

Glendenning Hamilton in the 1930s of ectoplasm reveal the substance to be made of tissue paper and magazine cut-outs of people. The famous photograph taken by Hamilton of the medium Mary Ann Marshall depicts tissue paper with a cut out of Arthur Conan Doyle's head from a newspaper. Skeptics have suspected that Hamilton may have been behind the hoax.[150]

Psychologists and researchers who studied Pearl Curran's automatic writings in the 1930s came to the conclusion Patience Worth was a fictitious creation of Curran.[151][152] In 1931 George Valiantine was exposed as a fraud in the séance room as it was discovered that he produced fraudulent "spirit" fingerprints in wax. The "spirit" thumbprint that Valiantine claimed belonged to Arthur Conan Doyle was revealed to be the print of his big toe on his right foot. It was also revealed that Valiantine made some of the prints with his elbow.[153]

The medium Frank Decker was exposed as a fraud in 1932. A magician and séance sitter who called himself M. Taylor presented a mail bag and Decker agreed to lock himself inside it. During the séance objects were moved around the room and it was claimed spirits had released Decker from the bag. It was later discovered to have been a trick as Martin Sunshine, a magic dealer admitted that he sold Decker a trick mail bag, such as stage escapologists use, and had acted as the medium's confederate by pretending to be M. Taylor, a magician.[154] The British medium Estelle Roberts claimed to materialize an Indian spirit guide called "Red Cloud". Researcher Melvin Harris who examined some photographs of Red Cloud wrote the face was the same as Roberts and she had dressed up in a feathered war-bonnet.[155]

In 1936, the psychical researcher Nandor Fodor tested the Hungarian apport medium Lajos Pap in London and during the séance a dead snake appeared. Pap was searched and was found to be wearing a device under his robe, where he had hidden the snake.[156] A photograph taken at a séance in 1937 in London shows the medium Colin Evans "levitating" in mid air. He claimed that spirits had lifted him. Evans was later discovered to be a fraud as a cord leading from a device in his hand has indicated that it was himself who triggered the flash-photograph and that all he had done was jump from his chair into the air and pretend he had levitated.[157]

According to the magician John Booth the stage mentalist David Devant managed to fool a number of people into believing he had genuine psychic ability who did not realize that his feats were magic tricks. At St. George's Hall, London he performed a fake "clairvoyant" act where he would read a message sealed inside an envelope. The spiritualist Oliver Lodge who was present in the audience was duped by the trick and claimed that Devant had used psychic powers. In 1936 Devant in his book *Secrets of My Magic* revealed the trick method he had used.[158]

The physicist Kristian Birkeland exposed the fraud of the direct voice medium Etta Wriedt. Birkeland turned on the lights during a séance, snatched her trumpets and discovered that the "spirit" noises were caused by chemical explosions induced by potassium and water and in other cases by lycopodium powder.[159] The British medium Isa Northage claimed to materialize the spirit of a surgeon known as Dr. Reynolds. When photographs taken of Reynolds were analyzed by researchers they discovered that Northage looked like Reynolds with a glued stage beard.[160]

The magician Julien Proskauer revealed that the levitating trumpet of Jack Webber was a trick. Close examination of photographs reveal Webber to be holding a telescopic reaching rod attached to the trumpet, and sitters in his séances only believed it to have levitated because the room was so dark they could not see the rod. Webber would cover the rod with crepe paper to disguise its real construction.[161]

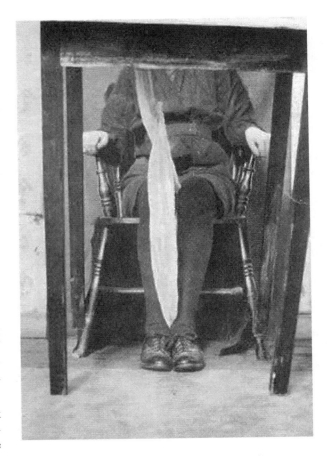

Kathleen Goligher with fake ectoplasm made of muslin.

In 1954, the psychical researcher Rudolf Lambert published a report revealing details about a case of fraud that was covered up by many early members of the Institute Metapsychique International (IMI).[162] Lambert who had studied Gustav Geley's files on the medium Eva Carrière discovered photographs depicting fraudulent ectoplasm taken by her companion Juliette Bisson.[162] Various "materializations" were artificially attached to Eva's hair by wires. The discovery was never published by Geley. Eugéne Osty (the director of the institute) and members Jean Meyer, Albert von Schrenck-Notzing and Charles Richet all knew about the fraudulent photographs but were firm believers in mediumship phenomena so demanded the scandal be kept secret.[162]

The fraudulent medium Ronald Edwin confessed he had duped his séance sitters and revealed the fraudulent methods he had used in his book *Clock Without Hands* (1955).[163] The psychical researcher Tony Cornell investigated the mediumship of Alec Harris in 1955. During the séance "spirit" materializations emerged from a cabinet and walked around the room. Cornell wrote that a stomach rumble, nicotine smelling breath and a pulse gave it away that all the spirit figures were in fact Harris and that he had dressed up as each one behind the cabinet.[164]

The British medium William Roy earned over £50,000 from his séance sitters. He confessed to fraud in 1958 revealing the microphone and trick-apparatus that he had used.[165] The automatic writings of the Irish medium Geraldine Cummins were analyzed by psychical researchers in 1960s and they revealed that she worked as a cataloguer at the National Library of Ireland and took information from various books that would appear in her automatic writings about ancient history.[166]

In 1960, psychic investigator Andrija Puharich and Tom O'Neill, publisher of the Spiritualist magazine *Psychic Observer*, arranged to film two seances at Camp Chesterfield, Indiana using infrared film, intending to procure scientific proof of spirit materializations. The medium was shown the camera beforehand, and was aware that she was being filmed. However, the film revealed obvious fraud on the part of the medium and her cabinet assistant. The expose was published in the 10 July 1960 issue of the *Psychic Observer*.[167]:96–97

In 1966 the son of Bishop Pike committed suicide. After his death, Pike contacted the British medium Ena Twigg for a series of séances and she claimed to have communicated with his son. Although Twigg denied formerly knowing anything about Pike and his son, the magician John Booth discovered that Twigg had already known information about the Pike family before the séances. Twigg had belonged to the same denomination of Bishop Pike, he had preached at a cathedral in Kent and she had known information about him and his deceased son from newspapers.[168]

In 1970 two psychical researchers investigated the direct-voice medium Leslie Flint and found that all the "spirit" voices in his séance sounded exactly like himself and attributed his mediumship to "second-rate ventriloquism".[169] The medium Arthur Ford died leaving specific instructions that all of his files should be burned. In 1971 after his death, psychical researchers discovered his files but instead of burning them they were examined and discovered to be filled with obituaries, newspaper articles and other information, which enabled Ford to research his séance sitters backgrounds.[170]

Ronald Pearsall in his book *Table-rappers: The Victorians and the Occult* (1972) documented how every Victorian medium investigated had been exposed as using trickery, in the book he revealed how mediums would even use acrobatic techniques during séances to convince audiences of spirit presences.[171]

In 1976, M. Lamar Keene, a medium in Florida and at the Spiritualist Camp Chesterfield in Indiana, confessed to defrauding the public in his book *The Psychic Mafia*. Keene detailed a multitude of common stage magic techniques uti-

lized by mediums which are supposed to give an appearance of paranormal powers or supernatural involvement.[172]

After her death in the 1980s the medium Doris Stokes was accused of fraud, by author and investigator Ian Wilson. Wilson stated that Mrs Stokes planted specific people in her audience and did prior research into her sitters.[173] Rita Goold a physical medium during the 1980s was accused of fraud, by the psychical researcher Tony Cornell. He claimed she would dress up as the spirits in her séances and would play music during them which provided cover for her to change clothes.[174]

The spirit guide Silver Belle was made from cardboard. Both Ethel Post-Parrish and the lady standing outside of the curtain were in on the hoax.

The British journalist Ruth Brandon published the book *The Spiritualists* (1983) which exposed the fraud of the Victorian mediums.[3] The book received positive reviews and has been influential to skeptics of spiritualism.[175] The British apport medium Paul McElhoney was exposed as a fraud during a séance in Osset, Yorkshire in 1983. The tape recorder that McElhoney took to his séances was investigated and a black tape was discovered bound around the battery compartment and inside carnation flowers were found as well as a key-ring torch and other objects.[176]

In 1988, the magician Bob Couttie criticized the paranormal author Brian Inglis for deliberately ignoring evidence of fraud in mediumship. Couttie wrote Inglis had not familiarized himself with magician techniques.[177] In 1990 the researcher Gordon Stein discovered that the levitation photograph of the medium Carmine Mirabelli was fraudulent. The photograph was a trick as there were signs of chemical retouching under Mirabelli's feet. The retouching showed that Mirabelli was not levitating but was standing on a ladder which was erased from the photograph.[178]

In 1991, Wendy Grossman in the *New Scientist* criticized the parapsychologist Stephen E. Braude for ignoring evidence of fraud in mediumship. According to Grossman "[Braude] accuses sceptics of ignoring the evidence he believes is solid, but himself ignores evidence that does not suit him. If a medium was caught cheating on some occasions, he says, the rest of that medium's phenomena were still genuine." Grossman came to the conclusion that Braude did not do proper research on the subject and should study "the art of conjuring."[179]

In 1992, Richard Wiseman analyzed the Feilding report of Eusapia Palladino and argued that she employed a secret accomplice that could enter the room by a fake door panel positioned near the séance cabinet. Wiseman discovered this trick was already mentioned in a book from 1851, he also visited a carpenter and skilled magician who constructed a door within an hour with a false panel. The accomplice was suspected to be her second husband, who insisted on bringing Palladino to the hotel where the séances took place.[180] Massimo Polidoro and Gian Marco Rinaldi also analyzed the Feilding report but came to the conclusion no secret accomplice was needed as Palladino during the 1908 Naples séances could have produced the phenomena by using her foot.[181]

Colin Fry was exposed in 1992 when during a séance the lights were unexpectedly turned on and he was seen holding a spirit trumpet in the air, which the audience had been led to believe was being levitated by spiritual energy.[182] In 1997, Massimo Polidoro and Luigi Garlaschelli produced wax-moulds directly from one's hand which were exactly the same copies as Gustav Geley obtained from Franek Kluski, which are kept at the Institute Metapsychique International.[183]

A series of mediumistic séances known as the Scole Experiment took place between 1993–98 in the presence of the researchers David Fontana, Arthur Ellison and Montague Keen. This has produced photographs, audio recordings and physical objects which appeared in the dark séance room (known as apports).[184] A criticism of the experiment was that it was flawed because it did not rule out the possibility of fraud. The skeptical investigator Brian Dunning wrote the Scole experiments fail in many ways. The séances were held in the basement of two of the mediums, only total darkness was allowed with no night vision apparatus as it might "frighten the spirits away". The box containing the film was not examined and could easily have been accessible to fraud. And finally, even though many years have passed, there has been no follow-up, no further research by any credible agency or published accounts.[184]

39.6.3 Recent

The VERITAS Research Program of the Laboratory for Advances in Consciousness and Health in the Department of Psychology at the University of Arizona, run by the parapsychologist Gary Schwartz, was created primarily to test

Joe Nickell a notable skeptic of mediumship. According to Nickell modern mediums use mentalist techniques such as cold reading.

the hypothesis that the consciousness (or identity) of a person survives physical death.[185] Schwartz claimed his experiments were indicative of survival, but do not yet provide conclusive proof.[186][187] The experiments described by Schwartz have received criticism from the scientific community for being inadequately designed and using poor controls.[188][189]

Ray Hyman discovered many methodological errors with Schwartz's research including; "Inappropriate control comparisons", "Failure to use double-blind procedures", "Creating non-falsifiable outcomes by reinterpreting failures as successes" and "Failure to independently check on facts the sitters endorsed as true". Hyman wrote "Even if the research program were not compromised by these defects, the claims being made would require replication by independent investigators." Hyman criticizes Schwartz's decision to publish his results without gathering "evidence for their hypothesis that would meet generally accepted scientific criteria... they have lost credibility."[190]

In 2003, skeptic investigator Massimo Polidoro in his book *Secrets of the Psychics* documented the history of fraud in mediumship and spiritualistic practices as well as the psychology of psychic deception.[51] Terence Hines in his book *Pseudoscience and the Paranormal* (2003) has written:

> Modern spiritualists and psychics keep detailed files on their victims. As might be expected, these files can be very valuable and are often passed on from one medium or psychic to another when one retires or dies. Even if a psychic doesn't use a private detective or have immediate access to driver's license records and such, there is still a very powerful technique that will al-

low the psychic to convince people that the psychic knows all about them, their problems, and their deep personal secrets, fears, and desires. The technique is called cold reading and is probably as old as charlatanism itself... If John Edward (or any of the other self-proclaimed speakers with the dead) really could communicate with the dead, it would be a trivial matter to prove it. All that would be necessary would be for him to contact any of the thousands of missing persons who are presumed dead—famous (e.g., Jimmy Hoffa, Judge Crater) or otherwise—and correctly report where the body is. Of course, this is never done. All we get, instead, are platitudes to the effect that Aunt Millie, who liked green plates, is happy on the other side.[191]

An experiment conducted by the British Psychological Society in 2005 suggests that under the controlled condition of the experiment, people who claimed to be professional mediums do not demonstrate the mediumistic ability. In the experiment, mediums were assigned to work the participants chosen to be "sitters." The mediums claimed to contact the deceased who were related to the sitters. The research gather the numbers of the statements made and have the sitters rate the accuracy of the statements. The readings that were considered to be somewhat accurate by the sitters were very generalized, and the ones that were considered inaccurate were the ones that were very specific.[192]

On Fox News on the Geraldo at Large show, October 6, 2007, Geraldo Rivera and other investigators accused Schwartz as a fraud as he had overstepped his position as a university researcher by requesting over three million dollars from a bereaved father who had lost his son. Schwartz claimed to have contacted the spirit of a 25-year-old man in the bathroom of his parents house and it is alleged he attempted to charge the family 3.5 million dollars for his mediumship services. Schwartz responded saying that the allegations were set up to destroy his science credibility.[193][194]

In 2013 Rose Marks and members of her family were convicted of fraud for a series of crimes spanning 20 years entailing between $20 and $45 million. They told vulnerable clients that to solve their problems they had to give the purported psychics money and valuables. Marks and family promised to return the cash and goods after "cleansing" them. Prosecutors established they had no intent to return the property.[195][196][197]

The exposures of fraudulent activity led to a rapid decline in ectoplasm and materialization séances.[198] Investigator Joe Nickell has written that modern self-proclaimed mediums like John Edward, Sylvia Browne, Rosemary Altea and James Van Praagh are avoiding the Victorian tradition

of dark rooms, spirit handwriting and flying tambourines as these methods risk exposure. They instead use "mental mediumship" tactics like cold reading or gleaning information from sitters before hand (hot reading). Group readings also improve hits by making general statements with conviction, which will fit at least one person in the audience. Shows are carefully edited before airing to show only what appears to be hits and removing anything that does not reflect well on the medium.[199]

Michael Shermer criticized mediums in Scientific American, saying, "mediums are unethical and dangerous: they prey on the emotions of the grieving. As grief counselors know, death is best faced head-on as a part of life." Shermer wrote that the human urge to seek connections between events that may form patterns meaningful for survival is a function of natural evolution, and called the alleged ability of mediums to talk to the dead "a well-known illusion of a meaningful pattern."[200]

According to James Randi, a skeptic who has debunked many claims of psychic ability and uncovered fraudulent practices,[201] mediums who do cold readings "fish, suggest possibilities, make educated guesses and give options." Randi has a standing offer of $1 million US dollars for anyone who can demonstrate psychic ability under controlled conditions. Most prominent psychics and mediums have not taken up his offer.[202]

The key role in mediumship of this sort is played by "effect of subjective confirmation" (see Barnum effect) — people are predisposed to consider reliable that information which though is casual coincidence or a guess, however it seems to them personally important and significant and answers their personal belief.[203]

The article about this phenomenon in Encyclopedia Britannica places emphasis that "... one by one spiritual mediums were convicted of fraud, sometimes using the tricks borrowed from scenic "magicians" to convince their paranormal abilities". In the article it is also noted that "... the opening of the wide ranging fraud happening on spiritualistic sessions caused serious damage to reputation of the movement of a Spiritualism and in the USA pushed it on the public periphery".[204]

39.7 See also

- Faith healing

- List of modern channelled texts

- List of topics characterized as pseudoscience

- *The Book on Mediums*

- *The Spirits Book*

- Theatrical seances

39.8   References

[1] Gilmore, Mernie (October 31, 2005). "A spiritual connection". *The Express* (London).

[2] Brandreth, Gyles (November 3, 2002). "Is Anybody There?". *The Sunday Telegraph* (London).

[3] Ruth Brandon. (1983). *The Spiritualists: The Passion for the Occult in the Nineteenth and Twentieth Centuries.* Alfred E. Knopf. ISBN 978-0394527406

[4] Milbourne Christopher. (1979). *Search for the Soul.* T. Y. Crowell. ISBN 978-0690017601

[5] Terence Hines. (2003). *Pseudoscience and the Paranormal.* Prometheus Books. ISBN 978-1573929790

[6] O'Keeffe, Ciaran (May 2005). "Testing Alleged Mediumship: Methods and Results". British Journal of Psychology. doi:10.1348/000712605X36361. ISSN 0007-1269.

[7] Thirty Years of Psychical Research by Charles Richet p. 38 The MacMillian Company 1923

[8] "Glossary of Key Words Frequently Used in Parapsychology", Parapsychological Association website. "Materialization: A phenomenon of physical mediumship in which living entities or inanimate objects are caused to take form, sometimes from ectoplasm." Retrieved January 24, 2006

[9] "Medium - Definition". *Dictionary.com.* Retrieved 23 March 2007.

[10] "Spiritism is not a religion but a science", as the famous French astronomer Camille Flammarion said in Allan Kardec's Eulogy on April 2, 1869, in *Death and Its Mystery - After Death. Manifestations and Apparitions of the Dead; The Soul After Death* Translated by Latrobe Carroll (London: Adelphi Terrace, 1923), archive version at Allan Kardec eulogy

[11] Brandon, Ruth. (1983). *Scientists and the Supernormal.* New Scientist. 16 June. pp. 783-786.

[12] Hines, Terence. (2003). *Pseudoscience and the Paranormal.* Prometheus Books. p. 52. ISBN 1-57392-979-4

[13] Anna Hurwic, *Pierre Curie,* translated by Lilananda Dasa and Joseph Cudnik, Paris, Flammarion, 1995, pp. 65, 66, 68, 247-48.

[14] "W.T. Stead and Spiritualism - The W.T. Stead Resource Site". *attackingthedevil.co.uk.*

[15] Jones, Kelvin I. (1989). *Conan Doyle and the Spirits: The Spiritualist Career of Arthur Conan Doyle.* Aquarian Press.

[16] Sutcliffe, Steven J. (2002). Children of the New Age. p. 35.

[17] "The SNU".

[18] *The Autobiography of a Fortune Teller* by C. Doreen Phillips, Vantage Press, 1958.

[19] Richard Castillo (1995) *Culture, Trance, and the Mind-Brain.* Anthropology of Consciousness. Volume 6, Issue 1, pages 17–34, March 1995.

[20] Braude, Anne, *Radical Spirits, Spiritualism and Women's Rights in Nineteenth Century America.* Bloomington: Indiana University Press, 2001.

[21] Deborah Blum. (2006). *Ghost Hunters, William James] and the Search for Scientic Proof of Life After Death.* The Penguin Press.

[22] Amy Tanner. (1994, originally published 1910). *Studies in Spiritism.* With an introduction by G. Stanley Hall. Prometheus Press. p. 18

[23] *God's World: A Treatise on Spiritualism Founded on Transcripts of Shorthand Notes Taken Down, Over a Period of Five Years, in the Seance-Room of the William T. Stead Memorial Center (a Religious Body Incorporated Under the Statutes of the State of Illinois), Mrs. Cecil M. Cook, Medium and Pastor. Compiled and Written by Lloyd Kenyon Jones. Chicago, Ill.: The William T. Stead Memorial Center, 1919.*

[24] "Ectoplasm" def. Merriam Webster dictionary, Retrieved 18 January 2007

[25] Somerlott, Robert, *Here, Mr. Splitfoot.* Viking, 1971.

[26] Connor, Steven (1999). "9. The Machine in the Ghost: Spiritualism, Technology and the 'Direct Voice'". In Buse, Peter; Stott, Andrew. *Ghosts: deconstruction, psychoanalysis, history.* Palgrave Macmillan. pp. 203–225. ISBN 978-0-312-21739-6.

[27] "What is a psychic?". UK Psychic Readings. Retrieved 30 July 2013.

[28] Wood, Matthew (2007). *Possession Power and the New Age: Ambiguities of Authority in Neoliberal Societies.* Ashgate Publishing, Limited. ISBN 0-7546-3339-X.

[29] LeCron, Leslie; Bordeaux, Jean (1970). *Hypnotism Today.* Wilshire Book Co. p. 278. ISBN 0-87980-081-X. When in a trance ... the medium seems to come under the control of another personality, purportedly the spirit of a departed soul, and a genuine medium undoubtedly believes the 'control' to be a spirit entity ... In the trance, the medium often enters a cataleptic state marked by extreme rigidity. The control then takes over, the voice may change completely ... and the supposed spirit answers the questions of the sitter, telling of things 'on the other plane' and gives messages from those who have 'passed over.'

[30] Brown, Michael F. (1999). *The Channeling Zone: American Spirituality in an Anxious Age.* Harvard University Press. ISBN 0-674-10883-3.

[31] Klimo, Jon (1998). *Channeling: Investigations on Receiving Information from Paranormal Sources.* North Atlantic Books. p. 100. ISBN 978-1-55643-248-4.

[32] Chalmers, Robert (8 July 2007). "Interview: The couple who claim they can make you rich beyond your wildest dreams". The Independent.

[33] Koven, Jean-Claude (2004). *Going Deeper: How to Make Sense of Your Life When Your Life Makes No Sense.* Prism House Press. p. 389. ISBN 0-972-39545-8.

[34] Wilcock, David (2014). *The Synchronicity Key: The Hidden Intelligence Guiding the Universe and You.* Plume. ISBN 0-142-18108-0.

[35] DifferenceBetween.net Retrieved 28 December 2011

[36] "Glossary of Key Words Frequently Used in Parapsychology", Parapsychological Association website, Retrieved January 29, 2007

[37] Ilya Vinitsky. (2009). *Ghostly Paradoxes: Modern Spiritualism and Russian Culture in the Age of Realism.* University of Toronto Press. p. 25. ISBN 978-0802099358

[38] Harvey J. Irwin, Caroline Watt. (2007). *An Introduction to Parapsychology.* McFarland. pp. 138-144. ISBN 978-0786430598

[39] Theodore Schick; Lewis Vaughn. (2013). *How to Think About Weird Things: Critical Thinking for a New Age.* McGraw-Hill Higher Education. ISBN 978-0-07-752631-3

[40] David Marks. (2000). *The Psychology of the Psychic.* Prometheus Books. ISBN 978-1573927987

[41] Nicola Holt, Christine Simmonds-Moore, David Luke, Christopher French. (2012). *Anomalistic Psychology (Palgrave Insights in Psychology).* Palgrave Macmillan. ISBN 978-0230301504

[42] Millais Culpin. (1920). *Spiritualism and the New Psychology, an Explanation of Spiritualist Phenomena and Beliefs in Terms of Modern Knowledge.* Kennelly Press. ISBN 978-1446056516

[43] Joseph Rinn. (1950). *Sixty Years of Psychical Research.* New York: Truth Seeker. pp. 200-205

[44] Wolffram, Heather. (2012). *'Trick', 'Manipulation' and 'Farce': Albert Moll's Critique of Occultism.* Medical History 56(2): 277-295.

[45] Leonard Zusne, Warren H. Jones. (1989). *Anomalistic Psychology: A Study of Magical Thinking.* Psychology Press. p. 221. ISBN 978-0805805086 "The spirits, controls, and guides of a medium are the products of the medium's own psychological dynamics. On the one hand, they personify the medium's hidden impulses and wish life. On the other, they are also shaped by the expectations of the medium's sitters, the medium's experience, the cultural background, and the spirit of the times."

[46] Ian Rowland. (1998). *The full facts book of cold reading.* London, England: Ian Roland. ISBN 978-0955847608

[47] Brad Clark (2002). *Spiritualism.* pp. 220-226. In Michael Shermer. *The Skeptic Encyclopedia of Pseudoscience.* ABC-CLIO. ISBN 978-1576076538

[48] Jonathan Smith. (2009). *Pseudoscience and Extraordinary Claims of the Paranormal: A Critical Thinker's Toolkit.* Wiley-Blackwell. pp. 141-241. ISBN 978-1405181228

[49] Richard Wiseman. (2011). *Paranormality: Why We See What Isn't There.* Macmillan. p. 38. ISBN 978-0-230-75298-6

[50] Wiseman, R., Greening, E., and Smith, M. (2003). *Belief in the paranormal and suggestion in the seance room.* British Journal of Psychology, 94 (3): 285-297.

[51] Massimo Polidoro. (2003). *Secrets of the Psychics: Investigating Paranormal Claims.* Prometheus Books. ISBN 978-1591020868

[52] James Houran. (2004). *From Shaman to Scientist: Essays on Humanity's Search for Spirits.* Scarecrow Press. p. 177. ISBN 978-0810850545 Also see Michael Shermer. (2002). *The Skeptic Encyclopedia of Pseudoscience.* ABC-CLIO. pp. 220-226. ISBN 978-1576076538

[53] Paul Kurtz. (1985). *A Skeptic's Handbook of Parapsychology.* Prometheus Books. ISBN 978-0879753009

[54] Lewis Spence. (2003). *An Encyclopaedia of Occultism.* Dover. p. 172

[55] Alan Gauld. (1968). *The Founders of Psychical Research.* Routledge & K. Paul.

[56] Janet Oppenheim. (1988). *The Other World: Spiritualism and Psychical Research in England, 1850-1914. Cambridge University Press.* ISBN 978-0521347679

[57] The Problem of Fraud by Paul Kurtz

[58] Chung Ling Soo. (1898). *Spirit Slate Writing and Kindred Phenomena.* Munn & Company. Henry Evans. (1897). *Hours With the Ghosts Or Nineteenth Century Witchcraft.* Kessinger Publishing. Julien Proskauer. (1932). *Spook crooks! Exposing the secrets of the prophet-eers who conduct our wickedest industry.* New York, A. L. Burt.

[59] Joseph Dunninger. (1935). *Inside the Medium's Cabinet.* New York, D. Kemp and Company. Harry Houdini. (1924). *A Magician Among the Spirits.* Cambridge University Press. Joseph Rinn. (1950). *Sixty Years Of Psychical Research: Houdini And I Among The Spiritualists.* Truth Seeker.

[60] *Preliminary Report of the Commission Appointed by the University of Pennsylvania,* The Seybert Commission, 1887. 1 April 2004.

[61] Spiritualism (religion) :: History - Britannica Online Encyclopedia

[62] Joseph McCabe. (1920). *Spiritualism: A Popular History from 1847*. Dodd, Mead and Company. pp. 110-112. A Mr. Merrifield was present at one of the sittings. Home's usual phenomena were messages, the moving of objects (presumably at a distance), and the playing of an accordion which he held with one hand under the shadow of the table. But from an early date in America he had been accustomed occasionally to "materialise" hands (as it was afterwards called). The sitters would, in the darkness, faintly see a ghostly hand and arm, or they might feel the touch of an icy limb. Mr. Merrifield and the other sitters saw a "spirit-hand" stretch across the faintly lit space of the window. But Mr. Merrifield says that Home sat, or crouched, low in a low chair, and that the "spirit-hand" was a false limb on the end of Home's arm. At other times, he says, he saw that Home was using his foot."

[63] Donald Serrell Thomas. (1989). *Robert Browning: A Life Within Life*. Weidenfeld and Nicolson. pp. 157-158. ISBN 978-0297796398

[64] Harry Houdini. (2011 reprint edition). Originally published in 1924. *A Magician Among the Spirits*. Cambridge University Press. p. 42. ISBN 978-1108027489

[65] John Casey. (2009). *After Lives: A Guide to Heaven, Hell and Purgatory*. Oxford. p. 373. ISBN 978-0199975037 "The poet attended one of Home's seances where a face was materialized, which, Home's spirit guide announced, was that of Browning's dead son. Browning seized the supposed materialized head, and it turned out to be the bare foot of Home. The deception was not helped by the fact that Browning never had lost a son in infancy."

[66] Joseph McCabe. (1920). *Is Spiritualism based on Fraud?: The Evidence Given by Sir A.C. Doyle and Others Drastically Examined*. London: Watts & Co. pp. 48-50. Also see the review of *The Enigma of Daniel Home: Medium or Fraud?* by Trevor H. Hall in F. B. Smith. (1986). Victorian Studies. Volume. 29, No. 4. pp. 613-614.

[67] Joe Nickell. (2001). *Real-Life X-Files: Investigating the Paranormal*. The University Press of Kentucky. pp. 267-268. ISBN 978-0813122106

[68] Sherrie Lynne Lyons. (2010). *Species, Serpents, Spirits, and Skulls: Science at the Margins in the Victorian Age*. State University of New York Press. p. 100. ISBN 978-1438427980

[69] Alex Owen. (2004). *The Darkened Room: Women, Power, and Spiritualism in Late Victorian England*. University Of Chicago Press. pp. 70-71. ISBN 978-0226642055

[70] Massimo Polidoro. (2000). *Anna Eva Fay: The Mentalist Who Baffled Sir William Crookes*. Skeptical Inquirer 24: 36-38.

[71] Georgess McHargue. (1972). *Facts, Frauds, and Phantasms: A Survey of the Spiritualist Movement*. Doubleday. p. 113. ISBN 978-0385053051

[72] Janet Oppenheim. (1985). *The Other World: Spiritualism and Psychical Research in England, 1850-1914*. Cambridge University Press. p. 19. ISBN 978-0521265058

[73] Paul Kurtz. (1985). *A Skeptic's Handbook of Parapsychology*. Prometheus Books. p. 29. ISBN 978-0879753009 "Florence Cook was caught cheating not only before her séances with Crookes but also afterward. Furthermore, she learned her trade from the mediums Frank Herne and Charles Williams, who were notorious for their cheating." Also see M. Lamar Keene. (1997). *The Psychic Mafia*. Prometheus Books. p. 64. ISBN 978-1573921619 "The most famous of materialization mediums, Florence Cook-- though she managed to convince a scientist, Sir William Crookes, that she was genuine-- was repeatedly exposed in fraud. Florence had been trained in the arts of the séance by Frank Herne, a well-known physical medium whose materializations were grabbed on more than one occasion and found to be the medium himself."

[74] Joseph McCabe. (1920). *Spiritualism: A Popular History from 1847*. Dodd, Mead and Company. pp. 160-161

[75] Chung Ling Soo. (1898). *Spirit Slate Writing and Kindred Phenomena*. Munn & Company. pp. 105-106

[76] Lewis Spence. (1991). *Encyclopedia of Occultism & Parapsychology*. Gale Research Company. p. 1106

[77] Adin Ballou. (2001). *The Rise of Victorian Spiritualism*. Routledge. p. 16

[78] Joseph McCabe. (1920). *Is Spiritualism based on Fraud?: The Evidence Given by Sir A.C. Doyle and Others Drastically Examined*. London: Watts & Co. p. 115

[79] Roy Stemman. (1976). *The Supernatural*. Danbury Press. p. 62

[80] Joseph McCabe. (1920). *Spiritualism: A Popular History From 1847*. T. F. Unwin Ltd. p. 167

[81] Trevor H. Hall. (1963). *The Spiritualists: The Story of Florence Cook and William Crookes*. Helix Press. p. 10

[82] Trevor H. Hall. (1980). *The Strange Case of Edmund Gurney*. Duckworth. p. 47

[83] Washington Irving Bishop. (1880). *Second Sight Explained: A Complete Exposition of Clairvoyance or Second Sight*. Edinburgh: John Menzies.

[84] Preliminary report of the Commission appointed by the University of Pennsylvania to investigate modern spiritualism, in accordance with the request of the late Henry Seybert (1887).

[85] Paul Boyer. *The Oxford Companion to United States History*. Oxford University Press. p. 738. ISBN 978-0195082098

[86] Rodger Anderson. (2006). *Psychics, Sensitives and Somnambules*. McFarland & Company. p. 90. ISBN 978-0786427703

[87] Will Goldston. (1942). *Tricks Of The Masters*. G. Routledge & Sons, Ltd. p. 4

[88] Melvin Harris. (2003). *Investigating the Unexplained: Psychic Detectives, the Amityville Horror-mongers, Jack the Ripper, and Other Mysteries of the Paranormal*. Prometheus Books. p. 21. ISBN 978-1591021087

[89] Samri Baldwin. (1895). *The Secrets of Mahatma Land Explained* Brooklyn, N.Y., Press of T. J. Dyson & Son.

[90] Harry Houdini. (2011). *A Magician Among the Spirits*. Cambridge University Press. p. 66. ISBN 978-1108027489

[91] Joe Nickell. (2001). *Real-Life X-Files: Investigating the Paranormal*. The University Press of Kentucky. pp. 260-261. Also see Joe Nickell. (2005). *Camera Clues: A Handbook for Photographic Investigation*. The University Press of Kentucky. p. 151

[92] Hereward Carrington. (1907). *The Physical Phenomena of Spiritualism*. Herbert B. Turner & Co. pp. 206-223

[93] Donald West. (1954). *Psychical Research Today*. Chapter Séance-Room Phenomena. Duckworth. p. 49

[94] Gordon Stein. (1996). *The Encyclopedia of the Paranormal*. Prometheus Books. p. 520. ISBN 978-1573920216

[95] Chung Ling Soo. (1898). *Spirit Slate Writing and Kindred Phenomena*. Munn & Company. pp. 101-104

[96] Ivor Lloyd Tuckett. (1911). *The Evidence for the Supernatural: A Critical Study Made with "Uncommon Sense"*. Kegan Paul, Trench, Trübner & Company. pp. 52-53

[97] Julian Franklyn. (1935). *A Survey of the Occult*. Kessinger Publishing. p. 248

[98] Joseph Jastrow. (1911). *Studies in Spiritism by Amy E. Tanner*. The American Journal of Psychology. Vol. 22, No. 1. pp. 122-124.

[99] Martin Gardner. *Are Universes Thicker Than Blackberries?* "How Mrs. Piper Bamboozled William James". *W. W. Norton & Company. pp. 252–62.*

[100] Ivor Lloyd Tuckett. (1911). *The Evidence for the Supernatural: A Critical Study Made with "Uncommon Sense"*. K. Paul, Trench, Trübner. pp. 321-395

[101] Corinna Treitel. (2004). *A Science for the Soul: Occultism and the Genesis of the German Modern*. The Johns Hopkins University Press. p. 165. ISBN 978-0801878121

[102] Harry Price. (1939). *Fifty Years of Psychical Research*. Kessinger Publishing. ISBN 978-0766142428

[103] Richard Wiseman. (1997). *Deception & Self-Deception: Investigating Psychics*. Prometheus Books. p. 23

[104] Richard Wiseman. (1997). *Deception & Self-Deception: Investigating Psychics*. Prometheus Books. p. 12

[105] William Hodson Brock. (2008). *William Crookes (1832-1919) and the Commercialization of Science*. Ashgate. p. 474. ISBN 978-0754663225

[106] Hereward Carrington. (1907). *The Physical Phenomena of Spiritualism*. Herbert B. Turner & Co.

[107] Rodger Anderson. (2006). *Psychics, Sensitives And Somnambules*. McFarland & Company. p. 26. ISBN 978-0786427703

[108] The New Paranatural Paradigm: Claims of Communicating with the Dead by Paul Kurtz

[109] Milbourne Christopher. (1971). *ESP, Seers & Psychics*. Crowell. pp. 188-204. ISBN 978-0690268157

• Everard Feilding, William Marriott. (1910). *Report on Further Series of Sittings with Eusapia Palladino at Naples*. Proceedings of the Society for Psychical Research. Volume 15. pp. 20–32.

[110] J. Gordon Melton. (2007). *The Encyclopedia of Religious Phenomena*. Visible Ink Press. p. 12. ISBN 978-1578592098

[111] Eric Dingwall. (1927). *How to Go to a Medium*. K. Paul, Trench, Trübner. pp. 31-32.

[112] Theodore Annemann. (1983). *Practical Mental Magic*. Dover Publications. pp. 7-11

[113] Pearson's Magazine. June 1910. C. Arthur Pearson Ltd. p. 615

[114] Joseph McCabe. (1920). *Is Spiritualism Based On Fraud? The Evidence Given By Sir A. C. Doyle and Others Drastically Examined*. London Watts & Co. pp. 33-34

[115] Edward Clodd. (1917). *The Question: A Brief History and Examination of Modern Spiritualism. Chapter Mrs. Leonard and Others*. pp. 215-241

[116] Charles Arthur Mercier. (1917). *Spiritualism and Sir Oliver Lodge*. London: Mental Culture Enterprise.

[117] Joseph Jastrow (1918). *The Psychology of Conviction*. Houghton Mifflin Company. pp. 101-127

[118] Fakebusters II: Scientific Detection of Fakery in Art and Philately

[119] Harry Price, *Fifty Years of Psychical Research*, chapter XI: The Mechanics of Spiritualism, F&W Media International, Ltd, 2012.

[120] Harry Price. (1939). Chapter *The Mechanics of Spiritualism* in *Fifty Years of Psychical Research*. Kessinger Publishing. ISBN 978-0766142428

[121] G. K. Nelson. (2013). *Spiritualism and Society*. Routledge. p. 159. ISBN 978-0415714624

[122] Clément Chéroux. (2005). *The Perfect Medium: Photography and the Occult.* Yale University Press. p. 268. ISBN 978-0300111361

[123] D. Scott Rogo. (1978). *Mind and Motion: The Riddle of Psychokinesis.* Taplinger Publishing. pp. 245-246. ISBN 978-0800824556

[124] Massimo Polidoro. (2001). *Final Séance: The Strange Friendship Between Houdini and Conan Doyle.* Prometheus Books. pp. 71-73. ISBN 978-1573928960

[125] Julian Franklyn. (2003). *A Survey of the Occult.* pp. 238-239. Kessinger Publishing. ISBN 978-0766130074

[126] Joseph McCabe. (1920). *Spiritualism: A Popular History from 1847.* Dodd, Mead and Company. p. 192

[127] Photos of Ghosts: The Burden of Believing the Unbelievable by Massimo Polidoro

[128] Edmund Edward Fournier d'Albe. (1922). *The Goligher Circle.* J. M. Watkins. p. 37

[129] Universitetskomiteen, Mediet Einer Nielsen, kontrolundersøkelser av universitetskomiteen i Kristiania. (Kristiania 1922). "Rapport fra den av Norsk Selskab for Psykisk Forskning nedsatte Kontrolkomité", Norsk Tidsskrift for Psykisk Forskning 1 (1921-22).

[130] Lewis Spence. (2003). *Encyclopedia of Occultism & Parapsychology.* Kessinger publishing. p. 399. ISBN 978-0766128156

[131] Eric Dingwall, Harry Price. (1922). *Revelations of a Spirit Medium.* Kegan Paul, Trench, Trübner & Co.

[132] Georgess McHargue. (1972). *Facts, Frauds, and Phantasms: A Survey of the Spiritualist Movement.* Doubleday. p. 158. ISBN 978-0385053051

[133] Carlos María de Heredia. (1923). *Spirit Hands, "ectoplasm," and Rubber Gloves.* Popular Mechanics. pp. 14-15

[134] Paul Tabori. (1961). *The Art of Folly.* Prentice-Hall International, Inc. pp. 178-179

[135] "Fraudulent Mediums". Lyceum Library.

[136] Julian Franklyn. (2003). *Dictionary of the Occult.* Kessinger Publishing. p. 228

[137] Harry Price. (1936). *Confessions of a Ghost-Hunter.* Putnam. p. 232

[138] Warren Jay Vinton. *The Famous Schneider Mediumship: A Critical Study of Alleged Supernormal Events.* No. 4 April 1927 in C. K. Ogden *Psyche: An Annual General and Linguistic Psychology.* 1920-1952 Routledge/Thoemmes Press, 1995.

[139] Further Tests of the Medium Rudi Schneider. (1934). Nature 134, 965-966.

[140] John Booth. (1986). *Psychic Paradoxes.* Prometheus Books. p. 8. ISBN 978-0879753580

[141] Bob Couttie. (1988). *Forbidden Knowledge: The Paranormal Paradox.* Lutterworth Press. pp. 104-105

[142] Brian Righi. (2008). *Ghosts, Apparitions and Poltergeists: An Exploration of the Supernatural through History.* Llewellyn Publications. Llewellyn Publications. p. 52. ISBN 978-0738713632 "One medium of the 1920s, Mina Crandon, became famous for producing ectoplasm during her sittings. At the height of the séance, she was even able to produce a tiny ectoplasmic hand from her navel, which waved about in the darkness. Her career ended when Harvard biologists were able to examine the tiny hand and found it to be nothing more than a carved piece of animal liver."

[143] E. Clephan Palmer. (2003). *The Riddle of Spiritualism.* Kessinger Publishing. pp. 35-39. ISBN 978-0766179318

[144] Lewis Spence. (1991). Encyclopedia of Occultism & Parapsychology. Gale Research Company. p. 1522. Massimo Polidoro. (2001). *Final Seance: The Strange Friendship Between Houdini and Conan Doyle.* Prometheus Books. p. 103. ISBN 978-1573928960

[145] Lewis Spence. (2003). *Encyclopedia of Occultism & Parapsychology.* Kessinger Publishing. p. 880

[146] Melvin Harris. (2003). *Investigating the Unexplained: Psychic Detectives, the Amityville Horror-mongers, Jack the Ripper, and Other Mysteries of the Paranormal.* Prometheus Books. p. 176. ISBN 978-1591021087

[147] Harry Price. (1931). *Regurgitation and the Duncan Mediumship.* (Bulletin I of the National Laboratory of Psychical Research, 120pp with 44 illustrations.)

[148] Marina Warner. (2008). *Phantasmagoria: Spirit Visions, Metaphors, and Media into the Twenty-first Century.* Oxford University Press. p. 299

[149] Jason Karl. (2007). *An Illustrated History of the Haunted World.* New Holland Publishers. p. 79

[150] Touching the Dead: Spooky Winnipeg by Tom Jokinen

[151] Joseph Jastrow. (1935). *Patience Worth: An Alter Ego* in *Wish and Wisdom: Episodes in the Vagaries of Belief.* D. Appleton-Century Company. pp. 78-92. Lyon Sprague de Camp. (1966). *Spirits, Stars, and Spells.* New York: Canaveral. p. 247. Robert Goldenson. (1973). *Mysteries of the Mind: The Drama of Human Behavior.* Doubleday. pp. 44-53. Milbourne Christopher. (1970). *ESP, Seers and Psychics.* New York: Crowell. pp. 128-129

[152] Patience Worth by Robert Todd Carroll

[153] Julian Franklyn. (2003). *A Survey of the Occult.* pp. 263-395. Kessinger Publishing. ISBN 978-0766130074

[154] M. Lamar Keene. (1997). *The Psychic Mafia.* Prometheus Books. p. 123. ISBN 978-1573921619

[155] Melvin Harris. (2003). *Investigating the Unexplained: Psychic Detectives, the Amityville Horror-mongers, Jack the Ripper, and Other Mysteries of the Paranormal.* Prometheus Books. p. 21. ISBN 978-0879753580

[156] Nandor Fodor. (1960). *The Haunted Mind: A Psychoanalyst Looks at the Supernatural.* Helix Press.

[157] Joe Nickell. (2005). *Camera Clues: A Handbook for Photographic Investigation.* The University Press of Kentucky. pp. 177-178. ISBN 978-0813191249

[158] John Booth. (1986). *Psychic Paradoxes.* Prometheus Books. pp. 15-16. ISBN 978-0879753580

[159] Joseph McCabe. (1920). *Is Spiritualism based on Fraud?: The Evidence Given by Sir A.C. Doyle and Others Drastically Examined.* London: Watts & CO. p. 126

[160] Melvin Harris. (2003). *Investigating the Unexplained: Psychic Detectives, the Amityville Horror-mongers, Jack the Ripper, and Other Mysteries of the Paranormal.* Prometheus Books. p. 22. ISBN 978-1591021087

[161] Julien Proskauer. (1946). *The Dead Do Not Talk.* Harper & Brothers. p. 94

[162] Sofie Lachapelle. (2011). *Investigating the Supernatural: From Spiritism and Occultism to Psychical Research and Metapsychics in France, 1853-1931.* Johns Hopkins University Press. pp. 144-145. ISBN 978-1421400136

[163] Ronald Edwin. (1955). *Clock Without Hands.* Sidgwick.

[164] Tony Cornell. (2002). *Investigating the Paranormal.* Helix Press New York. pp. 327-338. ISBN 978-0912328980

[165] Georgess McHargue. (1972). *Facts, Frauds, and Phantasms: A Survey of the Spiritualist Movement.* Doubleday. p. 250. ISBN 978-0385053051

[166] Eric Robertson Dodds. (2000). *Missing Persons: An Autobiography.* Oxford University Press. pp. 105-106. ISBN 978-0198120865

[167] Allen Spraggett, *The Unexplained,* (New York: New American Library, 1967).

[168] John Booth. (1986). *Psychic Paradoxes.* Prometheus Books. p. 148. ISBN 978-0879753580

[169] M. Lamar Keene. (1997). *The Psychic Mafia.* Prometheus Books. p 122. ISBN 978-1573921619 "A medium still riding high in England is Leslie Flint, famed as an exponent of direct voice. William Rauscher and Allen Spraggett, who attended a sitting Flint held in 1970 in New York, said that it was the most abysmal flop of any seance they had endured. All the spirit voices sounded exactly like the medium and displayed an incredible ignorance of nearly everything pertaining to the sitters. The "mediumship " was second-rate ventriloquism."

[170] Tim Madigan, David Goicoechea, Paul Kurtz. *Promethean Love: Paul Kurtz and the Humanistic Perspective on Love.* Cambridge Scholars Press. p. 293

[171] Ronald Pearsall. *Table-rappers: The Victorians and the Occult* The History Press Ltd; New Ed edition, 2004 ISBN 0-7509-3684-3

[172] Keene, Lamar (1997). *The Psychic Mafia.* Prometheus Books. ISBN 1-57392-161-0 (Republication of 1976 edition by St. Martin's Press.)

[173] Ian Wilson. (1989). *The After Death Experience.* William Morrow and Company. ISBN 978-0688080006

[174] Tony Cornell. (2002). *Investigating the Paranormal.* Helix Press New York. pp. 347-352. ISBN 978-0912328980

[175] Martin Gardner. (1988). *The New Age: Notes of a Fringe Watcher.* Prometheus Books. p. 175. ISBN 978-0879754327

[176] Melvin Harris. (2003). *Investigating the Unexplained: Psychic Detectives, the Amityville Horror-mongers, Jack the Ripper, and Other Mysteries of the Paranormal.* Prometheus Books. pp. 22-23. ISBN 978-1591021087

[177] Bob Couttie. (1988). *Forbidden Knowledge: The Paranormal Paradox.* Lutterworth Press. p. 24. ISBN 978-0718826864

[178] Joe Nickell. (2005). *Camera Clues: A Handbook for Photographic Investigation.* The University Press of Kentucky. p. 178. ISBN 978-0813191249

[179] Grossman, Wendy. (1991). *Dismissal is not disproof.* New Scientist. Vol. 130. Issue 1768, p. 53.

[180] Richard Wiseman. (1997). Chapter 3 *The Feilding Report: A Reconsideration.* In *Deception and Self-Deception: Investigating Psychics.* Prometheus Press. ISBN 1-57392-121-1

[181] Massimo Polidoro. (2003). *Secrets of the Psychics: Investigating Paranormal Claims.* Prometheus Books. pp. 65-95. ISBN 978-1591020868

[182] Colin Fry an Evaluation

[183] Massimo Polidoro. (2003). *Secrets of the Psychics: Investigating Paranormal Claims.* Prometheus Books. pp. 168-176. ISBN 978-1591020868

[184] "The Scole Experiment: Said to be the best evidence yet for the afterlife -- but how good is that evidence?". Skeptoid. 2009-11-10. Retrieved 2011-10-30.

[185] The VERITAS Research Program of the Laboratory for Advances in Consciousness and Health in the Department of Psychology at the University of Arizona

[186] newsnet5.com

[187] *The Truth about Medium* by Gary E. Schwartz, Ph. D., with William L. Simon, Hampton Books, 2005, page 119

[188] Book Review by Robert T. Carroll

[189] Gary Schwartz's Subjective Evaluation of Mediums: Veritas or Wishful Thinking by Robert Todd Carroll

[190] Hyman, Ray (Jan–Feb 2003). "How Not to Test Mediums: Critiquing the Afterlife Experiments". Skeptical Inquirer Magazine. Retrieved 2012-05-21.

[191] Terence Hines. (2003). *Pseudoscience and the Paranormal.* Prometheus Books. pp. 56-64. ISBN 978-1573929790

[192] O'Keeffe, Ciaran (May 2005). "Testing Alleged Mediumship: Methods and Results". British Journal of Psychology. doi:10.1348/000712605X36361. ISSN 0007-1269.

[193] Aykroyd, Peter. and Nart, Angela. (2009). *A History of Ghosts: the True Story of Seances, Mediums, Ghosts, and Ghostbusters.* Rodale. p. 216. ISBN 978-1605298757

[194] Geraldo at Large show, October 6, 2007

[195] "Jury Convicts Defendant in $25 Million Fraud Scheme" (Press release). Southern District of Florida, US Attorney's Office, US Department of Justice. 2013-09-26. Retrieved 2013-10-10.

[196] Musgrave, Jane (2013-09-27). "Psychic convicted on all fraud counts". *The Palm Beach Post* **105** (171) (First ed.). p. 1.

[197] Vasquez, Michael (2011-08-16). "Psychic scam a $40 million Fort Lauderdale - family affair, feds allege - A Fort Lauderdale family spent the last 20 years raking in millions as fake psychics, prosecutors allege in a newly unsealed indictment". *The Miami Herald.* – via NewsBank (subscription required) .

[198] J. Gordon Melton. (2007). *The Encyclopedia of Religious Phenomena.* Visible Ink Press. p. 96. ISBN 978-1578592098

[199] "Investigative Files: John Edward: Hustling the Bereaved". CSI. Nov–Dec 2001. Retrieved 2011-05-12.

[200] Shermer, Michael. "Deconstructing the Dead, "Crossing over" to expose the tricks of popular spirit mediums". *August 2001.* Scientific American. Retrieved 24 December 2011.

[201] "James Randi's Swift - April 21, 2006". Randi.org. Retrieved 2012-01-03.

[202] Woliver, Robbie (July 16, 2000). "An Encounter With a Television Psychic". *The New York Times.* Retrieved 24 December 2011.

[203] Robert T. Carroll. Subjective validation. // The Skeptic's Dictionary.

[204] Spiritualism (religion). www.britannica.com.

39.9   Further reading

- Ruth Brandon. (1983). *The Spiritualists: The Passion for the Occult in the Nineteenth and Twentieth Centuries.* Alfred E. Knopf. ISBN 978-0394527406

- Edward Clodd. (1917). *The Question: A Brief History and Examination of Modern Spiritualism.* Grant Richards, London.

- Stuart Cumberland. (1919). *Spiritualism: The Inside Truth.* London: Odhams.

- Joseph Dunninger. (1935). *Inside the Medium's Cabinet.* New York, D. Kemp and Company.

- Willis Dutcher. (1922). *On the Other Side of the Footlights: An Expose of Routines, Apparatus and Deceptions Resorted to by Mediums, Clairvoyants, Fortune Tellers and Crystal Gazers in Deluding the Public.* Berlin, WI: Heaney Magic.

- Walter Mann. (1919). *The Follies and Frauds of Spiritualism.* Rationalist Association. London: Watts & Co.

- Joseph McCabe. (1920). *Scientific Men and Spiritualism: A Skeptic's Analysis.* The Living Age. June 12. pp. 652–657. A skeptical look at SPR members who had supported Spiritualism, concludes they were duped by fraudulent mediums.

- Joseph McCabe. (1920). *Is Spiritualism Based On Fraud? The Evidence Given By Sir A. C. Doyle and Others Drastically Examined.* London: Watts & Co.

- Georgess McHargue. (1972). *Facts, Frauds, and Phantasms: A Survey of the Spiritualist Movement.* Doubleday. ISBN 978-0385053051

- Alex Owen. (2004). *The Darkened Room: Women, Power, and Spiritualism in Late Victorian England.* University Of Chicago Press. ISBN 978-0226642055

- Frank Podmore. (1911). *The Newer Spiritualism.* Henry Holt and Company.

- Massimo Polidoro. (2003). *Secrets of the Psychics: Investigating Paranormal Claims.* Prometheus Books. ISBN 978-1591020868

- Harry Price and Eric Dingwall. (1975). *Revelations of a Spirit Medium.* Arno Press. Reprint of 1891 edition by Charles F. Pidgeon. This rare, overlooked, and forgotten, book gives the "insider's knowledge" of 19th century deceptions.

- Joseph Rinn. (1950). *Sixty Years Of Psychical Research: Houdini And I Among The Spiritualists.* Truth Seeker.

- Chung Ling Soo. (1898). *Spirit Slate Writing and Kindred Phenomena. Munn & Company.*

- Richard Wiseman. (1997). *Deception & Self-Deception: Investigating Psychics.* Prometheus Books. ISBN 978-1573921213

39.10 External links

- Houdini v. The Blond Witch of Lime Street: A Historical Lesson in Skepticism - Massimo Polidoro

- How to Have a Séance: Tricks of the Fraudulent Mediums

- John Edward: Hustling the Bereaved - Joe Nickell

- Mediumship - Skeptic's Dictionary

- The 'Medium' Is Not the Messenger - James Randi

- Tricks of Fake Mediums - Harry Houdini

- Media related to Mediumship at Wikimedia Commons

- The dictionary definition of Mediumship at Wiktionary

39.11   Text and image sources, contributors, and licenses

39.11.1   Text

- **Neurotheology** *Source:* https://en.wikipedia.org/wiki/Neurotheology?oldid=707055211 *Contributors:* AxelBoldt, Vaughan, Paul A, Tregoweth, Jeandré du Toit, Charles Matthews, Altenmann, GreatWhiteNortherner, Cobaltbluetony, Carl Smotricz, Ojl, Mateuszica, Loremaster, Jack-davinci, FT2, Pjacobi, Bender235, Violetriga, Pietzsche, Kghose, Nectarflowed, Viriditas, I9Q79oL78KiL0QTFHgyc, Kensai, Famousdog, Jooyoonchung, Calton, Rtmyers, Memenen, Woohookitty, YHoshua, GregorB, Eras-mus, Porcher, Rjwilmsi, Josiah Rowe, AI, Ewlyahoocom, SteveBaker, Windharp, Gareth E. Kegg, GangofOne, Satanael, YurikBot, Flo98, A314268, Welsh, Epipelagic, Morgan Leigh, GeoffCapp, Varano, Tomisti, Wknight94, Igiffin, Emijrp, Harabanar, Whouk, NeilN, GrinBot~enwiki, Snottily, Yakudza, SmackBot, Pgk, Jtneill, Provelt, Portillo, Chris the speller, Stevenwagner, Solidusspriggan, Seamasmac, SheeEttin, Jacob Poon, Cybercobra, "alyosha", Dreadstar, BullRangifer, JorisvS, Makyen, Meco, Doczilla, Texas Dervish, Jodie44, Coffee Atoms, Nydas, Alankroeger, George100, Harold f, Shirahadasha, Cm-drObot, Insanephantom, Matthew Auger, Wargamer, Khatru2, Raoul NK, Mattisse, Keraunos, Headbomb, Sobreira, Kathovo, Cstreet, Colin MacLaurin, Mabim2002, Iris Vin, Researchfellow, Dekimasu, Swpb, Tonyfaull, Theroadislong, JaGa, CFCF, Maurice Carbonaro, Shawn in Montreal, CoreTechX, Rosenkreutz~enwiki, VolkovBot, Hamsaysitadakimasu, Guillaume2303, Loki~enwiki, Anarkistangel, EnviroGranny, Northfox, StAnselm, Dragondreams, Jojalozzo, Rjd0060, Bmlord, Editor2020, Asrghasrhiojadrhr, Addbot, Tassedethe, Lightbot, OlEnglish, Yobot, K2709, AnomieBOT, Mauro Lanari, Citation bot, Jburlinson, Jonesey95, Standardfact, Kered77, Kadilegho, MrX, RjwilmsiBot, Ster-rettc, Waithought, AriZonaRosa, Adrian-from-london, ChuispastonBot, Miradre, Neurorel, Doctor Ruud, Hamlet 2010a, Helpful Pixie Bot, Voyal, Pastorjamesmiller, Rendicase, Kid 007, Joshua Jonathan, BattyBot, Hypotha7, Ksirok, ElaineF423, BayBall2398, Fixuture, Monkbot, Robertlee79, Jerodlycett, Viliasenova and Anonymous: 97

- **Nervous system** *Source:* https://en.wikipedia.org/wiki/Nervous_system?oldid=708666176 *Contributors:* 0, Marj Tiefert, Mav, Graham Chap-man, SimonP, Peterlin~enwiki, Tox~enwiki, Bdesham, Lir, D, Mgmei, Lexor, Kku, Ixfd64, Karada, 168..., Mdebets, Ronz, Theresa knott, Snoyes, CatherineMunro, Angela, Statkit1, Salsa Shark, Glenn, Andres, Raven in Orbit, Finlay McWalter, Jeffq, Robbot, Moriori, May-ooranathan, Sylvienguyen, ToyAnh, Tonyng84, Alimon, Ducducpham, Hadal, Wikibot, Lupo, Diberri, Supapuerco, Dina, Marc Venot, Giftlite, Ævar Arnfjörð Bjarmason, Everyking, Bensaccount, Bird, Jfdwolff, Skagedal, Yekrats, Jackol, Erich gasboy, Knutux, SURIV, Quadell, Antan-drus, OverlordQ, PFHLai, Sayeth, Creidieki, Jh51681, Adashiel, Grunt, Safety Cap, Jacooks, Mike Rosoft, Discospinster, Rich Farmbrough, LindsayH, Ivan Bajlo, Jayc, Dbachmann, Bender235, Kaisershatner, Dpotter, MBisanz, Cedders, Lankiveil, Bobo192, Icut4you, Smalljim, Evolauxia, Shenme, Arcadian, Jag123, Chirag, La goutte de pluie, Jojit fb, Microtony, Daf, Benbread, Mdd, HasharBot~enwiki, Jumbuck, Storm Rider, Red Winged Duck, Alansohn, Matani2005~enwiki, Polarscribe, Civvi~enwiki, Penwhale, Andrewpmk, Algorhythm~enwiki, Walkerma, Hu, Snowolf, PaePae, Wtmitchell, Danaman5, Dirac1933, Sciurinæ, Kusma, Carlos Quesada, Stepheno, RyanGerbil10, Omnist, Stemonitis, George Hernandez, Mel Etitis, Woohookitty, TigerShark, Mathmo, Myleslong, Kurzon, Scjessey, Rend~enwiki, MONGO, Tabletop, Kaur-Jmeb, Bennetto, Grika, Bluemoose, SCEhardt, Isnow, TheAlphaWolf, MarcoTolo, Dysepsion, Mandarax, Magister Mathematicae, FreplySpang, Mendaliv, Chenxlee, Edison, Canderson7, Sjö, Rjwilmsi, Jake Wartenberg, Bill37212, Tawker, The wub, Bhadani, DoubleBlue, Yamamoto Ichiro, Revo331, FlaBot, Cless Alvein, Tordail, Latka, Winhunter, Nihiltres, Vsion, Nivix, Fragglet, RexNL, Gurch, ChongDae, Isuru~enwiki, Preslethe, King of Hearts, DVdm, WillMcC, Antiuser, Tone, Loco830, YurikBot, Wavelength, Themepark, Pip2andahalf, Phantomsteve, Reo On, Spaully, Hydrargyrum, Stephenb, Wimt, NawlinWiki, A314268, Dysmorodrepanis~enwiki, Wiki alf, Bachrach44, Howcheng, Irishguy, Daniel Mietchen, Darkmeerkat, Ruhrfisch, Moe Epsilon, Mlouns, Zzzzzzus, Alex43223, Epipelagic, JPMcGrath, Dbfirs, Bota47, Juicy fish-eye, Wknight94, Kelovy, 21655, Knotnic, Theda, Closedmouth, Arthur Rubin, Josh3580, Jesushaces, Dspradau, JoanneB, Rto, CopyEditing-Gal, Smurrayinchester, Willtron, Junglecat, SkerHawx, CIreland, Bibliomaniac15, NickelShoe, Luk, SpLoT, TravisTX, Joshbuddy, SmackBot, Bomac, Delldot, Hardyplants, Frymaster, RobotJcb, Gaff, Xaosflux, Yamaguchi⟦?⟧, Skizzik, Bluebot, Quinsareth, Gonzalo84, Persian Poet Gal, Master of Puppets, Fuzzform, Stellar-TO, Cross101020, SchfiftyThree, RayAYang, Baa, DHN-bot~enwiki, Darth Panda, Zachorious, De-thme0w, Can't sleep, clown will eat me, Joerite, Shalom Yechiel, Onorem, Snowmanradio, Addshore, Jmlk17, Flyguy649, Jaimie Henry, Nakon, Fullstop, T-borg, Dreadstar, KeithB, Shushruth, Where, Kukini, Clicketyclack, Thejerm, Bcasterline, Petr Kopač, Wvbailey, Ascend, Shlomke, Benesch, IronGargoyle, Extremophile, Ben Moore, Stwalkerster, Optimale, Mr Stephen, Dicklyon, Waggers, Eridani, Mets501, RichardF, EEP-ROM Eagle, David Souther, BranStark, Fan-1967, ILovePlankton, Iridescent, Kaarel, Wjejskenewr, Igoldste, Cbrown1023, Tony Fox, Cap-italR, Courcelles, Tawkerbot2, Dlohcierekim, Filelakeshoe, Lahiru k, DeEditor, MightyWarrior, JForget, Dycedarg, Halo89, Benwildeboer, Dgw, ShelfSkewed, MarsRover, Moreschi, Maxxicum, HalJor, Ryan, Alston2, Gogo Dodo, Anthonyhcole, JFreeman, Corpx, A Softer Answer, Skittleys, Clovis Sangrail, Christian75, DumbBOT, FastLizard4, JodyB, Vanished User jdksfajlasd, UberScienceNerd, DJBullfish, Epbr123, Cocoma, N5iln, 24fan24, Mojo Hand, Shadow Ninja, Mungomba, Headbomb, Marek69, John254, James086, Tellyaddict, TXiKi, FLarsen, InfernalPanda, CharlotteWebb, Natalie Erin, Dzubint, AntiVandalBot, Luna Santin, Seaphoto, Prolog, Jj137, TimVickers, LibLord, Danger, Chill doubt, BaxterG4, The man stephen, Gökhan, Joehall45, JAnDbot, Dan D. Ric, D99figge, Barek, Andonic, M@RIX, J-stan, Kirrages, LittleOldMe, Acroterion, Bencherlite, Pakkunthedog, Connormah, Bongwarrior, VoABot II, Crimsonseiko, Think outside the box, Rivertorch, Soulbot, Artlondon, Avicennasis, Faustnh, Animum, Mtd2006, 28421u2232nfenfcenc, Allstarecho, User A1, DerHexer, JaGa, Edward321, Khalid Mahmood, KenyaSong, TheRanger, Robin S, Erpbridge, Myrkkyhammas, The freddinator, MartinBot, BetBot~enwiki, NAHID, Nikpa-pag, Rettetast, Keith D, Tbone55, Autocratique, CommonsDelinker, AlexiusHoratius, Nono64, Frogdogz, PrestonH, 3dscience, Erkan Yilmaz, Rpclod, J.delanoy, Pharaoh of the Wizards, Trusilver, Bogey97, Numbo3, Peter Chastain, NightFalcon90909, Headinthedoor, StonedChip-munk, Extransit, Reedy Bot, Leif Halvorsen, Wandering Ghost, It Is Me Here, Katalaveno, Nemo bis, Jamesdivine, Bailo26, Mikael Häggström, David tipton, Gurchzilla, Jiu9, AntiSpamBot, Berserkerz Crit, LittleHow, NewEnglandYankee, SriMesh, Jimbodawg, Shshshsh, Juliancolton, Peepeedia, Cometstyles, Rymano, U.S.A.U.S.A.U.S.A., Treisijs, Bonadea, Doctoroxenbriery, Ja 62, Useight, Vinsfan368, JohnDoe0007, Much-clag, Idioma-bot, Xnuala, Wikieditor06, Boijunk, X!, Zougloub~enwiki, Deor, VolkovBot, CWii, ABF, Tbill92, Mrh30, Indubitably, Fences and windows, Joe5150, The All-Traq, Randomator, Philip Trueman, PNG crusade bot, TXiKiBoT, Oshwah, Azelor, Antoni Barau, Vipinhari, Captain Courageous, Free2live2104, Anonymous Dissident, Asianguy48, East of Lyra, Qxz, Naohiro19 revertvandal, Kuzman17, Dendodge, Martin451, JhsBot, Jackfork, LeaveSleaves, DoktorDec, Terryfying Terry Cooper, FFMG, Jfryan, Madhero88, Billgordon1099, Redacteur, Lova Falk, AgentCDE, Martin-Med, Temporaluser, Insanity Incarnate, Lew Zealand XIV, Legoktm, 26394march, Joethemanjoe, SieBot, Baddboy33, AC1, Tresiden, Tiddly Tom, Caulde, Scarian, SheepNotGoats, Cr3ation, Winchelsea, Dawn Bard, Caltas, Triwbe, Flyer22 Reborn, Tiptoety, Belinrahs, Oda Mari, Bookermorgan, Thelandof12, Wombatcat, Prestonmag, Oxymoron83, KoshVorlon, Conor Cliffe, Kudret abi, Svick, Stat-icGull, Mike2vil, Anchor Link Bot, Jacob.jose, Derfman24, Sean.hoyland, Mygerardromance, Heds, Gashane, Dabomb87, Indiaxxx manu,

GoingBatty, Hamedvahid, TuneyLoon, Wikipelli, Dooby Doo11, PatZilla13, Letsbeseriousguys, Ilikecake69, Mcmatter, Scythia, Cincybluffa, ClueBot NG, Rhain, Frietjes, Widr, JordoCo, North Atlanticist Usonian, Helpful Pixie Bot, Lionhead99, Jeraphine Gryphon, PhnomPencil, MusikAnimal, NukeofEarl, Androideditor, Adsad613, Mariraja2007, Forestfrolic, Mthoodhood, Johnjonesjr, MrBill3, Peace&Honesty, Mr. Guye, Aymankamelwiki, Lugia2453, Bidhan Singh, Jamesx12345, Dynomynoploo, Nessabug714, Howicus, Way2veers, Midroadstep, YiFei-Bot, Ginsuloft, Drcrazy102, Dwlover16, Fawnyyy, Monkbot, Jaz.C1234, Amortias, Mintyr2d2, BrianPansky, SuperWhoLock1967, Amymck 17, Jensen Quackles, Zgdgdhhdhe, Sarr Cat, Wailbinds7,8, Misshatt, UBI-et-ORBI, SocraticOath, Jerodlycett, Kayleighhjoness, KasparBot, Future Kick, Supfamiz, Satlinwillrise, Maureendepresident, Okdamn, Lillyfuzzy, CLCStudent, Danielaxoxlioxxoxo, Ferxthecat, GSS-1987, PhanSosTrash, Poopsnozle, Hehehefelicaia, Someone.XXXXXX, Satancriesallthetime, Phandomrules, Tel yari, SimSkeptic and Anonymous: 476

- **Religious experience** *Source:* https://en.wikipedia.org/wiki/Religious_experience?oldid=715646658 *Contributors:* Michael Hardy, Ahoerstemeier, Dimadick, Ashley Y, Blainster, Bradeos Graphon, Mateuszica, Sonjaaa, Jiy, Rich Farmbrough, Bender235, Closeapple, Stesmo, Troels Nybo~enwiki, Amorymeltzer, Pprevos~enwiki, Graham87, BD2412, Sjakkalle, Rjwilmsi, Pariah, TheRingess, Dangerous Angel, Heah, Bgwhite, RussBot, Tyenkrovy, Flo98, NawlinWiki, Bruguiea, GeoffCapp, Yeltensic42, Sardanaphalus, Veinor, SmackBot, Amatire, WilyD, Yamaguchi⁇⁇, Gilliam, Ohnoitsjamie, TimBentley, Daqu, Dreadstar, Hgilbert, Ixnayonthetimmay, CPMcE, Shadowlynk, A. Parrot, Iridescent, CuteWombat, Adriatikus, CmdrObot, Amalas, Neelix, Gregbard, Peterdjones, Gogo Dodo, Epbr123, Rsage, Ppaterson, Towopedia, NBeale, Aleksandros~enwiki, Matthew Fennell, Felix116, Magioladitis, Da baum, Bigdan201, Fletcher-Cook, Nposs, Lyonscc, JaGa, CliffC, CommonsDelinker, Tgeairn, AstroHurricane001, Adavidb, Moshe szweizer, Interestedindividual, DadaNeem, A. Ben-Shema, Moonksy29, Remi0o, VolkovBot, Athanasius28, ACEOREVIVED, Tommytocker, AlleborgoBot, StAnselm, Firefly322, ImageRemovalBot, MenoBot, Happynoodleboycey, ClueBot, Epsilon60198, TBRoberts, Jhananda, SchreiberBike, SoxBot III, Editor2020, Cminard, WikHead, Wordwebber, Addbot, Metagignosko, Tengu800, Verdeneon, Damiens.rf, PlankBot, Yobot, Legobot II, Samtar, K2709, AnomieBOT, Koliat, Jim1138, Cacala17, Ulric1313, Flewis, Materialscientist, 90 Auto, Citation bot, Xqbot, DSisyphBot, HRichman101, ReneVenegas95, Pinethicket, Jonesey95, Obscurasky, Xanx~enwiki, Kered77, An Anonymous Visitor, GoingBatty, ZéroBot, Sivasfriend, H3llBot, K kisses, Makecat, Sri0soma, Adaptions, Amplifying Life, ClueBot NG, Ambkj123, Dream of Nyx, K6cdb, Widr, Helpful Pixie Bot, BG19bot, Sri0soma1, Dpn saha, CitationCleanerBot, Joshua Jonathan, Croweml11, Iamtheyorkiemom, Khazar2, Nathanielfirst, Rleung12, Waqob, Dexbot, Happyseeu, Ispiritualawakening, Newthoughts34, Tentinator, JimRenge, AddWittyNameHere, Yellowmellow1, Monkbot, Nashe2000, AmbiVictoria and Anonymous: 104

- **Cognitive neuroscience** *Source:* https://en.wikipedia.org/wiki/Cognitive_neuroscience?oldid=707506366 *Contributors:* The Anome, Michael Hardy, Samw, Sunray, Washington irving, Dan aka jack, Rdsmith4, APH, Guppyfinsoup, Rich Farmbrough, Hippojazz, Kndiaye, Liberatus, Femto, Johnkarp, 4v4l0n42, Heida Maria, MIT Trekkie, Loxley~enwiki, Woohookitty, Dolfrog, Graham87, Qwertyus, Porcher, Zath42, RussBot, Stephenb, Gaius Cornelius, Salsb, Luuknam, A314268, Moe Epsilon, Sallison, Action potential, Mike Dillon, Arthur Rubin, AFdeCH, Sardanaphalus, SmackBot, InvictaHOG, Provelt, Ohnoitsjamie, BrotherGeorge, David Ludwig, Teemu08, Bluebot, Rogermw, Danielkueh, Cleanwiki, EPM, Suidafrikaan, Clicketyclack, Goodnightmush, Skapur, Aeternus, IvanLanin, Blehfu, Cogpsych, Jakelove, Penbat, Mattisse, Letranova, Epbr123, Ur land, Dmitri Lytov, Edhubbard, Darklilac, Cooper24, Soulbot, Sluox, Hifrommike65, WhatamIdoing, B9 hummingbird hovering, Smilingsuzy, Kpmiyapuram, Michael Daly, Splatek, Kenneth M Burke, Steel1943, TXiKiBoT, Noticket, Fyo, Wingedsubmariner, Planetnewbie, Lova Falk, Nwh5305, Zonuleofzinn, SieBot, JackSchmidt, Gordonofcartoon, Michaelhyphenpaul, Martarius, Sfan00 IMG, Niceguyedc, ChandlerMapBot, Sun Creator, XLinkBot, Ostracon, Brainmetric, Addbot, Adrian CZ, Fgnievinski, Looie496, Oakbell, AndersBot, Lightbot, Ettrig, Legobot, Chardar, Luckas-bot, Yobot, Ptbotgourou, Finereach, AnomieBOT, Rubinbot, Rjanag, LMBM2012, Citation bot, Xqbot, Anna Frodesiak, Aaron Kauppi, MultiPoly, FrescoBot, Dead goddess, I dream of horses, Acercyc, Kora09, EmausBot, Gcastellanos, Mark344, Octagon32, Steffenwerner, Access Denied, ChuispastonBot, ClueBot NG, Ronbo75, Rezabot, Amnerispgh, Titodutta, Criener, BG19bot, PhnomPencil, CitationCleanerBot, Sethlee003, Sam48823, MathewTownsend, Karol Alexandre, Gowerus, Ray.MacNeil, Iiropjaaskelainen, Elizabetho93, Bryn the human, Justincharnock, Lizia7, Brookscarla, Monkbot, SkateTier, Granta91, Refulgir, Fled From Nowhere and Anonymous: 113

- **Cognitive science of religion** *Source:* https://en.wikipedia.org/wiki/Cognitive_science_of_religion?oldid=718018727 *Contributors:* The Anome, William M. Connolley, Dimadick, Bearcat, David Gerard, Discospinster, DarTar, GregorB, Bobby1011, Muntuwandi, Welsh, Malcolma, SmackBot, Bpdlr, Snori, Rigadoun, Tktktk, Doczilla, Alaibot, Thijs!bot, Cjdowdeswell, Huanohk, David Couch, WereSpielChequers, Jalanb, Joelmort, Podzemnik, Mild Bill Hiccup, DragonBot, Tenellep, Editor2020, Neocultural, Addbot, Wingspeed, Proxima Centauri, Neapoli, Luckas-bot, Yobot, Bunnyhop11, AmeliorationBot, DOUG587, AnomieBOT, Shambalala, Materialscientist, Crzer07, AWElmwood, Norenzayan, FrescoBot, Allinthebrain, Machine Elf 1735, Codwiki, AvicAWB, Atrivo, Apollodisciple, K.Talmont, Zakhalesh, Helpful Pixie Bot, Joshua Jonathan, Académica Orientālis, Fixuture, Bookworm729, Jonntyler, HelenDeC, Djasonslone and Anonymous: 40

- **Psychology of religion** *Source:* https://en.wikipedia.org/wiki/Psychology_of_religion?oldid=714851334 *Contributors:* Fnielsen, Edward, Michael Hardy, Skysmith, Ahoerstemeier, Irmgard, Andres, Dcoetzee, Furrykef, Geraki, Stormie, Johnleemk, Lumos3, Goethean, Ashley Y, Markewilliams, Rursus, Blainster, Tom harrison, Fastfission, Bfinn, Volition, Kudz75, Andycjp, Sonjaaa, Piotrus, Sharavanabhava, Didactohedron, Lacrimosus, RevRagnarok, Sysy, Discospinster, Vsmith, LindsayH, Antaeus Feldspar, Bender235, ESkog, Jonathanischoice, Wareh, Cmdrjameson, Maureen, Famousdog, Tgr, MPerel, Merope, Munchkinguy, Calton, Mac Davis, Gpvos, Gmaxwell, Woohookitty, Wayward, Rjwilmsi, Zbxgscqf, Rafaelamonteiro80, AI, Paul foord, RussBot, Pippo2001, Icarus3, Pigman, Chris Capoccia, DanMS, SluggoOne, Ansell, Flo98, Sanguinity, Muntuwandi, Welsh, Cardamom, Todfox, Craigkbryant, Tomisti, Igiffin, Denisutku, Tevildo, Barry Wells, West Virginian, Sardanaphalus, SmackBot, Mcourtne199, Jtsang, Nihonjoe, Herostratus, DCDuring, Jtneill, Brossow, Edgar181, Chris the speller, Bluebot, TimBentley, DoctorW, Hoof Hearted, Hgilbert, DA3N, Scientizzle, A. Carl, Tim bates, Comicist, Meco, Doczilla, Scorpios, Aeternus, ACEO, Fming, CmdrObot, Dgw, Penbat, Kozuch, Iss246, Mattisse, Mbolo, Wikid77, Marek69, AstroFloyd, Qa Plar, Astavats, Wtfiv, Rothorpe, SiobhanHansa, Magioladitis, Alexander Domanda, Mbarbier, ***Ria777, Tonyfaull, Presearch, Adrian J. Hunter, JaGa, Edward321, GoodBooksMelbourne, CommonsDelinker, Jarhed, Tgeairn, Maurice Carbonaro, Nigholith, Memestream, Keeganwade, Belovedfreak, JoshuaEyer, Master shepherd, Pastordavid, Ingram, Xnuala, Cosmic Latte, Wassermann~enwiki, Nuloy, ACEOREVIVED, Burntsauce, Statesman 88, SieBot, Coastside, Caltas, ConfuciusOrnis, RucasHost, Flyer22 Reborn, Hello71, Fratrep, Ptr123, Eebahgum, ClueBot, Djacnov~enwiki, Matt434, Sting au, TBRoberts, AWCBoris, Tedlau, Apparition11, Editor2020, Jbeans, Addbot, DOI bot, SamatBot, Tassedethe, Lightbot, Neapoli, Luckas-bot, Yobot, Andersole, AnomieBOT, Tryptofish, Rubinbot, Jim1138, Cacala17, Citation bot, ArthurBot, Xqbot, Sionus, Nasnema, Makeswell, Crzer07, GrouchoBot, HRichman101, Tracyv811, FrescoBot, Citation bot 1, I dream of horses, Adlerbot, LittleWink, Canhelp, Obiwankinobi, Trappist the monk, Jonkerz, Theo10011, RjwilmsiBot, Tesseract2, EmausBot, Metacog, ZéroBot, Flies 1,

Alan347, Psych88, Cobaltcigs, Urbanco, TheAckademie, ClueBot NG, Dfarrell07, Snotbot, BL53J36, Helpful Pixie Bot, BG19bot, The Banner Turbo, PhnomPencil, Smcg8374, Joshua Jonathan, Mindheartinstitute, North911, Dobrich, Reiss7, Teddykra, CarlS23, Sapien Indamaze, Me, Myself, and I are Here, Lemnaminor, Newthoughts34, Sophia's aid, Wonkdonkhawk, Anrnusna, Ghan.lmurphy, Monkbot, Hubecos, Mercy-CAT211, Madisonwhite12, BlasianlovesVU, Ebisabeti, Chesivoirzr, Dr Graham PhD, Livetoedit1123, RMOxtoby, Davidrahat and Anonymous: 124

- **Altered state of consciousness** *Source:* https://en.wikipedia.org/wiki/Altered_state_of_consciousness?oldid=717319474 *Contributors:* Fubar Obfusco, Kwertii, Skysmith, Tregoweth, Angela, Cimon Avaro, Thseamon, Wikiborg, Pedant17, Maximus Rex, Martinphi, Chris Rodgers, PuzzletChung, Twang, Robbot, RedWolf, Goethean, Altenmann, Naddy, Andries, Kenny sh, Sonjaaa, Loremaster, Karol Langner, Lehi, Pie4all88, Florian Blaschke, Evice, El C, Skywalker, Arcadian, JYolkowski, Hu, Rebroad, SteinbDJ, Agguarx, Ceyockey, Loxley~enwiki, Alrik Fassbauer, Sparkit, BD2412, Johann Gambolputty~enwiki, Zoz, Rjwilmsi, TheRingess, Heah, Diza, DVdm, Flo98, Ihope127, Yeshua2000, Jessemerriman, DomenicDenicola, Athana, Light current, RDF, Arthur Rubin, NickelShoe, SmackBot, Prototime, Jimbo787, Portillo, Chris the speller, A. B., Zachorious, DJHasis, Prometheuspan, Lapaz, Scientizzle, Acitrano, Drwier, JorisvS, Lapiseyed, J freeman, Comicist, RichardF, Aeternus, R~enwiki, Vanisaac, Ibadibam, Spiritualheart, Gregbard, Jefchip, Void main, Lindsay658, Thijs!bot, Elaron, Headbomb, Doc pato, Neko18, Viniciuscb, AbstractClass, ReverendG, Rehnn83, Leuqarte, The Transhumanist, Batmagoo, Albany NY, Freshacconci, Bongwarrior, Reillyd, WLU, Pikolas, B9 hummingbird hovering, AstroHurricane001, AltiusBimm, TimofKingsland, Floaterfluss, NewEnglandYankee, Red Thrush, Squids and Chips, Hominidx, Dom Kaos, XVertigox, Carlvincent, IPSOS, Davin, Richwil, Lova Falk, Prodigyhk, Tiddly Tom, GreyTwilight, Martarius, TBRoberts, Obe19900, Jhananda, Thingg, JDPhD, Wednesday Next, XLinkBot, Indu, Nishmeh, Wordwebber, WikiDao, Monfornot, Q Valda, Addbot, CatAnna, Zeekythingy, FCSundae, Quercus solaris, OlEnglish, Yobot, K2709, AnomieBOT, Tryptofish, Citation bot, Omnipaedista, PeaceLoveHarmony, Aaron Kauppi, Custoo, Amit.amin, ServngU2, Citation bot 1, GreenZeb, NeuroWikiTyk, Gegik, Diannaa, EmausBot, John of Reading, Racerx11, GoingBatty, TheLastWordSword, Amitbalani, Demonkoryu, Urbanco, Sailsbystars, Senator2029, ClueBot NG, Евгений Пустошкин, MerlIwBot, Helpful Pixie Bot, Jeraphine Gryphon, BG19bot, Juro2351, Zimmygirl7, Smcg8374, Ohrnwuzler, Zephyr22, Joshua Jonathan, MrBill3, Ann112358, Madeleined2, ChrisGualtieri, Leonworld, Nusaybah, Dexbot, Geremy.Hebert, Makikobold, New worl, YiFeiBot, Jghapher, Kahtar, WPGA2345, Ithinkicahn, Vms77, Ybagby, Mayrapm128, Mjpolo15, OGanja, Monkbot, Kittenmittonz69, Gomail25, Johanna, Sizeofint, ErrorFixer007, Jerodlycett, Prolumbo, UY4Xe8VM5VYxaQQ, Sky of Burma and Anonymous: 180

- **Out-of-body experience** *Source:* https://en.wikipedia.org/wiki/Out-of-body_experience?oldid=713195306 *Contributors:* Mav, Tarquin, Lightning~enwiki, D, Chas zzz brown, Michael Hardy, Zocky, Spartacan, Liftarn, Wapcaplet, Lament, Kistaro, CesarB, TUF-KAT, Julesd, Timwi, Dino, Dysprosia, Wik, Haukurth, Martinphi, Chris Rodgers, Johnleemk, Robbot, Fredrik, Der Eberswalder, Doidimais Brasil, Hadal, JamesM-Lane, Tom harrison, Ich, Everyking, Chowbok, Nova77, Beland, WhiteDragon, PDH, Saucepan, Sam Hocevar, Aerion, JulieADriver, Gary D, Mrdectol, Cyprus2k1, SYSS Mouse, D6, NightMonkey, Freakofnurture, Discospinster, Rich Farmbrough, NeuronExMachina, Jordancpeterson, DS1953, Wfisher, Causa sui, Skywalker, Njyoder, Cayte, Fqsik, Forteanajones, Vanished user 19794758563875, Solar, Pearle, Hawol, Fbd, Gary, Mduvekot, Ben davison, Efortune, Hdeasy, DreamGuy, Fivetrees, Wtmitchell, Drat, Netkinetic, Ceyockey, Rodii, Mel Etitis, Havermayer, LOL, Marc K, GregorB, SCEhardt, Roysfree, Obe1989, Paxsimius, Mandarax, Ashmoo, Sparkit, BD2412, Zoz, Josh Parris, Funkymuskrat, Rjwilmsi, Jiohdi, Heah, NeonMerlin, Krash, Reinis, Dionyseus, Lsuff, Ewlyahoocom, Gurch, Choess, Consumed Crustacean, Reediewes, Kazuba, Visor, Benlisquare, DVdm, Bgwhite, YurikBot, RobotE, Pip2andahalf, Gaius Cornelius, CambridgeBayWeather, Garrick92, Yahya Abdal-Aziz, Ms2ger, Ronyclau, LoRa mei, 2over0, C h fleming, Open2universe, TheMadBaron, Teiladnam, Closedmouth, Brina700, CWenger, Booloo, Nealparr, Allens, Katieh5584, Carlosguitar, Sardanaphalus, SmackBot, Jclerman, Moeron, McGeddon, Jtneill, Pandion auk, Bragador, Portillo, Chris the speller, Bluebot, Zachorious, Can't sleep, clown will eat me, OrphanBot, Michael.Pohoreski, Metta Bubble, Topologyrob, Dreadstar, Vectrax, BullRangifer, Germandemat, Acdx, Kilnhanger, Ollj, The Ungovernable Force, ArglebargleIV, Perfectblue97, Brian Gunderson, RomanSpa, Ckatz, N1h1l, Kompere, Northmeister, Novangelis, JoeBot, Debeo Morium, Coffee Atoms, Tawkerbot2, Loxlie, Jack's Revenge, SkyWalker, Mattbr, WeggeBot, Cydebot, APCooper, DumbBOT, BOBKINSELLA, Khendra1984, Dyanega, Nicolette Erasmus, Thijs!bot, Omgfreshbeatsnap, Qwyrxian, Keraunos, Mojo Hand, Headbomb, Doc pato, Vileru, Amity150, Edhubbard, Hmrox, Robert Bushman, SummerPhD, Catherine Curran, Percevalles, Dougher, Leuqarte, JAnDbot, Husond, Epeefleche, AquinasProtocol, Meeples, Dekimasu, Yakushima, SineWave, Soulbot, Ranger2006, Mark PEA, Balloonguy, Schumi555, Romancer, Frotz, JaGa, Edward321, Waninge, Kayau, Hintswen, MartinBot, Xumm1du, Seer441546, Wimdw, Jorgepblank, AlexiusHoratius, Tgeairn, Kaesle, Isaac.tanner.madsen, Hans Dunkelberg, BashBrannigan, Cpiral, TimofKingsland, Thomas Larsen, Tarotcards, AntiSpamBot, Belovedfreak, Jorfer, XdonnieXdarkoX, Juliancolton, VolkovBot, Ryn78, Dchmelik, Ranilb5, Evansnf, Leafyplant, Natg 19, Waycool27, Agyle, OBEinter, Lova Falk, GlassFET, Cindamuse, Pjoef, Glst2, GirasoleDE, Dragondreams, Nubiatech, Dawn Bard, AlbertHall, Godfinger, Danelo, Cyfal, Wiknerd, Tandy1000tl2, Florentino floro, Sayspo, Maxschmelling, ReikiResearch, EPadmirateur, Johnhuk, Martarius, ClueBot, The Thing That Should Not Be, ScienceHealthGuy, William Ortiz, DragonBot, Jusdafax, Csferraro, Mikeumus, Craighp, Orlando098, Tired time, Johnuniq, DumZiBoT, XLinkBot, Good Olfactory, SweetNightmares, Addbot, Simonm223, Melab-1, Zellfaze, Jncraton, Cuaxdon, Livingsuccess, MrOllie, Download, Redheylin, سمرقندی, Theking17825, Madagascar periwinkle, Threxnova, Ecrone, Jarble, Jma0322, Quantumobserver, Luckas-bot, Yobot, K2709, AnomieBOT, Matt reltub, Jim1138, Abstruce, Ularevalo98, Mahmudmasri, Citation bot, Benhen1997, LilHelpa, Abesgabes, Coeur-Senechal, Aaron Kauppi, Abbyeagle, DoostdarWKP, Amosmoran, Lucidology, Sopher99, Calmer Waters, Skyerise, GreenZeb, MastiBot, Numinous2002, Severian79, Tim1357, Beht, Trappist the monk, SchreyP, MrX, PeHa, RjwilmsiBot, NameIsRon, Davidshaw69, Mashaunix, KHamsun, Slightsmile, Darkman101, Fæ, Tyblu, Scythia, Spongeboy443, Donner60, Cincybluffa, Ironrage, DASHBotAV, ClueBot NG, Iritakamas, Dream of Nyx, Brigadir~enwiki, Helpful Pixie Bot, BG19bot, Cthulhu Rising, PhnomPencil, Zimmygirl7, MusikAnimal, North911, MrBill3, GreenUniverse, Vanished user lt94ma34le12, Kusamura N, ChrisGualtieri, Khazar2, AlchemistOfJoy, Kilasic, Emmabayuk, Imjin138, Fodor Fan, Jayarava, Ghosts Ghouls, VanishedUser 2313214sad1, Tutweiler, DavidLeighEllis, BigCat82, Manul, OccultZone, Chiara Lawrence, MarilynnHughes, Monkbot, Goblin Face, Reward6, 卢伟明, Mabydont, Amywatson01, Jerodlycett, KasparBot, Future Kick, JuliaHunter, Sinhaabhijeet24, A little angry, Viliasenova, Alphabravotango and Anonymous: 443

- **Religious ecstasy** *Source:* https://en.wikipedia.org/wiki/Religious_ecstasy?oldid=717466193 *Contributors:* Netesq, Michael Hardy, Kwertii, Rossami, Jogloran, Astronautics~enwiki, Nilmerg, Andycjp, Beland, One Salient Oversight, O'Dea, Jiy, Bender235, Ceyockey, RichardWeiss, BD2412, Search4Lancer, Koavf, Vegaswikian, Eubot, Consumed Crustacean, RussBot, Briaboru, Rsrikanth05, Veledan, AdelaMae, RDF, Whobot, Br~enwiki, SmackBot, Dunestrider, Dreadstar, Kristenq, Kashmiri, Mr Stephen, Waggers, Sharnak, LadyofShalott, George100, Matthew Auger, Neelix, Jennifernol, Aristophanes68, Hebrides, Energyfreezer, Thijs!bot, Epbr123, WmRowan, Hele 7, VoABot II, Lucaas, Hoverfish, Stephenchou0722, CommonsDelinker, SJP, Sacredworld, Philip Trueman, Mayagaia, Henry Carrington, Shadowlapis, Billinghurst, Arpose, Faradayplank, Smilo Don, ClueBot, Hafspajen, Simon D M, ZuluPapa5, Editor2020, Addbot, OlEnglish, Yobot, Schuym1, SEM-

TEX85, Gerixau, AnomieBOT, AlexanderVanLoon, FrescoBot, IWMYS, Allinthebrain, ReneVenegas95, Aleister Wilson, RedBot, Simon Kidd, Obsidian Soul, Manytexts, ClueBot NG, Ambkj123, BG19bot, Smcg8374, Oct13, Joga inex Luce, Abpaudel, Sofia Koutsouveli, Iṣṭa Devatā, Narky Blert, TaqPol, Pixarh, SICDAMNOME and Anonymous: 56

- **Near-death experience** *Source:* https://en.wikipedia.org/wiki/Near-death_experience?oldid=717094307 *Contributors:* Kpjas, Chuck Smith, Lee Daniel Crocker, Zundark, The Anome, Ed Poor, Olivier, Frecklefoot, Edward, Chas zzz brown, Michael Hardy, Paul Barlow, Spartacan, Liftarn, Ixfd64, Angela, Julesd, Slusk, Nikai, Robertkeller, Malcohol, Silvonen, Peregrine981, David Shay, Martinphi, Mir Harven, Hawstom, Chris Rodgers, Lumos3, Robbot, Fredrik, Korath, Moondyne, Sam Spade, Academic Challenger, Rasmus Faber, Hadal, Wikibot, Wereon, Mushroom, Kent Wang, Diberri, Pengo, Smjg, Advance, Acampbell70, Bfinn, Everyking, StargateX1, Chinasaur, Jfdwolff, Khalid hassani, Wiki Wikardo, Andycjp, Nova77, Elembis, Saucepan, Jokestress, Sam Hocevar, Gary D, Jh51681, Kelsey Francis, Discospinster, Rich Farmbrough, Cacycle, Bumhoolery, Horsten, Bender235, Quietly, JoeSmack, Ben Standeven, Petersam, Pietzsche, El C, Cedders, RoyBoy, Perfecto, Sdaconsulting, Equanimity two, Thodu, I9Q79oL78KiL0QTFHgyc, Homerjay, IDX, Topher67, Aquillion, Forteanajones, Nk, Solar, Hawol, Alansohn, Eric Kvaalen, Arthena, Wiki-uk, Andrewpmk, Riana, ChaosFish, AzaToth, Bz2, Mlessard, NTK, Omphaloscope, Xpendersx, SteinbDJ, Redvers, Kazvorpal, Kitch, Kmorris1077, Woohookitty, FeanorStar7, Havermayer, Jeff3000, Miss Madeline, Hbdragon88, Waldir, Marudubshinki, Graham87, BD2412, Koavf, XP1, Scorpionman, FayssalF, Ian Pitchford, SiriusB, Hottentot, Phatmonkey, Gurch, NeoFreak, Axver, Str1977, Bgwhite, Straker, YurikBot, Wavelength, JarrahTree, Bhny, Splette, Gaius Cornelius, Eleassar, Neilbeach, TheMandarin, NawlinWiki, Wiki alf, Onias, RattleMan, JDoorjam, Truthdowser, MSJapan, Blue Danube, Pawyilee, Intershark, Smkolins, Echris1, Closedmouth, Chaleur, Fram, Booloo, ArielGold, Nealparr, Kungfuadam, Carlosguitar, Infinity0, Sardanaphalus, SmackBot, Elonka, KAtremer, Reedy, John Jackson, McGeddon, Gilliam, Portillo, Skizzik, Arthurchappell, Chris the speller, Tarayani, Rothery, (boxed), Neo-Jay, DHN-bot~enwiki, Colonies Chris, Can't sleep, clown will eat me, Crocker, Tharikrish, Nixeagle, JonHarder, Juandev, Timberlax, Kittybrewster, Maxt, VegaDark, THD3, RJBaran, Wizardman, FlyHigh, Ollj, Beyazid, TenPoundHammer, CIS, Nathanael Bar-Aur L., MrSharp, Soap, LDuplatt, Breno, Tktktk, Ruwolf, Tymothy, Ckatz, Plunge, JHunterJ, Wega14, Ivanbok, Big Smooth, Bryantjs6, Peyre, Turbokoala, Yugyug, Rnb, Deager, George100, ChrisCork, CmdrObot, Wraithcat, Janelle Young, W guice, Mudd1, Linus M., R9tgokunks, Ruslik0, ShelfSkewed, Hi There, Michael J. Mullany, Cydebot, UncleBubba, Bellerophon5685, DarthSidious, Hippypink, Doug Weller, Ysimonson, Instaurare, BishopBerkeley, Nicolette Erasmus, Barticus88, Wikid77, AntonioBu, Ppaterson, Mojo Hand, Luigifan, Second Quantization, AstroFloyd, Aquilosion, Davidsf6, Grayshi, Jasumi, Escarbot, PSKelligan, SummerPhD, Just Chilling, LuckyLouie, Percevalles, Shlomi Hillel, DagosNavy, Narssarssuaq, Igoruha, Andonic, VQts, Ophion, Magioladitis, VoABot II, Athanatis, Froid, Eiyuu Kou, Soursider21, $yD!, Spellmaster, Waninge, LinkLink~enwiki, ChaosE, Kayau, DGG, Gwern, Ztobor, Atmans, MartinBot, Nwcasebolt, V-Man737, TheEgyptian, R'n'B, Conundrumer, LedgendGamer, Dinkytown, Grazia11, J.delanoy, Codeye, Trusilver, AstroHurricane001, Pursey, All Is One, Extransit, WindAndConfusion, Tdadamemd, TomCat4680, Shawn in Montreal, Pmbcomm, Naniwako, SwordFishData, Rosenknospe, Jorfer, Shadow Android, Far Beyond, Tiggerjay, Tucansam420, Use the force, AndreaZ412, Aidoflight, Signalhead, Timotab, WithGoodReason, VolkovBot, Johnfos, TravellerDMT-07, Ryn78, AlnoktaBOT, Skeptic06, RunningAway, TXiKiBoT, Mercurywoodrose, Atsakiris, Ubzy, Foxjones, Brmerrick, IPSOS, Loubobcat, Ephix, Hepcat65, Suriel1981, Complex (de), Ar-wiki, Wasted Sapience, Lova Falk, Easyaspie, VanishedUserABC, Enviroboy, NinjaRobotPirate, Sardaka, Mehmet Karatay, Is Mise, Dannymoorjani, AngChenrui, John Stattic, Nubiatech, Nihil novi, Calabraxthis, Nickols k, Joe3600, Carling C., Flyer22 Reborn, Kvnmcinturff, Cablehorn, Wombatcat, Godfinger, Gayanp19, Lightmouse, Sunrise, OKBot, Dravecky, FluffyFlyingDog, Florentino floro, Denisarona, Maxschmelling, EPadmirateur, Johnhuk, ClueBot, Binksternet, Ds.mt, Saviour1979, Homer-at-Paris, Newzild, Kilo6, Abhinav, Trilobite12, Auntof6, Supportisp, Gareth Chamberlain, DragonBot, Millionsandbillions, Obiskatobis, Maryh1, Steven Evens, RedEagle07, Truth is relative, understanding is limited, Tired time, Yoman82, DumZiBoT, Barbaricino~enwiki, XLinkBot, Staticshakedown, Pichpich, DrOxacropheles, Mertozoro, Cinemind, EastTN, Nishmeh, Kimberli Webb, Saeed.Veradi, Fwapper, Good Olfactory, Maimai009, Addbot, C6541, Leszek Jańczuk, Looie496, MrOllie, Proxima Centauri, Glane23, Briggsja, Favonian, JordanParey, West.andrew.g, Tassedethe, Numbo3-bot, Bwrs, Hereford, Wikihelp1a, Verbal, Guyonthesubway, Zorrobot, Jarble, LuK3, Ben Ben, Yobot, Themfromspace, Senator Palpatine, K2709, Holg.Klein~enwiki, AnomieBOT, Jim1138, Totalizerz, Piano non troppo, AdjustShift, Mrmonkeymanofkintucket, Raven1977, ArthurBot, LilHelpa, Aquila89, Hspstudent, Anna Frodesiak, Thorn breaker, Unscented, Shadowjams, Aaron Kauppi, Ondeck1, Pinkypooky, FrescoBot, Surv1v4l1st, Kwiki, Ndespace, Viallet, Jasonflorida1, Periksson28, Rectec794613, Lifeobserver, Pinethicket, I dream of horses, Alonso de Mendoza, Sealpoint33, RedBot, Overkill82, Alanasings, Smijes08, Numinous2002, Mokumao24, Reconsider the static, Beht, Chico889, Nickyus, MrX, Hippal01, Minkchawla, Schwede66, Diannaa, Tbhotch, Masondickson, RjwilmsiBot, Carol McCormick, Jhonnyiitb, Beyond My Ken, EmausBot, John of Reading, WikitanvirBot, ViewWikiped, Psychonaut2010, 19maxx, Your Lord and Master, Cyberic71, ZéroBot, Mutomana, Evasivo, Alexygr07, EWikist, David J Johnson, Scoopczar, Erianna, Kirkurdu, Neardeathcom, Brandmeister, Donner60, J341933, SuperAtheist, Ironrage, ChuispastonBot, Ihardlythinkso, GermanJoe, GBRV, ClueBot NG, Gareth Griffith-Jones, Belayed Reasons, Amavroth, Lynnettian, Davidhweinstein, Dream of Nyx, FiachraByrne, CIGGSofWAR, Humbugling, Saberus, Acentury331, Nanapush, Helpful Pixie Bot, Danthekarateman2, Zenith Diamond, Jeraphine Gryphon, BG19bot, Redraven01, Consorveyapaaj2048394, Cthulhu Rising, Wbilly3814, Suescudder, The Almightey Drill, Harizotoh9, MrBill3, Johnny locks sudbury, Hamish59, אדר, Wikiz876, Wolfchance2012, Dking777, BattyBot, SkepticalRaptor, DoctorKubla, AlchemistOfJoy, Joelthegrey, Adamc1969, Dexbot, Kolega2357, SoledadKabocha, FiverFan65, Mogism, Pwnisher248, Tommy Pinball, Frosty, Contact1997, Kernsters, Fodor Fan, Joolzzt, 069952497a, Me, Myself, and I are Here, Greengreengreenred, Beatrice57, Melonkelon, Tutweiler, Distilled Truth, SonicFan7822, NC1051, GravRidr, Nvdvn, Frogger48, Tenepes, PeachRoses, Integrity001, Monkbot, Goblin Face, Ca2james, Jsd31977, IagoQnsi, The Editor's Apprentice, Mabydont, English Opening, Gravityseeker, Liance, Eteethan, Someguy3, Btrefethen, Ferrer1965, BlackOlive2, Raptor400, LegereScire, KasparBot, Ashley Cookie Love, Atanusen7, Piano Concerto in F Minor, Philosi4, JuliaHunter, Stratboy61, In veritas, Superior410 and Anonymous: 601

- **Near-death studies** *Source:* https://en.wikipedia.org/wiki/Near-death_studies?oldid=714371204 *Contributors:* Martinphi, StargateX1, Klemen Kocjancic, Bender235, Hooverbag, Cmdrjameson, Topher67, La goutte de pluie, Hawol, Alansohn, BD2412, Visor, Pigman, Shell Kinney, Smkolins, Blueyoshi321, PTSE, Ageekgal, SmackBot, Chris the speller, Bluebot, Breno, Wega14, Doczilla, CmdrObot, Wraithcat, Cydebot, Michaelas10, Mattisse, Second Quantization, DagosNavy, Waninge, Lusitanian, Jdaloner, Florentino floro, EPadmirateur, Twinsday, Niceguyedc, Pichpich, EastTN, Good Olfactory, Proxima Centauri, Favonian, Yobot, K2709, AnomieBOT, Eumolpo, Srich32977, I dream of horses, Numinous2002, Lapskingwiki, John of Reading, Dewritech, Erianna, Jeraphine Gryphon, BG19bot, Cthulhu Rising, Mark Arsten, Mogism, Galacxico, OccultZone and Anonymous: 39

- **Deathbed phenomena** *Source:* https://en.wikipedia.org/wiki/Deathbed_phenomena?oldid=699933349 *Contributors:* Timrollpickering, Beland, Art LaPella, Topher67, Wiki-uk, Stack, BD2412, Uruiamme, Magioladitis, Ryn78, EPadmirateur, Trivialist, Boneyard90, RedEagle07, SwisterTwister, AnomieBOT, Gilo1969, K1brain, Delusion23, Jeraphine Gryphon, Benzband, The Almightey Drill, MrBill3, Jihadcola, Dan skeptic,

StellaABC, Goblin Face, Departingvision, Steve the Skeptic and Anonymous: 5

- **God gene** *Source:* https://en.wikipedia.org/wiki/God_gene?oldid=711491629 *Contributors:* The Anome, Graft, JWSchmidt, Johnstone, Alan Liefting, Giftlite, Barbara Shack, Alison, Duncharris, OldakQuill, Andycjp, Beland, Icairns, Rich Farmbrough, Dbachmann, Guettarda, Irate~enwiki, Bobo192, Whosyourjudas, Billymac00, Thialfi, Velella, Tony Sidaway, Dan100, Ceyockey, Voldemort, GrundyCamellia, Rjwilmsi, JdforresterBot, Satanael, Muntuwandi, Mvsmith, Allens, Revtor07, AscendedAnathema, SmackBot, K-UNIT, Cooksey87, Hardyplants, Gilliam, IanDavies, Xiner, Fuhghettaboutit, Dreadstar, Mgiganteus1, Norm mit, Iridescent, RookZERO, Goldfritha, Sirmylesnagopaleentheda, Bobblehead, Doc Tropics, Nstarz, AniRaptor2001, LinkinPark, Magioladitis, Dekimasu, PelleSmith, Theroadislong, Adrian J. Hunter, EscapingLife, OWiseWun, Flyer22 Reborn, Jonathanstray, Manishearth, Alexbot, Mlaffs, Thingg, PotentialDanger, Johnuniq, DumZiBoT, XLinkBot, Swakkhar17~enwiki, Addbot, Yobot, Speedy la cucaracha, Cold ground, Mr. Muntuwandi, AnomieBOT, MindscapesGraphicDesign, Wapondaponda, DSisyphBot, Crzer07, GHJmover, Citation bot 1, RedBot, بداري, Alfredo Castro-Vazquez, Miradre, ClueBot NG, Goose friend, Helpful Pixie Bot, SARAGIANNINI, Pastorjamesmiller, Mark Arsten, DyslexicDNA, Cyberbot II, Chôji, Monkbot, Roshu Bangal, Rkk44, DavidJac and Anonymous: 54

- **God helmet** *Source:* https://en.wikipedia.org/wiki/God_helmet?oldid=693355915 *Contributors:* Fnielsen, Leandrod, Skysmith, Omegatron, Naddy, Dhodges, Dbenbenn, Jackdavinci, Klemen Kocjancic, O'Dea, Zenohockey, Viriditas, Famousdog, Clubmarx, Rjwilmsi, GangofOne, Ashleyisachild, Hillman, Chris Capoccia, Mccready, Morgan Leigh, Whouk, NeilN, SmackBot, Mitteldorf, Jtneill, Kledsky, Baldghoti, Solidusspriggan, Radagast83, Cybercobra, Tktktk, Doczilla, Phuzion, Alankroeger, Harold f, CmdrObot, Ibadibam, Mattisse, Headbomb, Luna Santin, Shirt58, KrijnMossel, ***Ria777, Dave Muscato, Saganaki-, STBot, CommonsDelinker, Maurice Carbonaro, Squids and Chips, Hy Brasil, Mercurywoodrose, UnitedStatesian, ClueBot, Badger Drink, MystBot, MatthewVanitas, Addbot, Debresser, Luckas-bot, Yobot, K2709, AnomieBOT, Materialscientist, Citation bot, Fingerz, FrescoBot, Mu Mind, Citation bot 1, Pinethicket, Jonesey95, Articulant, Scienceisgolden, Buddy23Lee, Difu Wu, RjwilmsiBot, John of Reading, ZéroBot, Ebehn, ClueBot NG, Hamlet 2010a, Antlersantlers, LizzardKitty, Evolve42, Adamglass3000, Tomfbake, Vouillamoz21, ChrisGualtieri, YFdyh-bot, Pik023, Ksirok, Thesassypenguin, Saectar, Monkbot, Robertlee79 and Anonymous: 74

- **G-LOC** *Source:* https://en.wikipedia.org/wiki/G-LOC?oldid=706232371 *Contributors:* Bearcat, Wolfkeeper, Golbez, Xezbeth, Rajneeshhegde, Interiot, Water Bottle, TaintedMustard, Gene Nygaard, GraemeLeggett, Graham87, Rjwilmsi, Eubot, AED, Spencerk, Chobot, Felsir, SmackBot, Thermalnoise, Bluebot, Wen D House, J.smith, Jaganath, Ex nihil, Heinous~enwiki, Lx45803, Bot-maru, Askari Mark, Naohiro19, Nono64, Ae020704, Zhar, OKBot, ClueBot, Pjotr ch, Alexbot, El bot de la dieta, Vybr8, DumZiBoT, Addbot, Zeugma fr, Yobot, AnomieBOT, Keystoneridin, FrescoBot, Tommy2010, Whoop whoop pull up, ClueBot NG, MerlIwBot, Saint Oliver, KLBot2, BattyBot, Reatlas, Jfimmano, Richie Sanders, HarryKernow and Anonymous: 31

- **Deep brain stimulation** *Source:* https://en.wikipedia.org/wiki/Deep_brain_stimulation?oldid=716479108 *Contributors:* AxelBoldt, JDG, Edward, Docu, Barak~enwiki, Tlotoxl, Pietro, Chris 73, Diberri, Oobopshark, Zigger, Alterego, Jfdwolff, Neutrality, Freakofnurture, CALR, Rich Farmbrough, Sladen, Roodog2k, SHARD, Smalljim, Duk, Arcadian, Zetawoof, Minority Report, SlimVirgin, HenkvD, Opherdonchin, Woohookitty, Urod, Jeff3000, Anaru, Johann Gambolputty~enwiki, Rjwilmsi, Koavf, Brighterorange, PaulWicks, YurikBot, Epolk, Deodar~enwiki, Nephron, Rmky87, Lipothymia, 2over0, Arthur Rubin, Wikimucker, Chriswaterguy, That Guy, From That Show!, Veinor, SmackBot, Stifle, Gilliam, Ohnoitsjamie, George Church, Raresel, Plustgarten, Wilfred Pau, Ohconfucius, Vgy7ujm, IronGargoyle, SandyGeorgia, Mfourman, Ginkgo100, Lujanjl, Psychofarm, Andymease, JForget, MeekMark, Jordan Brown, Cydebot, Was a bee, Anthonyhcole, Casliber, Thijs!bot, Elgati, Barticus88, Trevyn, AntiVandalBot, Kenahoo, Danger, SFairchild, MER-C, Sierrafarris, Magioladitis, GridEpsilon, Tomhannen, Brewhaha@edmc.net, MortenKringelbach, Rosco snappy, CFCF, Artmario2001, SJS1971, Psyklic, Belovedfreak, Remember the dot, MoodyGroove, Psamathos, VolkovBot, Yiorgos Stamoulis, Fences and windows, Mikebpac, Mark v1.0, Gnif global, Sciencewatcher, Jesin, Eubulides, Doc James, Legoktm, SieBot, NeuroWeb, Schlaepf~enwiki, Applebyb, Oxymoron83, Psychosomatic Tumor, Kopid03, Aechase1, Brushka, MikeVitale, Infrasonik, Desoto10, Bradka, DumZiBoT, XLinkBot, Jytdog, Ost316, Aeth909, Addbot, DOI bot, Neurostooge, Iirightii, Looie496, Anthonymsweeney, Dyuku, Jarble, Mrug, Yobot, Viking59, AnomieBOT, Shotcallerballerballer, Emerydora, Srich32977, FrescoBot, Jinja87, Hellerhoff, Nonlinearity, Citation bot 1, Slechte124, FergusRossFerrier, Trappist the monk, Angelito7, Tvashtar2919, EmausBot, John of Reading, WikitanvirBot, Sueli.f.lima, Basrblog, Alfredo ougaowen, Jeanpetr, Inniverse, Wikkieddit, ClueBot NG, ScipioWarrior, Widr, Helpful Pixie Bot, PDXNWWoman, BG19bot, Purielku, Kmpolacek, Meneswa, MiriamRGarcia, RodneyAnderson, Qetuth, BattyBot, Buffy a. summers, Me, Myself, and I are Here, Kejriwalv, Thevideodrome, Drchriswilliams, Brainiacal, Barneayg, Dylan.doggielama, Rperez831, Stormmeteo, Ejester, Monkbot, LeBassRobespierre, Strongylos, Mattgaidica, Medwriter55, Andreashorn, Doctor BW, Culturezoom, FrancoNeuro and Anonymous: 120

- **Consciousness after death** *Source:* https://en.wikipedia.org/wiki/Consciousness_after_death?oldid=716922074 *Contributors:* Ixfd64, Halibutt, Scottperry, Discospinster, Bishonen, Bender235, Lycurgus, Viriditas, Bobrayner, Rjwilmsi, Bgwhite, McGeddon, Gilliam, JorisvS, Wega14, S Marshall, Second Quantization, Matthew Proctor, Smartse, DagosNavy, Arifsaha, Magioladitis, BatteryIncluded, Ryn78, Kelapstick, Monty845, Stfg, EPadmirateur, Krapenhoeffer, Niceguyedc, Arjayay, Editor2020, Mitch Ames, Drlight11, Looie496, OlEnglish, Yobot, AnomieBOT, Machine Elf 1735, Crusoe8181, Trappist the monk, MrX, John of Reading, Ironrage, AndyTheGrump, Wakebrdkid, ClueBot NG, BG19bot, Smcg8374, MLearry, Falkirks, John Aiello, Dexbot, Everything Is Numbers, 93, Hakumaie, ?, Reatlas, Lemnaminor, I am One of Many, Amethyst1234, Alanhugenot, Caleb9849, Strecosaurus, Monkbot, Goblin Face, You're No Longer You, Rider ranger47, Horrorboy54, Potejohnson and Anonymous: 61

- **Monism** *Source:* https://en.wikipedia.org/wiki/Monism?oldid=717174045 *Contributors:* AxelBoldt, Wesley, William Avery, Ant, Ryguasu, Stevertigo, Michael Hardy, Palnatoke, Nixdorf, Kalki, Ellywa, Ahoerstemeier, William M. Connolley, Snoyes, AugPi, Poor Yorick, TonyClarke, Adam Conover, Peter Damian (original account), Reddi, Fuzheado, Selket, DJ Clayworth, Jjshapiro, Morwen, Shizhao, JorgeGG, Lumos3, Naturyl, Phil Boswell, Robbot, Goethean, Altenmann, Sam Spade, Mirv, Decumanus, Meursault2004, Marcika, Everyking, Elinnea, Joe Kress, Jfdwolff, Mboverload, Eequor, Mporch, LordSimonofShropshire, Andycjp, Kaldari, Jossi, Karol Langner, Rdsmith4, Sam Hocevar, Robin Hood~enwiki, Fintor, Takaitra, Mike Rosoft, Shahab, Venu62, Dbachmann, Bender235, ESkog, El C, Lycurgus, Kwamikagami, Liberatus, Visualerror, Felagund, Bobo192, Cmdrjameson, Tim Smith, Kjkolb, Terraist, Cherlin, Ogress, Jumbuck, Kentin, Raj2004, Alansohn, Wiki-uk, Gpvos, Grenavitar, Bsadowski1, HenryLi, Saxifrage, Zorblek, Daranz, WilliamKF, Kokoriko, Before My Ken, Ruud Koot, Jeff3000, Alfakim, Bdj, Ashmoo, BD2412, Anarchivist, Pranathi, Rjwilmsi, Tangotango, TheRingess, Feydey, Carvern, Juzer, FlaBot, Margosbot~enwiki, YurikBot, Wavelength, Hairy Dude, RussBot, Pigman, Gaius Cornelius, Wiki alf, Leutha, Cleared as filed, Tomisti, Deville, Lt-wiki-bot, RDF, TBadger, Caballero1967, Aryah, Infinity0, Sardanaphalus, SmackBot, RayBaxter, Mdiamante, AustinKnight, Srnec, David Ludwig, Go for it!,

Victoria h, DHN-bot~enwiki, Toughpigs, Dr. Dan, Vanished User 0001, Clinkophonist, Stevenmitchell, Ne0Freedom, Alister T, LoveMonkey, Lacatosias, Jklin, Salamurai, Nrgdocadams, Eliyak, Wtwilson3, Drivelhead, Fig wright, Taiwan boi, Feureau, NJA, MTSbot~enwiki, Vanished User 03, Chgwheeler, Keahapana, K, Fedro~enwiki, Harry Stoteles, Shoeofdeath, Beno1000, Zipz0p, Krishnamurthi, IronChris, Amalas, Makeemlighter, Black and White, Neelix, Gregbard, Babub, Verdy p, Viscious81, Roberta F., Coelacan, Mojo Hand, Who123, Marek69, Missvain, Zaiken, Nick Number, Monkeykiss, Gioto, Aletheia, Ste4k, Scepia, Colin MacLaurin, Peter Harriman, JAnDbot, Gordonnovak, Skomorokh, IanOsgood, Eurobas, Hut 8.5, Meic Crahart, Zghost, Antipodean Contributor, Valentinus~enwiki, Jatkins, Philosopher123, Gwern, STBot, Anarchia, R'n'B, VirtualDelight, Freeboson, Elfelix, Tyrianfishmonger, Numbo3, All Is One, Ian.thomson, 4ariadne, Jorfer, Mihilz, Shoessss, BrettAllen, Redtigerxyz, Alexgenaud, Yehoishophot Oliver, VolkovBot, RashmiPatel, TallNapoleon, CompRelProf, Chango369w, Aymatth2, IPSOS, Anna Lincoln, Irrationalgirl, Buddhipriya, Raymondwinn, Robert1947, Myscience, Synthebot, EmxBot, Sanchezdot, GoonerDP, SieBot, StAnselm, Nihil novi, Yintan, Nummer29, Commontater, Javierfv1212, Rickbrown9, Fratrep, Owlmonkey, WikipedianMarlith, Twinsday, ClueBot, Clivemacd, Mild Bill Hiccup, Boing! said Zebedee, Epsilon60198, Nymf, Alexbot, TaoChaChing, Torsmo, SchreiberBike, Muro Bot, Unmerklich, Yonskii, Vegetator, Editor2020, Wikidas, Ostinato2, Zenwhat, Wayne.sagon, Pichpich, Pfhorrest, Burningview, BodhisattvaBot, Mitsube, Saeed.Veradi, Addbot, Melab-1, Miskaton, Atethnekos, AnnaFrance, Favonian, Lightbot, Jarble, Arunpsmn, Yobot, Assika126, Sindhian, AnomieBOT, Dr. Günter Bechly, Orenshafir, Whitekingdom, VedicScience, GB fan, ArthurBot, Obersachsebot, DSisyphBot, Gilo1969, Jburlinson, Groovenstein, Makeswell, Omnipaedista, RibotBOT, SassoBot, Abd ul-Ghafoor Nicholas, Bo98, Jsp722, Isospin, Paine Ellsworth, Machine Elf 1735, HRoestBot, MastiBot, Pollinosisss, LilyKitty, Jigglyfidders, Diannaa, CLWSDW09, Jesse V., Gleaman, EmausBot, John of Reading, Leit... Leit... Leithammel, GoingBatty, Rarevogel, Jhaub420, EWikist, Stefan Milosevski, Mcc1789, Pandeist, ClueBot NG, Luxsolis, Gareth Griffith-Jones, Jack Greenmaven, Joefromrandb, Hiperfelix, Dream of Nyx, Widr, John M Brear, Hrugnir, Helpful Pixie Bot, Martin Berka, BG19bot, Imgaril, Davidiad, Marcocapelle, Jpacobb, Joshua Jonathan, Mootherfooker, BattyBot, Jeremy112233, Mediran, Khazar2, Tahc, Rockin It Loud, Asdfwasd, Hmainsbot1, Lightgraphs, TwoTwoHello, Lerr, K480b, Jwratner1, Mangostaniko, Petebot5, Ms Sarah Welch, The Green Man 21, SquashEngineer, KasparBot, IndologyScholar, DimensionQualm, Crawford88 and Anonymous: 267

- **Subitism** *Source:* https://en.wikipedia.org/wiki/Subitism?oldid=716834907 *Contributors:* Klemen Kocjancic, Ogress, BD2412, Rigadoun, Gregory Wonderwheel, CmdrObot, Cydebot, Alaibot, SusanLesch, KConWiki, NoychoH, B9 hummingbird hovering, Mind meal, IPSOS, WereSpielChequers, No essential nature, Redheylin, Yobot, AnomieBOT, Eugene-elgato, Shanghainese.ua, DrilBot, John of Reading, Klbrain, SporkBot, Helpful Pixie Bot, BG19bot, Joshua Jonathan, JimRenge, Srednuas Lenoroc and Anonymous: 9

- **Christian anthropology** *Source:* https://en.wikipedia.org/wiki/Christian_anthropology?oldid=716991277 *Contributors:* Cromwellt, BD2412, Marax, SouthernNights, TimNelson, SmackBot, Hmains, Jeffro77, Chris the speller, Mladifilozof, CmdrObot, Cydebot, Doug Weller, SteveMcCluskey, Vcg3rd, Vassilis78, Colin MacLaurin, Magioladitis, Tonicthebrown, StAnselm, Komusou, Ptolemy Caesarion, ClueBot, Jim Casy, PixelBot, Editor2020, DumZiBoT, WikHead, Addbot, Haruth, Luckas-bot, THEN WHO WAS PHONE?, AnomieBOT, Xqbot, GrouchoBot, RibotBOT, Hugetim, FrescoBot, Quodvultdeus, Alonso de Mendoza, Diannaa, RjwilmsiBot, WikitanvirBot, Jstovell, 8een4Tfor, Ludovica1, Styleset2001, Mhiji, ClueBot NG, Frietjes, WikiPuppies, Helpful Pixie Bot, Davidiad, Marcocapelle, Anthrophilos, Latarnia, ChrisGualtieri, Hmainsbot1, TheTahoeNatrLuvnYaho, Greaserpirate, Monkbot, Johnsoniensis, KasparBot, WannaBeEditor, Calebjbaker and Anonymous: 25

- **Hypergraphia** *Source:* https://en.wikipedia.org/wiki/Hypergraphia?oldid=715018477 *Contributors:* Isomorphic, Furrykef, Desmay, Robinoke, Gobeirne, Mporch, Discospinster, Purplefeltangel, Tronno, Rajah, Pharos, Officiallyover, Mac Davis, RJFJR, Guthrie, Graham87, Ryan Norton, Rjwilmsi, Koavf, MacRusgail, TexasAndroid, Aleichem, IceCreamAntisocial, MichaelCrawford, Trilemma, Pesematology, BorgQueen, DearPrudence, AeroIllini, SmackBot, Chewxy, BullRangifer, Argotechnica, SandyGeorgia, Doczilla, Fluppy, Ewulp, George100, Zotdragon, Cydebot, Rosser1954, Littlegeisha, Thijs!bot, Biruitorul, Qwyrxian, AgentPeppermint, Qwerty Binary, Madscribbler, AstroHurricane001, Naniwako, Ask123, Dookama, Rockdozen, BotMultichill, Mcfeisty, SoxBot III, Staticshakedown, Addbot, Looie496, LiteralKa, Yobot, AnomieBOT, Galoubet, LilHelpa, JensenInt, Lida Vorig, RjwilmsiBot, Minor4th, Erianna, Staszek Lem, ClueBot NG, Matthiaspaul, Helpful Pixie Bot, Zeke, the Mad Horrorist, BattyBot, Me, Myself, and I are Here, Mark viking, Oceoano, JimRenge, Hannahgrotz, Aly.neuro, Monkbot, Dyane Leshin-Harwood, Fastes12345, Dyane Leshin and Anonymous: 35

- **Geschwind syndrome** *Source:* https://en.wikipedia.org/wiki/Geschwind_syndrome?oldid=717774491 *Contributors:* Famousdog, Rjwilmsi, Gareth Jones, SmackBot, RDBrown, Pwjb, Filelakeshoe, Headbomb, Calaka, Brescd01, Matthew Fennell, Bonze blayk, Wingedsubmariner, DumZiBoT, Addbot, Looie496, Yobot, Rokeach, Jim1138, Jonesey95, Skyerise, Trappist the monk, EmausBot, ZéroBot, SporkBot, Atrivo, BG19bot, Joshua Jonathan, Dexbot, Tentinator, Clr324, BayBall2398, Tripleahg, Connor Beveridge, Monkbot, Rremus10, Knife-in-the-drawer and Anonymous: 20

- **Hypoactive sexual desire disorder** *Source:* https://en.wikipedia.org/wiki/Hypoactive_sexual_desire_disorder?oldid=716581516 *Contributors:* Jahsonic, Jpatokal, Conti, Furrykef, RedWolf, Der Eberswalder, Davodd, Hadal, Jfdwolff, Beland, Yayay, TonyW, Subsume, Abdull, Longhair, Arcadian, OGoncho, Malo, Markaci, Richard Arthur Norton (1958-), Pictureuploader, Graham87, Rjwilmsi, Koavf, FlaBot, Nihiltres, JdforresterBot, YurikBot, RobotE, Bhny, Pigman, Netscott, Zwobot, Arthur Rubin, Acctorp, Ephilei, SmackBot, Eskimbot, Shibidee, Drn8, Chris the speller, Shaggorama, RDBrown, Theone256, Thumperward, Fuzzform, Deli nk, Radagast83, Шизомби, Derek R Bullamore, Sashato-Bot, MTSbot~enwiki, Cooter227, Hu12, Antonio Prates, Xcentaur, Banzaimonkey, Penbat, Atomaton, SyntaxError55, Gogo Dodo, Thijs!bot, Faigl.ladislav, Alphachimpbot, JAnDbot, MER-C, Magioladitis, LeaHazel, Hurr1, WLU, RaccoonFox, CFCF, Osiris7, Oshwah, Coder Dan, Lova Falk, Doc James, AlleborgoBot, JJHeart, Flyer22 Reborn, Enti342, Callidior, Invertzoo, The Thing That Should Not Be, Enthusiast01, Siipikarja, Niceguyedc, Solar-Wind, Robertmuil, Alexbot, Leonard^Bloom, Ngebendi, Iohannes Animosus, Aitias, Nathan Johnson, Addbot, Freunlaven47, Elmondo21st, Diptanshu.D, Ccacsmss, Mightymax5672, דוד55, Jarble, Luckas-bot, Yobot, Yngvadottir, Triquetra, AnomieBOT, Citation bot, ArthurBot, Xqbot, Millahnna, Erik9, Thehelpfulbot, FrescoBot, Surv1v4l1st, OliverFL, HamburgerRadio, Serendipchic, LittleWink, MastiBot, Angelito7, Mcluver, RjwilmsiBot, Ripchip Bot, EmausBot, Hirsutism, MrGachapon, Mimabern, Infinette, Tellsbadjokes, ChuispastonBot, Helpful Pixie Bot, DBigXray, Pine, KateWishing, Ypp1987, F Maker, Amolbot, Bhzmr1, Mpranswers, BattyBot, Jeshleman, Morgantodd, Sensorsweep, Abbie.dodz, Goldkatze, Sachin.chitnis, Monkbot, Randomnessu, Medgirl131, Apmaples95 and Anonymous: 93

- **Syncope (medicine)** *Source:* https://en.wikipedia.org/wiki/Syncope_(medicine)?oldid=710993336 *Contributors:* AxelBoldt, Kpjas, Vicki Rosenzweig, Ap, Rgamble, Zadcat, Montrealais, Karada, Ellywa, Julesd, ShaunOfTheLive, Renato Caniatti~enwiki, Hankwang, Altenmann, Meelar, Acegikmo1, Diberri, DocWatson42, Gil Dawson, Wolfkeeper, Moshe~enwiki, Jfdwolff, Hugh2414, Gyrofrog, Beland, PFHLai, Jh51681, Now3d, Bender235, Kjoonlee, Petersam, Kwamikagami, Swillden, Arcadian, Phansen, Methegreat, PatrickFisher, Seans Potato Business, Mac Davis, TaintedMustard, Tainter, Markaci, Jak86, LOL, Pol098, MONGO, Eras-mus, Waldir, Graham87, Reisio, Jamesbateman, Jorunn, Rjwilmsi, Amire80, SMC, CannotResolveSymbol, Brighterorange, Eleazar~enwiki, Nandesuka, Ian Pitchford, AED, Arcimboldo,

Fresheneesz, Stevenfruitsmaak, Melanarchy, Preslethe, Samkass, Bgwhite, YurikBot, Hede2000, Chris Capoccia, Wikispork, Raquel Baranow, Stephenb, Eleassar, Rsrikanth05, Grafen, Trovatore, Maverick Leonhart, Occono, FlyingPenguins, Zephalis, Shralk, Codenamecuckoo, CharlesHBennett, Ligart, ChaseKiwi, Matt Heard, Luk, RichG, SmackBot, Gaff, Bloomingdedalus, Bidgee, Nabokovian, Yidisheryid, COMP-FUNK2, Thomaslau~enwiki, Cybercobra, Tiki2099, Dcamp314, Eristikophiles, Astroview120mm, Drphilharmonic, -Marcus-, Lambiam, Sbmehta, Cariniabean, 16@r, Ex nihil, Jared W, Beetstra, Hu12, IvanLanin, Blackhawk charlie2003, Octane, Gil Gamesh, Bentendo24, DangerousPanda, John Reed Riley, CBM, Smably, .Koen, Longshot.222, Founders4, Fluffy McNutter, Editor at Large, PamD, Thijs!bot, Skovorodkin, Fr00gy, Cyclonenim, Saimhe, Caledones, Firefeather, JEH, North Shoreman, DCman, Arx Fortis, Amberroom, Markthemac, JAnDbot, Deflective, Rick.Wicks, Vivacita, Conserrnd, Magioladitis, Bennybp, VoABot II, Meredyth, ***Ria777, WhatamIdoing, VegKilla, 28421u2232nfenfcenc, LorenzoB, JoergenB, DerHexer, JaGa, WLU, Yoni, CliffC, Chelmian, J.delanoy, CFCF, Silverxxx, Dolamite02, Mikael Häggström, Gurchzilla, Tjpravetz, WinterSpw, MoodyGroove, Station1, Tamayo2, TXiKiBoT, Skeggy ben, ArrhythmiaAlliance, A4bot, Reibot, Joybucket, Chrishibbard7, LeaveSleaves, Redsox04, Websurfer135, MajorHazard, Countincr, Doc James, Bluedenim, Andrewjlockley, Flyer22 Reborn, Spiinnniiaas, Naima.fatimi, RyanParis, ClueBot, Andrew Nutter, Snigbrook, Niceguyedc, PMDrive1061, Andrewshaman, RTaptap, Kaiba, ChrisHodgesUK, Versus22, Arlolra, Londonsista, XLinkBot, WikHead, SilvonenBot, Jkuo3, Fyrwoman49, Douvaine, Addbot, Grayfell, Betterusername, LaaknorBot, Ccacsmss, Glane23, דוד55, Jarble, Luckas-bot, Vedran12, Omino di carta, Legobot II, Killerz2222, Gongshow, Peterpeter13, Untrue Believer, AnomieBOT, Jim1138, GuyMontang, Formol, Blueasberry, Citation bot, ArthurBot, Addihockey10, Joneb, ArcadianOnUnsecuredLoc, Bradshaws1, Dr.PrabhuMD, GrouchoBot, Omnipaedista, RibotBOT, GenOrl, Edgars2007, FrescoBot, Citation bot 1, I dream of horses, LittleWink, RedBot, December21st2012Freak, كاشف عقیل, Angelito7, RjwilmsiBot, Doctoresbi, EmausBot, WikitanvirBot, Nothing149, Trinidade, Carrie9600, H3llBot, SporkBot, RoyBentley7, Salsabiel-NJITWILL, Teapeat, Spicemix, Miradre, ClueBot NG, Wonmean, XtrOrdinaryFilms, Manodragon, Thefeelingofwhathappens, Delusion23, Leefogel, Wbm1058, RZuljani, BG19bot, AvocatoBot, Altaïr, Liberty02, Illia Connell, Peter Jaschner, Dexbot, Mruwald, Ekips39, Wowzer42, BruceBlaus, Monkbot, Qwertyxp2000, Charlotte Aryanne, Kashish Arora, KasparBot and Anonymous: 220

- **Pedant** *Source:* https://en.wikipedia.org/wiki/Pedant?oldid=712907700 *Contributors:* SimonP, KF, Przepla, Johnleemk, Firebird, Francs2000, Fredrik, Moncrief, Geogre, Alan Liefting, Smjg, Barbara Shack, Eequor, Chameleon, Mkilly, Combuchan, Katherine Shaw, Femto, Devil Master, Smalljim, Neg, Scott Ritchie, RussBlau, Hanuman Das, Velella, SidP, Dirac1933, MickWest, Umofomia, Xiong Chiamiov, Jorunn, Josiah Rowe, Wahkeenah, MarnetteD, FlaBot, Unixan, Quuxplusone, Vonkje, YurikBot, Wavelength, Peregrine Fisher, Scott5834, Yamara, NawlinWiki, Elkman, FF2010, Light current, Bobryuu, Thnidu, Vicarious, Canadianism, SmackBot, Rikkyc, Flagmantho, Zephyrad, WikiPedant, Can't sleep, clown will eat me, Racklever, Stangbat, Flyguy649, Cybercobra, Nick125, Croyfan1, Rreuling, Glover, Tim riley, Lambiam, Albinoduck, Timdownie, Disavian, Robofish, Antonielly, Slakr, Shoeofdeath, Eastlaw, Requestion, Gogo Dodo, B, Tawkerbot4, DumbBOT, Al Lemos, Trevyn, TheTruthiness, Son of Somebody, Big Bird, AntiVandalBot, Paulannis, Qwerty Binary, Macaw 54, Davewho2, Marycontrary, Cwagstaff, Lizzysama, Irost, Valerius Tygart, Gasheadsteve, Aladdin Sane, Tgeairn, Jerry, McSly, Equazcion, Voxish, Squids and Chips, ACSE, Vranak, RasputinJSvengali, VolkovBot, Jeff G., Ccaggiano, Mcewan, TXiKiBoT, Mr. Nonsense, Jeremy Bolwell, Eubulides, Mtpandtlo, LinksWant2BeFree, Tiddly Tom, Veryfaststuff, Mockingbus, Hatmatbbat10, Jpeeler, ClueBot, Jeanarock, Morel, SchreiberBike, DumZiBoT, Moorestep45, MystBot, Addbot, ConicProjection, Fieldday-sunday, LaaknorBot, Favonian, SpBot, Doniago, Ehrenkater, Tide rolls, OlEnglish, Jarble, Yobot, Kan8eDie, Jesus022090, Amicon, AdjustShift, ErikTheBikeMan, Ubwergeek, Materialscientist, 90 Auto, Xqbot, Bihco, LivingBot, Samsmasam, Tsblloyd, Dougofborg, Garygateaux, Sallyannw, Anterior1, Marlieman, Infinity Tr0n, Lotje, Onel5969, Ripchip Bot, GoingBatty, Tinytn, EleferenBot, Jg2904, Tiredartist, Thine Antique Pen, ChuispastonBot, Resgug, Didlix, ClueBot NG, Joefromrandb, Dobby18, Chisme, BG19bot, Seanylynch, Davidiad, BattyBot, Cyberbot II, Makecat-bot, K Y Mckay, Writerzblock, AmericanDad86, Alarty, Crispulop, Horatio Snickers, Sam Sailor, Mutantvirus, Aspaa, Hoyanakis, Nøkkenbuer, NowWD and Anonymous: 213

- **Neuroimaging** *Source:* https://en.wikipedia.org/wiki/Neuroimaging?oldid=717783523 *Contributors:* The Anome, Rsabbatini, Michael Hardy, Vaughan, Karada, Stan Shebs, Brinticus, Charles Matthews, Wikiborg, Dysprosia, Mandark~enwiki, Omegatron, Thue, Paranoid, Nilmerg, Hadal, Xanzzibar, Giftlite, Jfdwolff, Mboverload, Foobar, Khalid hassani, Erich gasboy, Tothebarricades.tk, Sayeth, Marcos, Mike Rosoft, RedWordSmith, NeuronExMachina, Pjacobi, Raistlinjones, Mal~enwiki, O lara o, Xiggelee, El C, Ascorbic, Smalljim, AllyUnion, Arcadian, Mdd, Jumbuck, Alansohn, Silver hr, Mykej, Wouterstomp, AjAldous, Ringbang, Vadim Makarov, Simetrical, Rjwilmsi, Dloeckx, SanGatiche, FlaBot, Fresheneesz, Bgwhite, YurikBot, Stephenb, A314268, Daniel Mietchen, Rjlabs, Action potential, Kkmurray, Closedmouth, Sardanaphalus, Veinor, SmackBot, Hydrogen Iodide, Ze miguel, DCDuring, Fabrice.Rossi, Delldot, Kslays, Gcmarino, Chris the speller, Thumperward, Sbharris, Danielkueh, DR04, Aeternus, CmdrObot, Jakebroadhurst, Was a bee, Dancter, Tawkerbot4, John.d.van.horn, Kozuch, Thijs!bot, SusanLesch, Dawnseeker2000, Escarbot, The Transhumanist, Ph.eyes, VoABot II, Appraiser, Scottalter, Schmloof, CommonsDelinker, Genesis12~enwiki, Erkan Yilmaz, Mindgames11, Trusilver, Maurice Carbonaro, Kpmiyapuram, Louislemieux, Junior Brian, Ipigott, Warut, Torstenrohlfing, Guillaume2303, Maxim, Gfariello, Lova Falk, Doc James, Typofier, Friedrich K., FSHL, Faradayplank, Rythmcubed, Mygerardromance, ImageRemovalBot, DragonBot, Redrocketboy, BáthoryPéter, Aitias, N.vanstrien, MarkSCohen, Poocat, EEng, Afiller, GyroMagician, Diptanshu.D, Looie496, SpBot, Aviados, Dwayne Reed, Fryed-peach, Yobot, Fraggle81, Suntag, Tryptofish, Rjanag, Blueasberry, Materialscientist, Citation bot, Kirigiri, Frajolex, J04n, Omnipaedista, Chriss789, FrescoBot, Full-date unlinking bot, Bento00, Tesseract2, EmausBot, John of Reading, Gcastellanos, AnonymousVex, K6ka, CheeseCake109, Gsarwa, Yurypetrov, FeatherPluma, BG19bot, Kollamrajeshr, Amygdulus, Rob Hurt, BattyBot, Kodiologist, Jmjamet, Dexbot, Amorrissette3, Soueumxm, Wikiuserresuikiw, FelixRosch, Anishpotnis, Monkbot, Dmrwikiprof, Love.short.stops, Prof ater, Dorasteel, Jamal Abdalla and Anonymous: 106

- **Return from Tomorrow** *Source:* https://en.wikipedia.org/wiki/Return_from_Tomorrow?oldid=699347173 *Contributors:* Art LaPella, Grenavitar, Jenblower, Pegship, Bluebot, Macwiki, CmdrObot, Neelix, Cydebot, Alaibot, Gatorsong, Foxjones, EPadmirateur, Wkharrisjr, Carriearchdale, Borock, Good Olfactory, AnomieBOT, FrescoBot, Bigweeboy, Justlettersandnumbers, Titodutta, BattyBot, Frogger48 and Anonymous: 3

- **Life After Life (book)** *Source:* https://en.wikipedia.org/wiki/Life_After_Life_(book)?oldid=705400937 *Contributors:* Ed Poor, Karen Johnson, Michael Hardy, Angela, Sunray, YUL89YYZ, Number 0, Mairi, Sasquatch, Mdd, BDD, Abanima, GregorB, Ketiltrout, Koavf, TheMandarin, Pegship, Meditationguru, Katieh5584, SmackBot, Syarzhuk, Gobonobo, George100, Ruslik0, Cydebot, Thijs!bot, Vmadeira, TAnthony, Johnfos, WatchAndObserve, Godfinger, EPadmirateur, Kilo6, Alexbot, Addbot, Verbal, Yobot, Vini 17bot5, ArthurBot, Xqbot, Srich32977, LivingBot, Angelito7, AvicAWB, Colapeninsula, Helpful Pixie Bot, CitationCleanerBot, Goblin Face, Spcoastal and Anonymous: 8

- **Betty Eadie** *Source:* https://en.wikipedia.org/wiki/Betty_Eadie?oldid=703178022 *Contributors:* Ed Poor, Frecklefoot, Chris Rodgers, Rursus, Bensaccount, Gary D, Kate, InShaneee, DreamGuy, Sfacets, Sesmith, Rtdrury, SDC, Secfan fucker, Bgwhite, RussBot, Tony1, Arundhati bakshi, Allens, SmackBot, Gigs, Vanished User 0001, Blake-, Andrew c, Jetman, CmdrObot, Cydebot, Julia Rossi, Tjmayerinsf, Bluetooth954, ARTEST4ECHO, Waacstats, Prestonmcconkie, Missclaire, Foxjones, Mr.Z-bot, Niceguyedc, Snocrates, XLinkBot, Good Olfactory, Addbot, Lightbot, Stokar, Yunshui, RjwilmsiBot, Beyond My Ken, EmausBot, Fishspill, Helpful Pixie Bot, Jojemi1, DarafshBot, Mimzy210, VIAFbot, Frogger48, MagicatthemovieS, Cathygaul, KasparBot and Anonymous: 17

- **Saved by the Light** *Source:* https://en.wikipedia.org/wiki/Saved_by_the_Light?oldid=711830191 *Contributors:* Alan Liefting, Popefauvexxiii, Mytildebang, GregorB, Ricardo Carneiro Pires, Pegship, SmackBot, Bluebot, Cydebot, DarthSidious, Mercurywoodrose, Foxjones, NinjaRobot-Pirate, EPadmirateur, Good Olfactory, ArmbrustBot and Anonymous: 6

- **Placebo (at funeral)** *Source:* https://en.wikipedia.org/wiki/Placebo_(at_funeral)?oldid=639993118 *Contributors:* Choster, Anthony Appleyard, Uucp, Eubot, RussBot, BullRangifer, Rwflammang, Cydebot, Gzhanstong, Nitin.i.azam, Cobaltcigs, Marcocapelle, Mogism and Anonymous: 8

- **90 Minutes in Heaven** *Source:* https://en.wikipedia.org/wiki/90_Minutes_in_Heaven?oldid=704949066 *Contributors:* Zoe, Phil Boswell, Bearcat, Karl Dickman, Calton, Rjwilmsi, Metropolitan90, Welsh, Mikeblas, Pegship, Crystallina, SmackBot, Ser Amantio di Nicolao, Gobonobo, Robofish, Grumpyyoungman01, Basawala, Bbagot, Cydebot, Bellerophon5685, Doug Weller, LuckyLouie, Albany NY, Magioladitis, Michael10127, DadaNeem, Donmike10, Bovineboy2008, Bigboy1069, Michaelsbll, Dr78, KoshVorlon, EPadmirateur, Binksternet, Drmies, Trivialist, Callinus, Good Olfactory, Gongshow, AnomieBOT, Hornymanatee, Trappist the monk, RjwilmsiBot, Wikienlight, Δ, ClueBot NG, Jeraphine Gryphon, BG19bot, Falkirks, Krystaleen, Aussiechildpsychiatrist, Frogger48, Factsforus, Ozzeyo, Landingdude13, Valentinois26, Caliburn and Anonymous: 49

- **Heaven Is for Real** *Source:* https://en.wikipedia.org/wiki/Heaven_Is_for_Real?oldid=717543274 *Contributors:* Darrell Greenwood, Deselms, Auric, HangingCurve, Andycjp, ESkog, Mr. Billion, Orbst, Gary, Walter Görlitz, GregorB, Mandarax, Rjwilmsi, Nightscream, Koavf, Bgwhite, Ezia, Dmaestoso, Dbfirs, Caballero1967, Katieh5584, Gilliam, Ser Amantio di Nicolao, Gobonobo, Tktktk, IronGargoyle, Taram, Cydebot, Instaurare, Bf2002, Matthew Fennell, Joshua, Magioladitis, KConWiki, Cgingold, Torchiest, Poetdancer, Edward321, Paulmcdonald, Cadwaladr, Kmzundel, Vmaldia, Finarfen, WOSlinker, Oshwah, StAnselm, Annasdottir, Happysailor, Nebbel, EPadmirateur, Binksternet, All Hallow's Wraith, Trivialist, Arjayay, Elizium23, Badmintonhist, DoctorEric, Callinus, Editor2020, XLinkBot, Mitch Ames, Addbot, Grayfell, Proxima Centauri, Glane23, RichLindvall, Luckas-bot, WikiDan61, Fraggle81, AnomieBOT, Ipatrol, Materialscientist, Cameron Scott, Xqbot, Gorge-CustersSabre, Mark Schierbecker, Sunshinesquad, Dutchmonkey9000, Aoidh, Cirrus Editor, RjwilmsiBot, Petermcelwee, EmausBot, Domesticenginerd, Winner 42, K6ka, AvicBot, ZéroBot, Josve05a, Tolly4bolly, Captain Assassin!, Petrb, ClueBot NG, Jack Greenmaven, Widr, IgnorantArmies, Helpful Pixie Bot, HMSSolent, Wiki13, MusikAnimal, Maksymilian Sielicki, BattyBot, Cyberbot II, 009o9, Kendallschmidt15, Booklover84, JustAMuggle, Mgraunikar, Michipedian, FiredanceThroughTheNight, Doorknobby, LahmacunKebab, Pluperfectionist2, Frogger48, MagicatthemovieS, SpiritedMichelle, LFtcG, RunninFree, Crazynyancat, TerryAlex, Ankitbko, ChamithN, Socjerm, Angel d Dios, Ferretsrock, Katecooper 11, Erictuffendsam, Klafz, Art & SoulWorks, Dilidor, White Arabian Filly, FixDefunktDomain and Anonymous: 132

- **Parallel Universes: A Memoir from the Edges of Space and Time** *Source:* https://en.wikipedia.org/wiki/Parallel_Universes%3A_A_Memoir_from_the_Edges_of_Space_and_Time?oldid=689119889 *Contributors:* JamesAM, Heroeswithmetaphors, Robina Fox, TAnthony, GrahamHardy, Logan, 1ForTheMoney, Good Olfactory, Drpickem, Yobot, FrescoBot, I dream of horses, ViewWikiped, Chris857, Helpful Pixie Bot, Khazar2, Frogger48, PeachRoses, Michaeljdjackson and Anonymous: 2

- **Eben Alexander (author)** *Source:* https://en.wikipedia.org/wiki/Eben_Alexander_(author)?oldid=717319404 *Contributors:* AxelBoldt, JackofOz, Mdmcginn, Macrakis, Dbachmann, Wiki-uk, FeanorStar7, GregorB, Koavf, Bgwhite, Tony1, Crisco 1492, Pawyilee, Gaborgulya, Ser Amantio di Nicolao, Doug Weller, Relhager, Second Quantization, Ekabhishek, Postcard Cathy, Albany NY, Edward321, Valerius Tygart, Johnpacklambert, 5Q5, Thismightbezach, Hugo999, Dawn Bard, Arbor to SJ, EPadmirateur, Binksternet, Jusdafax, Callinus, Addbot, Shiva321, Ealexander3, Yobot, AnomieBOT, Must We, Trappist the monk, Chico889, Kilfio, RjwilmsiBot, Dewritech, GoingBatty, ZéroBot, Illegitimate Barrister, SporkBot, Liuthar, ClueBot NG, Andrewpatrickc, Joefromrandb, Mannanan51, Jeraphine Gryphon, BG19bot, Brian Tomasik, Drjetfuel, Monkelese, DarafshBot, MahdiBot, Cyberbot II, Makecat-bot, Malerooster, Epicgenius, Frogger48, Tshuva, Manul, MagicatthemovieS, Nikolozik, Tina9 81, EbenAlexander, Skr15081997, LeBassRobespierre, Jahendr, Sackandsugar, Phdinall, KasparBot, Thomas Deen, Wikipedia Wonderful 698-D, Yeardley5335 and Anonymous: 43

- **Beyond and Back** *Source:* https://en.wikipedia.org/wiki/Beyond_and_Back?oldid=684088098 *Contributors:* Michael Hardy, Herzen, SiriusB, Pigman, Welsh, Drboisclair, Jogers, SmackBot, Gjs238, Chris the speller, Bluebot, ProfessorPaul, Cydebot, Lugnuts, STBot, Shawn in Montreal, WOSlinker, Polbot, TubularWorld, Martarius, RWardy, Mild Bill Hiccup, Tnxman307, Good Olfactory, Lightbot, Yobot, AnomieBOT, LowSelfEstidle, DirtyFrank68, Surv1v4l1st, Tim1357, Jonkerz, SporkBot, Grizzlyadamsmichelle.tv, Ldavid1985, Frogger48 and Anonymous: 12

- **Lazarus syndrome** *Source:* https://en.wikipedia.org/wiki/Lazarus_syndrome?oldid=717663545 *Contributors:* Michael Hardy, Auric, Alanyst, Alan Liefting, StuartDouglas, Circeus, Pauli133, Guy M, Waldir, Dwaipayanc, Coemgenus, Stevenfruitsmaak, Bgwhite, Wavelength, TheDoober, Jo3y~enwiki, BorgQueen, DearPrudence, SmackBot, Rogermw, IronGargoyle, Dr.K., Dl2000, Joseph Solis in Australia, Olaf Davis, Ken Gallager, Mack2, TAnthony, Manticore, Tdadamemd, Olegwiki, Magnvss, FergusM1970, Phjellming, Radiooperator, Marcwiki9, Doc James, Angelastic, Dough4872, Musicandnintendo, Denisarona, Sterlsilver, TheRedPenOfDoom, CaptainVideo890, SilvonenBot, Sgpsaros, Good Olfactory, Addbot, Queenmomcat, Sillyfolkboy, PersOnLine, Luckas-bot, Yobot, Opus 17, Piano non troppo, Citation bot, BeforeTheFoundation, Carlsotr, Xqbot, Srich32977, Timofp, Omnipaedista, Alex60466176, 6th Happiness, Citation bot 1, RjwilmsiBot, KinkyLipids, Medeis, Ctsinclair, Unreal7, TyA, Smartie2thaMaxXx, ClueBot NG, FLHerne, Widr, Blahdenoma, UAwiki, Tito Reinaldo, BattyBot, Jimw338, Joejudy2, TylerDurden8823, Dexbot, Frosty, Oneultralamewhiteboy, Govgovgov, Triavalon, Mandruss, SuperHypercane, Monkbot, Paruski24246, Amortias, BraveByDefault, WD5858 and Anonymous: 93

- **Mediumship** *Source:* https://en.wikipedia.org/wiki/Mediumship?oldid=717159560 *Contributors:* The Anome, Ed Poor, Infrogmation, Martinphi, Hoopes, Dale Arnett, Lowellian, Xanzzibar, Graeme Bartlett, DocWatson42, IStuart, Alison, Bluejay Young, Elembis, Ukexpat, Eep², Discospinster, MBisanz, El C, Sdaconsulting, I9Q79oL78KiL0QTFHgyc, Famousdog, DCEdwards1966, Riana, DreamGuy, Amorymeltzer, New Age Retro Hippie, Ceyockey, Steven S. Mair, Woohookitty, RHaworth, Kosher Fan, Pepsi90919, Obersachse, Graham87, BD2412, Mendaliv, Josh Parris, Rjwilmsi, Amire80, HappyCamper, Djrobgordon, Ewlyahoocom, Wgfcrafty, Kazuba, RussBot, Bhny, Pigman, Hydrargyrum, David Woodward, Arichnad, Irishguy, PhilipO, RUL3R, Epa101, CorbieVreccan, Wknight94, 2over0, Tyrenius, Nealparr, Sarah, Otheus, True Pagan Warrior, SmackBot, McGeddon, Ominae, Gregory j, Eaglizard, Ohnoitsjamie, Hmains, Skizzik, Bluebot, Audacity, MartinPoulter, Ultiam, Silly rabbit, Colonies Chris, Sct72, Onorem, Clinkophonist, MaxMangel, Anthon.Eff, Decltype, Nakon, Dreadstar, BullRangifer,

39.11.2 Images

- **File:Creation_of_Adam.jpg** *Source:* https://upload.wikimedia.org/wikipedia/commons/f/f2/Creation_of_Adam.jpg *License:* Public domain *Contributors:* From English Wikipedia: en:Image:Creation of Adam.jpg *Original artist:* Michelangelo

- **File:Deep_brain_stimulation_electrode_placement_reconstruction.png** *Source:* https://upload.wikimedia.org/wikipedia/commons/d/de/ Deep_brain_stimulation_electrode_placement_reconstruction.png *License:* CC BY-SA 4.0 *Contributors:* Own work *Original artist:* Andreashorn

- **File:Descartes-reflex.JPG** *Source:* https://upload.wikimedia.org/wikipedia/commons/8/8a/Descartes-reflex.JPG *License:* Public domain *Contributors:* Copied from a 345 year old book, Traite de l'homme *Original artist:* René Descartes

- **File:Development_of_the_neural_tube.png** *Source:* https://upload.wikimedia.org/wikipedia/commons/4/4c/Development_of_the_neural_ tube.png *License:* Public domain *Contributors:* Figure 6 (p. 24) of "The anatomy of the nervous system" by Stephen Walter Ranson, published W.B. Saunders, 1920 *Original artist:* user:Looie496 created file, original artist unknown

- **File:Dharma_Wheel.svg** *Source:* https://upload.wikimedia.org/wikipedia/commons/d/df/Dharma_Wheel.svg *License:* CC-BY-SA-3.0 *Contributors:* Own work *Original artist:* Shazz, Esteban.barahona

- **File:Dualism-vs-Monism.png** *Source:* https://upload.wikimedia.org/wikipedia/commons/7/79/Dualism-vs-Monism.png *License:* CC0 *Contributors:* Own work *Original artist:* Dustin Dewynne

- **File:Earthworm_nervous_system.png** *Source:* https://upload.wikimedia.org/wikipedia/commons/4/43/Earthworm_nervous_system.png *License:* Public domain *Contributors:* scanned from figure 12 (p. 86) of the book *The mental and physical life of school children* by Peter Sandiford, published by Longmans, Green and compay, 1913 *Original artist:* image created by user:Looie496; original artist unknown

- **File:Edit-clear.svg** *Source:* https://upload.wikimedia.org/wikipedia/en/f/f2/Edit-clear.svg *License:* Public domain *Contributors:* The *Tango! Desktop Project. Original artist:*
  The people from the Tango! project. And according to the meta-data in the file, specifically: "Andreas Nilsson, and Jakub Steiner (although minimally)."

- **File:FMRIscan.jpg** *Source:* https://upload.wikimedia.org/wikipedia/en/d/d1/FMRIscan.jpg *License:* Fair use *Contributors:* ? *Original artist:* ?

- **File:Falun_Dafa_fifth_meditation_exercise.jpg** *Source:* https://upload.wikimedia.org/wikipedia/commons/9/9c/Falun_Dafa_fifth_ meditation_exercise.jpg *License:* CC BY 3.0 *Contributors:* Falun Dafa fifth meditation exercise (in Bangkok) *Original artist:* longtrekhome

- **File:Folder_Hexagonal_Icon.svg** *Source:* https://upload.wikimedia.org/wikipedia/en/4/48/Folder_Hexagonal_Icon.svg *License:* Cc-by-sa-3.0 *Contributors:* ? *Original artist:* ?

- **File:Gaius_Julius_Caesar_(100-44_BC).JPG** *Source:* https://upload.wikimedia.org/wikipedia/commons/2/26/Gaius_Julius_Caesar_ %28100-44_BC%29.JPG *License:* Public domain *Contributors:* H. F. Helmolt (ed.): *History of the World.* New York, 1902 (University of Texas Library Portrait Gallery) *Original artist:* ?

- **File:Gforce_demo2.webm** *Source:* https://upload.wikimedia.org/wikipedia/en/0/0f/Gforce_demo2.webm *License:* CC0 *Contributors:* ? *Original artist:* ?

- **File:Gnome-searchtool.svg** *Source:* https://upload.wikimedia.org/wikipedia/commons/1/1e/Gnome-searchtool.svg *License:* LGPL *Contributors:* http://ftp.gnome.org/pub/GNOME/sources/gnome-themes-extras/0.9/gnome-themes-extras-0.9.0.tar.gz *Original artist:* David Vignoni

- **File:Gray17.png** *Source:* https://upload.wikimedia.org/wikipedia/commons/9/95/Gray17.png *License:* Public domain *Contributors:* Henry Gray (1918) *Anatomy of the Human Body*, invalid ID (See "Book" section below)
  Original artist: Henry Vandyke Carter

- **File:Gray518.png** *Source:* https://upload.wikimedia.org/wikipedia/commons/3/35/Gray518.png *License:* Public domain *Contributors:* Henry Gray (1918) *Anatomy of the Human Body*, invalid ID (See "Book" section below)
  Original artist: Henry Vandyke Carter

- **File:Gray728.svg** *Source:* https://upload.wikimedia.org/wikipedia/commons/1/1a/Gray728.svg *License:* Public domain *Contributors:* Henry Gray (1918) *Anatomy of the Human Body*, invalid ID (See "Book" section below)
  Original artist: Henry Vandyke Carter

- **File:Gray739.png** *Source:* https://upload.wikimedia.org/wikipedia/commons/9/96/Gray739.png *License:* Public domain *Contributors:* Henry Gray (1918) *Anatomy of the Human Body*, invalid ID (See "Book" section below)
  Original artist: Henry Vandyke Carter

- **File:Gray797.png** *Source:* https://upload.wikimedia.org/wikipedia/commons/3/38/Gray797.png *License:* Public domain *Contributors:* Henry Gray (1918) *Anatomy of the Human Body*, invalid ID (See "Book" section below)
  Original artist: Henry Vandyke Carter

- **File:Hall_Freud_Jung_in_front_of_Clark_1909.jpg** *Source:* https://upload.wikimedia.org/wikipedia/commons/e/e1/Hall_Freud_Jung_in_ front_of_Clark_1909.jpg *License:* Public domain *Contributors:* Jung's First Visit to America *Original artist:* Unknown<a href='//www.wikidata. org/wiki/Q4233718' title='wikidata:Q4233718'><img alt='wikidata:Q4233718' src='https://upload.wikimedia.org/wikipedia/commons/thumb/ f/ff/Wikidata-logo.svg/20px-Wikidata-logo.svg.png' width='20' height='11' srcset='https://upload.wikimedia.org/wikipedia/commons/thumb/ f/ff/Wikidata-logo.svg/30px-Wikidata-logo.svg.png 1.5x, https://upload.wikimedia.org/wikipedia/commons/thumb/f/ff/Wikidata-logo.svg/ 40px-Wikidata-logo.svg.png 2x' data-file-width='1050' data-file-height='590' /></a>

- **File:Helen-duncan-platexi.jpg** *Source:* https://upload.wikimedia.org/wikipedia/commons/c/c5/Helen-duncan-platexi.jpg *License:* Public domain *Contributors:* Harry Price (1931) Regurgitation and the Duncan Mediumship (Bulletin I of the National Laboratory of Psychical Research, 120pp with 44 illustrations.) *Original artist:* Harry Price

- **File:Helen_Duncan_fake_ectoplasm.jpg** *Source:* https://upload.wikimedia.org/wikipedia/commons/c/cf/Helen_Duncan_fake_ectoplasm. jpg *License:* Public domain *Contributors:* Harry Price. Leaves from a Psychist's Case-Book (Victor Gollancz Ltd, 1933) *Original artist:* Harvey Metcalfe

39.11.3 Content license

43507426R00150

Made in the USA
San Bernardino, CA
20 December 2016